Garfield
FAT CAT 3-PACK
VOLUME 12

BY
JIM DAVIS

BALLANTINE BOOKS · NEW YORK

2019 Ballantine Books Trade Paperback Edition

GARFIELD LIFE TO THE FULLEST copyright © 1999, 2017 by PAWS, Inc. All Rights Reserved.
GARFIELD FEEDS THE KITTY copyright © 1999, 2018 by PAWS, Inc. All Rights Reserved.
GARFIELD HOGS THE SPOTLIGHT copyright © 2000, 2018 by PAWS, Inc. All Rights Reserved.
"GARFIELD" and the GARFIELD characters are trademarks of PAWS, Inc.

Published in the United States by Ballantine Books, an imprint of Random House,
a division of Penguin Random House LLC, New York.

BALLANTINE and the HOUSE colophon are registered trademarks of Penguin Random House LLC.

GARFIELD LIFE TO THE FULLEST was originally published separately in 1999 and in a colorized version in
2017, GARFIELD FEEDS THE KITTY was originally published separately in 1999 and in a colorized version in
2018, and GARFIELD HOGS THE SPOTLIGHT was originally published separately in 2000 and in a colorized
version in 2018 by Ballantine Books, an imprint of Random House, a division of Penguin Random House LLC.

ISBN 978-0-425-28578-7

Printed in China on acid-free paper

randomhousebooks.com

9 8 7 6 5 4 3 2 1

Garfield
life to
the fullest

BY JIM DAVIS

Ballantine Books ● New York

THINGS GARFIELD WOULD NEVER SAY...

Do you think these jeans make my butt look big?

Odie—I love ya, man!

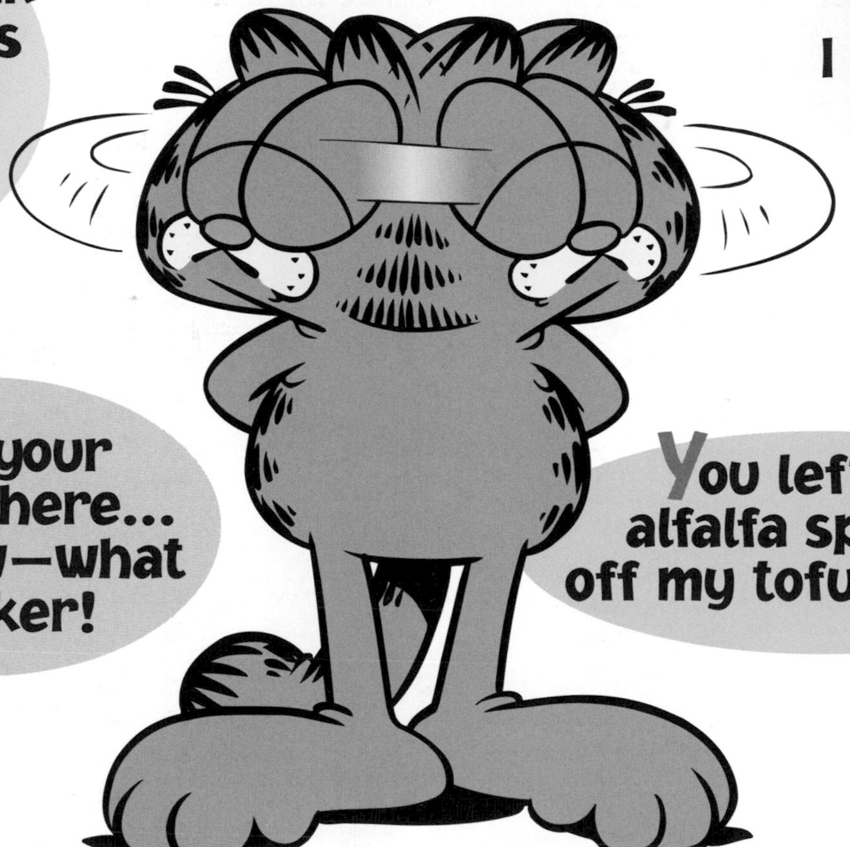

Jon, your date's here... and wow—what a looker!

You left the alfalfa sprouts off my tofu burger.

Cats...dogs... spiders...can't we all just get along?

Anyone wanna go "halvsies" on that last piece of double-fudge banana cheesecake?

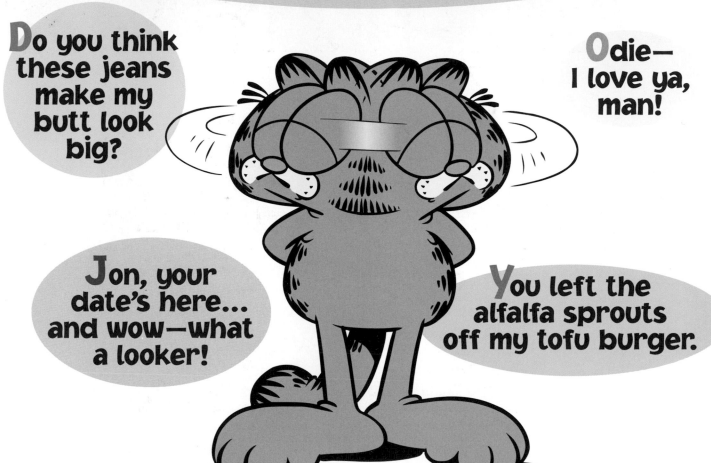

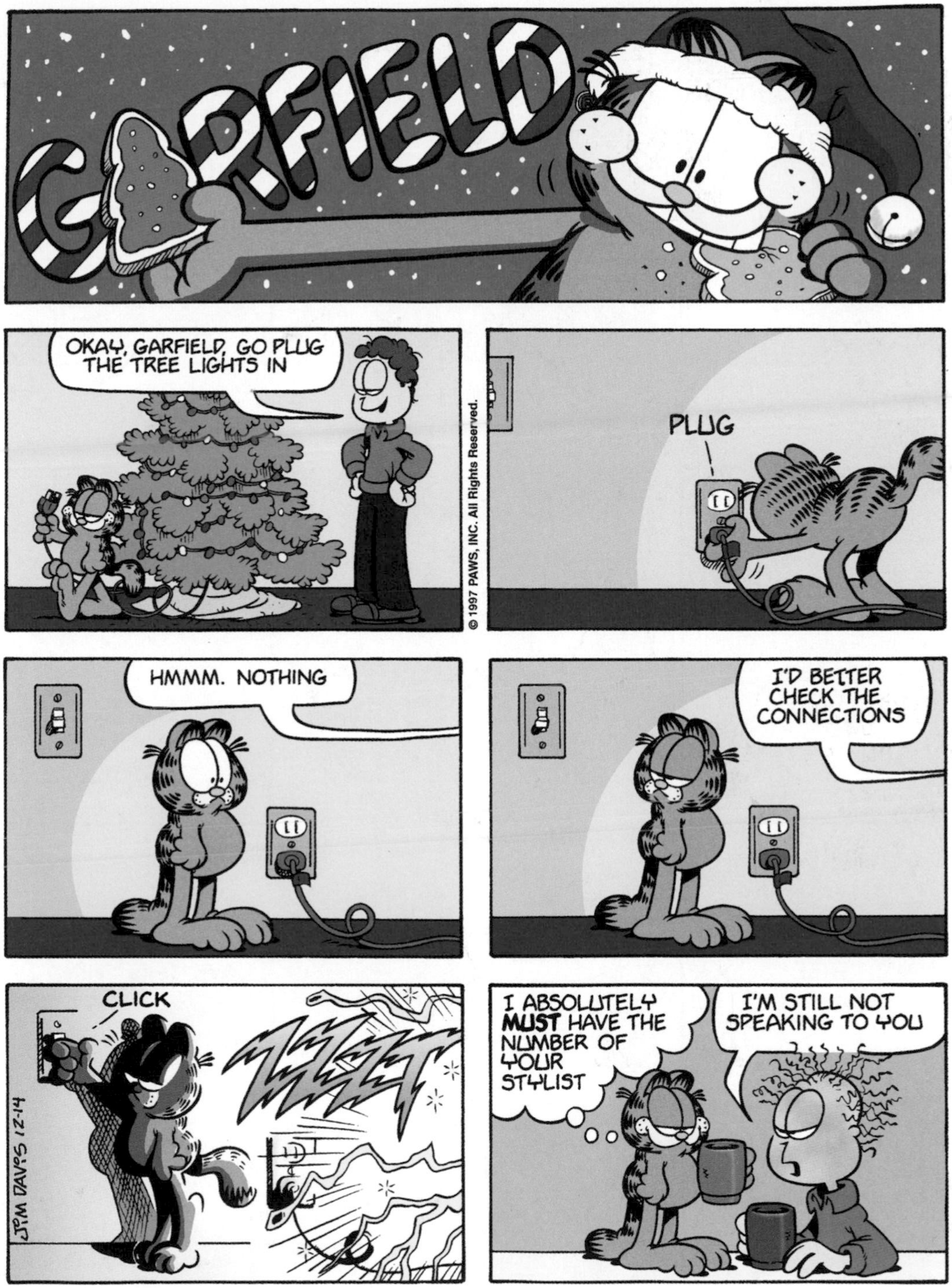
GARFIELD
OKAY, GARFIELD, GO PLUG THE TREE LIGHTS IN
© 1997 PAWS, INC. All Rights Reserved.
PLUG
HMMM. NOTHING
I'D BETTER CHECK THE CONNECTIONS
CLICK
JIM DAVIS 12-14
I ABSOLUTELY **MUST** HAVE THE NUMBER OF YOUR STYLIST
I'M STILL NOT SPEAKING TO YOU

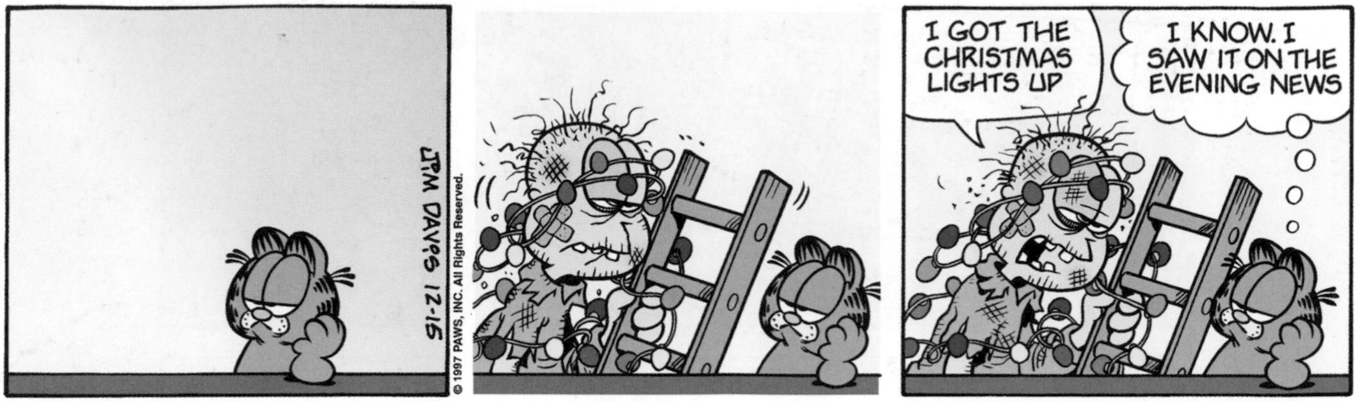
JIM DAVIS 12-15
© 1997 PAWS, INC. All Rights Reserved.
I GOT THE CHRISTMAS LIGHTS UP
I KNOW. I SAW IT ON THE EVENING NEWS

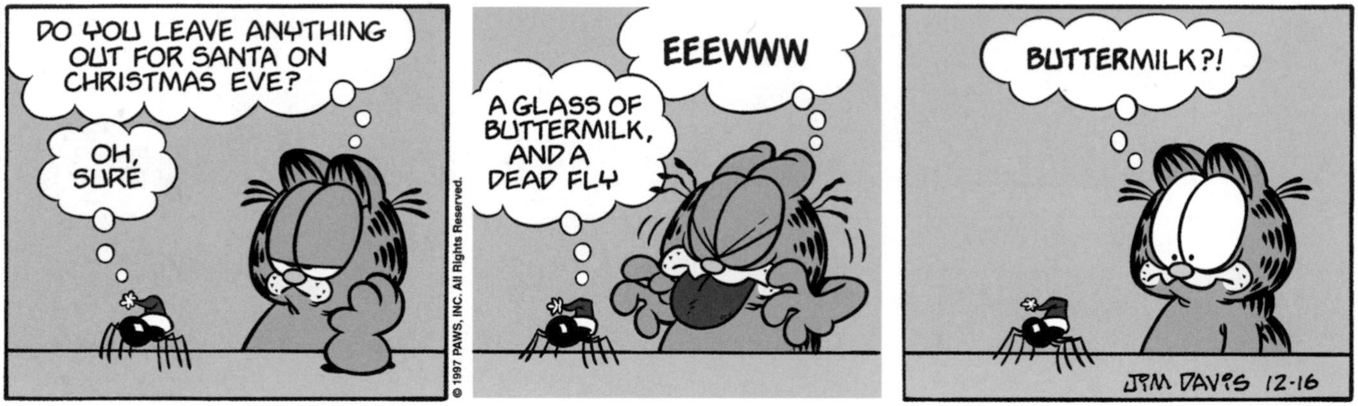
DO YOU LEAVE ANYTHING OUT FOR SANTA ON CHRISTMAS EVE?
OH, SURE
© 1997 PAWS, INC. All Rights Reserved.
A GLASS OF BUTTERMILK, AND A DEAD FLY
EEEWWW
BUTTERMILK?!
JIM DAVIS 12-16

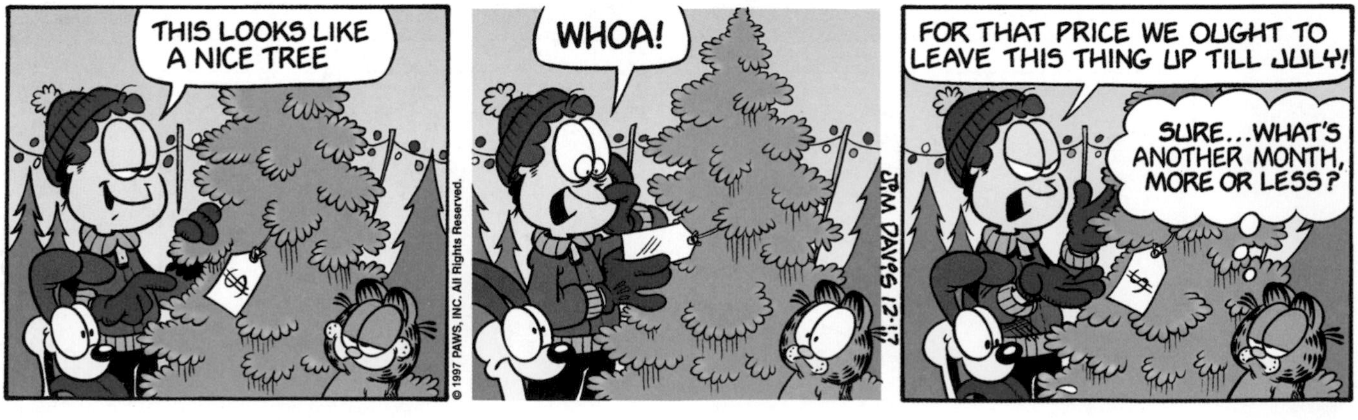
THIS LOOKS LIKE A NICE TREE
© 1997 PAWS, INC. All Rights Reserved.
WHOA!
JIM DAVIS 12-17
FOR THAT PRICE WE OUGHT TO LEAVE THIS THING UP TILL JULY!
SURE... WHAT'S ANOTHER MONTH, MORE OR LESS?

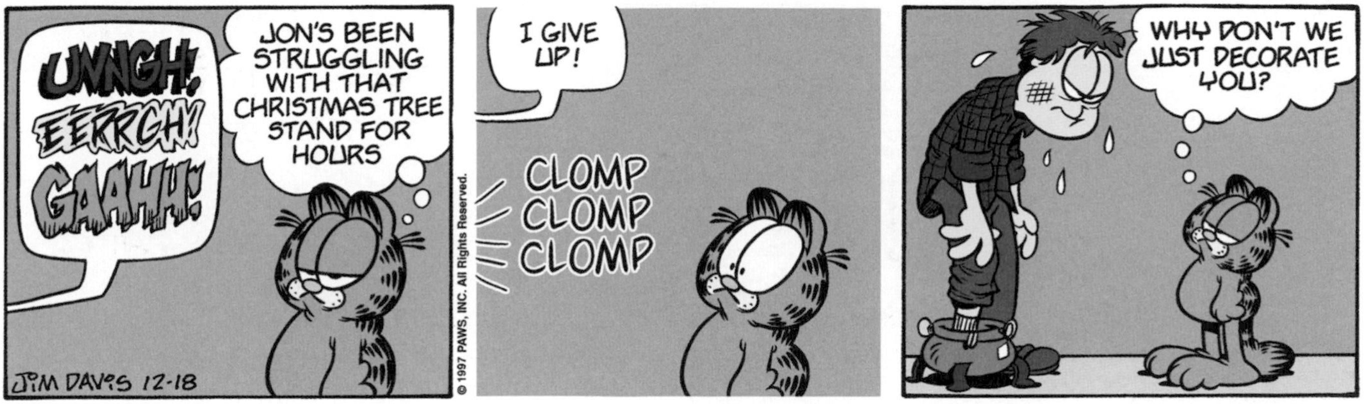
UNNGH! EERRGH! GAAHH!
JON'S BEEN STRUGGLING WITH THAT CHRISTMAS TREE STAND FOR HOURS
JIM DAVIS 12-18
© 1997 PAWS, INC. All Rights Reserved.
I GIVE UP!
CLOMP CLOMP CLOMP
WHY DON'T WE JUST DECORATE YOU?

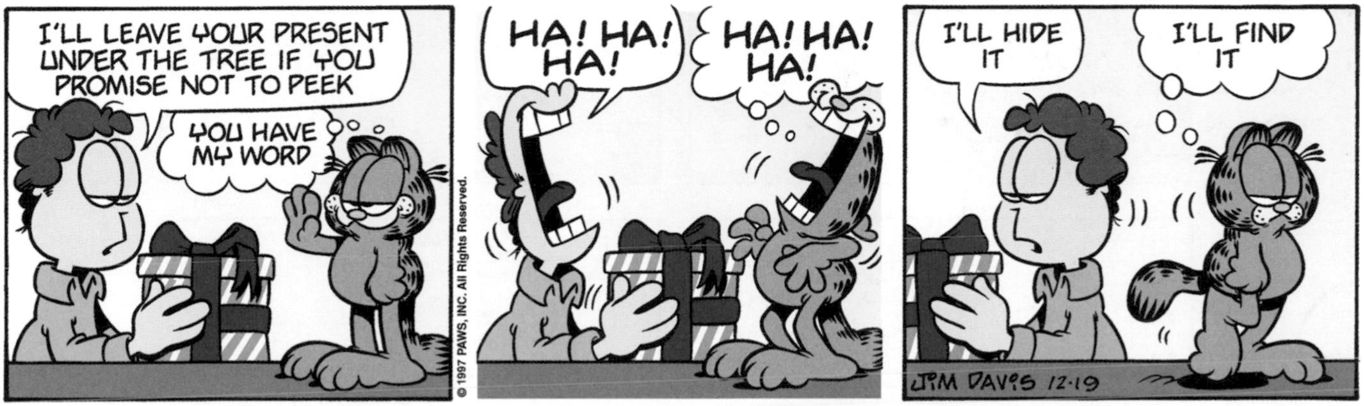
I'LL LEAVE YOUR PRESENT UNDER THE TREE IF YOU PROMISE NOT TO PEEK
YOU HAVE MY WORD
© 1997 PAWS, INC. All Rights Reserved.
HA! HA! HA!
HA! HA! HA!
I'LL HIDE IT
I'LL FIND IT
JIM DAVIS 12-19

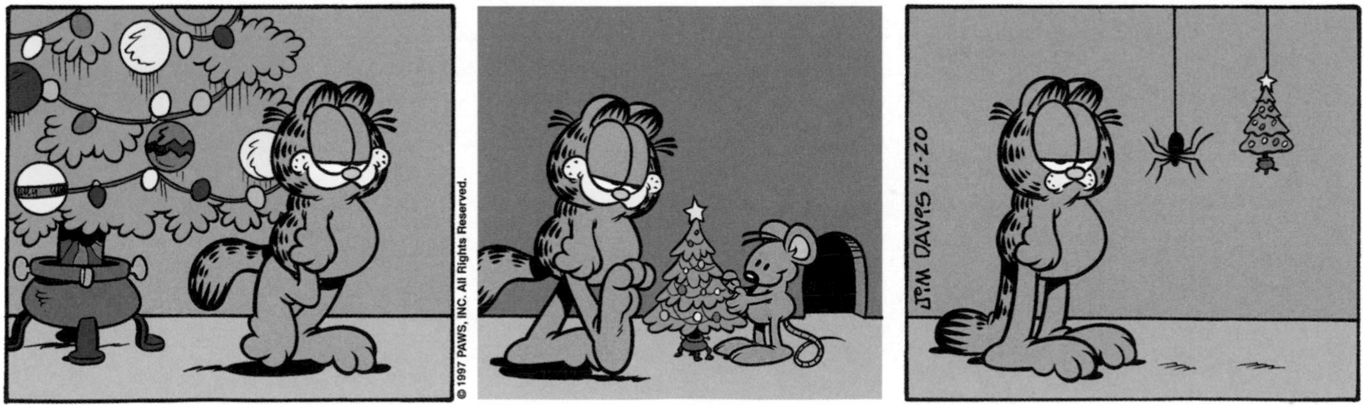
© 1997 PAWS, INC. All Rights Reserved.
JIM DAVIS 12-20

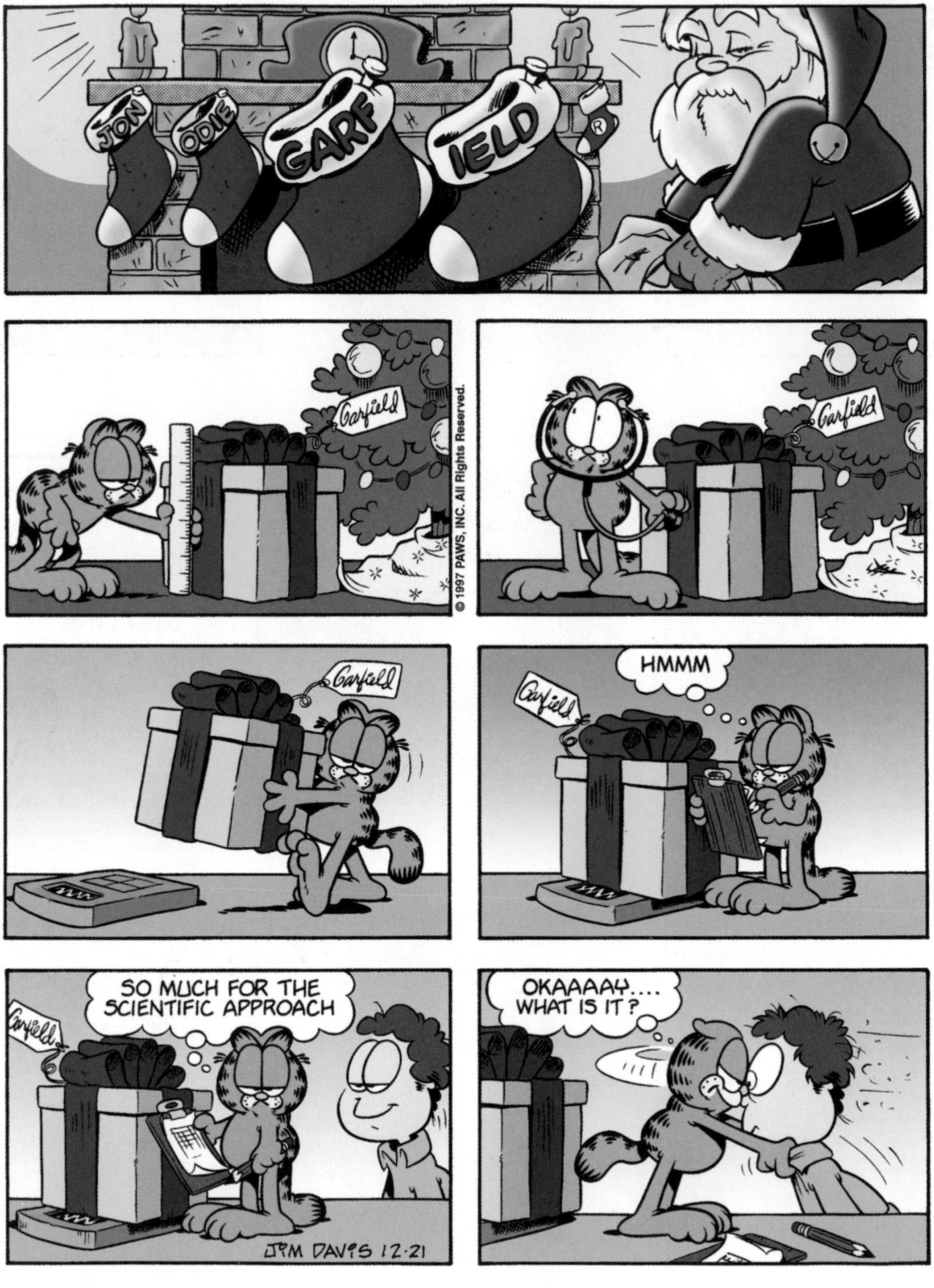
JON
ODIE
GARF
IELD
Garfield
© 1997 PAWS, INC. All Rights Reserved.
Garfield
Garfield
HMMM
Garfield
Garfield
SO MUCH FOR THE SCIENTIFIC APPROACH
JIM DAVIS 12·21
OKAAAAY....
WHAT IS IT?

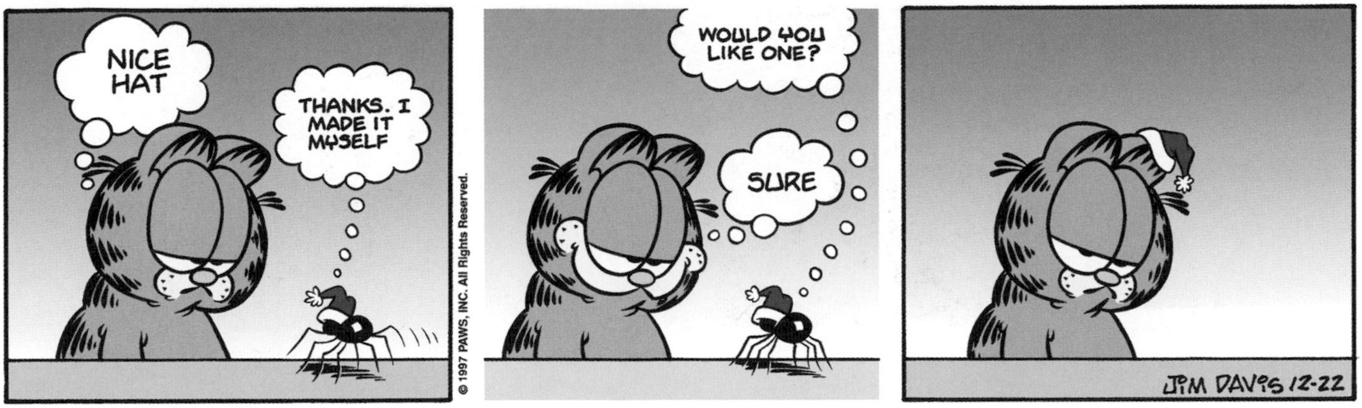
NICE HAT
THANKS. I MADE IT MYSELF
© 1997 PAWS, INC. All Rights Reserved.
WOULD YOU LIKE ONE?
SURE
JIM DAVIS 12-22

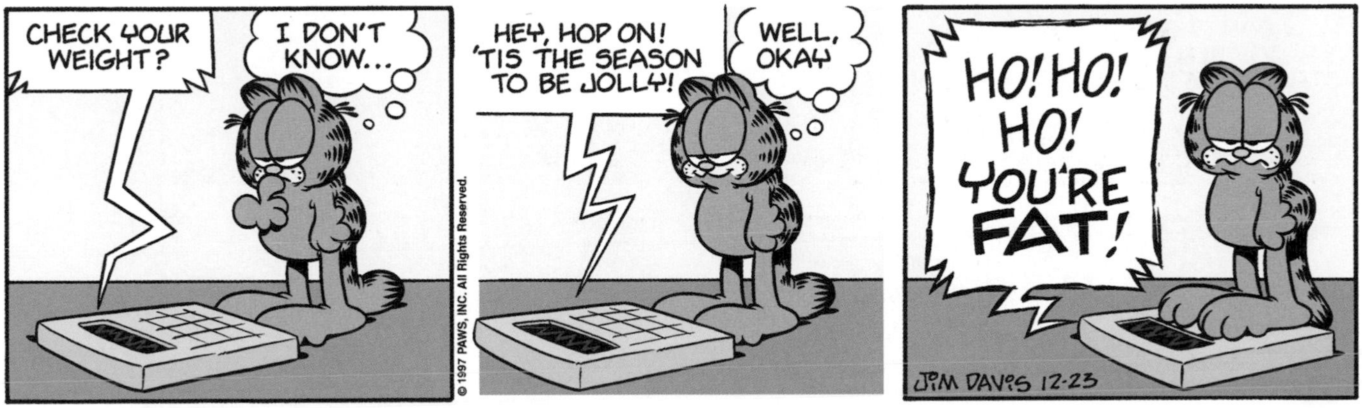
CHECK YOUR WEIGHT?
I DON'T KNOW...
© 1997 PAWS, INC. All Rights Reserved.
HEY, HOP ON! 'TIS THE SEASON TO BE JOLLY!
WELL, OKAY
HO! HO! HO! YOU'RE FAT!
JIM DAVIS 12-23

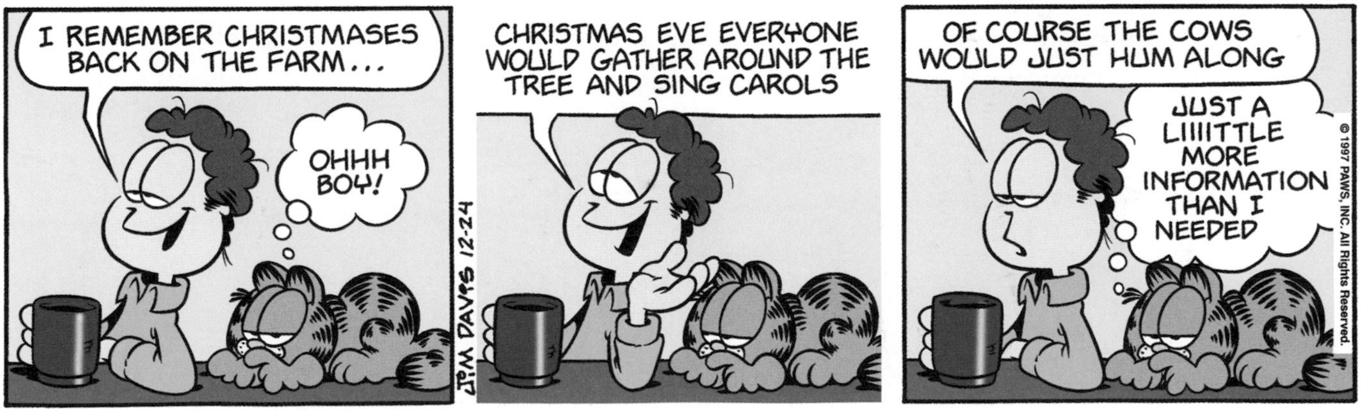
I REMEMBER CHRISTMASES BACK ON THE FARM...
OHHH BOY!
JIM DAVIS 12-24
CHRISTMAS EVE EVERYONE WOULD GATHER AROUND THE TREE AND SING CAROLS
OF COURSE THE COWS WOULD JUST HUM ALONG
JUST A LIIIITTLE MORE INFORMATION THAN I NEEDED
© 1997 PAWS, INC. All Rights Reserved.

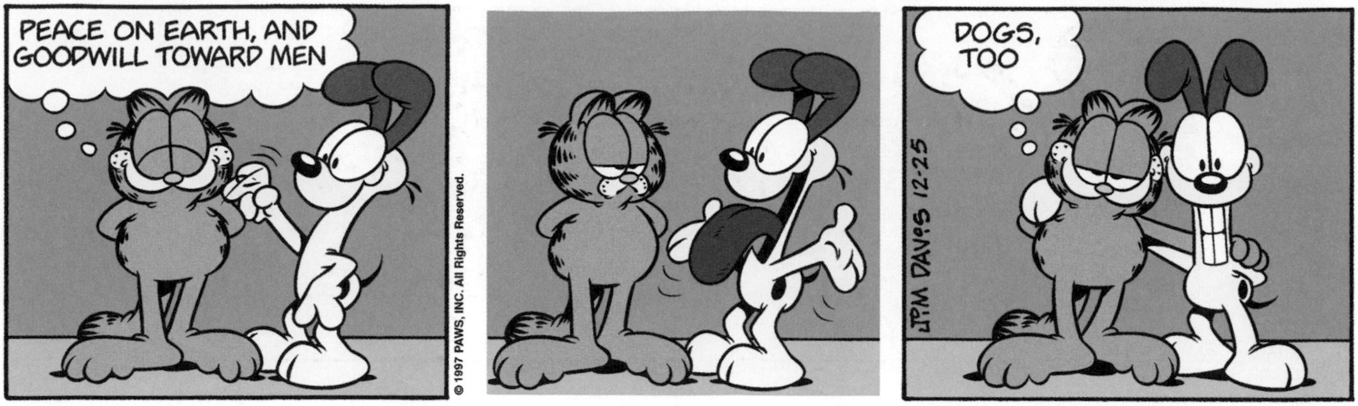
PEACE ON EARTH, AND GOODWILL TOWARD MEN
DOGS, TOO
JIM DAVIS 12-25

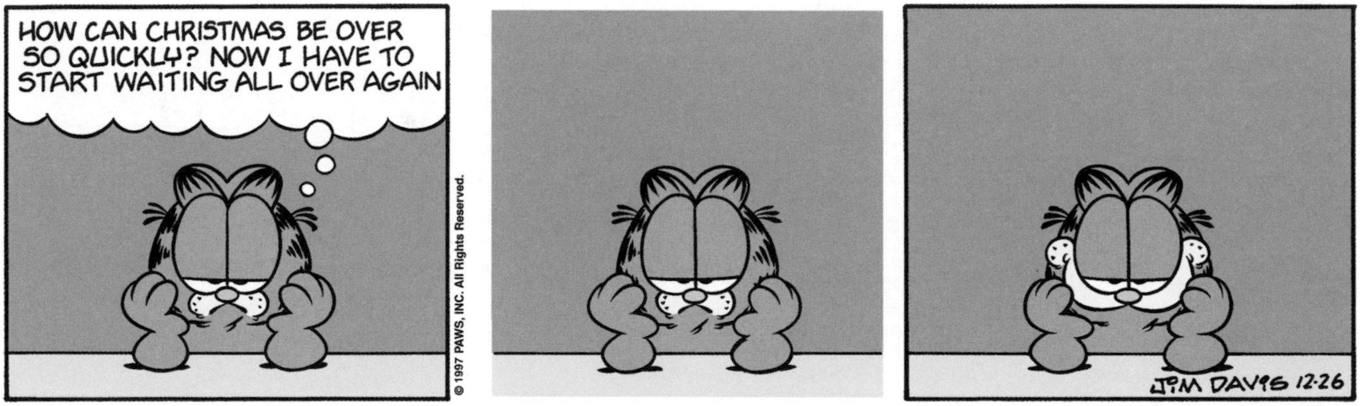
HOW CAN CHRISTMAS BE OVER SO QUICKLY? NOW I HAVE TO START WAITING ALL OVER AGAIN
JIM DAVIS 12-26

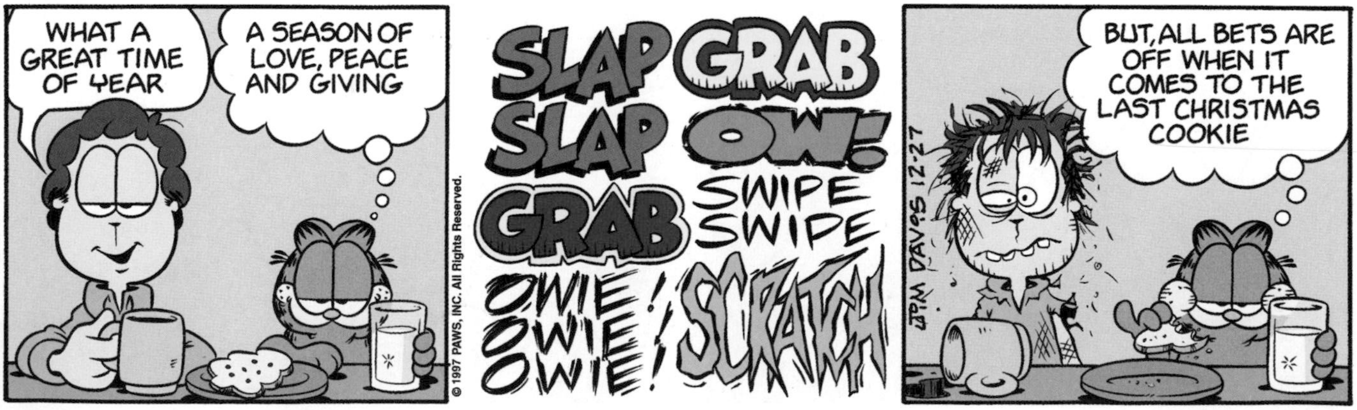
WHAT A GREAT TIME OF YEAR
A SEASON OF LOVE, PEACE AND GIVING
SLAP GRAB
SLAP OW!
GRAB SWIPE SWIPE
OWIE! OWIE! OWIE! SCRATCH
BUT, ALL BETS ARE OFF WHEN IT COMES TO THE LAST CHRISTMAS COOKIE
JIM DAVIS 12-27

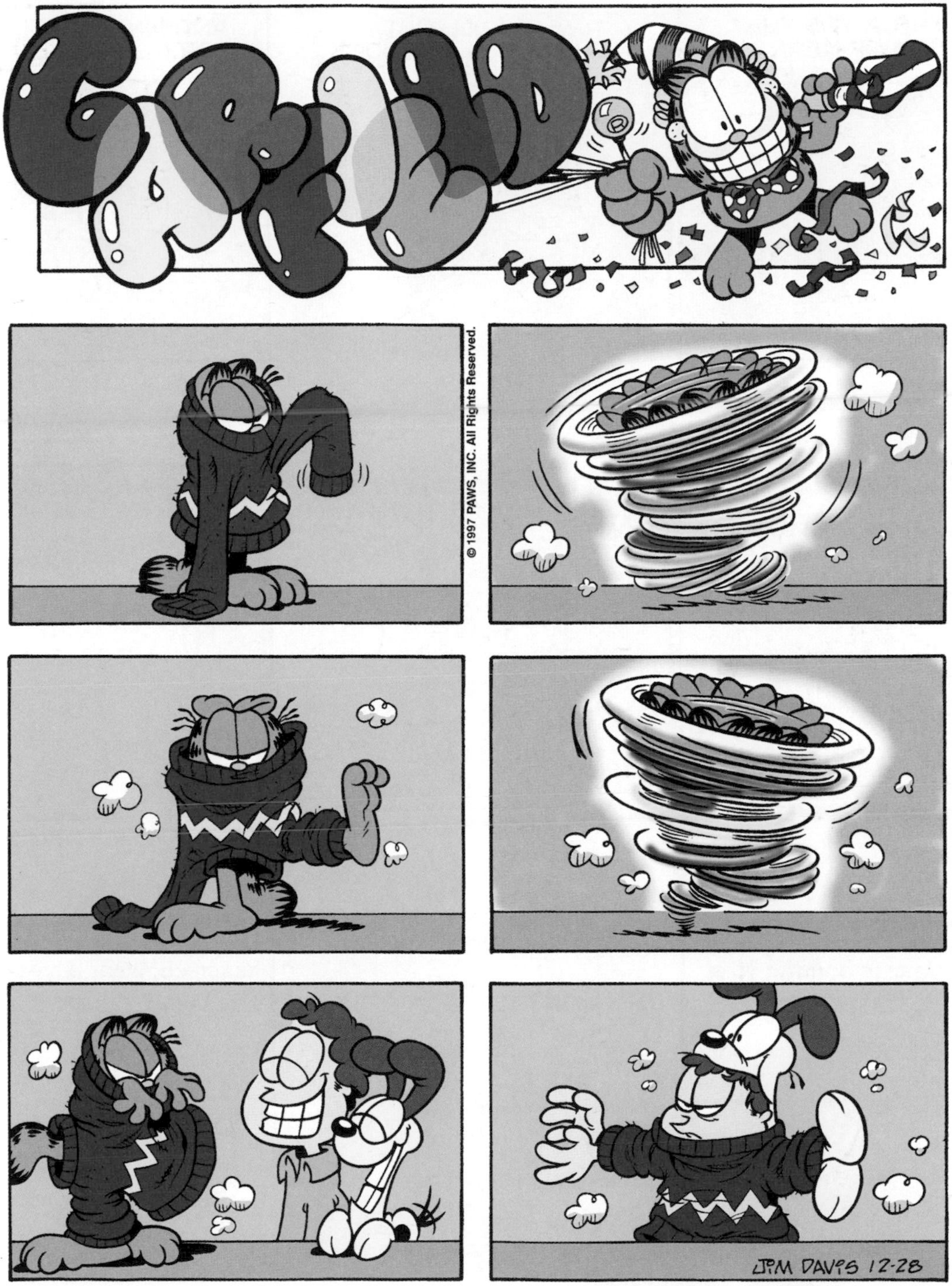
GARFIELD
© 1997 PAWS, INC. All Rights Reserved.
JIM DAVIS 12-28

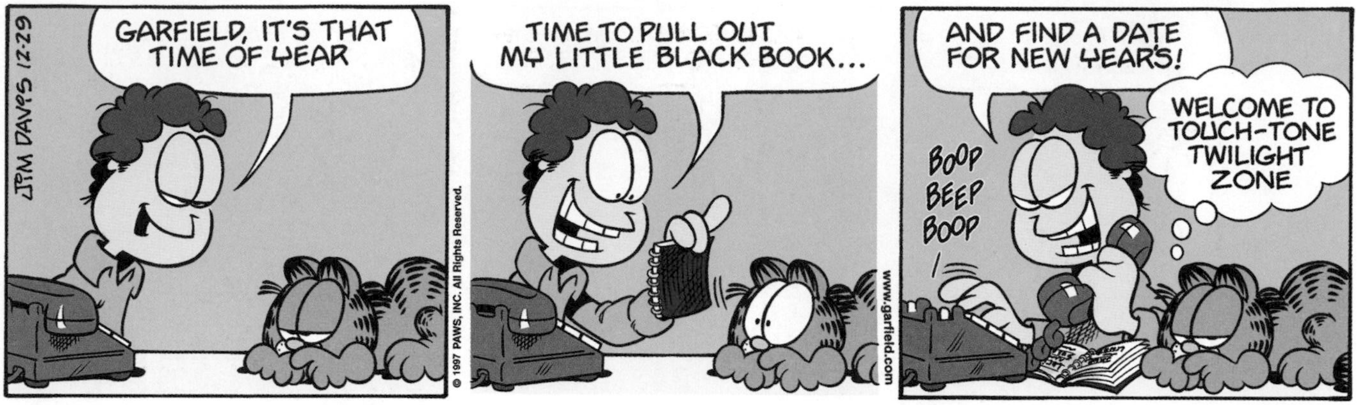
JIM DAVIS 12-29
GARFIELD, IT'S THAT TIME OF YEAR
TIME TO PULL OUT MY LITTLE BLACK BOOK...
© 1997 PAWS, INC. All Rights Reserved.
AND FIND A DATE FOR NEW YEAR'S!
BOOP BEEP BOOP
WELCOME TO TOUCH-TONE TWILIGHT ZONE
www.garfield.com

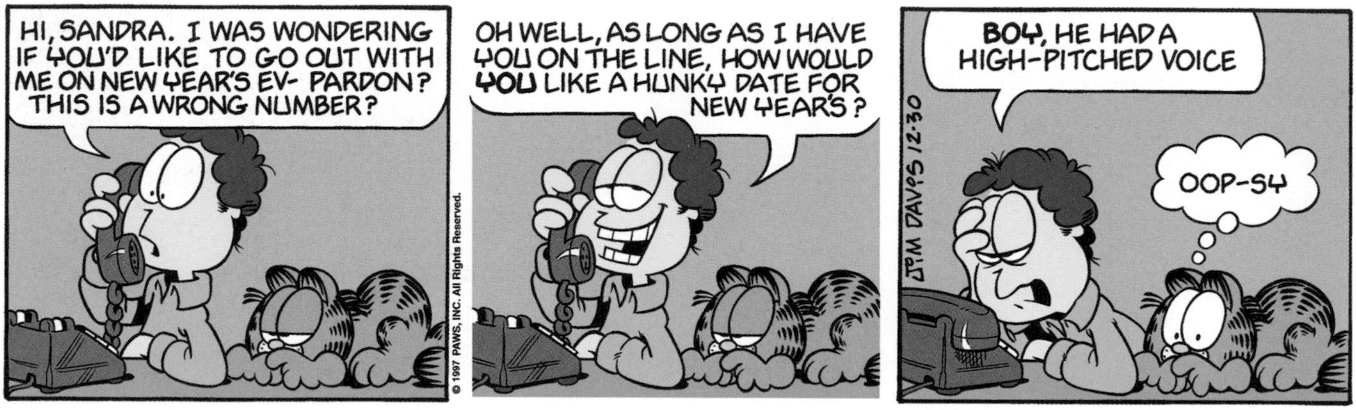
HI, SANDRA. I WAS WONDERING IF YOU'D LIKE TO GO OUT WITH ME ON NEW YEAR'S EV- PARDON? THIS IS A WRONG NUMBER?
© 1997 PAWS, INC. All Rights Reserved.
OH WELL, AS LONG AS I HAVE YOU ON THE LINE, HOW WOULD YOU LIKE A HUNKY DATE FOR NEW YEAR'S?
JIM DAVIS 12-30
BOY, HE HAD A HIGH-PITCHED VOICE
OOP-SY

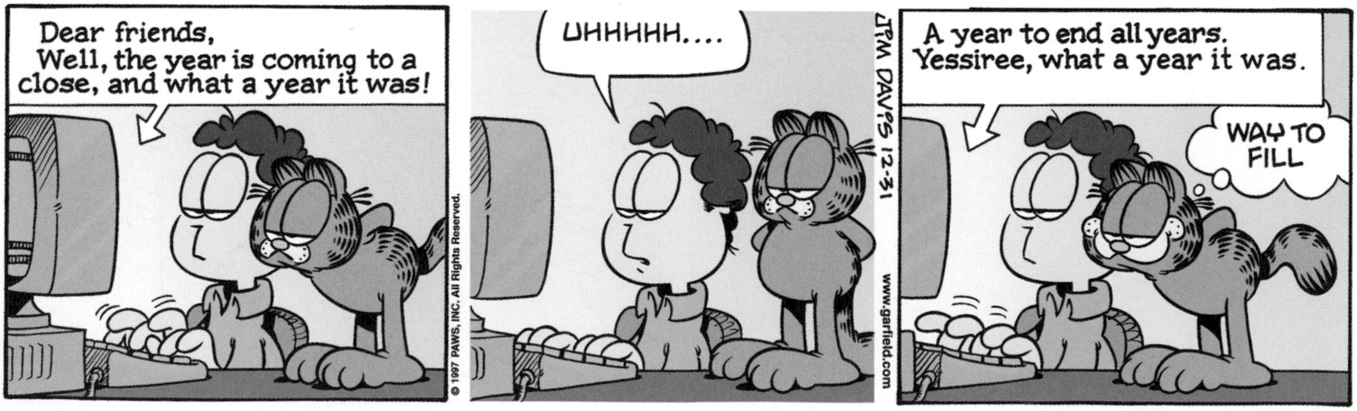
Dear friends,
Well, the year is coming to a close, and what a year it was!
© 1997 PAWS, INC. All Rights Reserved.
UHHHHH....
JIM DAVIS 12-31
www.garfield.com
A year to end all years. Yessiree, what a year it was.
WAY TO FILL

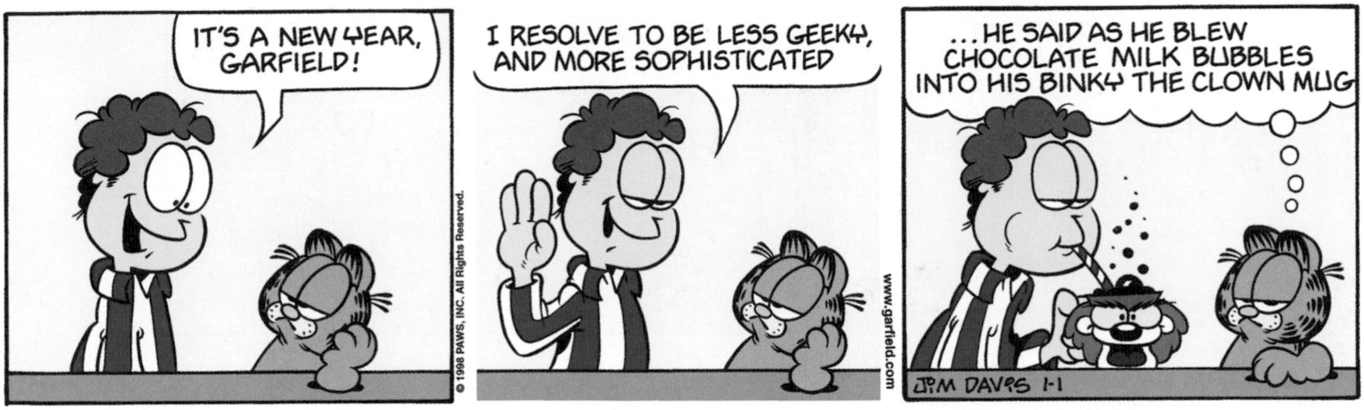
IT'S A NEW YEAR, GARFIELD!
© 1998 PAWS, INC. All Rights Reserved.
I RESOLVE TO BE LESS GEEKY, AND MORE SOPHISTICATED
www.garfield.com
...HE SAID AS HE BLEW CHOCOLATE MILK BUBBLES INTO HIS BINKY THE CLOWN MUG
JIM DAVIS 1-1

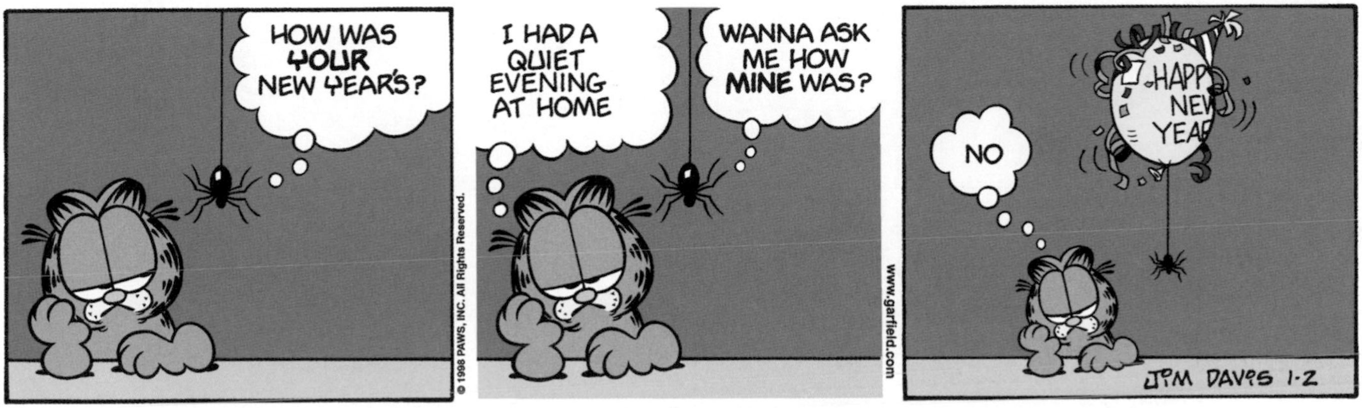
HOW WAS **YOUR** NEW YEAR'S?
© 1998 PAWS, INC. All Rights Reserved.
I HAD A QUIET EVENING AT HOME
WANNA ASK ME HOW **MINE** WAS?
www.garfield.com
NO
JIM DAVIS 1-2

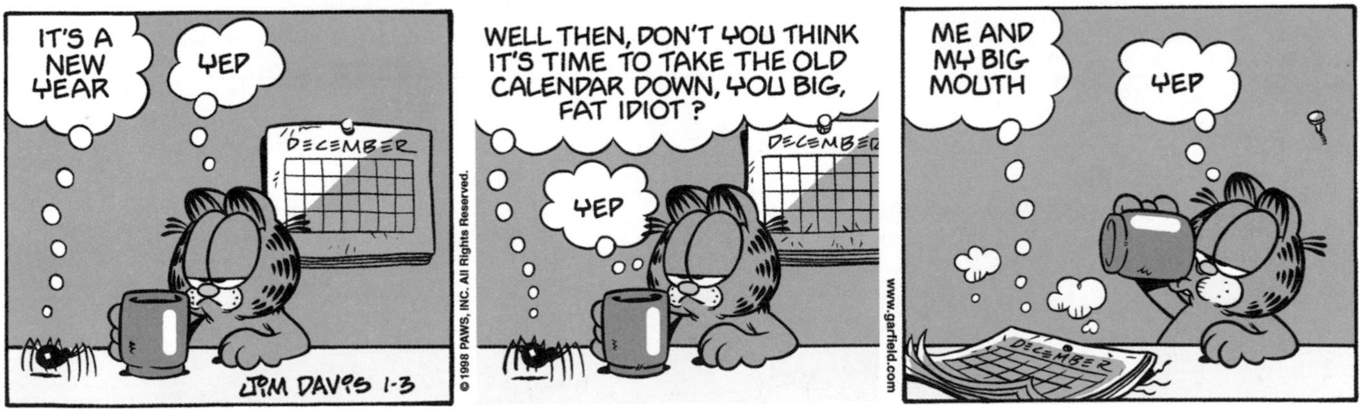
IT'S A NEW YEAR
YEP
DECEMBER
JIM DAVIS 1-3
© 1998 PAWS, INC. All Rights Reserved.
WELL THEN, DON'T YOU THINK IT'S TIME TO TAKE THE OLD CALENDAR DOWN, YOU BIG, FAT IDIOT?
YEP
www.garfield.com
ME AND MY BIG MOUTH
YEP
DECEMBER

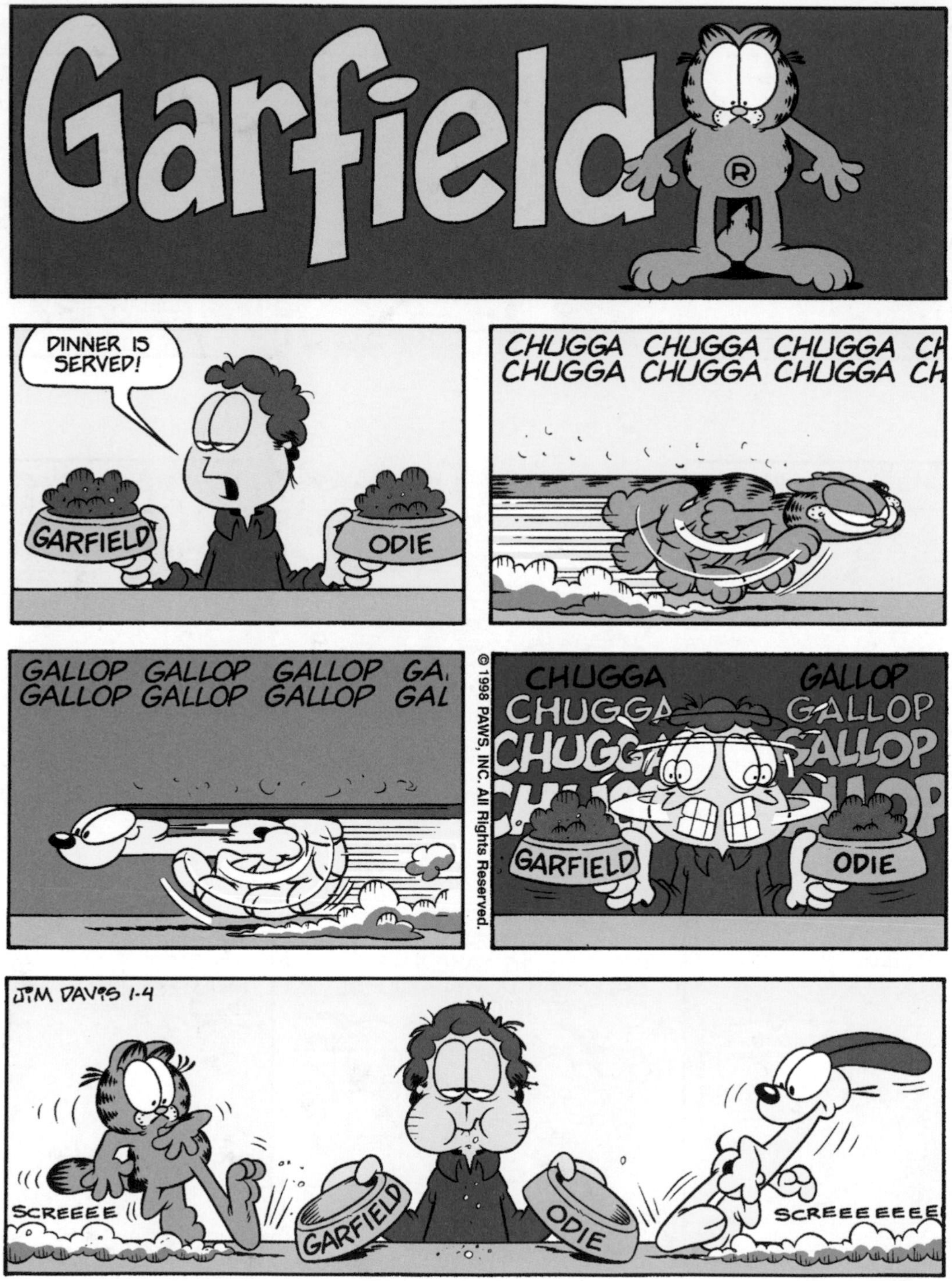
Garfield
DINNER IS SERVED!
GARFIELD
ODIE
CHUGGA CHUGGA CHUGGA
CHUGGA CHUGGA CHUGGA
GALLOP GALLOP GALLOP
GALLOP GALLOP GALLOP
CHUGGA
GALLOP
CHUGGA
GALLOP
GARFIELD
ODIE
JIM DAVIS 1-4
SCREEEE
GARFIELD
ODIE
SCREEEEEEEE

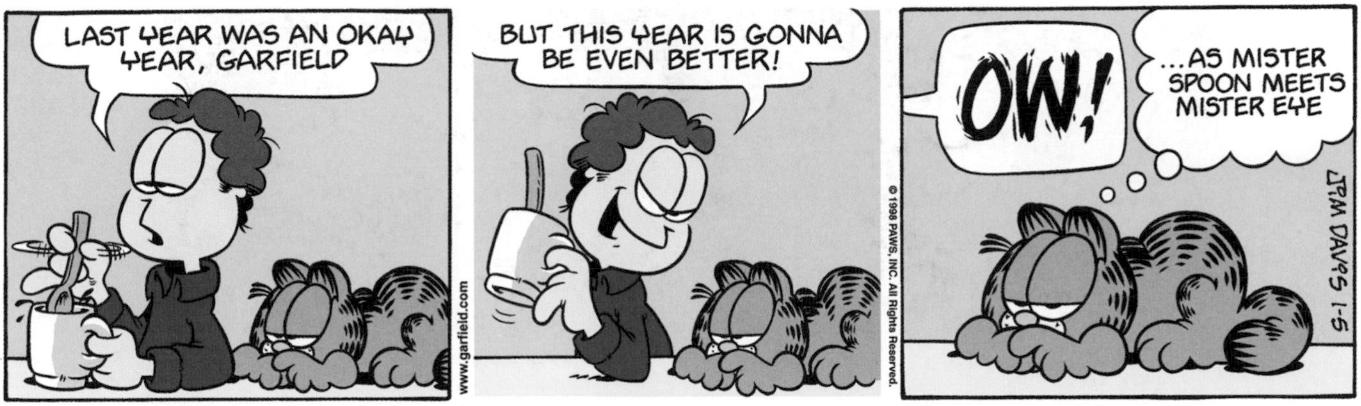
LAST YEAR WAS AN OKAY YEAR, GARFIELD
www.garfield.com
BUT THIS YEAR IS GONNA BE EVEN BETTER!
© 1998 PAWS, INC. All Rights Reserved.
OW!
...AS MISTER SPOON MEETS MISTER EYE
JIM DAVIS 1-5

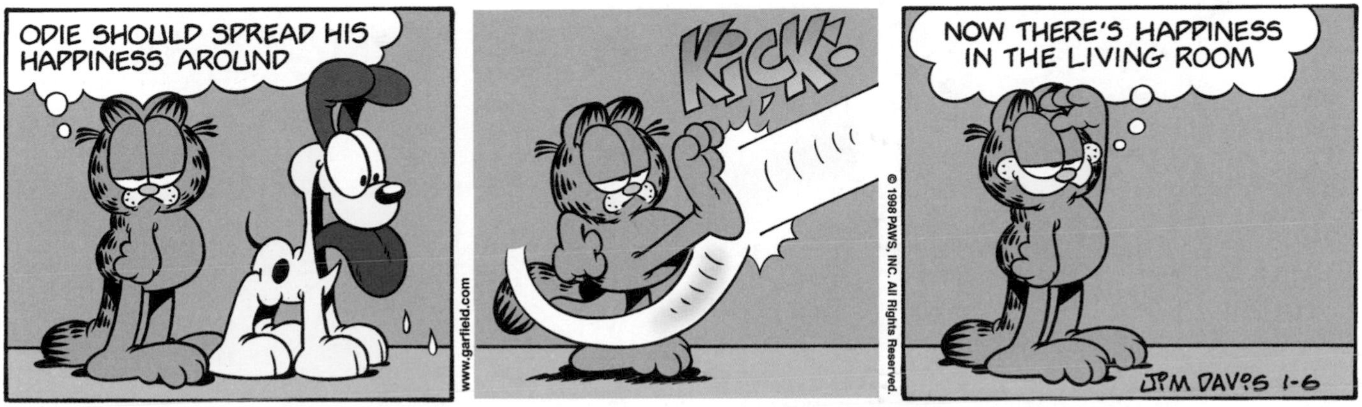
ODIE SHOULD SPREAD HIS HAPPINESS AROUND
www.garfield.com
KICK!
© 1998 PAWS, INC. All Rights Reserved.
NOW THERE'S HAPPINESS IN THE LIVING ROOM
JIM DAVIS 1-6

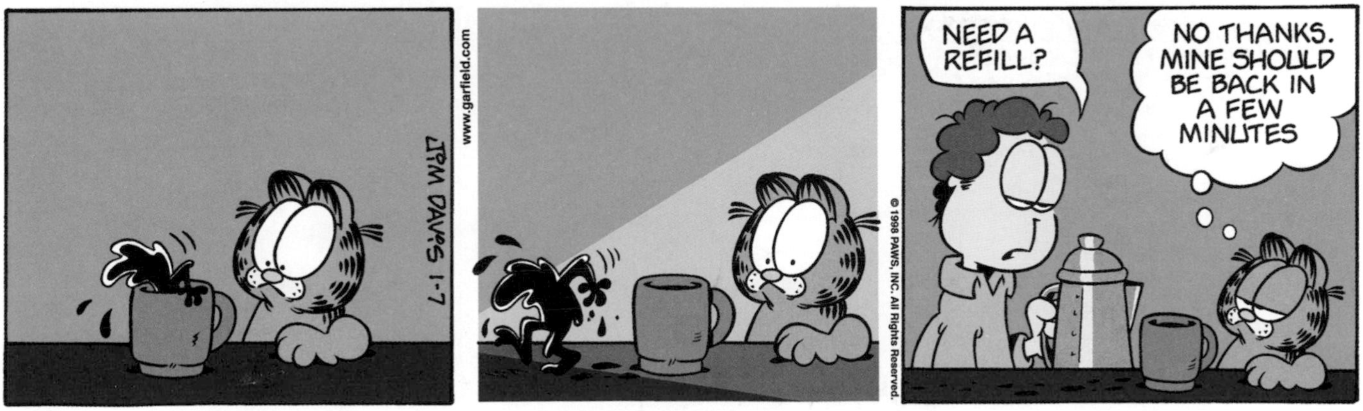
JIM DAVIS 1-7
www.garfield.com
© 1998 PAWS, INC. All Rights Reserved.
NEED A REFILL?
NO THANKS. MINE SHOULD BE BACK IN A FEW MINUTES

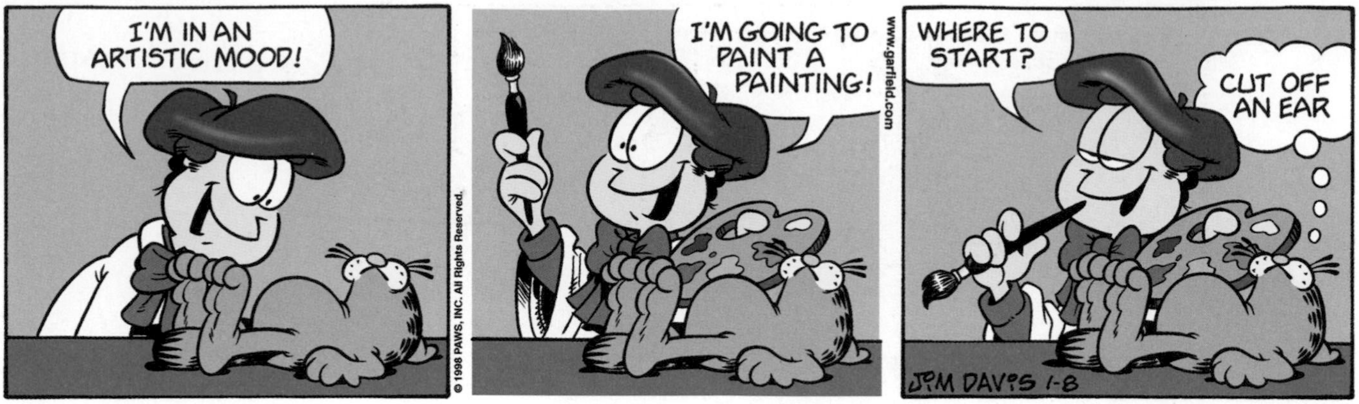
I'M IN AN ARTISTIC MOOD!
I'M GOING TO PAINT A PAINTING!
WHERE TO START?
CUT OFF AN EAR

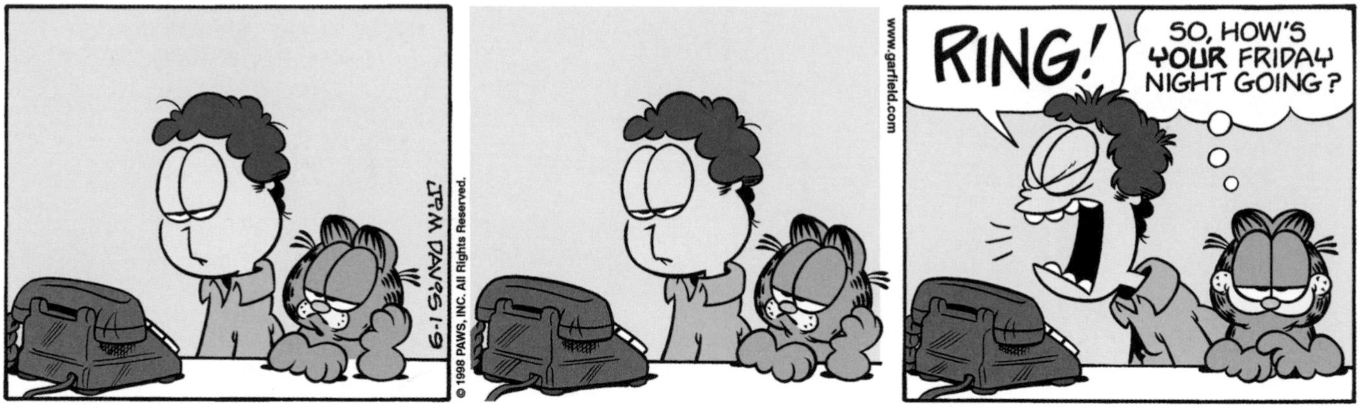
RING!
SO, HOW'S **YOUR** FRIDAY NIGHT GOING?

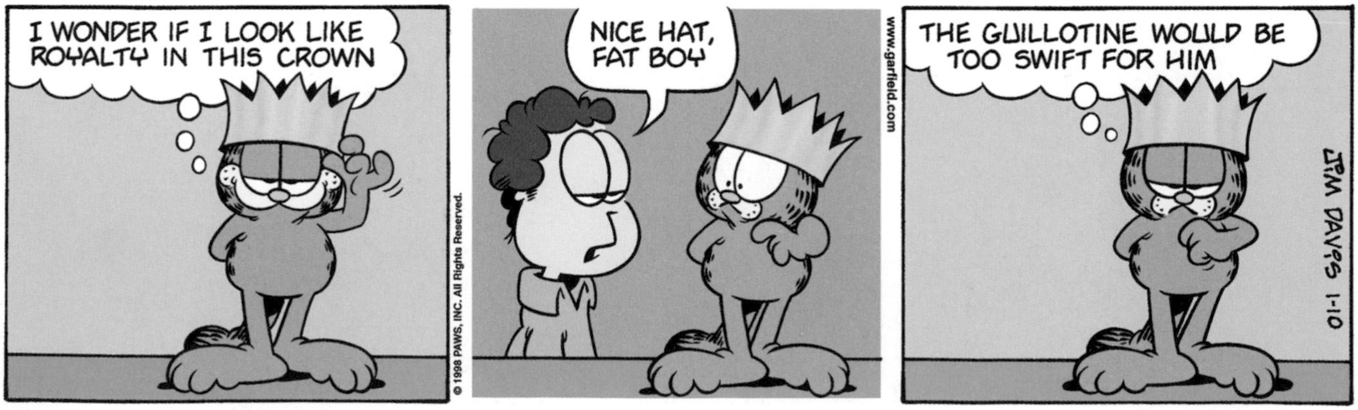
I WONDER IF I LOOK LIKE ROYALTY IN THIS CROWN
NICE HAT, FAT BOY
THE GUILLOTINE WOULD BE TOO SWIFT FOR HIM

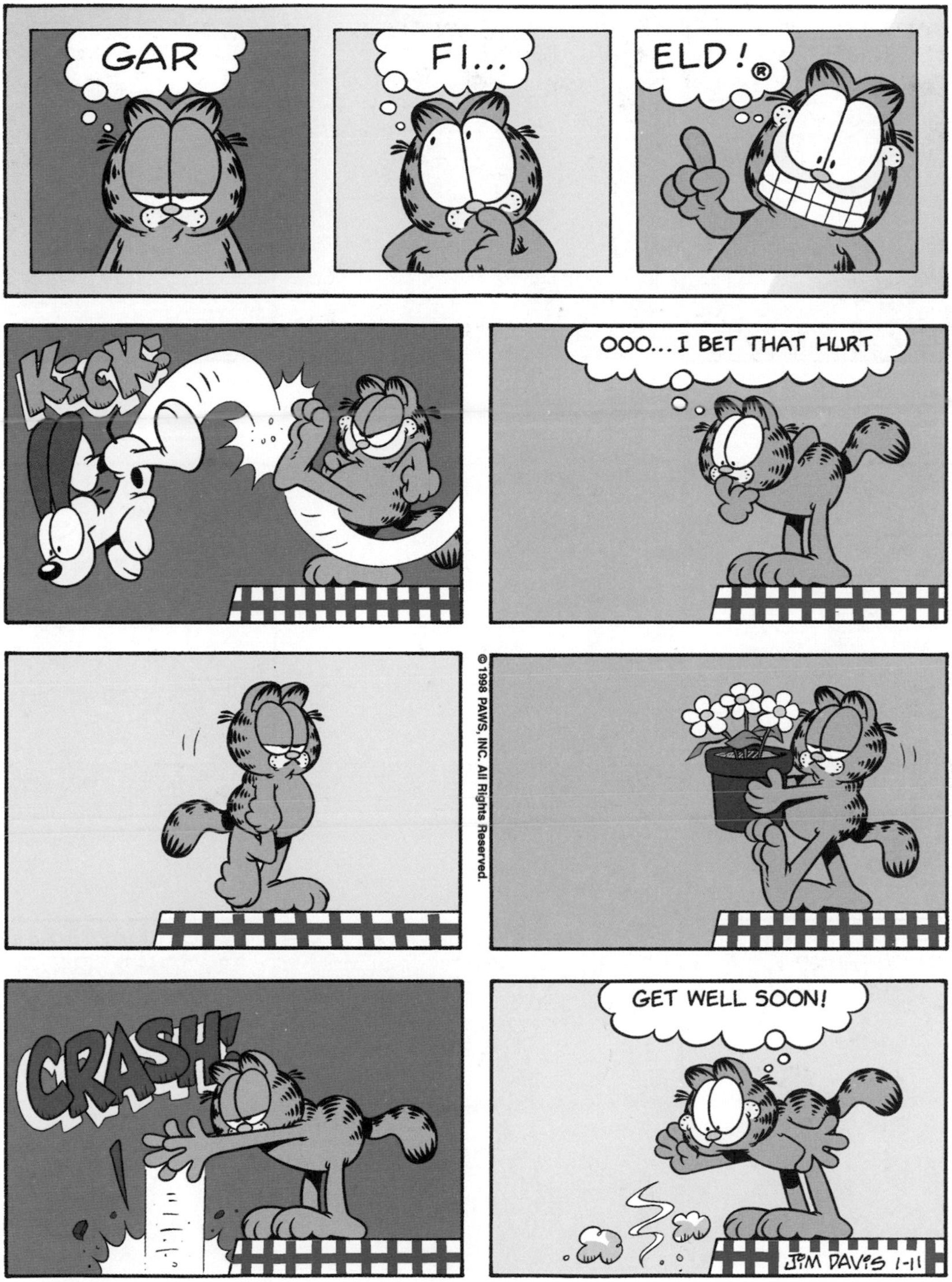
GAR
FI...
ELD! ®
KICK!
OOO... I BET THAT HURT
CRASH!
GET WELL SOON!
JIM DAVIS 1-11

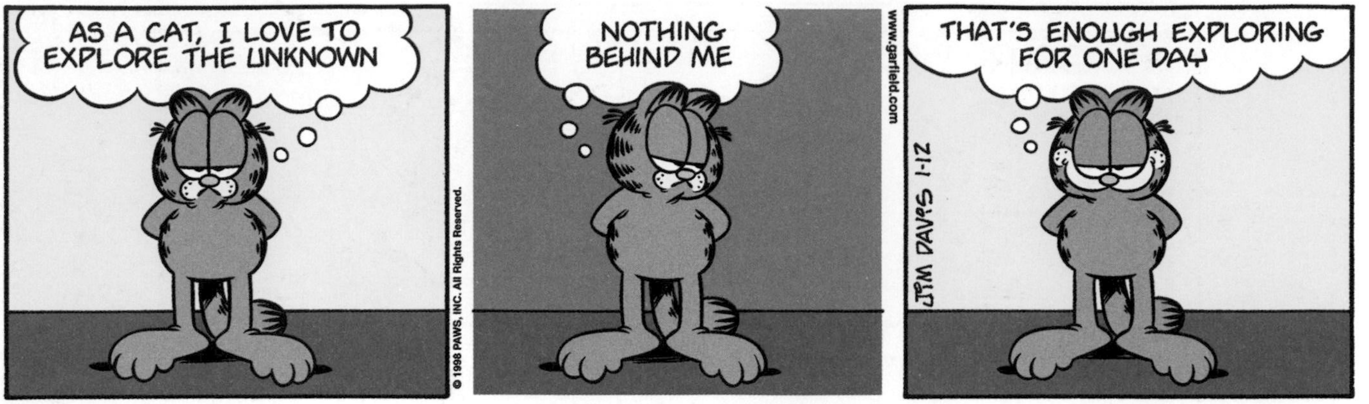
AS A CAT, I LOVE TO EXPLORE THE UNKNOWN
© 1998 PAWS, INC. All Rights Reserved.
NOTHING BEHIND ME
www.garfield.com
THAT'S ENOUGH EXPLORING FOR ONE DAY
JIM DAVIS 1-12

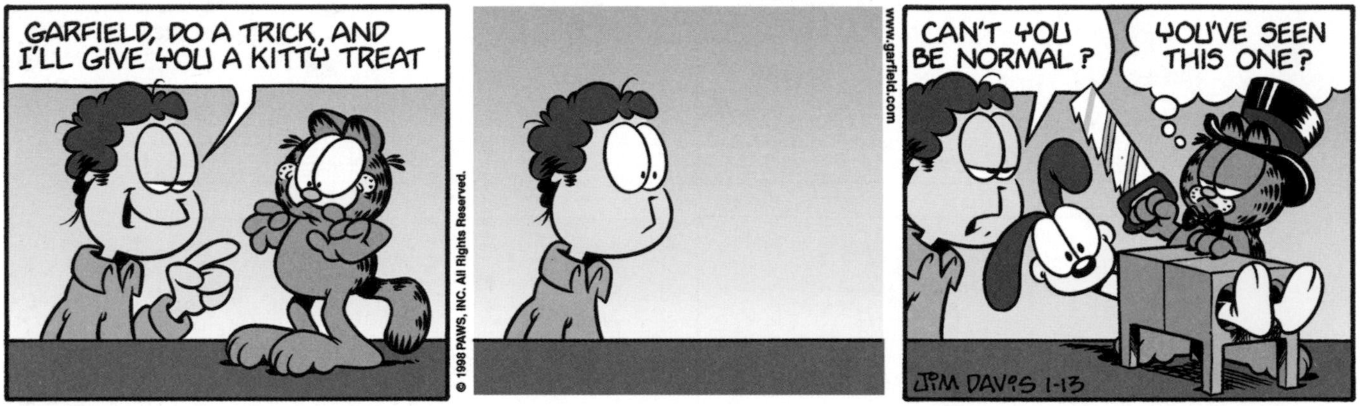
GARFIELD, DO A TRICK, AND I'LL GIVE YOU A KITTY TREAT
© 1998 PAWS, INC. All Rights Reserved.
www.garfield.com
CAN'T YOU BE NORMAL ?
YOU'VE SEEN THIS ONE ?
JIM DAVIS 1-13

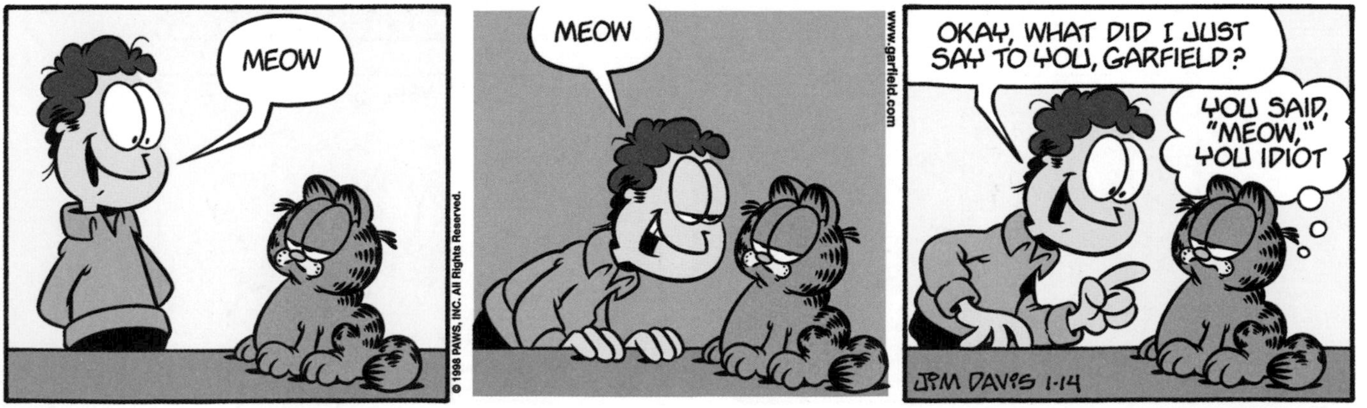
MEOW
© 1998 PAWS, INC. All Rights Reserved.
MEOW
www.garfield.com
OKAY, WHAT DID I JUST SAY TO YOU, GARFIELD ?
YOU SAID, "MEOW," YOU IDIOT
JIM DAVIS 1-14

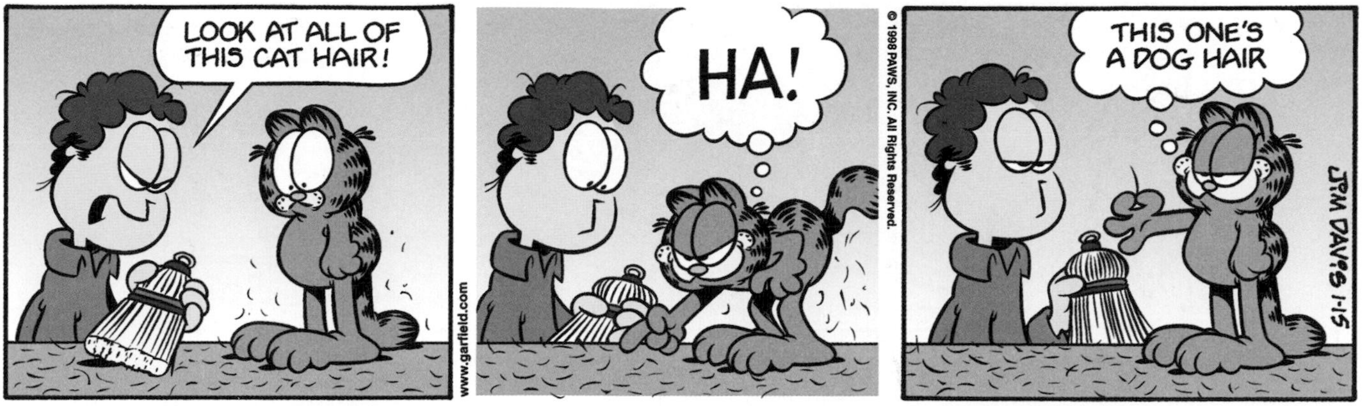
LOOK AT ALL OF THIS CAT HAIR!
www.garfield.com
HA!
© 1998 PAWS, INC. All Rights Reserved.
THIS ONE'S A DOG HAIR
JIM DAVIS 1-15

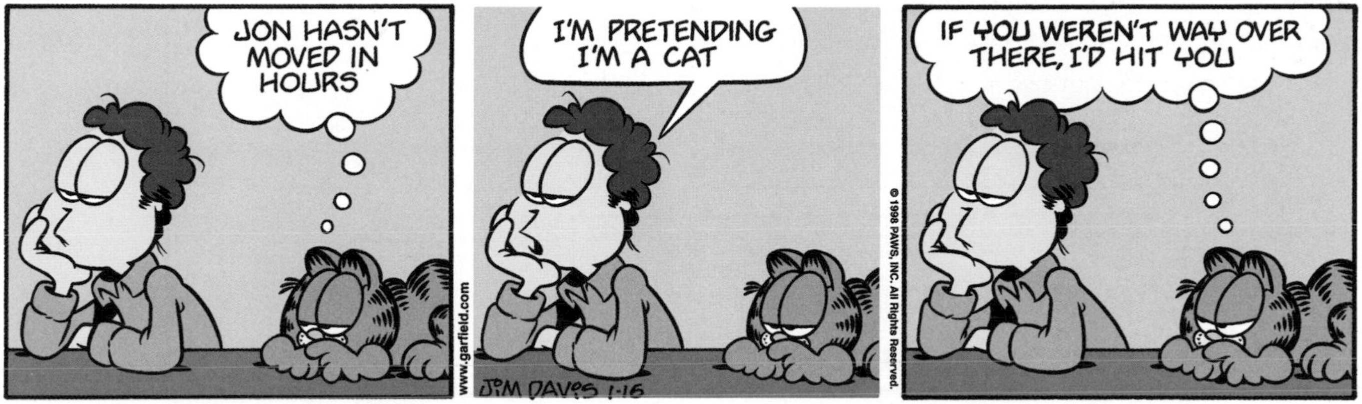
JON HASN'T MOVED IN HOURS
www.garfield.com
I'M PRETENDING I'M A CAT
JIM DAVIS 1-16
© 1998 PAWS, INC. All Rights Reserved.
IF YOU WEREN'T WAY OVER THERE, I'D HIT YOU

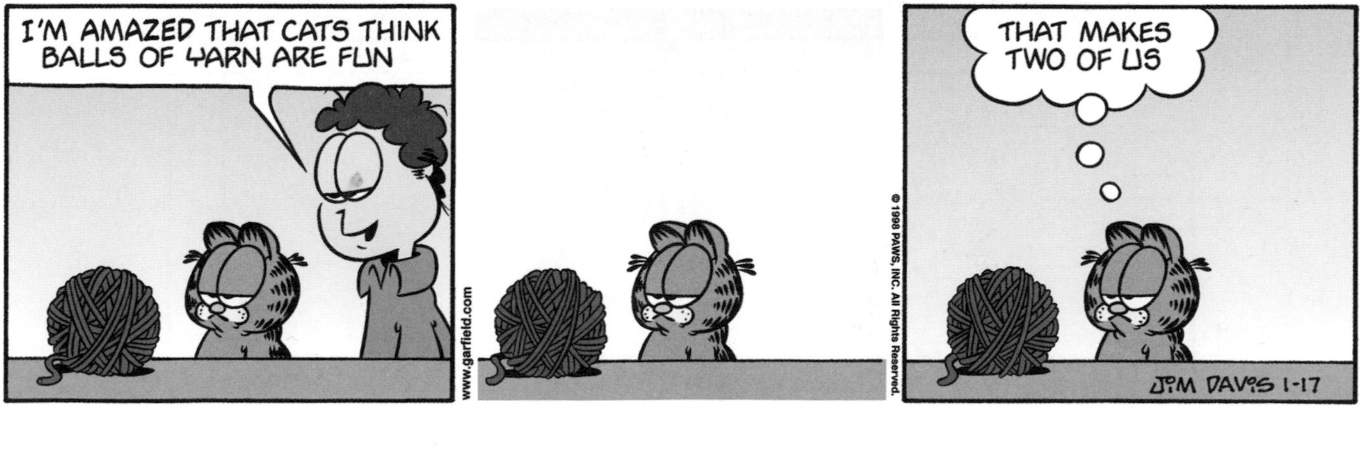
I'M AMAZED THAT CATS THINK BALLS OF YARN ARE FUN
www.garfield.com
© 1998 PAWS, INC. All Rights Reserved.
THAT MAKES TWO OF US
JIM DAVIS 1-17

GARFIELD
JIM DAVIS 1-18
© 1998 PAWS, INC. All Rights Reserved.
NYAH! NYAH! NYAH!
DOG IN A PICKUP TRUCK

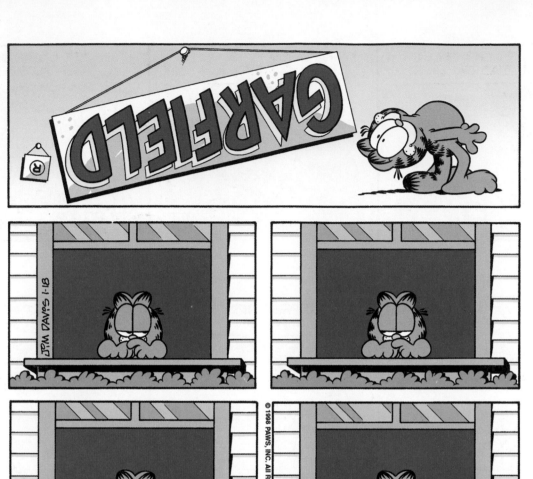

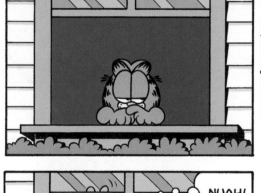

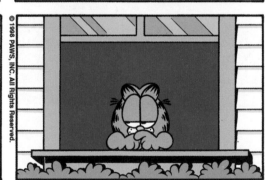

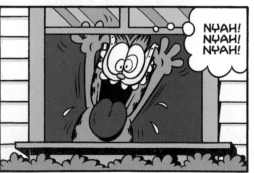

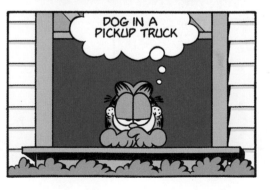

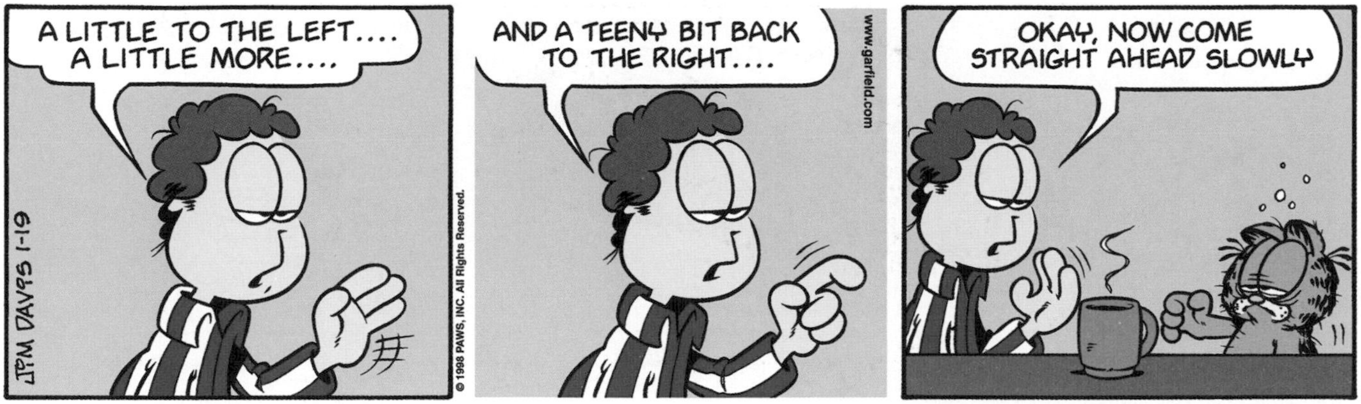
A LITTLE TO THE LEFT.... A LITTLE MORE....
JIM DAVIS 1-19
© 1998 PAWS, INC. All Rights Reserved.
AND A TEENY BIT BACK TO THE RIGHT....
www.garfield.com
OKAY, NOW COME STRAIGHT AHEAD SLOWLY

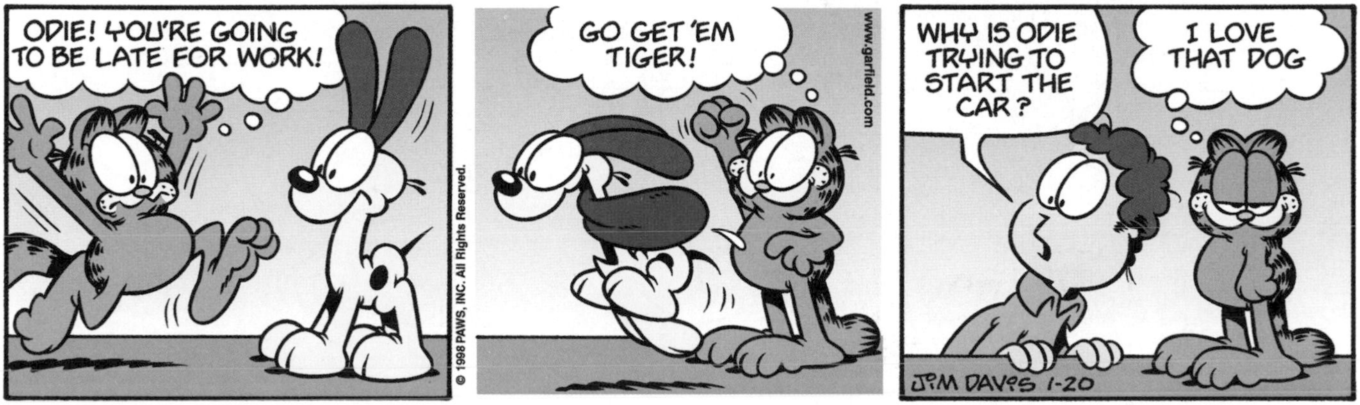
ODIE! YOU'RE GOING TO BE LATE FOR WORK!
© 1998 PAWS, INC. All Rights Reserved.
GO GET 'EM TIGER!
www.garfield.com
WHY IS ODIE TRYING TO START THE CAR?
I LOVE THAT DOG
JIM DAVIS 1-20

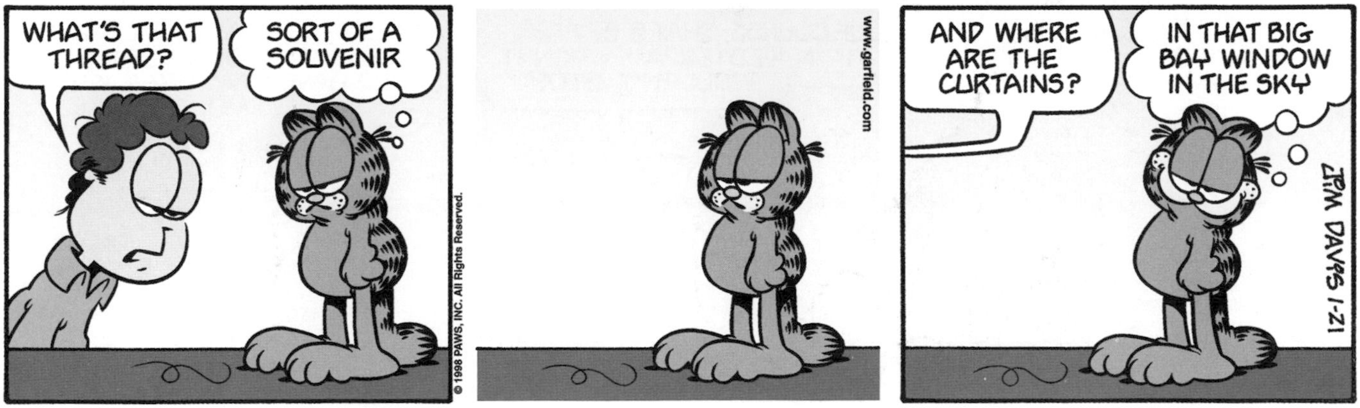
WHAT'S THAT THREAD?
SORT OF A SOUVENIR
© 1998 PAWS, INC. All Rights Reserved.
www.garfield.com
AND WHERE ARE THE CURTAINS?
IN THAT BIG BAY WINDOW IN THE SKY
JIM DAVIS 1-21

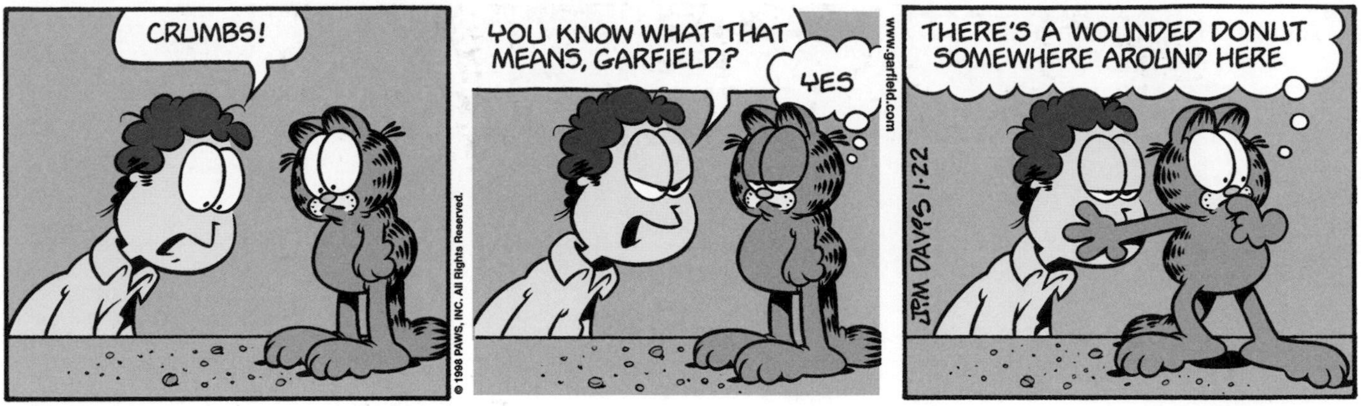
CRUMBS!
YOU KNOW WHAT THAT MEANS, GARFIELD?
YES
THERE'S A WOUNDED DONUT SOMEWHERE AROUND HERE
© 1998 PAWS, INC. All Rights Reserved.
www.garfield.com
JIM DAVIS 1-22

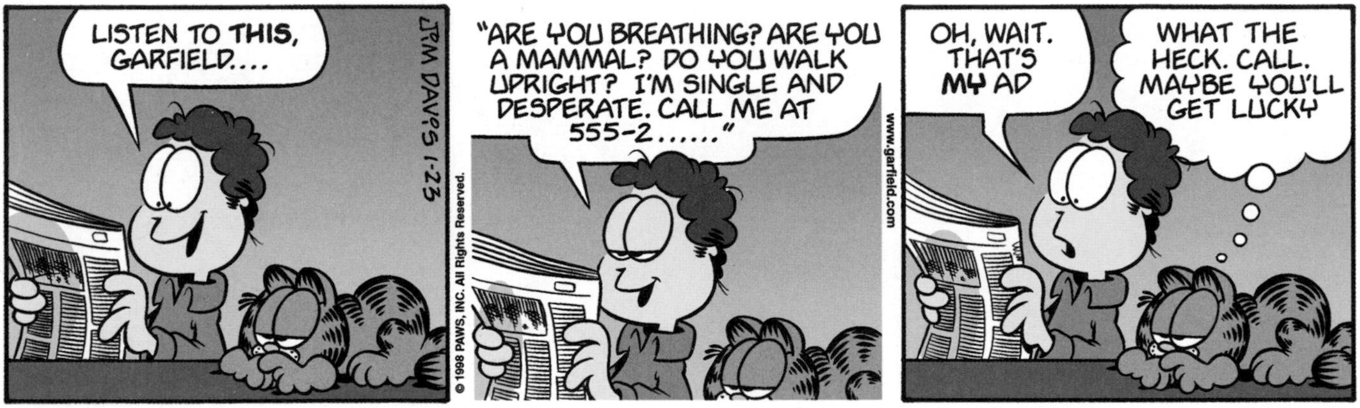
LISTEN TO **THIS**, GARFIELD....
"ARE YOU BREATHING? ARE YOU A MAMMAL? DO YOU WALK UPRIGHT? I'M SINGLE AND DESPERATE. CALL ME AT 555-2......"
OH, WAIT. THAT'S **MY** AD
WHAT THE HECK. CALL. MAYBE YOU'LL GET LUCKY
JIM DAVIS 1-23
© 1998 PAWS, INC. All Rights Reserved.
www.garfield.com

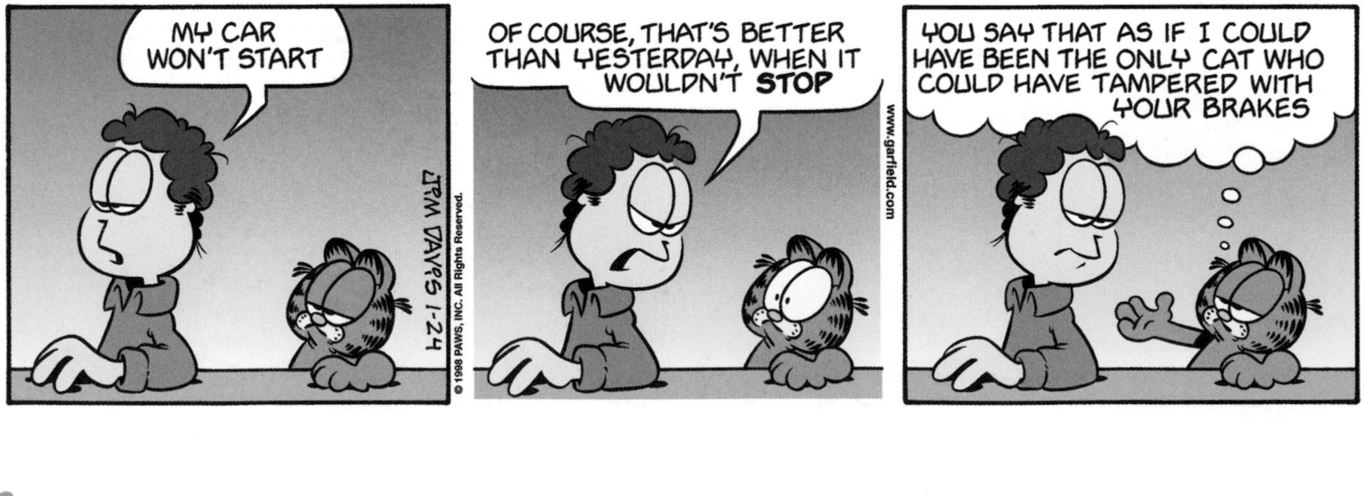
MY CAR WON'T START
OF COURSE, THAT'S BETTER THAN YESTERDAY, WHEN IT WOULDN'T **STOP**
YOU SAY THAT AS IF I COULD HAVE BEEN THE ONLY CAT WHO COULD HAVE TAMPERED WITH YOUR BRAKES
JIM DAVIS 1-24
© 1998 PAWS, INC. All Rights Reserved.
www.garfield.com

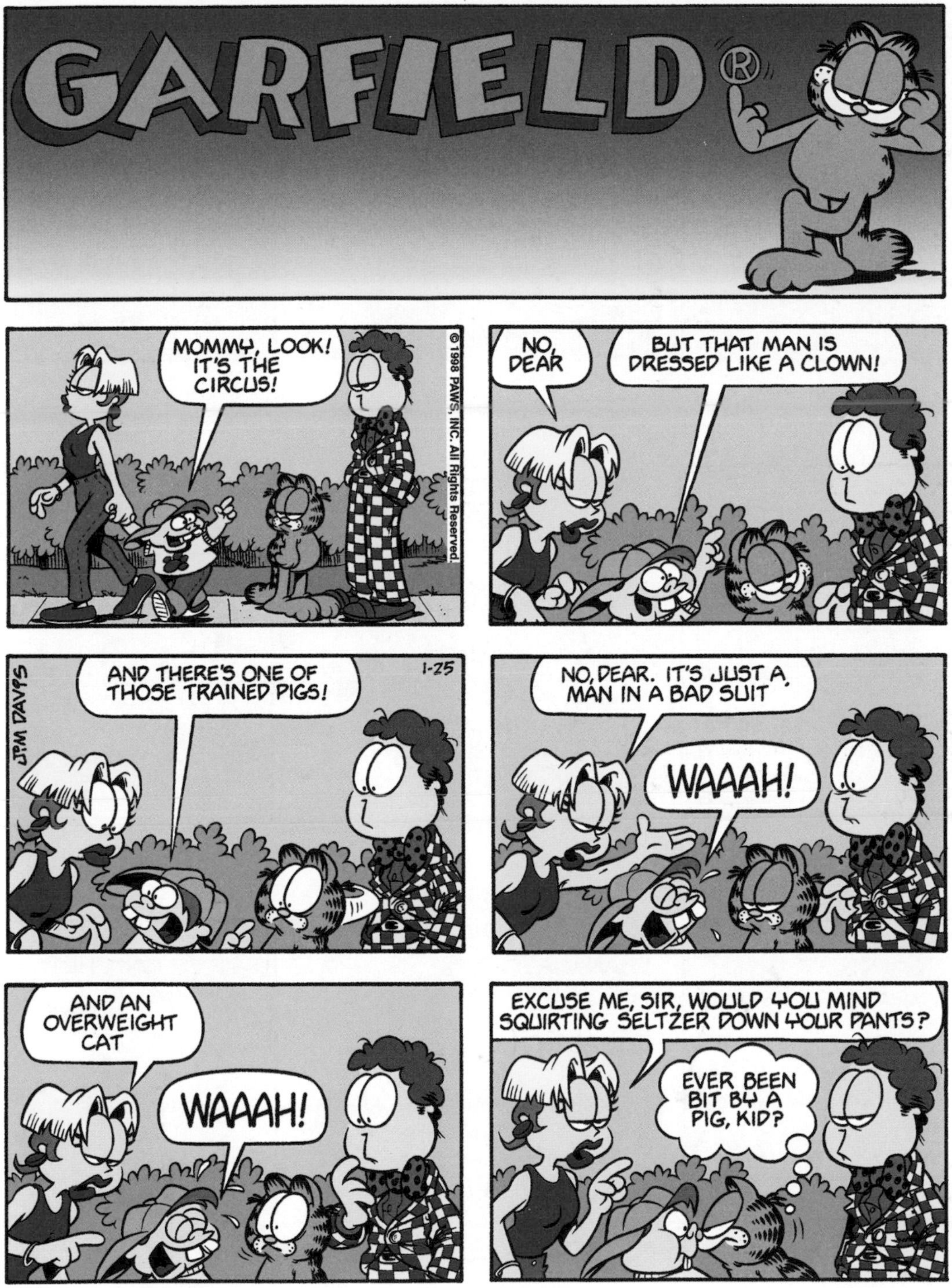
GARFIELD®
MOMMY, LOOK! IT'S THE CIRCUS!
© 1998 PAWS, INC. All Rights Reserved.
NO, DEAR
BUT THAT MAN IS DRESSED LIKE A CLOWN!
JPM DAVPS
1-25
AND THERE'S ONE OF THOSE TRAINED PIGS!
NO, DEAR. IT'S JUST A MAN IN A BAD SUIT
WAAAH!
AND AN OVERWEIGHT CAT
WAAAH!
EXCUSE ME, SIR, WOULD YOU MIND SQUIRTING SELTZER DOWN YOUR PANTS?
EVER BEEN BIT BY A PIG, KID?

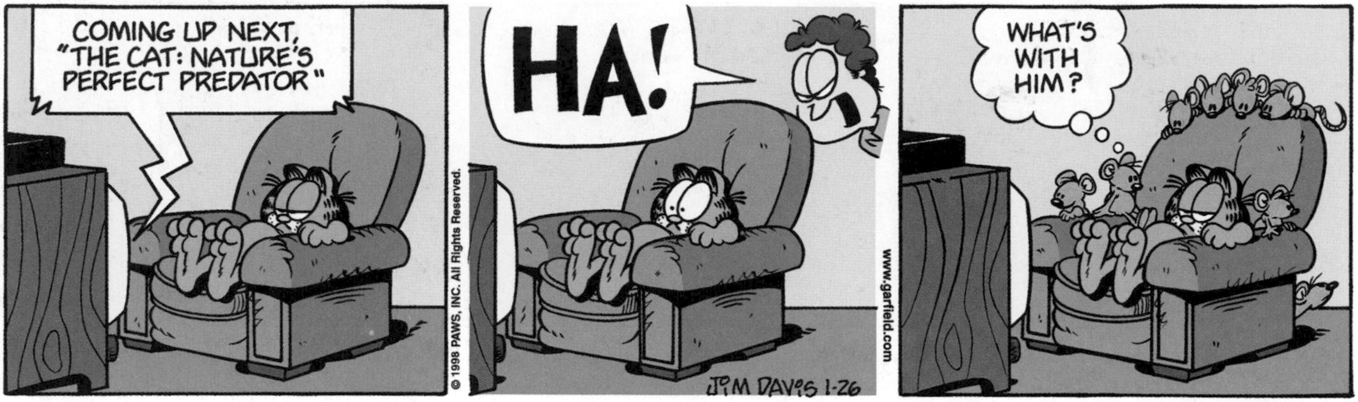
COMING UP NEXT, "THE CAT: NATURE'S PERFECT PREDATOR"
© 1998 PAWS, INC. All Rights Reserved.
HA!
JIM DAVIS 1-26
www.garfield.com
WHAT'S WITH HIM?

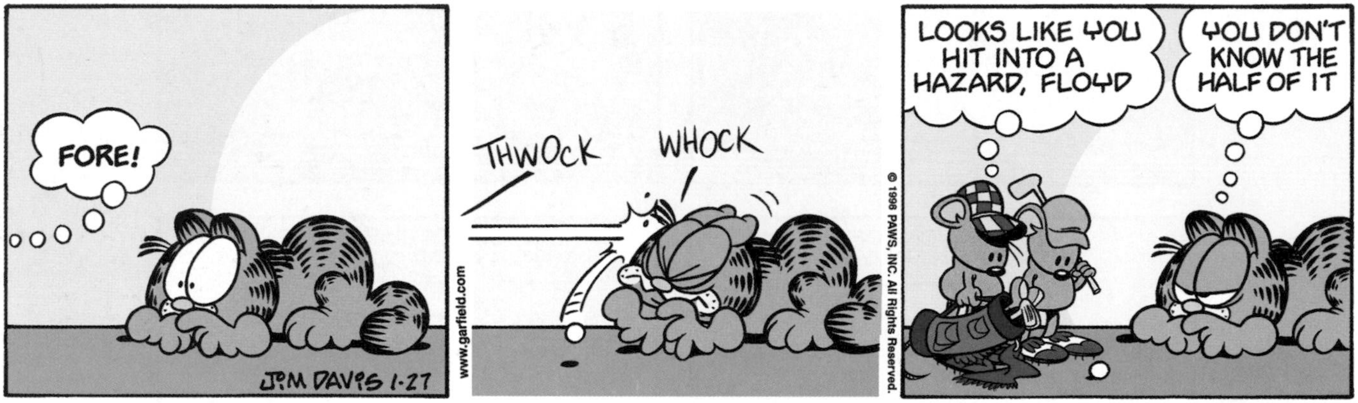
FORE!
JIM DAVIS 1-27
www.garfield.com
THWOCK
WHOCK
© 1998 PAWS, INC. All Rights Reserved.
LOOKS LIKE YOU HIT INTO A HAZARD, FLOYD
YOU DON'T KNOW THE HALF OF IT

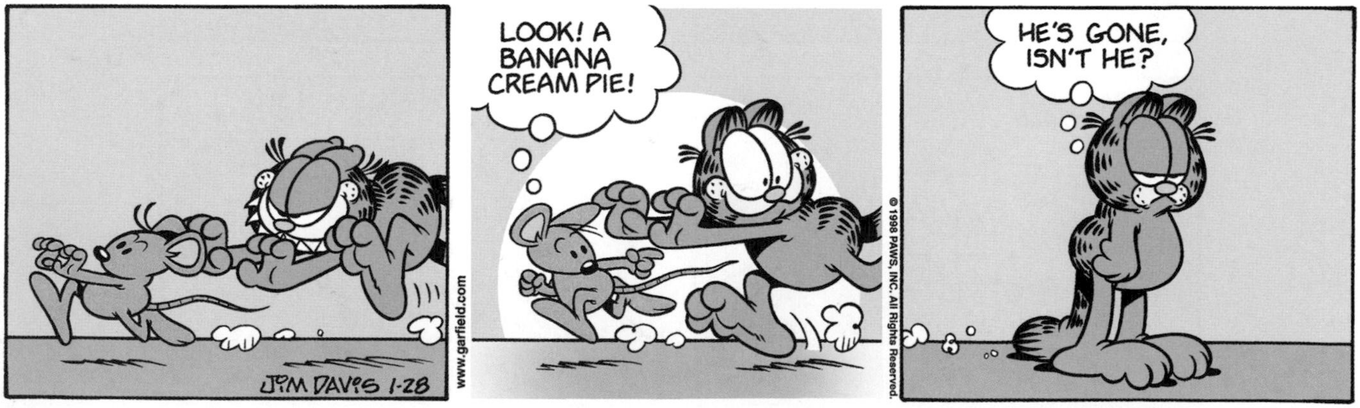
JIM DAVIS 1-28
www.garfield.com
LOOK! A BANANA CREAM PIE!
© 1998 PAWS, INC. All Rights Reserved.
HE'S GONE, ISN'T HE?

SOMEONE HAS BEEN STEALING MY CHOCOLATES
AND I WANT TO KNOW WHO!
YOU THERE!... WITH THE ZITS!
JIM DAVIS 1-29
www.garfield.com
© 1998 PAWS, INC. All Rights Reserved.

'NIGHT
'NIGHT
GARFIELD!
JIM DAVIS 1-30
© 1998 PAWS, INC. All Rights Reserved.
www.garfield.com

WHAT HAPPENED TO YOU?
I LOST A CONTACT LENS
YOU'RE GONNA HAVE TO RETURN THE SALAD BOWL
JIM DAVIS 1-31
© 1998 PAWS, INC. All Rights Reserved.
www.garfield.com

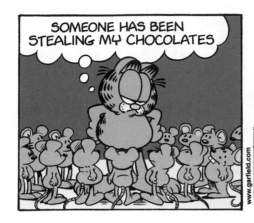

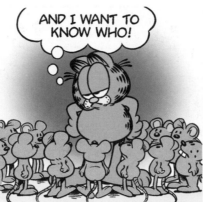

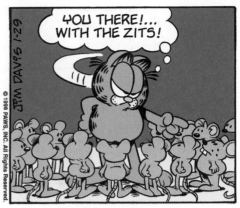

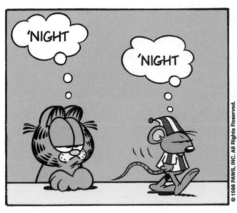

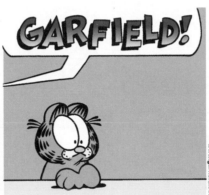

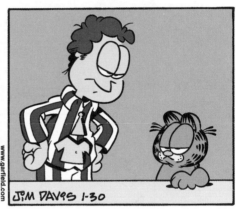

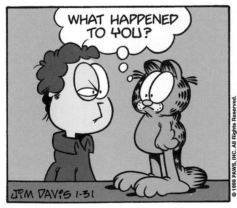

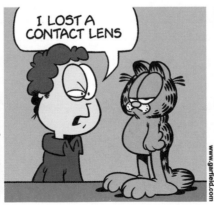

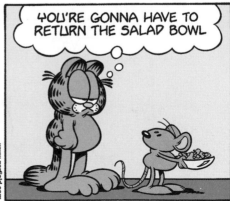

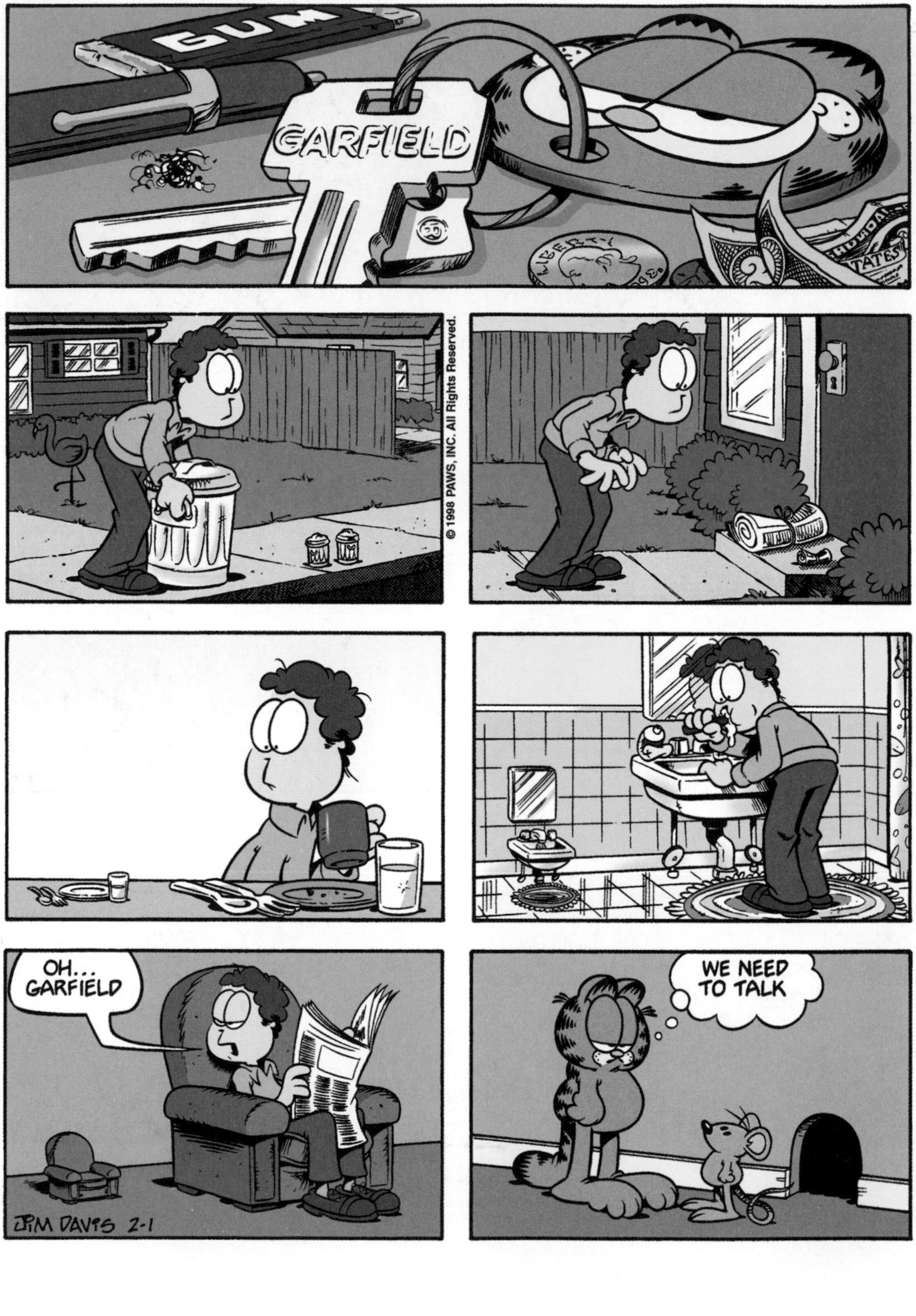
GUM
GARFIELD
© 1998 PAWS, INC. All Rights Reserved.
OH... GARFIELD
WE NEED TO TALK
JIM DAVIS 2-1

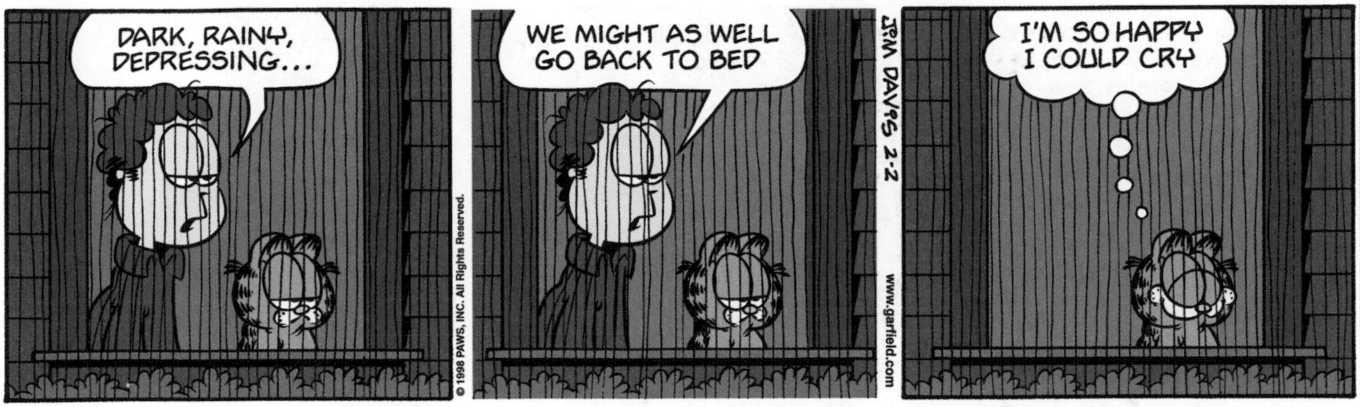
DARK, RAINY, DEPRESSING...
© 1998 PAWS, INC. All Rights Reserved.
WE MIGHT AS WELL GO BACK TO BED
JIM DAVIS 2-2
www.garfield.com
I'M SO HAPPY I COULD CRY

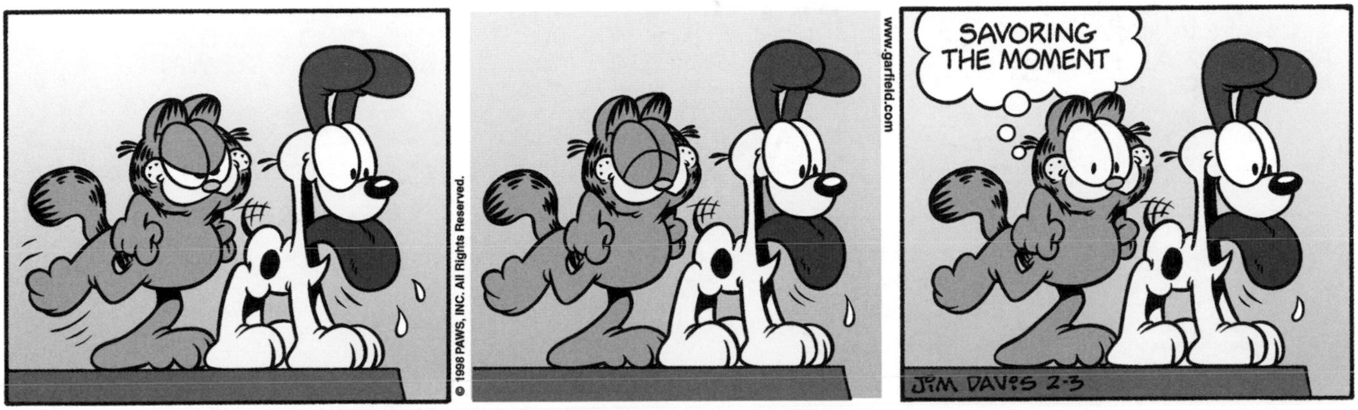
© 1998 PAWS, INC. All Rights Reserved.
www.garfield.com
SAVORING THE MOMENT
JIM DAVIS 2-3

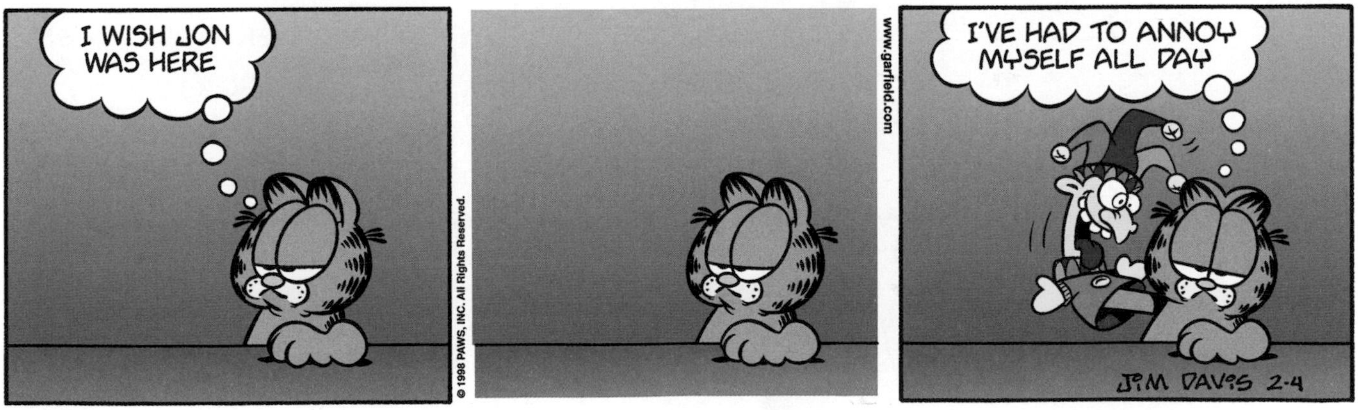
I WISH JON WAS HERE
© 1998 PAWS, INC. All Rights Reserved.
www.garfield.com
I'VE HAD TO ANNOY MYSELF ALL DAY
JIM DAVIS 2-4

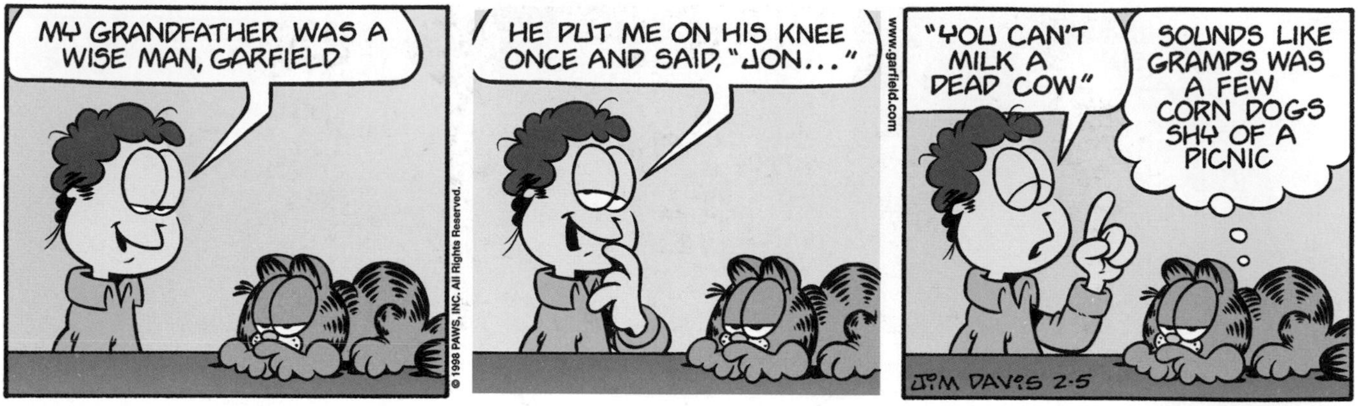
MY GRANDFATHER WAS A WISE MAN, GARFIELD
© 1998 PAWS, INC. All Rights Reserved.
HE PUT ME ON HIS KNEE ONCE AND SAID, "JON..."
www.garfield.com
"YOU CAN'T MILK A DEAD COW"
SOUNDS LIKE GRAMPS WAS A FEW CORN DOGS SHY OF A PICNIC
JIM DAVIS 2-5

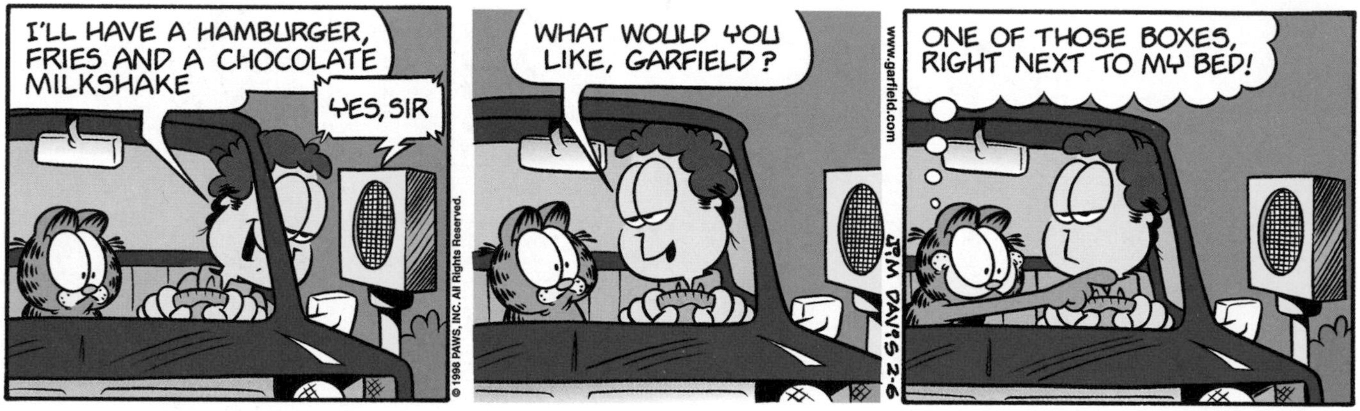
I'LL HAVE A HAMBURGER, FRIES AND A CHOCOLATE MILKSHAKE
YES, SIR
© 1998 PAWS, INC. All Rights Reserved.
WHAT WOULD YOU LIKE, GARFIELD?
JIM DAVIS 2-6
www.garfield.com
ONE OF THOSE BOXES, RIGHT NEXT TO MY BED!

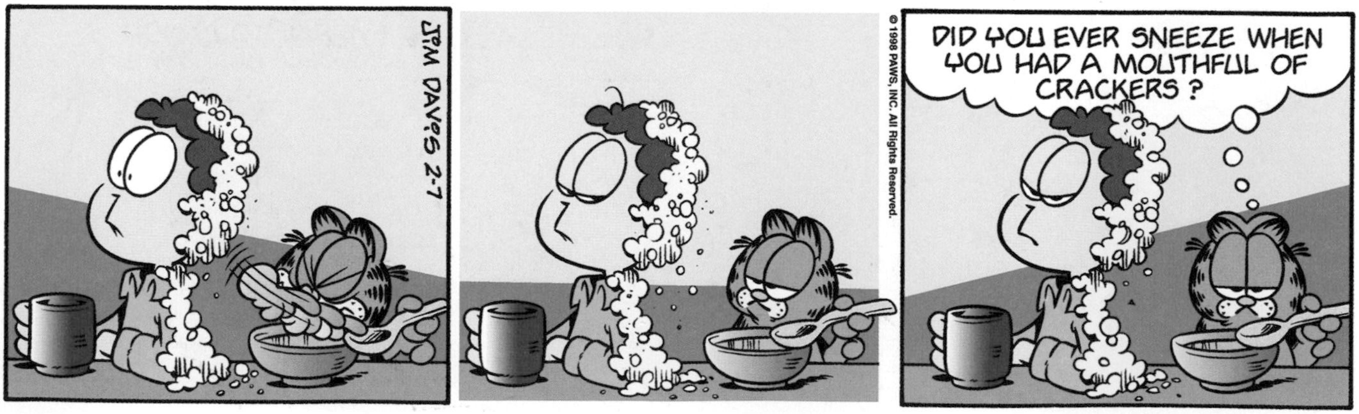
JIM DAVIS 2-7
© 1998 PAWS, INC. All Rights Reserved.
DID YOU EVER SNEEZE WHEN YOU HAD A MOUTHFUL OF CRACKERS?

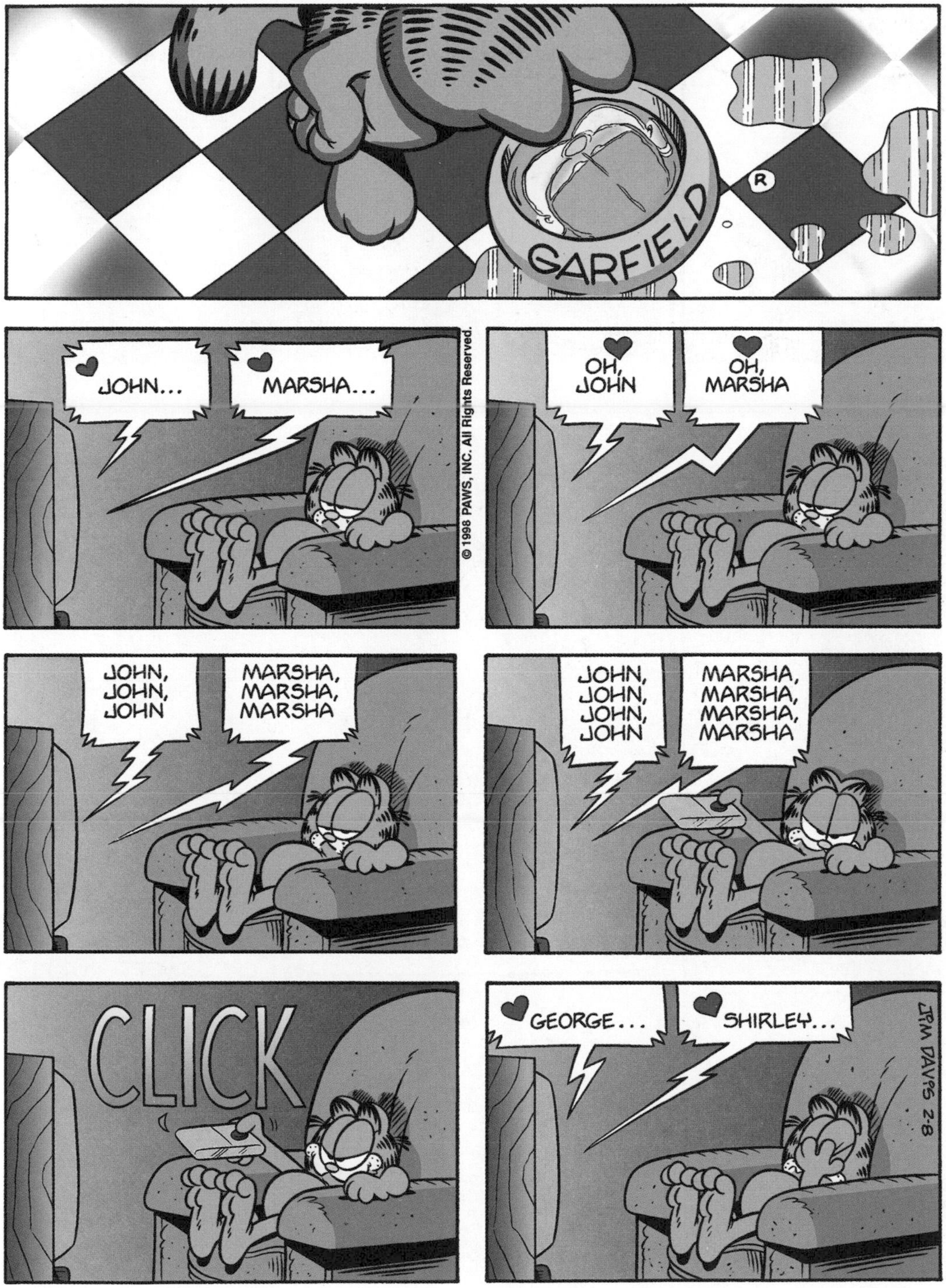
GARFIELD
JOHN...
MARSHA...
OH, JOHN
OH, MARSHA
JOHN, JOHN, JOHN
MARSHA, MARSHA, MARSHA
JOHN, JOHN, JOHN, JOHN
MARSHA, MARSHA, MARSHA, MARSHA
CLICK
GEORGE...
SHIRLEY...
JIM DAVIS 2-8

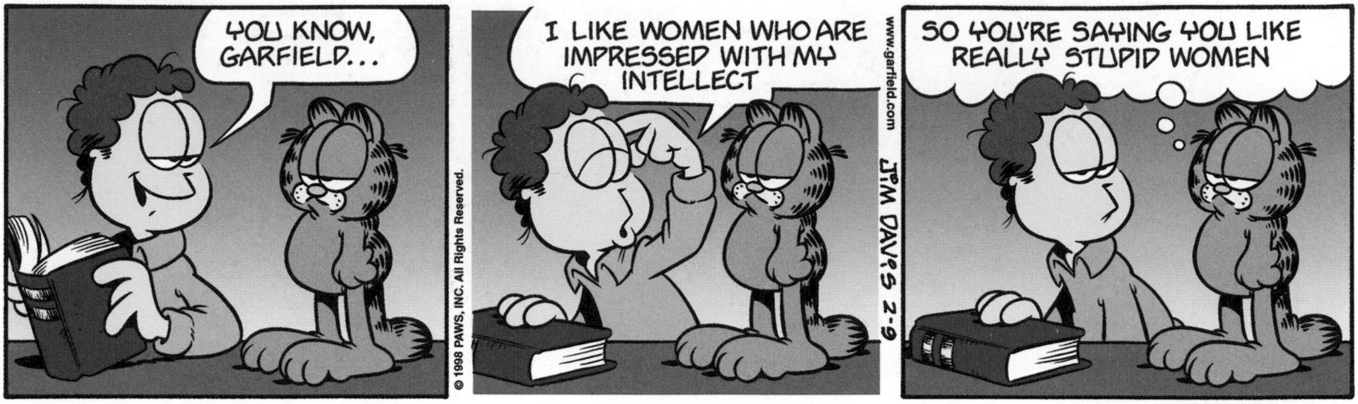
YOU KNOW, GARFIELD...
© 1998 PAWS, INC. All Rights Reserved.
I LIKE WOMEN WHO ARE IMPRESSED WITH MY INTELLECT
JIM DAVIS 2-9
www.garfield.com
SO YOU'RE SAYING YOU LIKE REALLY STUPID WOMEN

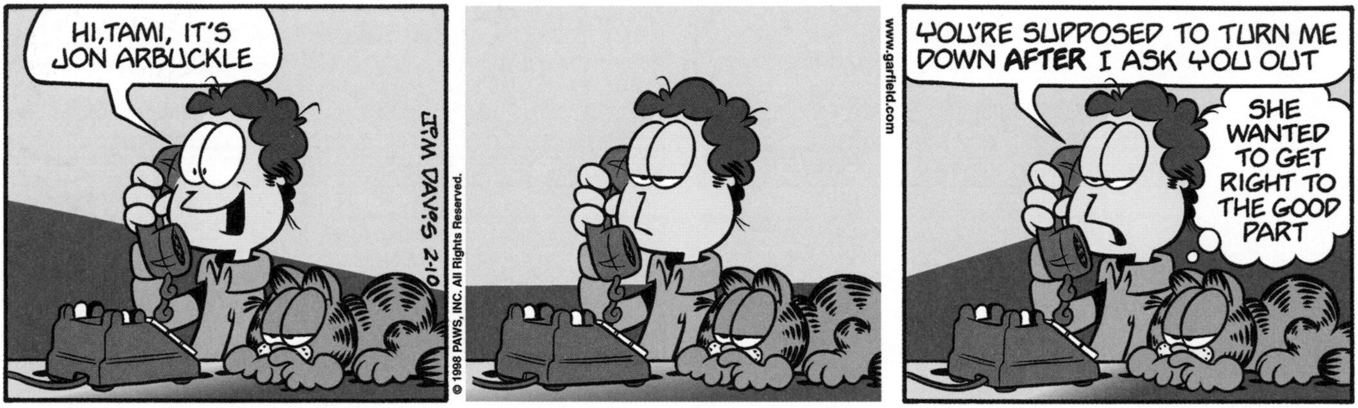
HI, TAMI, IT'S JON ARBUCKLE
JIM DAVIS 2-10
© 1998 PAWS, INC. All Rights Reserved.
www.garfield.com
YOU'RE SUPPOSED TO TURN ME DOWN **AFTER** I ASK YOU OUT
SHE WANTED TO GET RIGHT TO THE GOOD PART

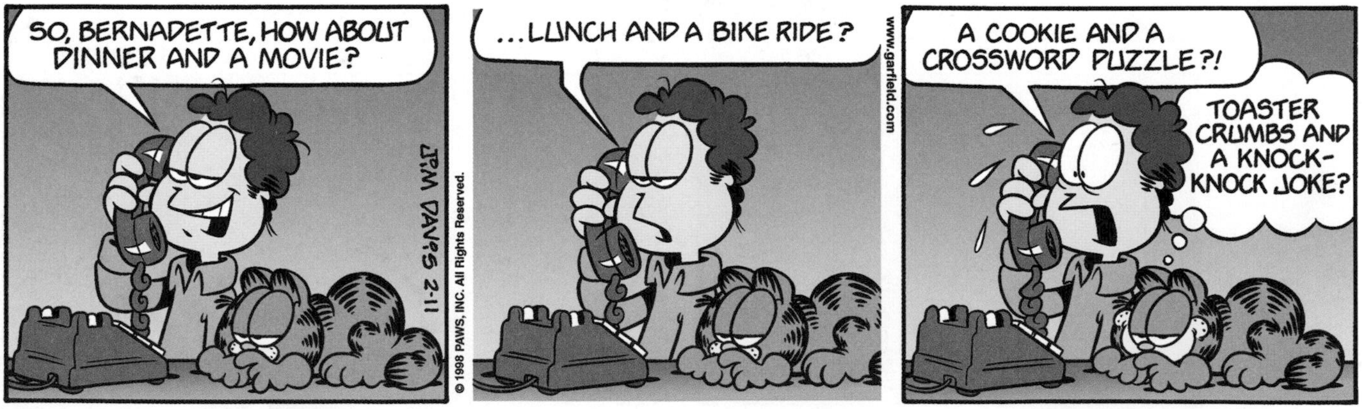
SO, BERNADETTE, HOW ABOUT DINNER AND A MOVIE?
JIM DAVIS 2-11
© 1998 PAWS, INC. All Rights Reserved.
...LUNCH AND A BIKE RIDE?
www.garfield.com
A COOKIE AND A CROSSWORD PUZZLE?!
TOASTER CRUMBS AND A KNOCK-KNOCK JOKE?

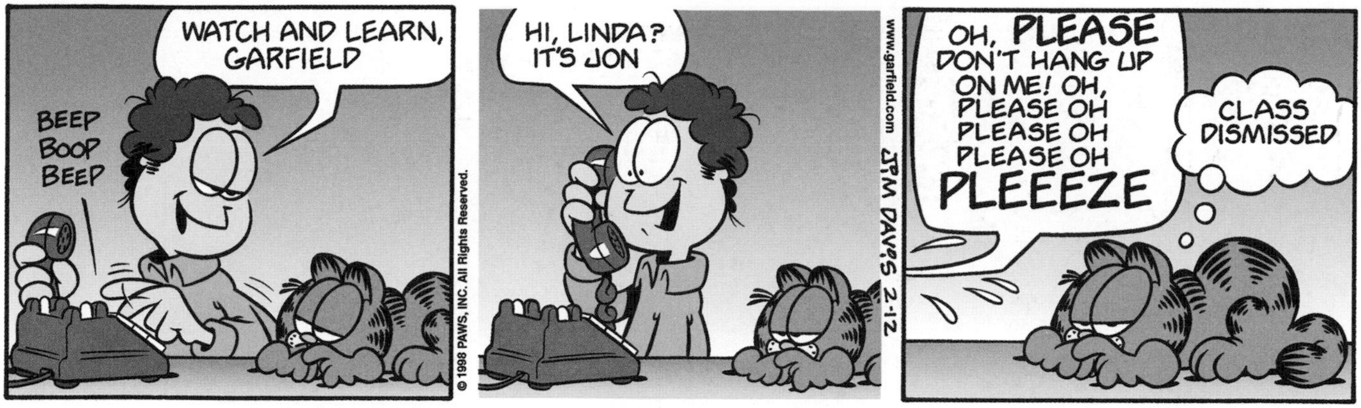
WATCH AND LEARN, GARFIELD
BEEP BOOP BEEP
© 1998 PAWS, INC. All Rights Reserved.
HI, LINDA? IT'S JON
JIM DAVIS 2-12
www.garfield.com
OH, PLEASE DON'T HANG UP ON ME! OH, PLEASE OH PLEASE OH PLEASE OH PLEEEZE
CLASS DISMISSED

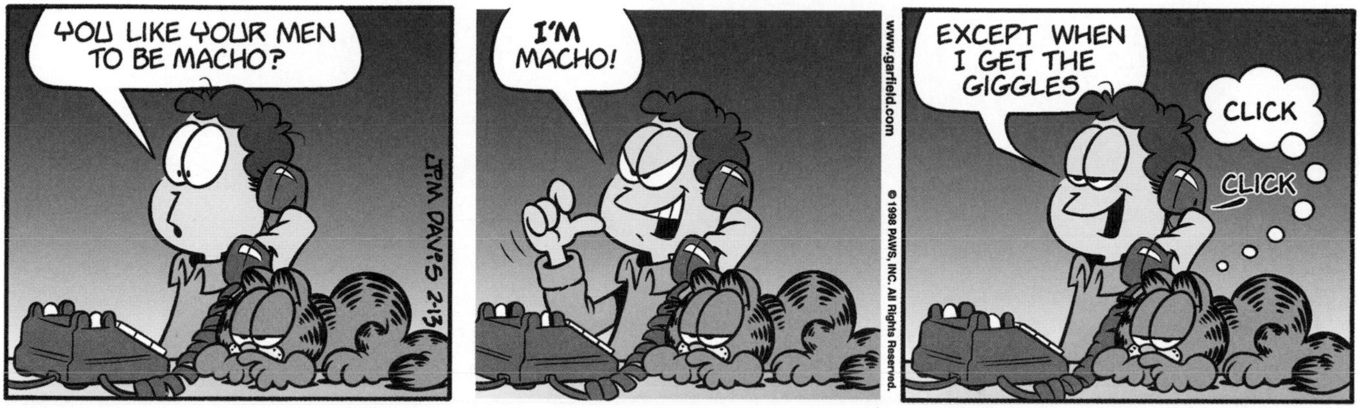
YOU LIKE YOUR MEN TO BE MACHO?
JIM DAVIS 2-13
I'M MACHO!
www.garfield.com
© 1998 PAWS, INC. All Rights Reserved.
EXCEPT WHEN I GET THE GIGGLES
CLICK
CLICK

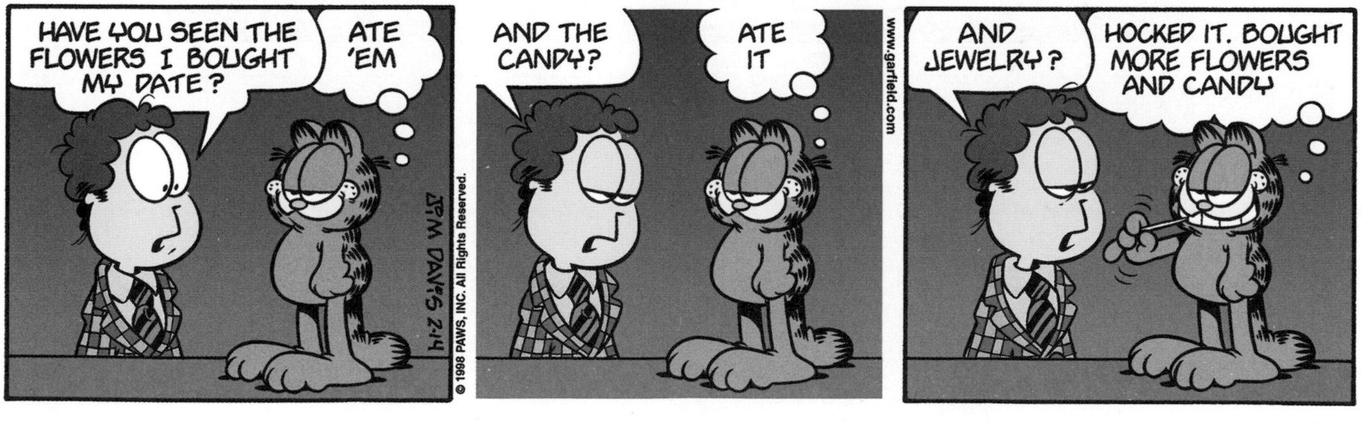
HAVE YOU SEEN THE FLOWERS I BOUGHT MY DATE?
ATE 'EM
JIM DAVIS 2-14
© 1998 PAWS, INC. All Rights Reserved.
AND THE CANDY?
ATE IT
www.garfield.com
AND JEWELRY?
HOCKED IT. BOUGHT MORE FLOWERS AND CANDY

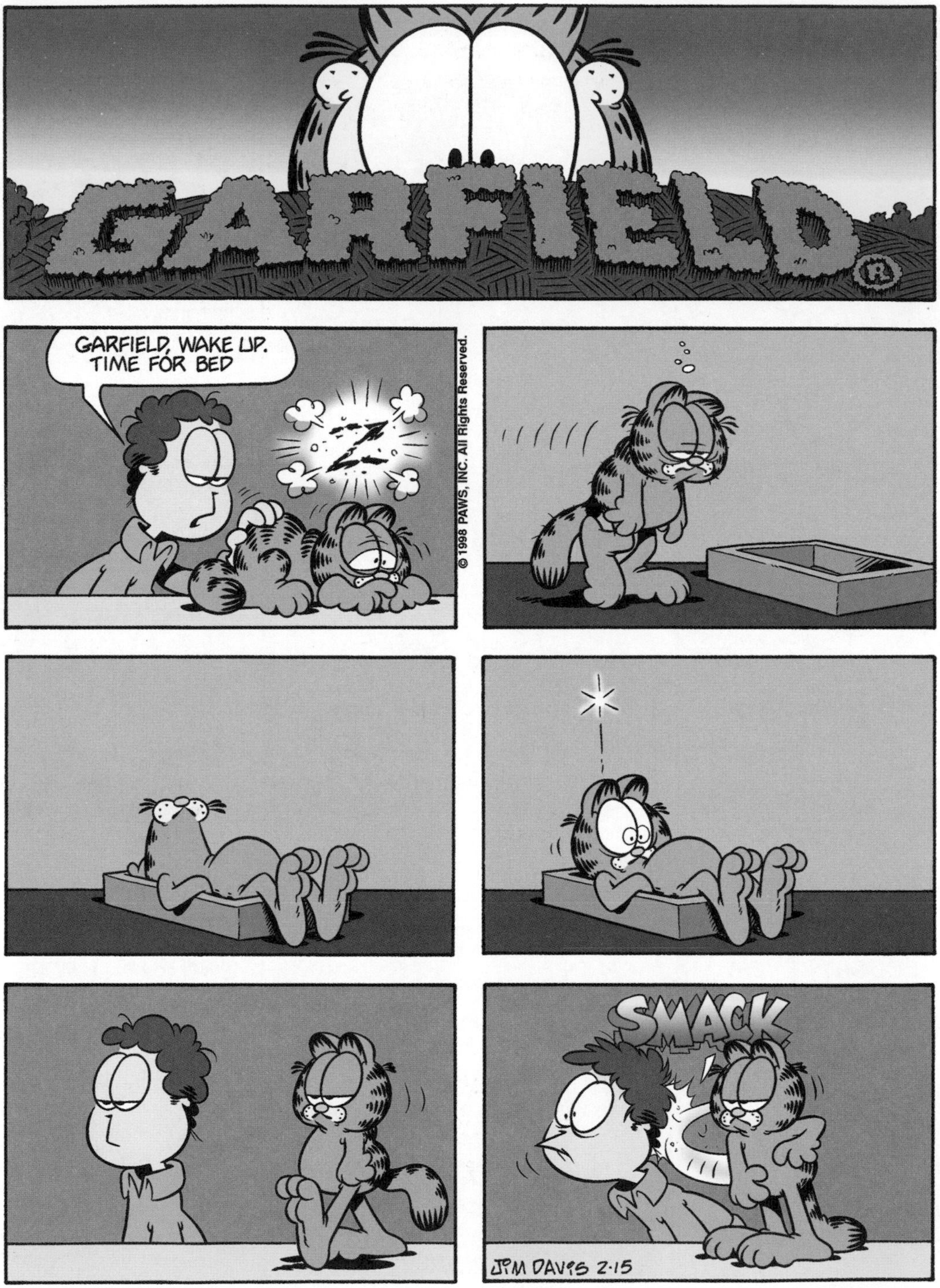
GARFIELD®
GARFIELD, WAKE UP. TIME FOR BED
Z
© 1998 PAWS, INC. All Rights Reserved.
SMACK
JIM DAVIS 2·15

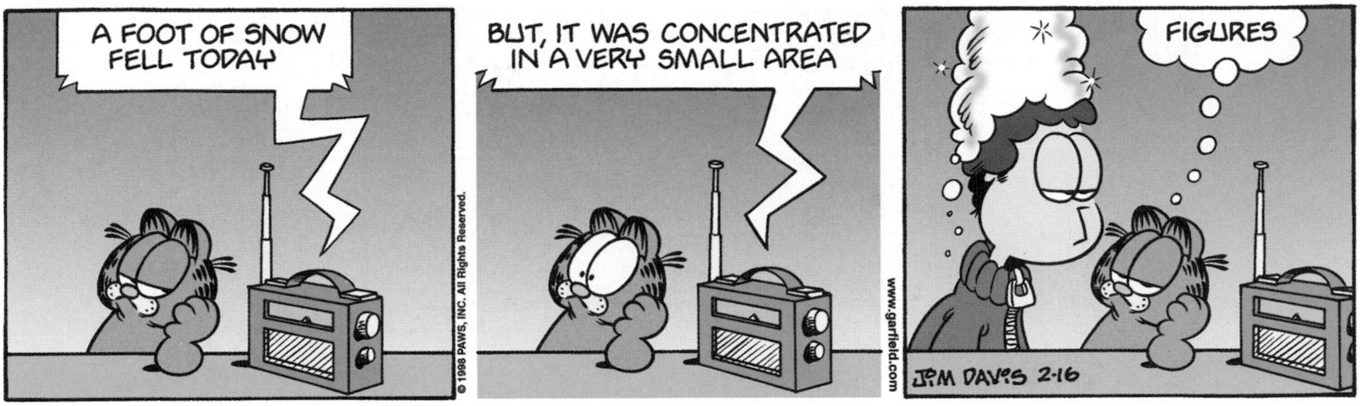
A FOOT OF SNOW FELL TODAY
BUT, IT WAS CONCENTRATED IN A VERY SMALL AREA
FIGURES
© 1998 PAWS, INC. All Rights Reserved.
www.garfield.com
JIM DAVIS 2-16

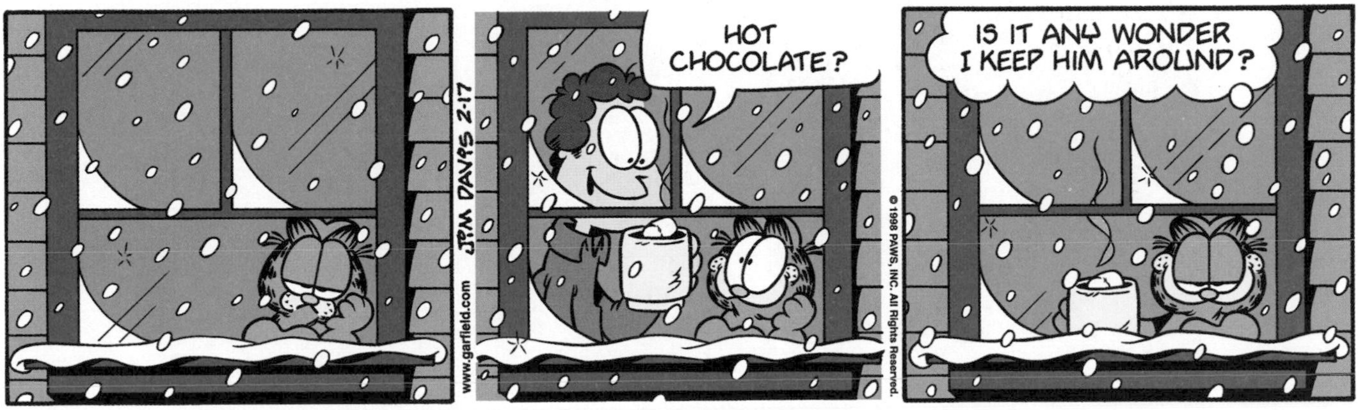
JIM DAVIS 2-17
www.garfield.com
HOT CHOCOLATE?
© 1998 PAWS, INC. All Rights Reserved.
IS IT ANY WONDER I KEEP HIM AROUND?

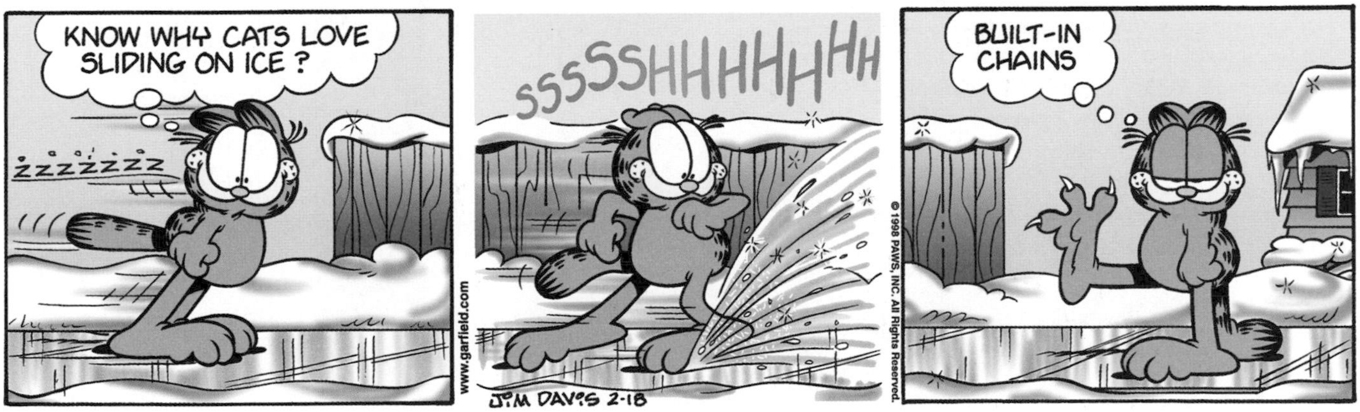
KNOW WHY CATS LOVE SLIDING ON ICE?
ZZZZZZZ
www.garfield.com
SSSSSHHHHHHHH
JIM DAVIS 2-18
© 1998 PAWS, INC. All Rights Reserved.
BUILT-IN CHAINS

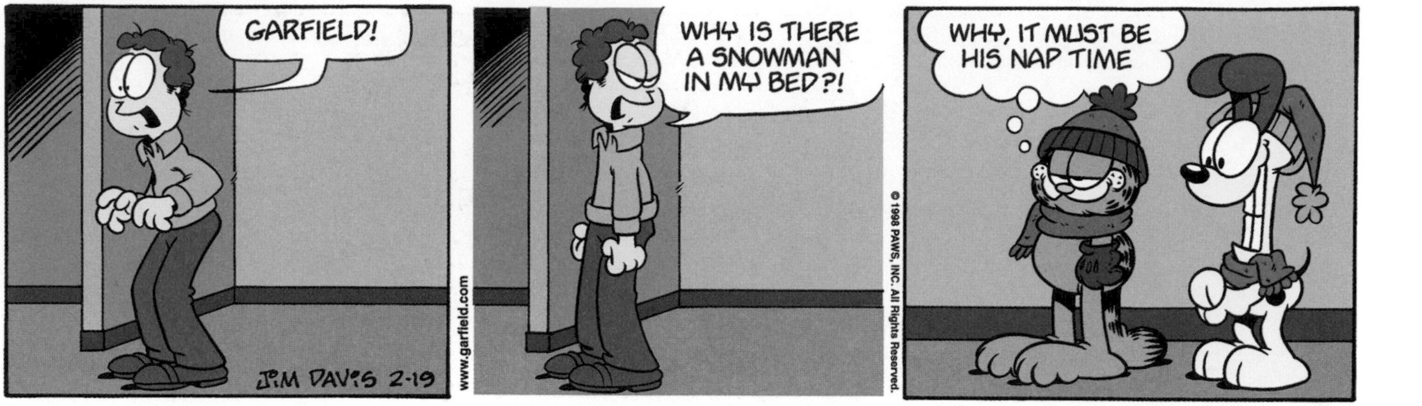
GARFIELD!
JIM DAVIS 2-19
www.garfield.com
WHY IS THERE A SNOWMAN IN MY BED?!
© 1998 PAWS, INC. All Rights Reserved.
WHY, IT MUST BE HIS NAP TIME

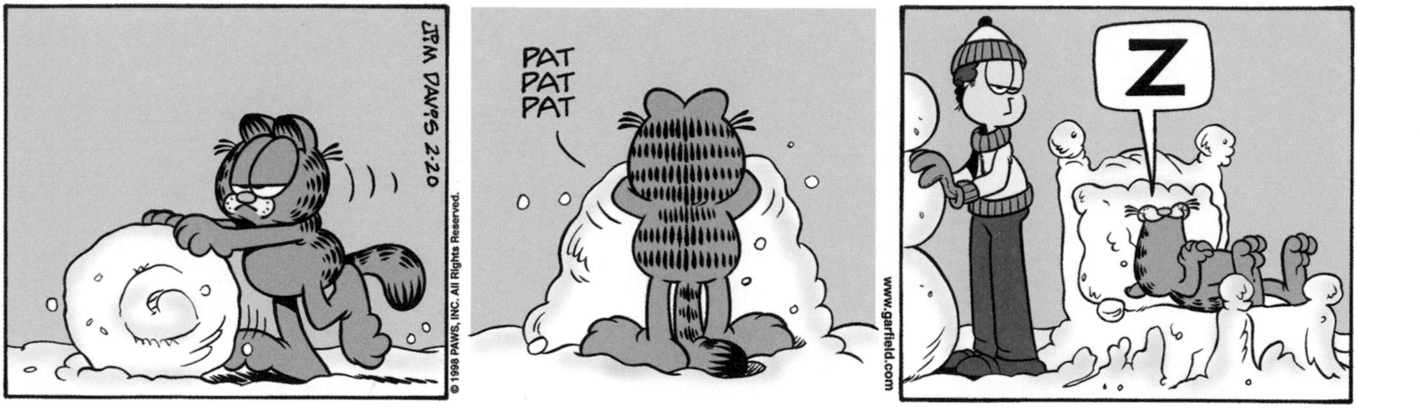
JIM DAVIS 2-20
© 1998 PAWS, INC. All Rights Reserved.
PAT PAT PAT
www.garfield.com
Z

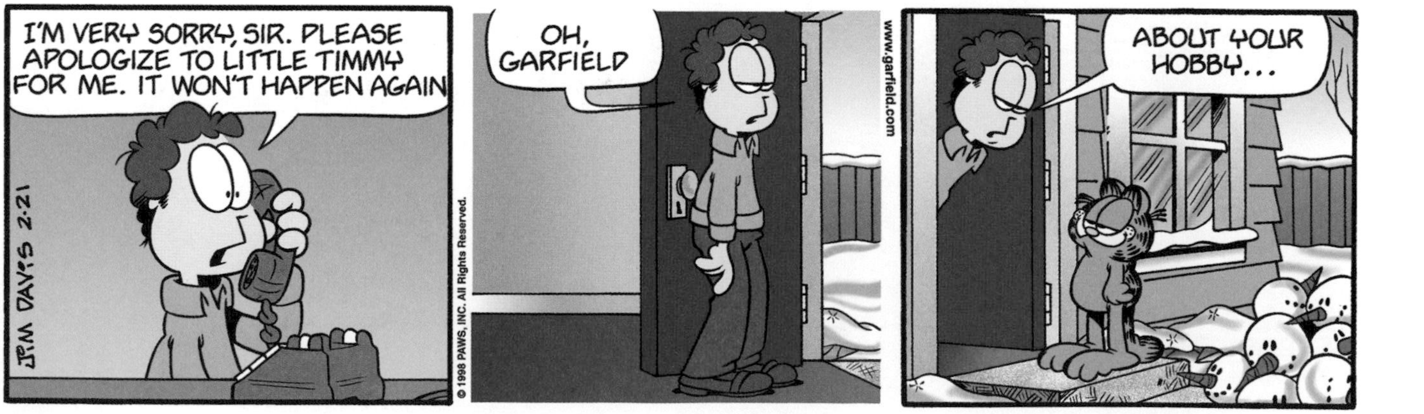
I'M VERY SORRY, SIR. PLEASE APOLOGIZE TO LITTLE TIMMY FOR ME. IT WON'T HAPPEN AGAIN
JIM DAVIS 2-21
© 1998 PAWS, INC. All Rights Reserved.
OH, GARFIELD
www.garfield.com
ABOUT YOUR HOBBY...

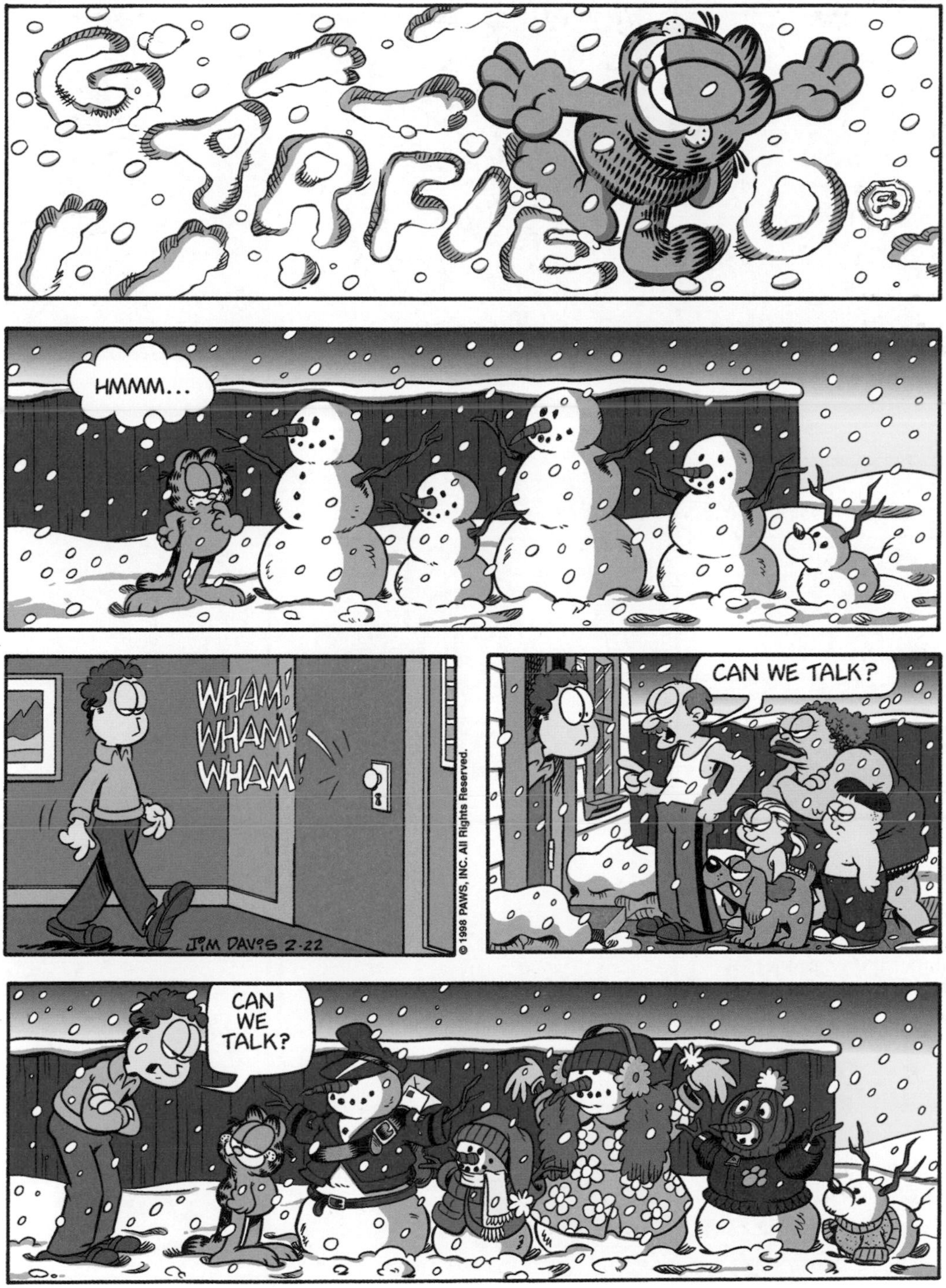
GARFIELD®
HMMM...
WHAM! WHAM! WHAM!
JIM DAVIS 2-22
© 1998 PAWS, INC. All Rights Reserved.
CAN WE TALK?
CAN WE TALK?

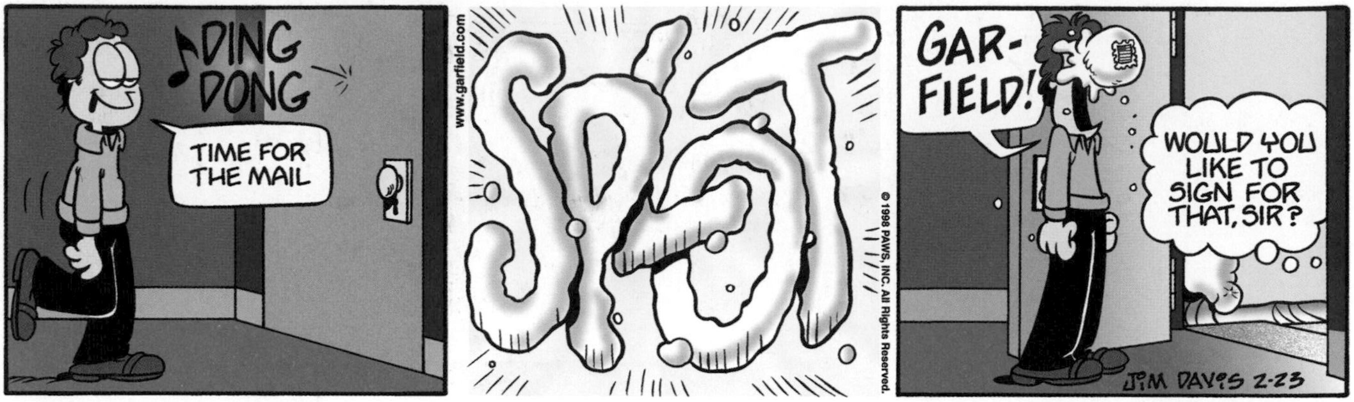
DING DONG
TIME FOR THE MAIL
www.garfield.com
SPLAT
© 1998 PAWS, INC. All Rights Reserved.
GAR-FIELD!
WOULD YOU LIKE TO SIGN FOR THAT, SIR?
JIM DAVIS 2-23

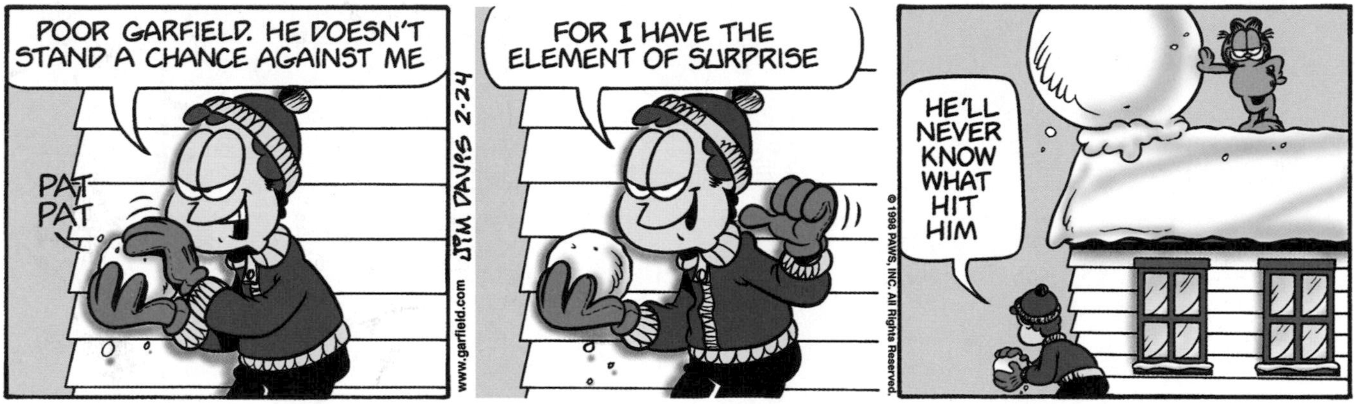
POOR GARFIELD. HE DOESN'T STAND A CHANCE AGAINST ME
PAT PAT
JIM DAVIS 2-24
www.garfield.com
FOR I HAVE THE ELEMENT OF SURPRISE
© 1998 PAWS, INC. All Rights Reserved.
HE'LL NEVER KNOW WHAT HIT HIM

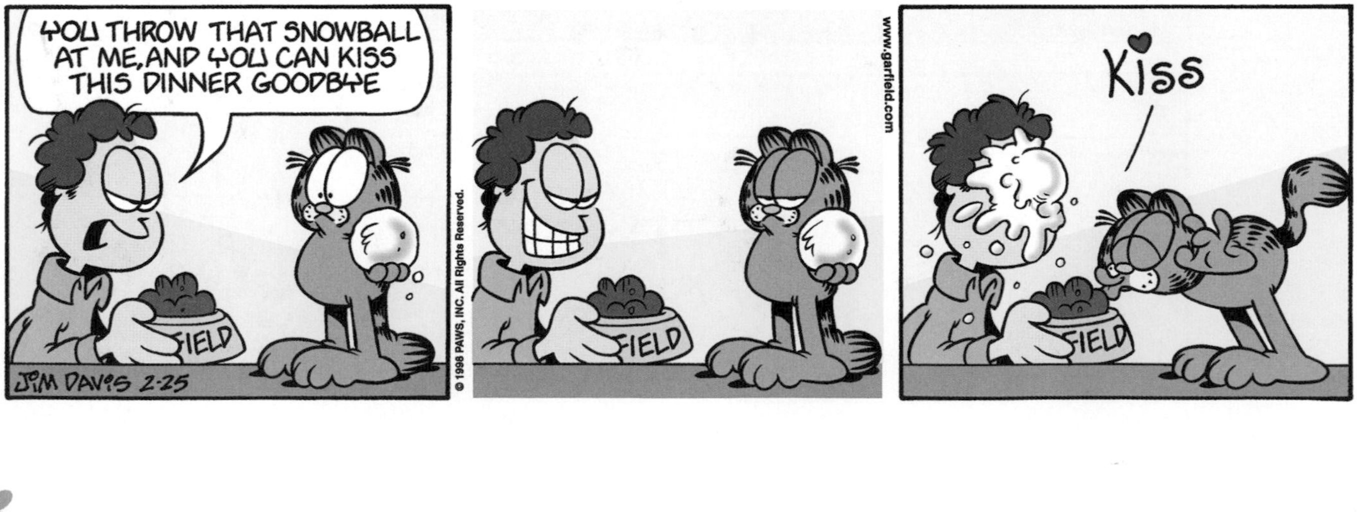
YOU THROW THAT SNOWBALL AT ME, AND YOU CAN KISS THIS DINNER GOODBYE
FIELD
JIM DAVIS 2-25
© 1998 PAWS, INC. All Rights Reserved.
FIELD
www.garfield.com
Kiss
FIELD

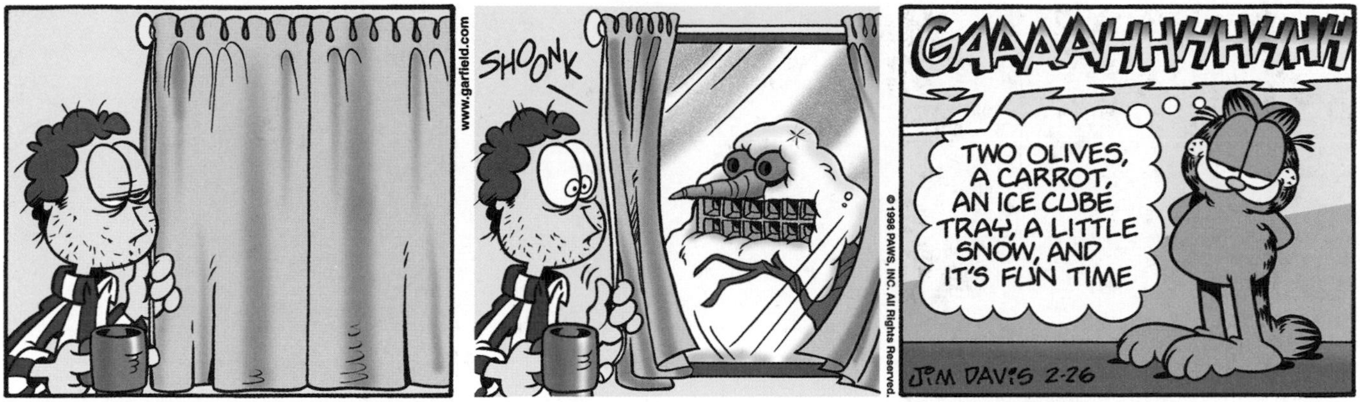
www.garfield.com
SHOONK
© 1998 PAWS, INC. All Rights Reserved.
GAAAAHHHHHHH
TWO OLIVES, A CARROT, AN ICE CUBE TRAY, A LITTLE SNOW, AND IT'S FUN TIME
JIM DAVIS 2-26

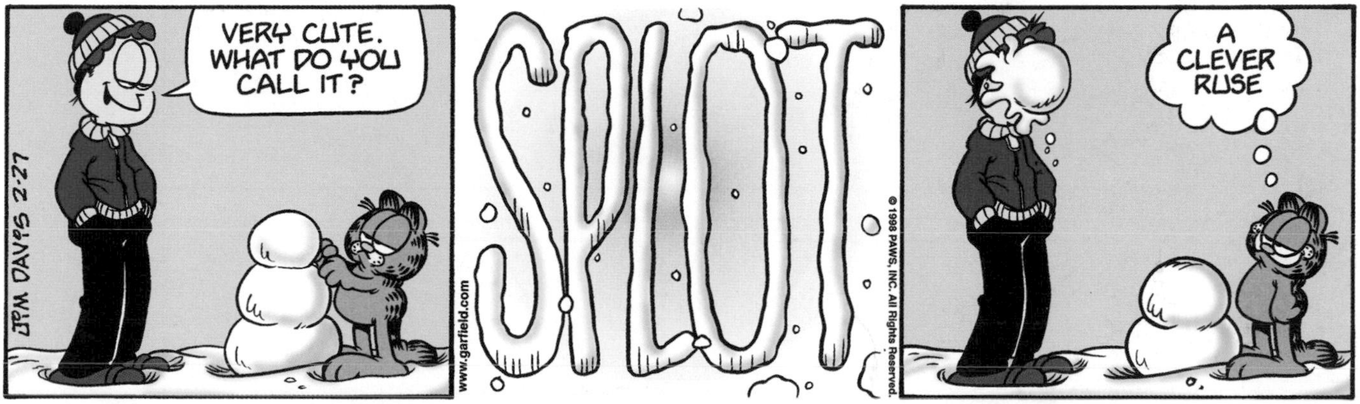
VERY CUTE. WHAT DO YOU CALL IT?
JIM DAVIS 2-27
www.garfield.com
SPLOT
© 1998 PAWS, INC. All Rights Reserved.
A CLEVER RUSE

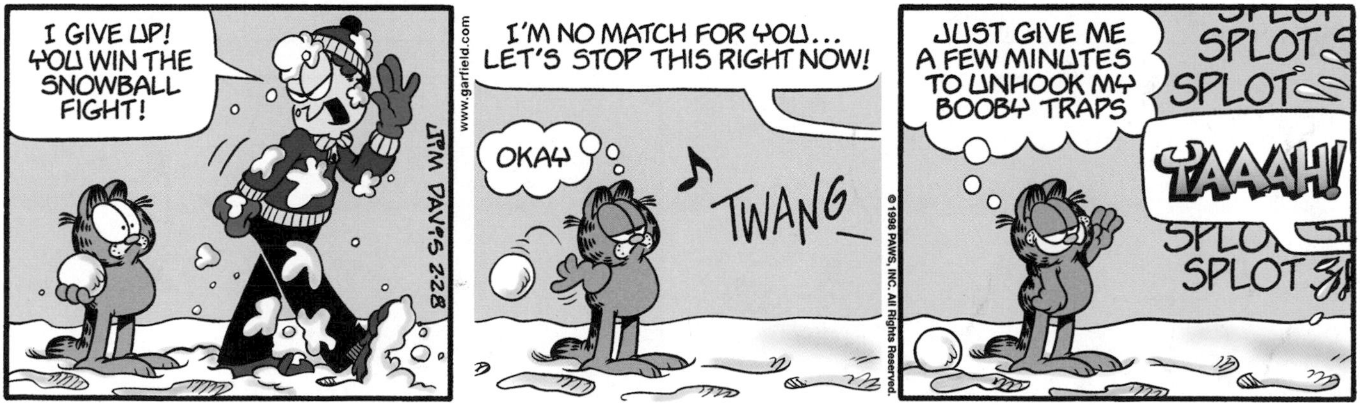
I GIVE UP! YOU WIN THE SNOWBALL FIGHT!
JIM DAVIS 2-28
www.garfield.com
I'M NO MATCH FOR YOU... LET'S STOP THIS RIGHT NOW!
OKAY
TWANG
© 1998 PAWS, INC. All Rights Reserved.
JUST GIVE ME A FEW MINUTES TO UNHOOK MY BOOBY TRAPS
SPLOT
SPLOT
YAAAH!
SPLOT

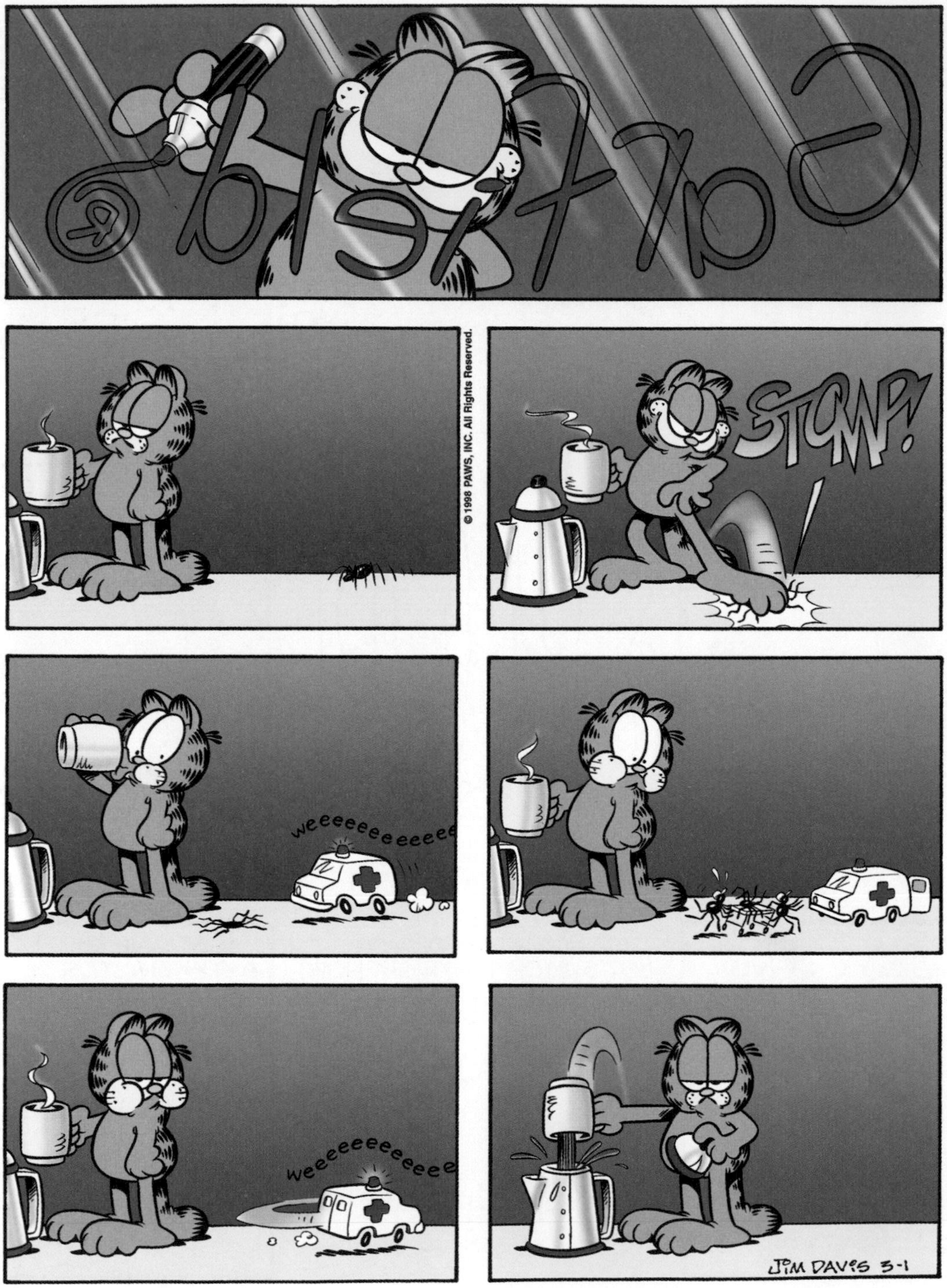
Garfield
STOMP!
weeeeeeeeeeee
weeeeeeeeeeee
JIM DAVIS 3-1

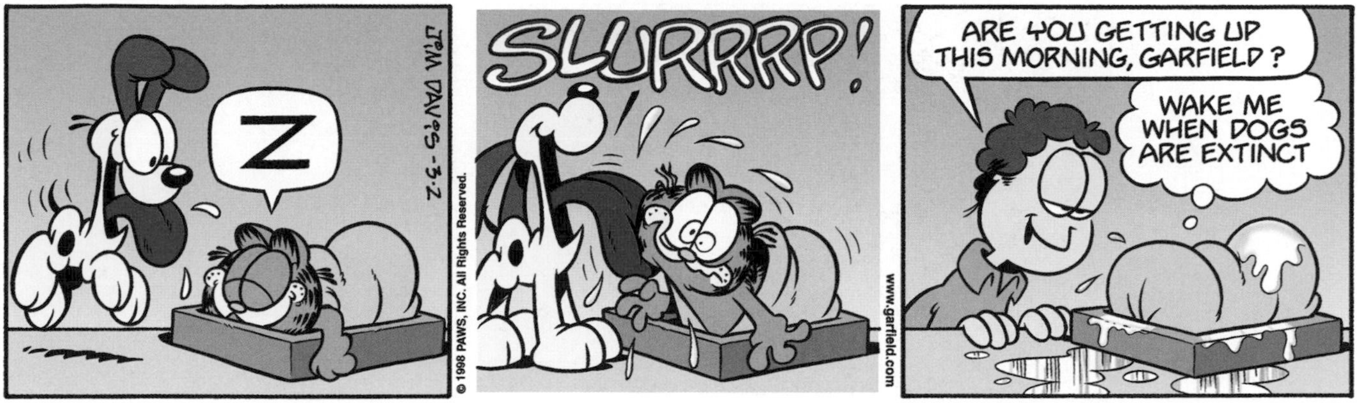
JIM DAVIS 3-2
Z
© 1998 PAWS, INC. All Rights Reserved.
SLURRRP!
www.garfield.com
ARE YOU GETTING UP THIS MORNING, GARFIELD?
WAKE ME WHEN DOGS ARE EXTINCT

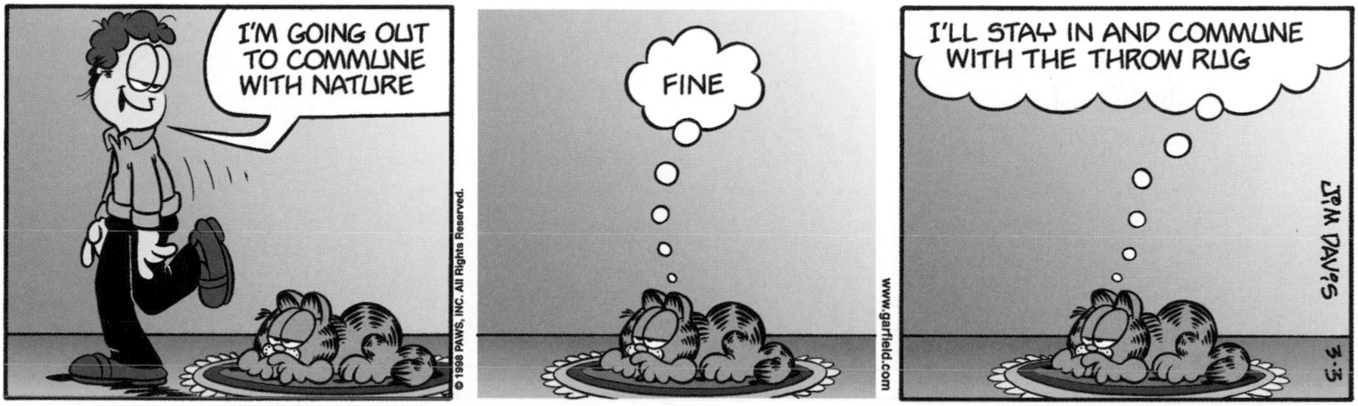
I'M GOING OUT TO COMMUNE WITH NATURE
© 1998 PAWS, INC. All Rights Reserved.
FINE
www.garfield.com
I'LL STAY IN AND COMMUNE WITH THE THROW RUG
JIM DAVIS 3-3

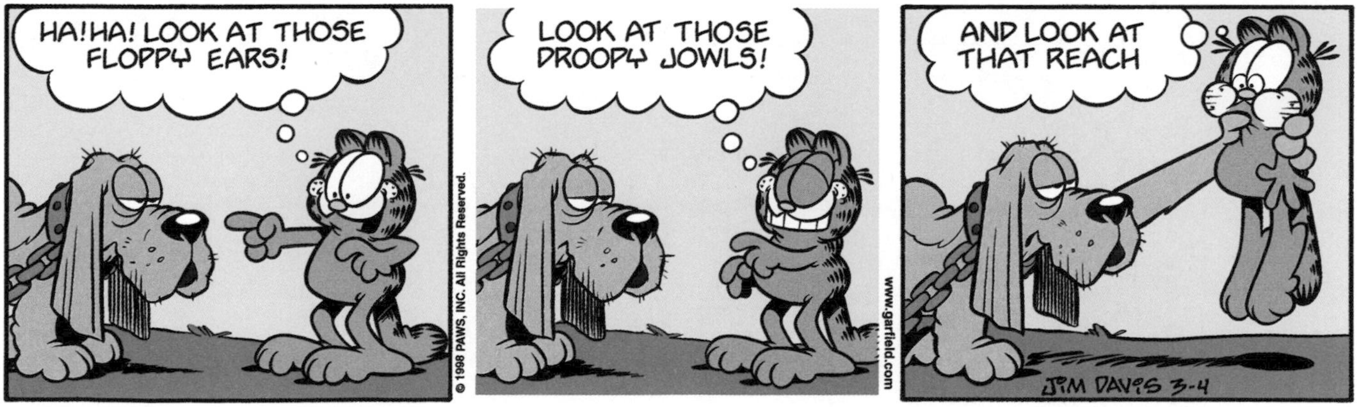
HA! HA! LOOK AT THOSE FLOPPY EARS!
© 1998 PAWS, INC. All Rights Reserved.
LOOK AT THOSE DROOPY JOWLS!
www.garfield.com
AND LOOK AT THAT REACH
JIM DAVIS 3-4

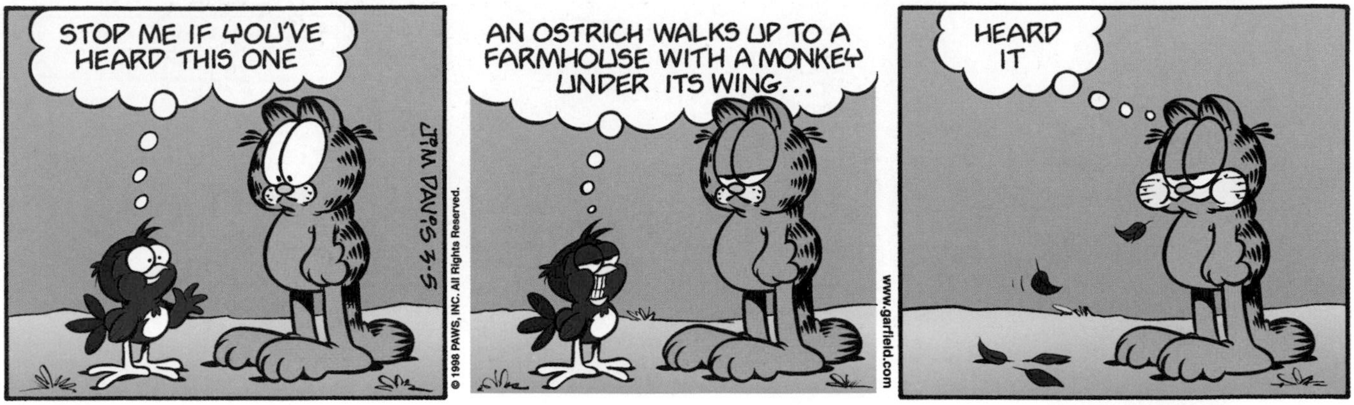
STOP ME IF YOU'VE HEARD THIS ONE
JIM DAVIS 3-5
© 1998 PAWS, INC. All Rights Reserved.
AN OSTRICH WALKS UP TO A FARMHOUSE WITH A MONKEY UNDER ITS WING...
www.garfield.com
HEARD IT

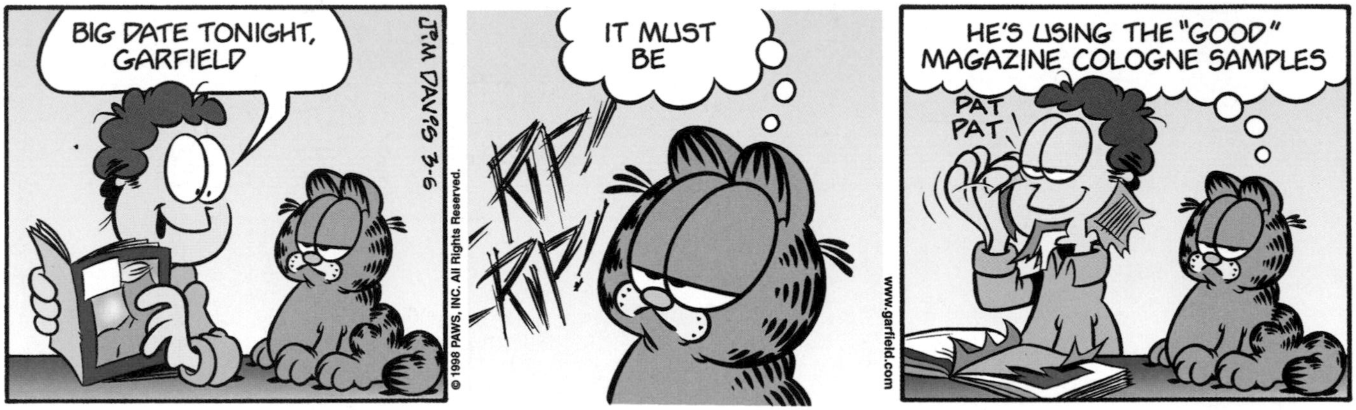
BIG DATE TONIGHT, GARFIELD
JIM DAVIS 3-6
© 1998 PAWS, INC. All Rights Reserved.
RIP! RIP!
IT MUST BE
www.garfield.com
PAT PAT
HE'S USING THE "GOOD" MAGAZINE COLOGNE SAMPLES

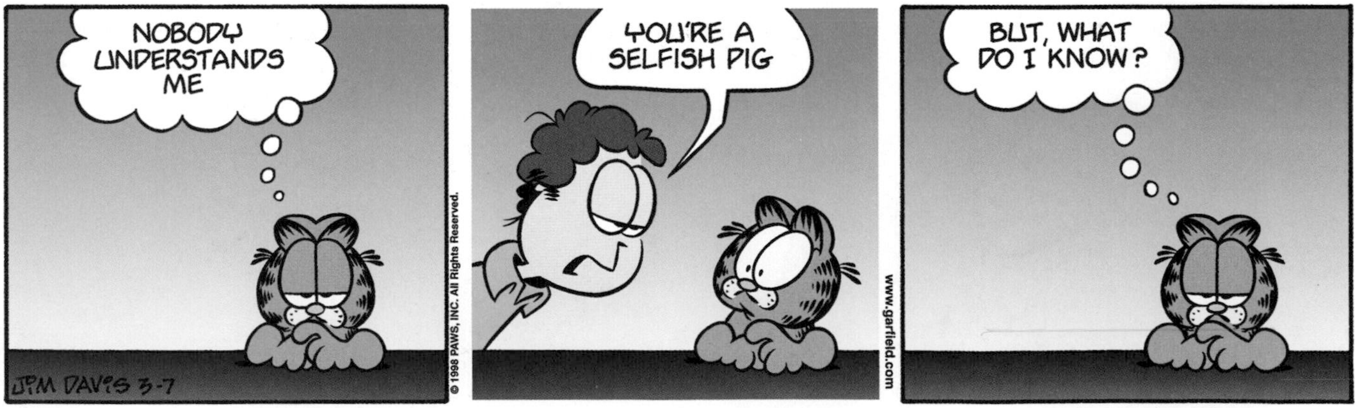
NOBODY UNDERSTANDS ME
JIM DAVIS 3-7
© 1998 PAWS, INC. All Rights Reserved.
YOU'RE A SELFISH PIG
www.garfield.com
BUT, WHAT DO I KNOW?

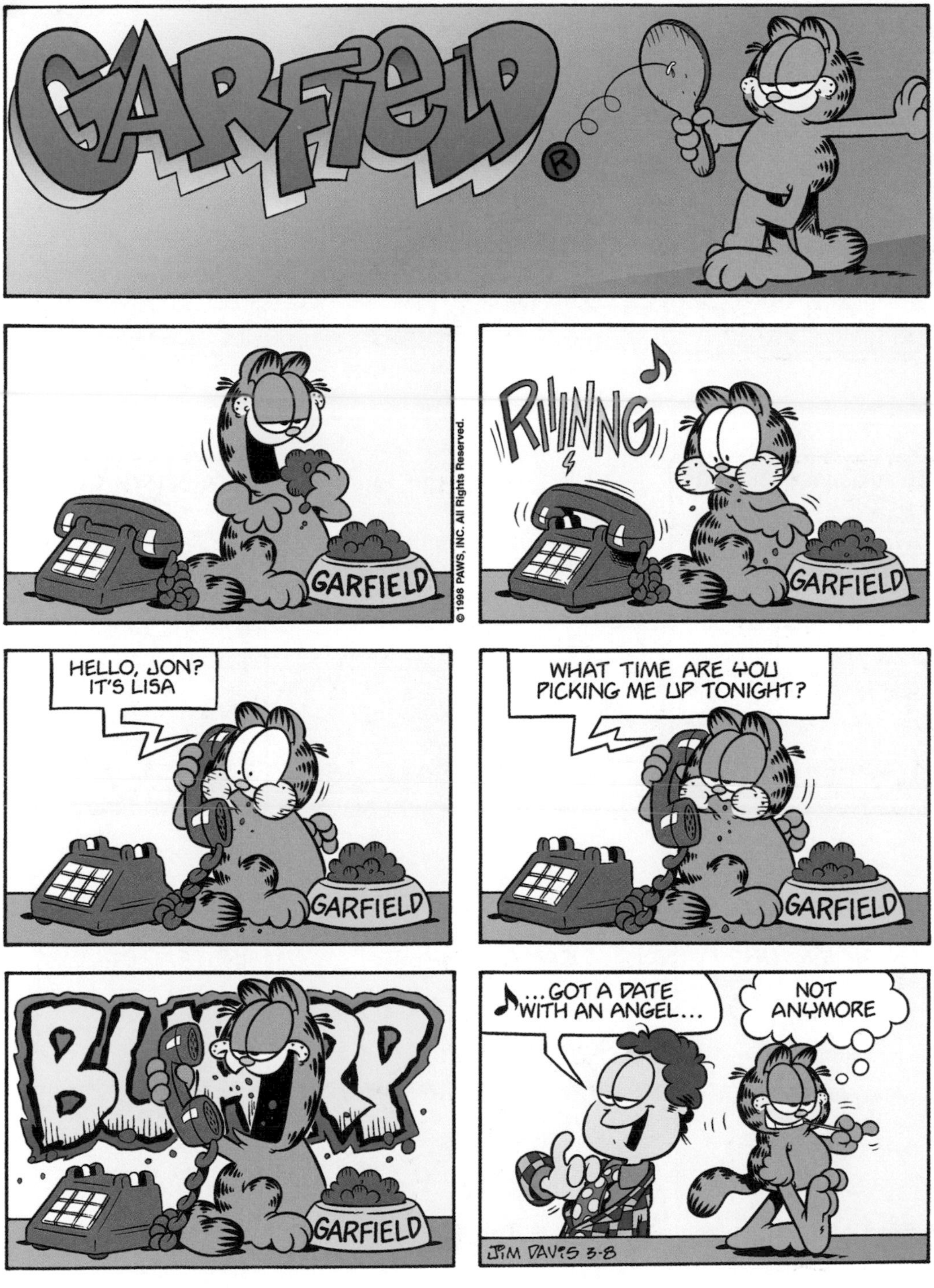
GARFIELD
© 1998 PAWS, INC. All Rights Reserved.
RIIINNG
GARFIELD
HELLO, JON? IT'S LISA
WHAT TIME ARE YOU PICKING ME UP TONIGHT?
...GOT A DATE WITH AN ANGEL...
NOT ANYMORE
JIM DAVIS 3-8

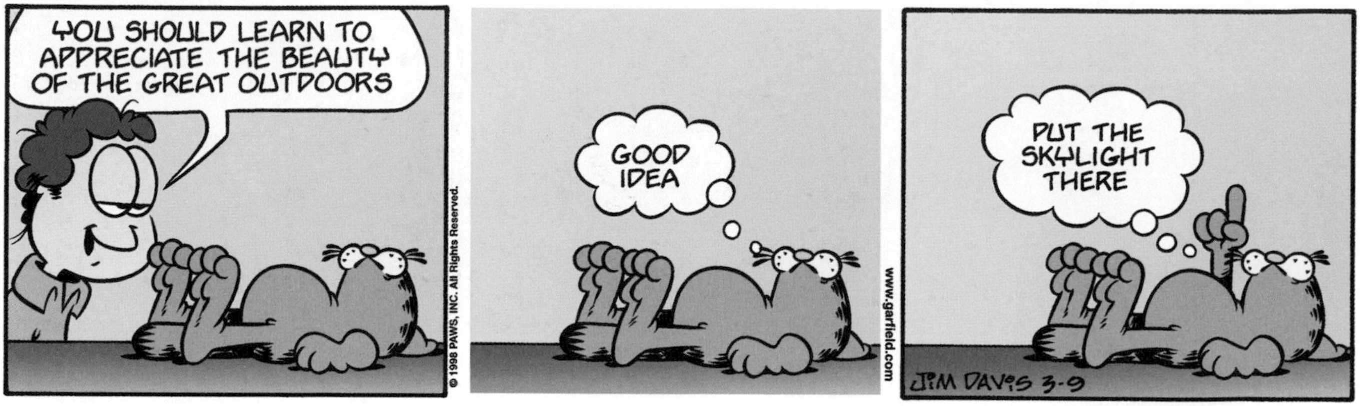
YOU SHOULD LEARN TO APPRECIATE THE BEAUTY OF THE GREAT OUTDOORS
GOOD IDEA
PUT THE SKYLIGHT THERE
© 1998 PAWS, INC. All Rights Reserved.
www.garfield.com
JIM DAVIS 3-9

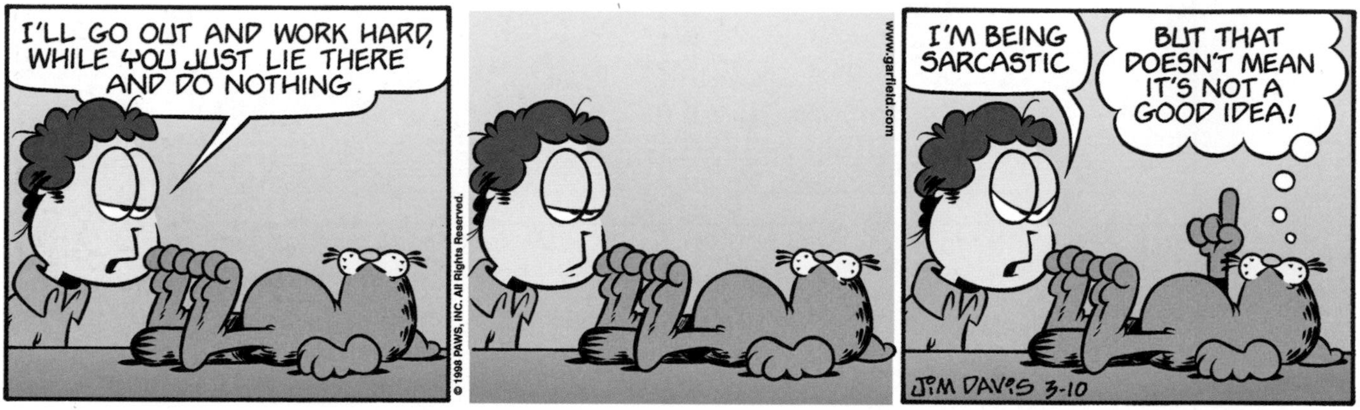
I'LL GO OUT AND WORK HARD, WHILE YOU JUST LIE THERE AND DO NOTHING
I'M BEING SARCASTIC
BUT THAT DOESN'T MEAN IT'S NOT A GOOD IDEA!
© 1998 PAWS, INC. All Rights Reserved.
www.garfield.com
JIM DAVIS 3-10

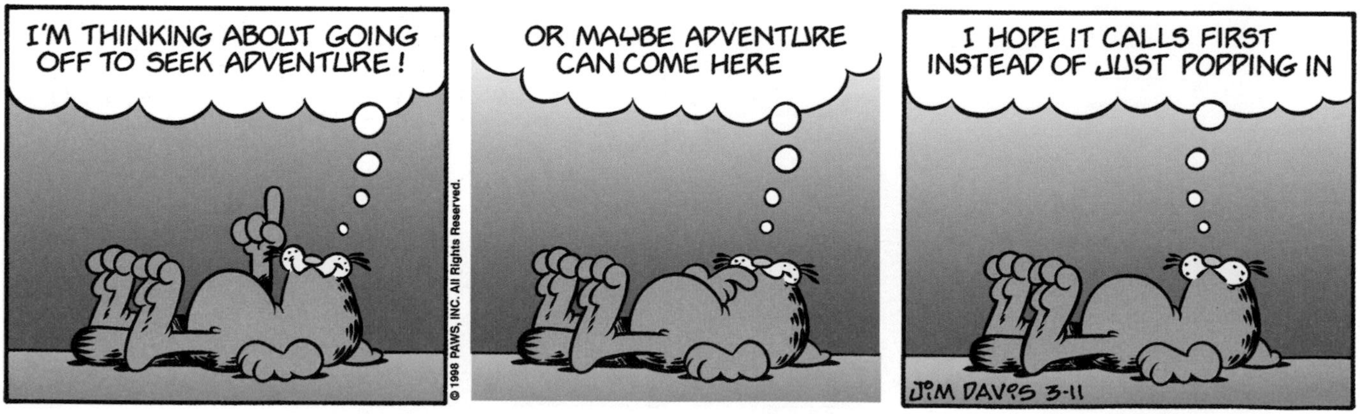
I'M THINKING ABOUT GOING OFF TO SEEK ADVENTURE!
OR MAYBE ADVENTURE CAN COME HERE
I HOPE IT CALLS FIRST INSTEAD OF JUST POPPING IN
© 1998 PAWS, INC. All Rights Reserved.
JIM DAVIS 3-11

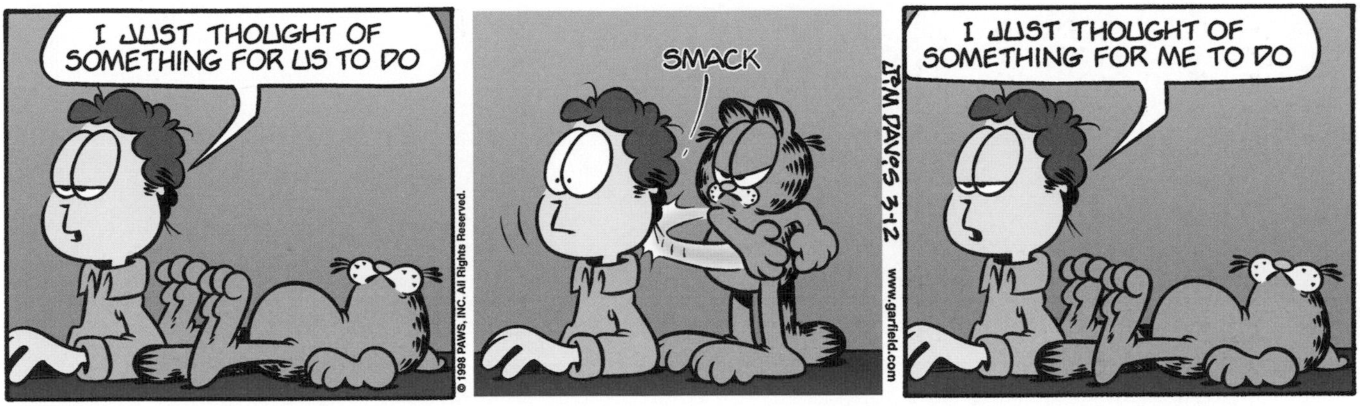
I JUST THOUGHT OF SOMETHING FOR US TO DO
© 1998 PAWS, INC. All Rights Reserved.
SMACK
JIM DAVIS 3-12
www.garfield.com
I JUST THOUGHT OF SOMETHING FOR ME TO DO

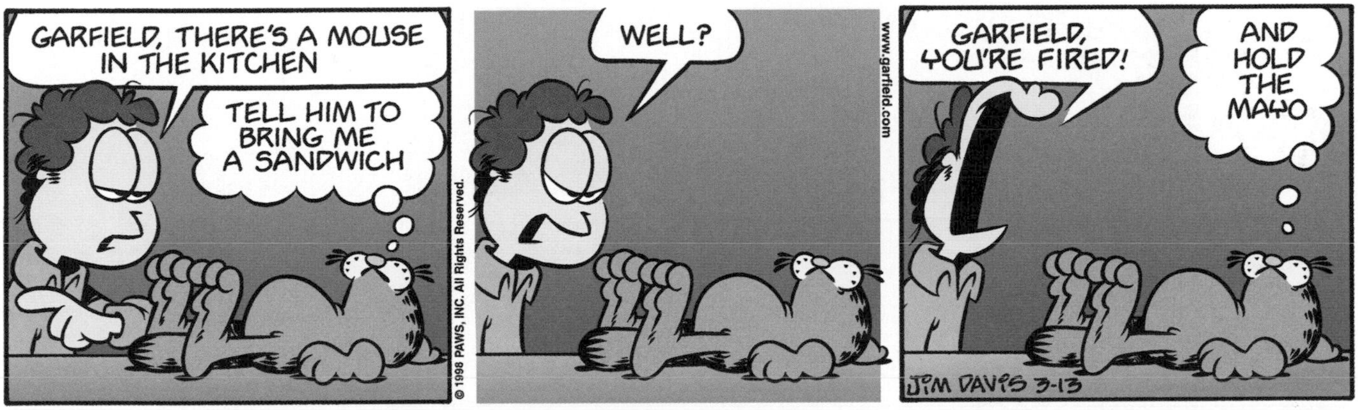
GARFIELD, THERE'S A MOUSE IN THE KITCHEN
TELL HIM TO BRING ME A SANDWICH
© 1998 PAWS, INC. All Rights Reserved.
WELL?
www.garfield.com
GARFIELD, YOU'RE FIRED!
AND HOLD THE MAYO
JIM DAVIS 3-13

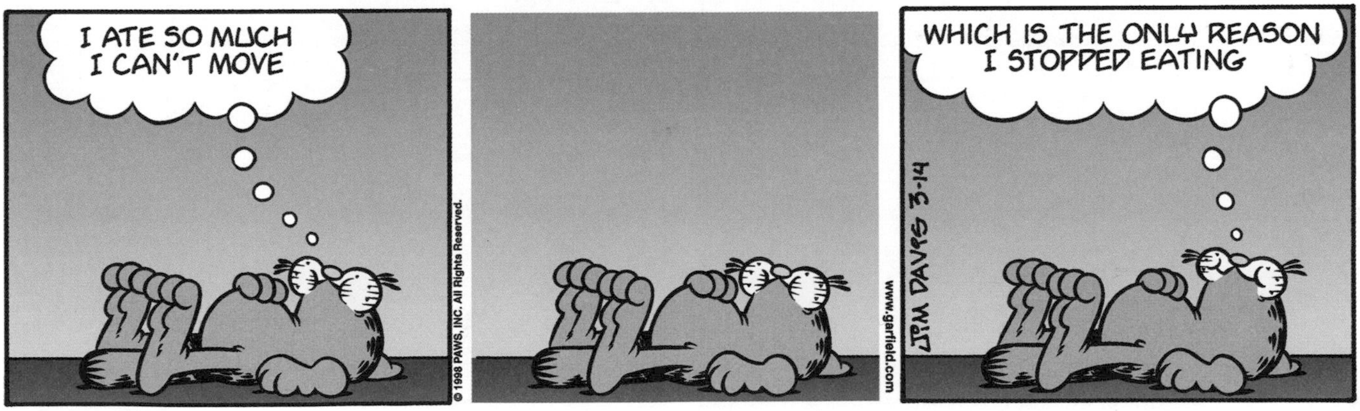
I ATE SO MUCH I CAN'T MOVE
© 1998 PAWS, INC. All Rights Reserved.
www.garfield.com
JIM DAVIS 3-14
WHICH IS THE ONLY REASON I STOPPED EATING

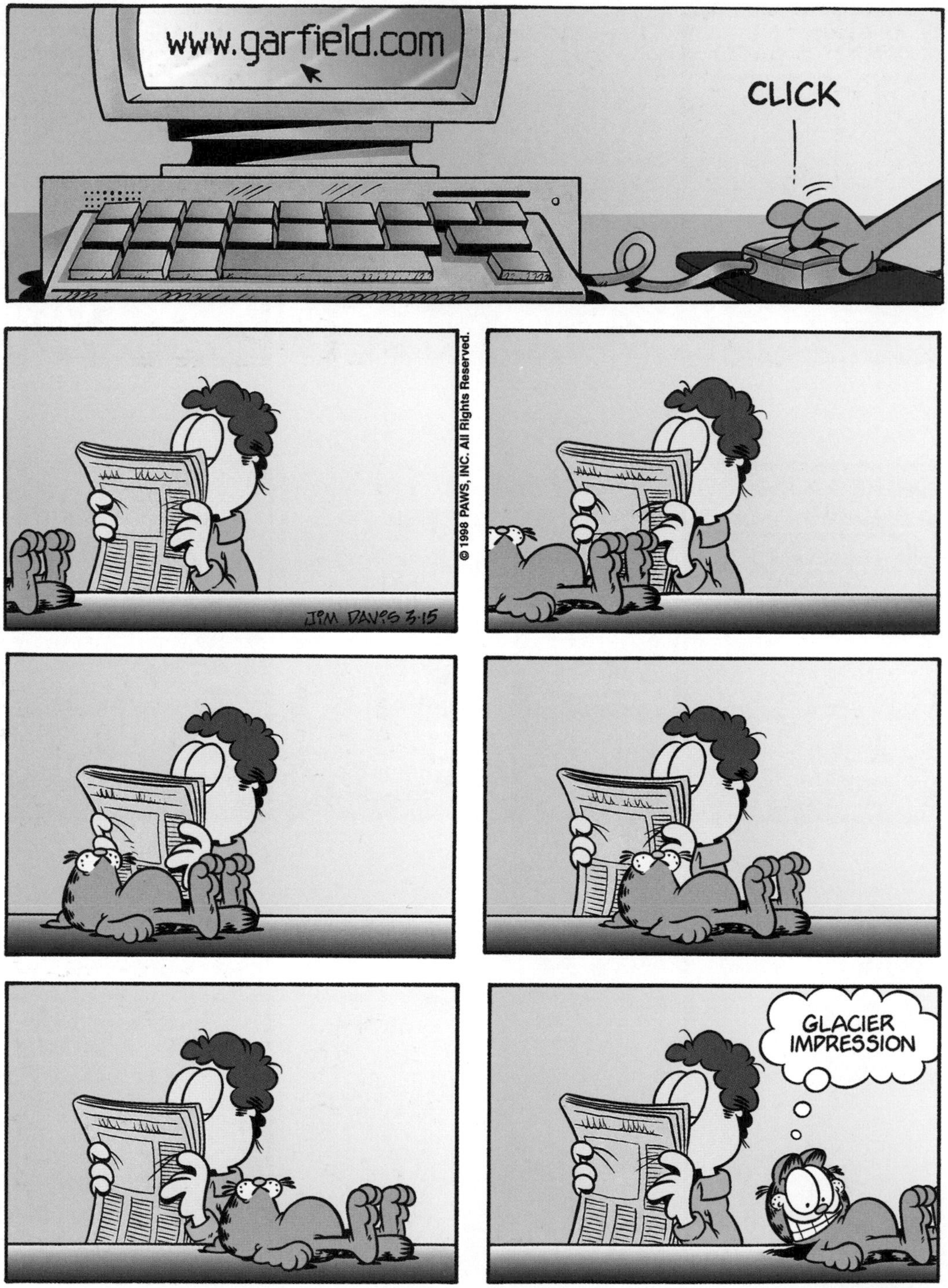
www.garfield.com
CLICK
© 1998 PAWS, INC. All Rights Reserved.
JIM DAVIS 3-15
GLACIER IMPRESSION

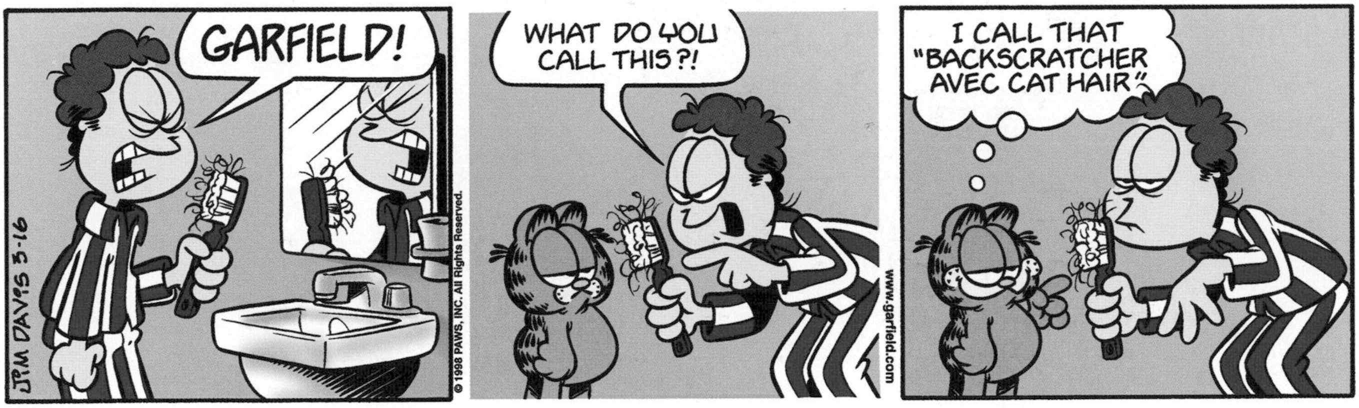
GARFIELD!
JIM DAVIS 3-16
© 1998 PAWS, INC. All Rights Reserved.
WHAT DO YOU CALL THIS?!
www.garfield.com
I CALL THAT "BACKSCRATCHER AVEC CAT HAIR"

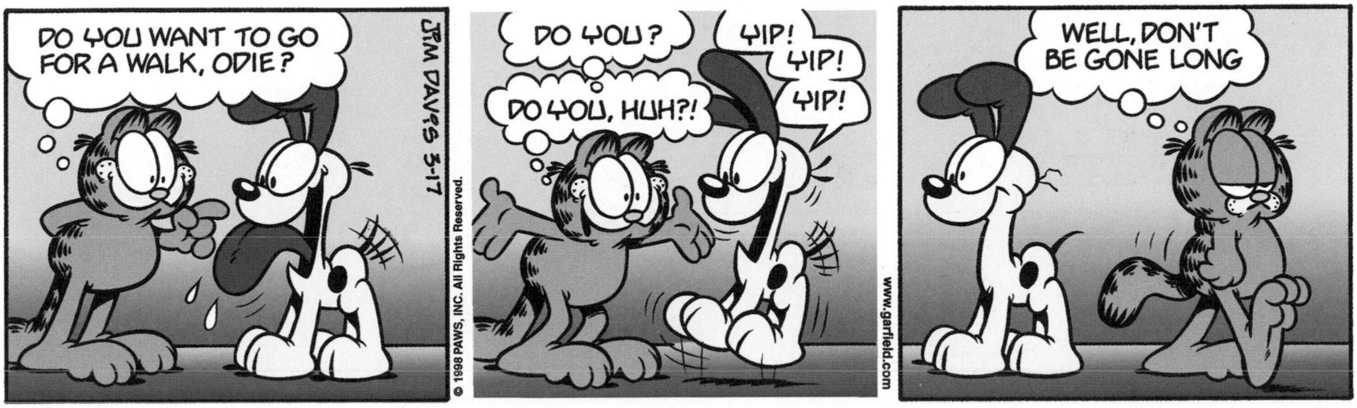
DO YOU WANT TO GO FOR A WALK, ODIE?
JIM DAVIS 3-17
© 1998 PAWS, INC. All Rights Reserved.
DO YOU?
DO YOU, HUH?!
YIP!
YIP!
YIP!
www.garfield.com
WELL, DON'T BE GONE LONG

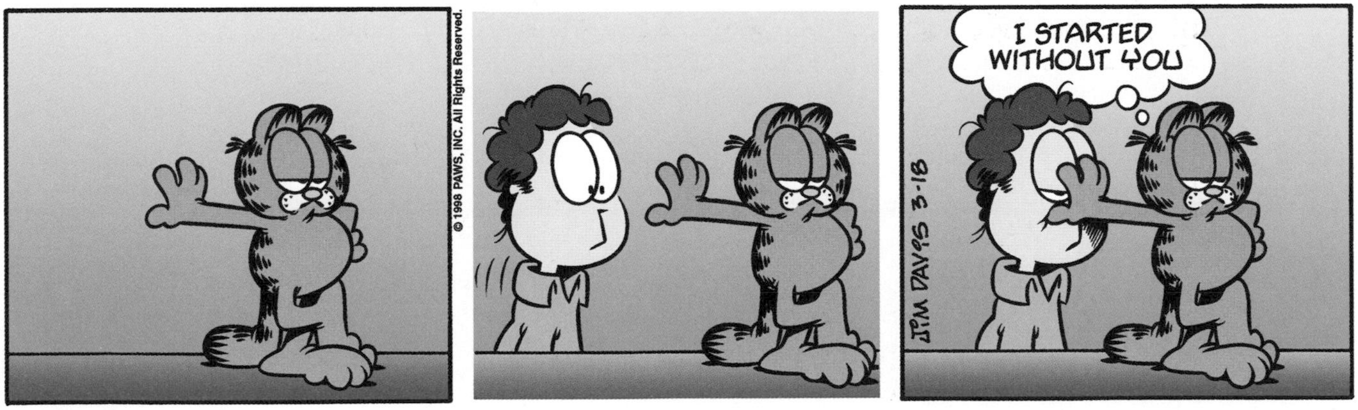
© 1998 PAWS, INC. All Rights Reserved.
JIM DAVIS 3-18
I STARTED WITHOUT YOU

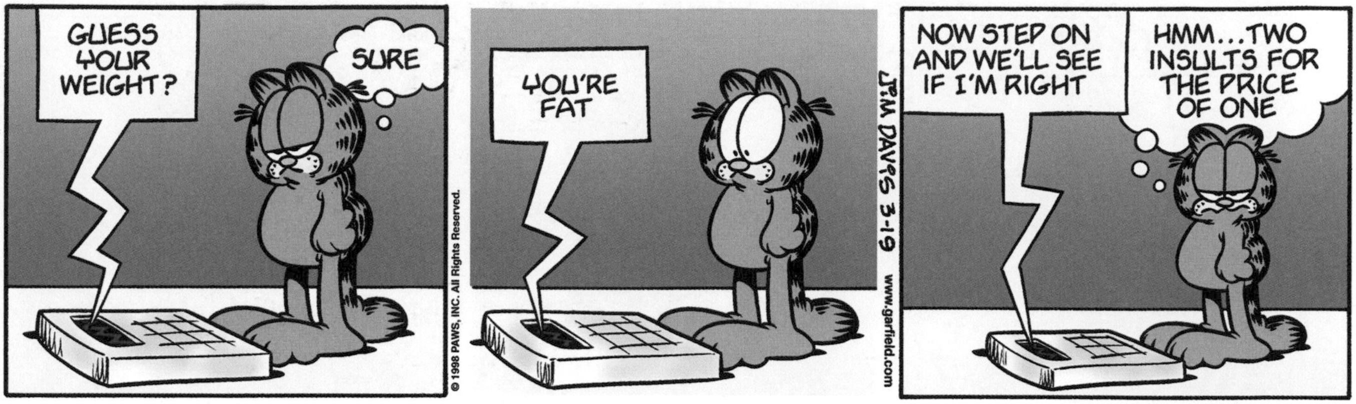
GUESS YOUR WEIGHT?
SURE
YOU'RE FAT
NOW STEP ON AND WE'LL SEE IF I'M RIGHT
HMM...TWO INSULTS FOR THE PRICE OF ONE
© 1998 PAWS, INC. All Rights Reserved.
JIM DAVIS 3-19
www.garfield.com

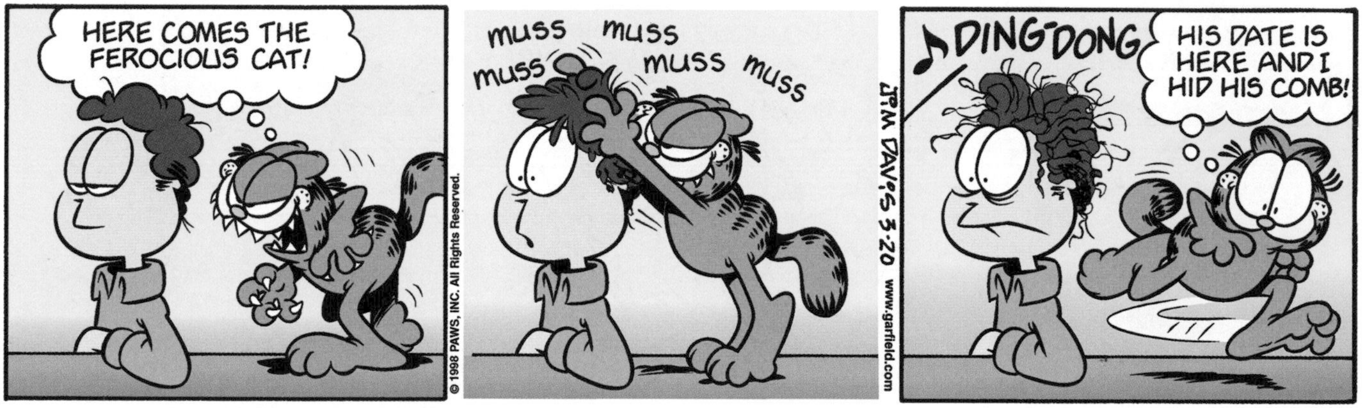
HERE COMES THE FEROCIOUS CAT!
muss muss
muss muss muss
DING-DONG
HIS DATE IS HERE AND I HID HIS COMB!
© 1998 PAWS, INC. All Rights Reserved.
JIM DAVIS 3-20
www.garfield.com

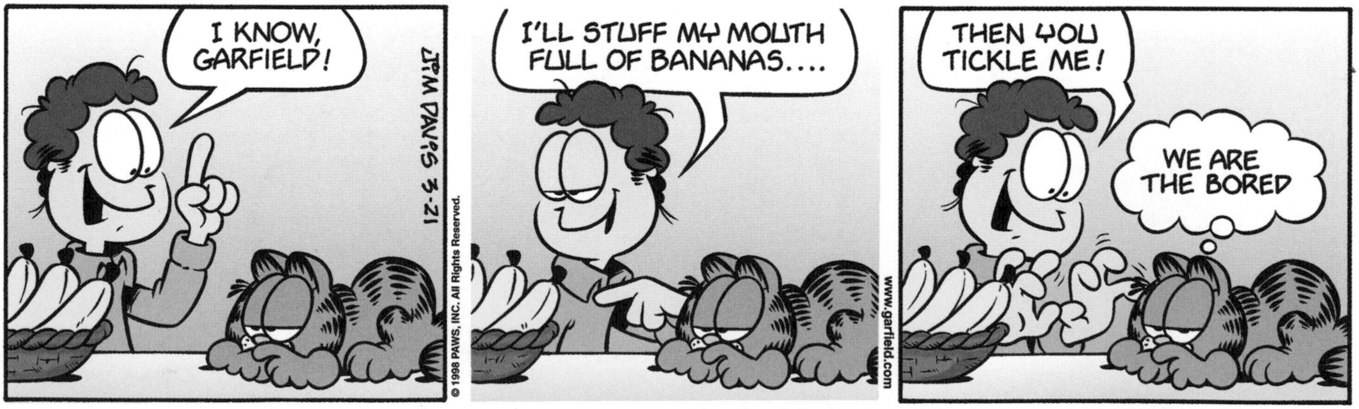
I KNOW, GARFIELD!
I'LL STUFF MY MOUTH FULL OF BANANAS....
THEN YOU TICKLE ME!
WE ARE THE BORED
JIM DAVIS 3-21
© 1998 PAWS, INC. All Rights Reserved.
www.garfield.com

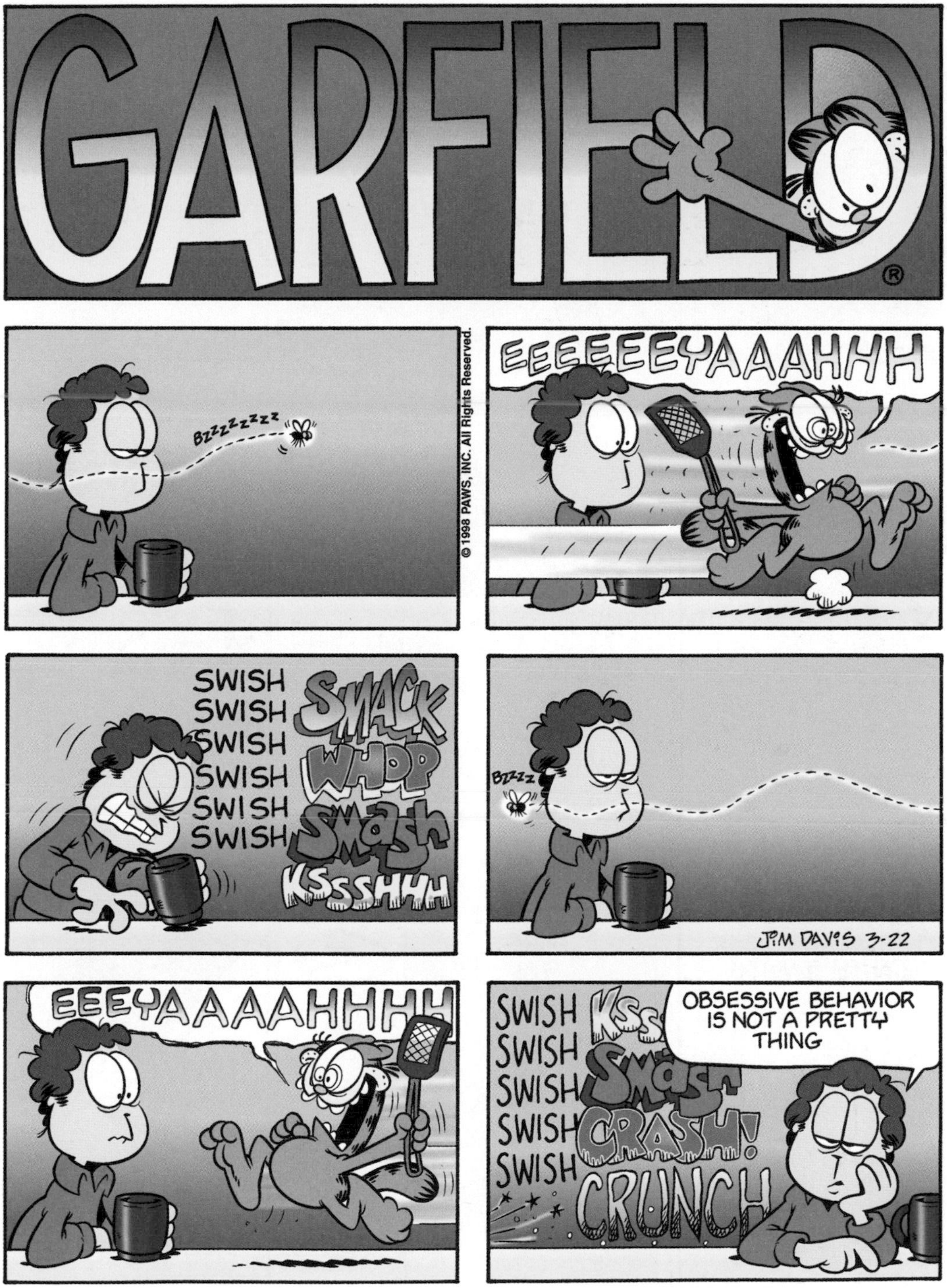
GARFIELD®
© 1998 PAWS, INC. All Rights Reserved.
BZZZZZZZZ
EEEEEEEYAAAHHH
SWISH SWISH SWISH SWISH SWISH SWISH
SMACK
WHOP
SMASH
KSSSHHH
BZZZZ
JIM DAVIS 3-22
EEEYAAAAHHHH
SWISH SWISH SWISH SWISH SWISH
SMASH
CRASH!
CRUNCH
OBSESSIVE BEHAVIOR IS NOT A PRETTY THING

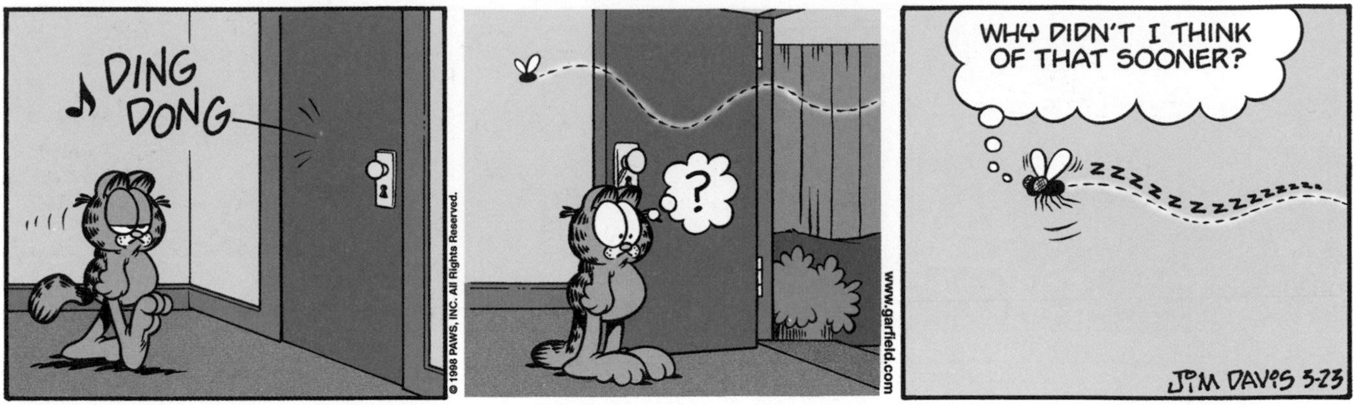
DING DONG
?
WHY DIDN'T I THINK OF THAT SOONER?
ZZZZZZZZZZZZZZ
JIM DAVIS 3-23
© 1998 PAWS, INC. All Rights Reserved.
www.garfield.com

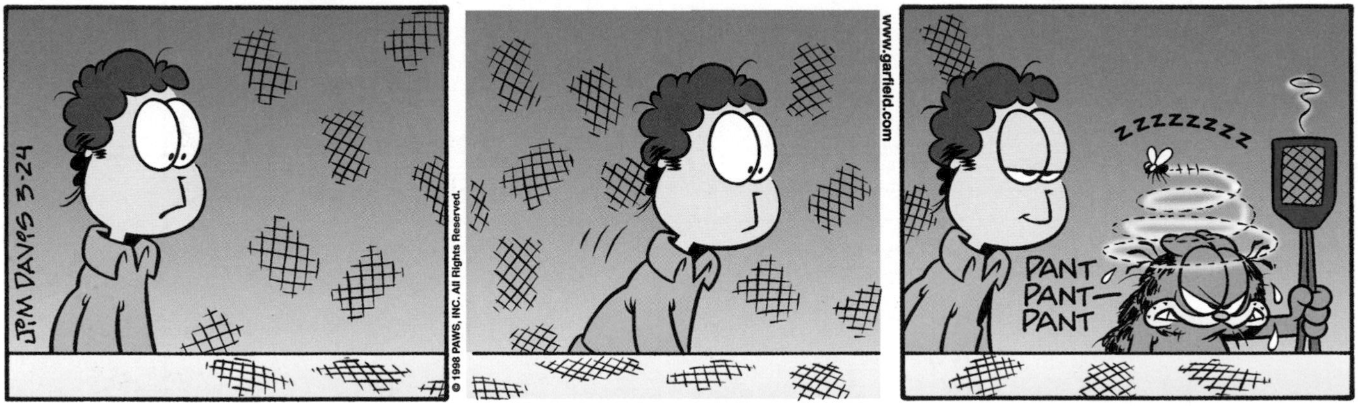
JIM DAVIS 3-24
© 1998 PAWS, INC. All Rights Reserved.
www.garfield.com
ZZZZZZZZ
PANT PANT PANT

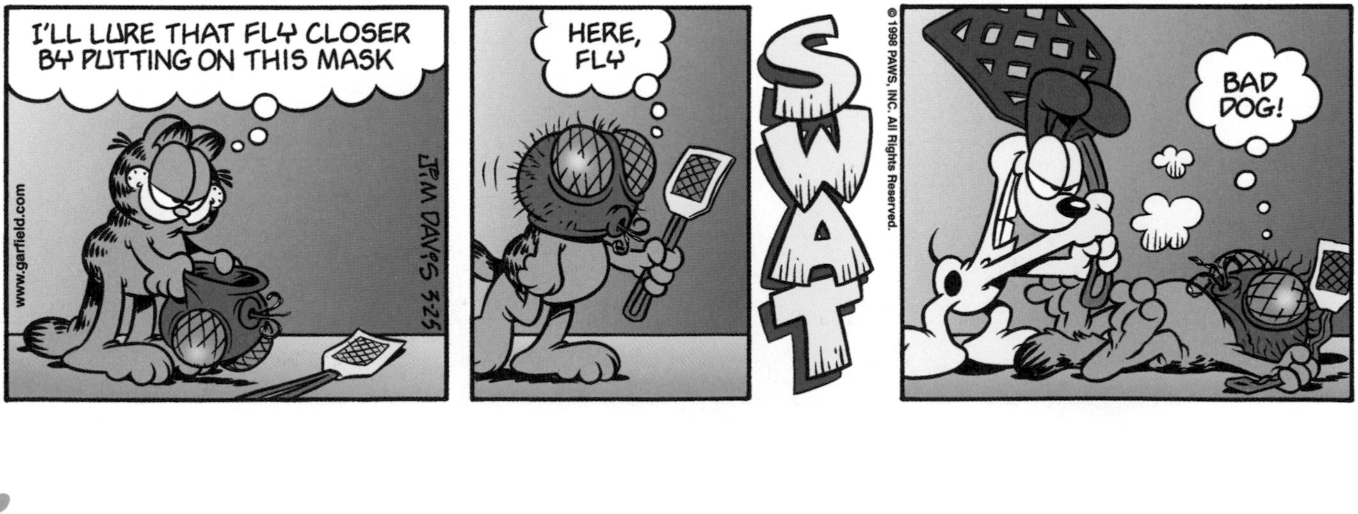
I'LL LURE THAT FLY CLOSER BY PUTTING ON THIS MASK
JIM DAVIS 3-25
www.garfield.com
HERE, FLY
SWAT
© 1998 PAWS, INC. All Rights Reserved.
BAD DOG!

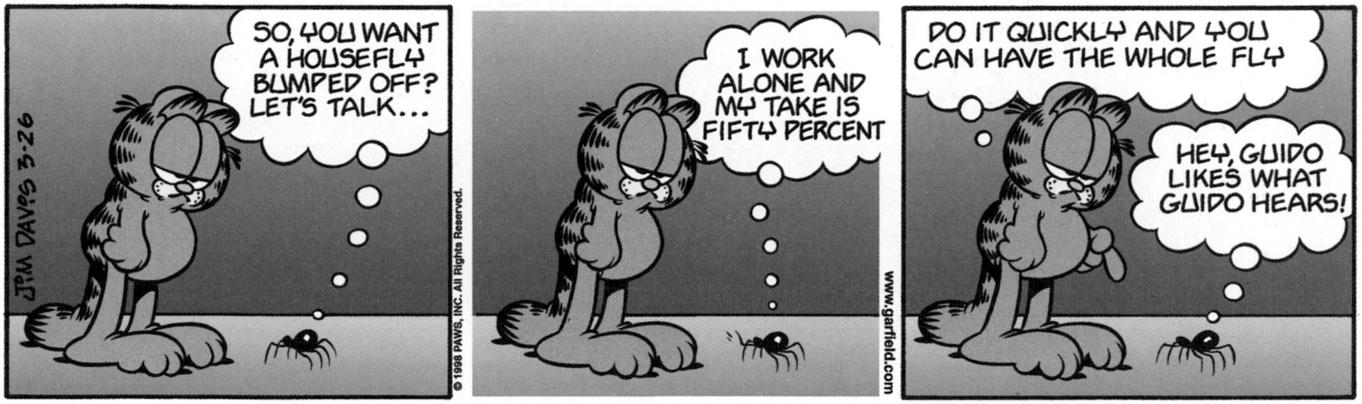
JIM DAVIS 3-26
SO, YOU WANT A HOUSEFLY BUMPED OFF? LET'S TALK...
© 1998 PAWS, INC. All Rights Reserved.
I WORK ALONE AND MY TAKE IS FIFTY PERCENT
www.garfield.com
DO IT QUICKLY AND YOU CAN HAVE THE WHOLE FLY
HEY, GUIDO LIKES WHAT GUIDO HEARS!

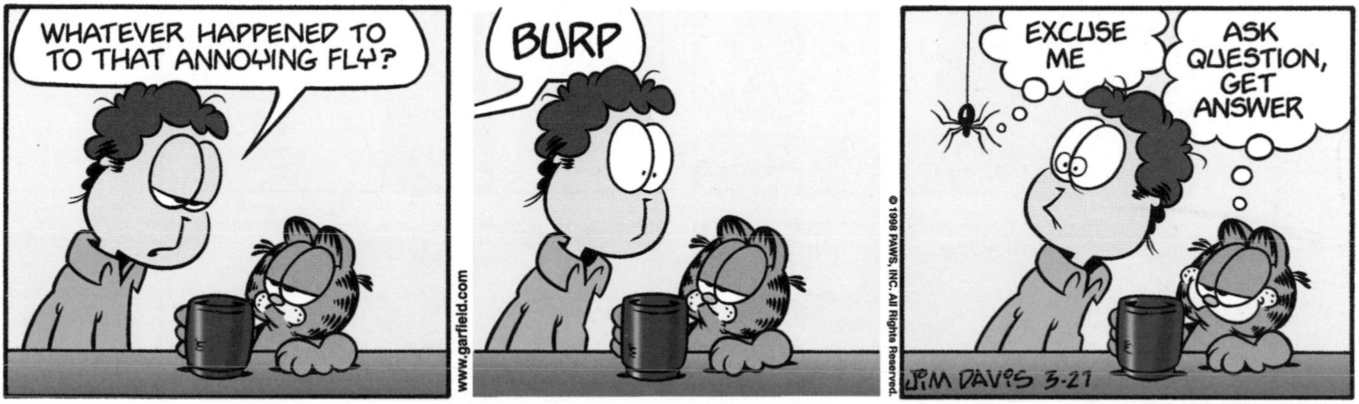
WHATEVER HAPPENED TO TO THAT ANNOYING FLY?
www.garfield.com
BURP
© 1998 PAWS, INC. All Rights Reserved.
EXCUSE ME
ASK QUESTION, GET ANSWER
JIM DAVIS 3-27

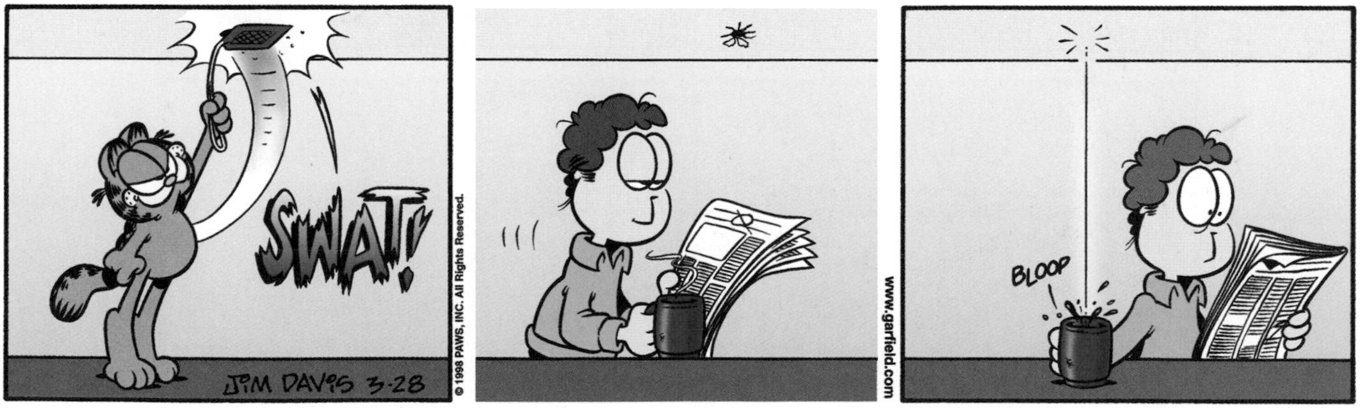
SWAT!
JIM DAVIS 3-28
© 1998 PAWS, INC. All Rights Reserved.
www.garfield.com
BLOOP

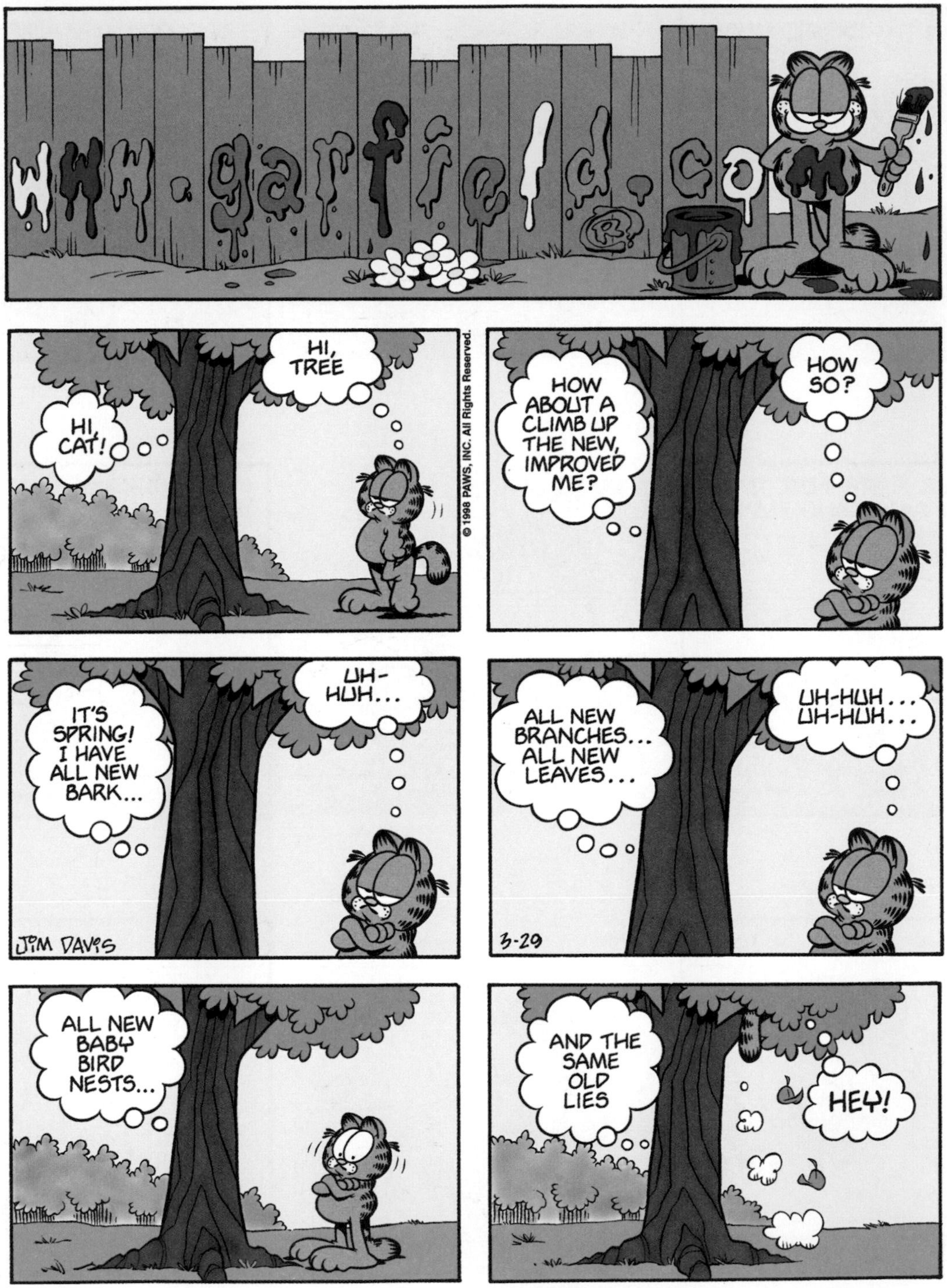

www.garfield.com®
HI, CAT!
HI, TREE
© 1998 PAWS, INC. All Rights Reserved.
HOW ABOUT A CLIMB UP THE NEW, IMPROVED ME?
HOW SO?
IT'S SPRING! I HAVE ALL NEW BARK...
UH-HUH...
JIM DAVIS
ALL NEW BRANCHES... ALL NEW LEAVES...
UH-HUH... UH-HUH...
3-29
ALL NEW BABY BIRD NESTS...
AND THE SAME OLD LIES
HEY!

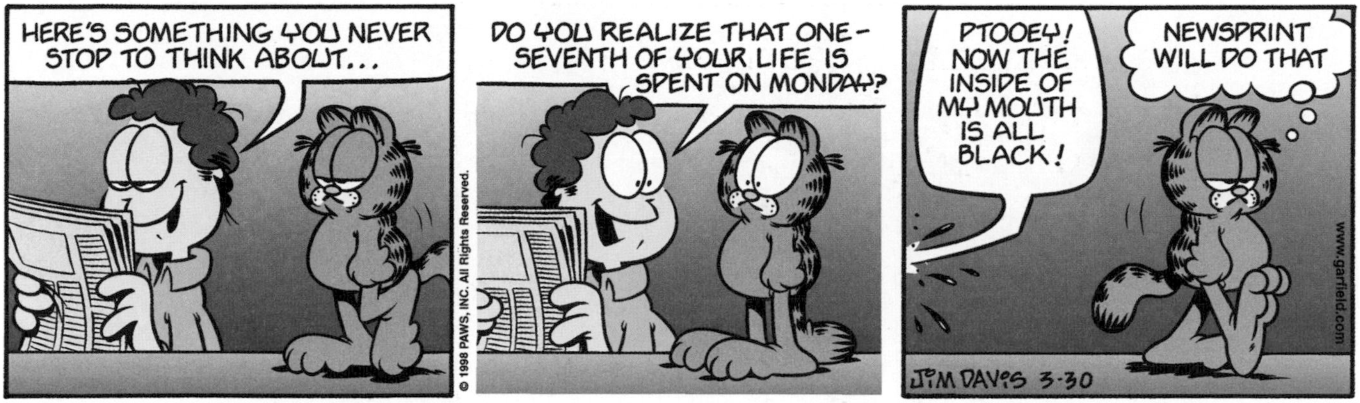
HERE'S SOMETHING YOU NEVER STOP TO THINK ABOUT...
© 1998 PAWS, INC. All Rights Reserved.
DO YOU REALIZE THAT ONE-SEVENTH OF YOUR LIFE IS SPENT ON MONDAY?
PTOOEY! NOW THE INSIDE OF MY MOUTH IS ALL BLACK!
NEWSPRINT WILL DO THAT
www.garfield.com
JIM DAVIS 3-30

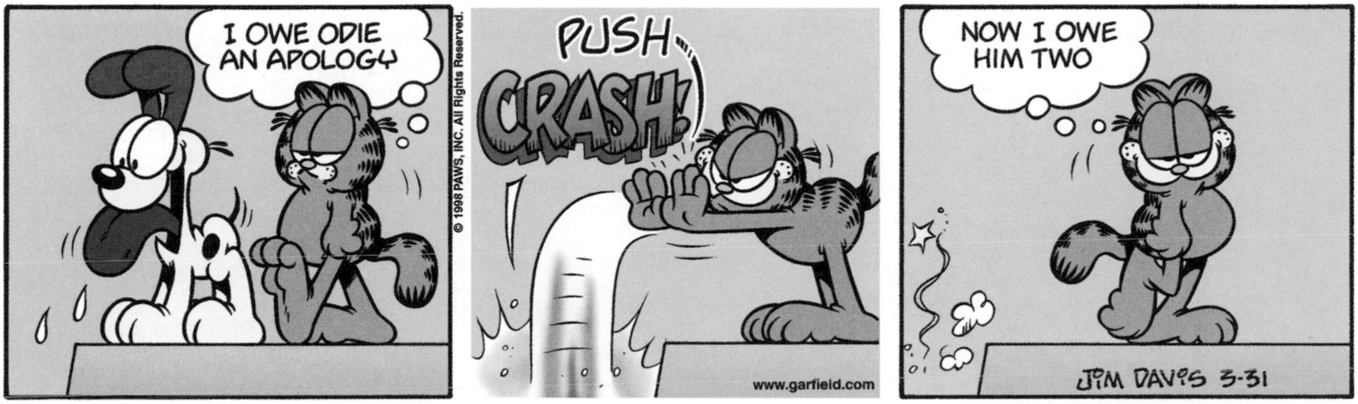
I OWE ODIE AN APOLOGY
© 1998 PAWS, INC. All Rights Reserved.
PUSH
CRASH!
www.garfield.com
NOW I OWE HIM TWO
JIM DAVIS 3-31

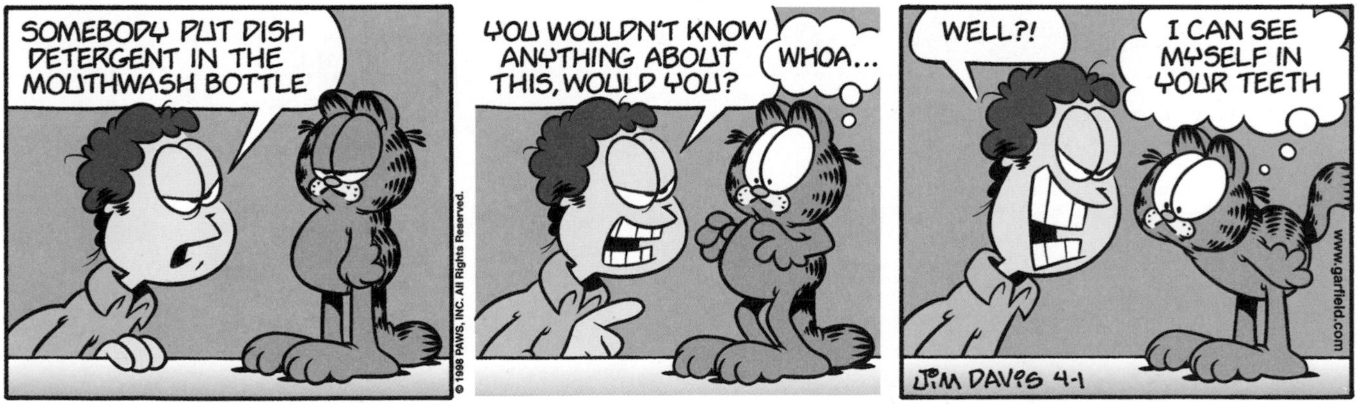
SOMEBODY PUT DISH DETERGENT IN THE MOUTHWASH BOTTLE
© 1998 PAWS, INC. All Rights Reserved.
YOU WOULDN'T KNOW ANYTHING ABOUT THIS, WOULD YOU?
WHOA...
WELL?!
I CAN SEE MYSELF IN YOUR TEETH
www.garfield.com
JIM DAVIS 4-1

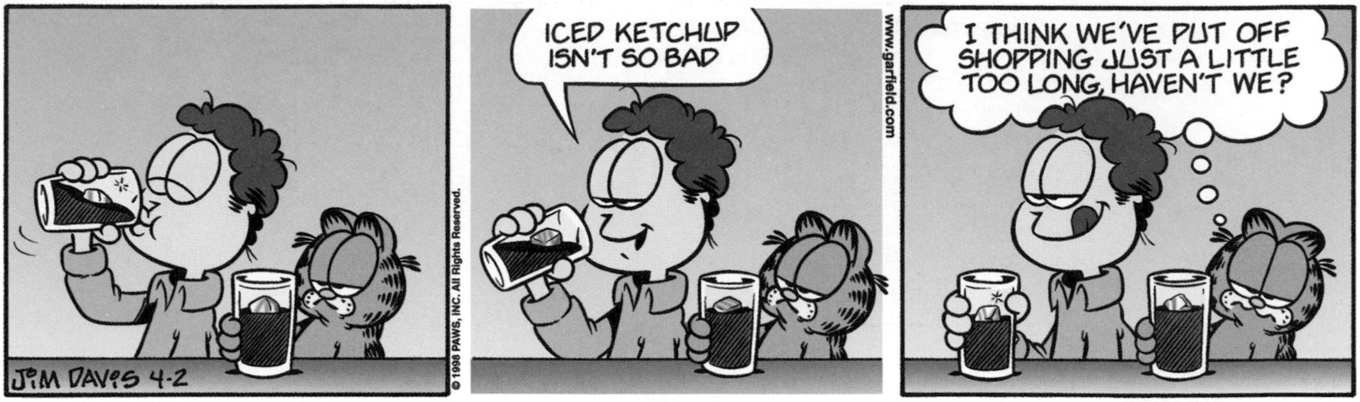
JIM DAVIS 4-2
© 1998 PAWS, INC. All Rights Reserved.
ICED KETCHUP ISN'T SO BAD
www.garfield.com
I THINK WE'VE PUT OFF SHOPPING JUST A LITTLE TOO LONG, HAVEN'T WE?

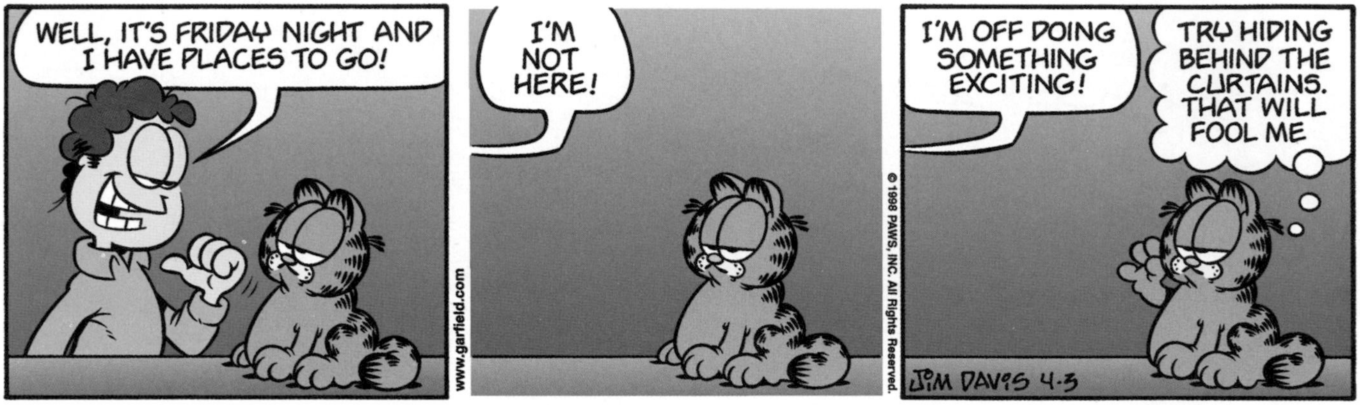
WELL, IT'S FRIDAY NIGHT AND I HAVE PLACES TO GO!
www.garfield.com
I'M NOT HERE!
© 1998 PAWS, INC. All Rights Reserved.
I'M OFF DOING SOMETHING EXCITING!
TRY HIDING BEHIND THE CURTAINS. THAT WILL FOOL ME
JIM DAVIS 4-3

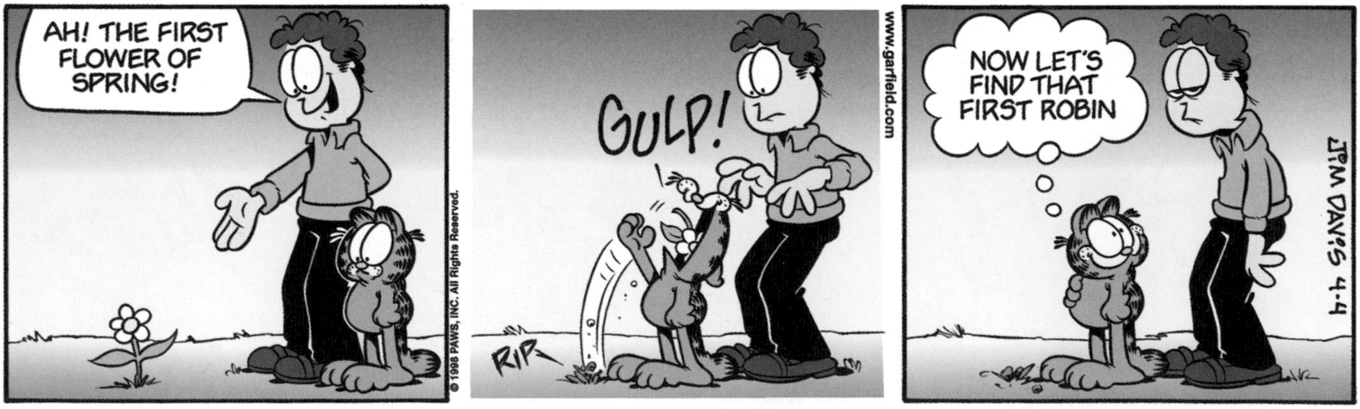
AH! THE FIRST FLOWER OF SPRING!
© 1998 PAWS, INC. All Rights Reserved.
GULP!
RIP
www.garfield.com
NOW LET'S FIND THAT FIRST ROBIN
JIM DAVIS 4-4

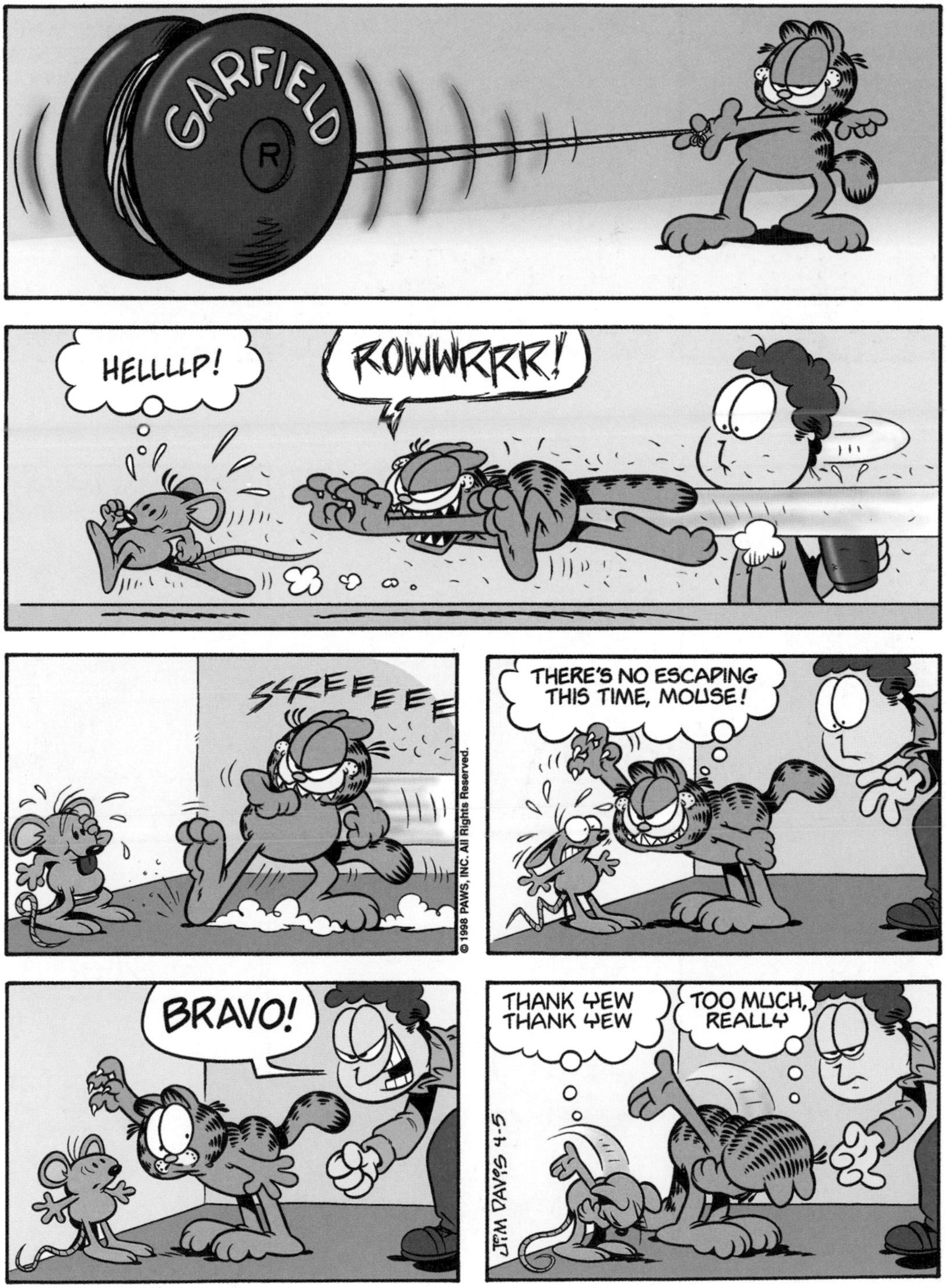
GARFIELD
HELLLLP!
ROWWRRR!
SCREEEEEEE
© 1998 PAWS, INC. All Rights Reserved.
THERE'S NO ESCAPING THIS TIME, MOUSE!
BRAVO!
JIM DAVIS 4-5
THANK YEW THANK YEW
TOO MUCH, REALLY

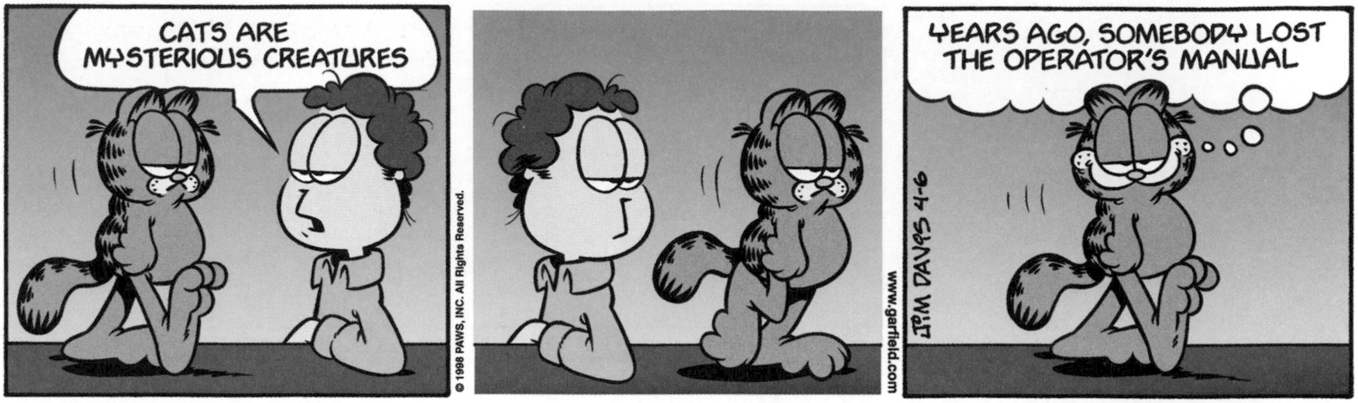
CATS ARE MYSTERIOUS CREATURES
YEARS AGO, SOMEBODY LOST THE OPERATOR'S MANUAL

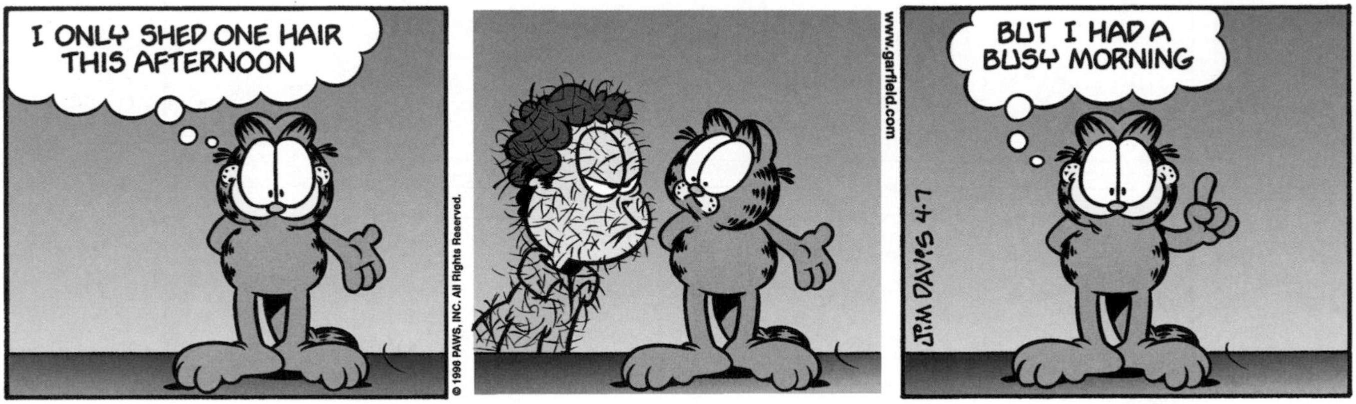
I ONLY SHED ONE HAIR THIS AFTERNOON
BUT I HAD A BUSY MORNING

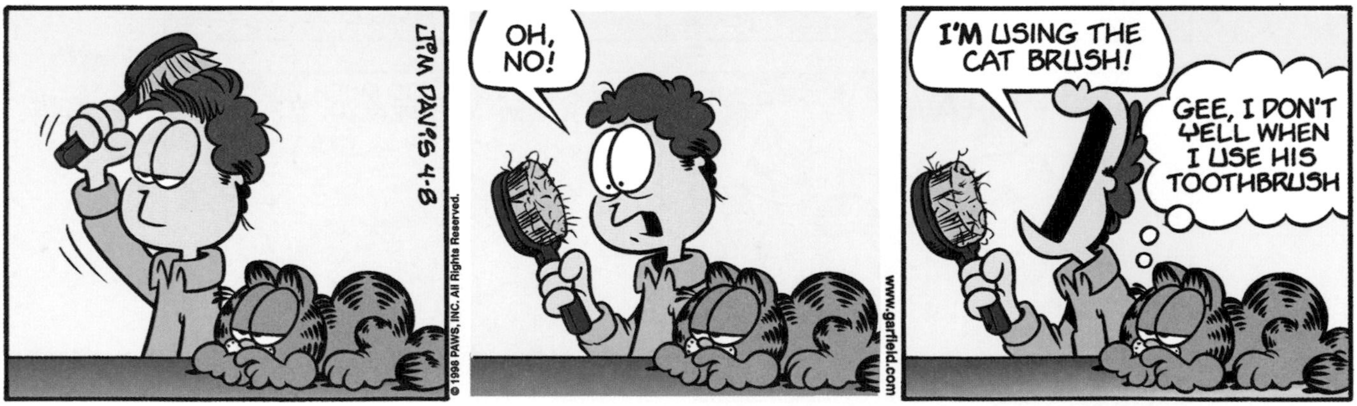
OH, NO!
I'M USING THE CAT BRUSH!
GEE, I DON'T YELL WHEN I USE HIS TOOTHBRUSH

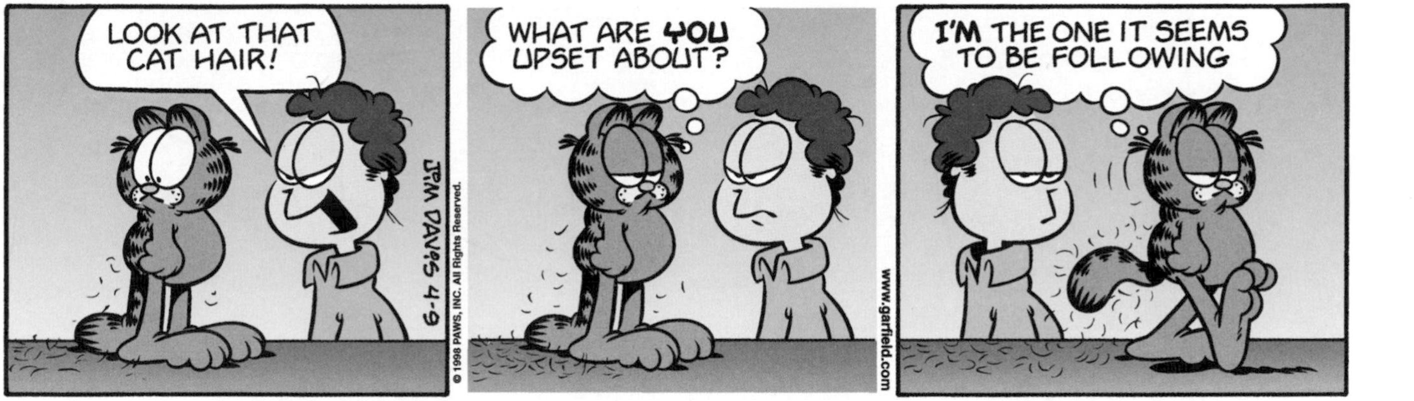
LOOK AT THAT CAT HAIR!
JIM DAVIS 4-9
© 1998 PAWS, INC. All Rights Reserved.
WHAT ARE YOU UPSET ABOUT?
www.garfield.com
I'M THE ONE IT SEEMS TO BE FOLLOWING

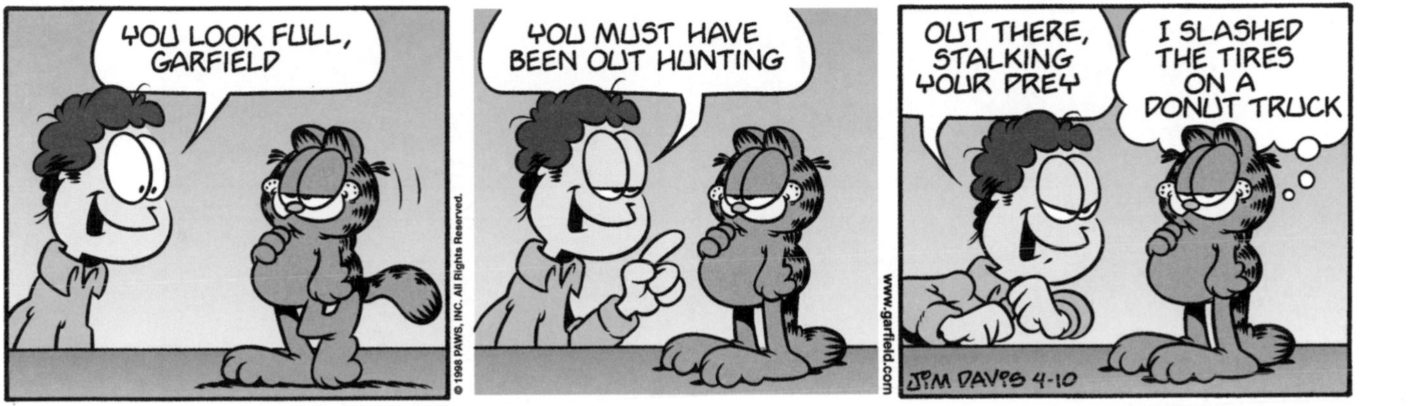
YOU LOOK FULL, GARFIELD
© 1998 PAWS, INC. All Rights Reserved.
YOU MUST HAVE BEEN OUT HUNTING
www.garfield.com
OUT THERE, STALKING YOUR PREY
I SLASHED THE TIRES ON A DONUT TRUCK
JIM DAVIS 4-10

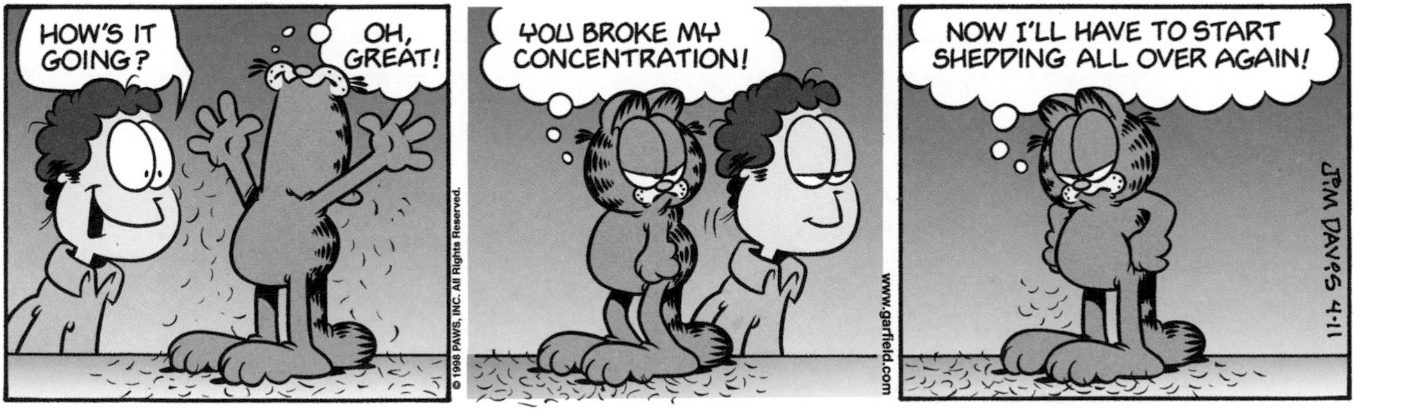
HOW'S IT GOING?
OH, GREAT!
© 1998 PAWS, INC. All Rights Reserved.
YOU BROKE MY CONCENTRATION!
www.garfield.com
NOW I'LL HAVE TO START SHEDDING ALL OVER AGAIN!
JIM DAVIS 4-11

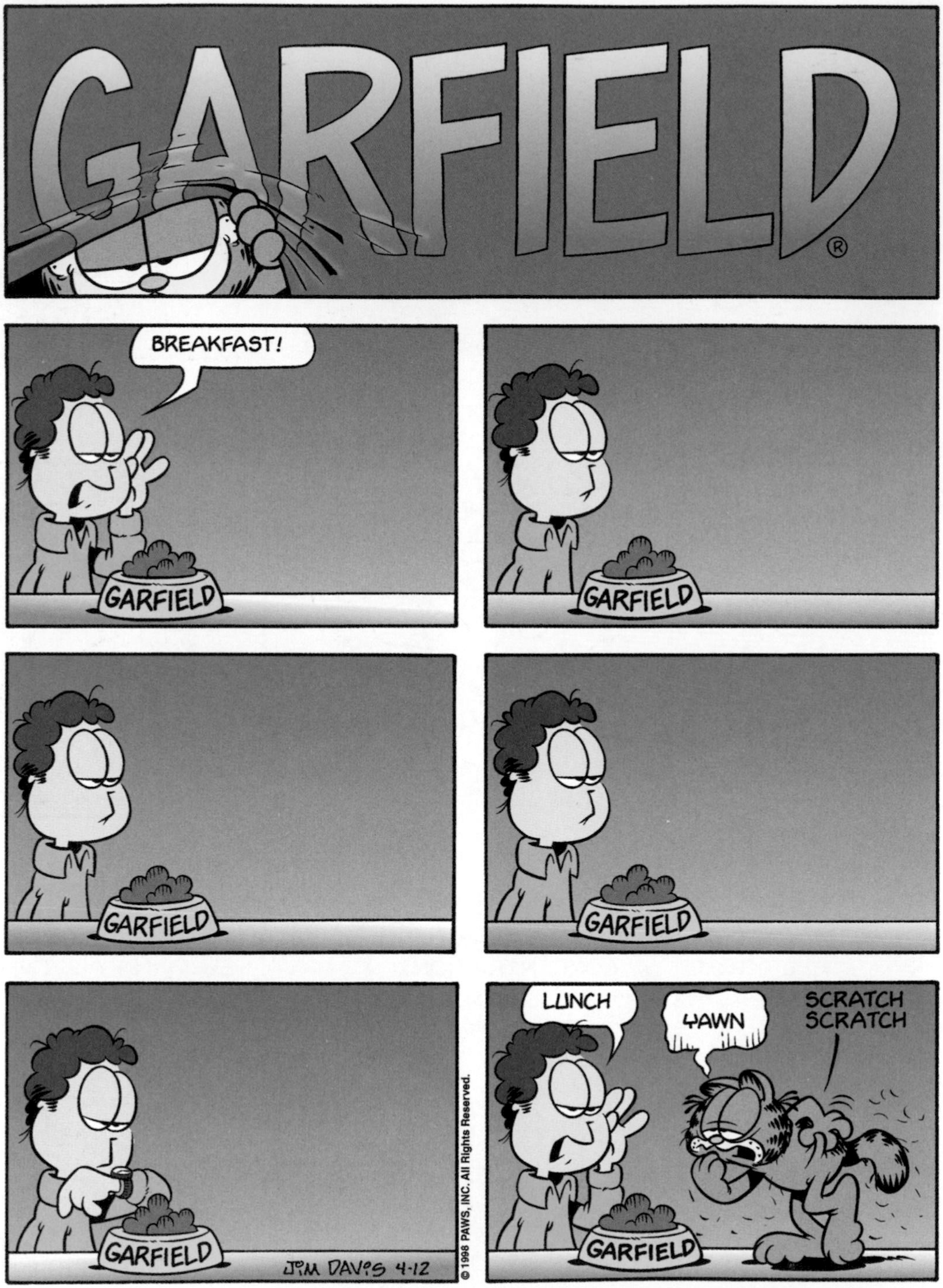
GARFIELD
BREAKFAST!
GARFIELD
GARFIELD
GARFIELD
GARFIELD
GARFIELD
JIM DAVIS 4-12
LUNCH
YAWN
SCRATCH SCRATCH
GARFIELD

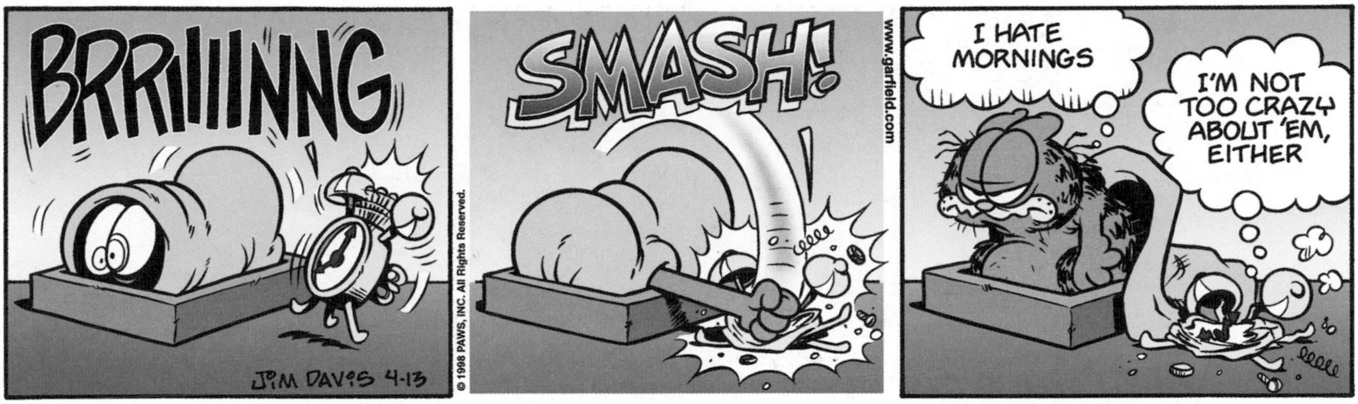
BRRIIIINNG
JIM DAVIS 4-13
© 1998 PAWS, INC. All Rights Reserved.
SMASH!
www.garfield.com
I HATE MORNINGS
I'M NOT TOO CRAZY ABOUT 'EM, EITHER

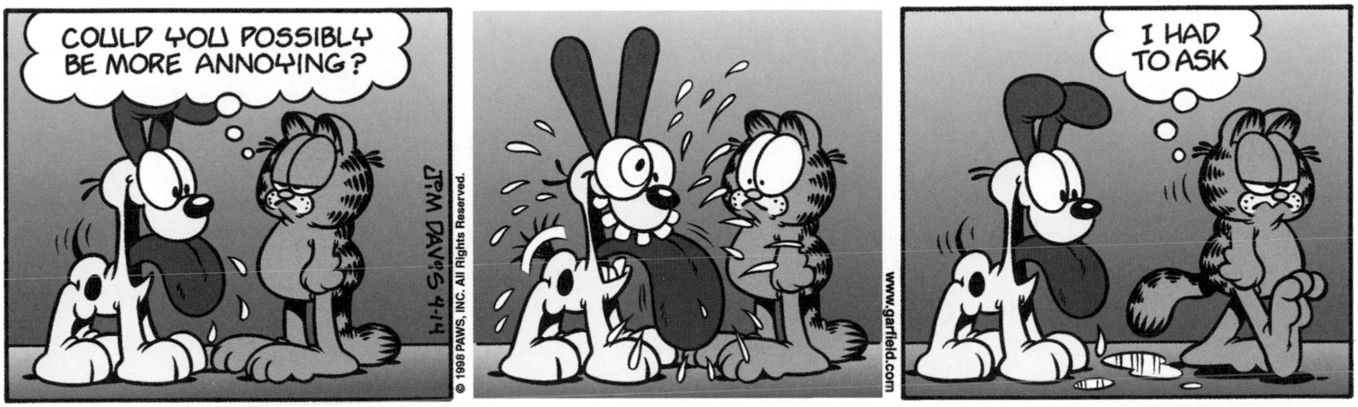
COULD YOU POSSIBLY BE MORE ANNOYING?
JIM DAVIS 4-14
© 1998 PAWS, INC. All Rights Reserved.
www.garfield.com
I HAD TO ASK

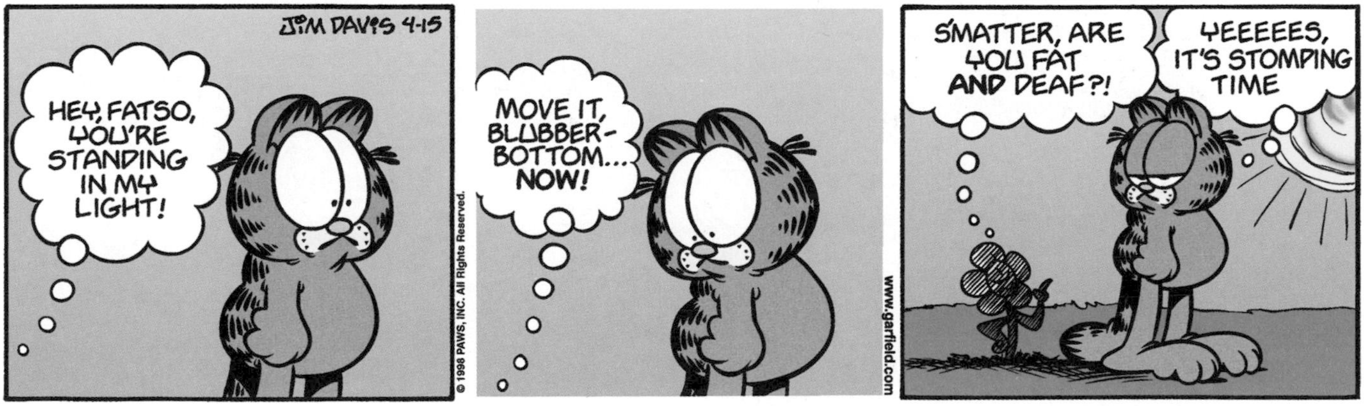
JIM DAVIS 4-15
HEY, FATSO, YOU'RE STANDING IN MY LIGHT!
© 1998 PAWS, INC. All Rights Reserved.
MOVE IT, BLUBBER-BOTTOM... NOW!
www.garfield.com
S'MATTER, ARE YOU FAT AND DEAF?!
YEEEEES, IT'S STOMPING TIME

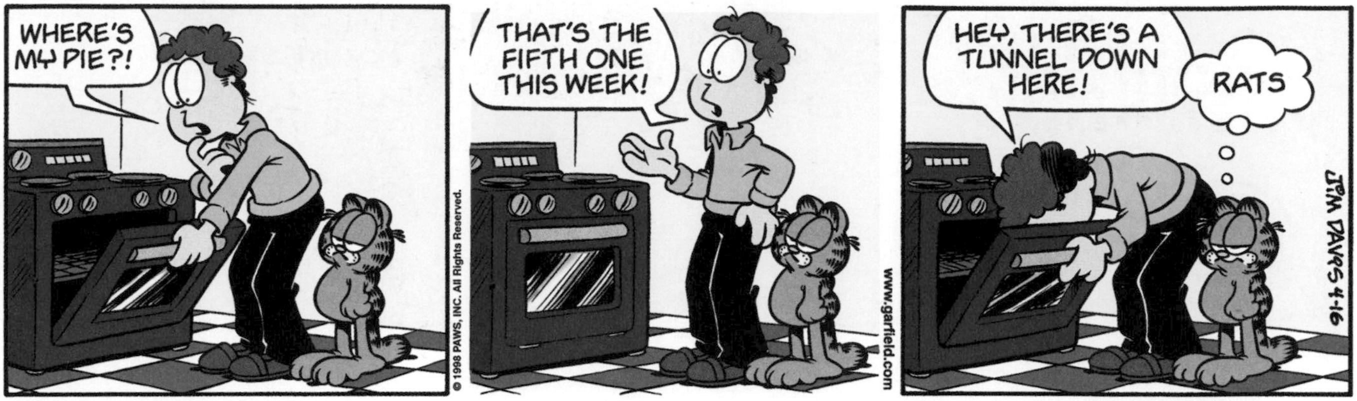
WHERE'S MY PIE?!
THAT'S THE FIFTH ONE THIS WEEK!
HEY, THERE'S A TUNNEL DOWN HERE!
RATS
© 1998 PAWS, INC. All Rights Reserved.
www.garfield.com
JIM DAVIS 4-16

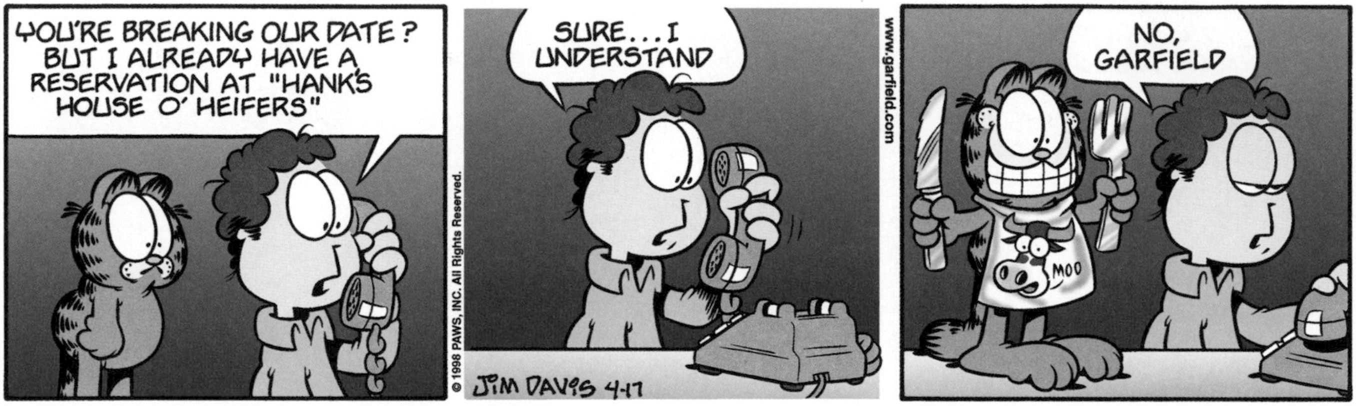
YOU'RE BREAKING OUR DATE? BUT I ALREADY HAVE A RESERVATION AT "HANK'S HOUSE O' HEIFERS"
SURE... I UNDERSTAND
NO, GARFIELD
MOO
© 1998 PAWS, INC. All Rights Reserved.
www.garfield.com
JIM DAVIS 4-17

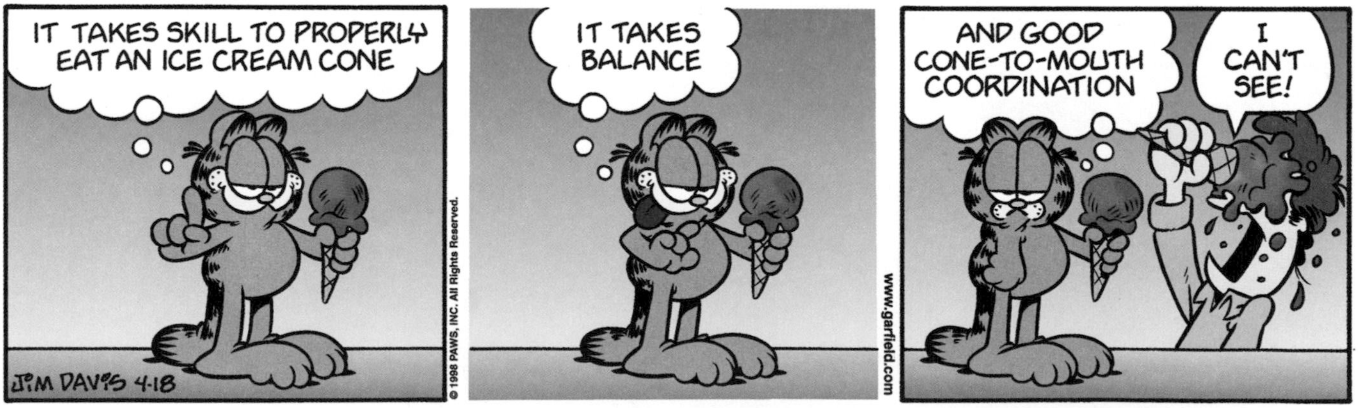
IT TAKES SKILL TO PROPERLY EAT AN ICE CREAM CONE
IT TAKES BALANCE
AND GOOD CONE-TO-MOUTH COORDINATION
I CAN'T SEE!
JIM DAVIS 4-18
© 1998 PAWS, INC. All Rights Reserved.
www.garfield.com

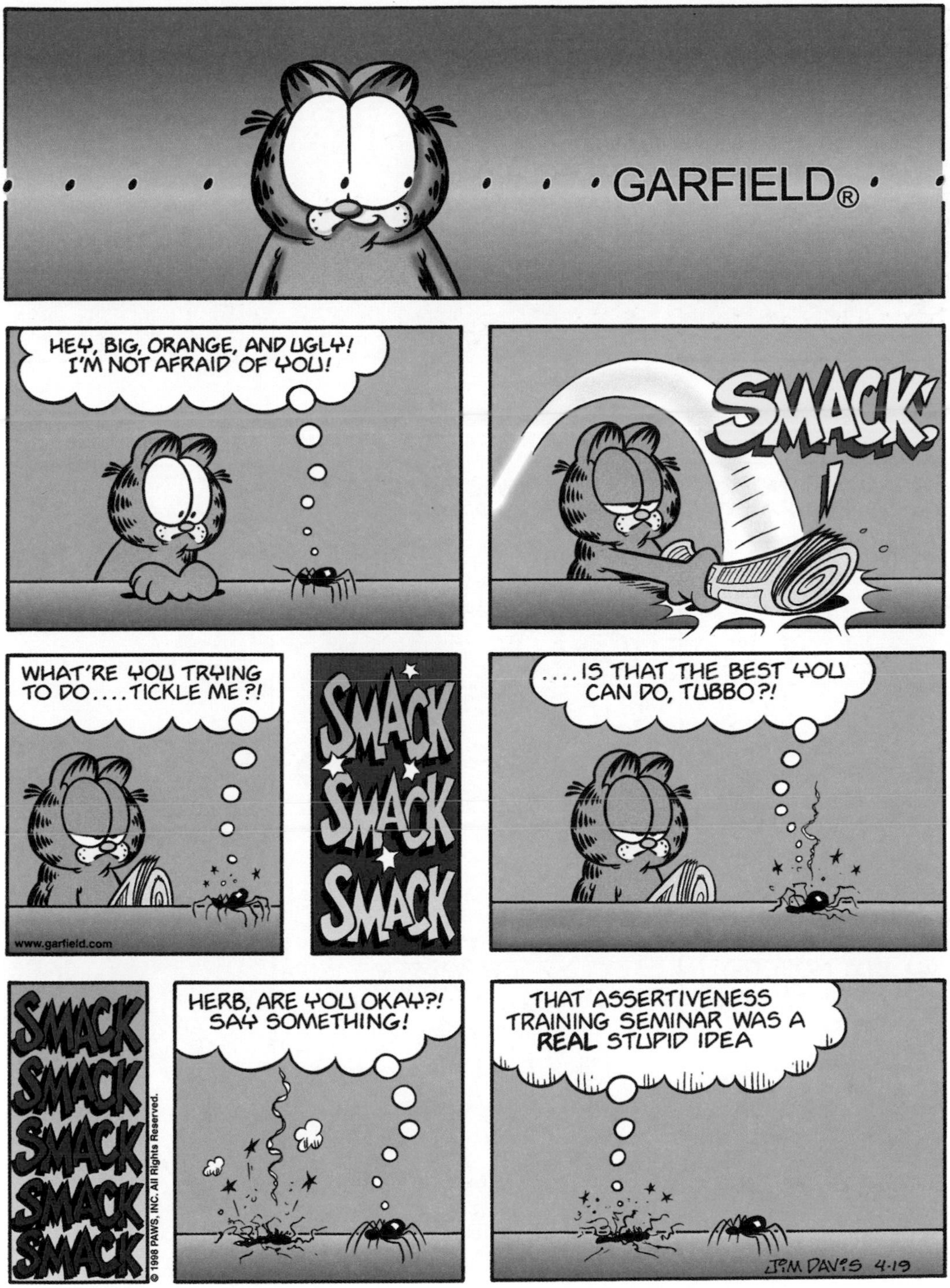
GARFIELD®
HEY, BIG, ORANGE, AND UGLY! I'M NOT AFRAID OF YOU!
SMACK!
WHAT'RE YOU TRYING TO DO....TICKLE ME?!
www.garfield.com
SMACK SMACK SMACK
....IS THAT THE BEST YOU CAN DO, TUBBO?!
SMACK SMACK SMACK SMACK SMACK
© 1998 PAWS, INC. All Rights Reserved.
HERB, ARE YOU OKAY?! SAY SOMETHING!
THAT ASSERTIVENESS TRAINING SEMINAR WAS A **REAL** STUPID IDEA
JIM DAVIS 4-19

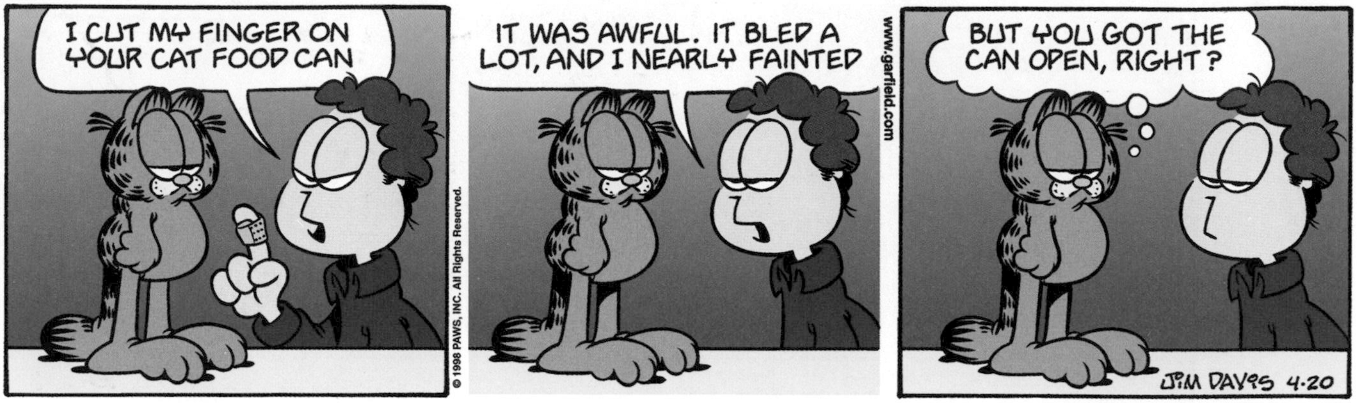
I CUT MY FINGER ON YOUR CAT FOOD CAN
© 1998 PAWS, INC. All Rights Reserved.
IT WAS AWFUL. IT BLED A LOT, AND I NEARLY FAINTED
www.garfield.com
BUT YOU GOT THE CAN OPEN, RIGHT?
JIM DAVIS 4-20

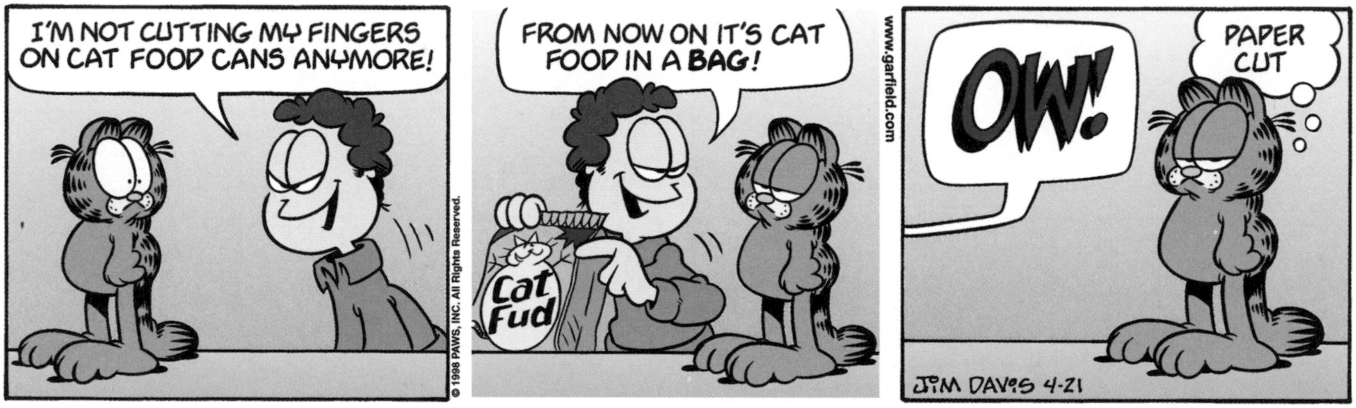
I'M NOT CUTTING MY FINGERS ON CAT FOOD CANS ANYMORE!
© 1998 PAWS, INC. All Rights Reserved.
FROM NOW ON IT'S CAT FOOD IN A BAG!
Cat Fud
www.garfield.com
OW!
PAPER CUT
JIM DAVIS 4-21

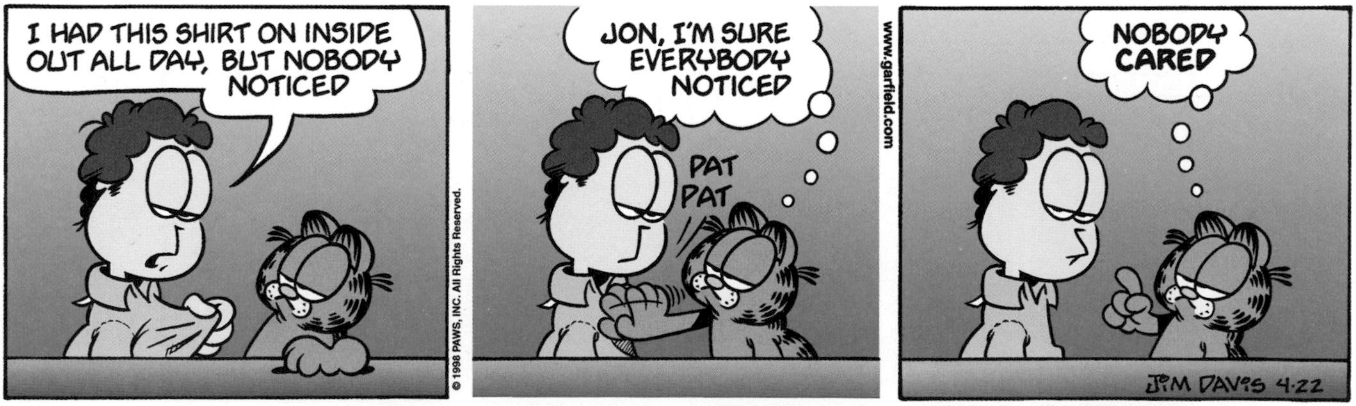
I HAD THIS SHIRT ON INSIDE OUT ALL DAY, BUT NOBODY NOTICED
© 1998 PAWS, INC. All Rights Reserved.
JON, I'M SURE EVERYBODY NOTICED
PAT PAT
www.garfield.com
NOBODY CARED
JIM DAVIS 4-22

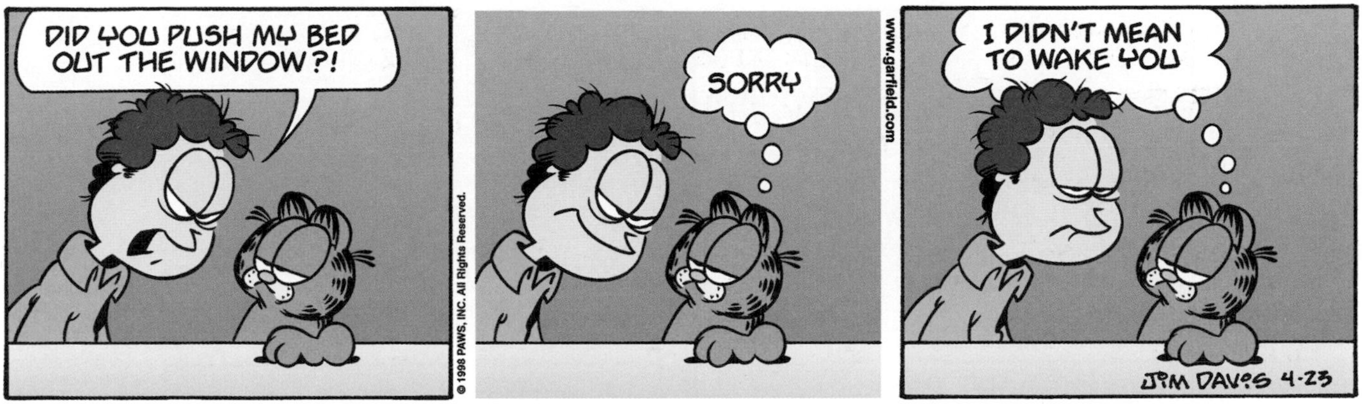
DID YOU PUSH MY BED OUT THE WINDOW?!
© 1998 PAWS, INC. All Rights Reserved.
SORRY
www.garfield.com
I DIDN'T MEAN TO WAKE YOU
JIM DAVIS 4-23

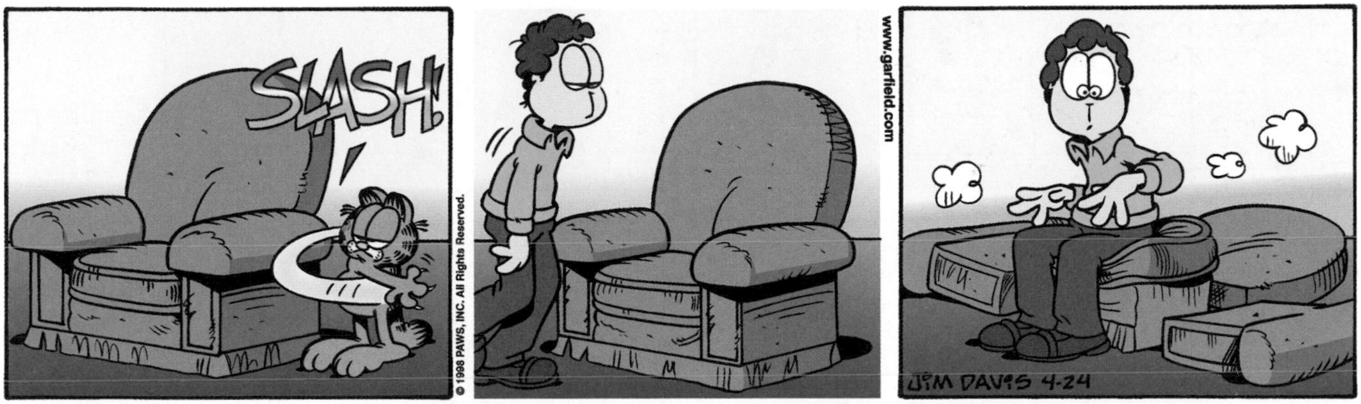
SLASH!
© 1998 PAWS, INC. All Rights Reserved.
www.garfield.com
JIM DAVIS 4-24

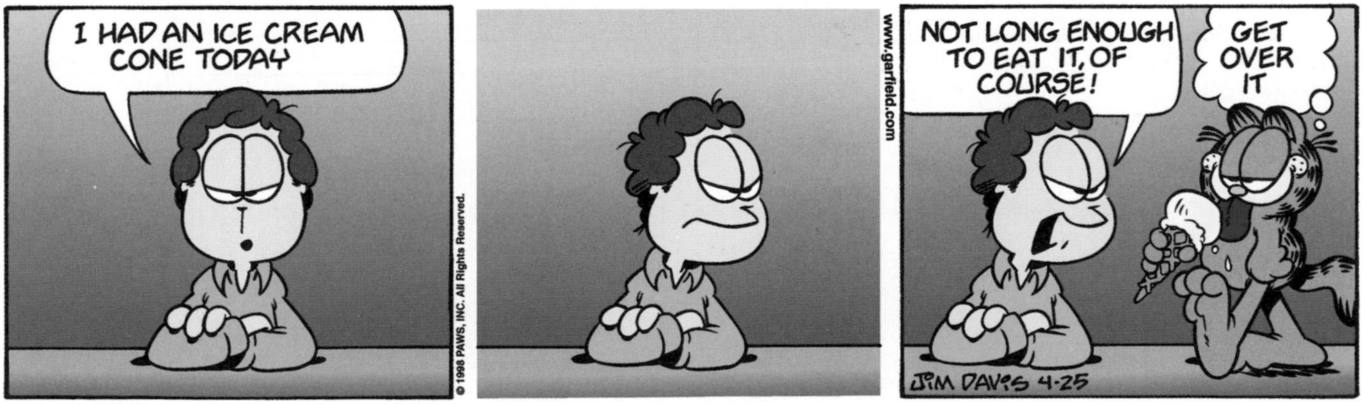
I HAD AN ICE CREAM CONE TODAY
© 1998 PAWS, INC. All Rights Reserved.
www.garfield.com
NOT LONG ENOUGH TO EAT IT, OF COURSE!
GET OVER IT
JIM DAVIS 4-25

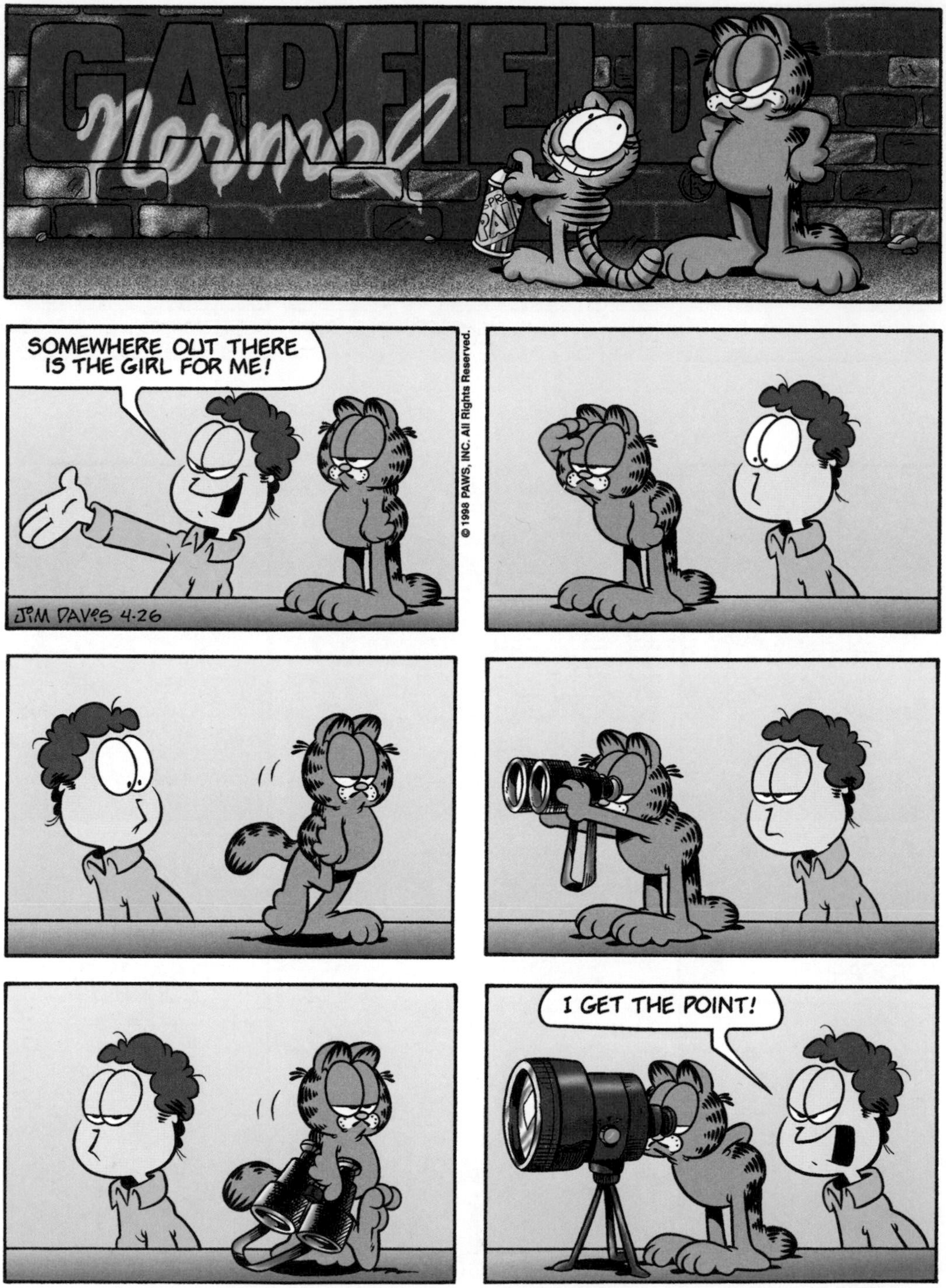
GARFIELD
Normal
PAINT
SOMEWHERE OUT THERE IS THE GIRL FOR ME!
JIM DAVIS 4-26
© 1998 PAWS, INC. All Rights Reserved.
I GET THE POINT!

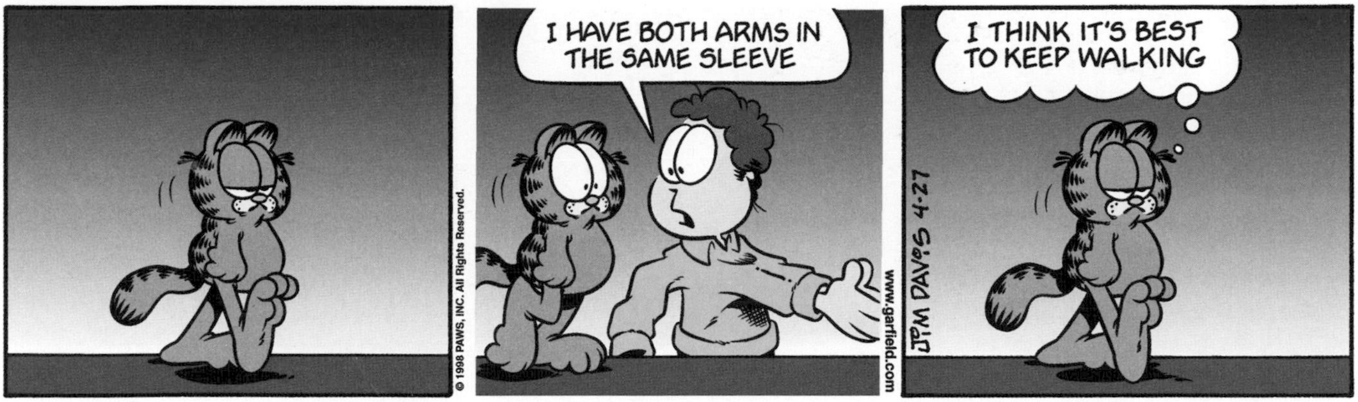
I HAVE BOTH ARMS IN THE SAME SLEEVE
I THINK IT'S BEST TO KEEP WALKING
© 1998 PAWS, INC. All Rights Reserved.
www.garfield.com
JIM DAVIS 4-27

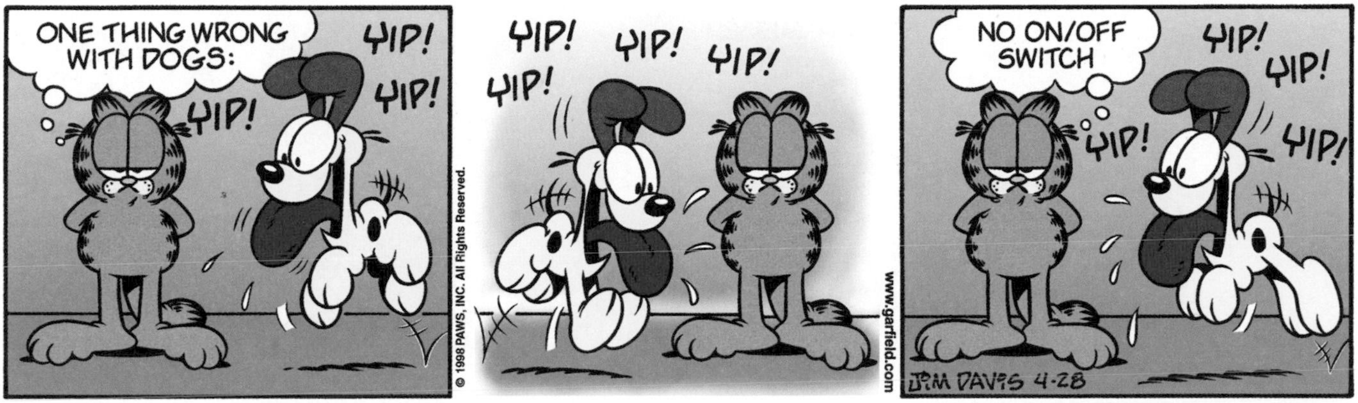
ONE THING WRONG WITH DOGS:
YIP! YIP! YIP!
YIP! YIP! YIP! YIP!
NO ON/OFF SWITCH
YIP! YIP! YIP! YIP!
© 1998 PAWS, INC. All Rights Reserved.
www.garfield.com
JIM DAVIS 4-28

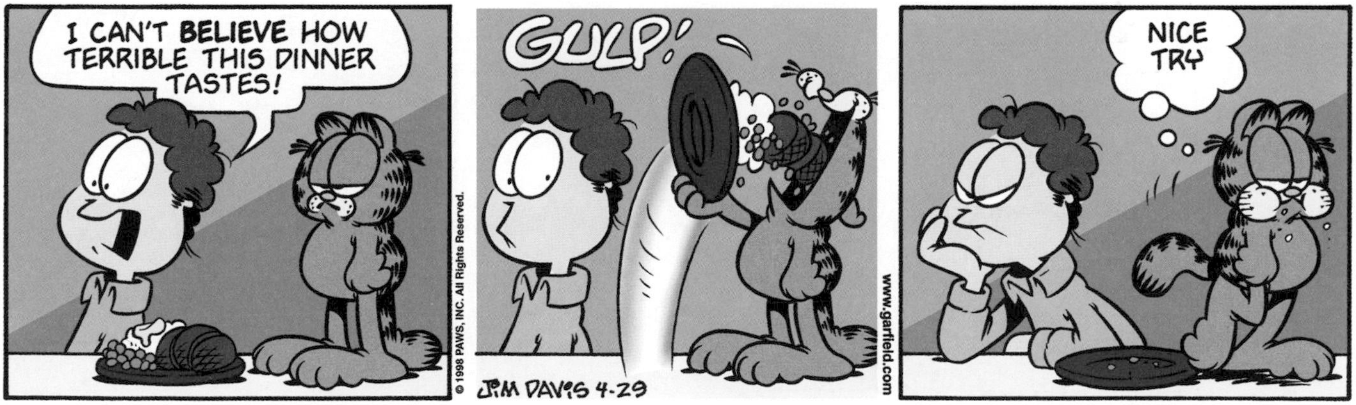
I CAN'T **BELIEVE** HOW TERRIBLE THIS DINNER TASTES!
GULP!
NICE TRY
© 1998 PAWS, INC. All Rights Reserved.
www.garfield.com
JIM DAVIS 4-29

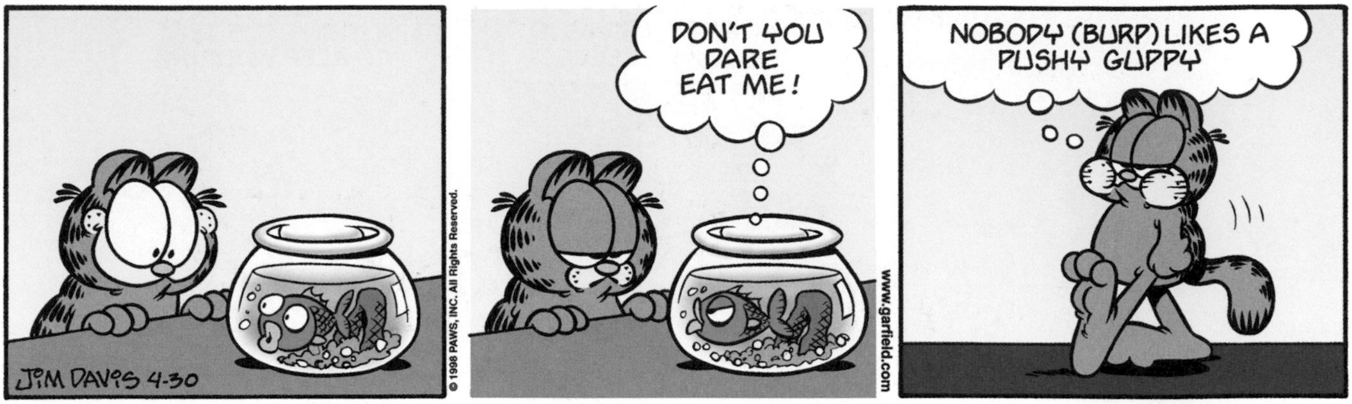
JIM DAVIS 4-30
© 1998 PAWS, INC. All Rights Reserved.
DON'T YOU DARE EAT ME!
www.garfield.com
NOBODY (BURP) LIKES A PUSHY GUPPY

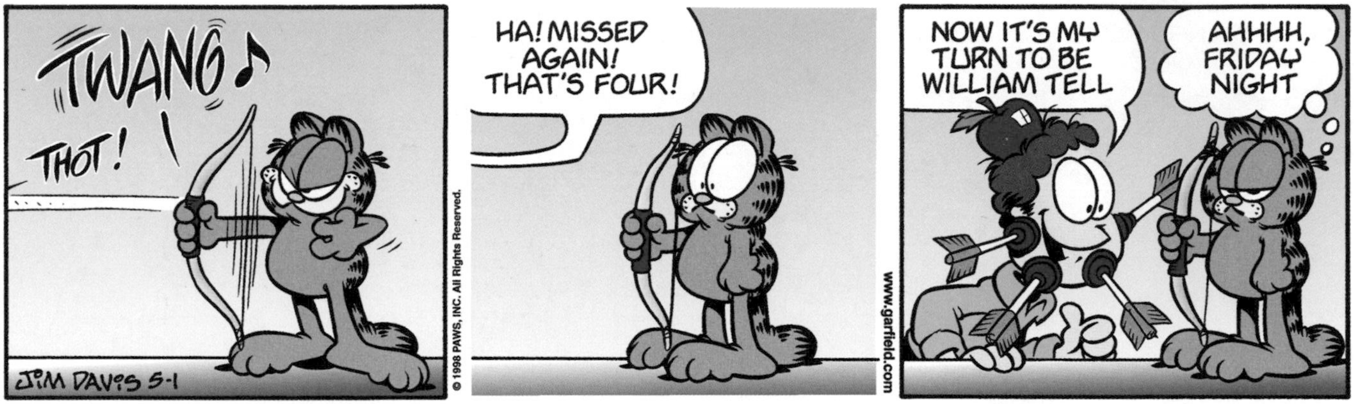
TWANG♪
THOT!
JIM DAVIS 5-1
© 1998 PAWS, INC. All Rights Reserved.
HA! MISSED AGAIN! THAT'S FOUR!
www.garfield.com
NOW IT'S MY TURN TO BE WILLIAM TELL
AHHHH, FRIDAY NIGHT

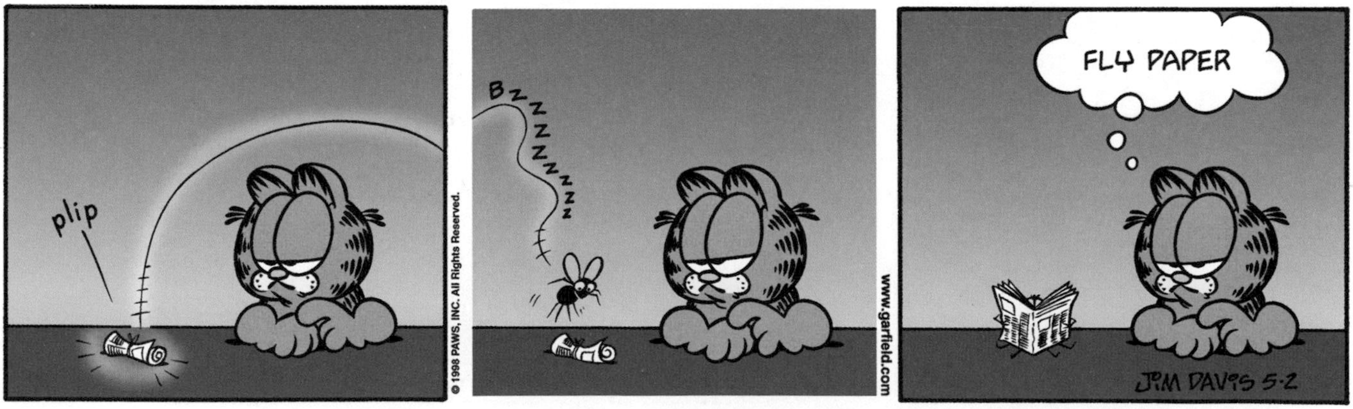
plip
© 1998 PAWS, INC. All Rights Reserved.
BZZZZZZZZZ
www.garfield.com
FLY PAPER
JIM DAVIS 5-2

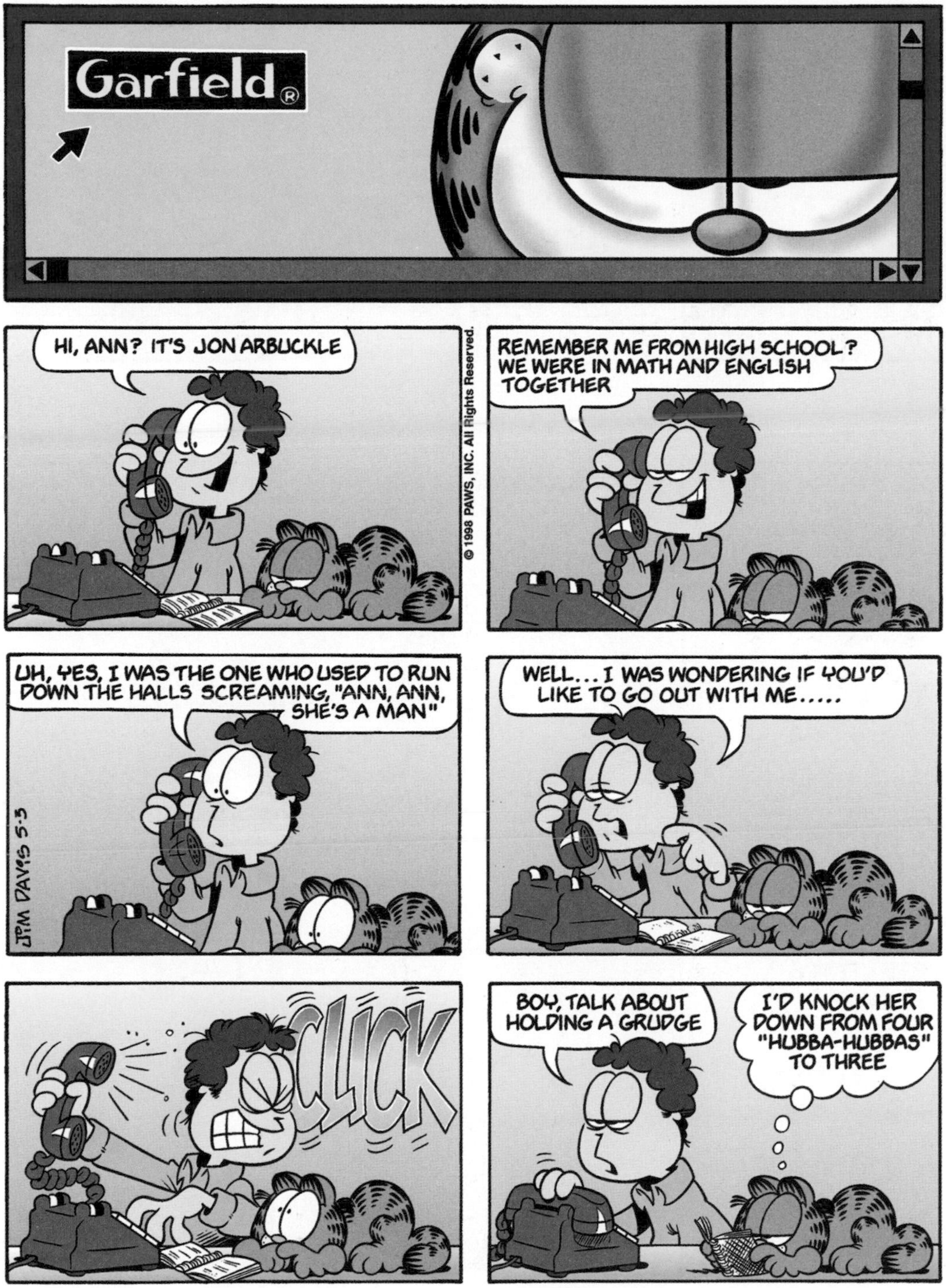
Garfield®
HI, ANN? IT'S JON ARBUCKLE
© 1998 PAWS, INC. All Rights Reserved.
REMEMBER ME FROM HIGH SCHOOL? WE WERE IN MATH AND ENGLISH TOGETHER
UH, YES, I WAS THE ONE WHO USED TO RUN DOWN THE HALLS SCREAMING, "ANN, ANN, SHE'S A MAN"
JIM DAVIS 5-3
WELL... I WAS WONDERING IF YOU'D LIKE TO GO OUT WITH ME.....
CLICK
BOY, TALK ABOUT HOLDING A GRUDGE
I'D KNOCK HER DOWN FROM FOUR "HUBBA-HUBBAS" TO THREE

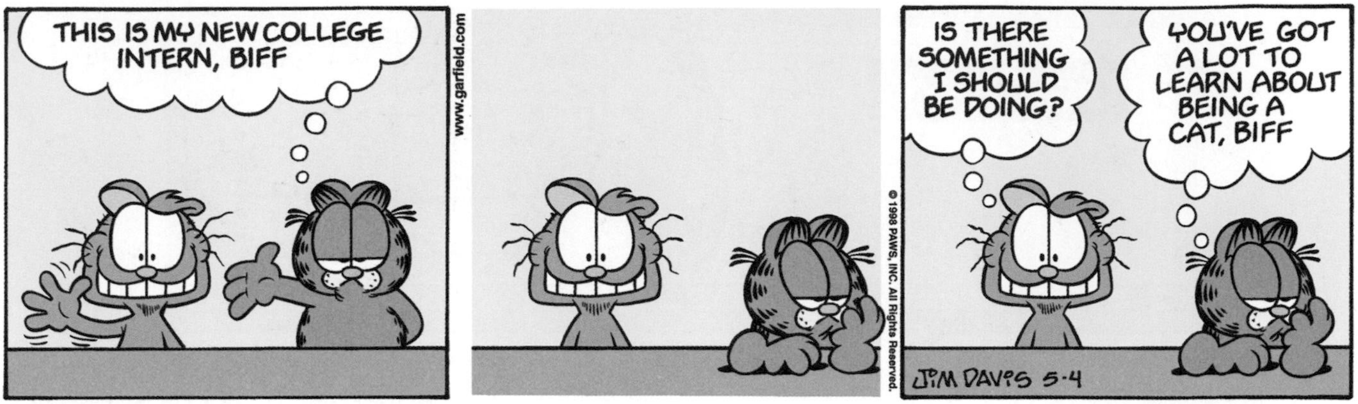
THIS IS MY NEW COLLEGE INTERN, BIFF
www.garfield.com
© 1998 PAWS, INC. All Rights Reserved.
IS THERE SOMETHING I SHOULD BE DOING?
YOU'VE GOT A LOT TO LEARN ABOUT BEING A CAT, BIFF
JIM DAVIS 5-4

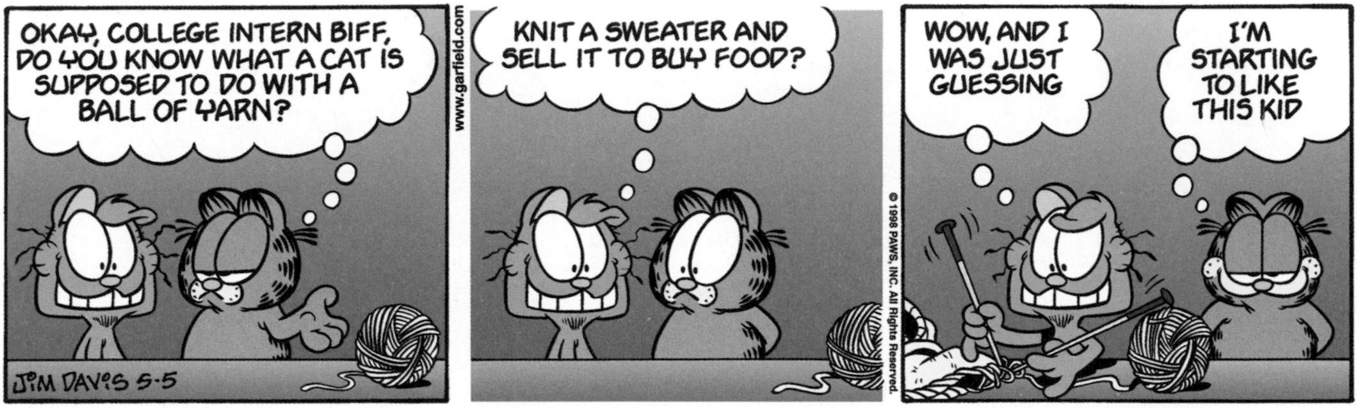
OKAY, COLLEGE INTERN BIFF, DO YOU KNOW WHAT A CAT IS SUPPOSED TO DO WITH A BALL OF YARN?
JIM DAVIS 5-5
www.garfield.com
KNIT A SWEATER AND SELL IT TO BUY FOOD?
© 1998 PAWS, INC. All Rights Reserved.
WOW, AND I WAS JUST GUESSING
I'M STARTING TO LIKE THIS KID

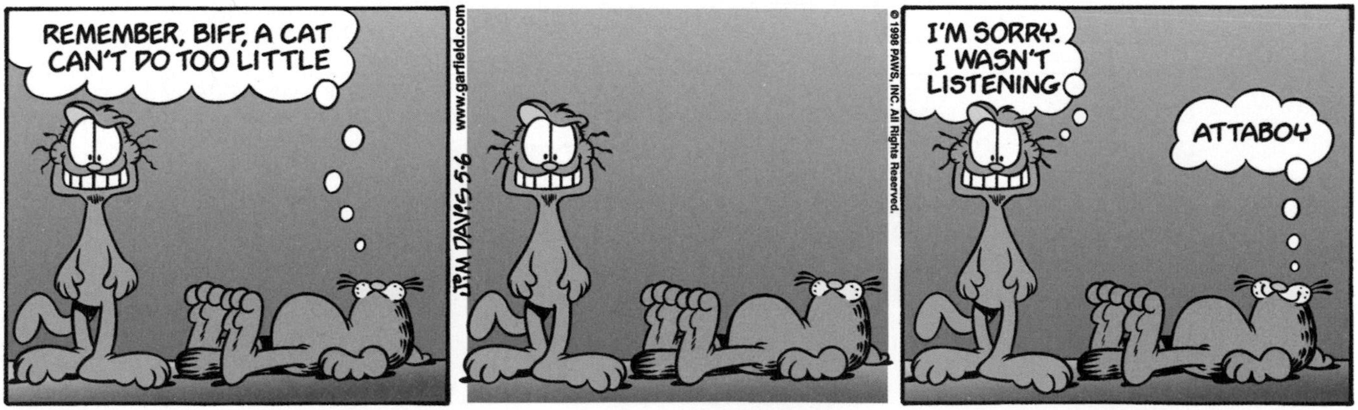
REMEMBER, BIFF, A CAT CAN'T DO TOO LITTLE
www.garfield.com
JIM DAVIS 5-6
© 1998 PAWS, INC. All Rights Reserved.
I'M SORRY. I WASN'T LISTENING
ATTABOY

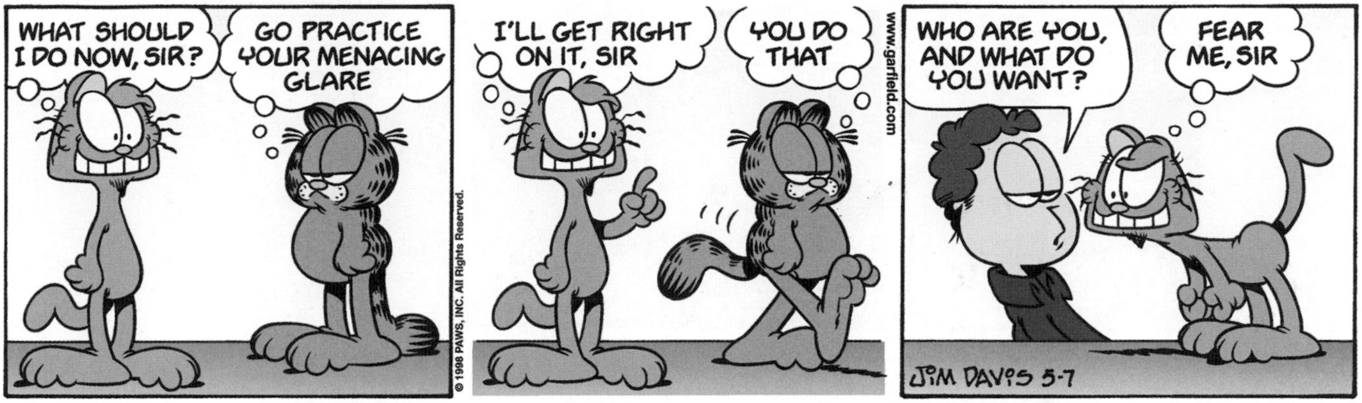
WHAT SHOULD I DO NOW, SIR?
GO PRACTICE YOUR MENACING GLARE
© 1998 PAWS, INC. All Rights Reserved.
I'LL GET RIGHT ON IT, SIR
YOU DO THAT
www.garfield.com
WHO ARE YOU, AND WHAT DO YOU WANT?
FEAR ME, SIR
JIM DAVIS 5-7

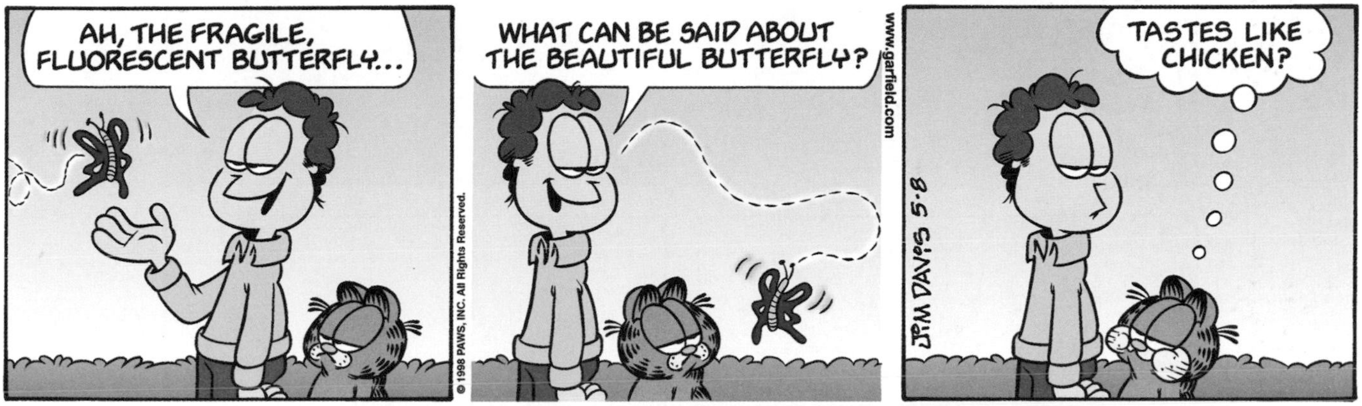
AH, THE FRAGILE, FLUORESCENT BUTTERFLY...
© 1998 PAWS, INC. All Rights Reserved.
WHAT CAN BE SAID ABOUT THE BEAUTIFUL BUTTERFLY?
www.garfield.com
TASTES LIKE CHICKEN?
JIM DAVIS 5-8

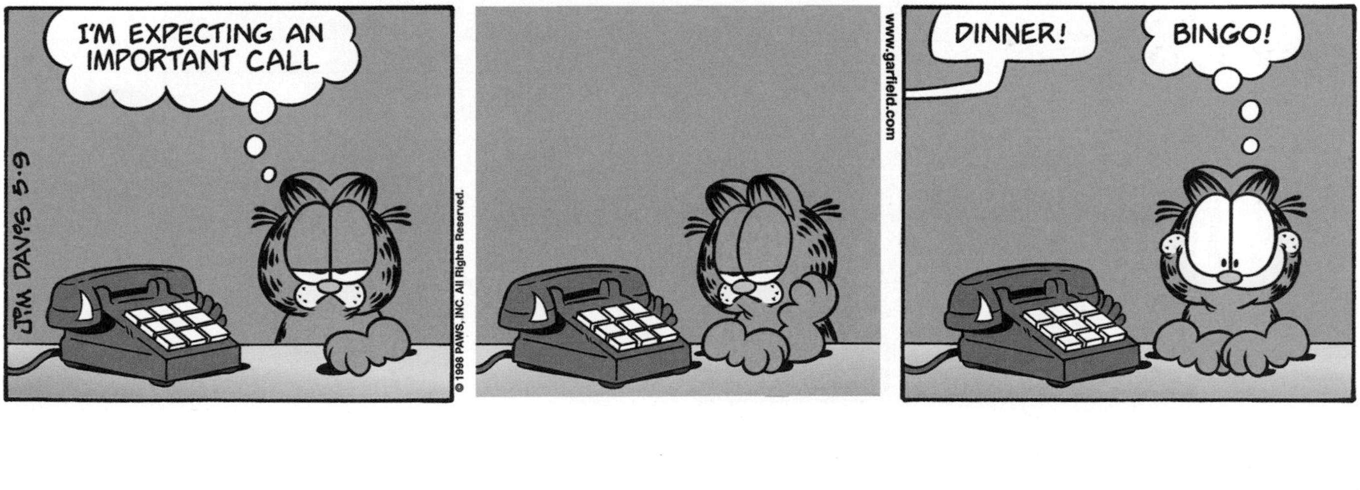
I'M EXPECTING AN IMPORTANT CALL
JIM DAVIS 5-9
© 1998 PAWS, INC. All Rights Reserved.
www.garfield.com
DINNER!
BINGO!

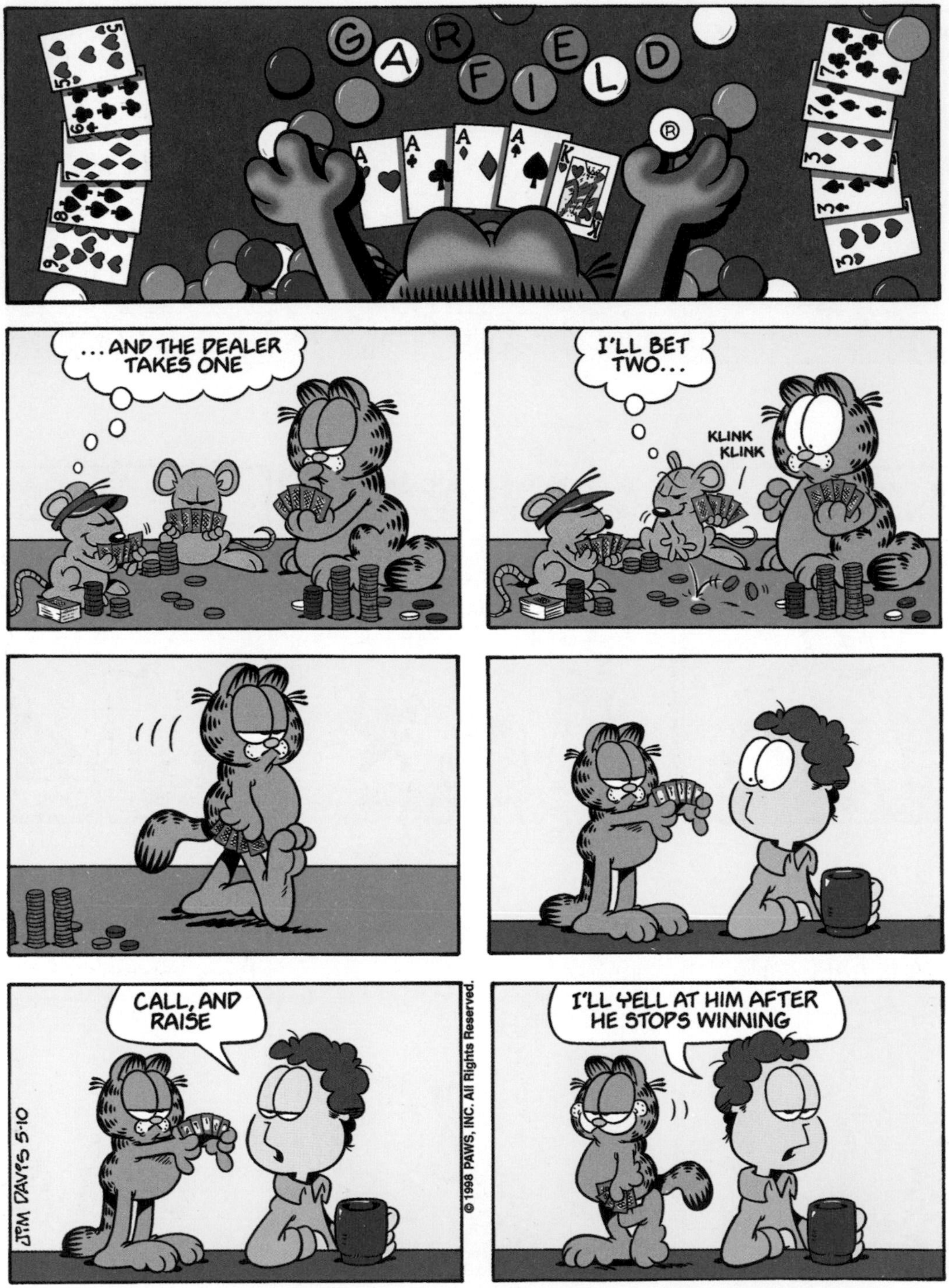
GARFIELD®
...AND THE DEALER TAKES ONE
I'LL BET TWO...
KLINK KLINK
CALL, AND RAISE
JIM DAVIS 5-10
© 1998 PAWS, INC. All Rights Reserved.
I'LL YELL AT HIM AFTER HE STOPS WINNING

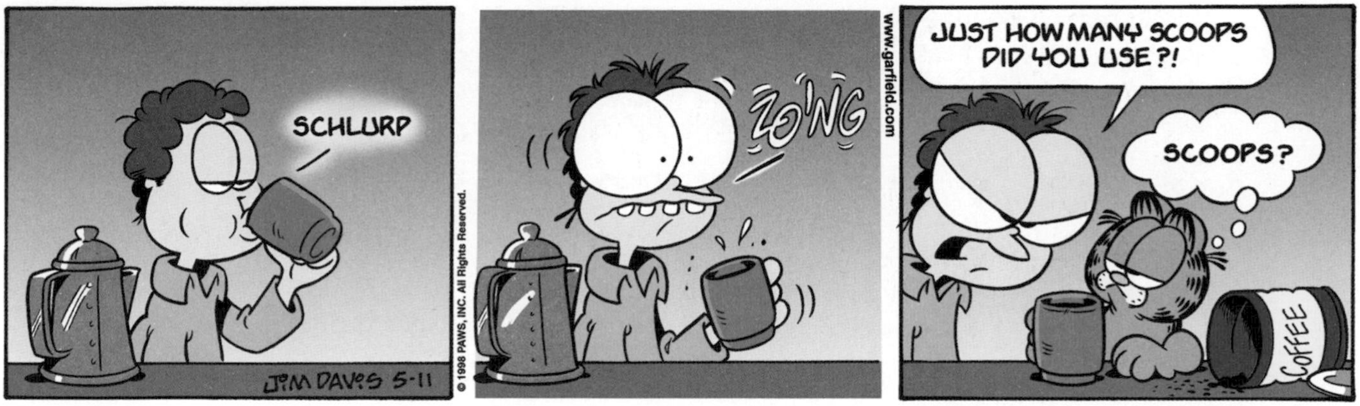
SCHLURP
JIM DAVIS 5-11
© 1998 PAWS, INC. All Rights Reserved.
ZO'NG
www.garfield.com
JUST HOW MANY SCOOPS DID YOU USE?!
SCOOPS?
COFFEE

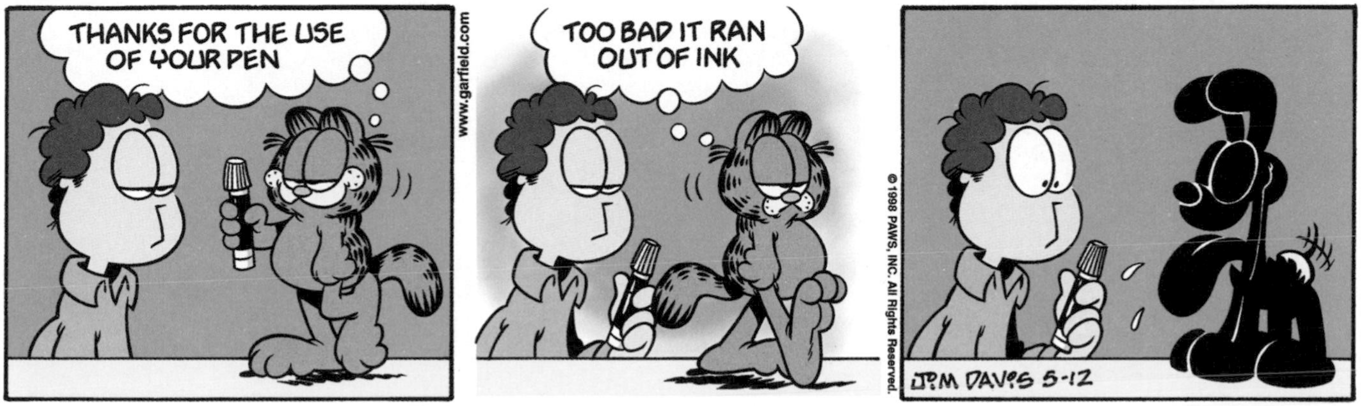
THANKS FOR THE USE OF YOUR PEN
www.garfield.com
TOO BAD IT RAN OUT OF INK
© 1998 PAWS, INC. All Rights Reserved.
JIM DAVIS 5-12

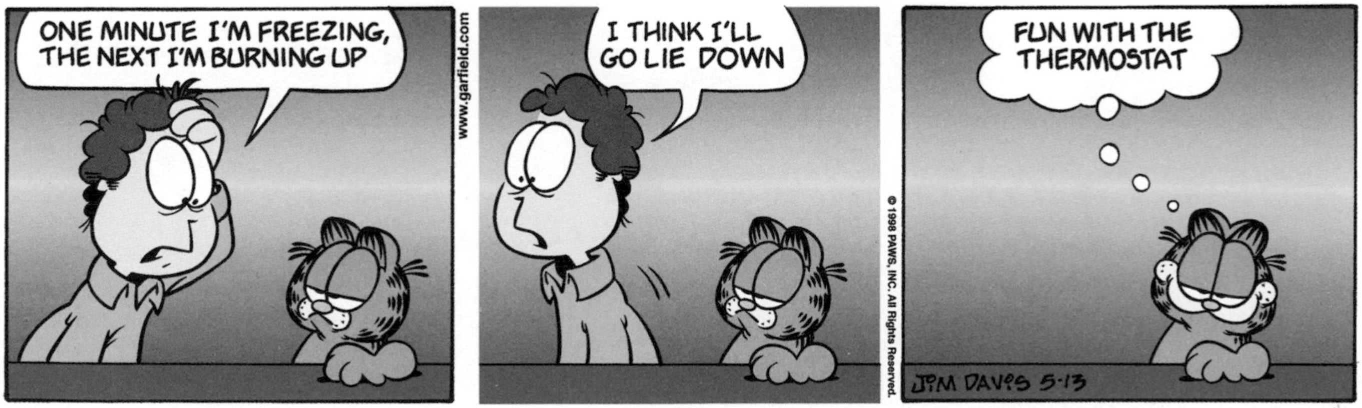
ONE MINUTE I'M FREEZING, THE NEXT I'M BURNING UP
www.garfield.com
I THINK I'LL GO LIE DOWN
© 1998 PAWS, INC. All Rights Reserved.
FUN WITH THE THERMOSTAT
JIM DAVIS 5-13

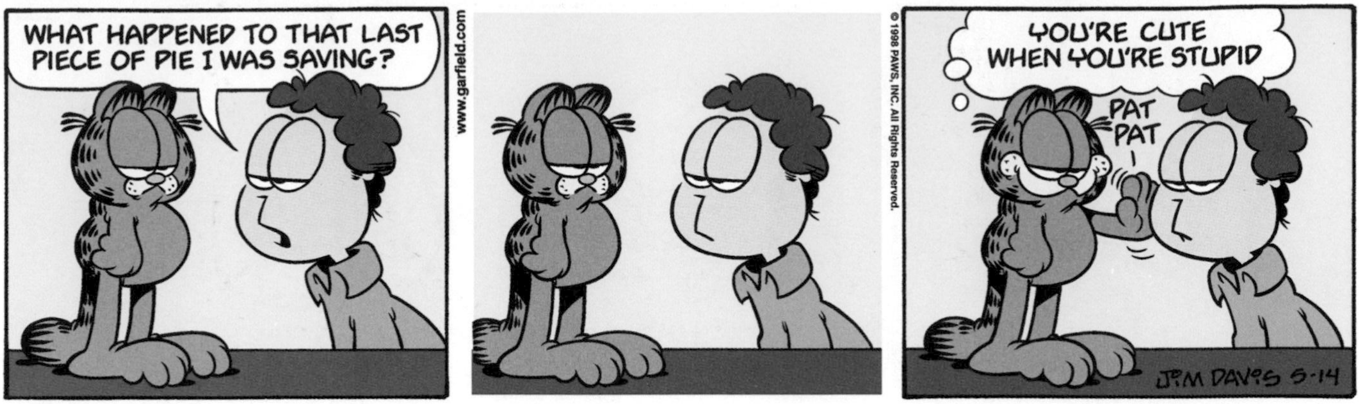
WHAT HAPPENED TO THAT LAST PIECE OF PIE I WAS SAVING?
www.garfield.com
© 1998 PAWS, INC. All Rights Reserved.
YOU'RE CUTE WHEN YOU'RE STUPID
PAT PAT
JIM DAVIS 5-14

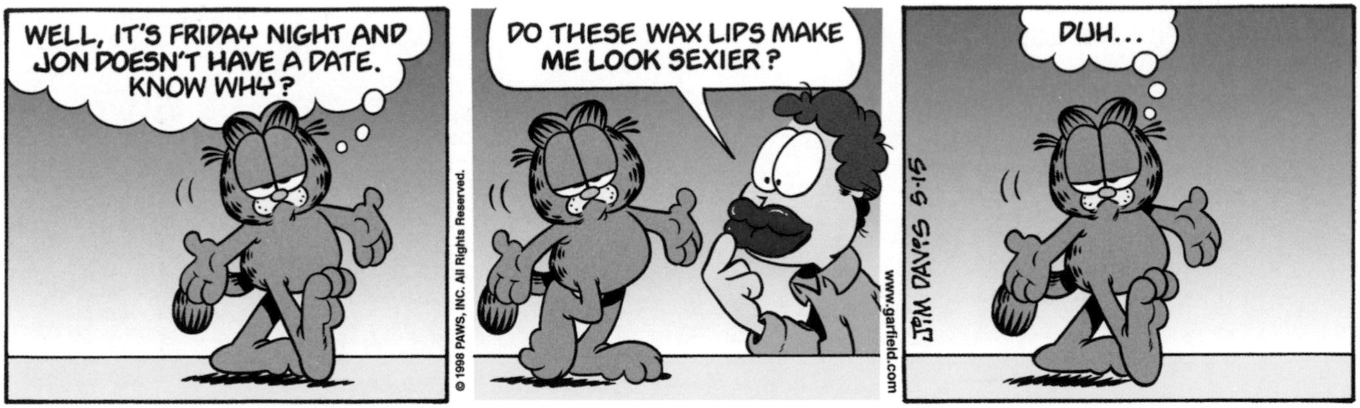
WELL, IT'S FRIDAY NIGHT AND JON DOESN'T HAVE A DATE. KNOW WHY?
© 1998 PAWS, INC. All Rights Reserved.
DO THESE WAX LIPS MAKE ME LOOK SEXIER?
www.garfield.com
JIM DAVIS 5-15
DUH...

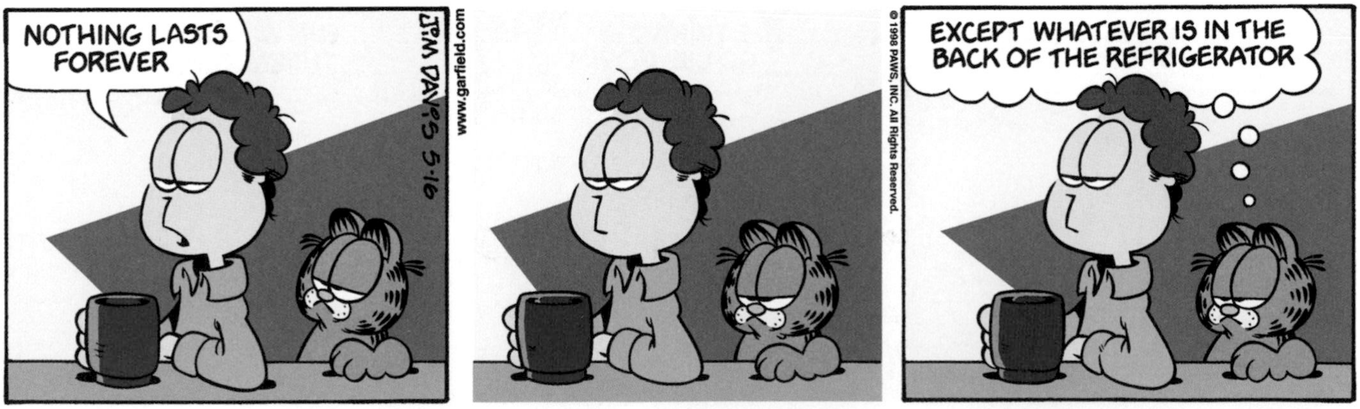
NOTHING LASTS FOREVER
JIM DAVIS 5-16
www.garfield.com
© 1998 PAWS, INC. All Rights Reserved.
EXCEPT WHATEVER IS IN THE BACK OF THE REFRIGERATOR

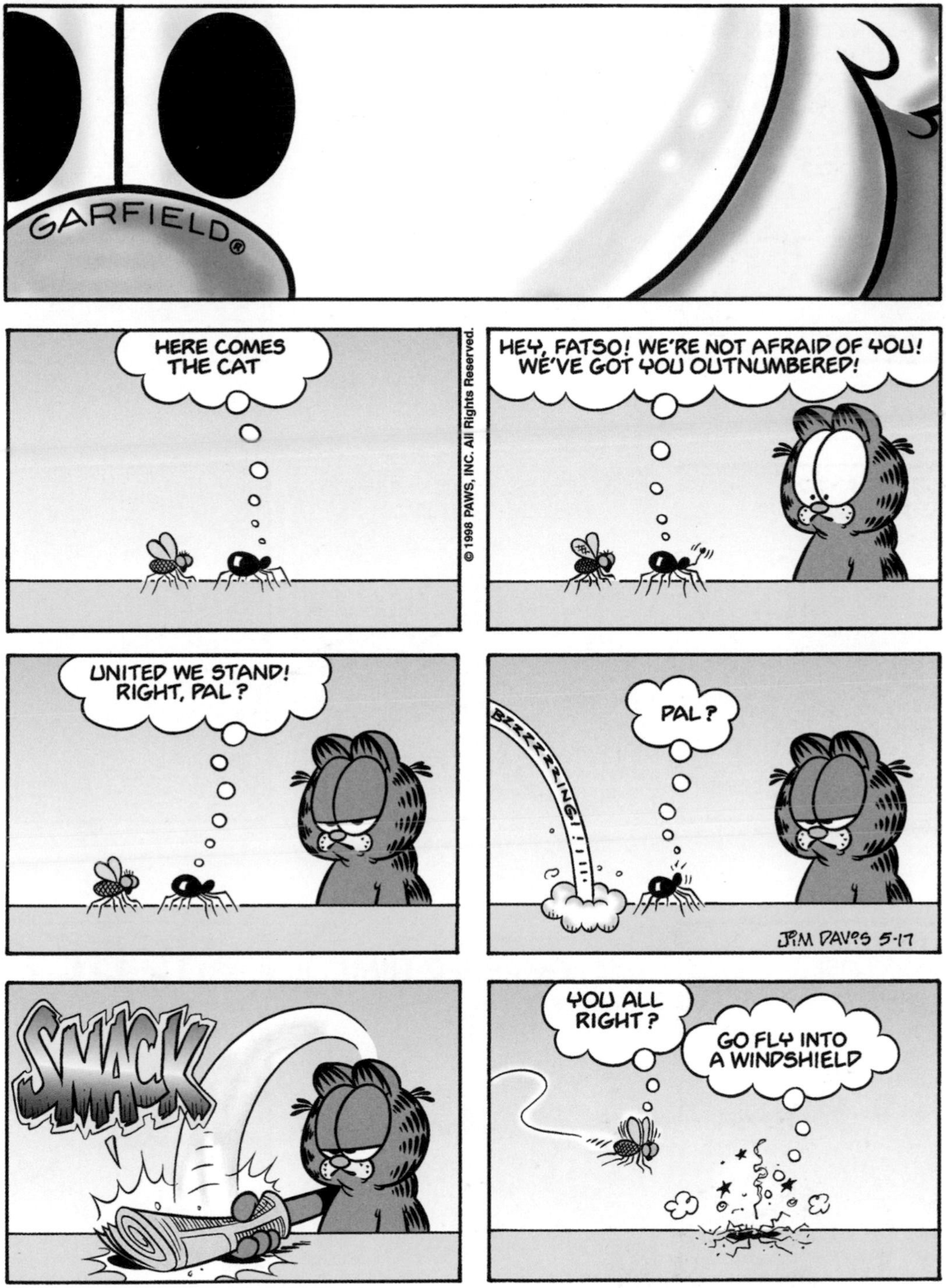
GARFIELD®
© 1998 PAWS, INC. All Rights Reserved.
HERE COMES THE CAT
HEY, FATSO! WE'RE NOT AFRAID OF YOU! WE'VE GOT YOU OUTNUMBERED!
UNITED WE STAND! RIGHT, PAL?
PAL?
JIM DAVIS 5-17
SMACK
YOU ALL RIGHT?
GO FLY INTO A WINDSHIELD

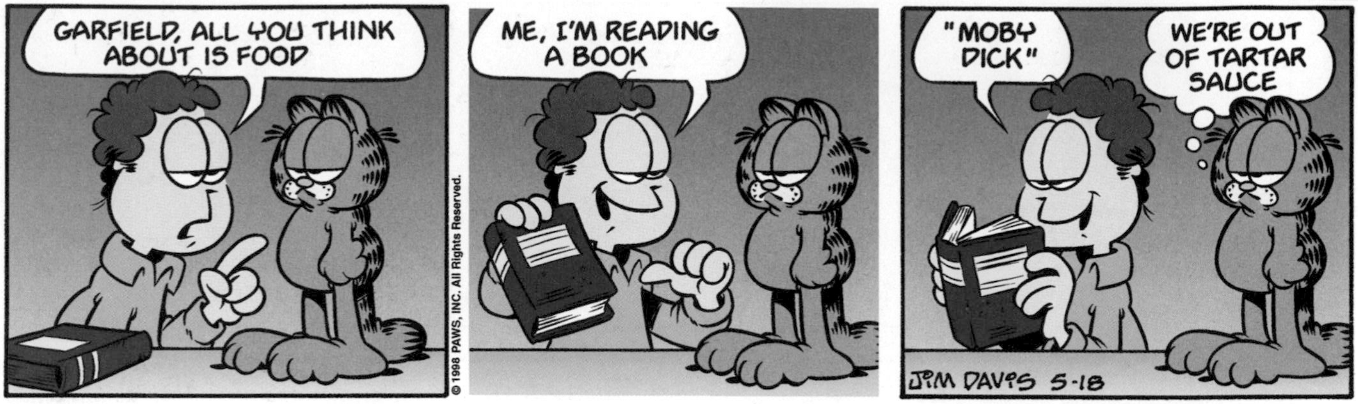
GARFIELD, ALL YOU THINK ABOUT IS FOOD
© 1998 PAWS, INC. All Rights Reserved.
ME, I'M READING A BOOK
"MOBY DICK"
WE'RE OUT OF TARTAR SAUCE
JIM DAVIS 5-18

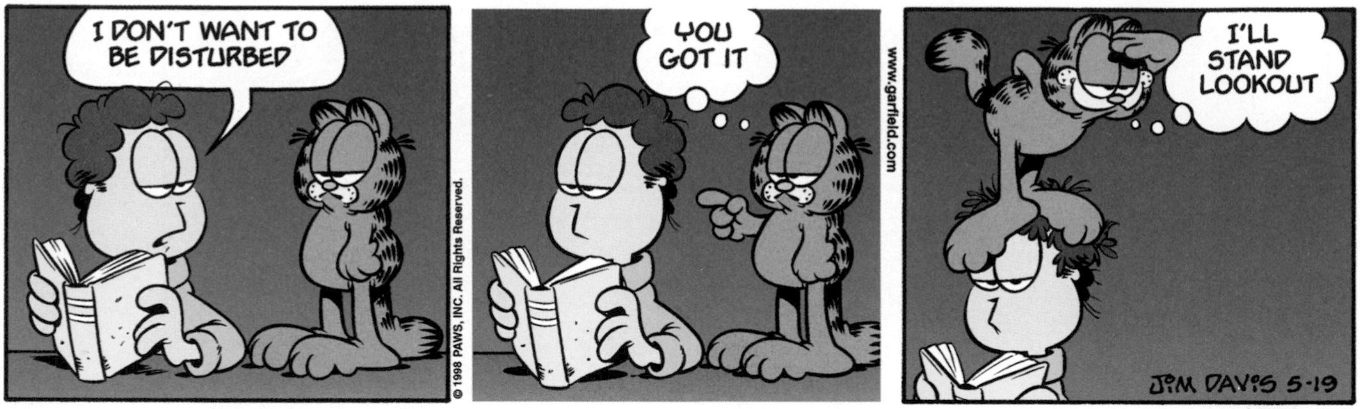
I DON'T WANT TO BE DISTURBED
© 1998 PAWS, INC. All Rights Reserved.
YOU GOT IT
www.garfield.com
I'LL STAND LOOKOUT
JIM DAVIS 5-19

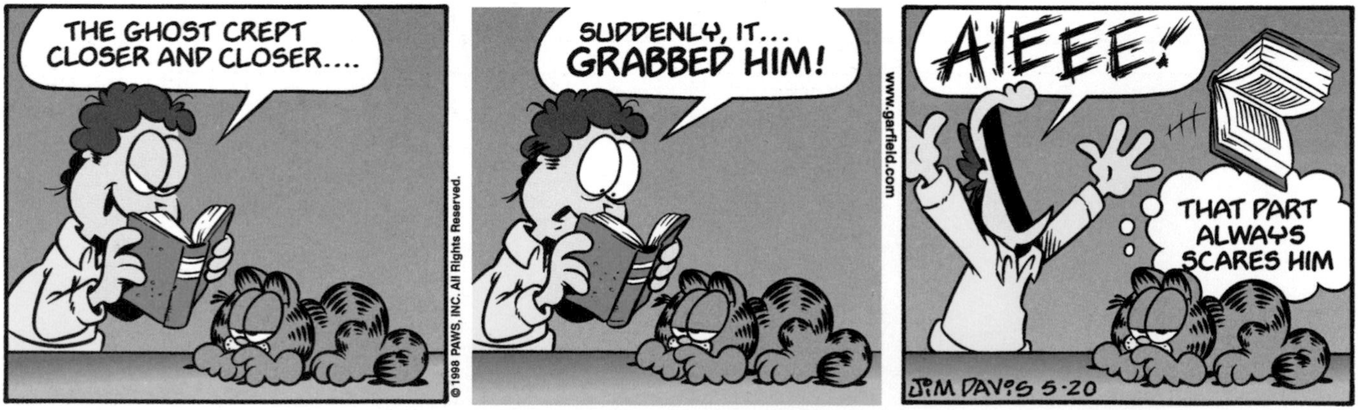
THE GHOST CREPT CLOSER AND CLOSER....
© 1998 PAWS, INC. All Rights Reserved.
SUDDENLY, IT... GRABBED HIM!
www.garfield.com
AIEEE!
THAT PART ALWAYS SCARES HIM
JIM DAVIS 5-20

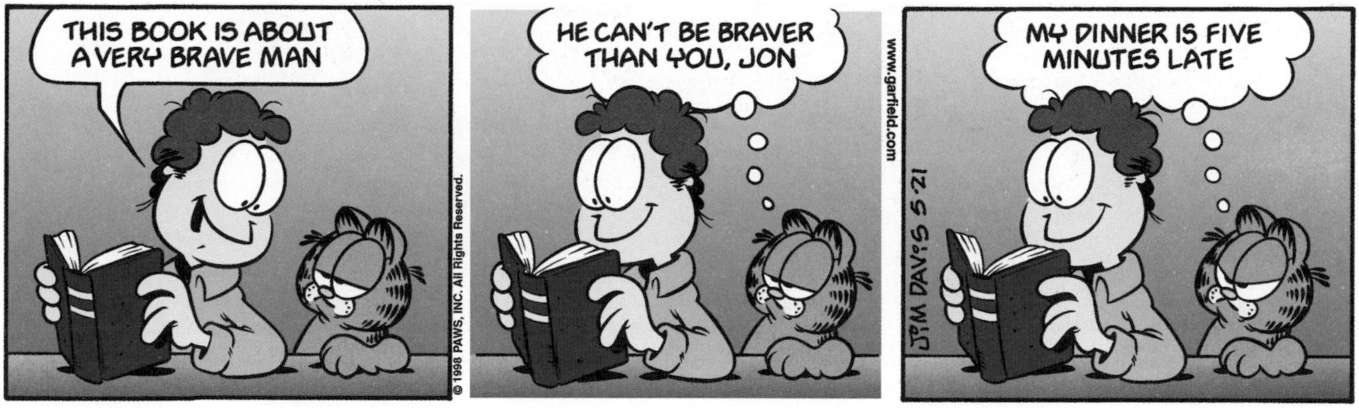
THIS BOOK IS ABOUT A VERY BRAVE MAN
HE CAN'T BE BRAVER THAN YOU, JON
MY DINNER IS FIVE MINUTES LATE
© 1998 PAWS, INC. All Rights Reserved.
www.garfield.com
JIM DAVIS 5-21

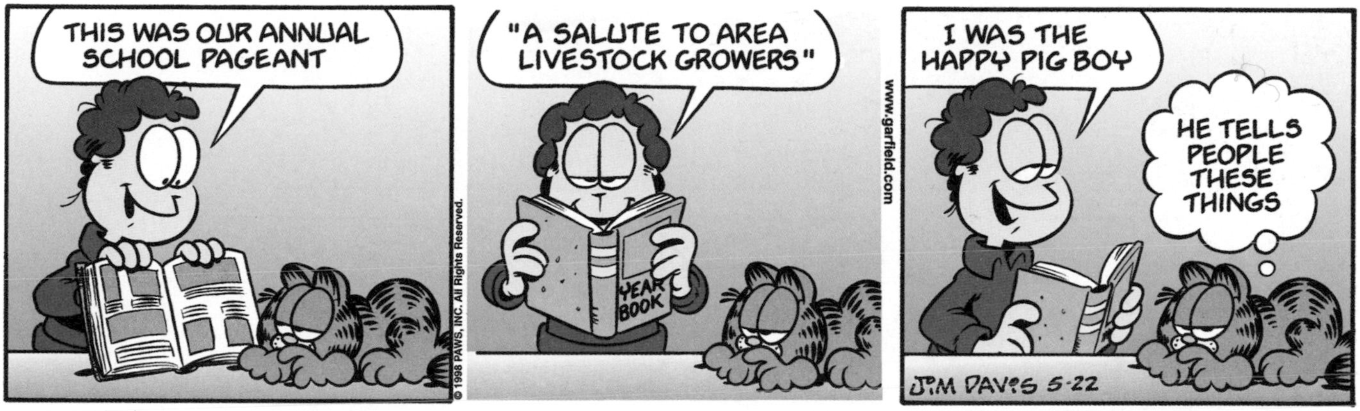
THIS WAS OUR ANNUAL SCHOOL PAGEANT
"A SALUTE TO AREA LIVESTOCK GROWERS"
YEAR BOOK
I WAS THE HAPPY PIG BOY
HE TELLS PEOPLE THESE THINGS
© 1998 PAWS, INC. All Rights Reserved.
www.garfield.com
JIM DAVIS 5-22

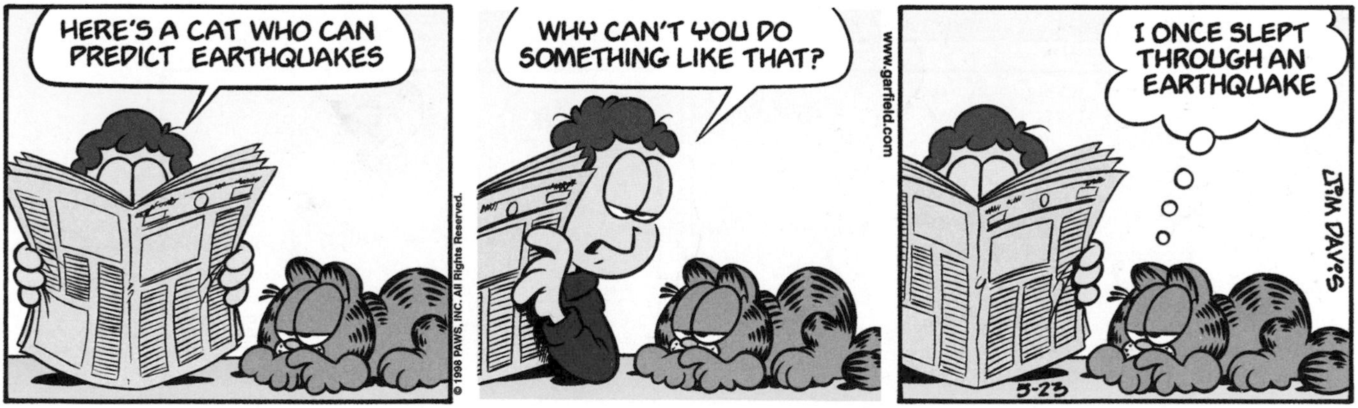
HERE'S A CAT WHO CAN PREDICT EARTHQUAKES
WHY CAN'T YOU DO SOMETHING LIKE THAT?
I ONCE SLEPT THROUGH AN EARTHQUAKE
© 1998 PAWS, INC. All Rights Reserved.
www.garfield.com
JIM DAVIS
5-23

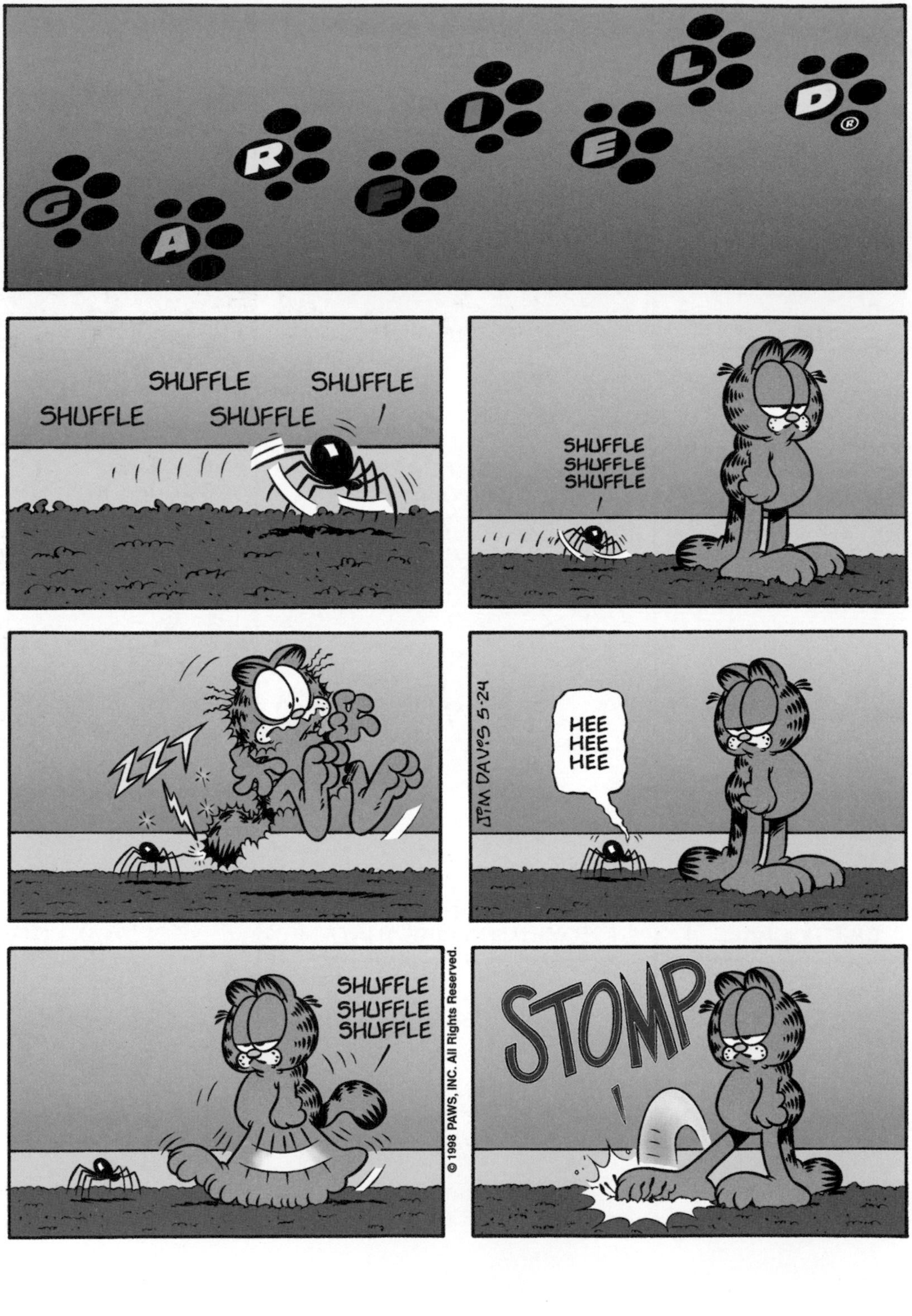
GARFIELD®
SHUFFLE SHUFFLE SHUFFLE SHUFFLE
SHUFFLE SHUFFLE SHUFFLE
ZZZT
HEE HEE HEE
JPM DAVIS 5-24
SHUFFLE SHUFFLE SHUFFLE
© 1998 PAWS, INC. All Rights Reserved.
STOMP

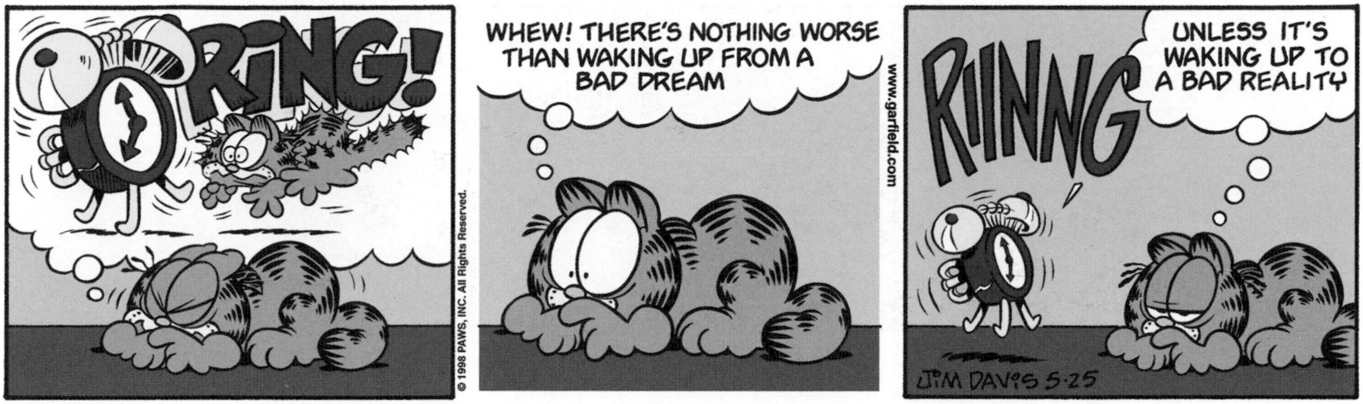
RING!
© 1998 PAWS, INC. All Rights Reserved.
WHEW! THERE'S NOTHING WORSE THAN WAKING UP FROM A BAD DREAM
www.garfield.com
RIINNG
UNLESS IT'S WAKING UP TO A BAD REALITY
JIM DAVIS 5-25

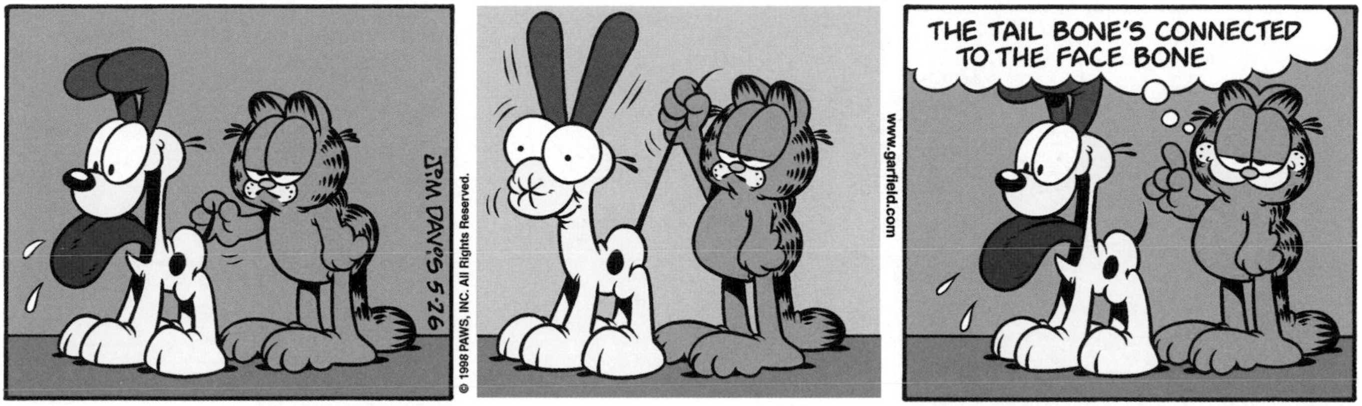
JIM DAVIS 5-26
© 1998 PAWS, INC. All Rights Reserved.
www.garfield.com
THE TAIL BONE'S CONNECTED TO THE FACE BONE

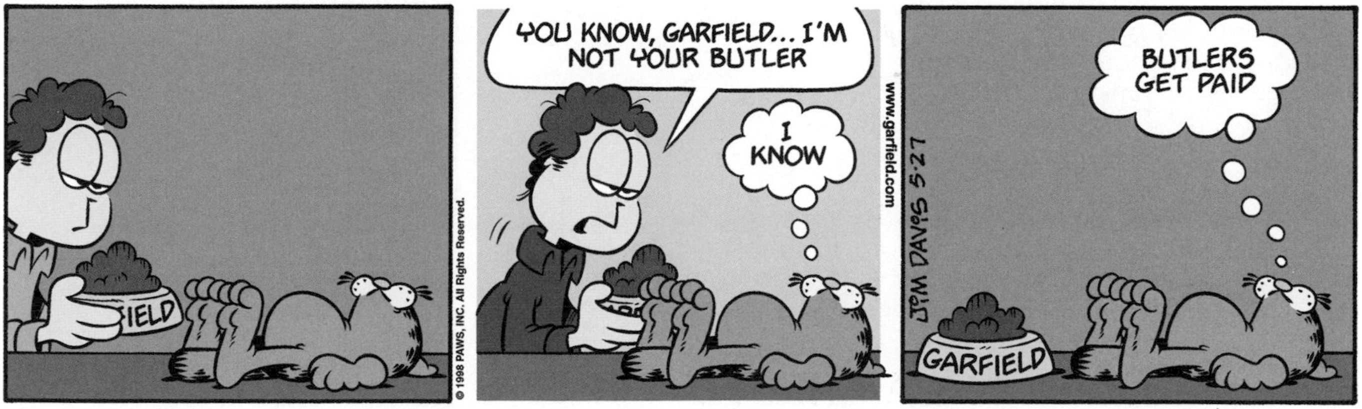
© 1998 PAWS, INC. All Rights Reserved.
YOU KNOW, GARFIELD... I'M NOT YOUR BUTLER
I KNOW
www.garfield.com
JIM DAVIS 5-27
BUTLERS GET PAID
GARFIELD

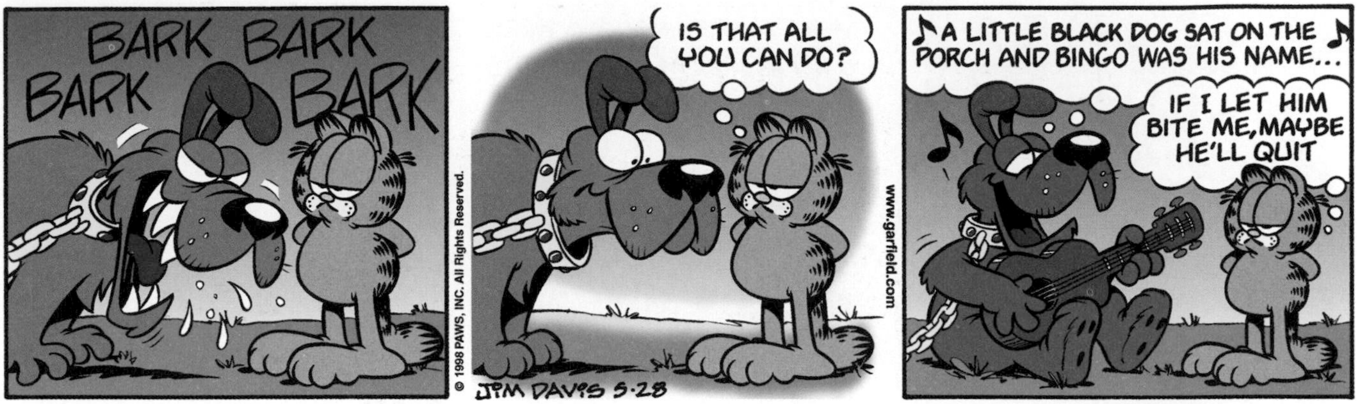
BARK BARK
BARK BARK
IS THAT ALL YOU CAN DO?
A LITTLE BLACK DOG SAT ON THE PORCH AND BINGO WAS HIS NAME...
IF I LET HIM BITE ME, MAYBE HE'LL QUIT
© 1998 PAWS, INC. All Rights Reserved.
www.garfield.com
JIM DAVIS 5-28

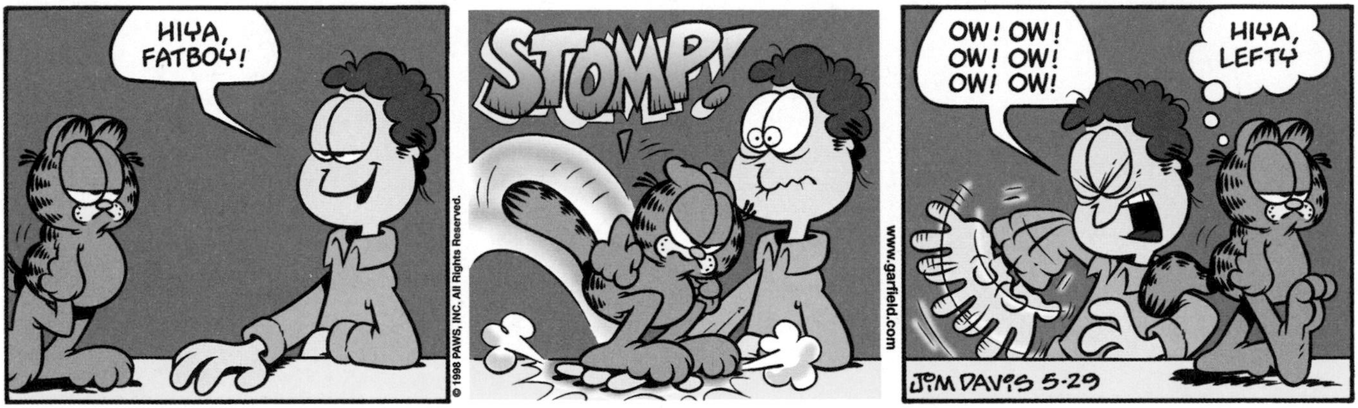
HIYA, FATBOY!
STOMP!
OW! OW! OW! OW! OW! OW!
HIYA, LEFTY
© 1998 PAWS, INC. All Rights Reserved.
www.garfield.com
JIM DAVIS 5-29

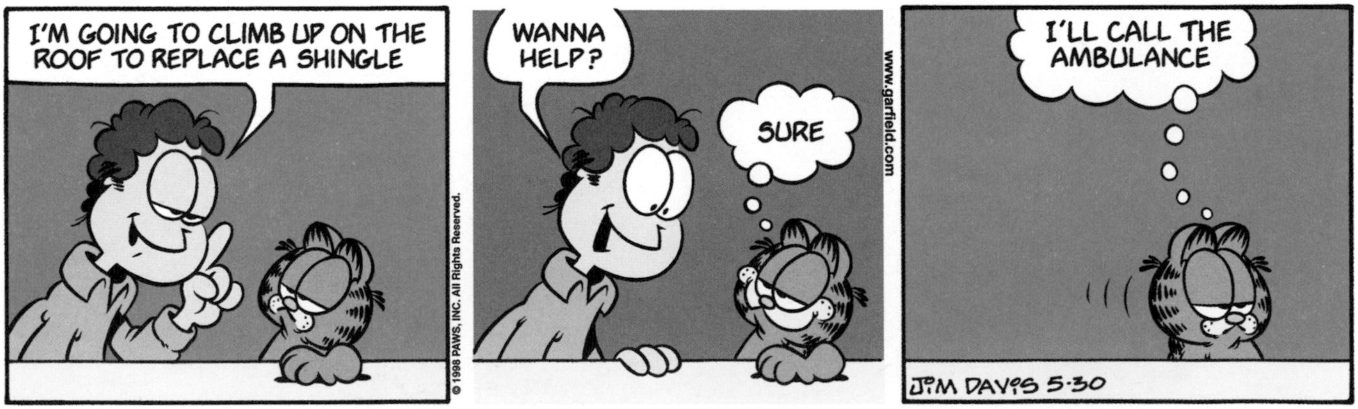
I'M GOING TO CLIMB UP ON THE ROOF TO REPLACE A SHINGLE
WANNA HELP?
SURE
I'LL CALL THE AMBULANCE
© 1998 PAWS, INC. All Rights Reserved.
www.garfield.com
JIM DAVIS 5-30

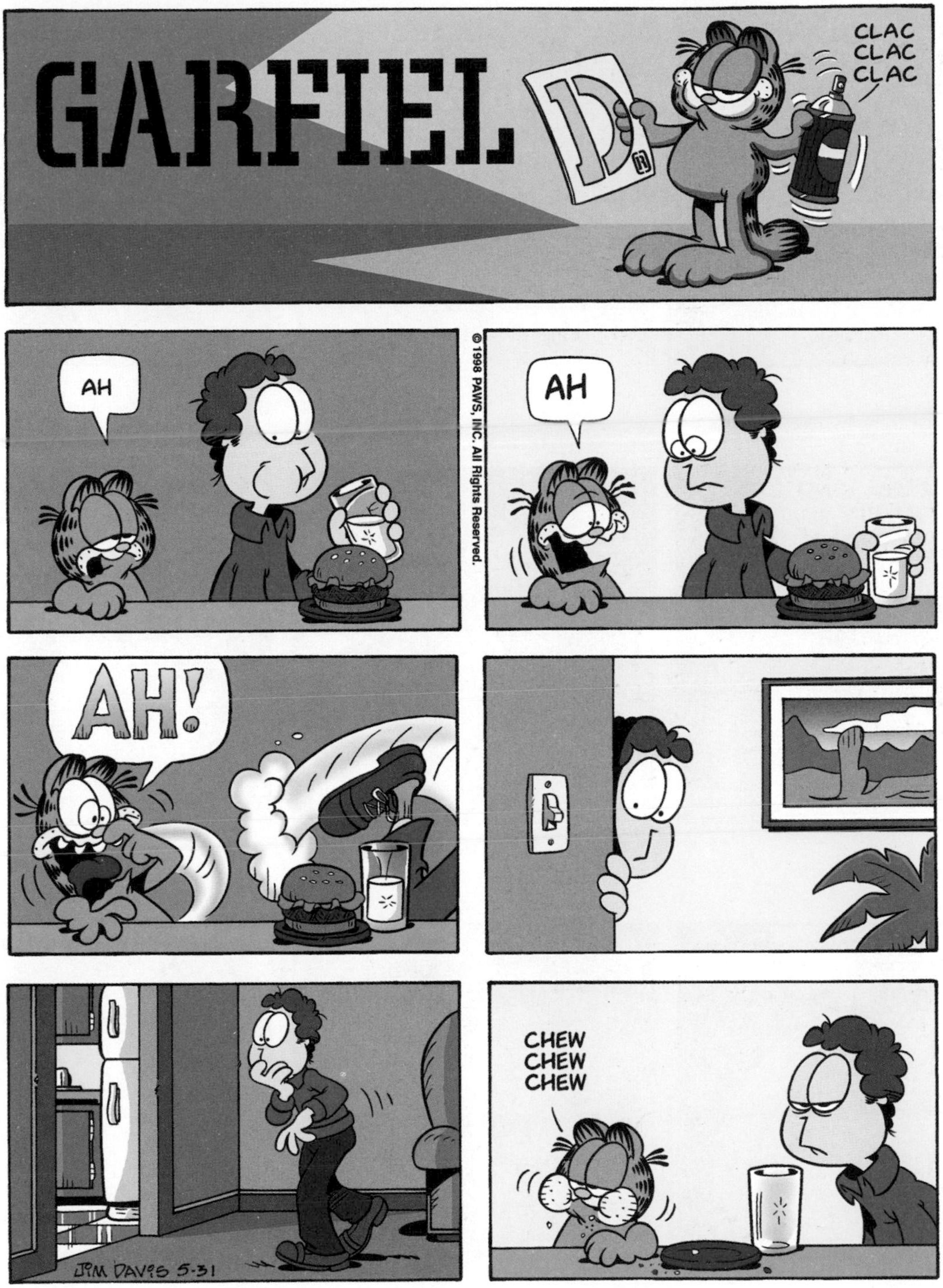
GARFIEL
CLAC
CLAC
CLAC
AH
AH
AH!
JIM DAVIS 5-31
CHEW
CHEW
CHEW

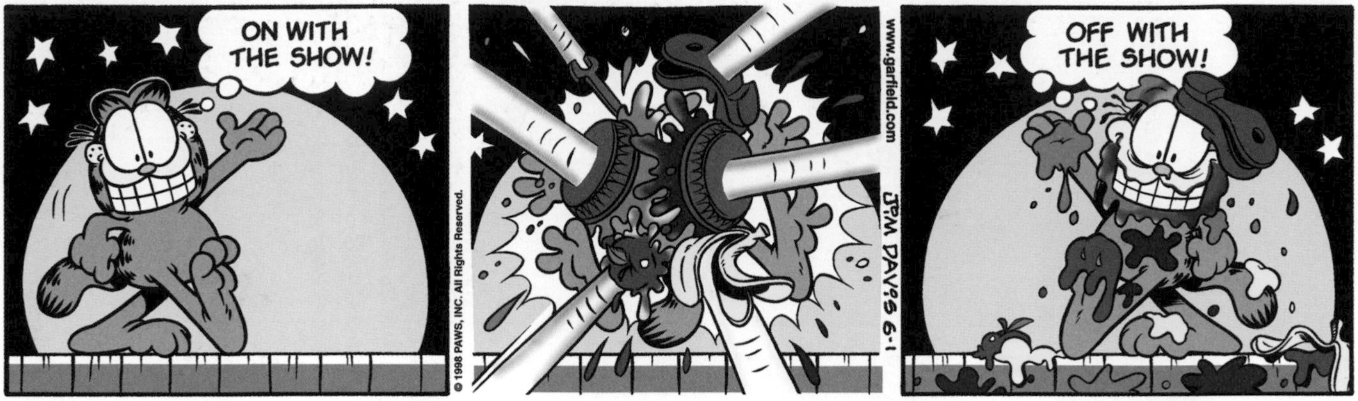
ON WITH THE SHOW!
© 1998 PAWS, INC. All Rights Reserved.
www.garfield.com
JPM DAVPS 6-1
OFF WITH THE SHOW!

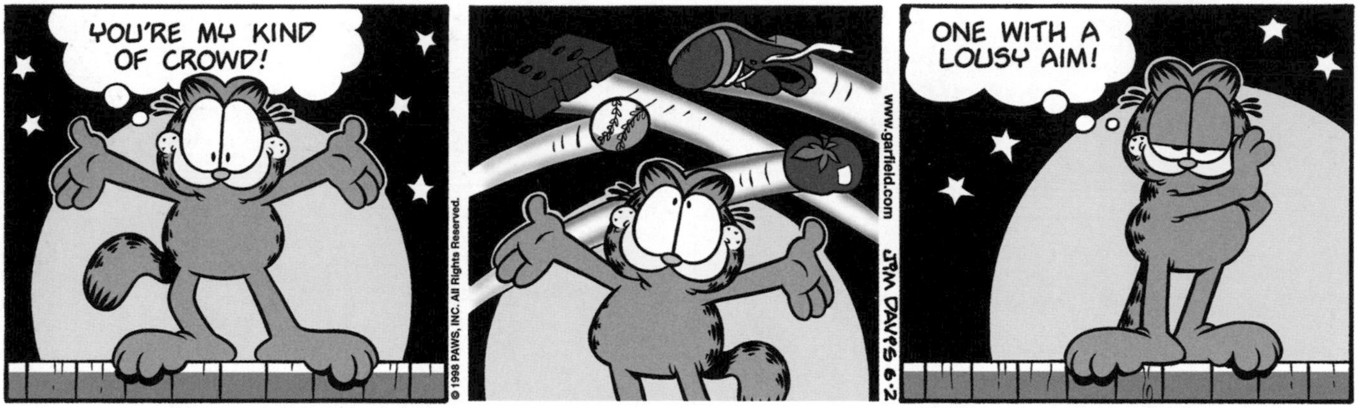
YOU'RE MY KIND OF CROWD!
© 1998 PAWS, INC. All Rights Reserved.
www.garfield.com
JPM DAVPS 6-2
ONE WITH A LOUSY AIM!

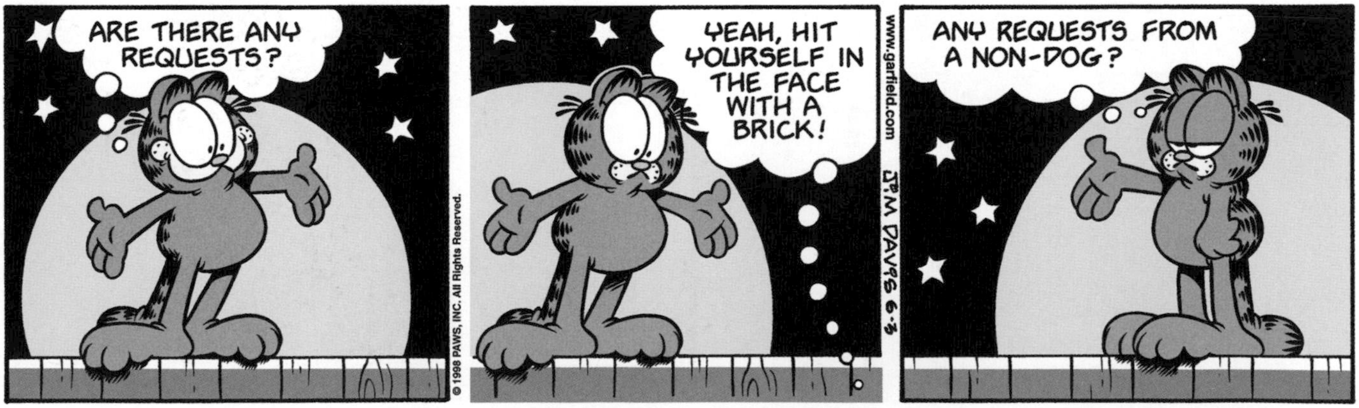
ARE THERE ANY REQUESTS?
© 1998 PAWS, INC. All Rights Reserved.
YEAH, HIT YOURSELF IN THE FACE WITH A BRICK!
www.garfield.com
JPM DAVPS 6-3
ANY REQUESTS FROM A NON-DOG?

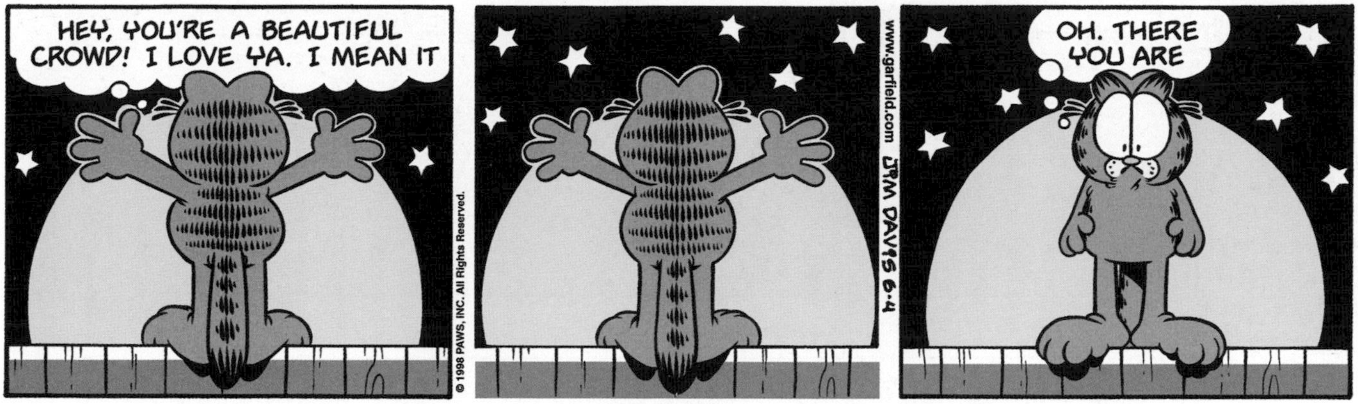
HEY, YOU'RE A BEAUTIFUL CROWD! I LOVE YA. I MEAN IT
© 1998 PAWS, INC. All Rights Reserved.
www.garfield.com
JIM DAVIS 6-4
OH. THERE YOU ARE

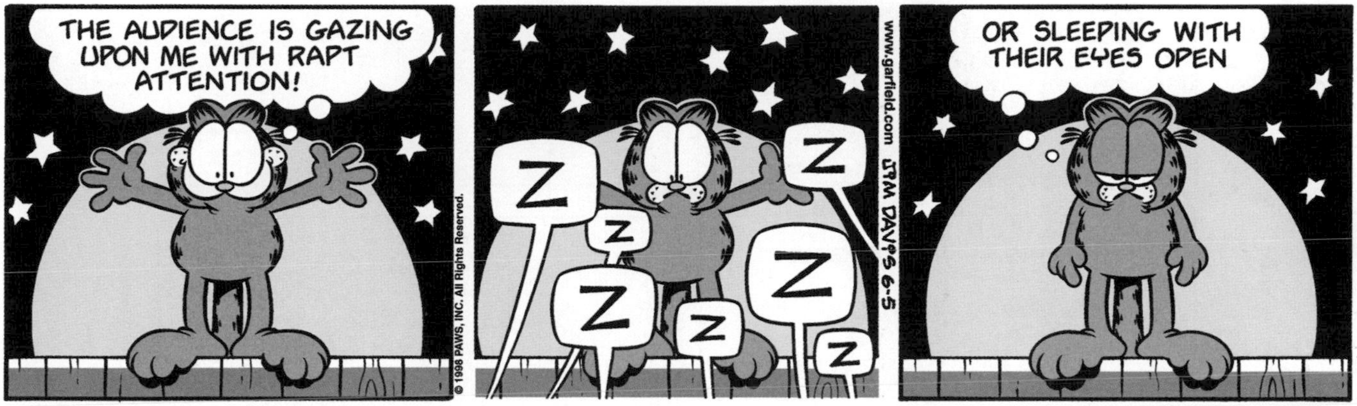
THE AUDIENCE IS GAZING UPON ME WITH RAPT ATTENTION!
© 1998 PAWS, INC. All Rights Reserved.
Z
Z
Z
Z
Z
Z
Z
www.garfield.com
JIM DAVIS 6-5
OR SLEEPING WITH THEIR EYES OPEN

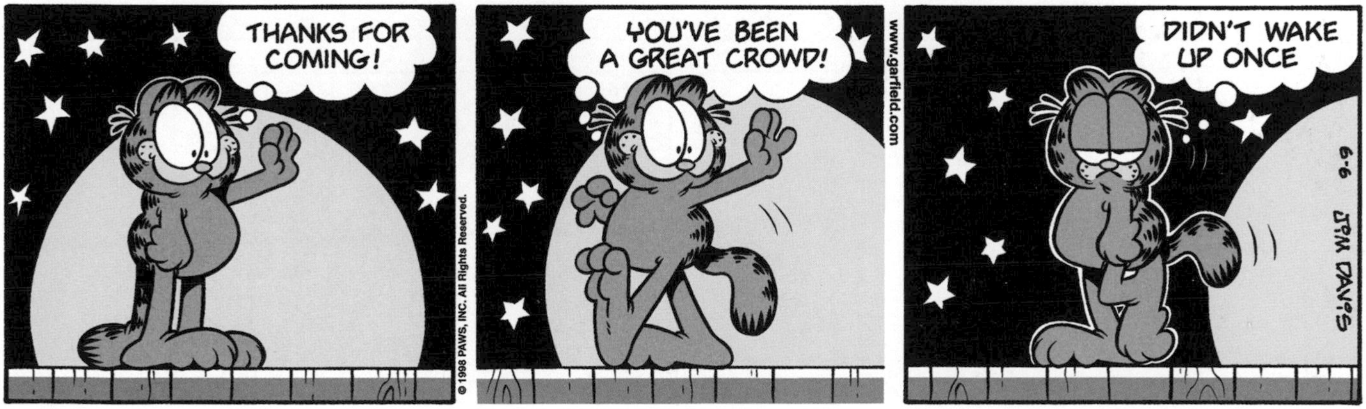
THANKS FOR COMING!
© 1998 PAWS, INC. All Rights Reserved.
YOU'VE BEEN A GREAT CROWD!
www.garfield.com
DIDN'T WAKE UP ONCE
6-6
JIM DAVIS

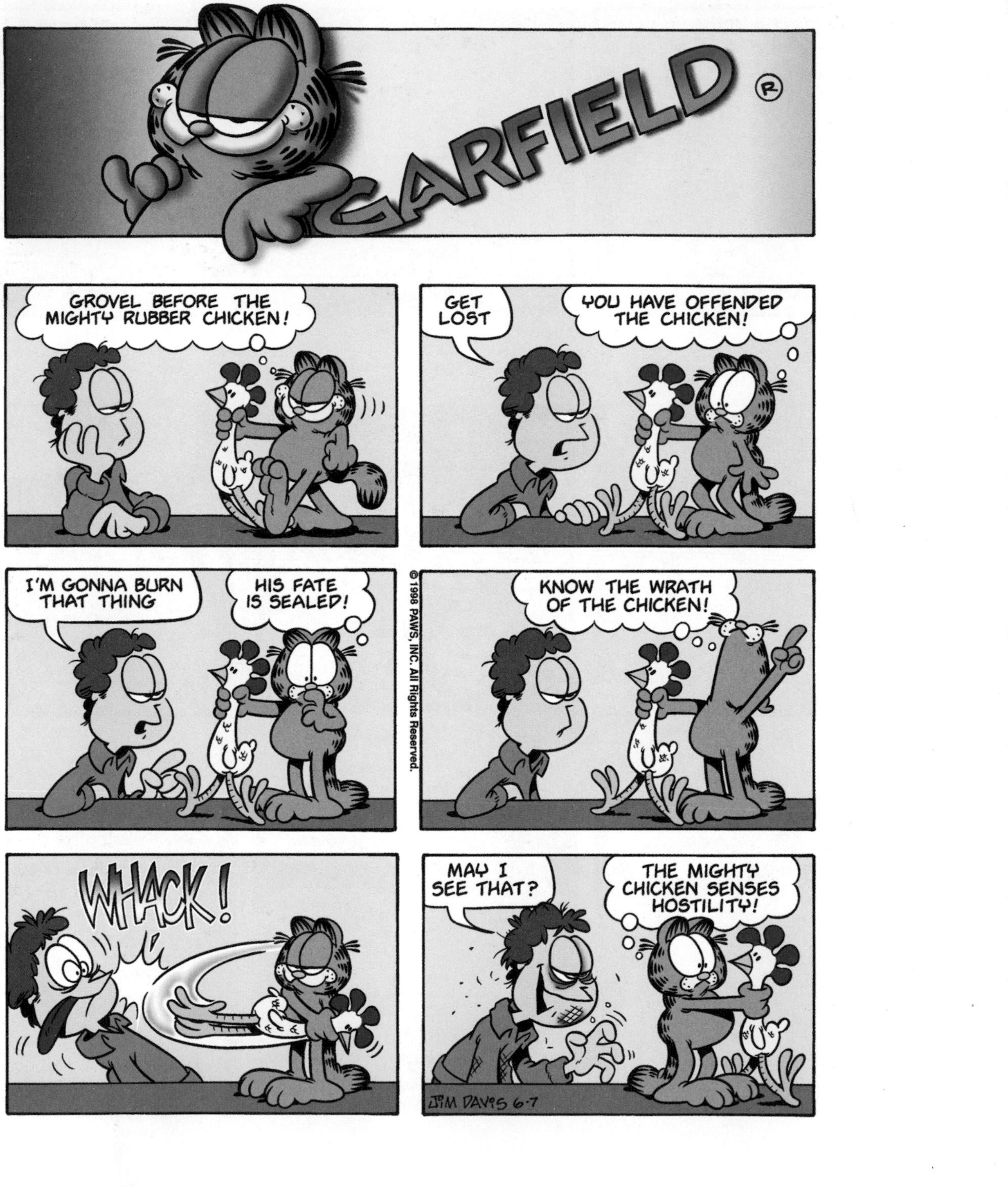
GARFIELD ®
GROVEL BEFORE THE MIGHTY RUBBER CHICKEN!
GET LOST
YOU HAVE OFFENDED THE CHICKEN!
I'M GONNA BURN THAT THING
HIS FATE IS SEALED!
KNOW THE WRATH OF THE CHICKEN!
WHACK!
MAY I SEE THAT?
THE MIGHTY CHICKEN SENSES HOSTILITY!
JIM DAVIS 6-7

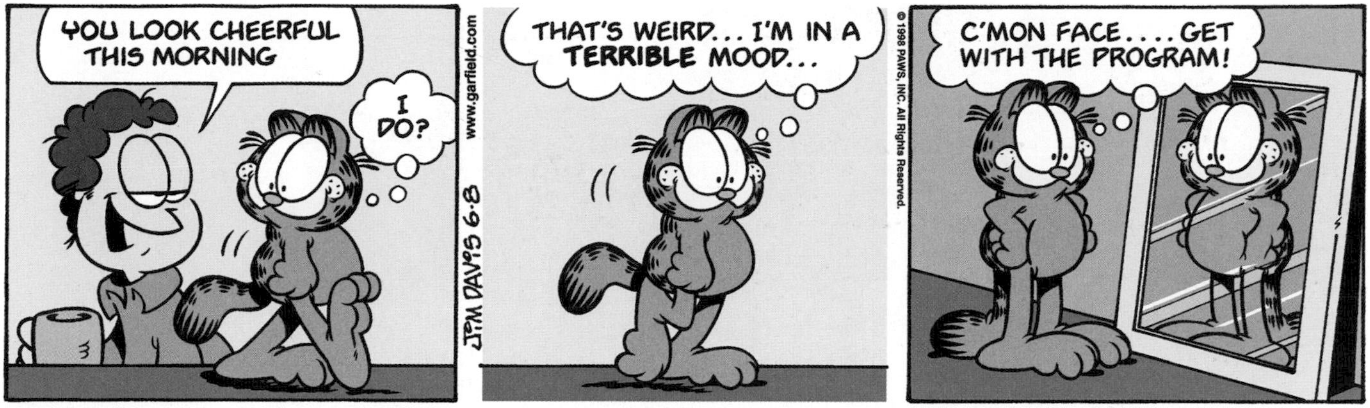
YOU LOOK CHEERFUL THIS MORNING
I DO?
JIM DAVIS 6-8
www.garfield.com
THAT'S WEIRD... I'M IN A **TERRIBLE** MOOD...
© 1998 PAWS, INC. All Rights Reserved.
C'MON FACE.... GET WITH THE PROGRAM!

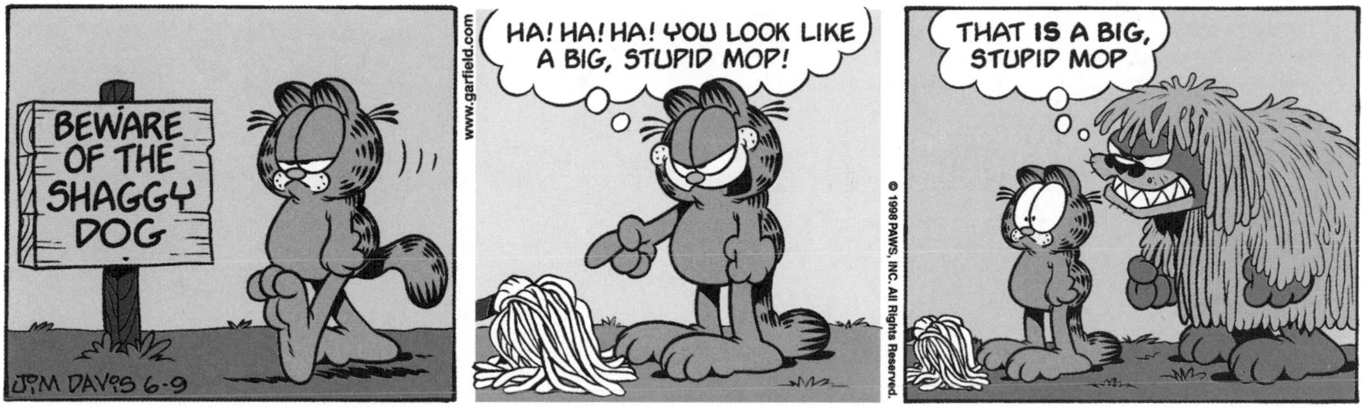
BEWARE OF THE SHAGGY DOG
JIM DAVIS 6-9
www.garfield.com
HA! HA! HA! YOU LOOK LIKE A BIG, STUPID MOP!
© 1998 PAWS, INC. All Rights Reserved.
THAT **IS** A BIG, STUPID MOP

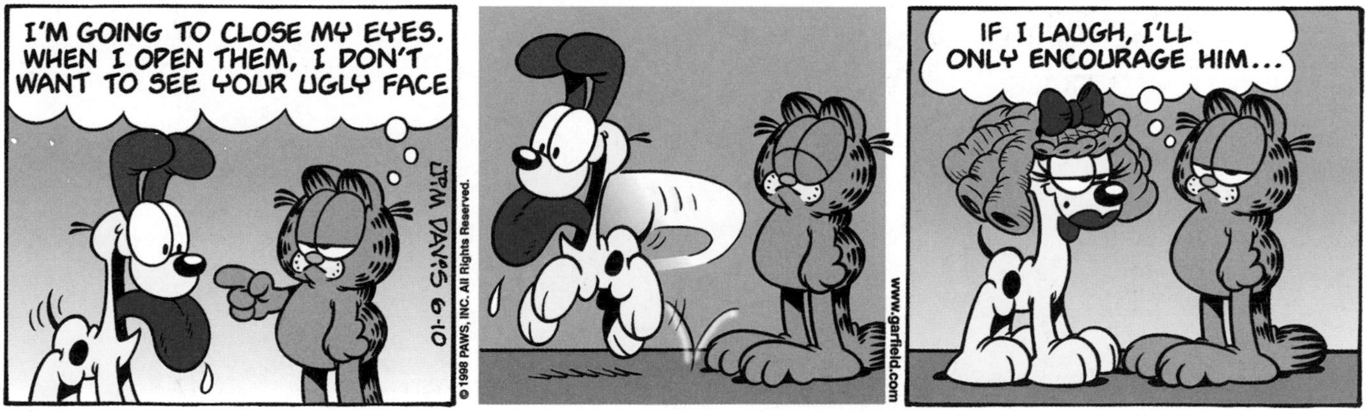
I'M GOING TO CLOSE MY EYES. WHEN I OPEN THEM, I DON'T WANT TO SEE YOUR UGLY FACE
JIM DAVIS 6-10
© 1998 PAWS, INC. All Rights Reserved.
www.garfield.com
IF I LAUGH, I'LL ONLY ENCOURAGE HIM...

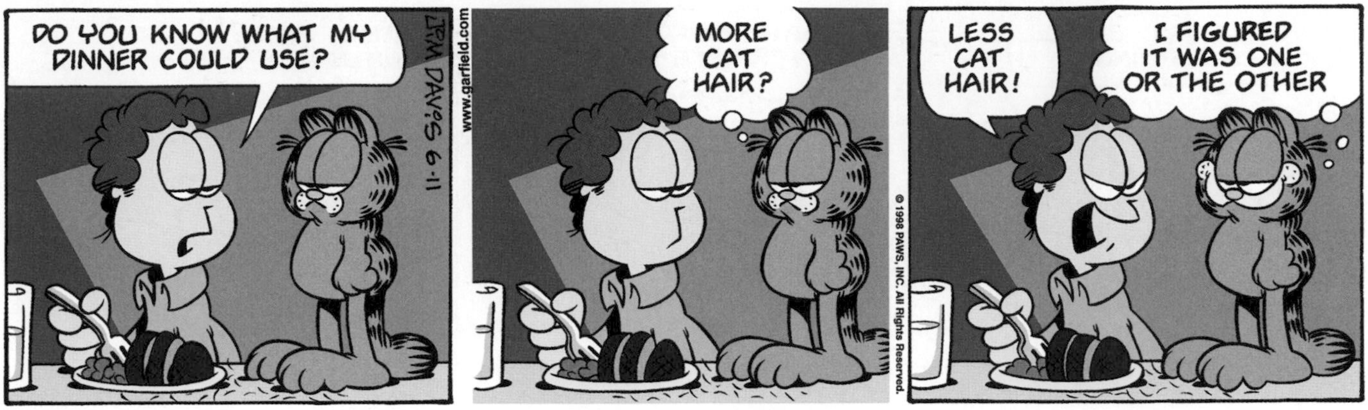
DO YOU KNOW WHAT MY DINNER COULD USE?
JIM DAVIS 6-11
www.garfield.com
MORE CAT HAIR?
© 1998 PAWS, INC. All Rights Reserved.
LESS CAT HAIR!
I FIGURED IT WAS ONE OR THE OTHER

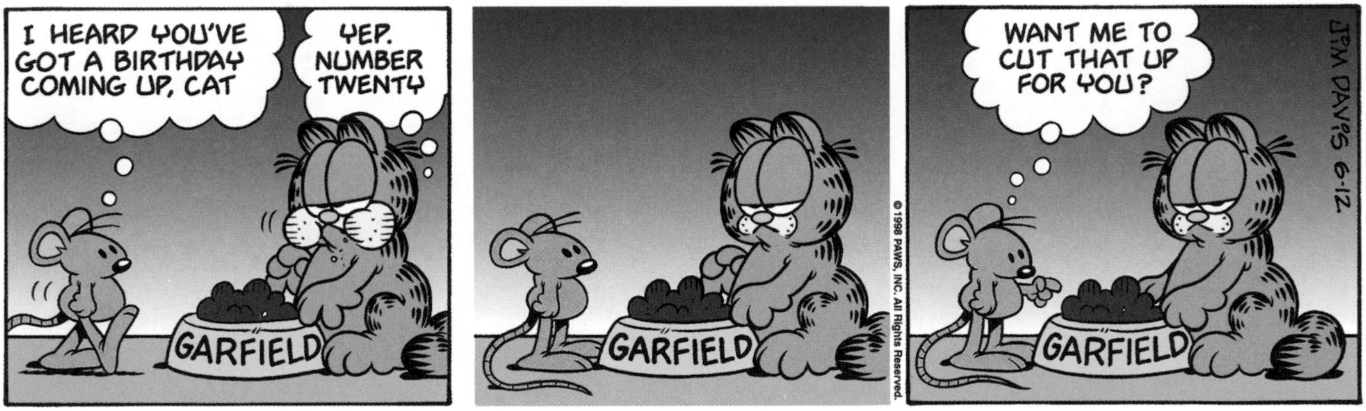
I HEARD YOU'VE GOT A BIRTHDAY COMING UP, CAT
YEP. NUMBER TWENTY
GARFIELD
GARFIELD
© 1998 PAWS, INC. All Rights Reserved.
WANT ME TO CUT THAT UP FOR YOU?
GARFIELD
JIM DAVIS 6-12

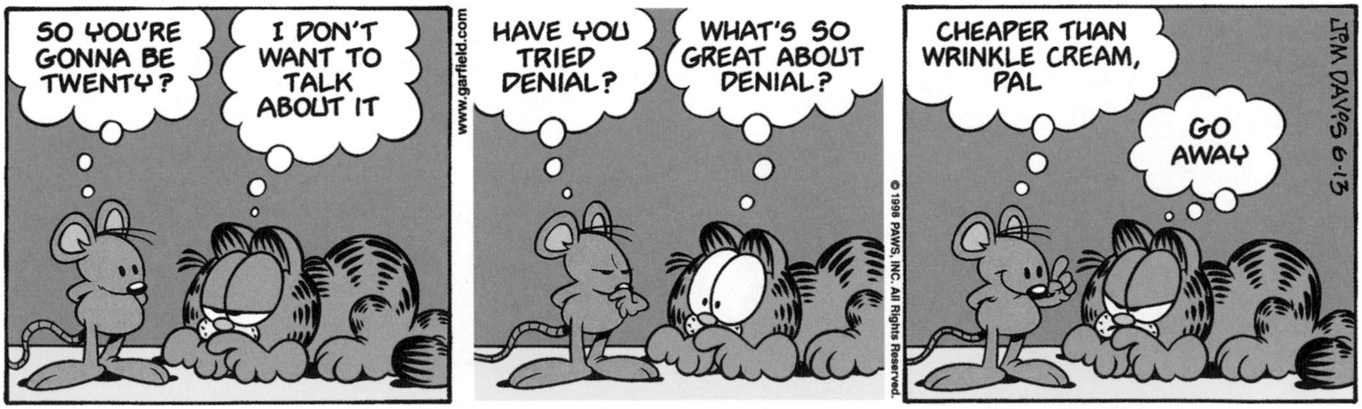
SO YOU'RE GONNA BE TWENTY?
I DON'T WANT TO TALK ABOUT IT
www.garfield.com
HAVE YOU TRIED DENIAL?
WHAT'S SO GREAT ABOUT DENIAL?
© 1998 PAWS, INC. All Rights Reserved.
CHEAPER THAN WRINKLE CREAM, PAL
GO AWAY
JIM DAVIS 6-13

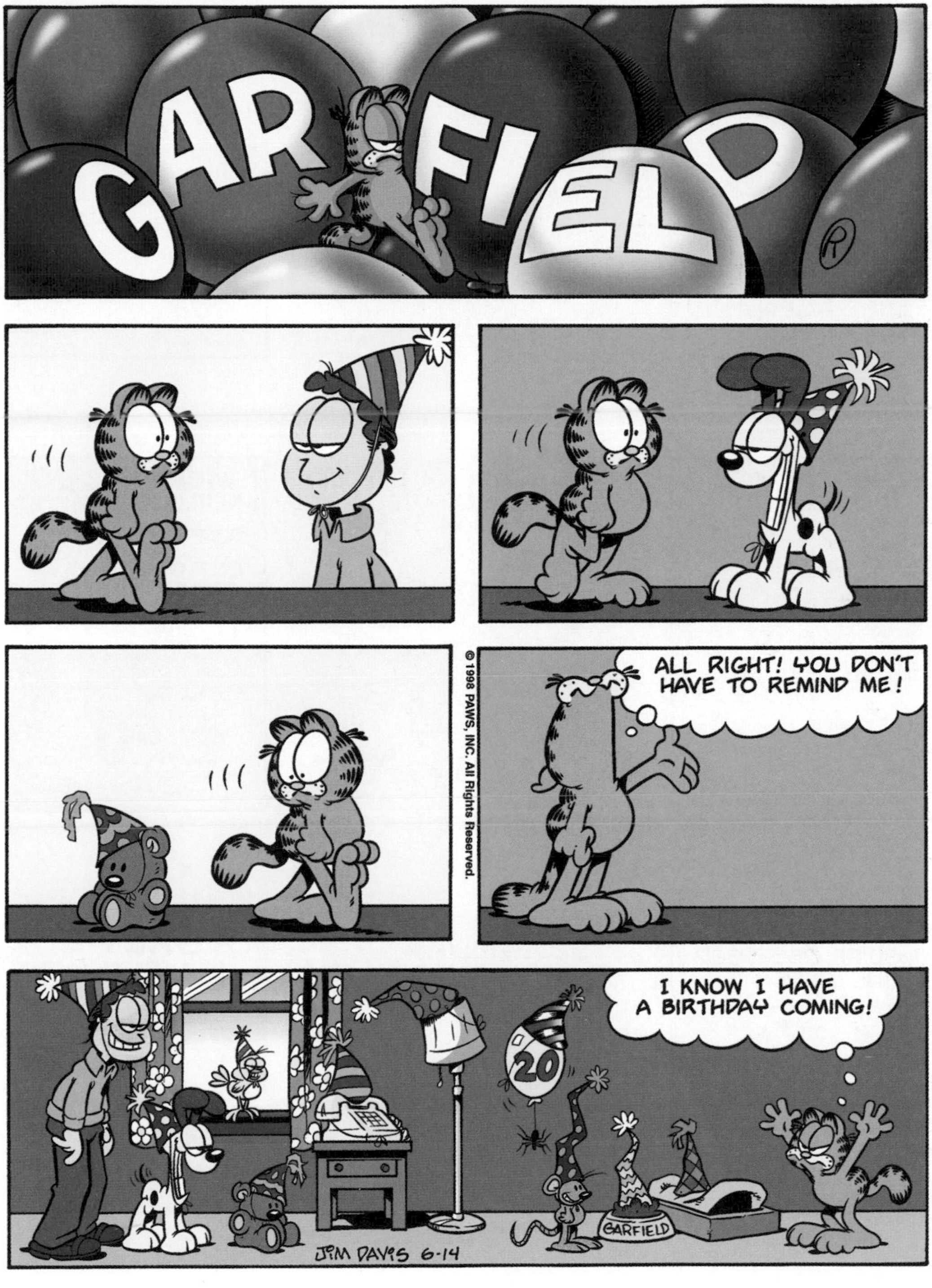
GARFIELD®
© 1998 PAWS, INC. All Rights Reserved.
ALL RIGHT! YOU DON'T HAVE TO REMIND ME!
I KNOW I HAVE A BIRTHDAY COMING!
GARFIELD
JIM DAVIS 6-14

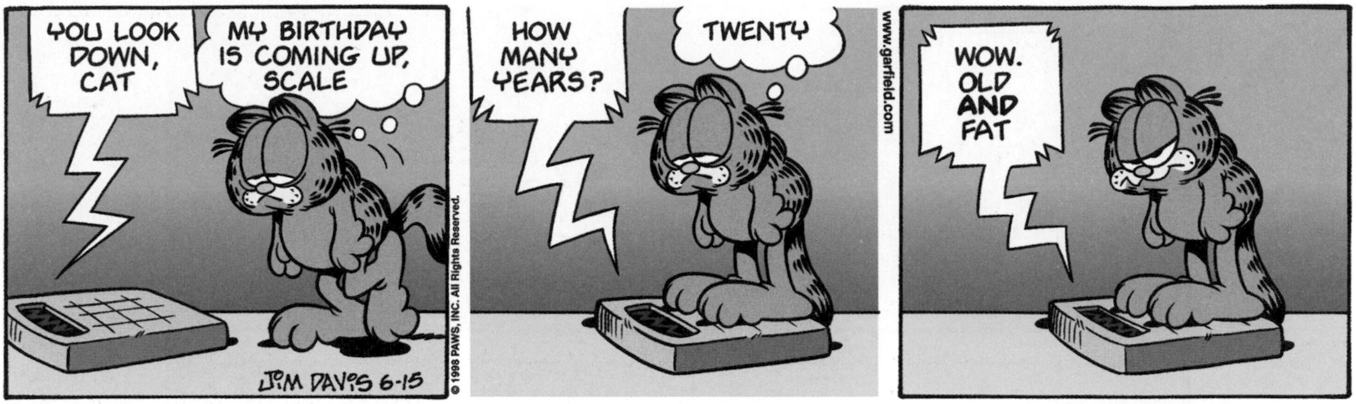
YOU LOOK DOWN, CAT
MY BIRTHDAY IS COMING UP, SCALE
JIM DAVIS 6-15
© 1998 PAWS, INC. All Rights Reserved.
HOW MANY YEARS?
TWENTY
www.garfield.com
WOW. OLD AND FAT

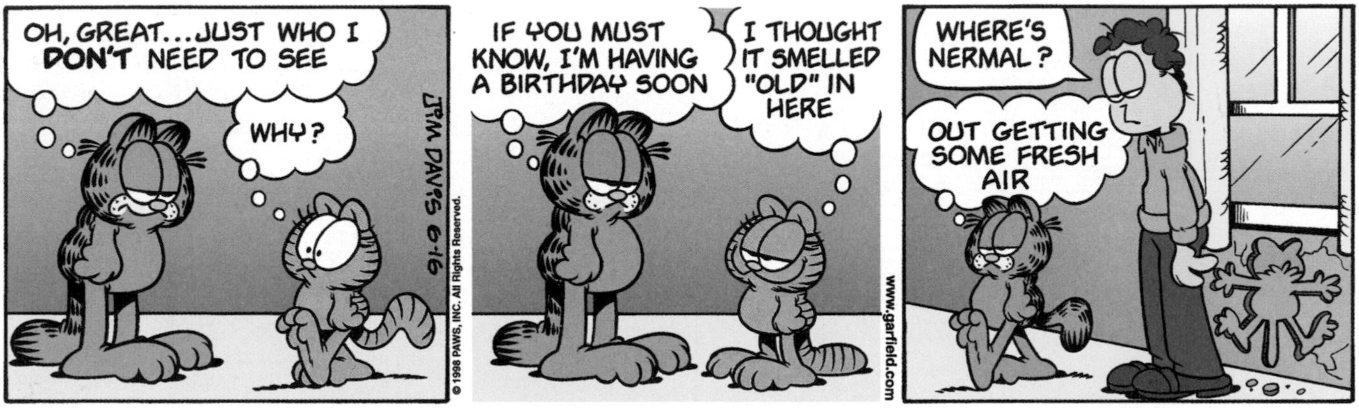
OH, GREAT...JUST WHO I DON'T NEED TO SEE
WHY?
JIM DAVIS 6-16
© 1998 PAWS, INC. All Rights Reserved.
IF YOU MUST KNOW, I'M HAVING A BIRTHDAY SOON
I THOUGHT IT SMELLED "OLD" IN HERE
www.garfield.com
WHERE'S NERMAL?
OUT GETTING SOME FRESH AIR

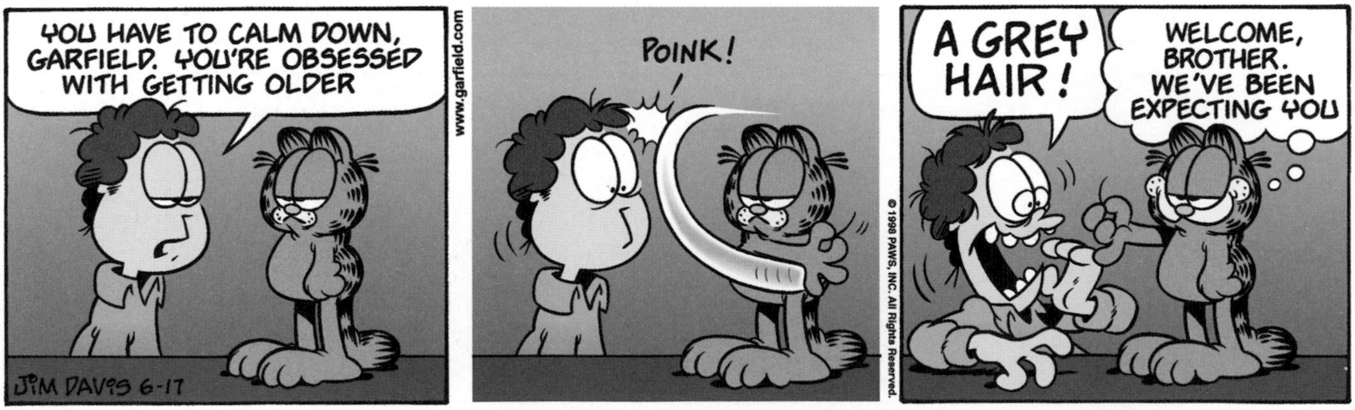
YOU HAVE TO CALM DOWN, GARFIELD. YOU'RE OBSESSED WITH GETTING OLDER
JIM DAVIS 6-17
www.garfield.com
POINK!
A GREY HAIR!
WELCOME, BROTHER. WE'VE BEEN EXPECTING YOU
© 1998 PAWS, INC. All Rights Reserved.

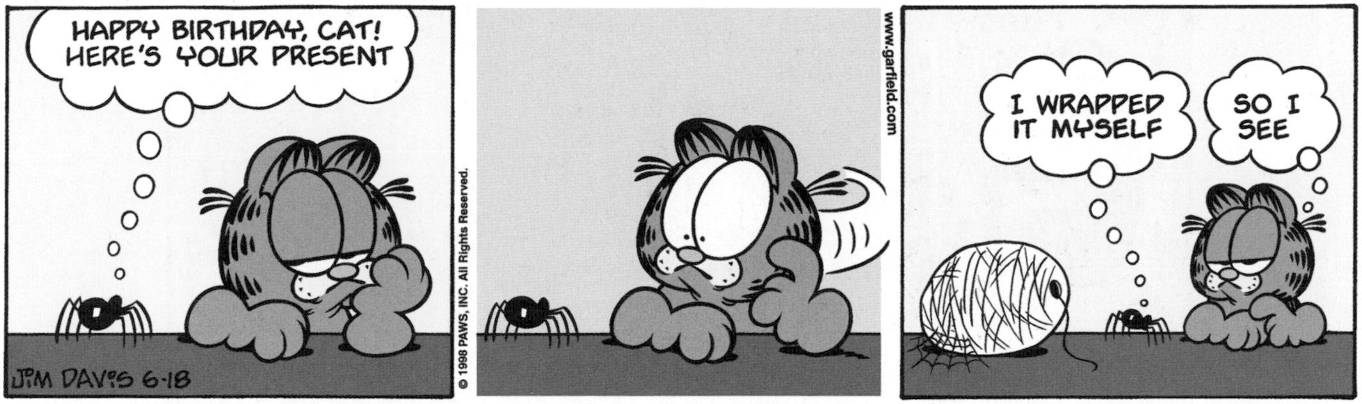
HAPPY BIRTHDAY, CAT! HERE'S YOUR PRESENT
JIM DAVIS 6-18
© 1998 PAWS, INC. All Rights Reserved.
www.garfield.com
I WRAPPED IT MYSELF
SO I SEE

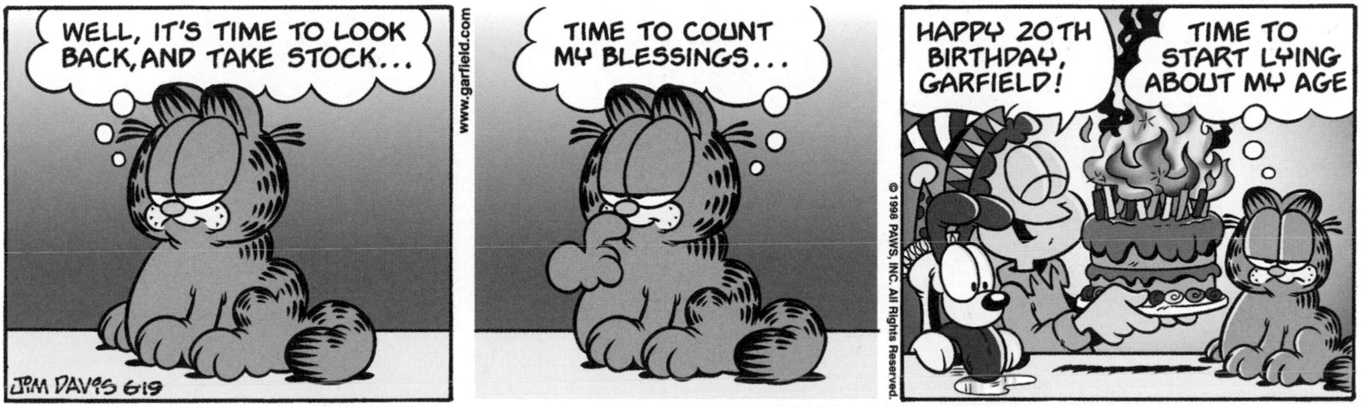
WELL, IT'S TIME TO LOOK BACK, AND TAKE STOCK...
JIM DAVIS 6-19
www.garfield.com
TIME TO COUNT MY BLESSINGS...
© 1998 PAWS, INC. All Rights Reserved.
HAPPY 20TH BIRTHDAY, GARFIELD!
TIME TO START LYING ABOUT MY AGE

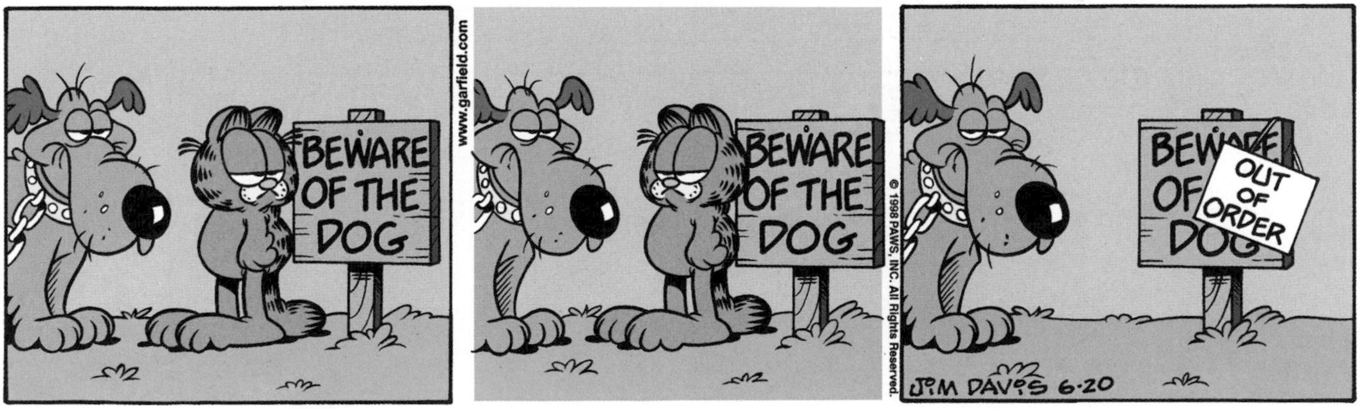
BEWARE OF THE DOG
www.garfield.com
BEWARE OF THE DOG
© 1998 PAWS, INC. All Rights Reserved.
OUT OF ORDER
JIM DAVIS 6-20

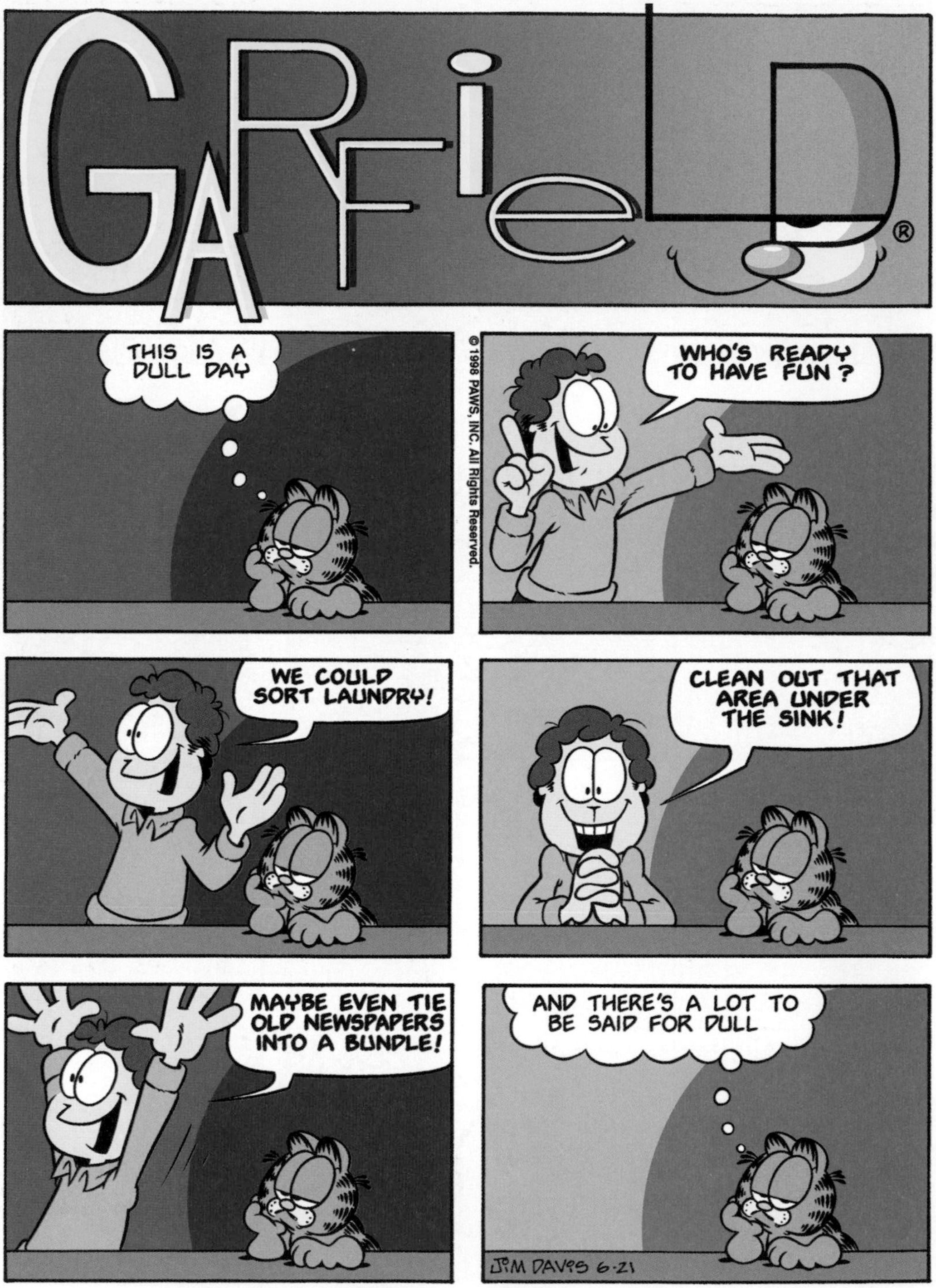
GARFIELD®
THIS IS A DULL DAY
© 1998 PAWS, INC. All Rights Reserved.
WHO'S READY TO HAVE FUN?
WE COULD SORT LAUNDRY!
CLEAN OUT THAT AREA UNDER THE SINK!
MAYBE EVEN TIE OLD NEWSPAPERS INTO A BUNDLE!
AND THERE'S A LOT TO BE SAID FOR DULL
JIM DAVIS 6-21

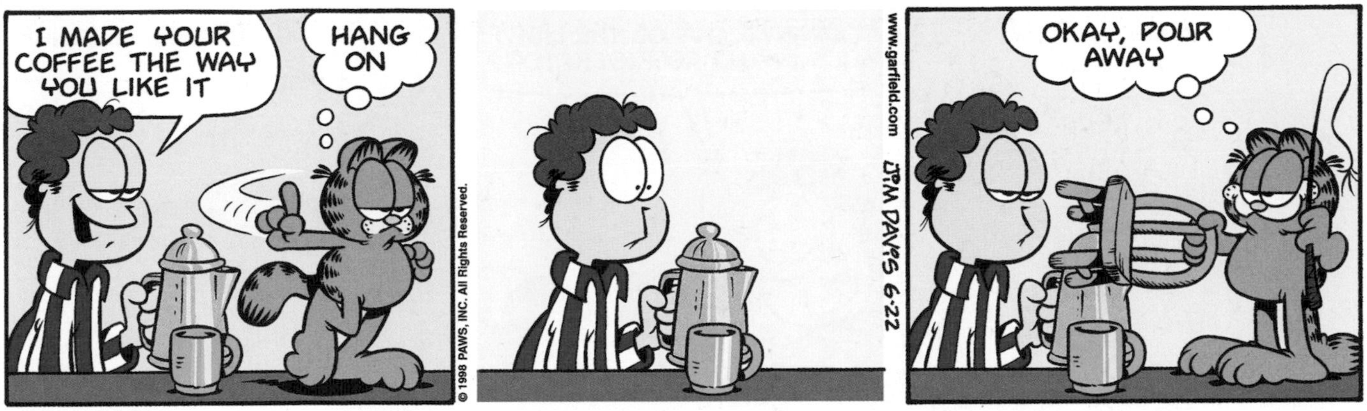
I MADE YOUR COFFEE THE WAY YOU LIKE IT
HANG ON
© 1998 PAWS, INC. All Rights Reserved.
www.garfield.com
JIM DAVIS 6-22
OKAY, POUR AWAY

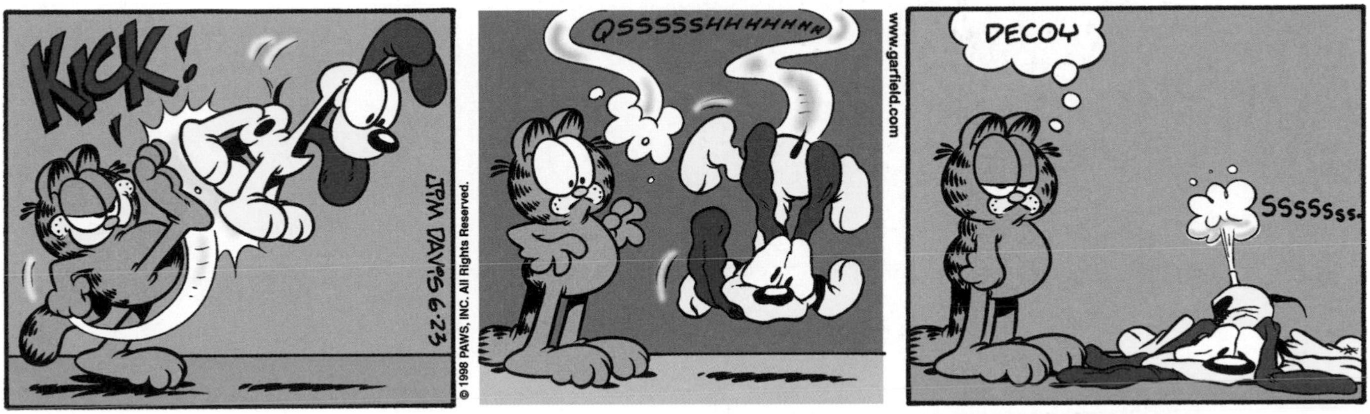
KICK!
JIM DAVIS 6-23
© 1998 PAWS, INC. All Rights Reserved.
QSSSSSHHHHHHH
www.garfield.com
DECOY
SSSSSss.

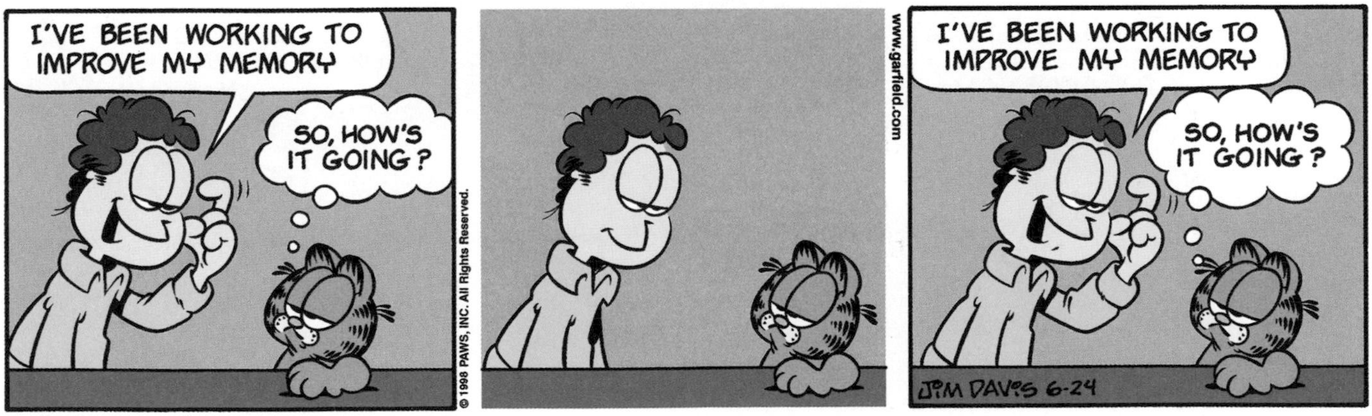
I'VE BEEN WORKING TO IMPROVE MY MEMORY
SO, HOW'S IT GOING?
© 1998 PAWS, INC. All Rights Reserved.
www.garfield.com
I'VE BEEN WORKING TO IMPROVE MY MEMORY
SO, HOW'S IT GOING?
JIM DAVIS 6-24

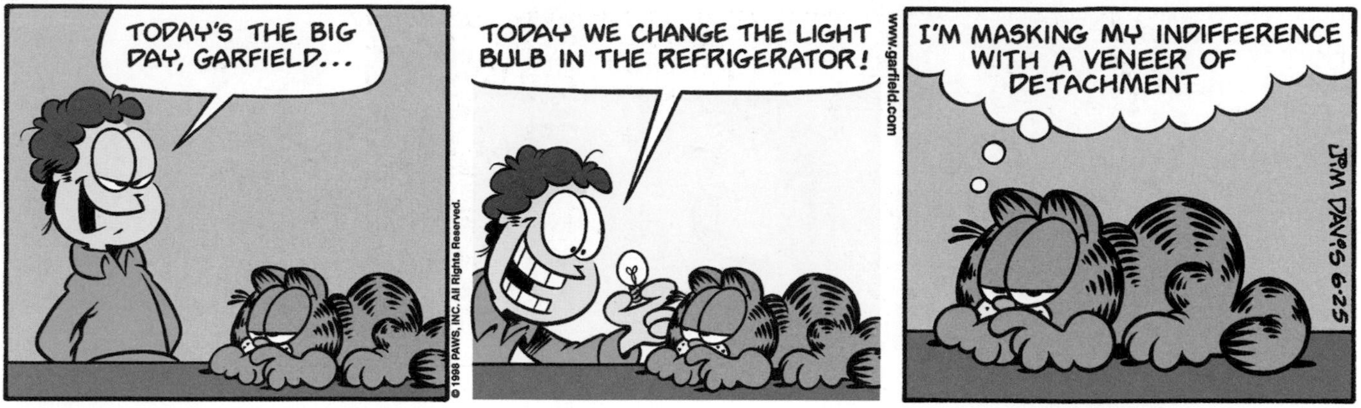
TODAY'S THE BIG DAY, GARFIELD...
TODAY WE CHANGE THE LIGHT BULB IN THE REFRIGERATOR!
I'M MASKING MY INDIFFERENCE WITH A VENEER OF DETACHMENT
© 1998 PAWS, INC. All Rights Reserved.
www.garfield.com
JIM DAVIS 6-25

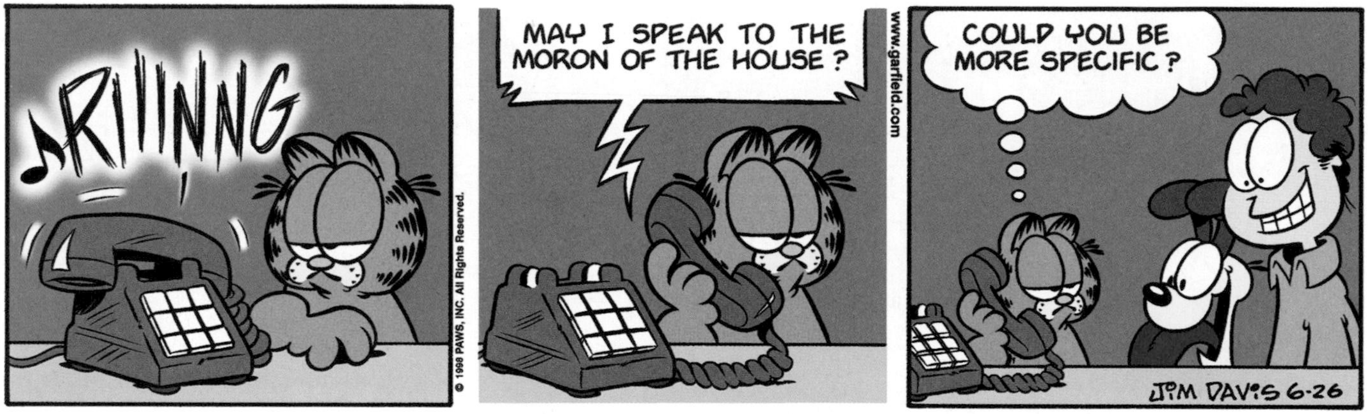
RIIINNG
MAY I SPEAK TO THE MORON OF THE HOUSE?
COULD YOU BE MORE SPECIFIC?
© 1998 PAWS, INC. All Rights Reserved.
www.garfield.com
JIM DAVIS 6-26

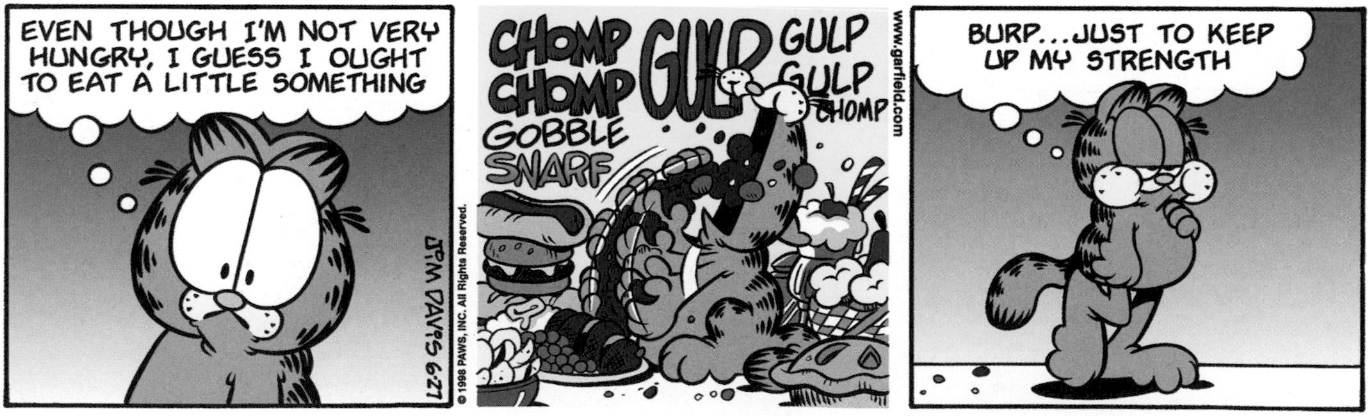
EVEN THOUGH I'M NOT VERY HUNGRY, I GUESS I OUGHT TO EAT A LITTLE SOMETHING
CHOMP CHOMP GULP GULP GULP GULP CHOMP GOBBLE SNARF
BURP...JUST TO KEEP UP MY STRENGTH
© 1998 PAWS, INC. All Rights Reserved.
www.garfield.com
JIM DAVIS 6-27

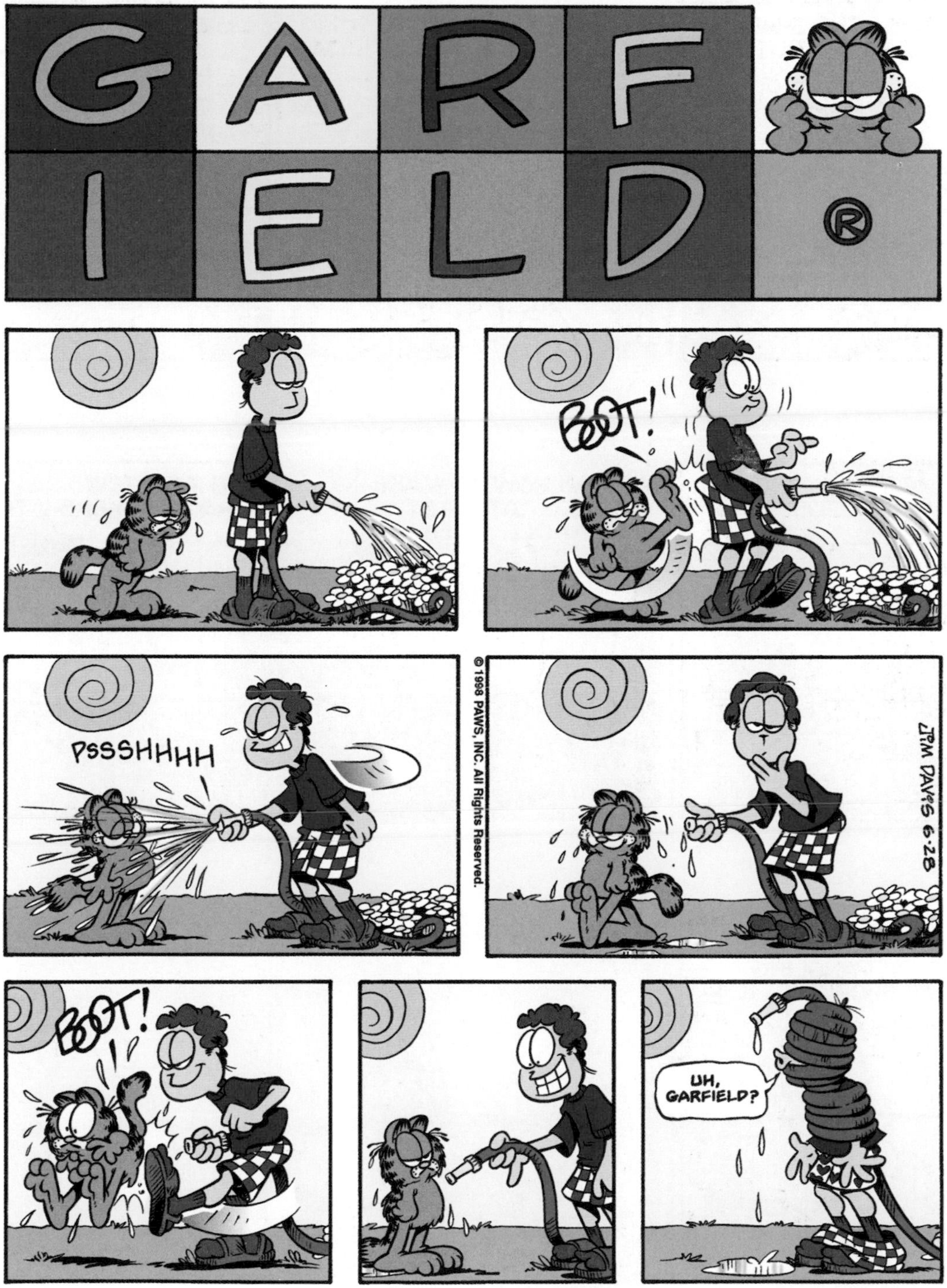
GARFIELD®
BOOT!
PSSSHHHH
© 1998 PAWS, INC. All Rights Reserved.
JIM DAVIS 6-28
BOOT!
UH, GARFIELD?

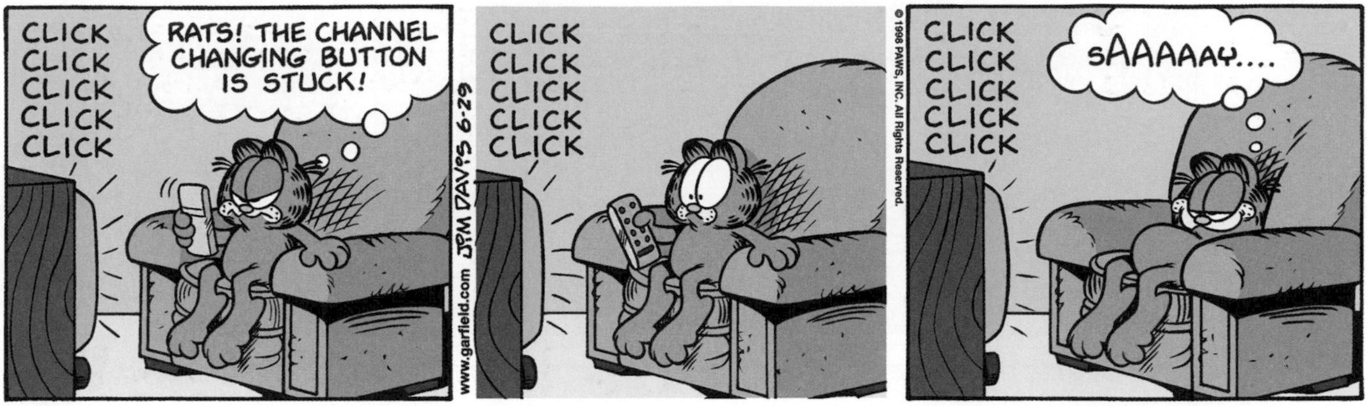
CLICK CLICK CLICK CLICK CLICK
RATS! THE CHANNEL CHANGING BUTTON IS STUCK!
JIM DAVIS 6-29
www.garfield.com
CLICK CLICK CLICK CLICK CLICK
© 1998 PAWS, INC. All Rights Reserved.
CLICK CLICK CLICK CLICK CLICK
sAAAAAY....

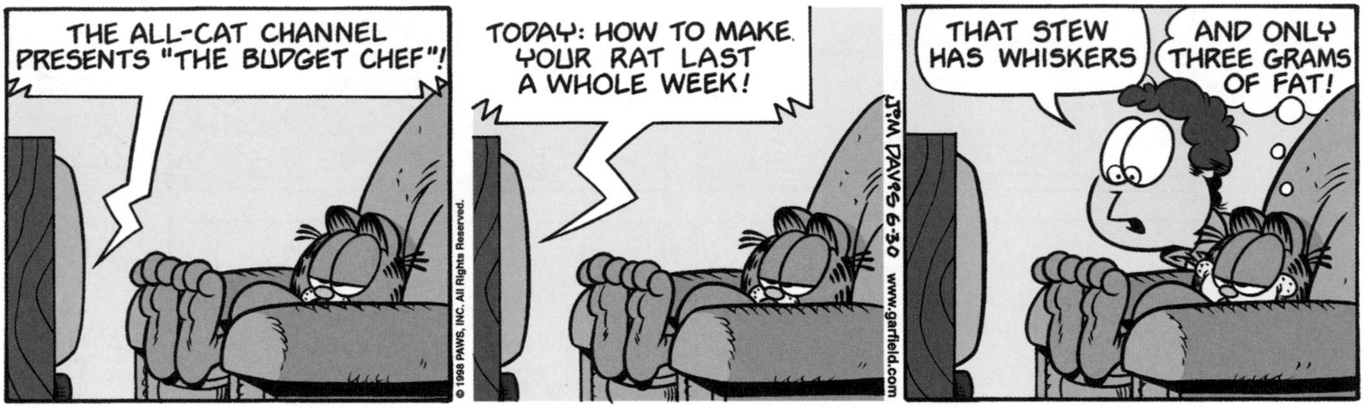
THE ALL-CAT CHANNEL PRESENTS "THE BUDGET CHEF"!
© 1998 PAWS, INC. All Rights Reserved.
TODAY: HOW TO MAKE YOUR RAT LAST A WHOLE WEEK!
JIM DAVIS 6-30
www.garfield.com
THAT STEW HAS WHISKERS
AND ONLY THREE GRAMS OF FAT!

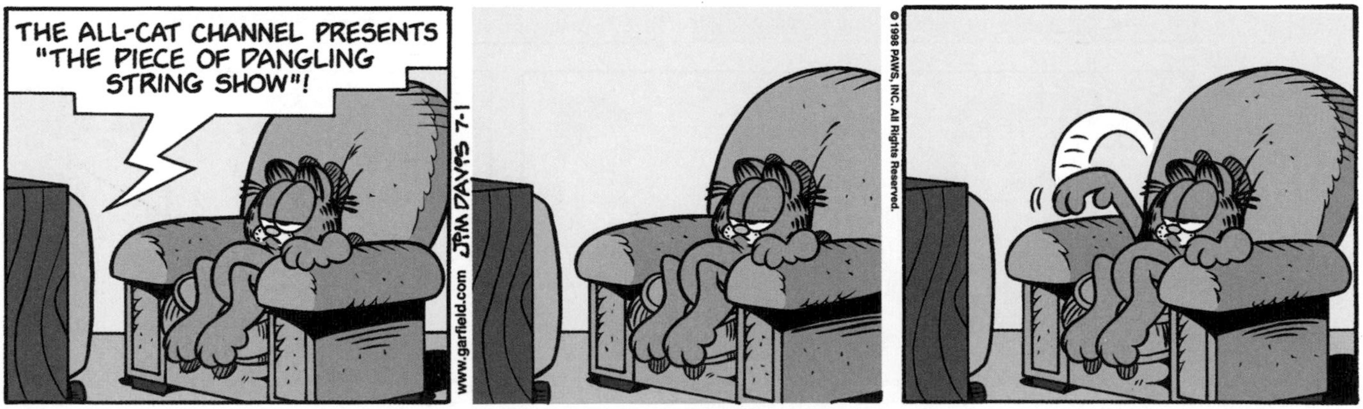
THE ALL-CAT CHANNEL PRESENTS "THE PIECE OF DANGLING STRING SHOW"!
JIM DAVIS 7-1
www.garfield.com
© 1998 PAWS, INC. All Rights Reserved.

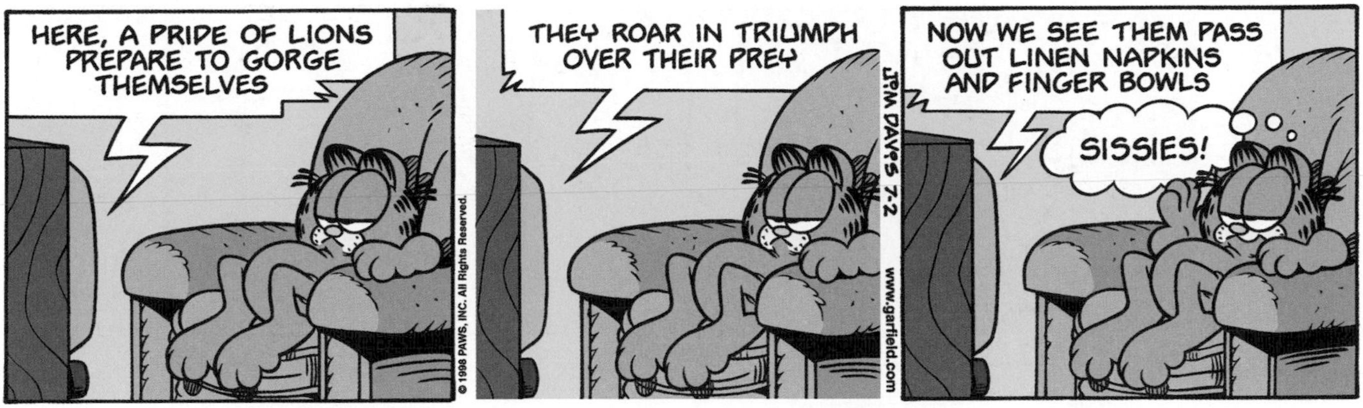
HERE, A PRIDE OF LIONS PREPARE TO GORGE THEMSELVES
© 1998 PAWS, INC. All Rights Reserved.
THEY ROAR IN TRIUMPH OVER THEIR PREY
JPM DAVIS 7-2
www.garfield.com
NOW WE SEE THEM PASS OUT LINEN NAPKINS AND FINGER BOWLS
SISSIES!

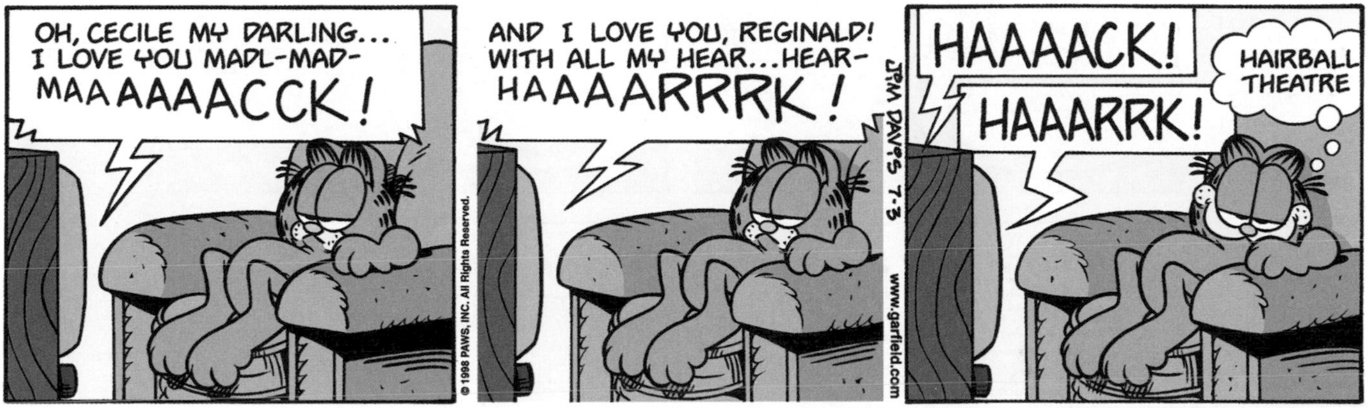
OH, CECILE MY DARLING... I LOVE YOU MADL-MAD-MAAAAAACCK!
© 1998 PAWS, INC. All Rights Reserved.
AND I LOVE YOU, REGINALD! WITH ALL MY HEAR...HEAR-HAAAARRRK!
JPM DAVIS 7-3
www.garfield.com
HAAAACK!
HAAARRK!
HAIRBALL THEATRE

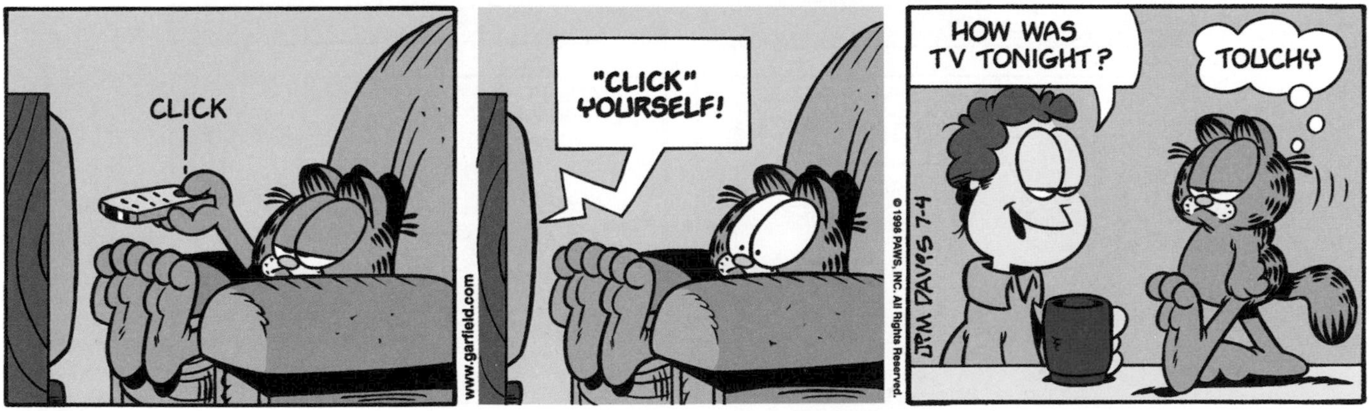
CLICK
www.garfield.com
"CLICK" YOURSELF!
© 1998 PAWS, INC. All Rights Reserved.
JPM DAVIS 7-4
HOW WAS TV TONIGHT?
TOUCHY

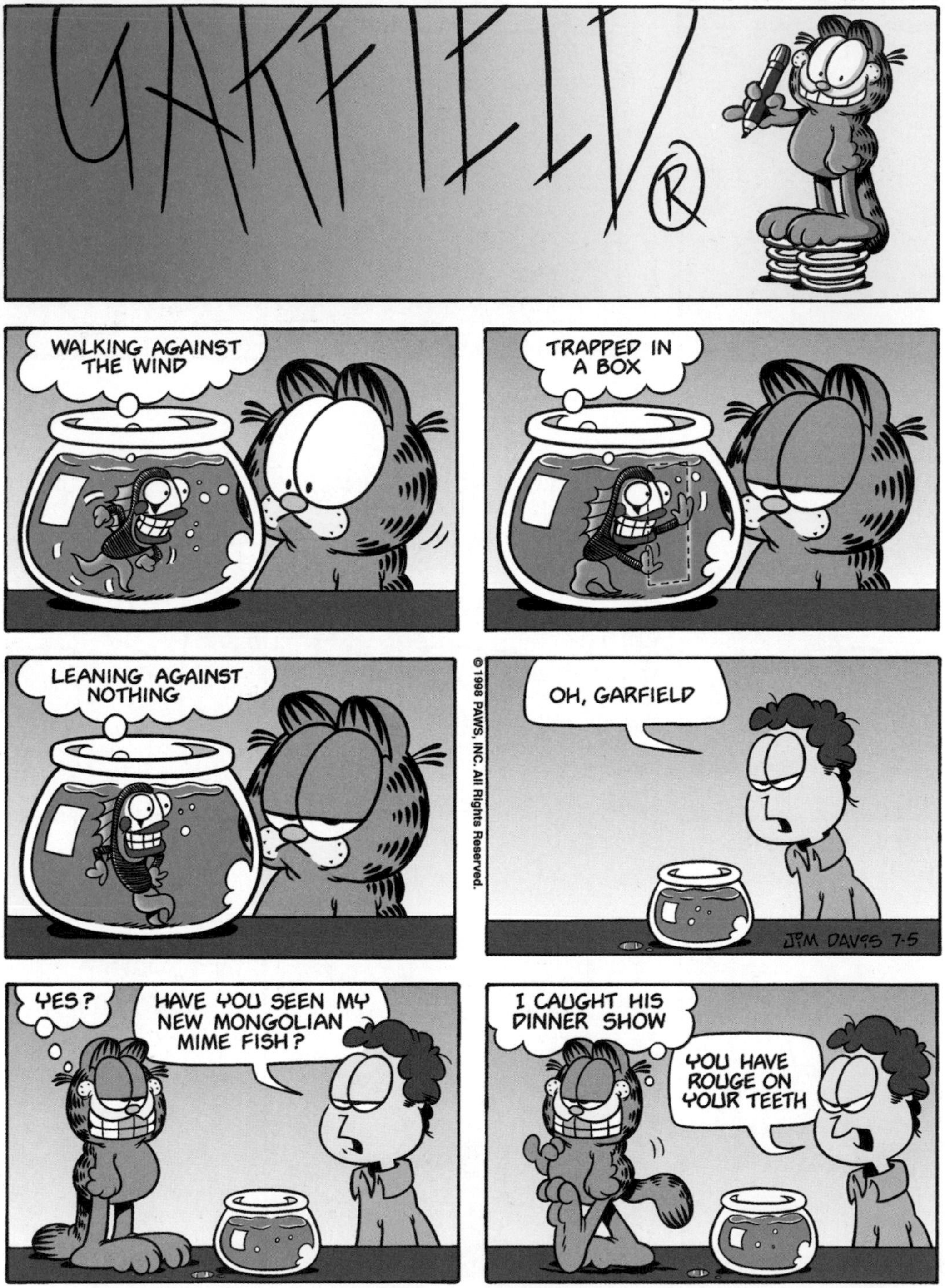
GARFIELD®
WALKING AGAINST THE WIND
TRAPPED IN A BOX
LEANING AGAINST NOTHING
© 1998 PAWS, INC. All Rights Reserved.
OH, GARFIELD
JIM DAVIS 7-5
YES?
HAVE YOU SEEN MY NEW MONGOLIAN MIME FISH?
I CAUGHT HIS DINNER SHOW
YOU HAVE ROUGE ON YOUR TEETH

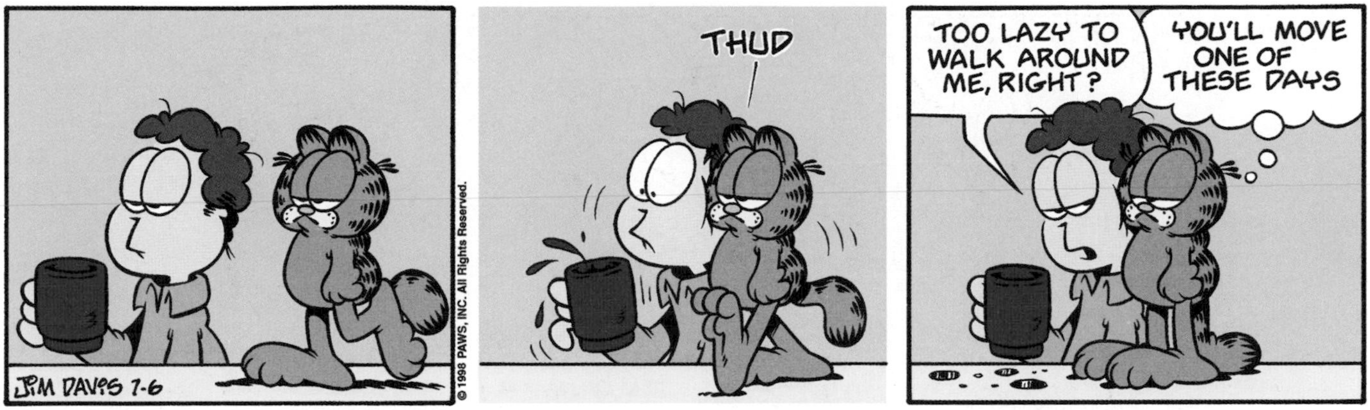
JIM DAVIS 7-6
© 1998 PAWS, INC. All Rights Reserved.
THUD
TOO LAZY TO WALK AROUND ME, RIGHT?
YOU'LL MOVE ONE OF THESE DAYS

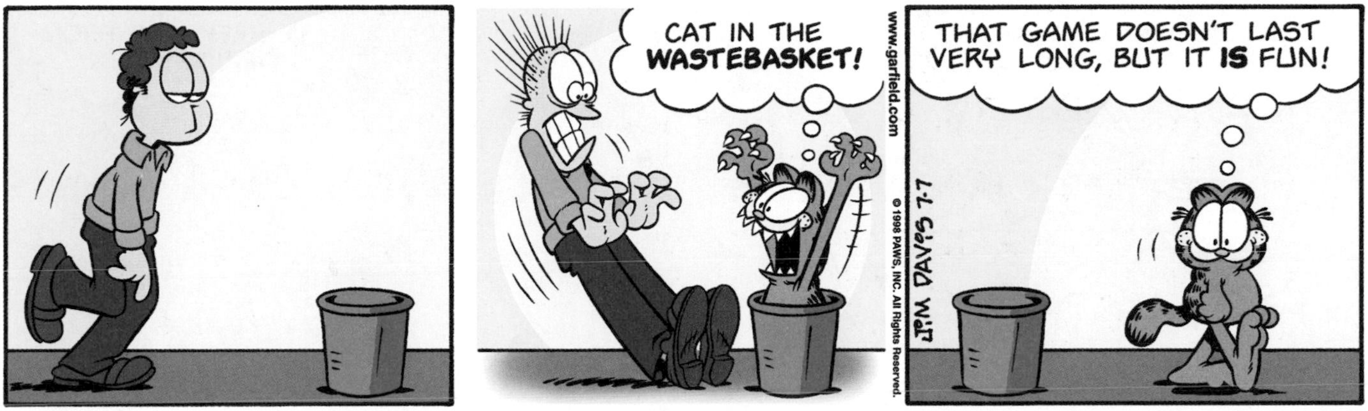
CAT IN THE **WASTEBASKET!**
www.garfield.com
© 1998 PAWS, INC. All Rights Reserved.
JIM DAVIS 7-7
THAT GAME DOESN'T LAST VERY LONG, BUT IT **IS** FUN!

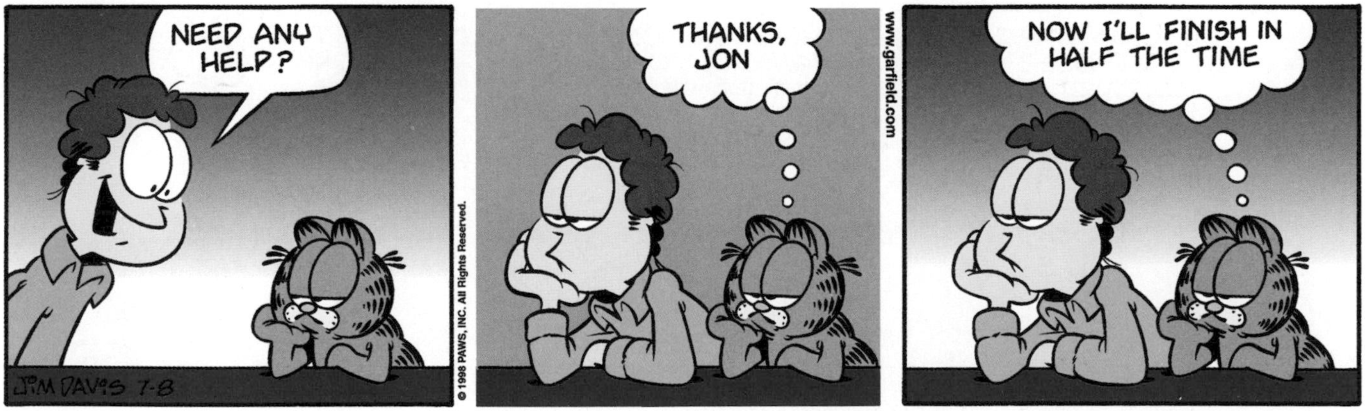
NEED ANY HELP?
JIM DAVIS 7-8
© 1998 PAWS, INC. All Rights Reserved.
THANKS, JON
www.garfield.com
NOW I'LL FINISH IN HALF THE TIME

I'M TAKING ODIE FOR A WALK
© 1998 PAWS, INC. All Rights Reserved.
JIM DAVIS 7-9
www.garfield.com
COULDN'T FIND A LEASH

WHY DO YOU HAVE A TAIL?
JIM DAVIS 7-10
© 1998 PAWS, INC. All Rights Reserved.
JON, JON, JON
www.garfield.com
IT KEEPS ME FROM TIPPING OVER

YOU KNOW WHAT I COULD USE?
JIM DAVIS 7-11
www.garfield.com
THREE GALLONS OF STRAWBERRY MACADAMIA NUT ICE CREAM?
© 1998 PAWS, INC. All Rights Reserved.
SOME TIME ALONE
MORE FOR ME

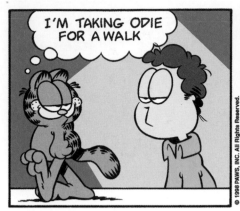

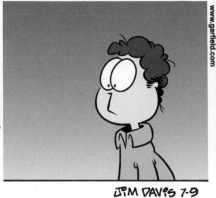

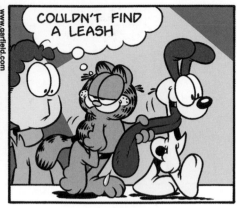

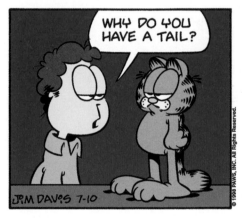

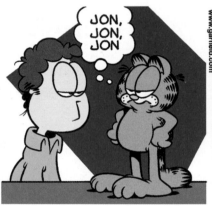

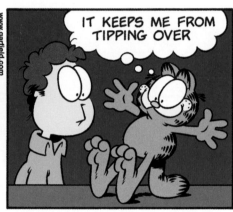

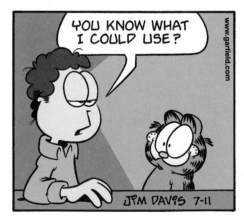

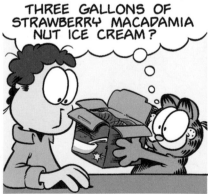

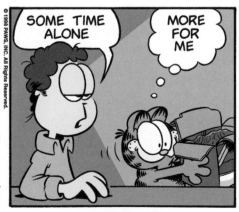

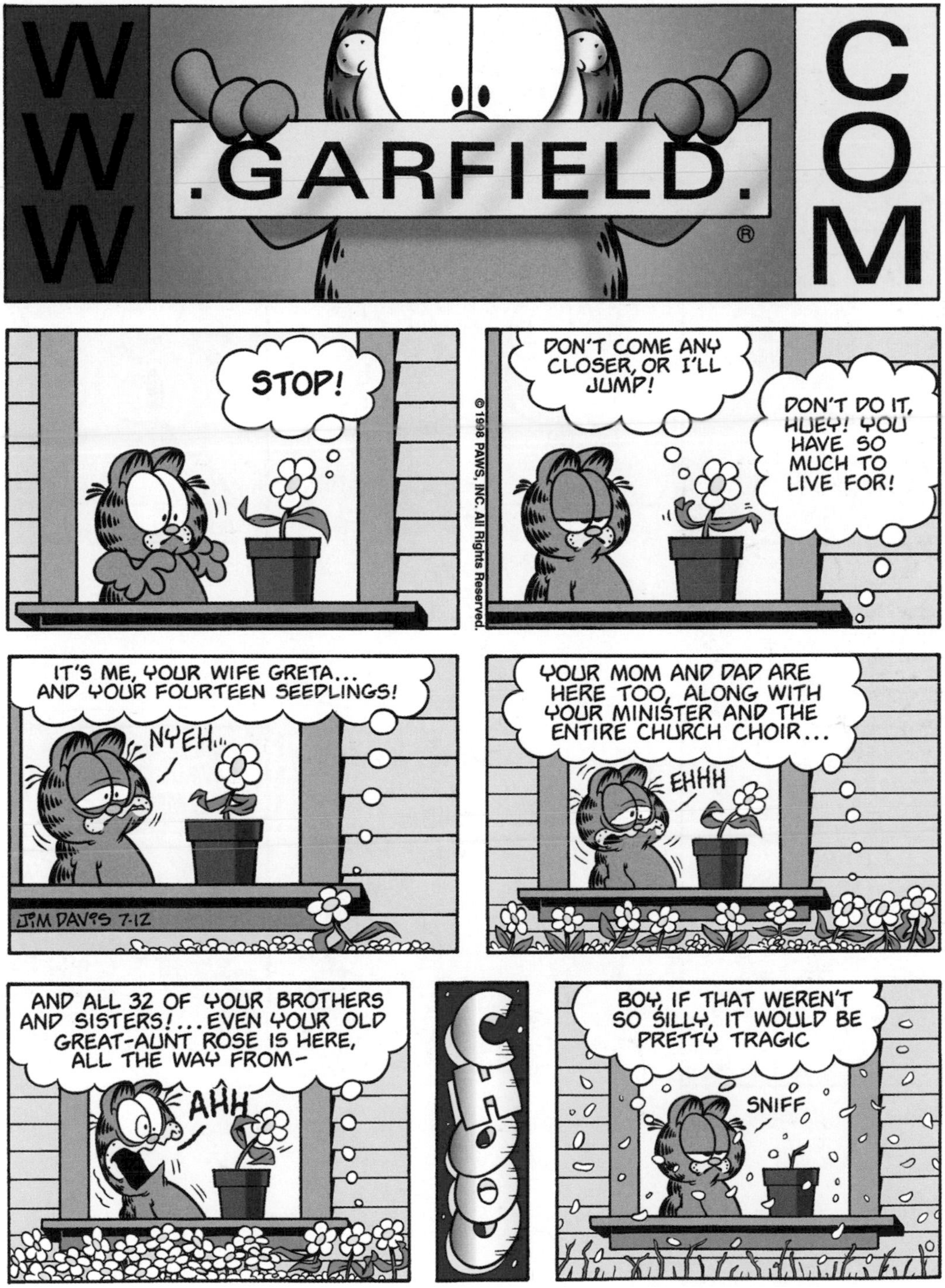
WWW.GARFIELD.COM
STOP!
© 1998 PAWS, INC. All Rights Reserved.
DON'T COME ANY CLOSER, OR I'LL JUMP!
DON'T DO IT, HUEY! YOU HAVE SO MUCH TO LIVE FOR!
IT'S ME, YOUR WIFE GRETA... AND YOUR FOURTEEN SEEDLINGS!
NYEH...
JIM DAVIS 7-12
YOUR MOM AND DAD ARE HERE TOO, ALONG WITH YOUR MINISTER AND THE ENTIRE CHURCH CHOIR...
EHHH
AND ALL 32 OF YOUR BROTHERS AND SISTERS!... EVEN YOUR OLD GREAT-AUNT ROSE IS HERE, ALL THE WAY FROM-
AHH
CHOOO
BOY, IF THAT WEREN'T SO SILLY, IT WOULD BE PRETTY TRAGIC
SNIFF

LIFE HAS ITS UPS AND DOWNS
© 1998 PAWS, INC. All Rights Reserved.
www.garfield.com
I HAVE UPS!
I DIDN'T SAY ANYTHING
JIM DAVIS 7-13

JIM DAVIS 7-14
CHEW
CHEW
CHEW
CHEW
CHEW
GARFIELD
© 1998 PAWS, INC. All Rights Reserved.
CHEW CHEW
CHEW
CHEW
CHEW CHEW
GARFIELD
www.garfield.com
WILL YOU SWALLOW?!
ONLY IF THERE'S MORE FOOD
CHEW
CHEW
CHEW
CHEW
CHEW
GARFIELD

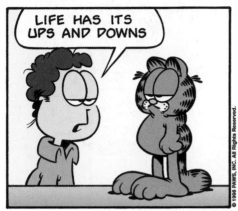

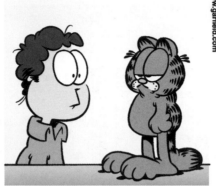

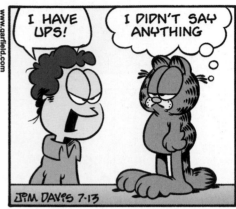

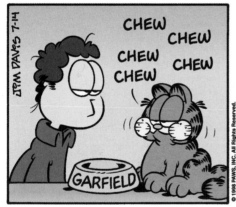

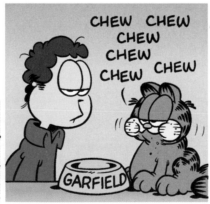

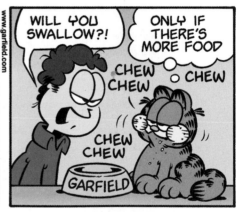

JON'S SCARIEST DATES

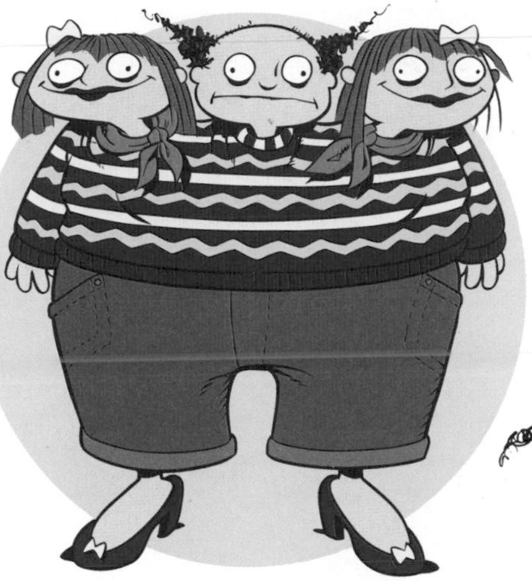

Gertie, Greta, and Bob, Siamese Triplets

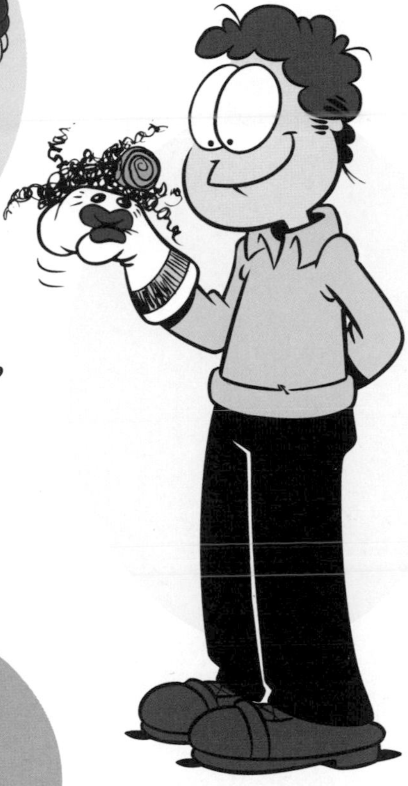

"Señorita Del Fuego"

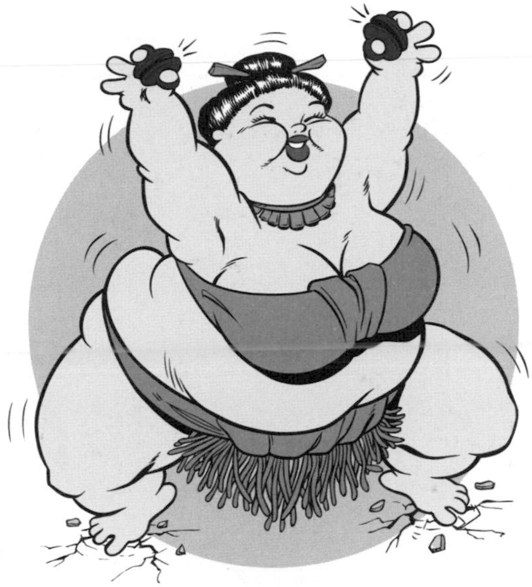

Suki the Sumo Belly Dancer

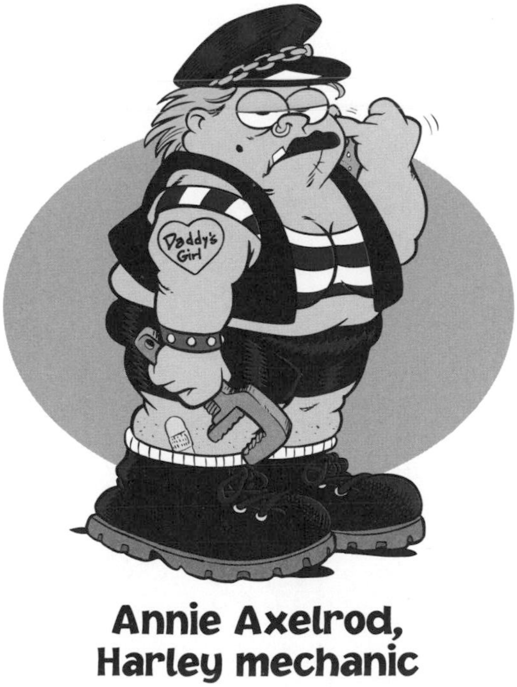
Daddy's Girl

Annie Axelrod, Harley mechanic

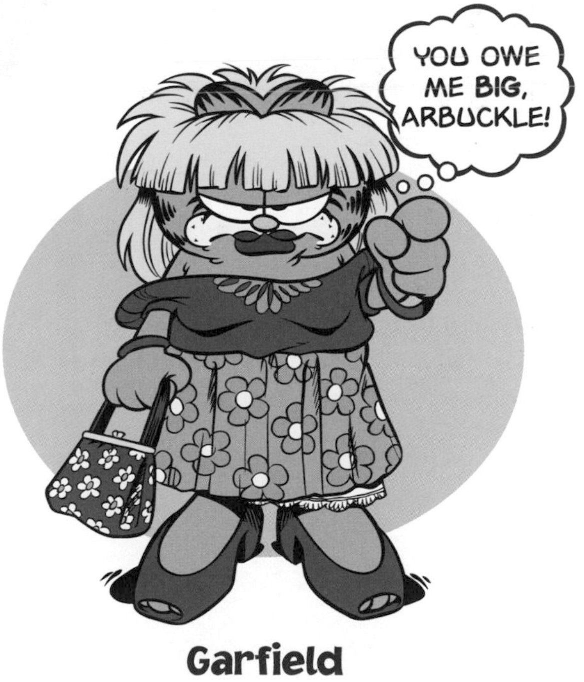
YOU OWE ME BIG, ARBUCKLE!

Garfield

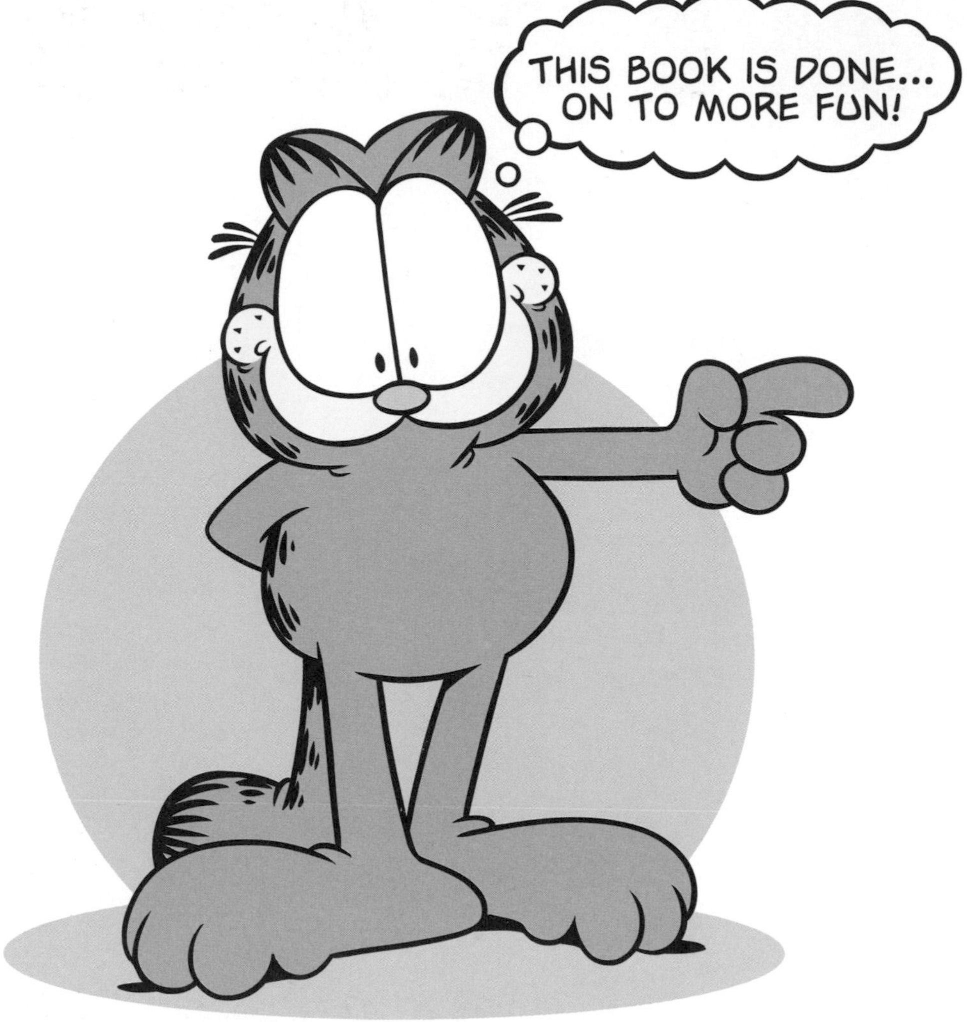
THIS BOOK IS DONE...
ON TO MORE FUN!

Garfield
feeds the kitty

BY JIM DAVIS

Ballantine Books ● New York

PRACTICAL USES FOR GARFIELD'S HAIRBALLS

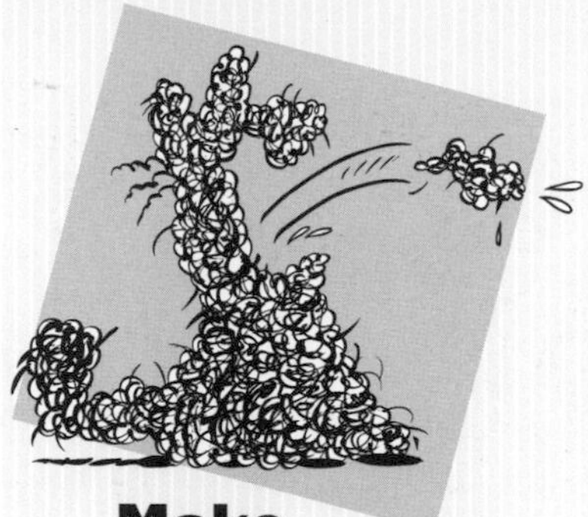

Make Another Cat

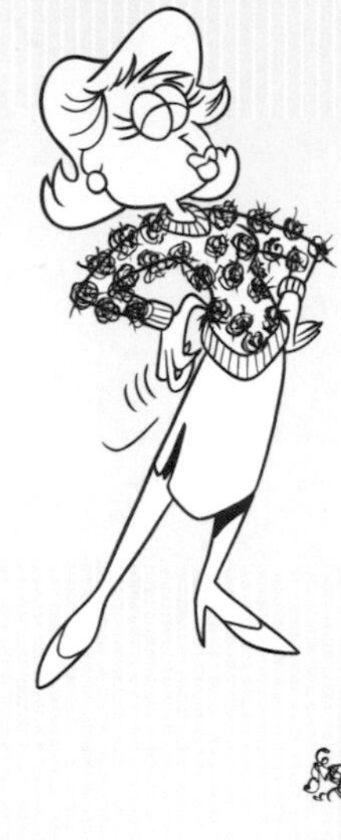

Unique Sweaters

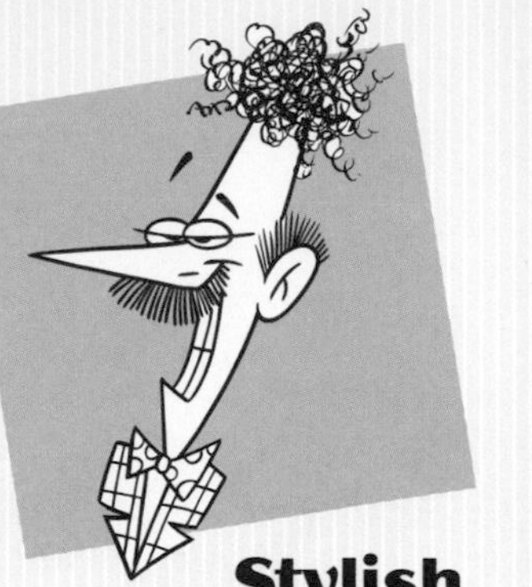

Stylish Toupees

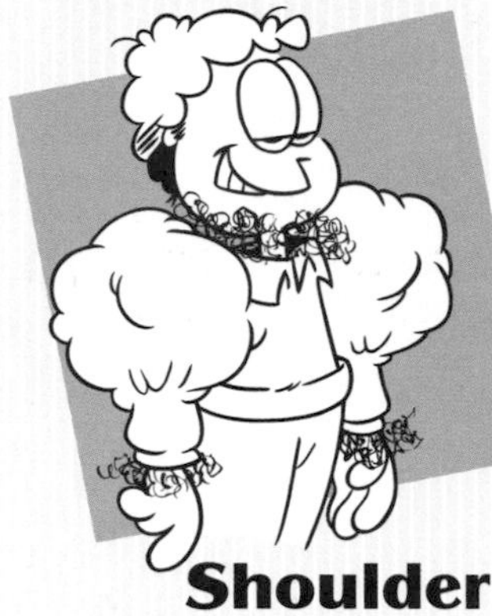

Shoulder Pads

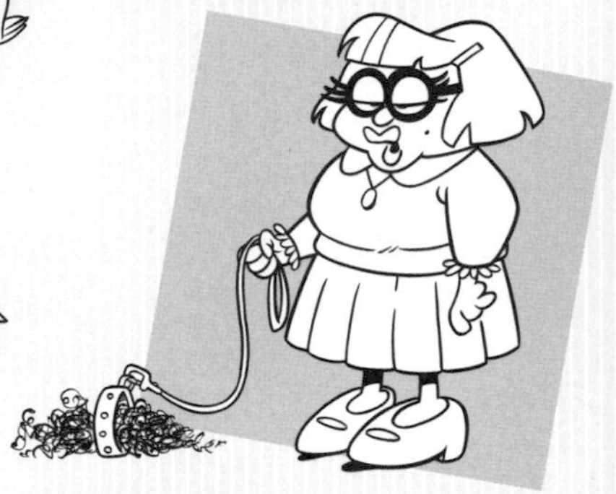

Maintenance-Free Pets

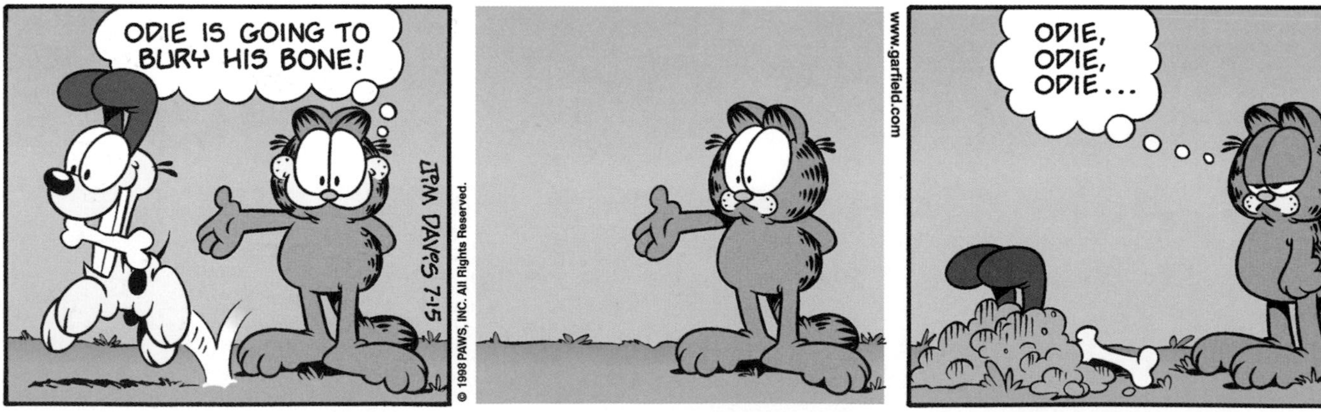
ODIE IS GOING TO BURY HIS BONE!
JPM DAVIS 7-15
© 1998 PAWS, INC. All Rights Reserved.
www.garfield.com
ODIE, ODIE, ODIE...

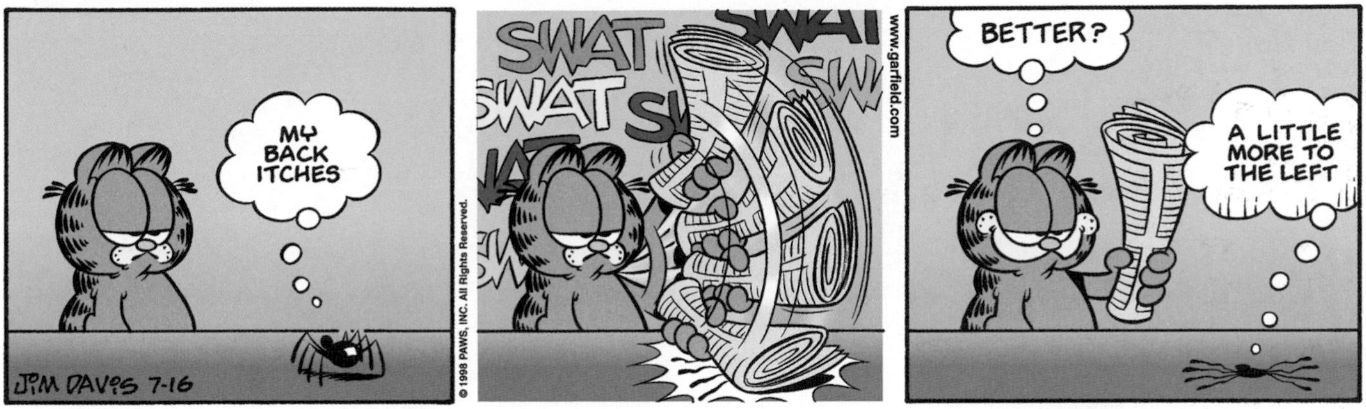
MY BACK ITCHES
JIM DAVIS 7-16
SWAT
SWAT
© 1998 PAWS, INC. All Rights Reserved.
www.garfield.com
BETTER?
A LITTLE MORE TO THE LEFT

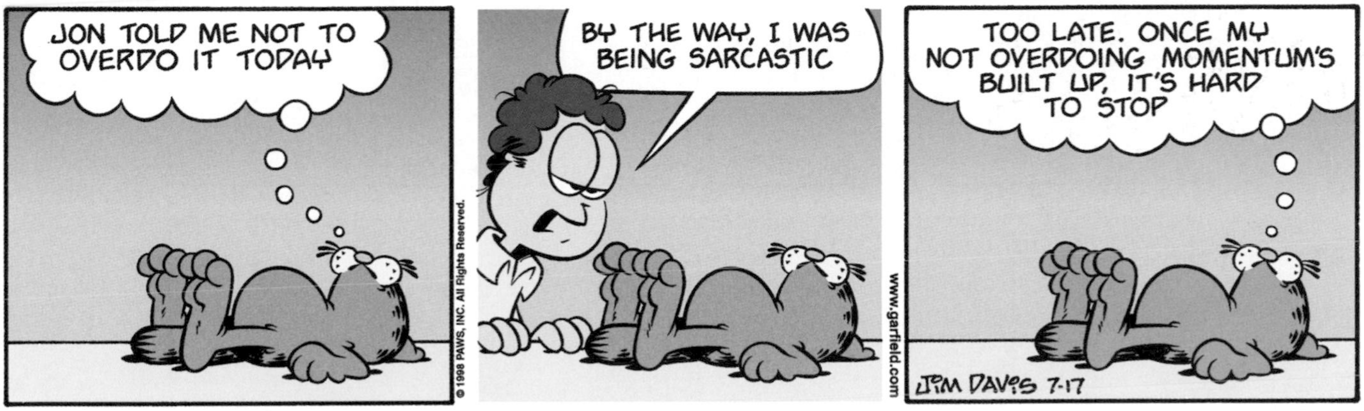
JON TOLD ME NOT TO OVERDO IT TODAY
© 1998 PAWS, INC. All Rights Reserved.
BY THE WAY, I WAS BEING SARCASTIC
www.garfield.com
TOO LATE. ONCE MY NOT OVERDOING MOMENTUM'S BUILT UP, IT'S HARD TO STOP
JIM DAVIS 7-17

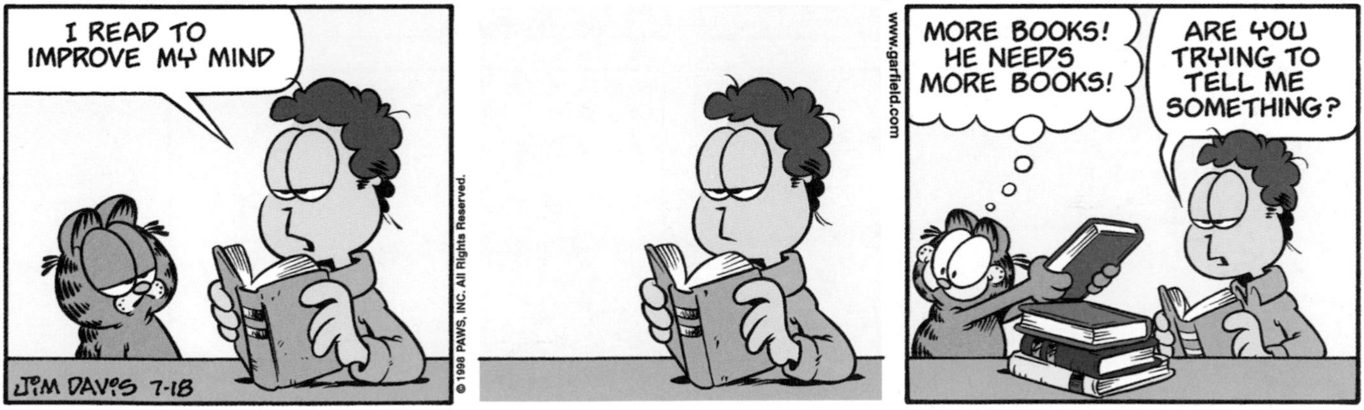
I READ TO IMPROVE MY MIND
JIM DAVIS 7-18
© 1998 PAWS, INC. All Rights Reserved.
www.garfield.com
MORE BOOKS! HE NEEDS MORE BOOKS!
ARE YOU TRYING TO TELL ME SOMETHING?

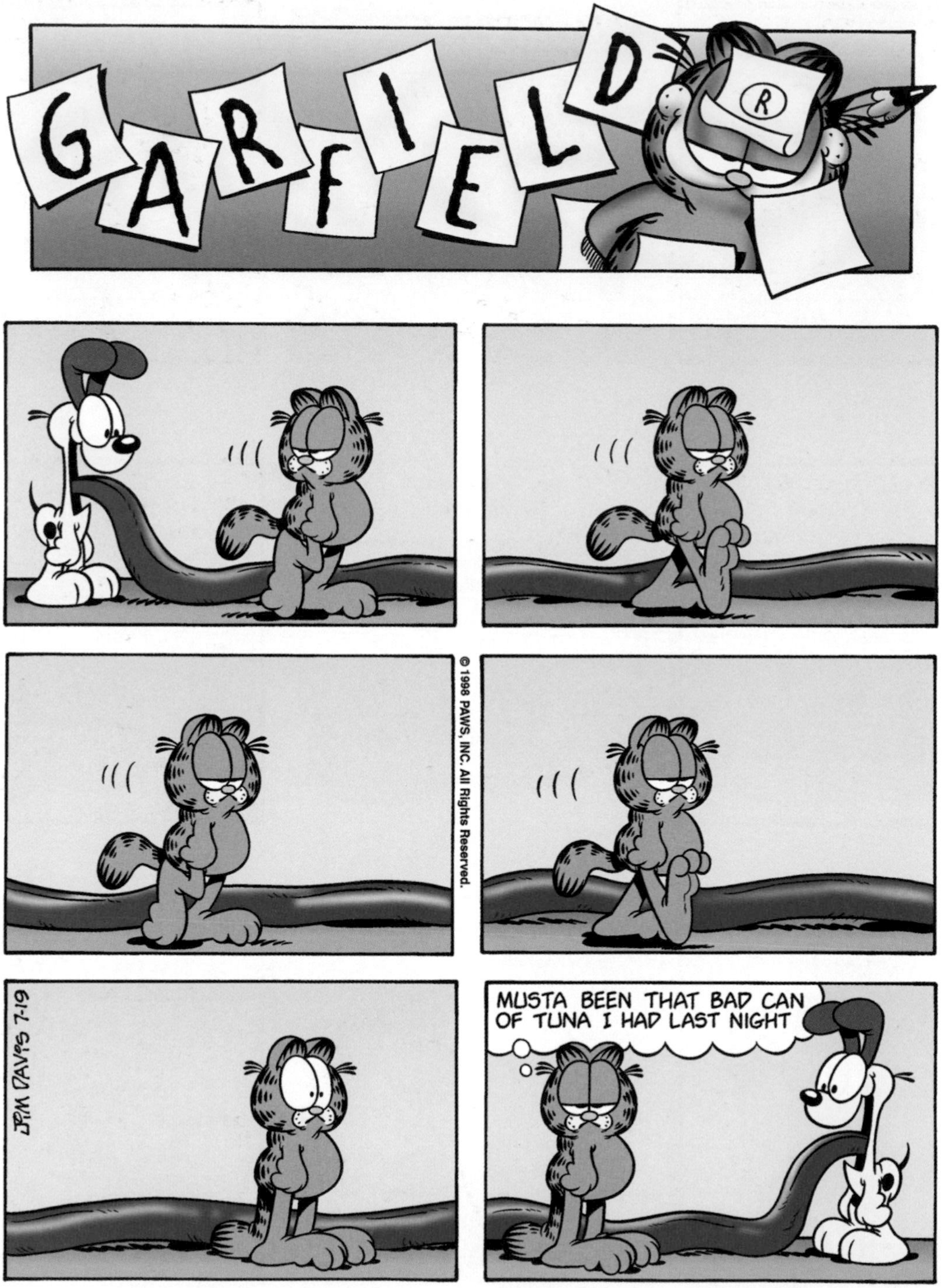
GARFIELD
JIM DAVIS 7-19
MUSTA BEEN THAT BAD CAN OF TUNA I HAD LAST NIGHT

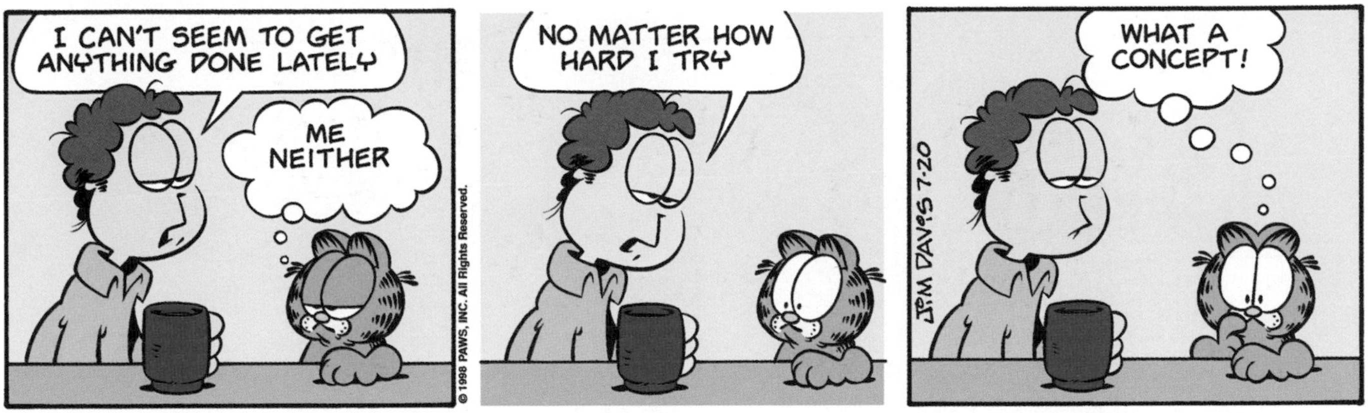
I CAN'T SEEM TO GET ANYTHING DONE LATELY
ME NEITHER
© 1998 PAWS, INC. All Rights Reserved.
NO MATTER HOW HARD I TRY
JIM DAVIS 7-20
WHAT A CONCEPT!

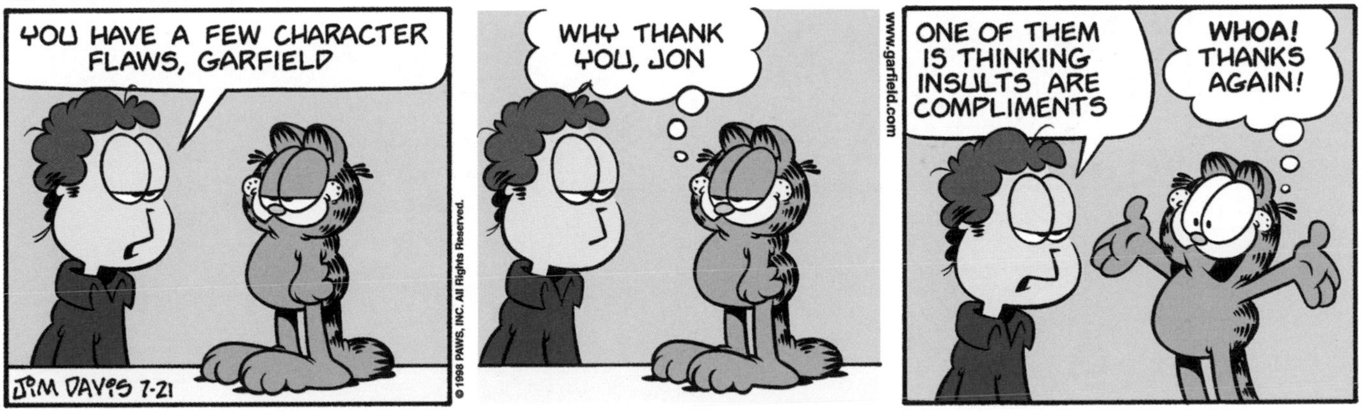
YOU HAVE A FEW CHARACTER FLAWS, GARFIELD
JIM DAVIS 7-21
© 1998 PAWS, INC. All Rights Reserved.
WHY THANK YOU, JON
www.garfield.com
ONE OF THEM IS THINKING INSULTS ARE COMPLIMENTS
WHOA! THANKS AGAIN!

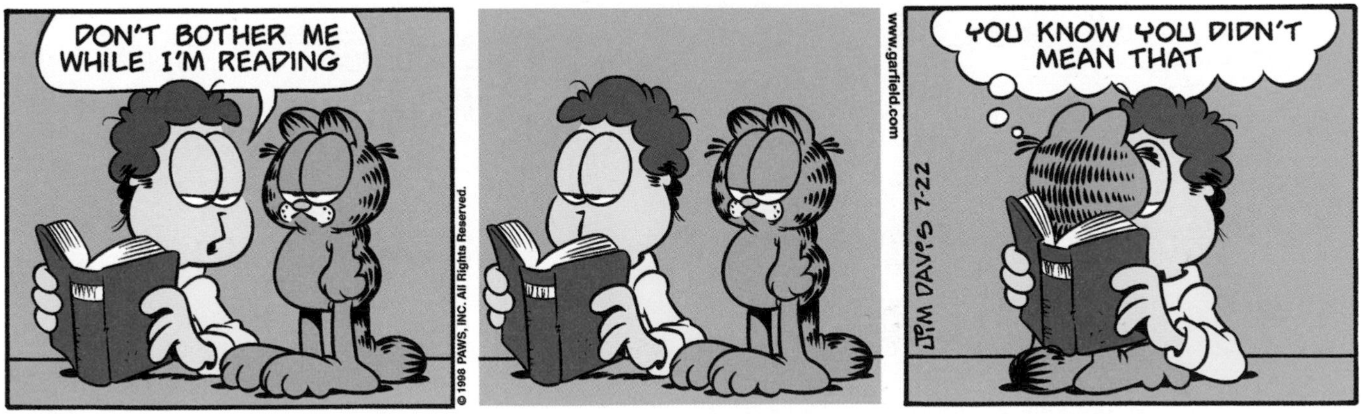
DON'T BOTHER ME WHILE I'M READING
© 1998 PAWS, INC. All Rights Reserved.
www.garfield.com
JIM DAVIS 7-22
YOU KNOW YOU DIDN'T MEAN THAT

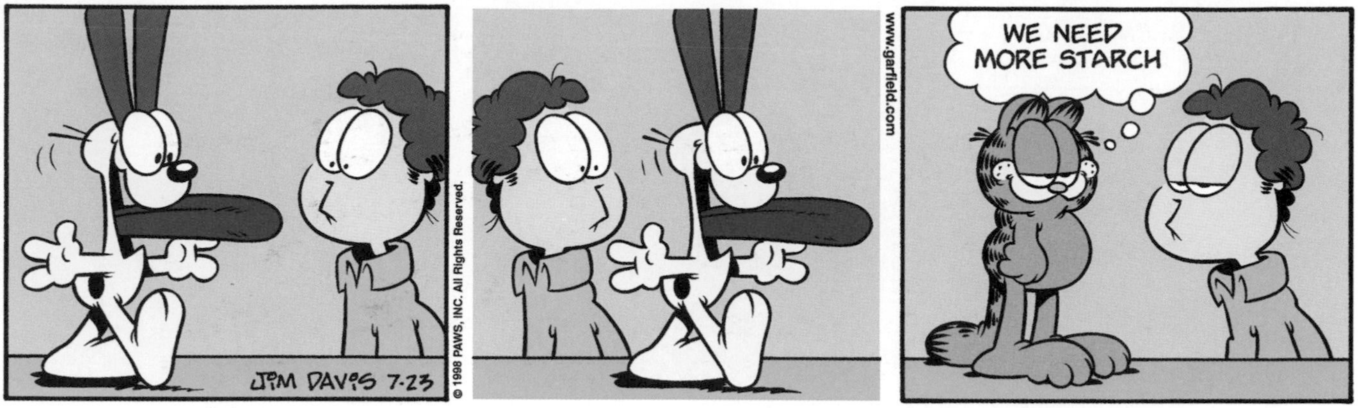
JIM DAVIS 7-23
© 1998 PAWS, INC. All Rights Reserved.
www.garfield.com
WE NEED MORE STARCH

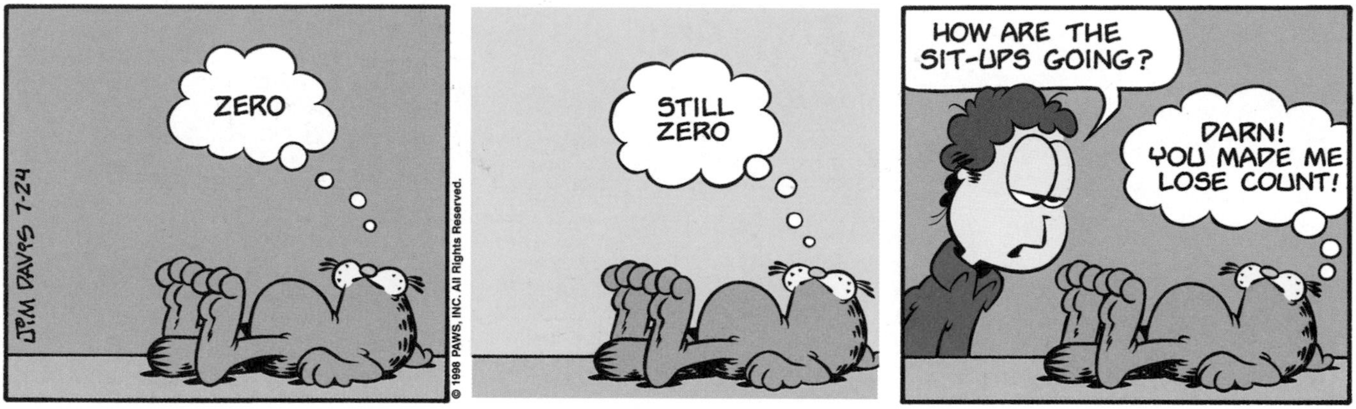
JIM DAVIS 7-24
ZERO
© 1998 PAWS, INC. All Rights Reserved.
STILL ZERO
HOW ARE THE SIT-UPS GOING?
DARN! YOU MADE ME LOSE COUNT!

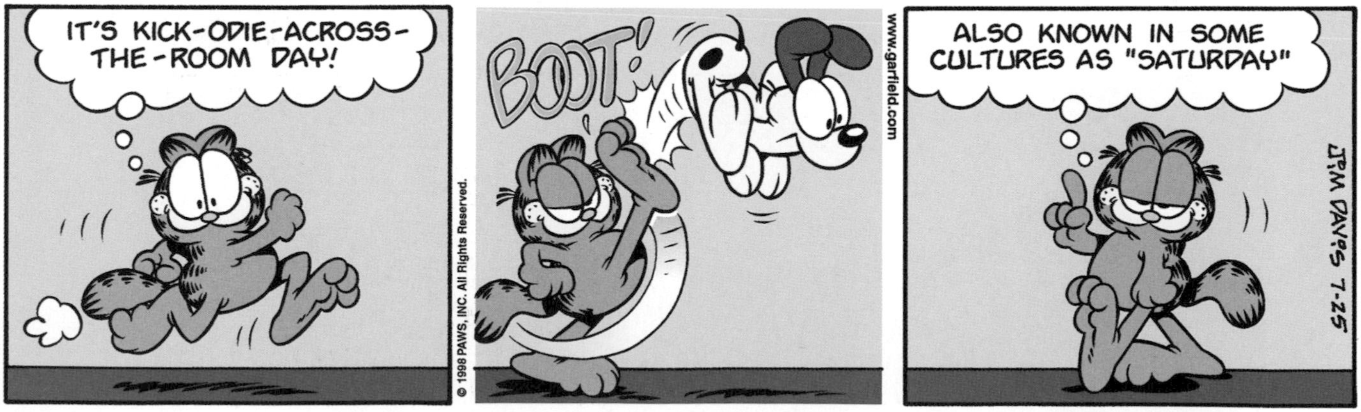
IT'S KICK-ODIE-ACROSS-THE-ROOM DAY!
© 1998 PAWS, INC. All Rights Reserved.
BOOT!
www.garfield.com
ALSO KNOWN IN SOME CULTURES AS "SATURDAY"
JIM DAVIS 7-25

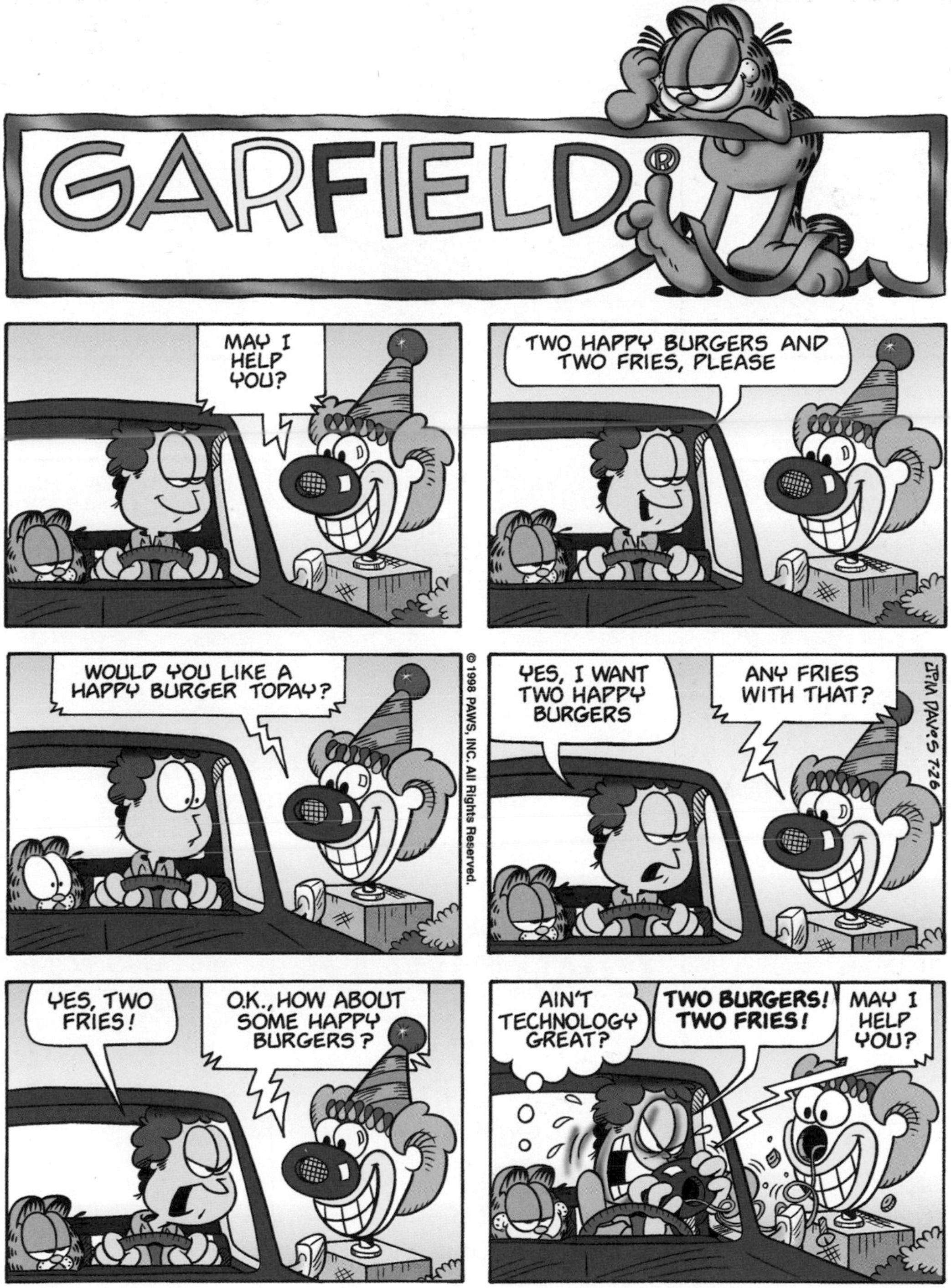
GARFIELD®
MAY I HELP YOU?
TWO HAPPY BURGERS AND TWO FRIES, PLEASE
WOULD YOU LIKE A HAPPY BURGER TODAY?
© 1998 PAWS, INC. All Rights Reserved.
YES, I WANT TWO HAPPY BURGERS
ANY FRIES WITH THAT?
JPM DAVIS 7-26
YES, TWO FRIES!
O.K., HOW ABOUT SOME HAPPY BURGERS?
AIN'T TECHNOLOGY GREAT?
TWO BURGERS! TWO FRIES!
MAY I HELP YOU?

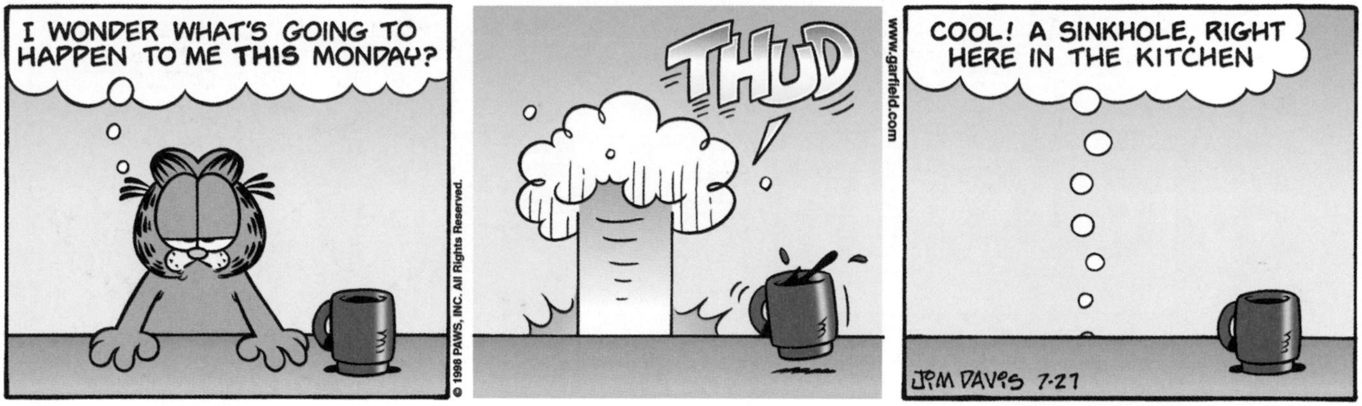
I WONDER WHAT'S GOING TO HAPPEN TO ME THIS MONDAY?
© 1998 PAWS, INC. All Rights Reserved.
THUD
www.garfield.com
COOL! A SINKHOLE, RIGHT HERE IN THE KITCHEN
JIM DAVIS 7-27

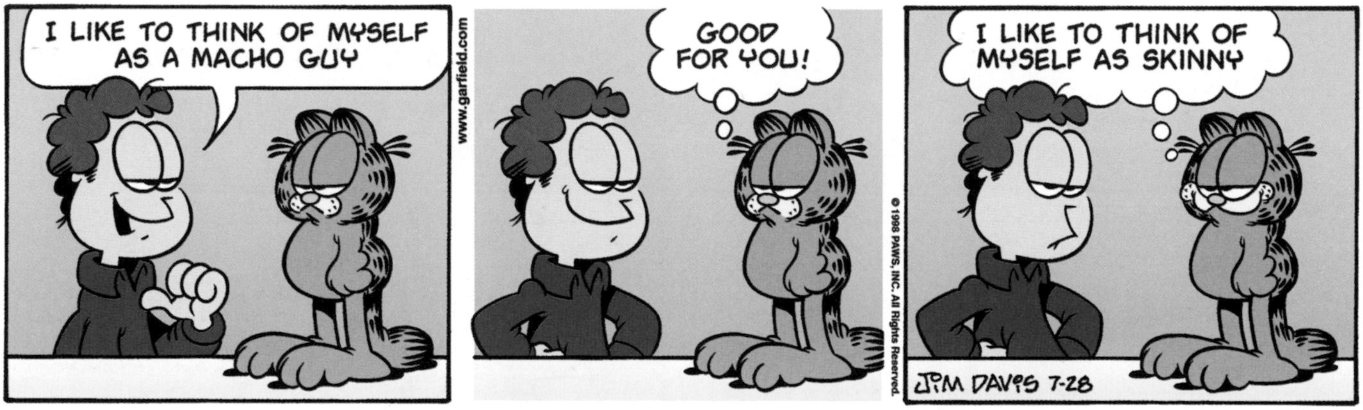
I LIKE TO THINK OF MYSELF AS A MACHO GUY
www.garfield.com
GOOD FOR YOU!
© 1998 PAWS, INC. All Rights Reserved.
I LIKE TO THINK OF MYSELF AS SKINNY
JIM DAVIS 7-28

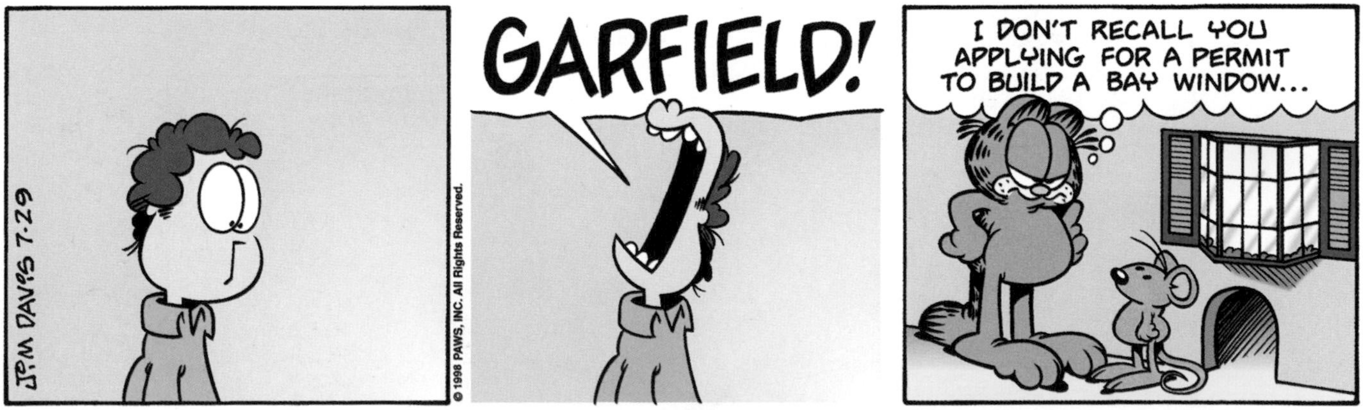
JIM DAVIS 7-29
© 1998 PAWS, INC. All Rights Reserved.
GARFIELD!
I DON'T RECALL YOU APPLYING FOR A PERMIT TO BUILD A BAY WINDOW...

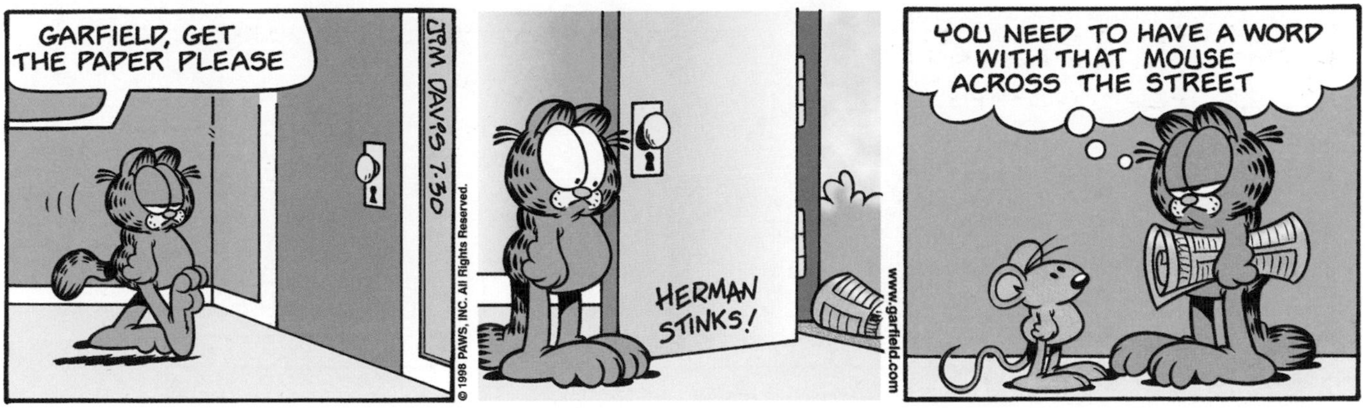
GARFIELD, GET THE PAPER PLEASE
JIM DAVIS 7-30
© 1998 PAWS, INC. All Rights Reserved.
HERMAN STINKS!
www.garfield.com
YOU NEED TO HAVE A WORD WITH THAT MOUSE ACROSS THE STREET

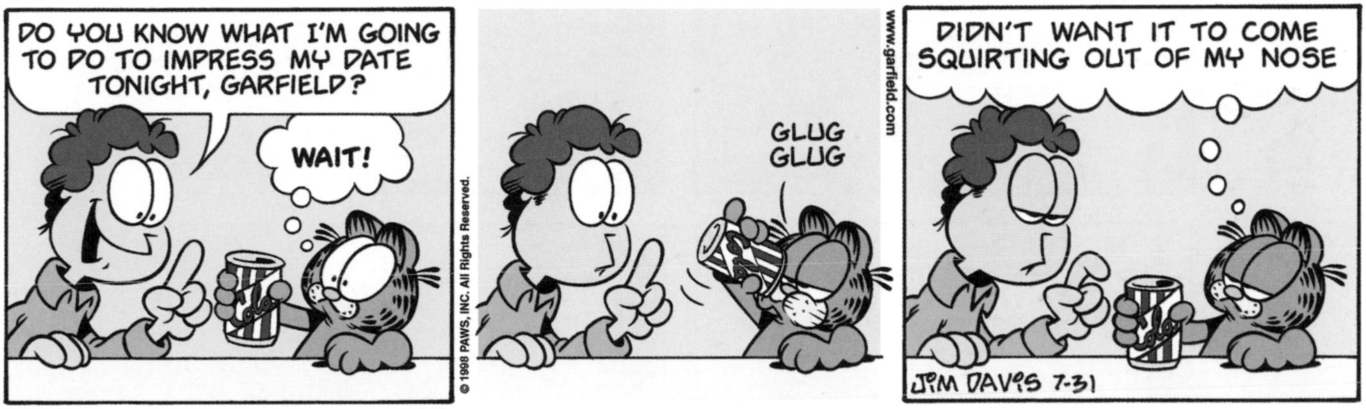
DO YOU KNOW WHAT I'M GOING TO DO TO IMPRESS MY DATE TONIGHT, GARFIELD?
WAIT!
© 1998 PAWS, INC. All Rights Reserved.
GLUG GLUG
www.garfield.com
DIDN'T WANT IT TO COME SQUIRTING OUT OF MY NOSE
JIM DAVIS 7-31

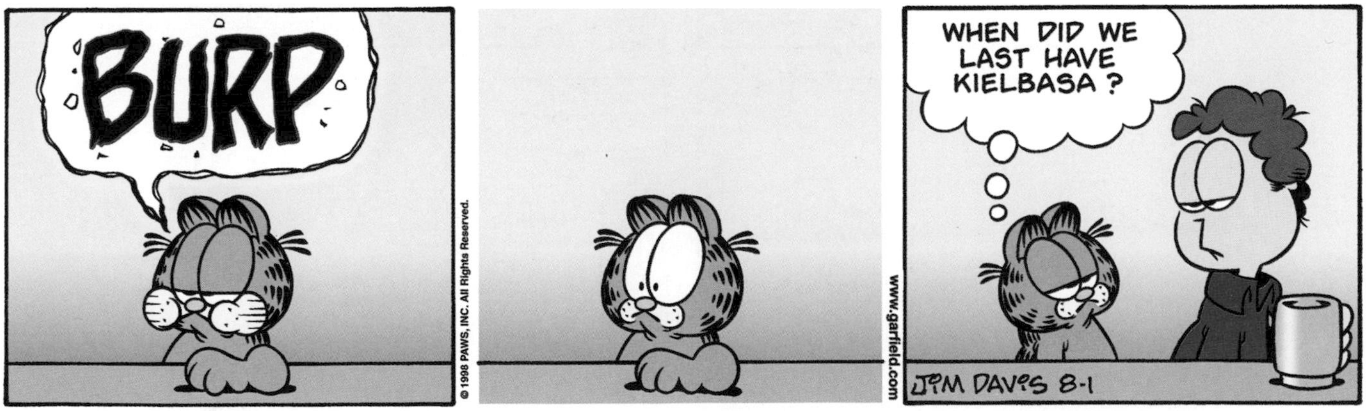
BURP
© 1998 PAWS, INC. All Rights Reserved.
www.garfield.com
WHEN DID WE LAST HAVE KIELBASA?
JIM DAVIS 8-1

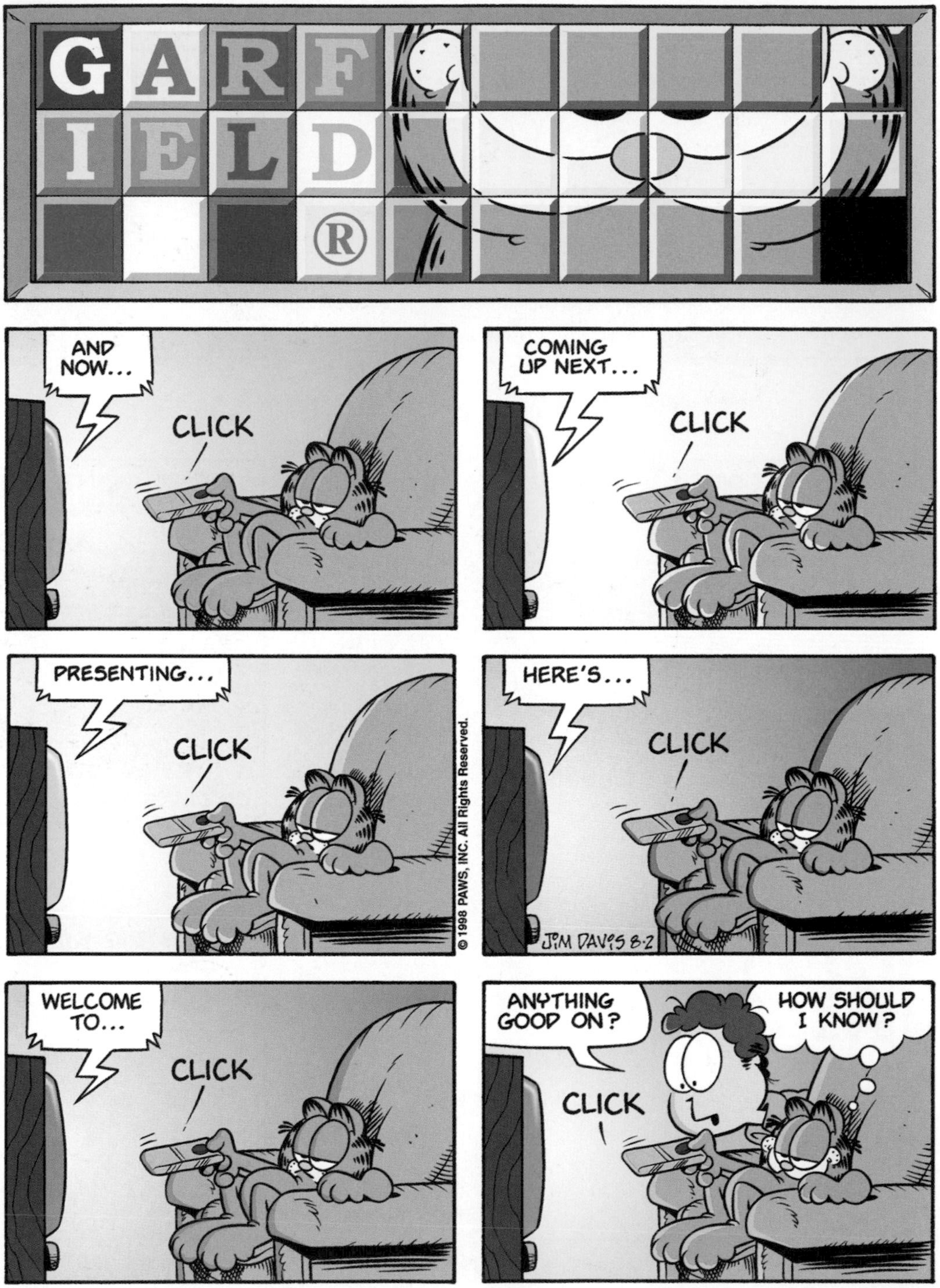
GARFIELD®
AND NOW...
CLICK
COMING UP NEXT...
CLICK
PRESENTING...
CLICK
HERE'S...
CLICK
JIM DAVIS 8-2
WELCOME TO...
CLICK
ANYTHING GOOD ON?
CLICK
HOW SHOULD I KNOW?

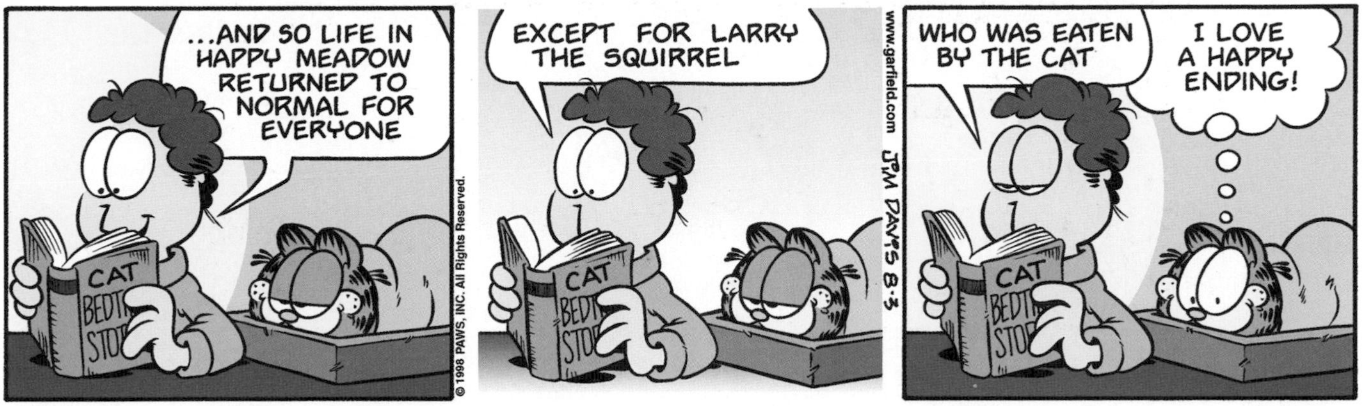
...AND SO LIFE IN HAPPY MEADOW RETURNED TO NORMAL FOR EVERYONE
CAT BEDTI STO
© 1998 PAWS, INC. All Rights Reserved.
EXCEPT FOR LARRY THE SQUIRREL
www.garfield.com
JIM DAVIS 8-3
WHO WAS EATEN BY THE CAT
I LOVE A HAPPY ENDING!

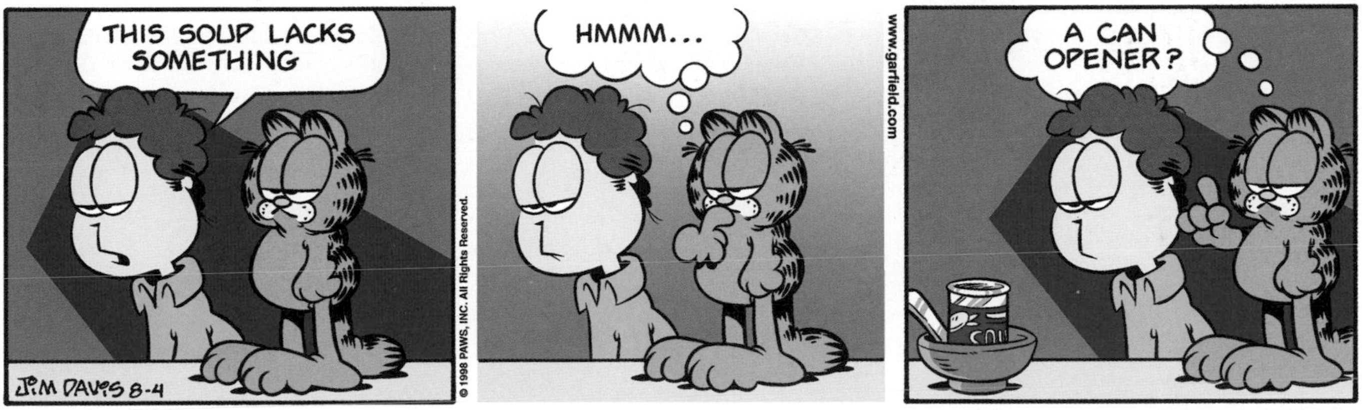
THIS SOUP LACKS SOMETHING
JIM DAVIS 8-4
© 1998 PAWS, INC. All Rights Reserved.
HMMM...
www.garfield.com
A CAN OPENER?

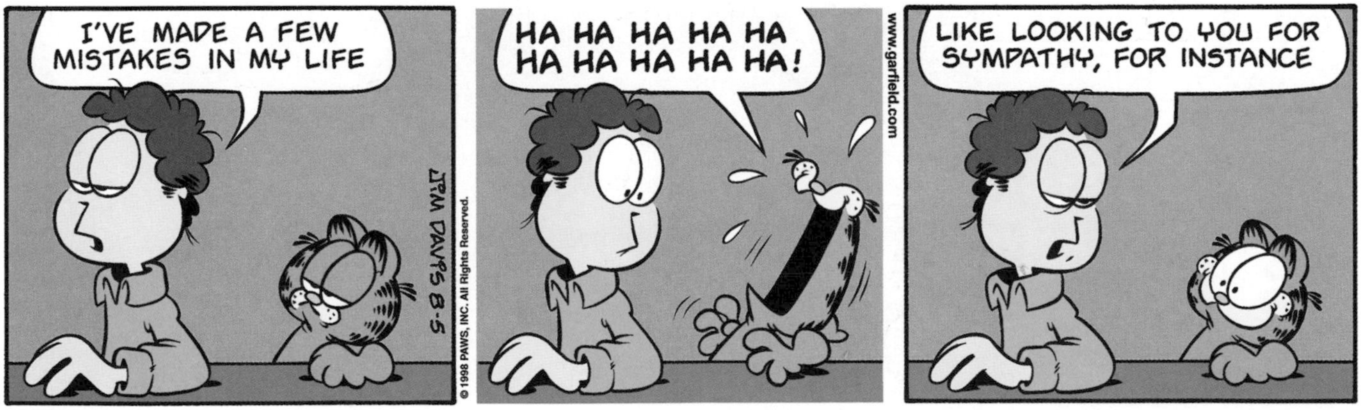
I'VE MADE A FEW MISTAKES IN MY LIFE
JIM DAVIS 8-5
© 1998 PAWS, INC. All Rights Reserved.
HA HA HA HA HA HA HA HA HA HA!
www.garfield.com
LIKE LOOKING TO YOU FOR SYMPATHY, FOR INSTANCE

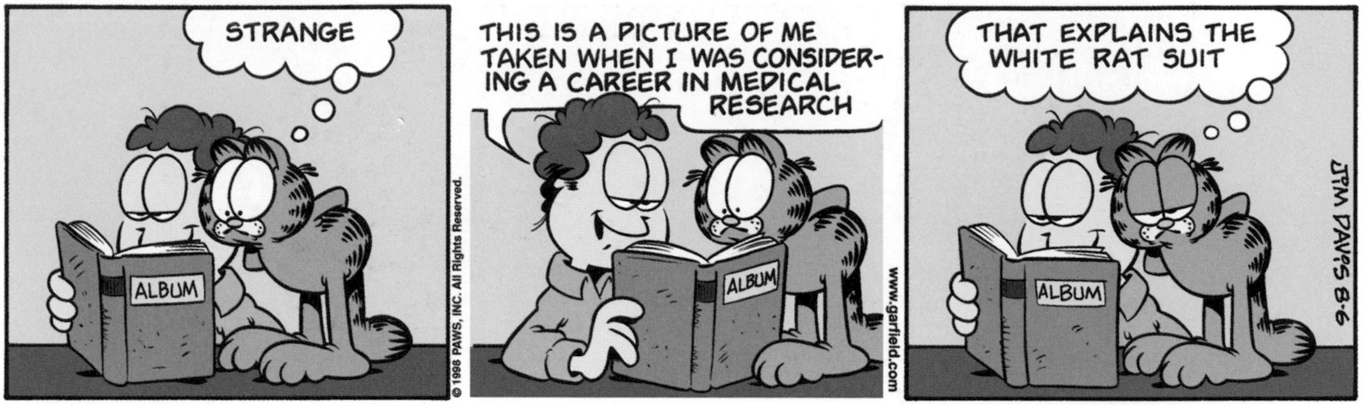
STRANGE
THIS IS A PICTURE OF ME TAKEN WHEN I WAS CONSIDERING A CAREER IN MEDICAL RESEARCH
THAT EXPLAINS THE WHITE RAT SUIT
ALBUM
© 1998 PAWS, INC. All Rights Reserved.
www.garfield.com
JIM DAVIS 8-6

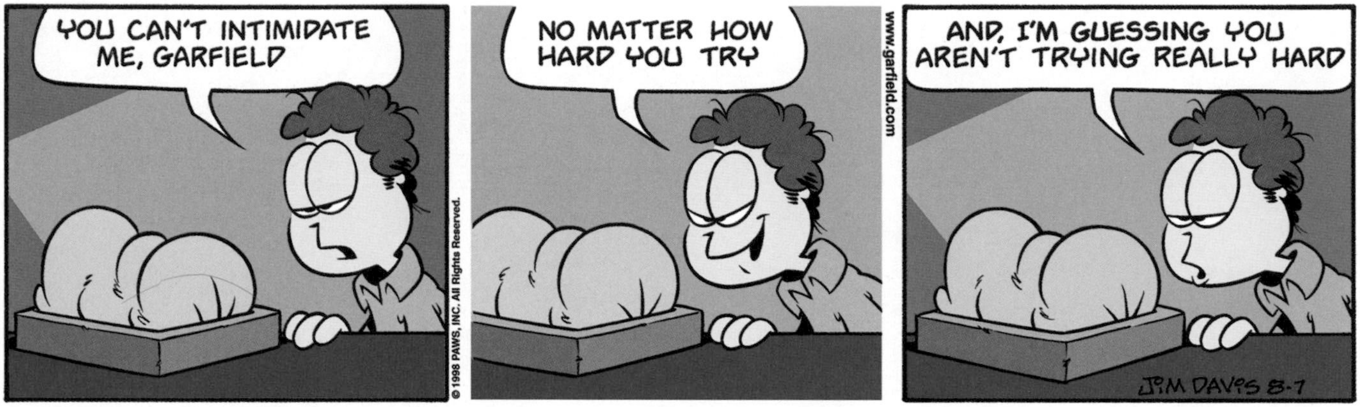
YOU CAN'T INTIMIDATE ME, GARFIELD
NO MATTER HOW HARD YOU TRY
AND, I'M GUESSING YOU AREN'T TRYING REALLY HARD
© 1998 PAWS, INC. All Rights Reserved.
www.garfield.com
JIM DAVIS 8-7

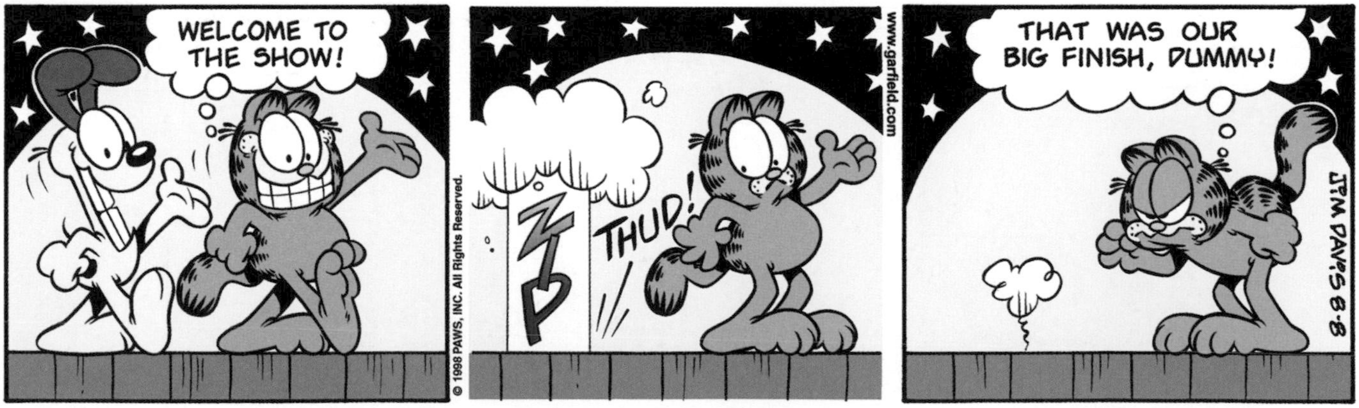
WELCOME TO THE SHOW!
ZIP
THUD!
THAT WAS OUR BIG FINISH, DUMMY!
© 1998 PAWS, INC. All Rights Reserved.
www.garfield.com
JIM DAVIS 8-8

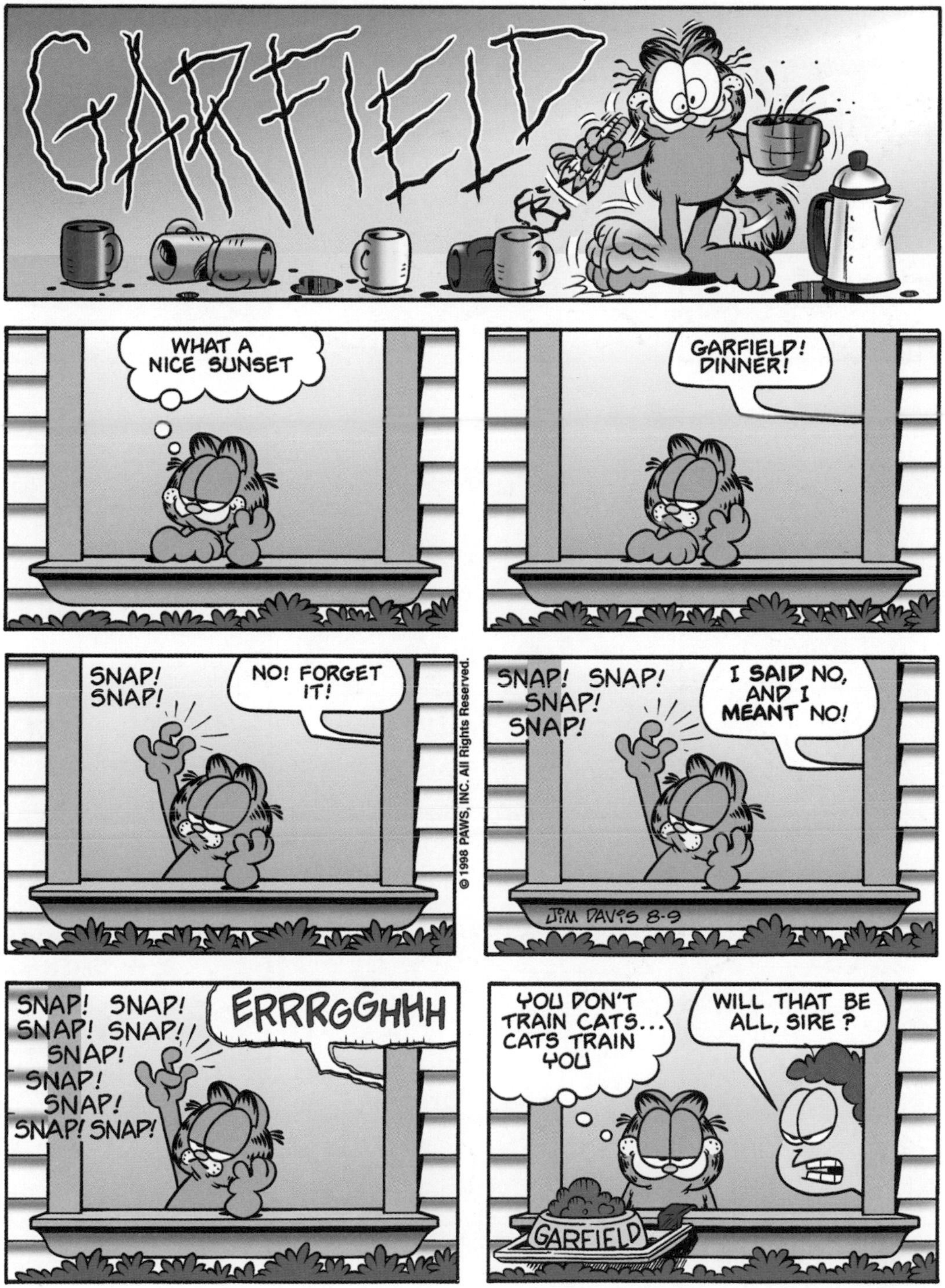
GARFIELD
WHAT A NICE SUNSET
GARFIELD! DINNER!
SNAP! SNAP!
NO! FORGET IT!
© 1998 PAWS, INC. All Rights Reserved.
SNAP! SNAP! SNAP! SNAP!
I SAID NO, AND I MEANT NO!
JIM DAVIS 8-9
SNAP! SNAP! SNAP! SNAP! SNAP! SNAP! SNAP! SNAP! SNAP!
ERRRGGHHH
YOU DON'T TRAIN CATS... CATS TRAIN YOU
WILL THAT BE ALL, SIRE ?
GARFIELD

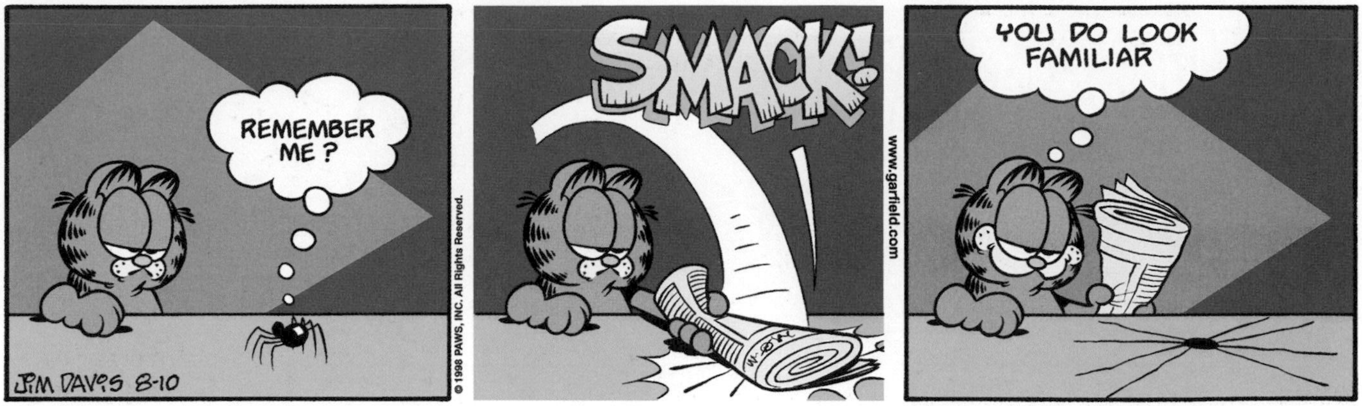
REMEMBER ME?
JIM DAVIS 8-10
© 1998 PAWS, INC. All Rights Reserved.
SMACK!
www.garfield.com
YOU DO LOOK FAMILIAR

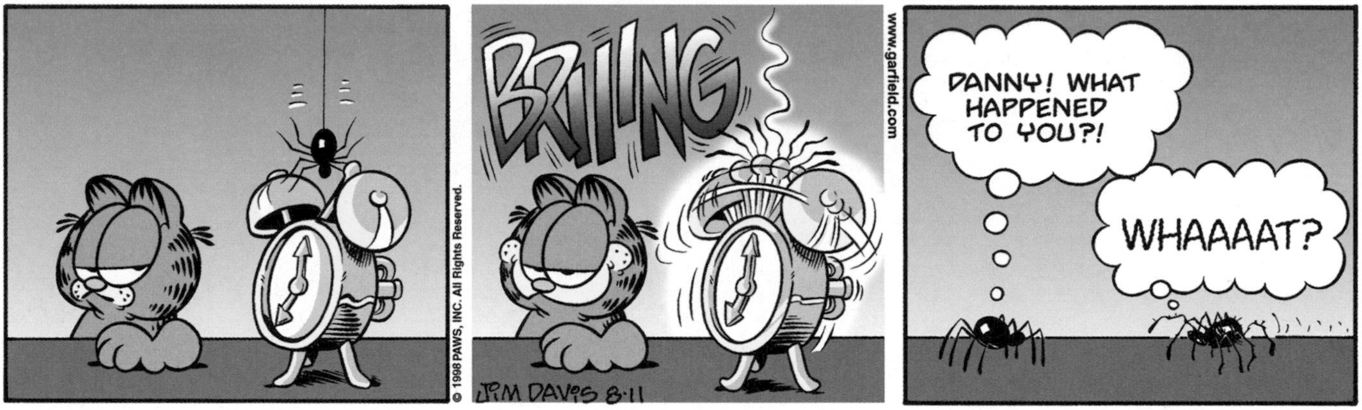
© 1998 PAWS, INC. All Rights Reserved.
BRIIING
JIM DAVIS 8-11
www.garfield.com
DANNY! WHAT HAPPENED TO YOU?!
WHAAAAT?

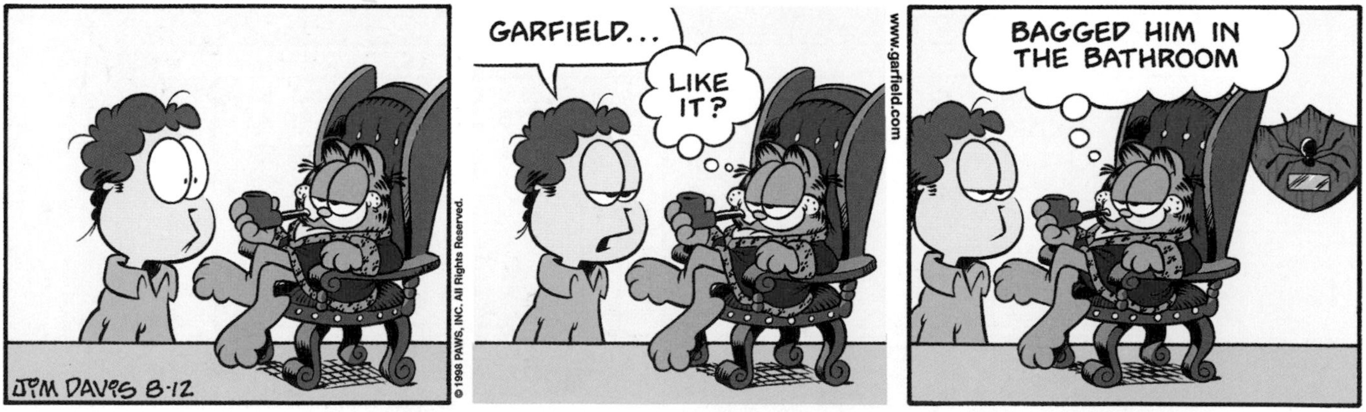
JIM DAVIS 8-12
© 1998 PAWS, INC. All Rights Reserved.
GARFIELD...
LIKE IT?
www.garfield.com
BAGGED HIM IN THE BATHROOM

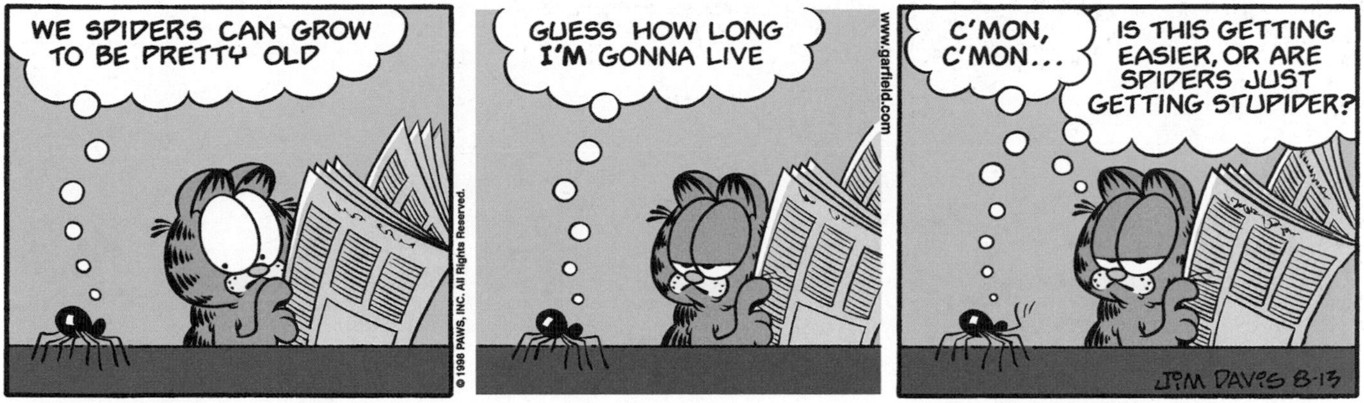
WE SPIDERS CAN GROW TO BE PRETTY OLD
GUESS HOW LONG I'M GONNA LIVE
C'MON, C'MON...
IS THIS GETTING EASIER, OR ARE SPIDERS JUST GETTING STUPIDER?
© 1998 PAWS, INC. All Rights Reserved.
www.garfield.com
JIM DAVIS 8-13

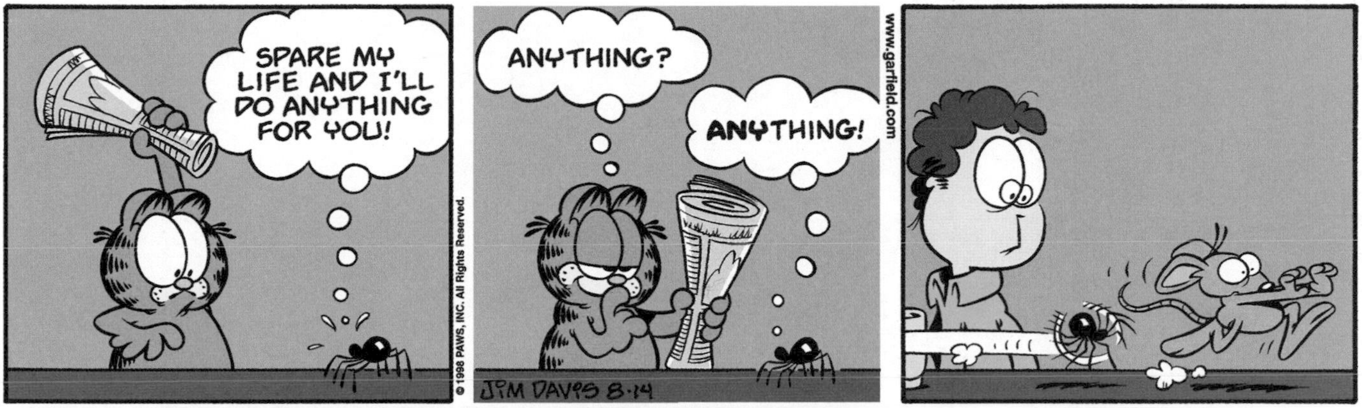
SPARE MY LIFE AND I'LL DO ANYTHING FOR YOU!
ANYTHING?
ANYTHING!
© 1998 PAWS, INC. All Rights Reserved.
www.garfield.com
JIM DAVIS 8-14

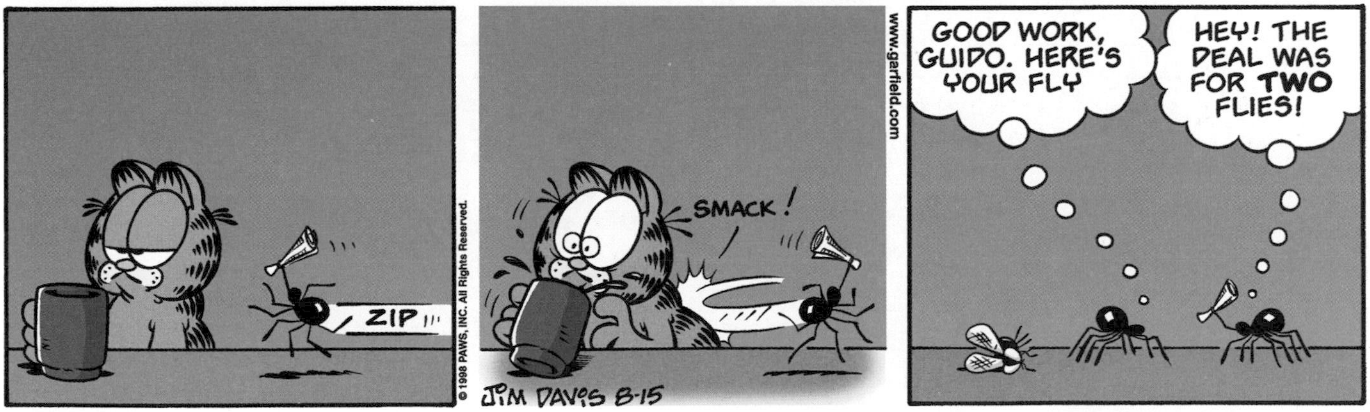
ZIP
SMACK!
GOOD WORK, GUIDO. HERE'S YOUR FLY
HEY! THE DEAL WAS FOR TWO FLIES!
© 1998 PAWS, INC. All Rights Reserved.
www.garfield.com
JIM DAVIS 8-15

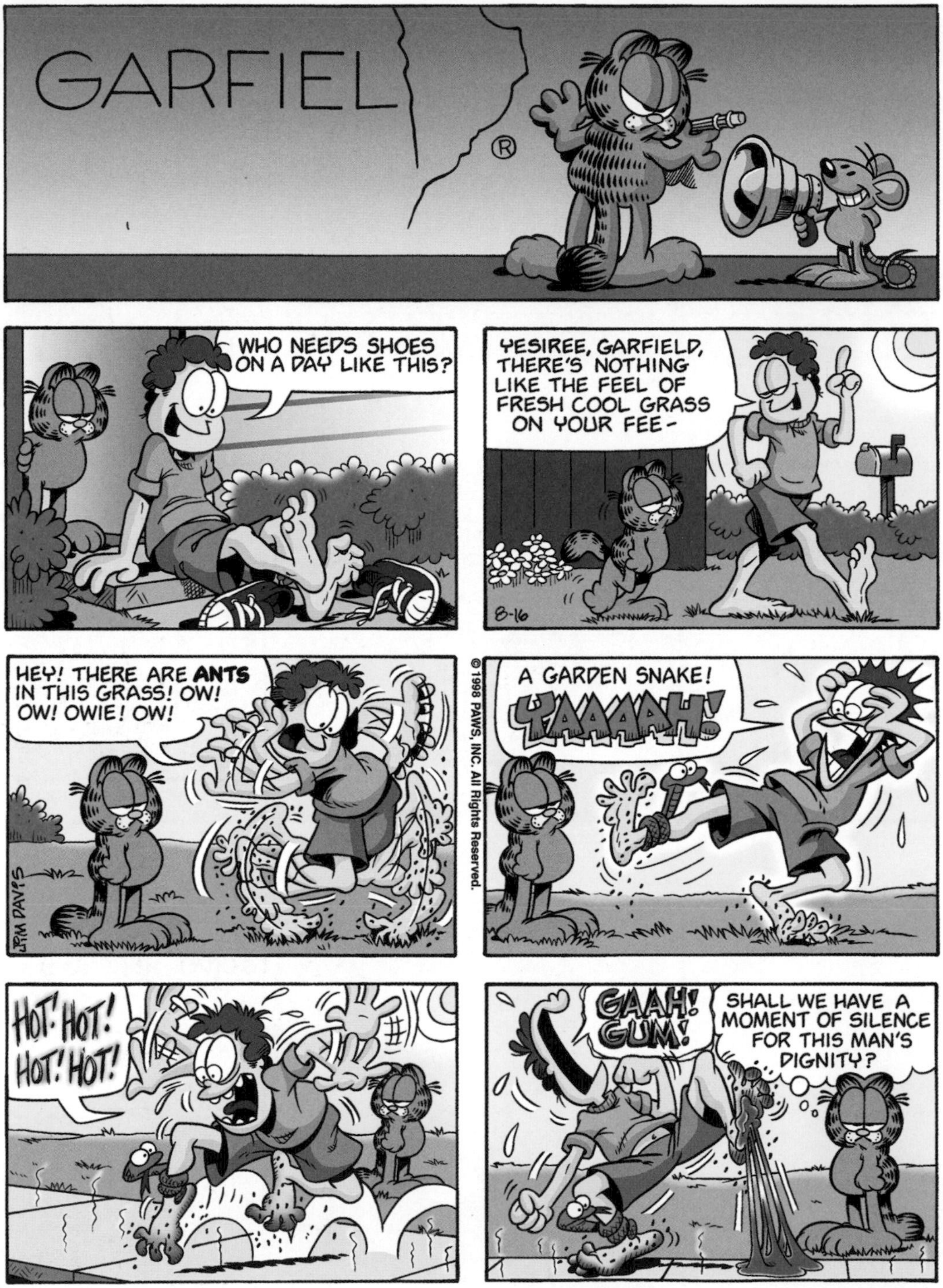
GARFIEL
WHO NEEDS SHOES ON A DAY LIKE THIS?
YESIREE, GARFIELD, THERE'S NOTHING LIKE THE FEEL OF FRESH COOL GRASS ON YOUR FEE-
8-16
© 1998 PAWS, INC. All Rights Reserved.
HEY! THERE ARE ANTS IN THIS GRASS! OW! OW! OWIE! OW!
JPM DAVIS
A GARDEN SNAKE! YAAAAH!
HOT! HOT! HOT! HOT!
GAAH! GUM!
SHALL WE HAVE A MOMENT OF SILENCE FOR THIS MAN'S DIGNITY?

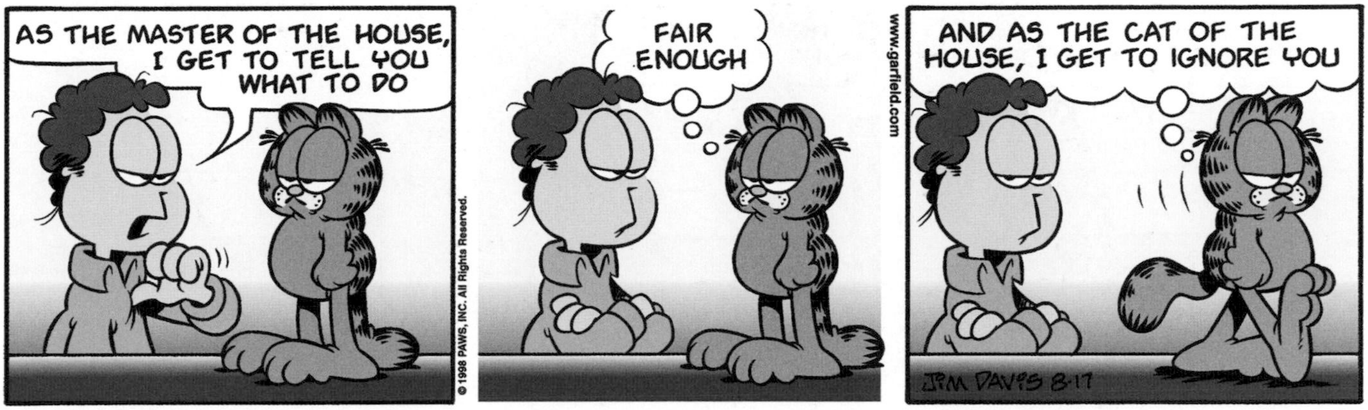
AS THE MASTER OF THE HOUSE, I GET TO TELL YOU WHAT TO DO
© 1998 PAWS, INC. All Rights Reserved.
FAIR ENOUGH
www.garfield.com
AND AS THE CAT OF THE HOUSE, I GET TO IGNORE YOU
JIM DAVIS 8-17

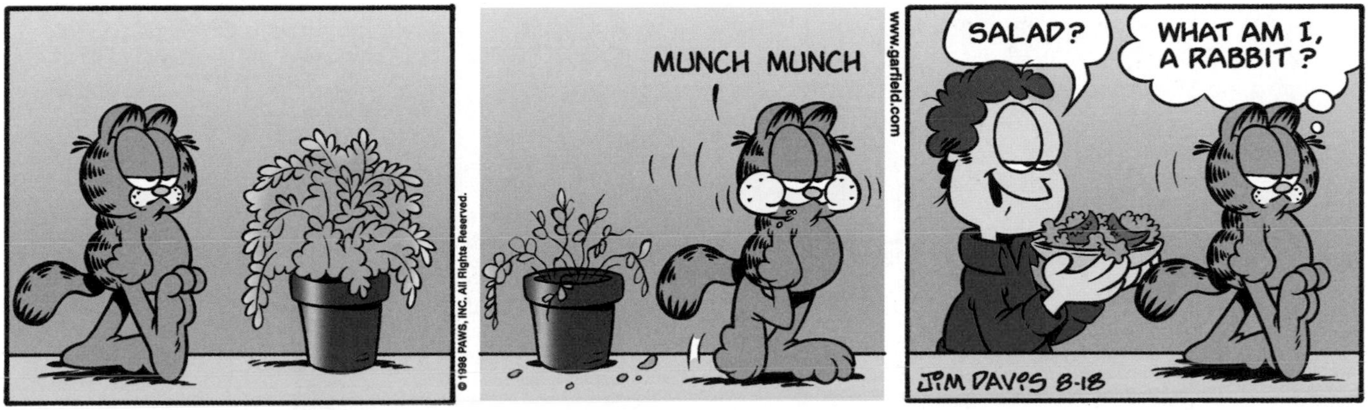
© 1998 PAWS, INC. All Rights Reserved.
MUNCH MUNCH
www.garfield.com
SALAD?
WHAT AM I, A RABBIT?
JIM DAVIS 8-18

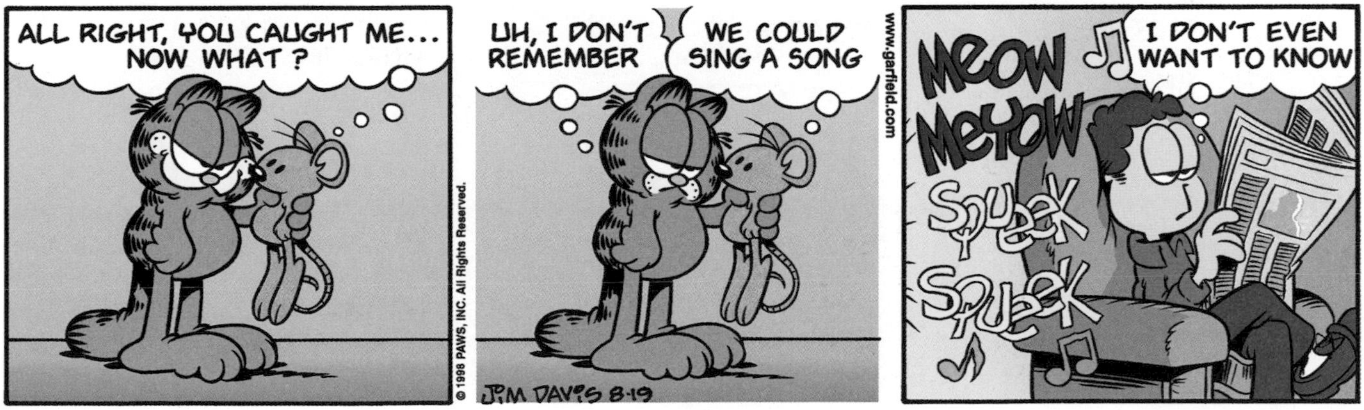
ALL RIGHT, YOU CAUGHT ME... NOW WHAT?
© 1998 PAWS, INC. All Rights Reserved.
UH, I DON'T REMEMBER
WE COULD SING A SONG
JIM DAVIS 8-19
www.garfield.com
MEOW
MEYOW
SQUEEK
SQUEEK
I DON'T EVEN WANT TO KNOW

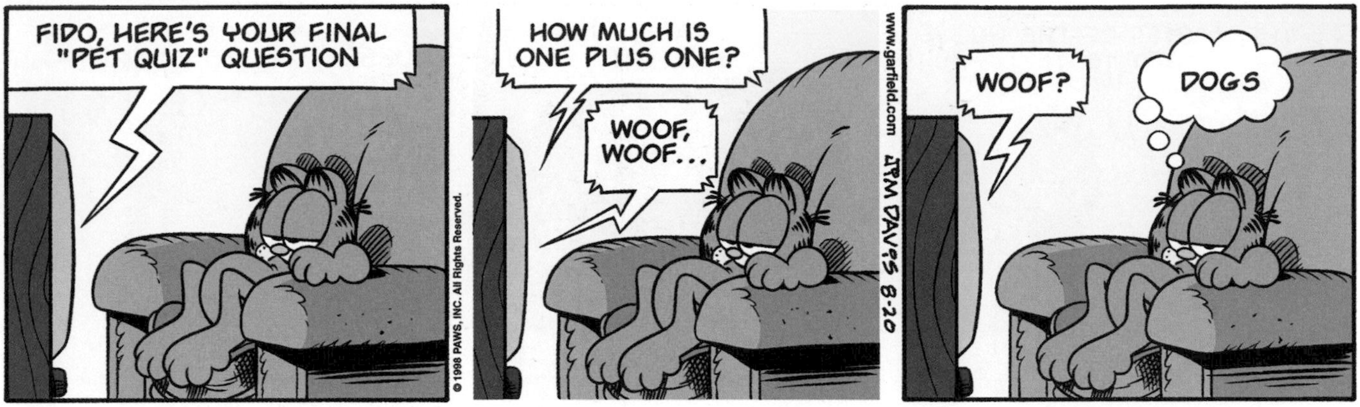
FIDO, HERE'S YOUR FINAL "PET QUIZ" QUESTION
© 1998 PAWS, INC. All Rights Reserved.
HOW MUCH IS ONE PLUS ONE?
WOOF, WOOF...
www.garfield.com
JIM DAVIS 8-20
WOOF?
DOGS

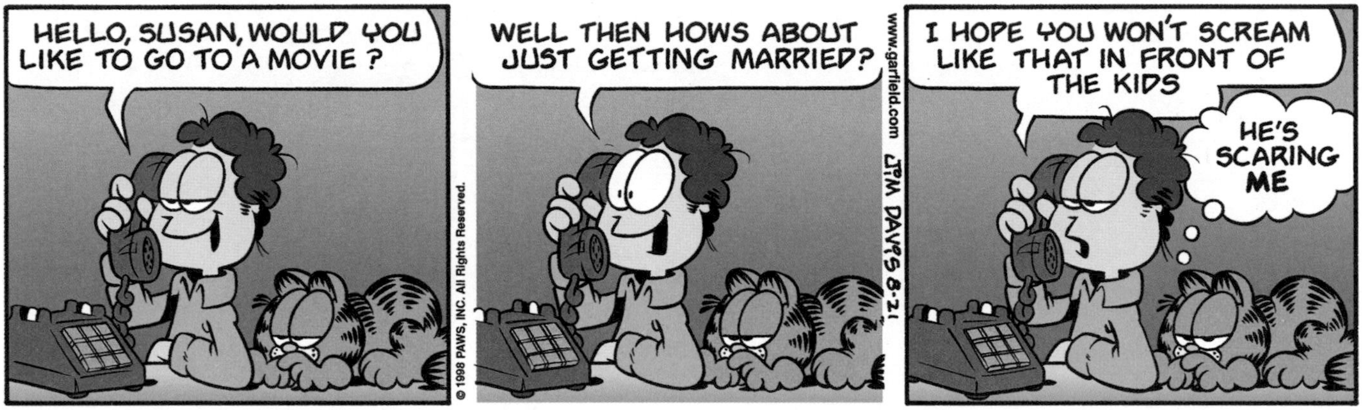
HELLO, SUSAN, WOULD YOU LIKE TO GO TO A MOVIE ?
© 1998 PAWS, INC. All Rights Reserved.
WELL THEN HOWS ABOUT JUST GETTING MARRIED?
www.garfield.com
JIM DAVIS 8-21
I HOPE YOU WON'T SCREAM LIKE THAT IN FRONT OF THE KIDS
HE'S SCARING ME

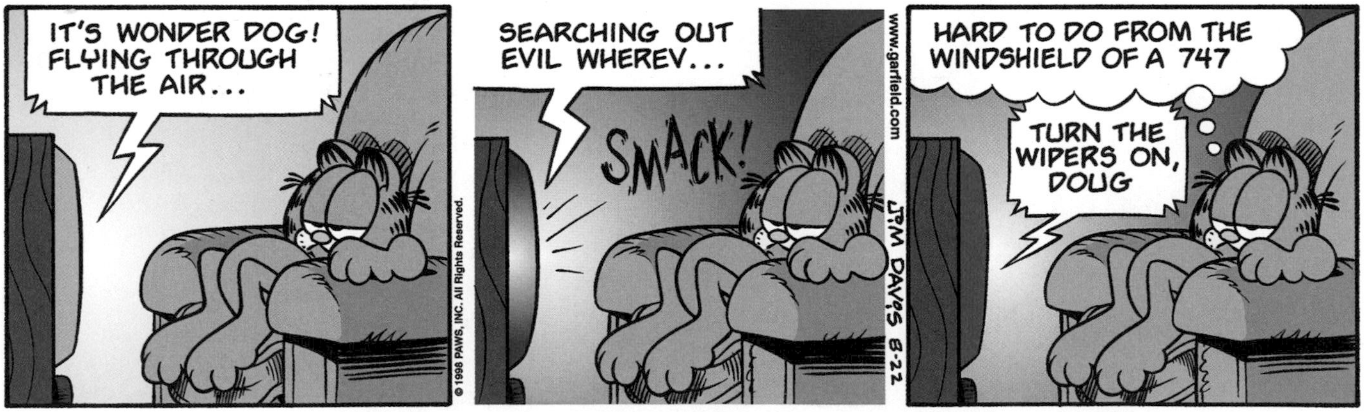
IT'S WONDER DOG! FLYING THROUGH THE AIR...
© 1998 PAWS, INC. All Rights Reserved.
SEARCHING OUT EVIL WHEREV...
SMACK!
www.garfield.com
JIM DAVIS 8-22
HARD TO DO FROM THE WINDSHIELD OF A 747
TURN THE WIPERS ON, DOUG

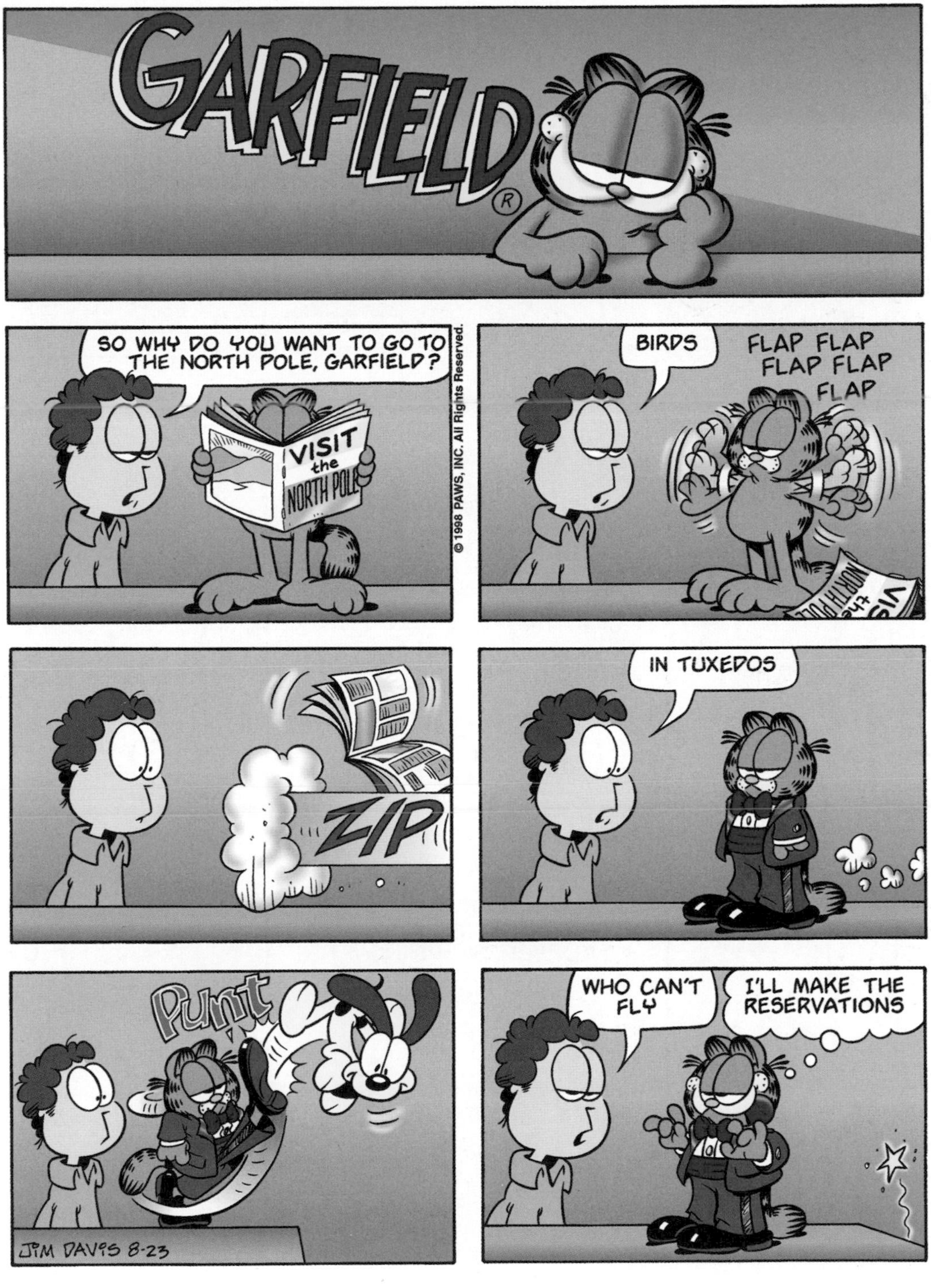
GARFIELD
SO WHY DO YOU WANT TO GO TO THE NORTH POLE, GARFIELD?
VISIT the NORTH POLE
© 1998 PAWS, INC. All Rights Reserved.
BIRDS
FLAP FLAP FLAP FLAP FLAP
ZIP
IN TUXEDOS
PUNT
JIM DAVIS 8-23
WHO CAN'T FLY
I'LL MAKE THE RESERVATIONS

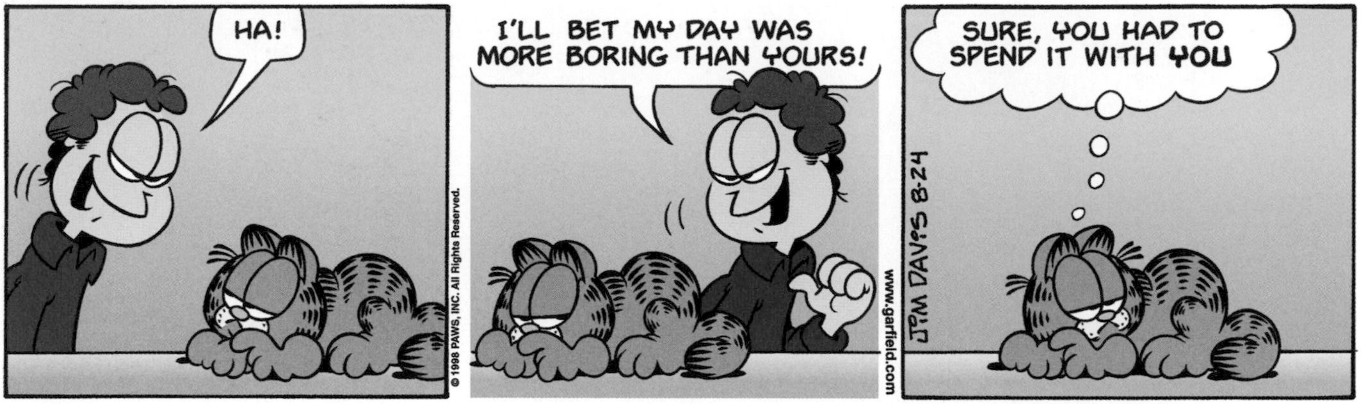
HA!
I'LL BET MY DAY WAS MORE BORING THAN YOURS!
SURE, YOU HAD TO SPEND IT WITH YOU
© 1998 PAWS, INC. All Rights Reserved.
www.garfield.com
JIM DAVIS 8-24

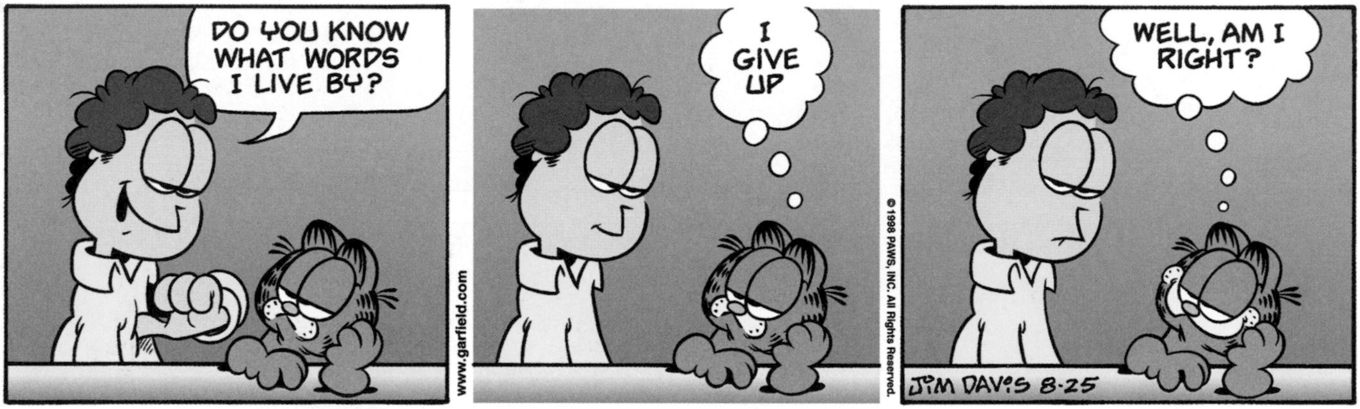
DO YOU KNOW WHAT WORDS I LIVE BY?
I GIVE UP
WELL, AM I RIGHT?
www.garfield.com
© 1998 PAWS, INC. All Rights Reserved.
JIM DAVIS 8-25

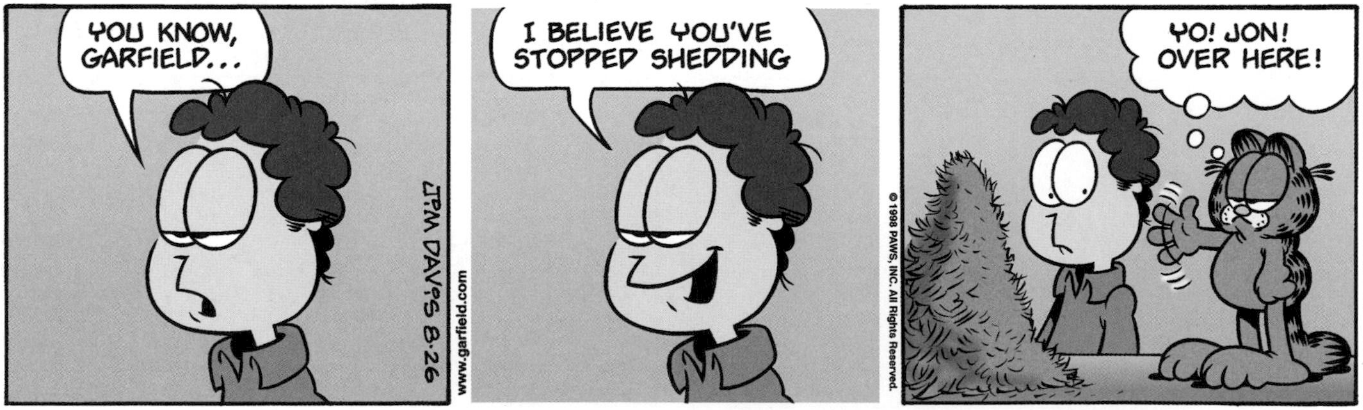
YOU KNOW, GARFIELD...
I BELIEVE YOU'VE STOPPED SHEDDING
YO! JON! OVER HERE!
JIM DAVIS 8-26
www.garfield.com
© 1998 PAWS, INC. All Rights Reserved.

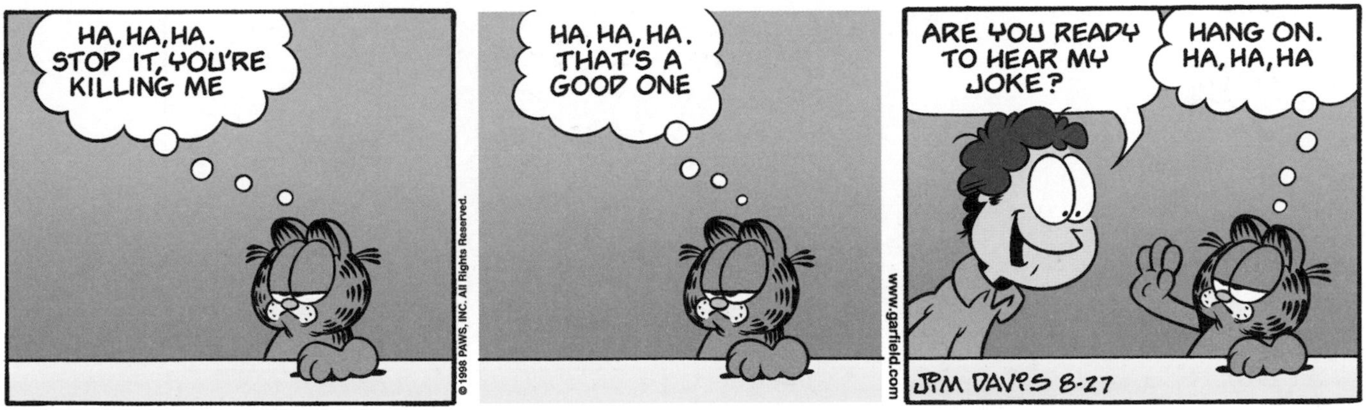
HA, HA, HA. STOP IT, YOU'RE KILLING ME
HA, HA, HA. THAT'S A GOOD ONE
© 1998 PAWS, INC. All Rights Reserved.
ARE YOU READY TO HEAR MY JOKE?
HANG ON. HA, HA, HA
www.garfield.com
JIM DAVIS 8-27

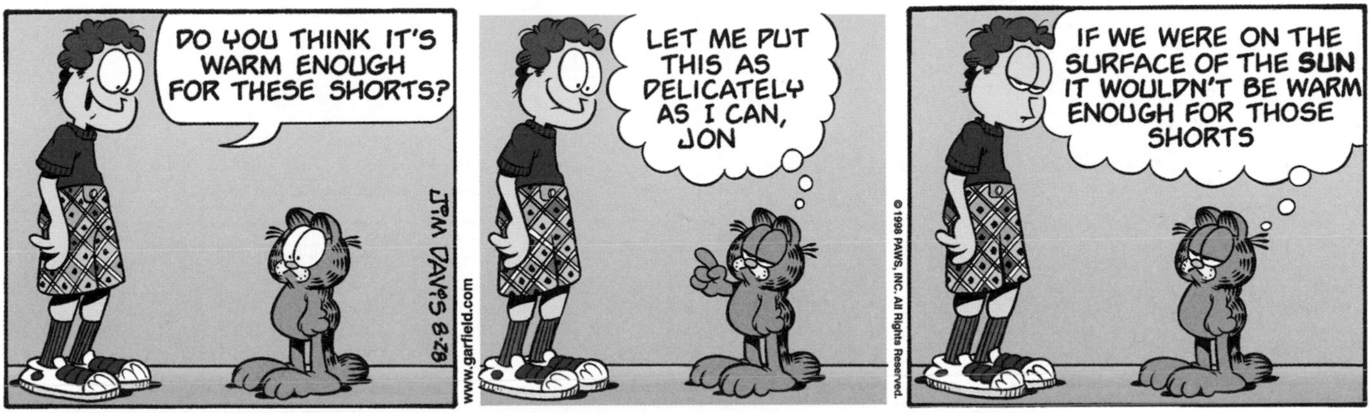
DO YOU THINK IT'S WARM ENOUGH FOR THESE SHORTS?
JIM DAVIS 8-28
www.garfield.com
LET ME PUT THIS AS DELICATELY AS I CAN, JON
© 1998 PAWS, INC. All Rights Reserved.
IF WE WERE ON THE SURFACE OF THE **SUN** IT WOULDN'T BE WARM ENOUGH FOR THOSE SHORTS

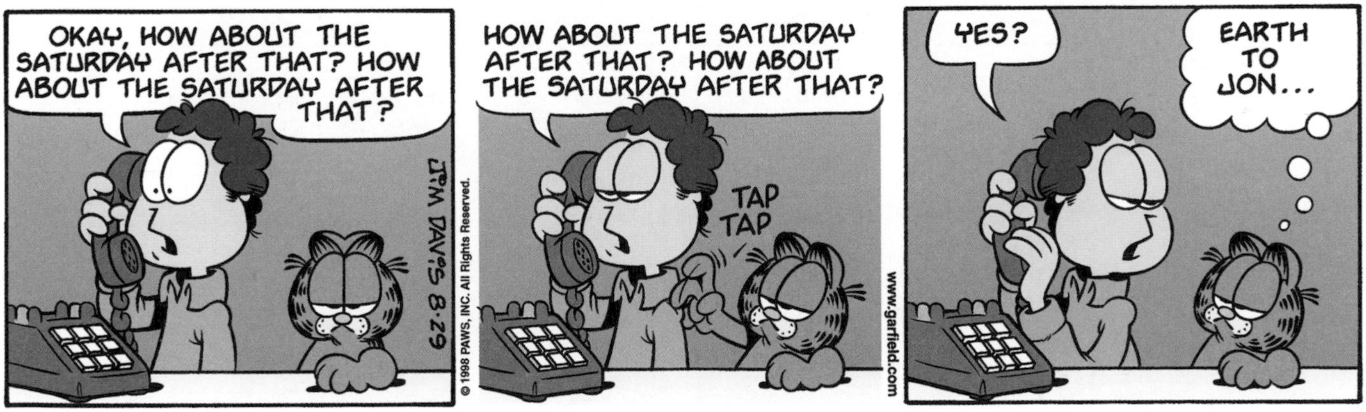
OKAY, HOW ABOUT THE SATURDAY AFTER THAT? HOW ABOUT THE SATURDAY AFTER THAT?
JIM DAVIS 8-29
© 1998 PAWS, INC. All Rights Reserved.
HOW ABOUT THE SATURDAY AFTER THAT? HOW ABOUT THE SATURDAY AFTER THAT?
TAP TAP
www.garfield.com
YES?
EARTH TO JON...

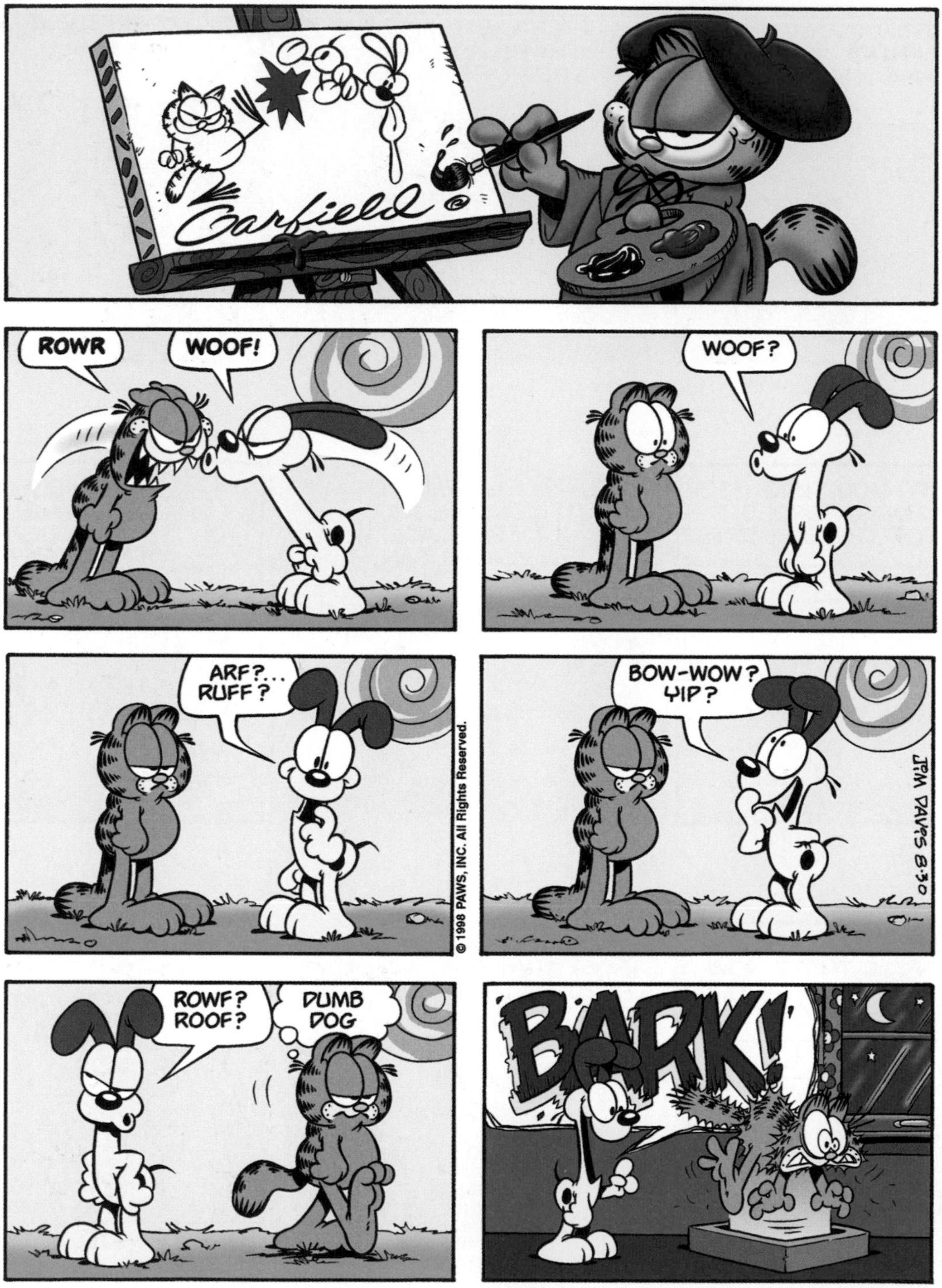
Garfield
ROWR
WOOF!
WOOF?
ARF?...
RUFF?
BOW-WOW?
YIP?
JPM DAVPS 8-30
ROWF?
ROOF?
DUMB
DOG
BARK!

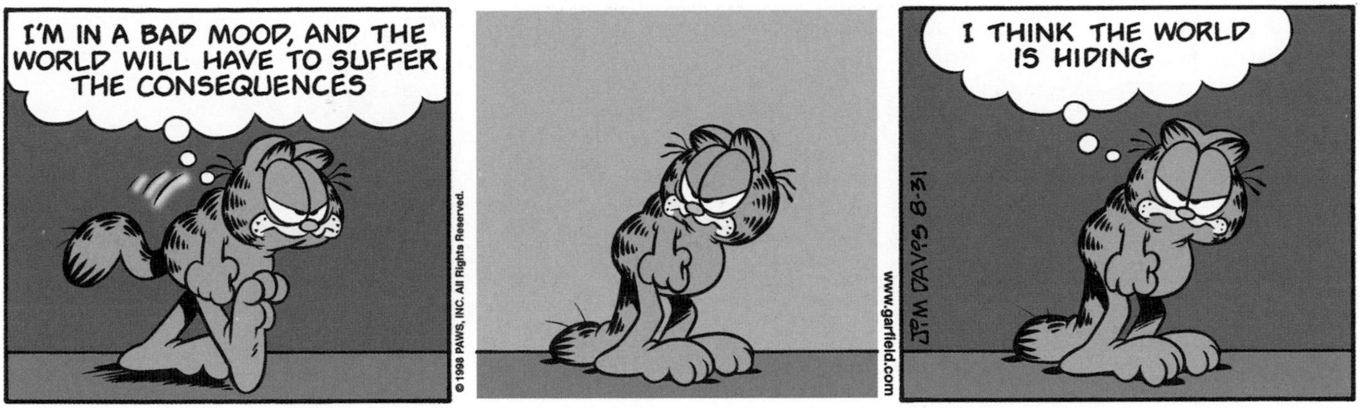
I'M IN A BAD MOOD, AND THE WORLD WILL HAVE TO SUFFER THE CONSEQUENCES
© 1998 PAWS, INC. All Rights Reserved.
www.garfield.com
JIM DAVIS 8-31
I THINK THE WORLD IS HIDING

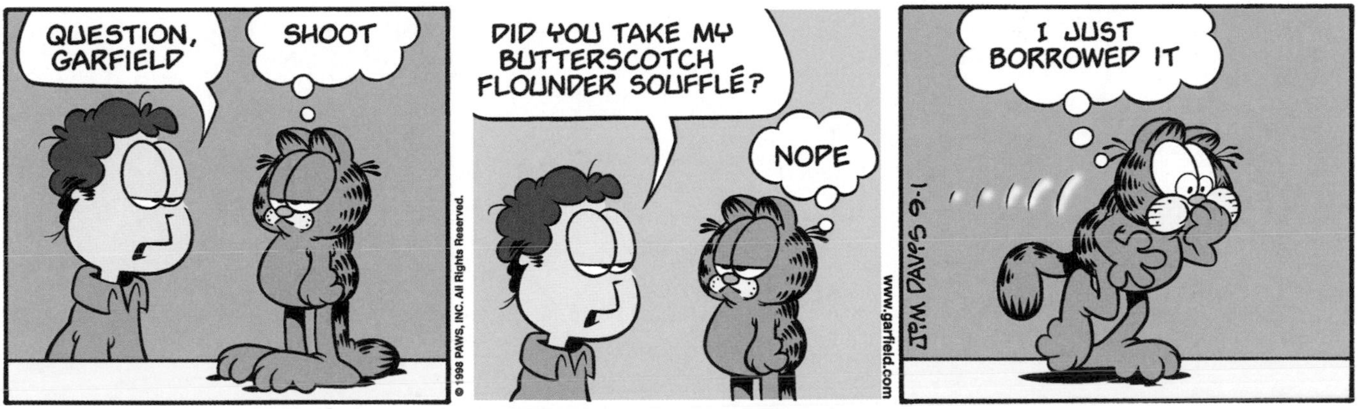
QUESTION, GARFIELD
SHOOT
© 1998 PAWS, INC. All Rights Reserved.
DID YOU TAKE MY BUTTERSCOTCH FLOUNDER SOUFFLÉ?
NOPE
www.garfield.com
JIM DAVIS 9-1
I JUST BORROWED IT

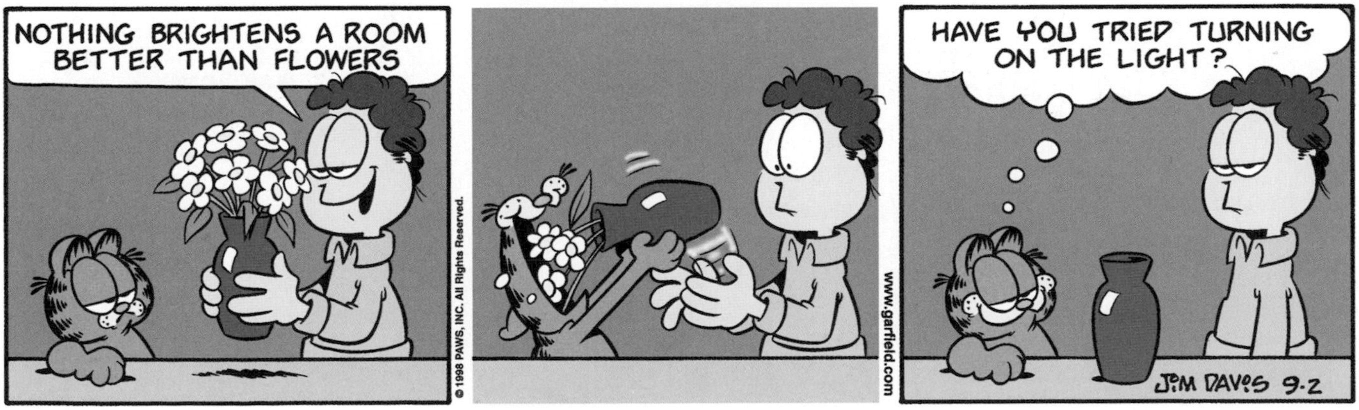
NOTHING BRIGHTENS A ROOM BETTER THAN FLOWERS
© 1998 PAWS, INC. All Rights Reserved.
www.garfield.com
HAVE YOU TRIED TURNING ON THE LIGHT?
JIM DAVIS 9-2

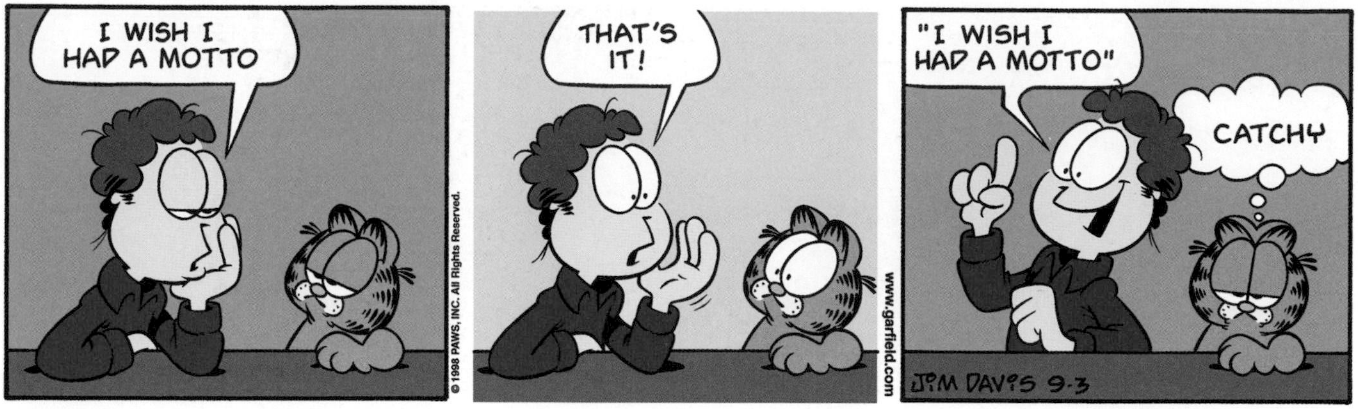
I WISH I HAD A MOTTO
© 1998 PAWS, INC. All Rights Reserved.
THAT'S IT!
www.garfield.com
"I WISH I HAD A MOTTO"
CATCHY
JIM DAVIS 9-3

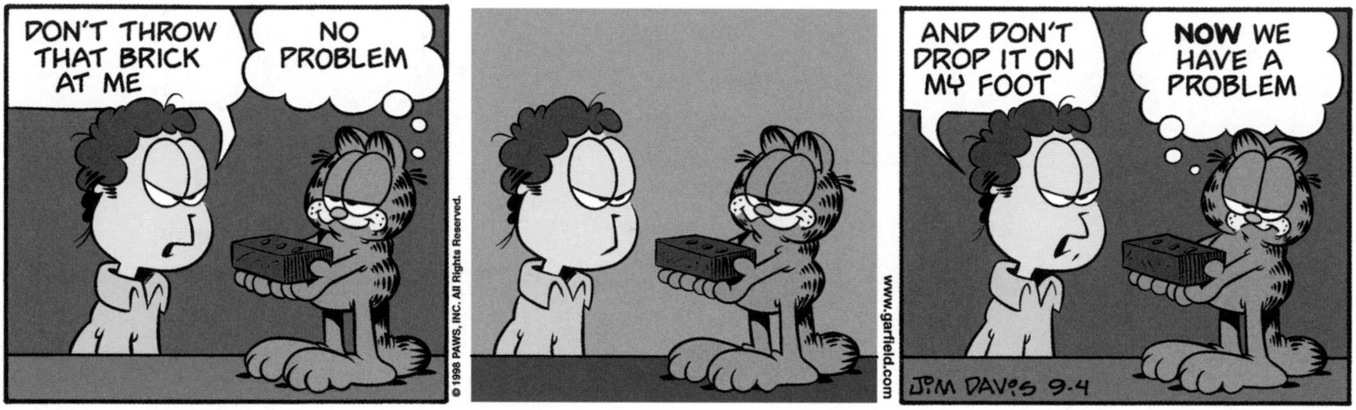
DON'T THROW THAT BRICK AT ME
NO PROBLEM
© 1998 PAWS, INC. All Rights Reserved.
www.garfield.com
AND DON'T DROP IT ON MY FOOT
NOW WE HAVE A PROBLEM
JIM DAVIS 9-4

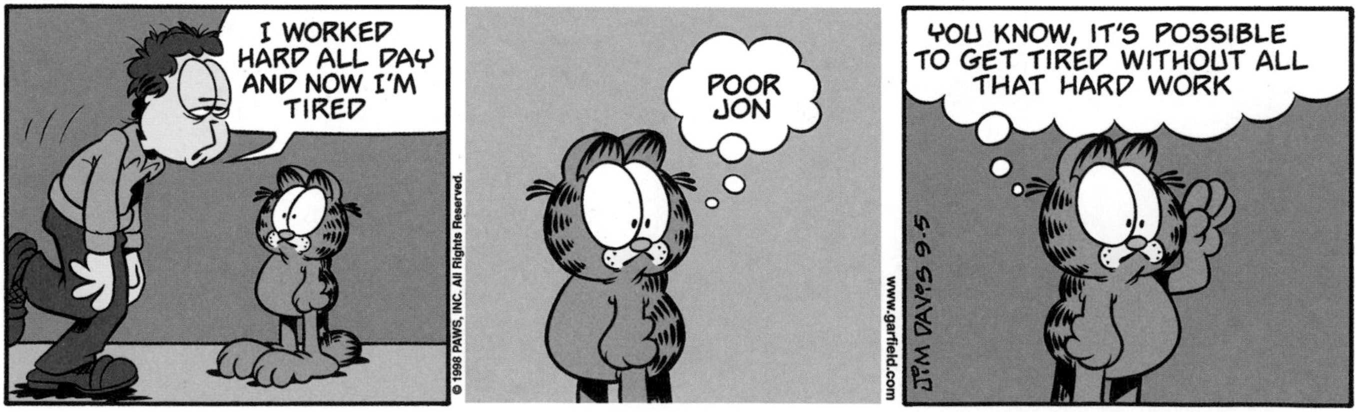
I WORKED HARD ALL DAY AND NOW I'M TIRED
© 1998 PAWS, INC. All Rights Reserved.
POOR JON
www.garfield.com
JIM DAVIS 9-5
YOU KNOW, IT'S POSSIBLE TO GET TIRED WITHOUT ALL THAT HARD WORK

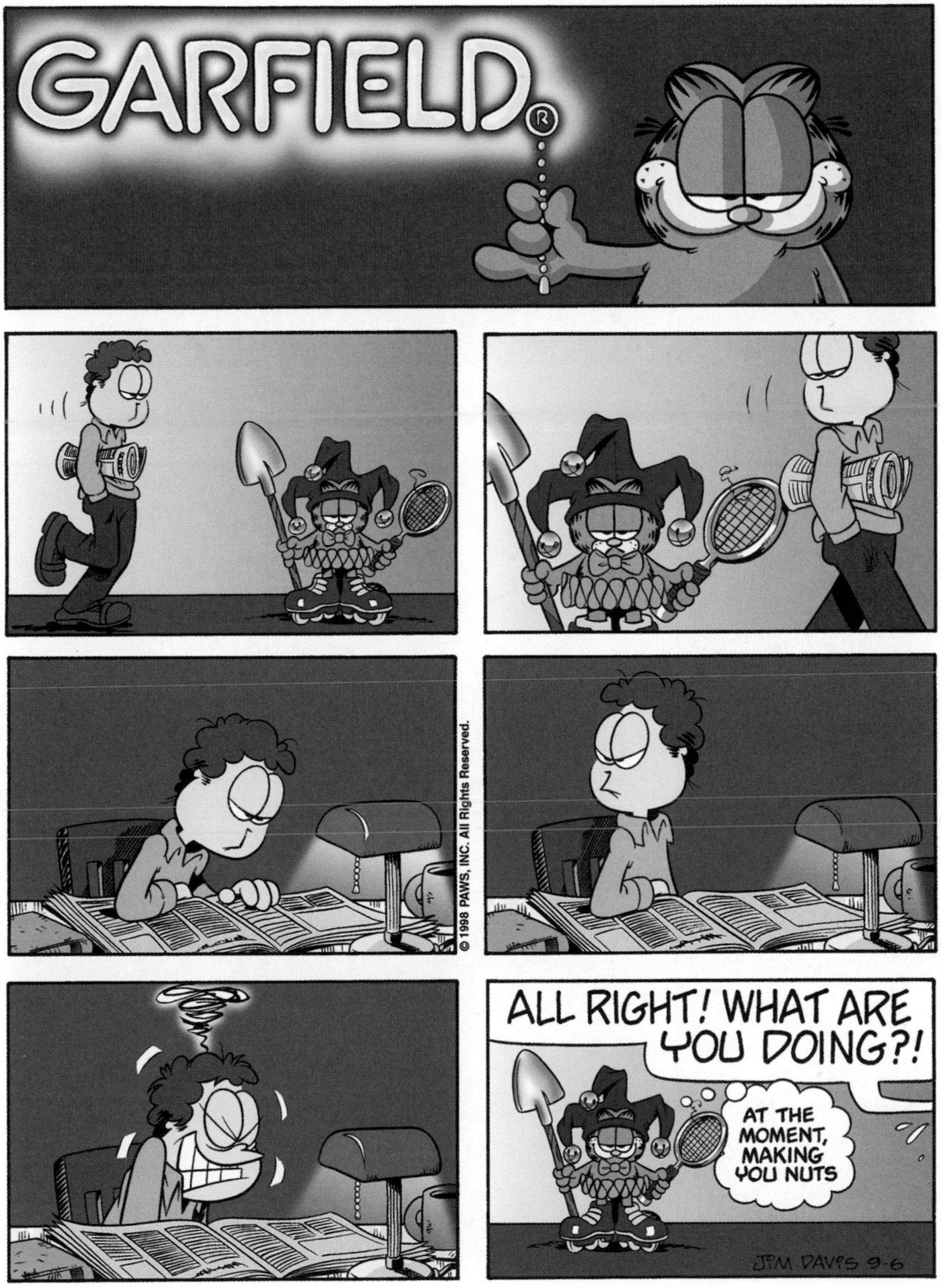
GARFIELD
© 1998 PAWS, INC. All Rights Reserved.
ALL RIGHT! WHAT ARE YOU DOING?!
AT THE MOMENT, MAKING YOU NUTS
JIM DAVIS 9-6

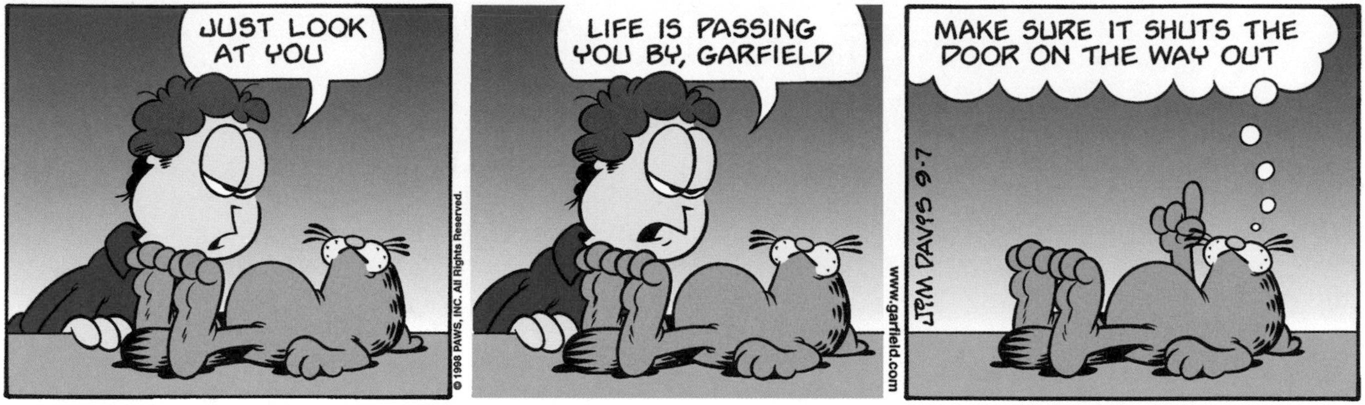
JUST LOOK AT YOU
© 1998 PAWS, INC. All Rights Reserved.
LIFE IS PASSING YOU BY, GARFIELD
www.garfield.com
MAKE SURE IT SHUTS THE DOOR ON THE WAY OUT
JIM DAVIS 9-7

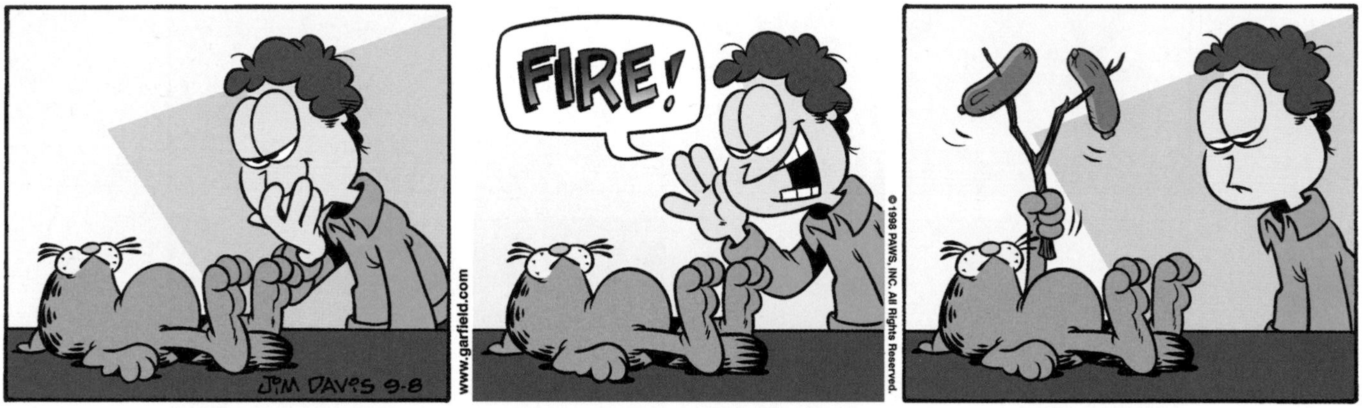
JIM DAVIS 9-8
www.garfield.com
FIRE!
© 1998 PAWS, INC. All Rights Reserved.

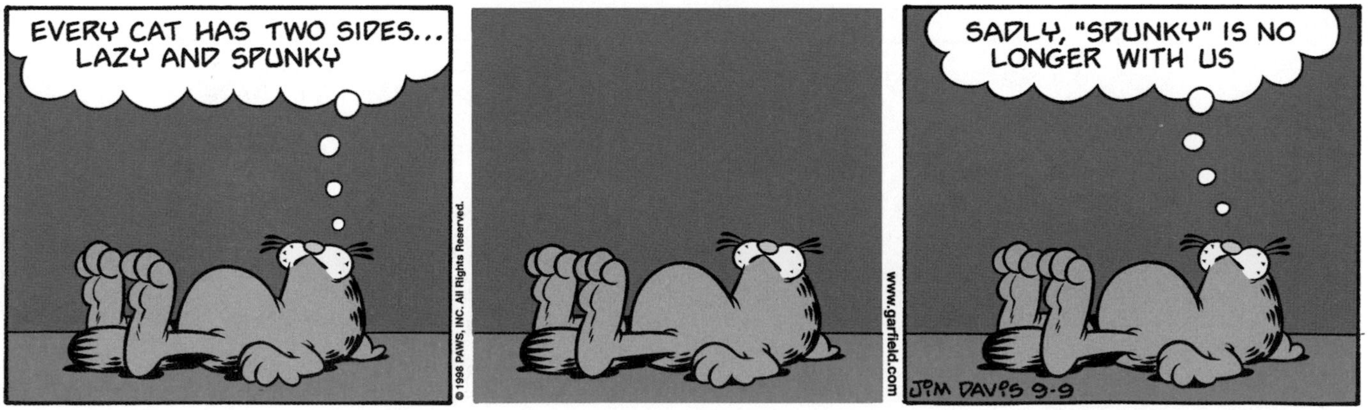
EVERY CAT HAS TWO SIDES... LAZY AND SPUNKY
© 1998 PAWS, INC. All Rights Reserved.
www.garfield.com
SADLY, "SPUNKY" IS NO LONGER WITH US
JIM DAVIS 9-9

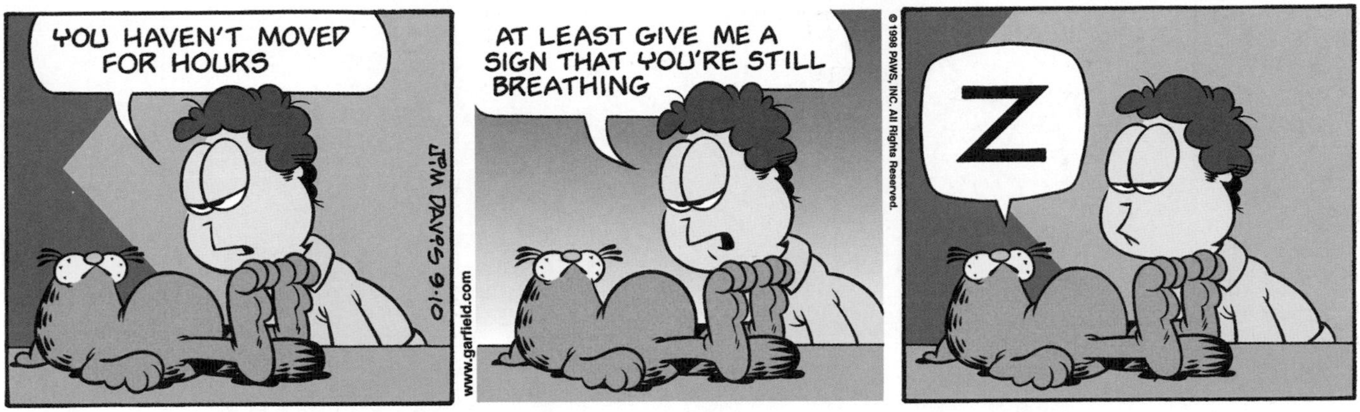
YOU HAVEN'T MOVED FOR HOURS
JIM DAVIS 9-10
www.garfield.com
AT LEAST GIVE ME A SIGN THAT YOU'RE STILL BREATHING
© 1998 PAWS, INC. All Rights Reserved.
Z

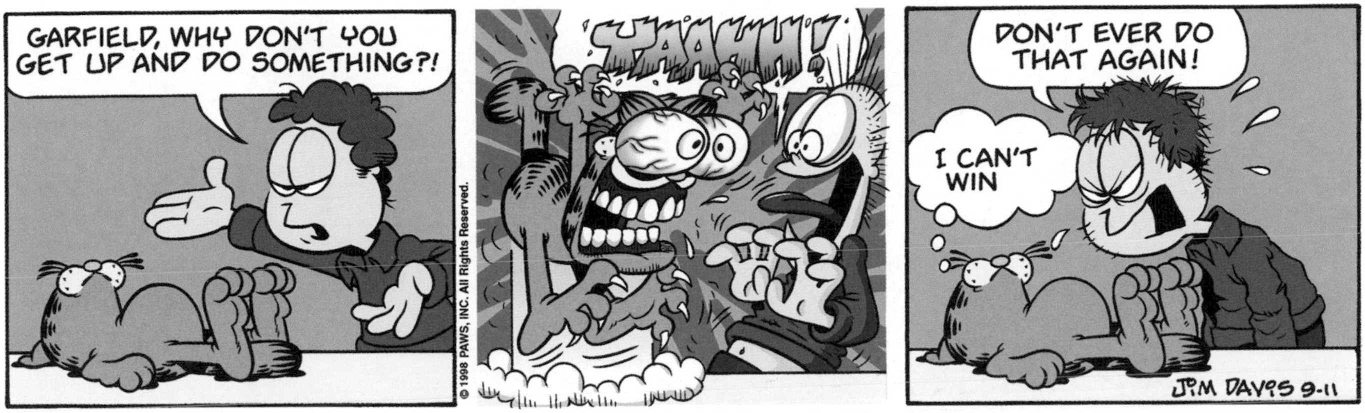
GARFIELD, WHY DON'T YOU GET UP AND DO SOMETHING?!
© 1998 PAWS, INC. All Rights Reserved.
YAAHH!
DON'T EVER DO THAT AGAIN!
I CAN'T WIN
JIM DAVIS 9-11

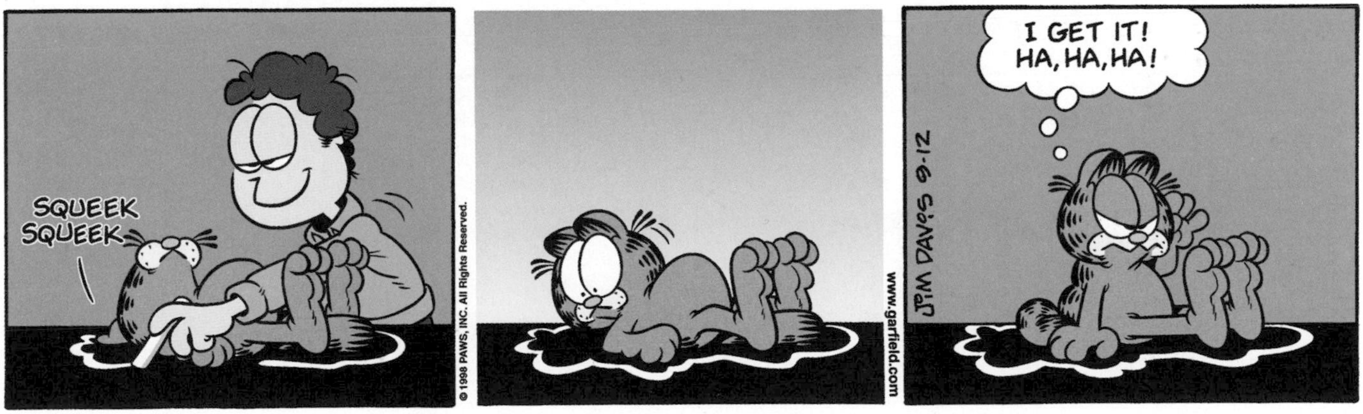
SQUEEK SQUEEK
© 1998 PAWS, INC. All Rights Reserved.
JIM DAVIS 9-12
www.garfield.com
I GET IT! HA, HA, HA!

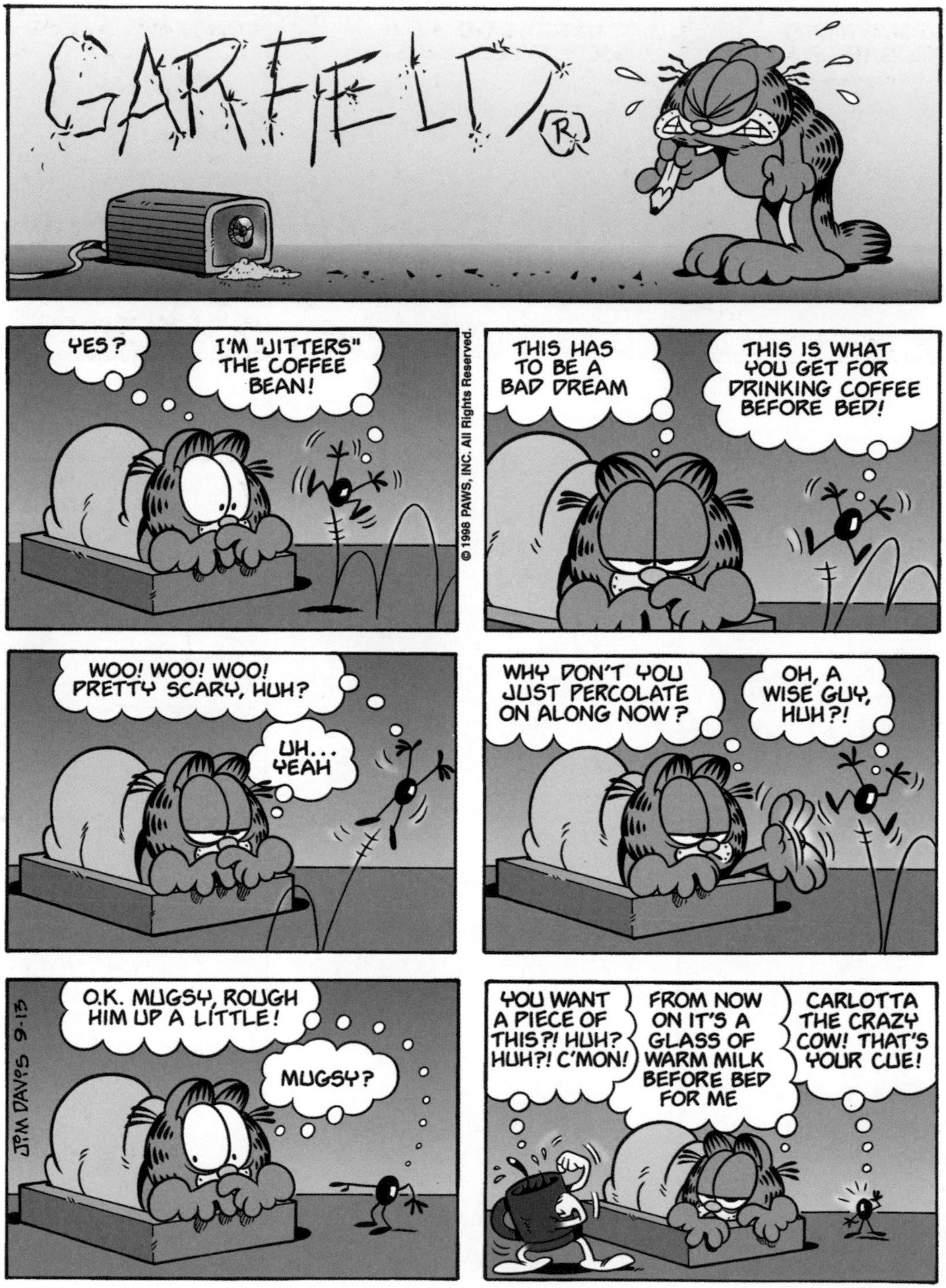
GARFIELD®
YES?
I'M "JITTERS" THE COFFEE BEAN!
© 1998 PAWS, INC. All Rights Reserved.
THIS HAS TO BE A BAD DREAM
THIS IS WHAT YOU GET FOR DRINKING COFFEE BEFORE BED!
WOO! WOO! WOO! PRETTY SCARY, HUH?
UH... YEAH
WHY DON'T YOU JUST PERCOLATE ON ALONG NOW?
OH, A WISE GUY, HUH?!
O.K. MUGSY, ROUGH HIM UP A LITTLE!
MUGSY?
JIM DAVIS 9-13
YOU WANT A PIECE OF THIS?! HUH? HUH?! C'MON!
FROM NOW ON IT'S A GLASS OF WARM MILK BEFORE BED FOR ME
CARLOTTA THE CRAZY COW! THAT'S YOUR CUE!

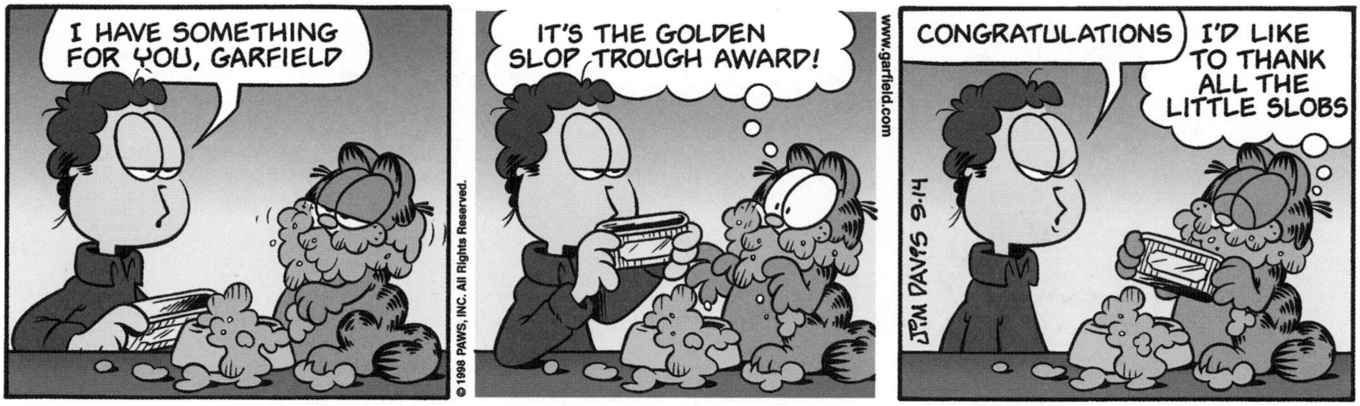
I HAVE SOMETHING FOR YOU, GARFIELD
© 1998 PAWS, INC. All Rights Reserved.
IT'S THE GOLDEN SLOP TROUGH AWARD!
www.garfield.com
CONGRATULATIONS
I'D LIKE TO THANK ALL THE LITTLE SLOBS
JIM DAVIS 9-14

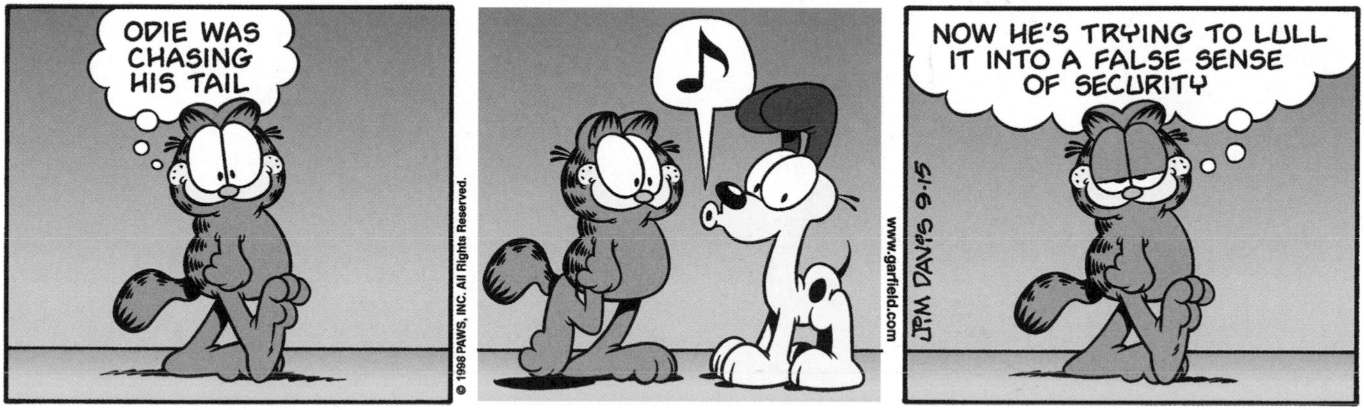
ODIE WAS CHASING HIS TAIL
© 1998 PAWS, INC. All Rights Reserved.
www.garfield.com
NOW HE'S TRYING TO LULL IT INTO A FALSE SENSE OF SECURITY
JIM DAVIS 9-15

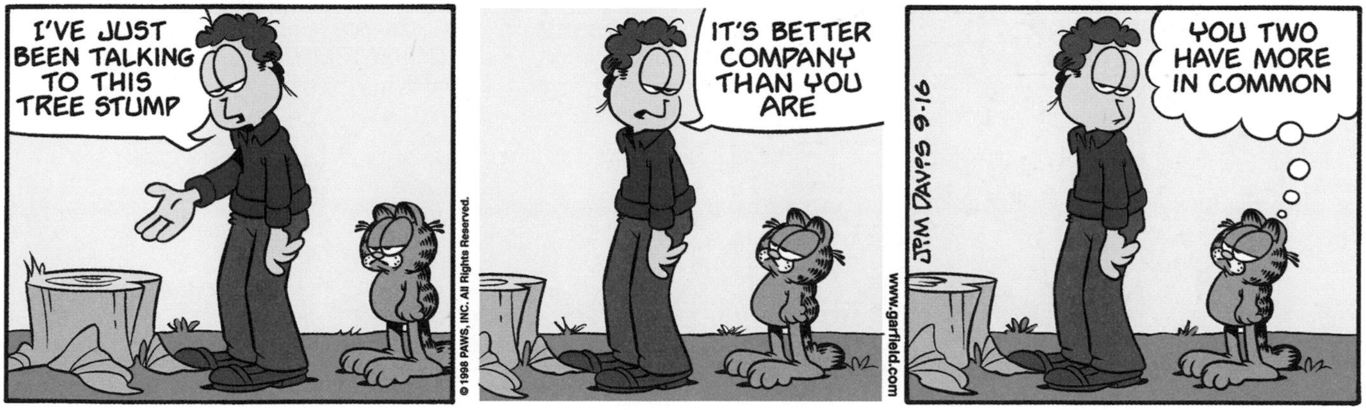
I'VE JUST BEEN TALKING TO THIS TREE STUMP
© 1998 PAWS, INC. All Rights Reserved.
IT'S BETTER COMPANY THAN YOU ARE
www.garfield.com
JIM DAVIS 9-16
YOU TWO HAVE MORE IN COMMON

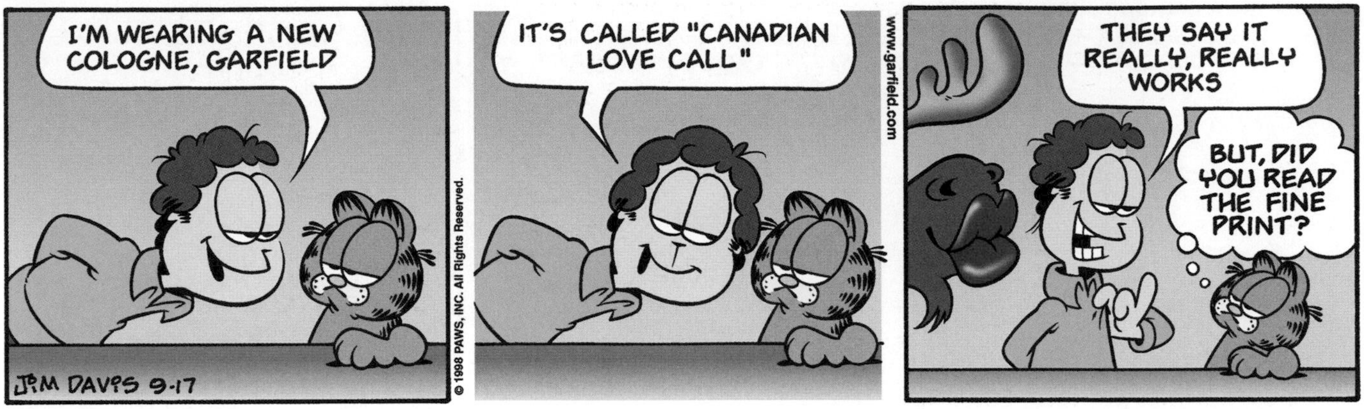
I'M WEARING A NEW COLOGNE, GARFIELD
JIM DAVIS 9-17
© 1998 PAWS, INC. All Rights Reserved.
IT'S CALLED "CANADIAN LOVE CALL"
www.garfield.com
THEY SAY IT REALLY, REALLY WORKS
BUT, DID YOU READ THE FINE PRINT?

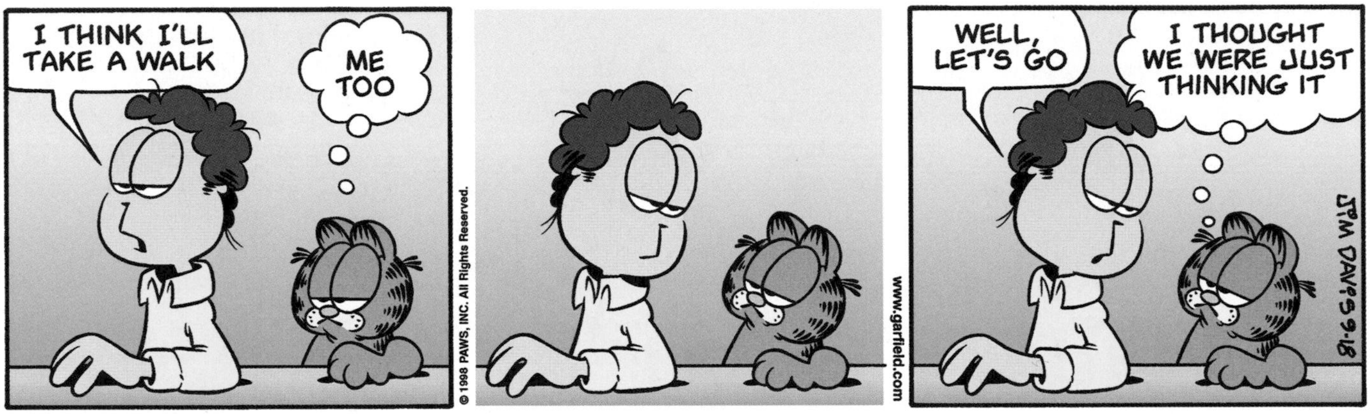
I THINK I'LL TAKE A WALK
ME TOO
© 1998 PAWS, INC. All Rights Reserved.
www.garfield.com
WELL, LET'S GO
I THOUGHT WE WERE JUST THINKING IT
JIM DAVIS 9-18

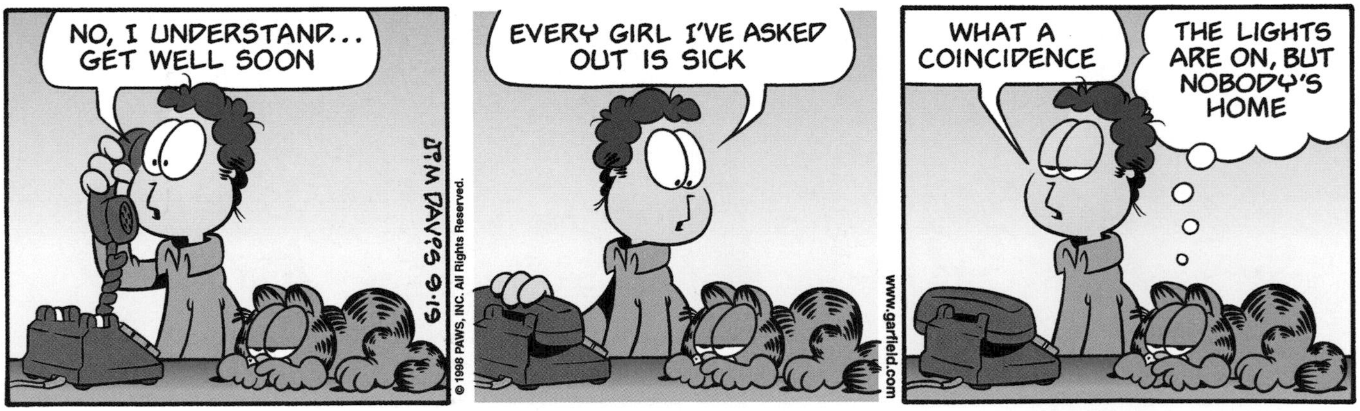
NO, I UNDERSTAND... GET WELL SOON
JIM DAVIS 9-19
© 1998 PAWS, INC. All Rights Reserved.
EVERY GIRL I'VE ASKED OUT IS SICK
www.garfield.com
WHAT A COINCIDENCE
THE LIGHTS ARE ON, BUT NOBODY'S HOME

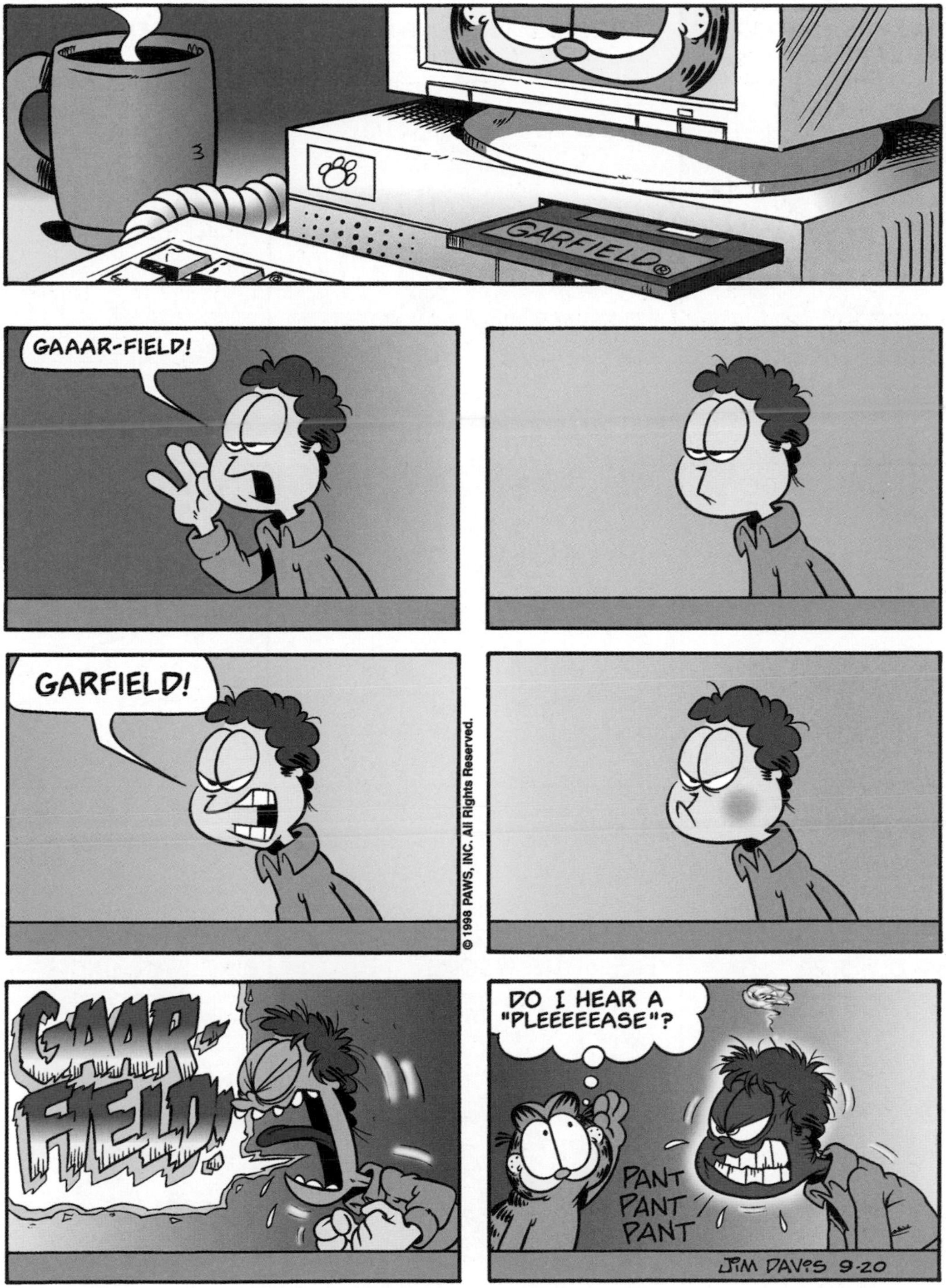
GARFIELD®
GAAAR-FIELD!
GARFIELD!
GAAR-FIELD!
DO I HEAR A "PLEEEEEASE"?
PANT PANT PANT
JIM DAVIS 9-20

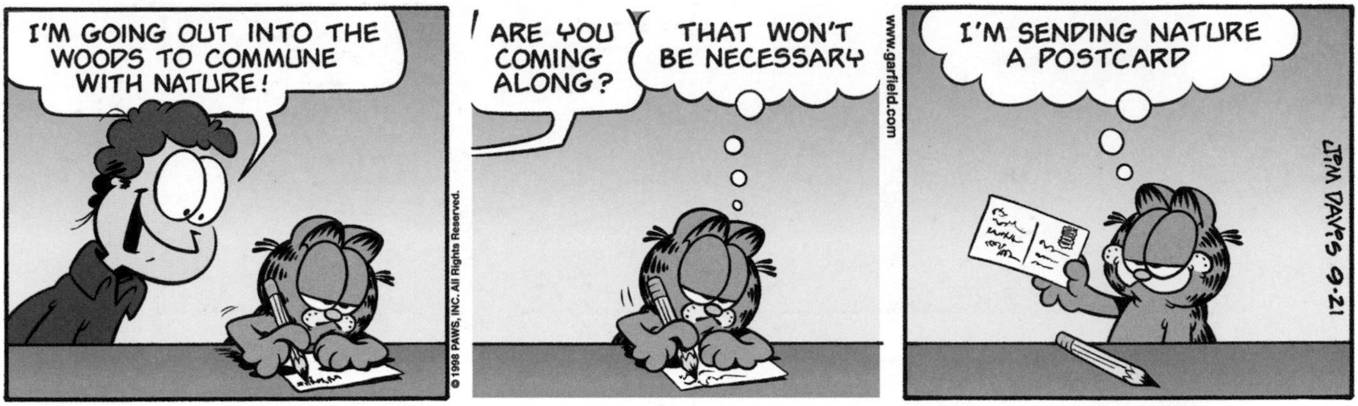
I'M GOING OUT INTO THE WOODS TO COMMUNE WITH NATURE!
© 1998 PAWS, INC. All Rights Reserved.
ARE YOU COMING ALONG?
THAT WON'T BE NECESSARY
www.garfield.com
I'M SENDING NATURE A POSTCARD
JIM DAVIS 9-21

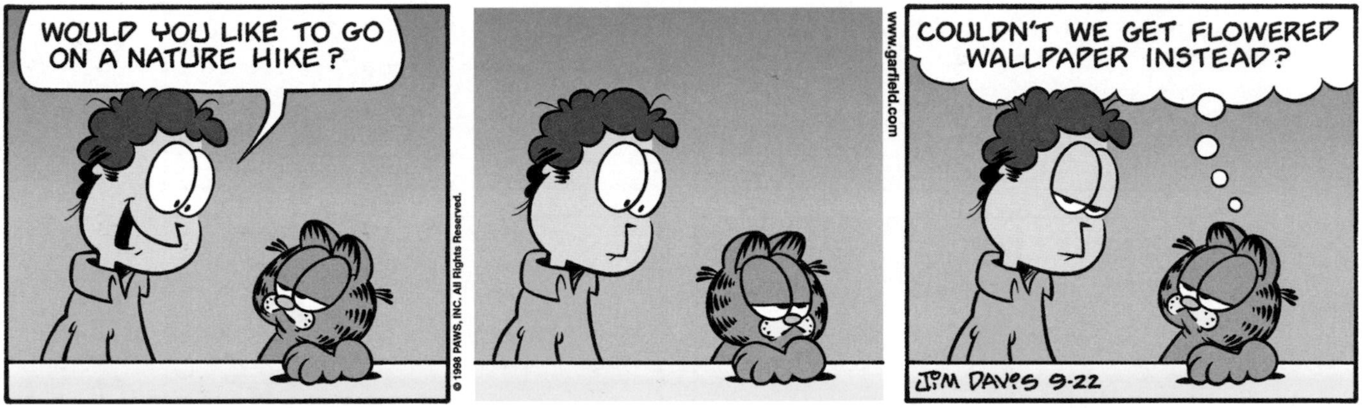
WOULD YOU LIKE TO GO ON A NATURE HIKE?
© 1998 PAWS, INC. All Rights Reserved.
www.garfield.com
COULDN'T WE GET FLOWERED WALLPAPER INSTEAD?
JIM DAVIS 9-22

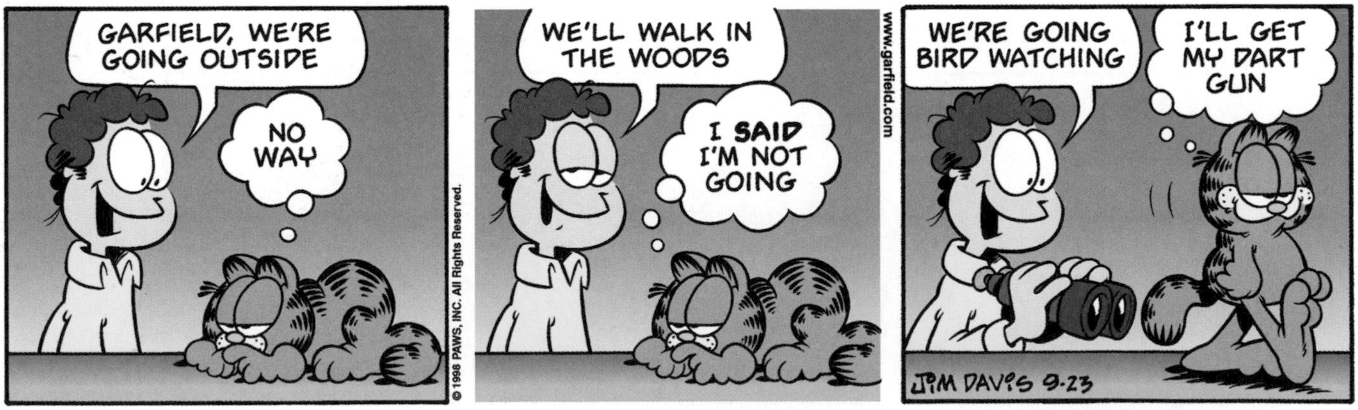
GARFIELD, WE'RE GOING OUTSIDE
NO WAY
© 1998 PAWS, INC. All Rights Reserved.
WE'LL WALK IN THE WOODS
I **SAID** I'M NOT GOING
www.garfield.com
WE'RE GOING BIRD WATCHING
I'LL GET MY DART GUN
JIM DAVIS 9-23

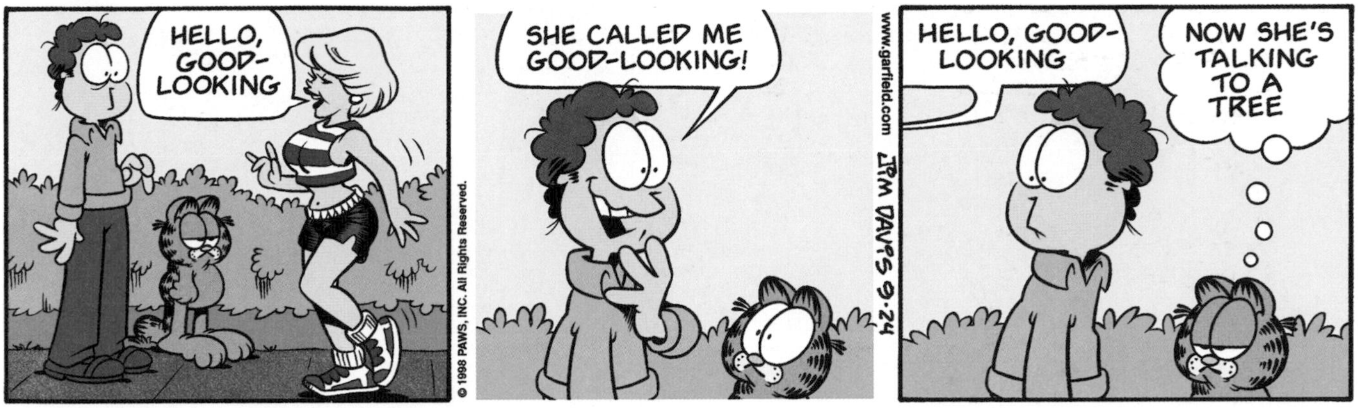
HELLO, GOOD-LOOKING
© 1998 PAWS, INC. All Rights Reserved.
SHE CALLED ME GOOD-LOOKING!
www.garfield.com
JIM DAVIS 9-24
HELLO, GOOD-LOOKING
NOW SHE'S TALKING TO A TREE

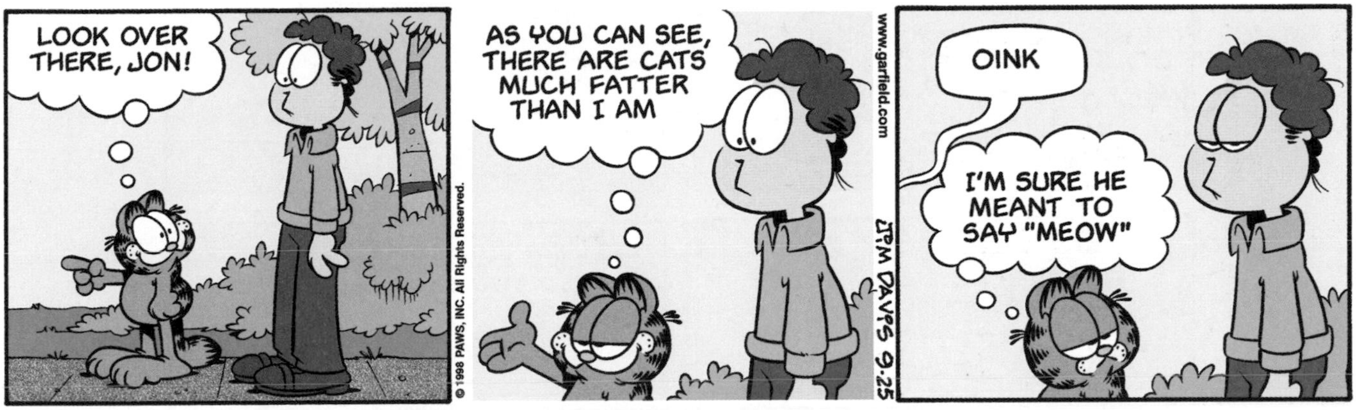
LOOK OVER THERE, JON!
© 1998 PAWS, INC. All Rights Reserved.
AS YOU CAN SEE, THERE ARE CATS MUCH FATTER THAN I AM
www.garfield.com
JIM DAVIS 9-25
OINK
I'M SURE HE MEANT TO SAY "MEOW"

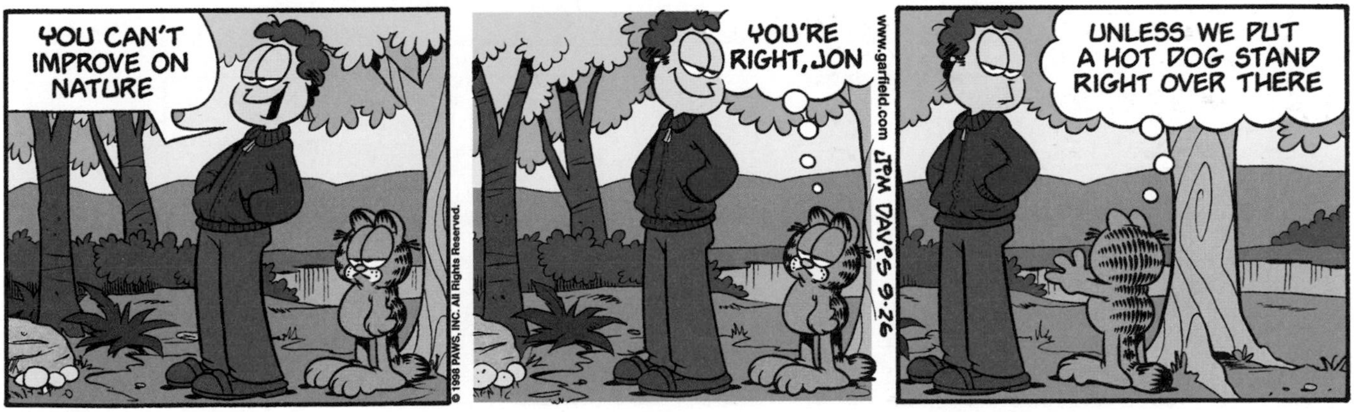
YOU CAN'T IMPROVE ON NATURE
© 1998 PAWS, INC. All Rights Reserved.
YOU'RE RIGHT, JON
www.garfield.com
JIM DAVIS 9-26
UNLESS WE PUT A HOT DOG STAND RIGHT OVER THERE

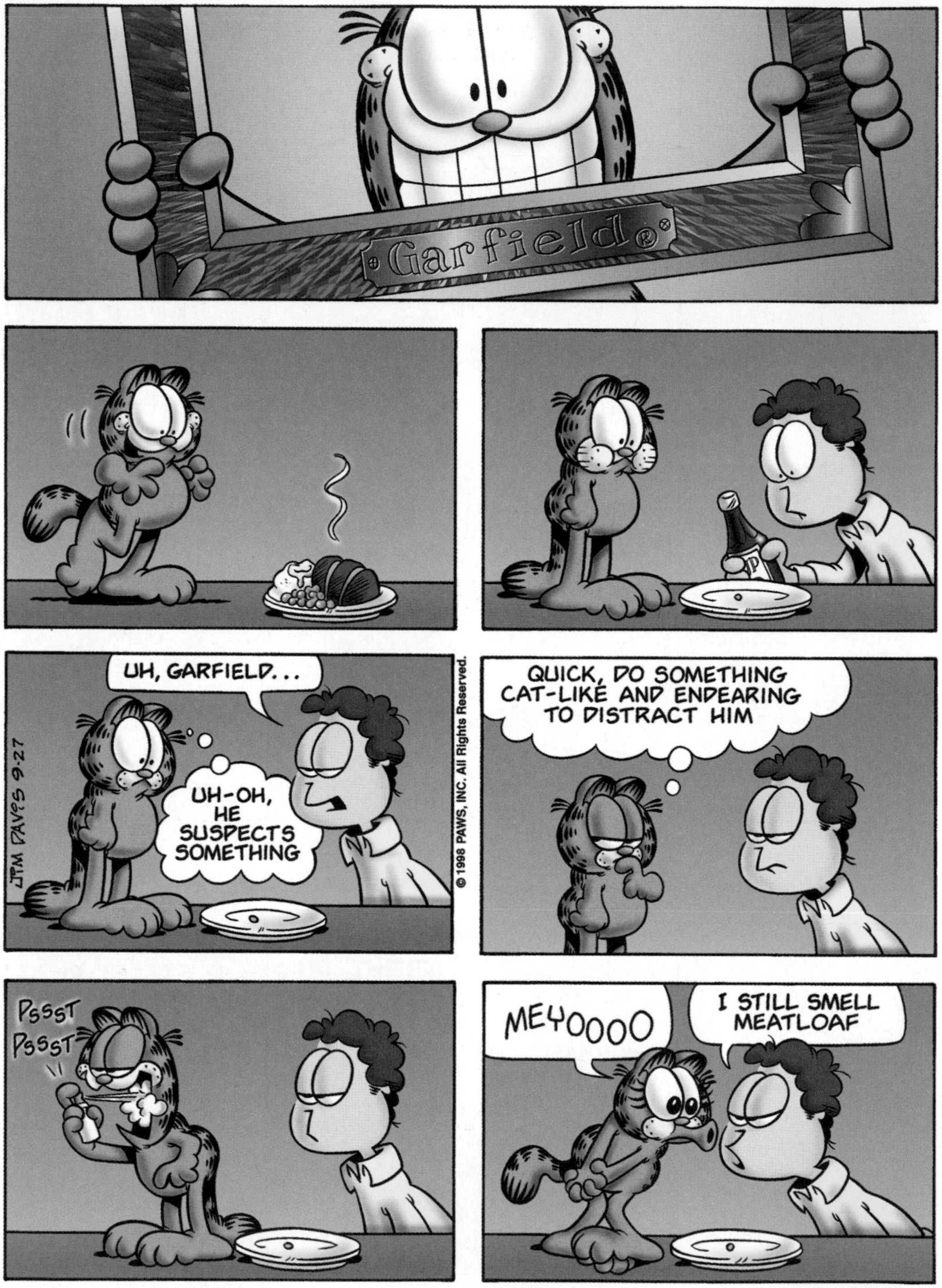
Garfield®
UH, GARFIELD...
UH-OH, HE SUSPECTS SOMETHING
JPM DAVPS 9·27
© 1998 PAWS, INC. All Rights Reserved.
QUICK, DO SOMETHING CAT-LIKE AND ENDEARING TO DISTRACT HIM
PSSST PSSST
MEYOOOO
I STILL SMELL MEATLOAF

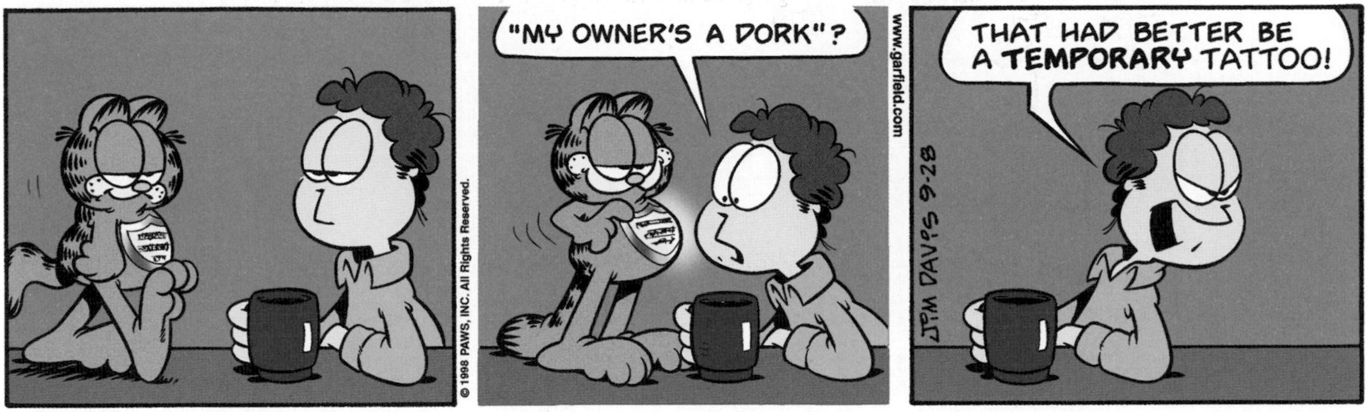
"MY OWNER'S A DORK"?
THAT HAD BETTER BE A **TEMPORARY** TATTOO!
JIM DAVIS 9-28
© 1998 PAWS, INC. All Rights Reserved.
www.garfield.com

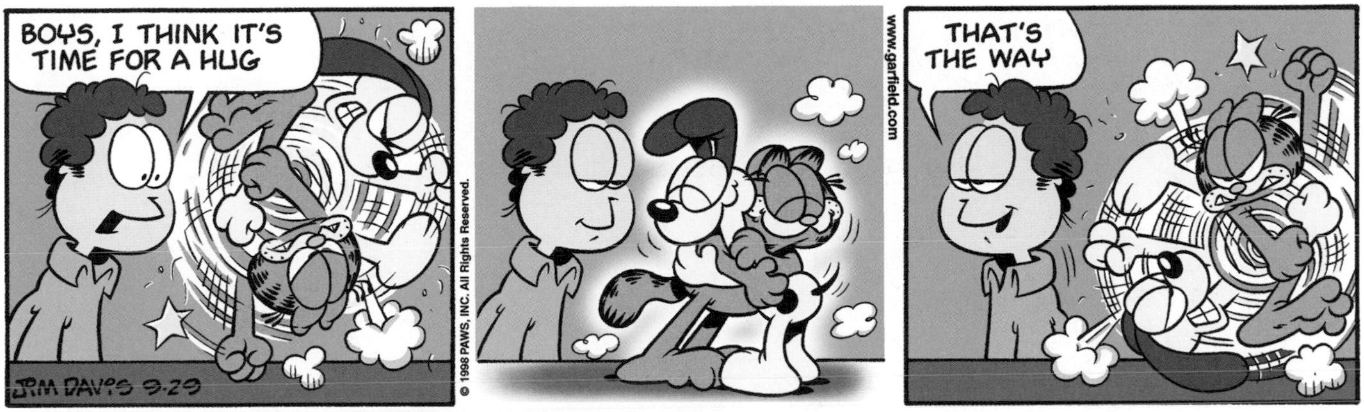
BOYS, I THINK IT'S TIME FOR A HUG
THAT'S THE WAY
JIM DAVIS 9-29
© 1998 PAWS, INC. All Rights Reserved.
www.garfield.com

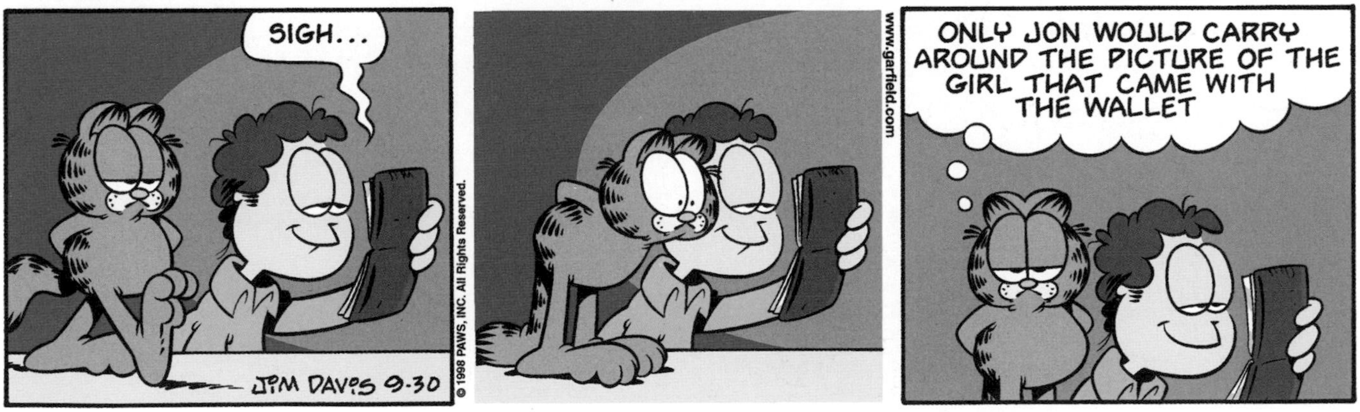
SIGH...
ONLY JON WOULD CARRY AROUND THE PICTURE OF THE GIRL THAT CAME WITH THE WALLET
JIM DAVIS 9-30
© 1998 PAWS, INC. All Rights Reserved.
www.garfield.com

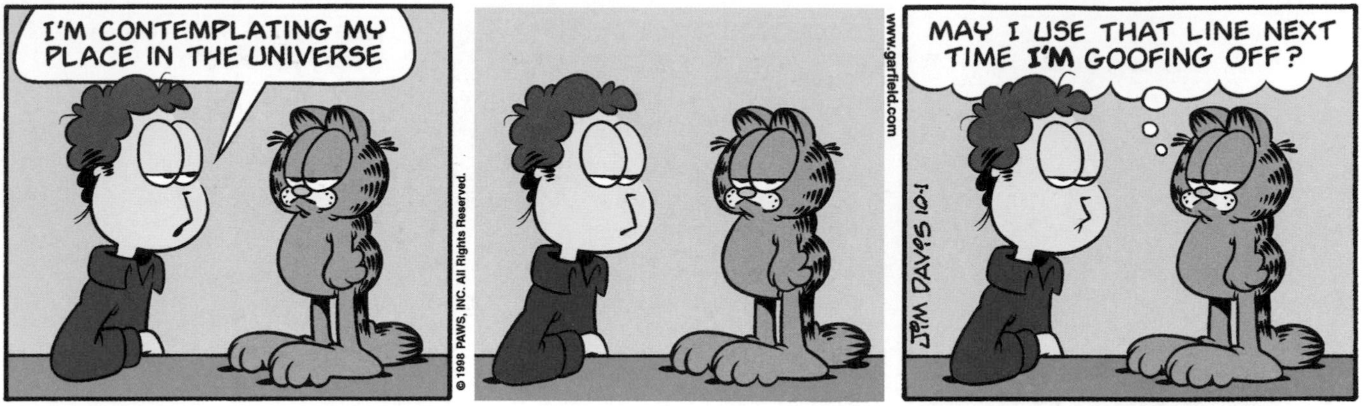
I'M CONTEMPLATING MY PLACE IN THE UNIVERSE
© 1998 PAWS, INC. All Rights Reserved.
www.garfield.com
JIM DAVIS 10-1
MAY I USE THAT LINE NEXT TIME I'M GOOFING OFF?

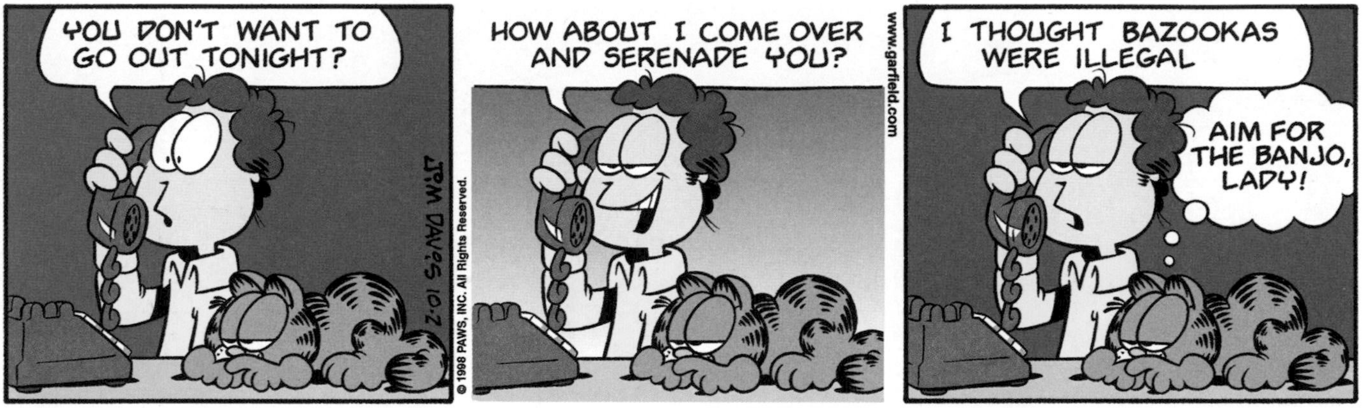
YOU DON'T WANT TO GO OUT TONIGHT?
JIM DAVIS 10-2
© 1998 PAWS, INC. All Rights Reserved.
HOW ABOUT I COME OVER AND SERENADE YOU?
www.garfield.com
I THOUGHT BAZOOKAS WERE ILLEGAL
AIM FOR THE BANJO, LADY!

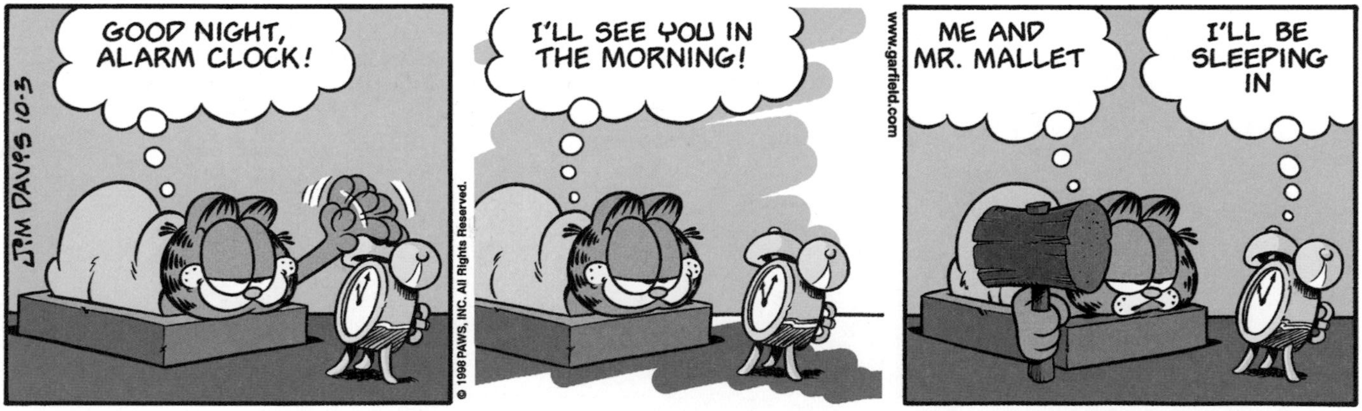
GOOD NIGHT, ALARM CLOCK!
JIM DAVIS 10-3
© 1998 PAWS, INC. All Rights Reserved.
I'LL SEE YOU IN THE MORNING!
www.garfield.com
ME AND MR. MALLET
I'LL BE SLEEPING IN

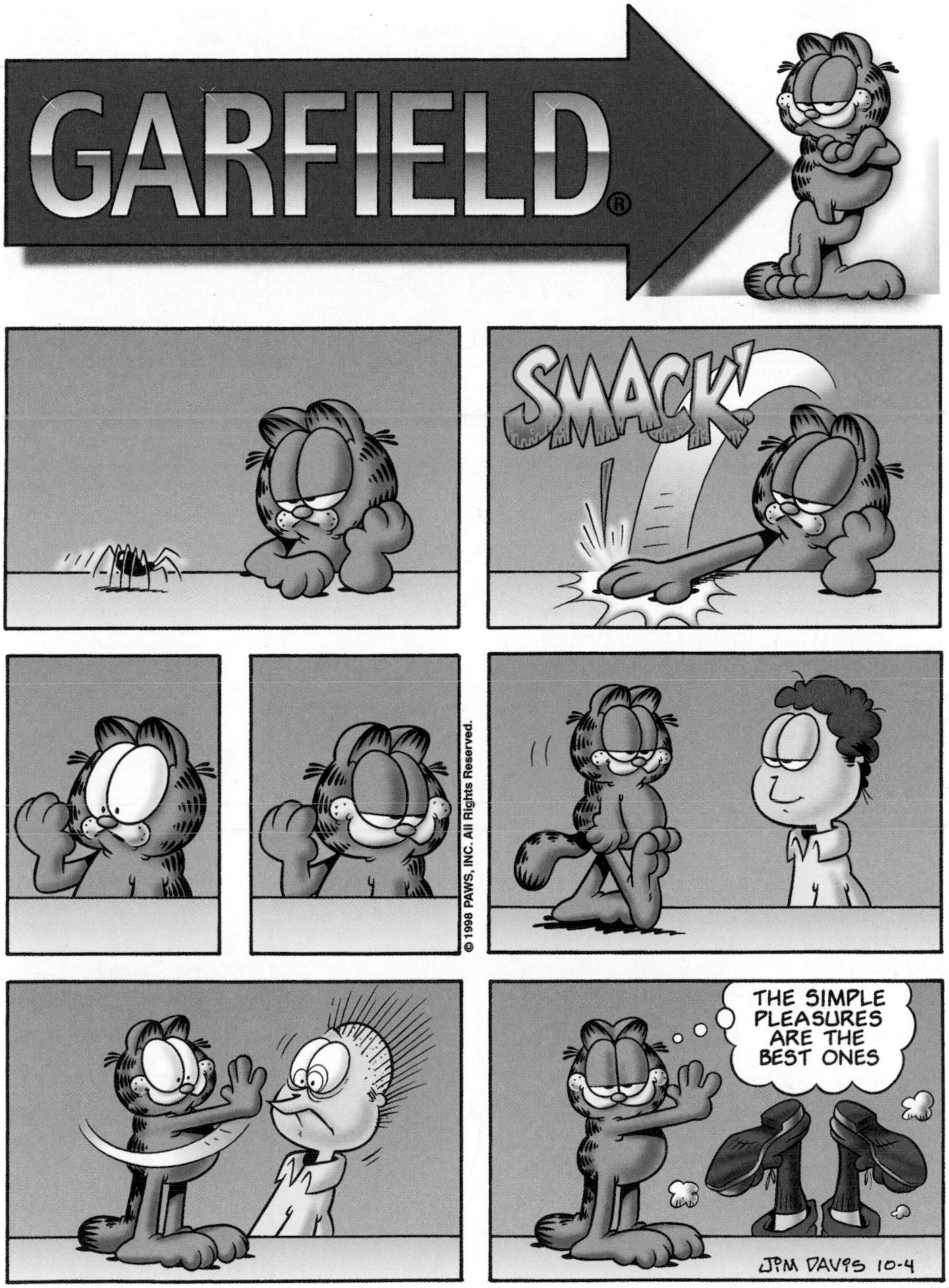
GARFIELD®
SMACK!
© 1998 PAWS, INC. All Rights Reserved.
THE SIMPLE PLEASURES ARE THE BEST ONES
JIM DAVIS 10-4

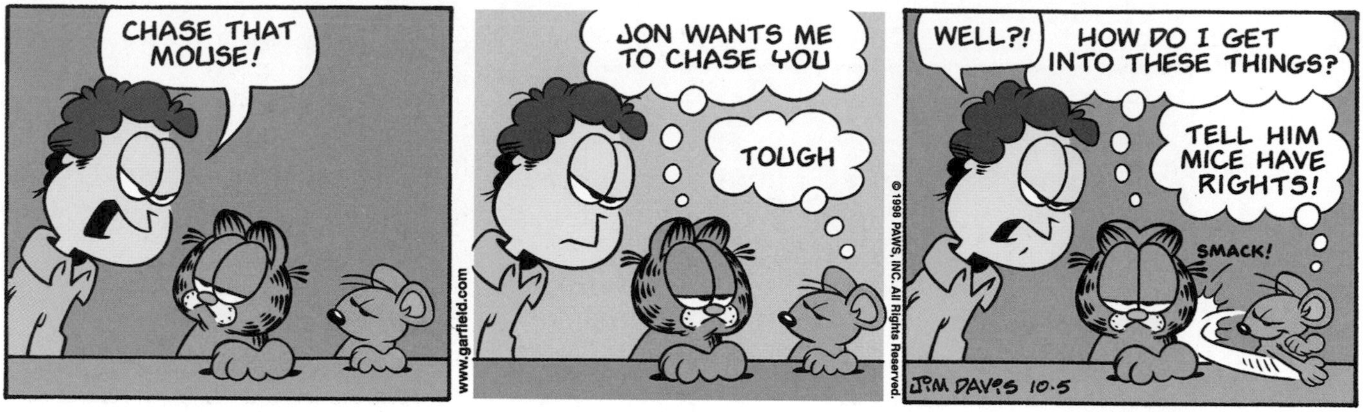
CHASE THAT MOUSE!
JON WANTS ME TO CHASE YOU
TOUGH
WELL?!
HOW DO I GET INTO THESE THINGS?
TELL HIM MICE HAVE RIGHTS!
SMACK!
www.garfield.com
© 1998 PAWS, INC. All Rights Reserved.
JIM DAVIS 10-5

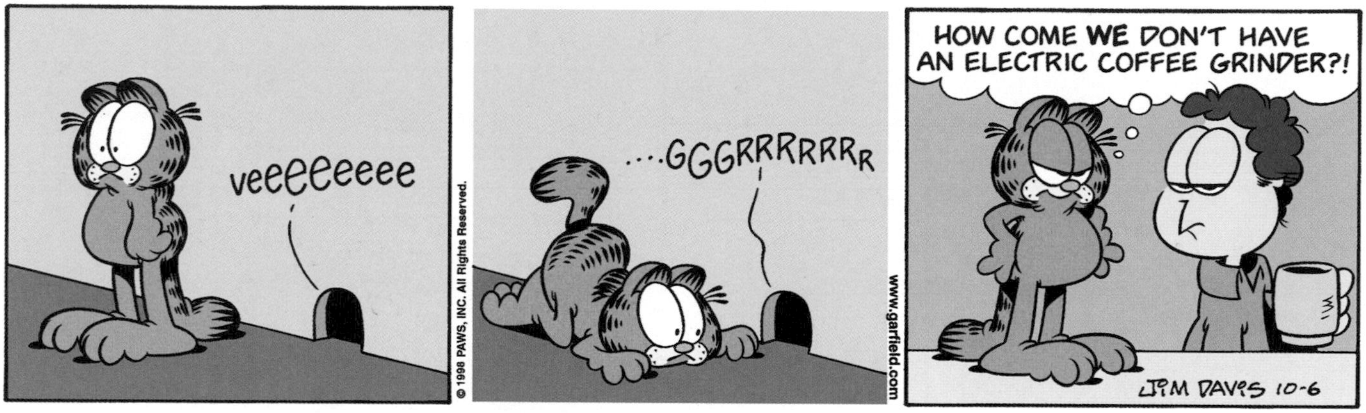
veeeeeeee
....GGGRRRRRRR
HOW COME WE DON'T HAVE AN ELECTRIC COFFEE GRINDER?!
© 1998 PAWS, INC. All Rights Reserved.
www.garfield.com
JIM DAVIS 10-6

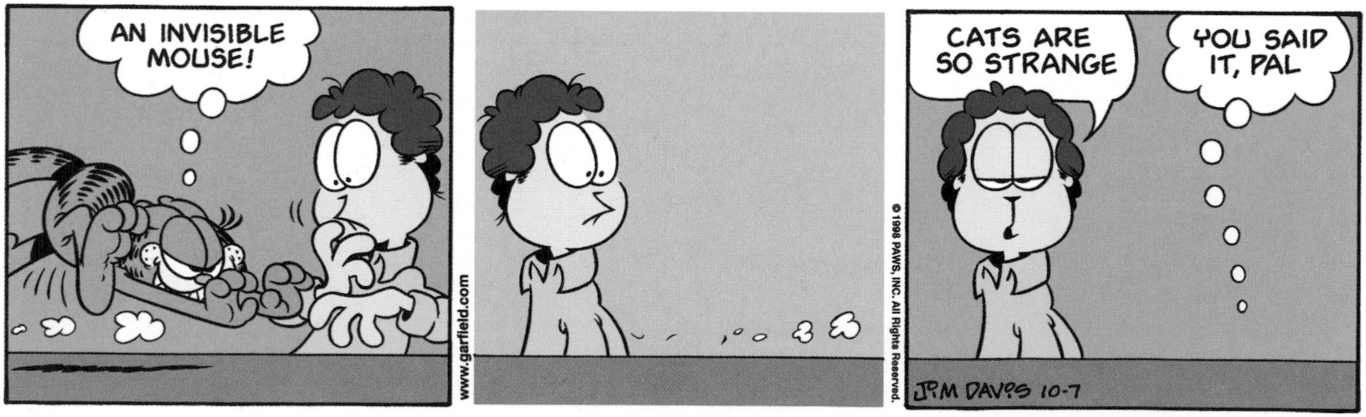
AN INVISIBLE MOUSE!
CATS ARE SO STRANGE
YOU SAID IT, PAL
www.garfield.com
© 1998 PAWS, INC. All Rights Reserved.
JIM DAVIS 10-7

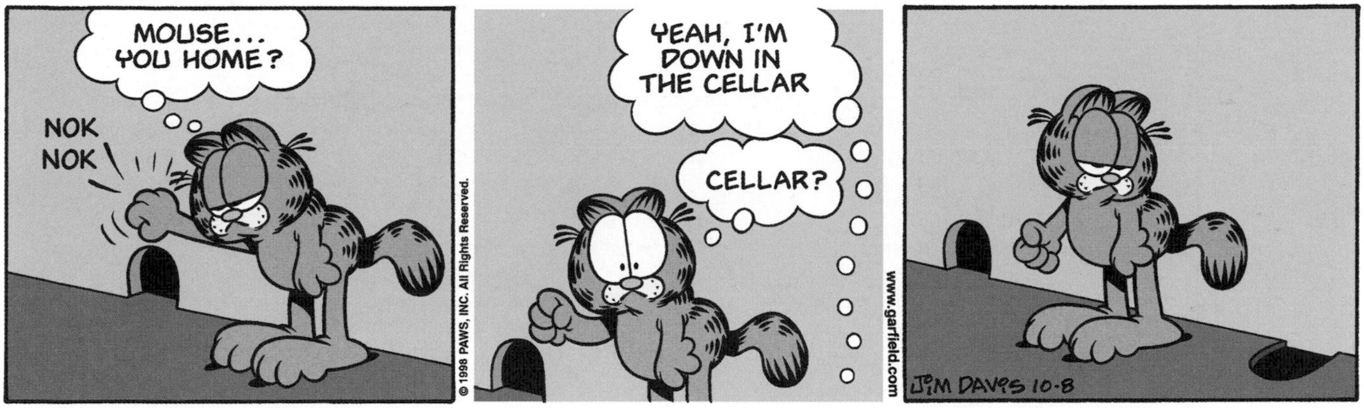
MOUSE... YOU HOME?
NOK NOK
© 1998 PAWS, INC. All Rights Reserved.
YEAH, I'M DOWN IN THE CELLAR
CELLAR?
www.garfield.com
JIM DAVIS 10-8

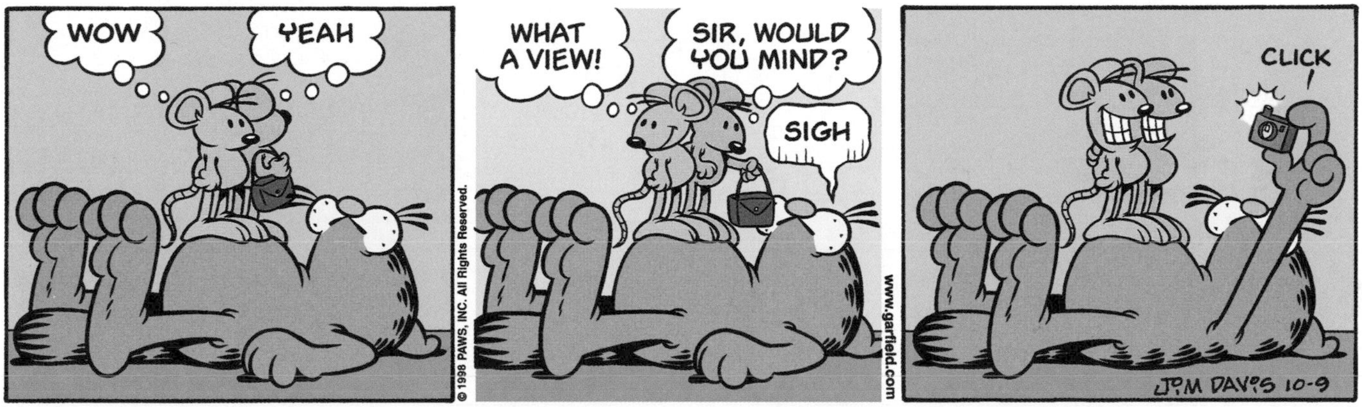
WOW
YEAH
© 1998 PAWS, INC. All Rights Reserved.
WHAT A VIEW!
SIR, WOULD YOU MIND?
SIGH
www.garfield.com
CLICK
JIM DAVIS 10-9

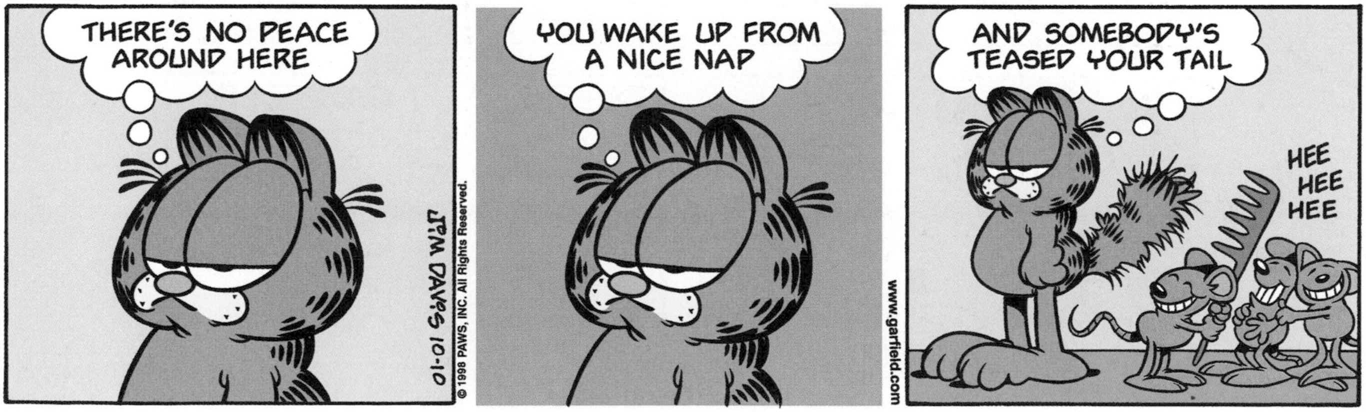
THERE'S NO PEACE AROUND HERE
JIM DAVIS 10-10
© 1998 PAWS, INC. All Rights Reserved.
YOU WAKE UP FROM A NICE NAP
www.garfield.com
AND SOMEBODY'S TEASED YOUR TAIL
HEE HEE HEE

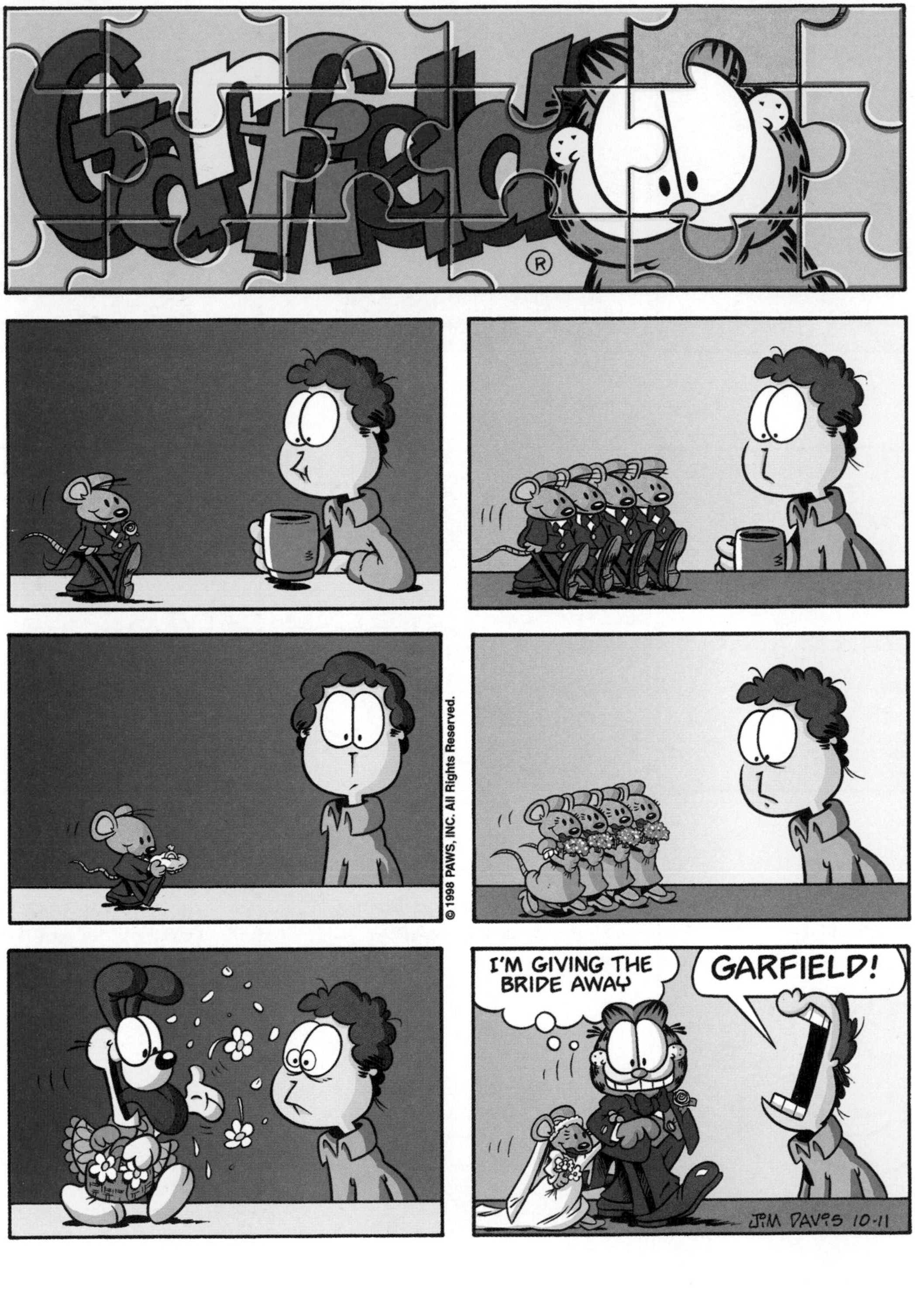
Garfield®
© 1998 PAWS, INC. All Rights Reserved.
I'M GIVING THE BRIDE AWAY
GARFIELD!
JIM DAVIS 10-11

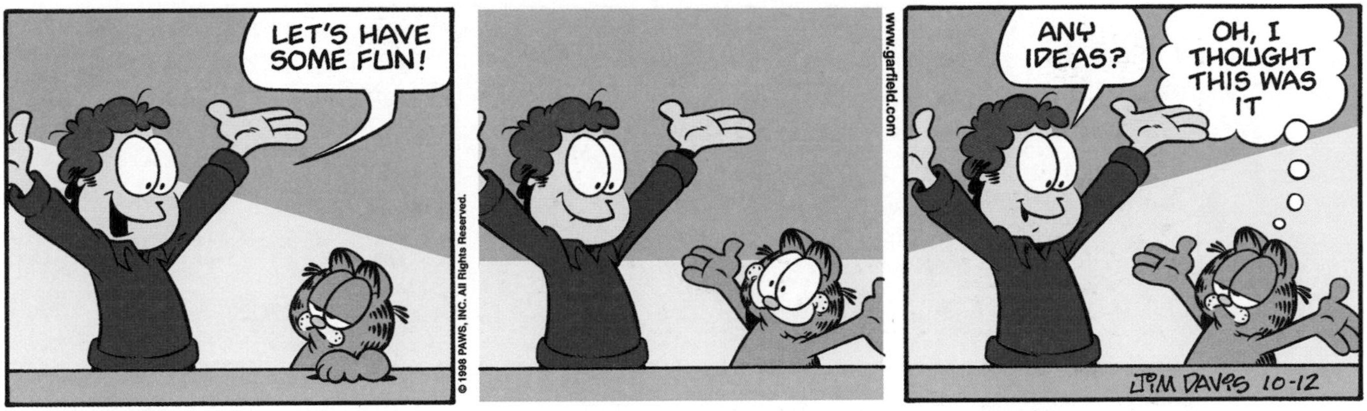
LET'S HAVE SOME FUN!
© 1998 PAWS, INC. All Rights Reserved.
www.garfield.com
ANY IDEAS?
OH, I THOUGHT THIS WAS IT
JIM DAVIS 10-12

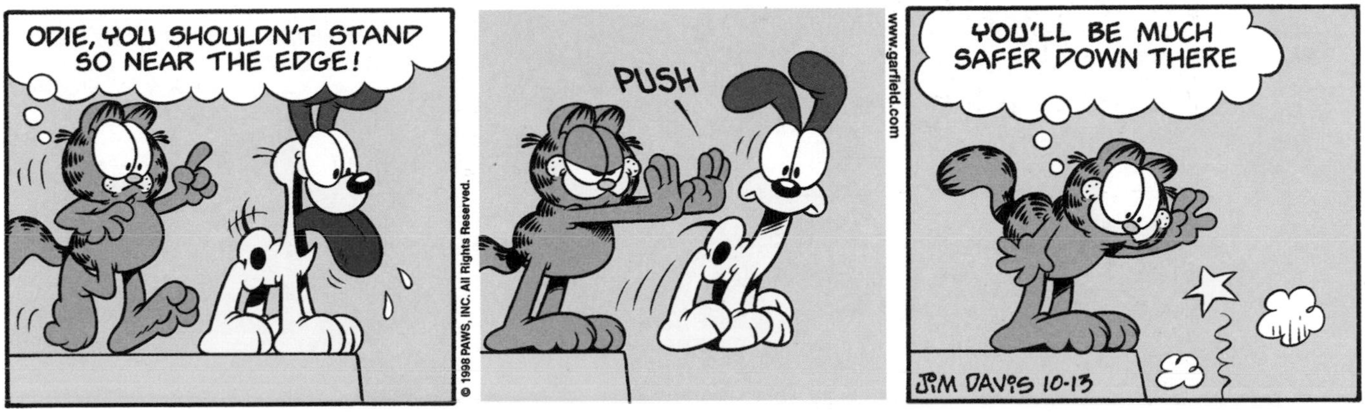
ODIE, YOU SHOULDN'T STAND SO NEAR THE EDGE!
© 1998 PAWS, INC. All Rights Reserved.
PUSH
www.garfield.com
YOU'LL BE MUCH SAFER DOWN THERE
JIM DAVIS 10-13

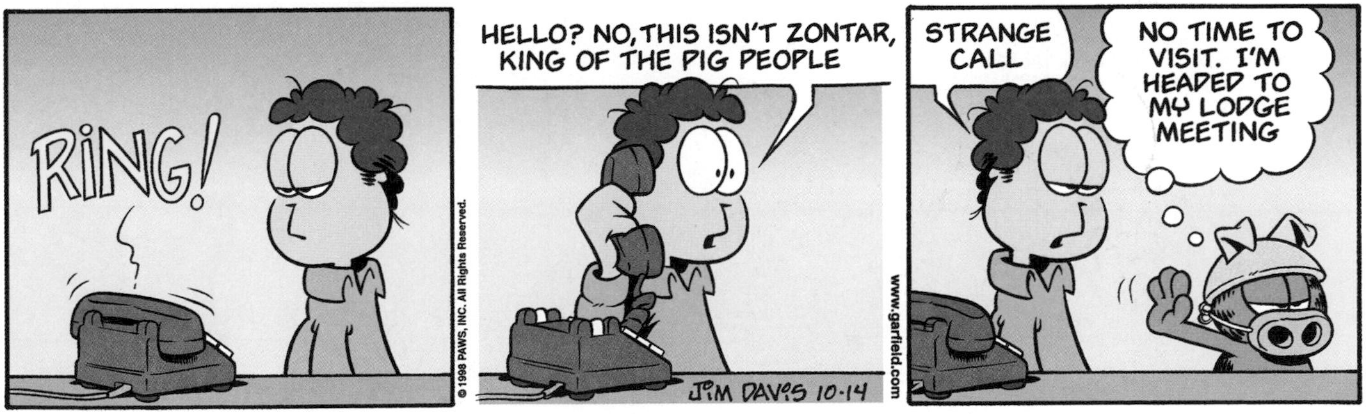
RING!
© 1998 PAWS, INC. All Rights Reserved.
HELLO? NO, THIS ISN'T ZONTAR, KING OF THE PIG PEOPLE
JIM DAVIS 10-14
www.garfield.com
STRANGE CALL
NO TIME TO VISIT. I'M HEADED TO MY LODGE MEETING

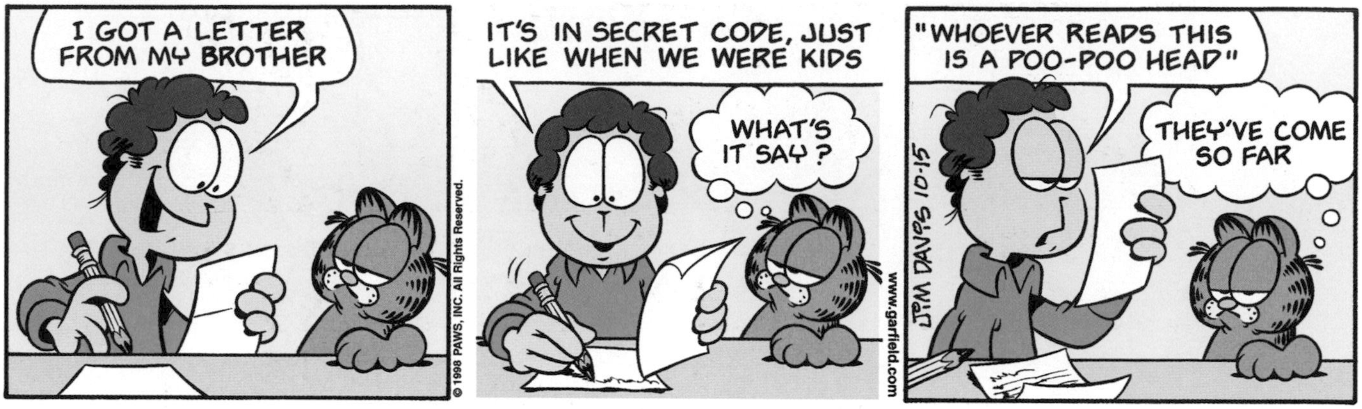
I GOT A LETTER FROM MY BROTHER
IT'S IN SECRET CODE, JUST LIKE WHEN WE WERE KIDS
WHAT'S IT SAY ?
"WHOEVER READS THIS IS A POO-POO HEAD"
THEY'VE COME SO FAR
JIM DAVIS 10-15
© 1998 PAWS, INC. All Rights Reserved.
www.garfield.com

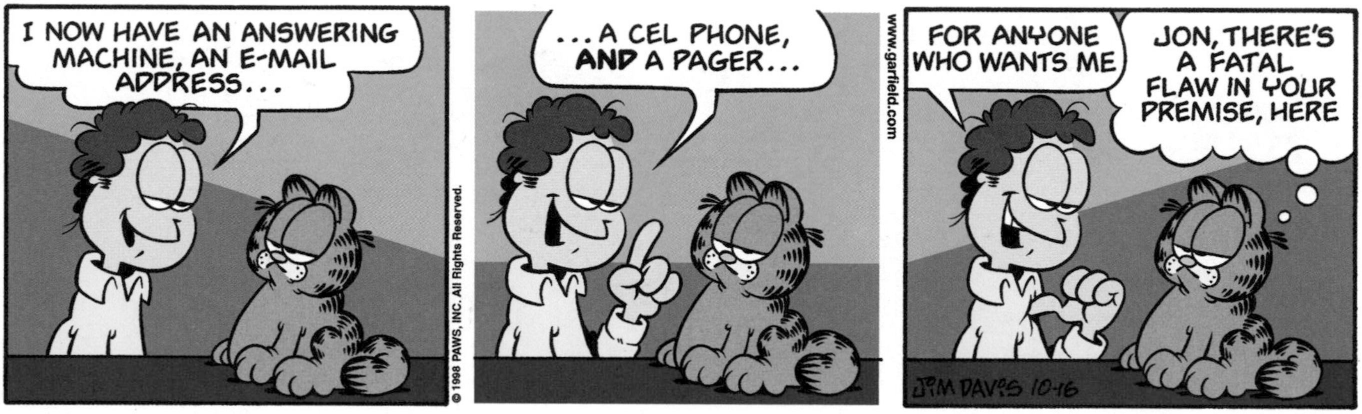
I NOW HAVE AN ANSWERING MACHINE, AN E-MAIL ADDRESS...
...A CEL PHONE, AND A PAGER...
FOR ANYONE WHO WANTS ME
JON, THERE'S A FATAL FLAW IN YOUR PREMISE, HERE
JIM DAVIS 10-16
© 1998 PAWS, INC. All Rights Reserved.
www.garfield.com

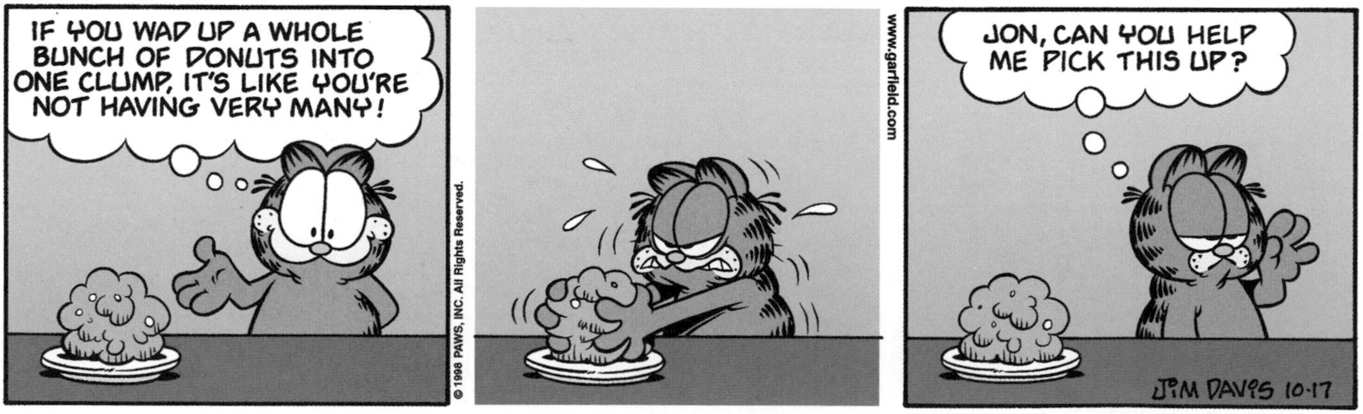
IF YOU WAD UP A WHOLE BUNCH OF DONUTS INTO ONE CLUMP, IT'S LIKE YOU'RE NOT HAVING VERY MANY!
JON, CAN YOU HELP ME PICK THIS UP?
JIM DAVIS 10-17
© 1998 PAWS, INC. All Rights Reserved.
www.garfield.com

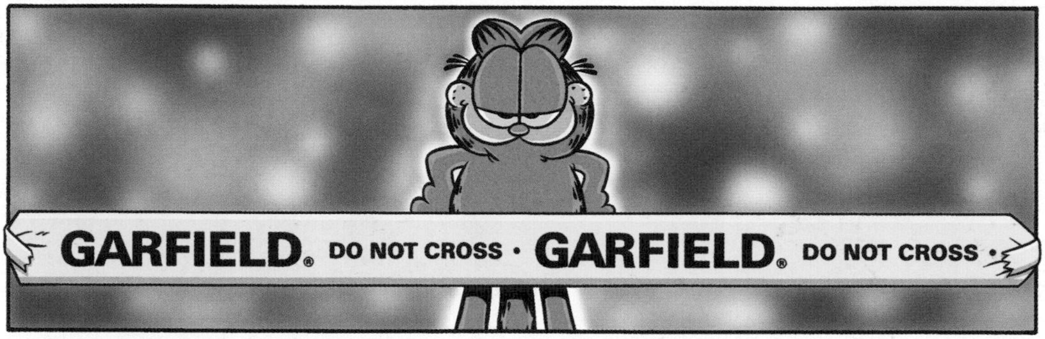
GARFIELD. DO NOT CROSS · GARFIELD. DO NOT CROSS ·

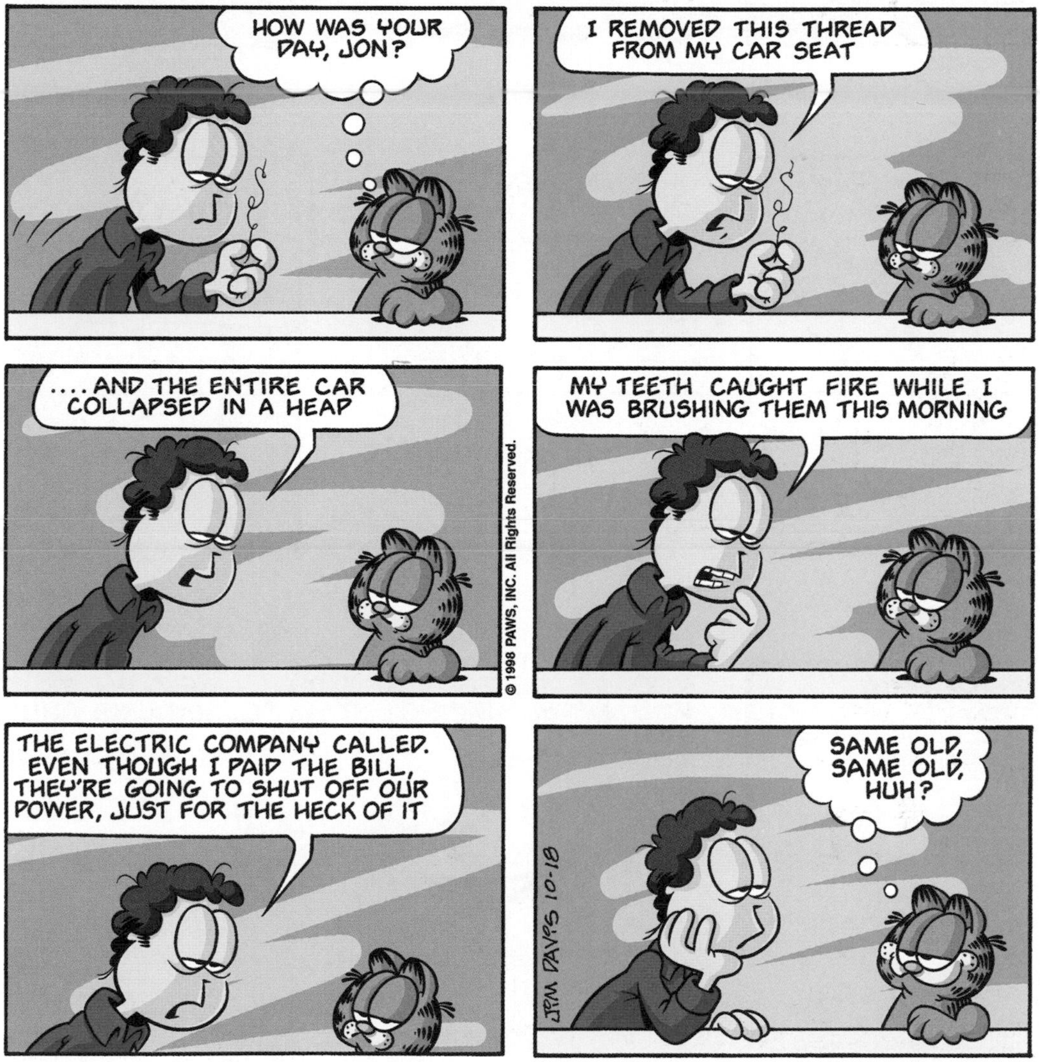
HOW WAS YOUR DAY, JON?
I REMOVED THIS THREAD FROM MY CAR SEAT
....AND THE ENTIRE CAR COLLAPSED IN A HEAP
MY TEETH CAUGHT FIRE WHILE I WAS BRUSHING THEM THIS MORNING
THE ELECTRIC COMPANY CALLED. EVEN THOUGH I PAID THE BILL, THEY'RE GOING TO SHUT OFF OUR POWER, JUST FOR THE HECK OF IT
SAME OLD, SAME OLD, HUH?
JPM DAVPS 10-18

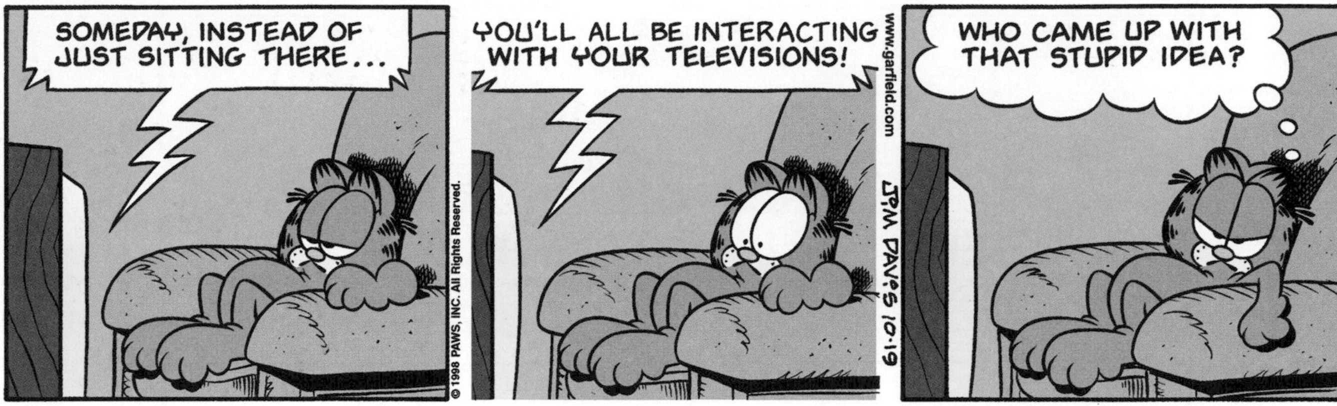
SOMEDAY, INSTEAD OF JUST SITTING THERE...
YOU'LL ALL BE INTERACTING WITH YOUR TELEVISIONS!
WHO CAME UP WITH THAT STUPID IDEA?
© 1998 PAWS, INC. All Rights Reserved.
www.garfield.com
JIM DAVIS 10-19

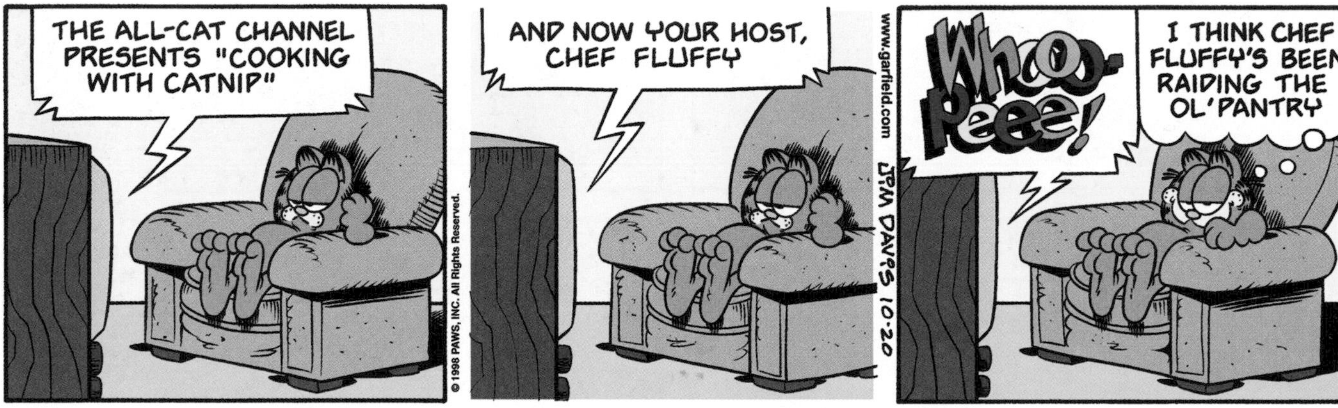
THE ALL-CAT CHANNEL PRESENTS "COOKING WITH CATNIP"
AND NOW YOUR HOST, CHEF FLUFFY
Whoo-Peee!
I THINK CHEF FLUFFY'S BEEN RAIDING THE OL' PANTRY
© 1998 PAWS, INC. All Rights Reserved.
www.garfield.com
JIM DAVIS 10-20

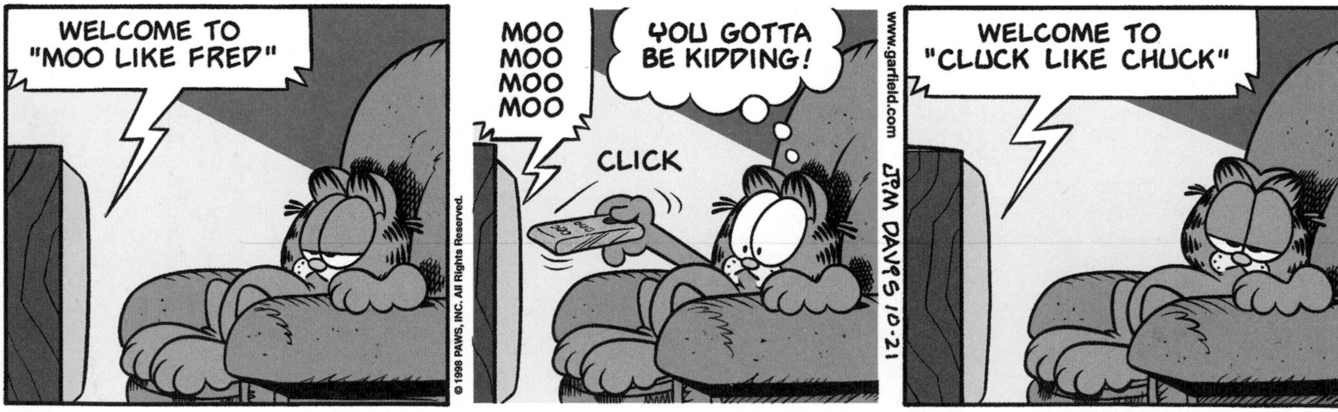
WELCOME TO "MOO LIKE FRED"
MOO MOO MOO MOO
YOU GOTTA BE KIDDING!
CLICK
WELCOME TO "CLUCK LIKE CHUCK"
© 1998 PAWS, INC. All Rights Reserved.
www.garfield.com
JIM DAVIS 10-21

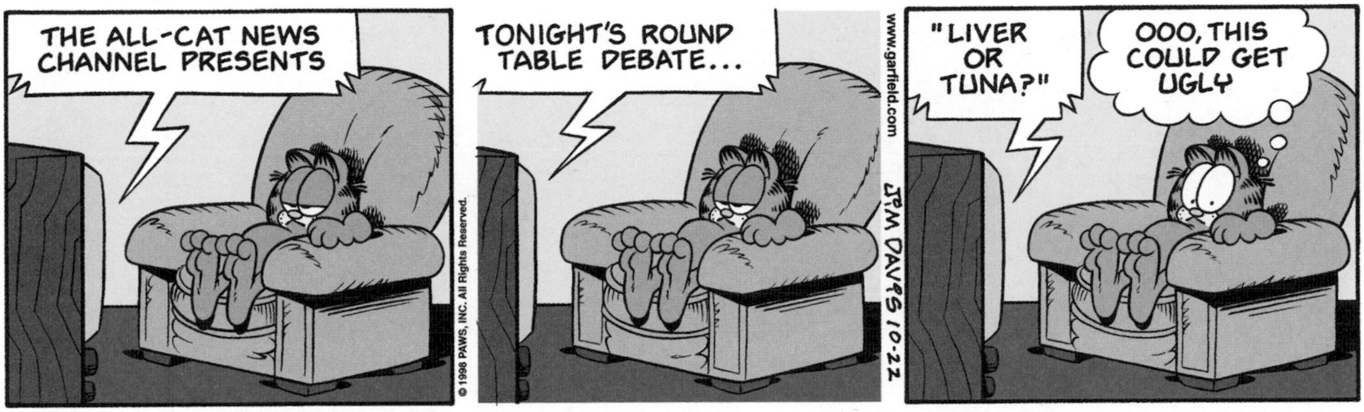
THE ALL-CAT NEWS CHANNEL PRESENTS
© 1998 PAWS, INC. All Rights Reserved.
TONIGHT'S ROUND TABLE DEBATE...
JIM DAVIS 10-22
www.garfield.com
"LIVER OR TUNA?"
OOO, THIS COULD GET UGLY

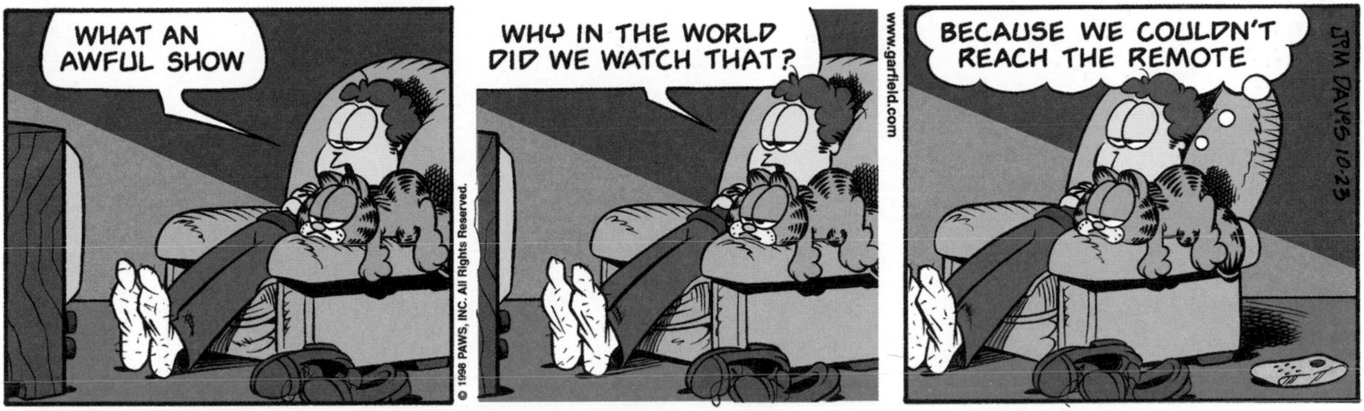
WHAT AN AWFUL SHOW
© 1998 PAWS, INC. All Rights Reserved.
WHY IN THE WORLD DID WE WATCH THAT?
www.garfield.com
BECAUSE WE COULDN'T REACH THE REMOTE
JIM DAVIS 10-23

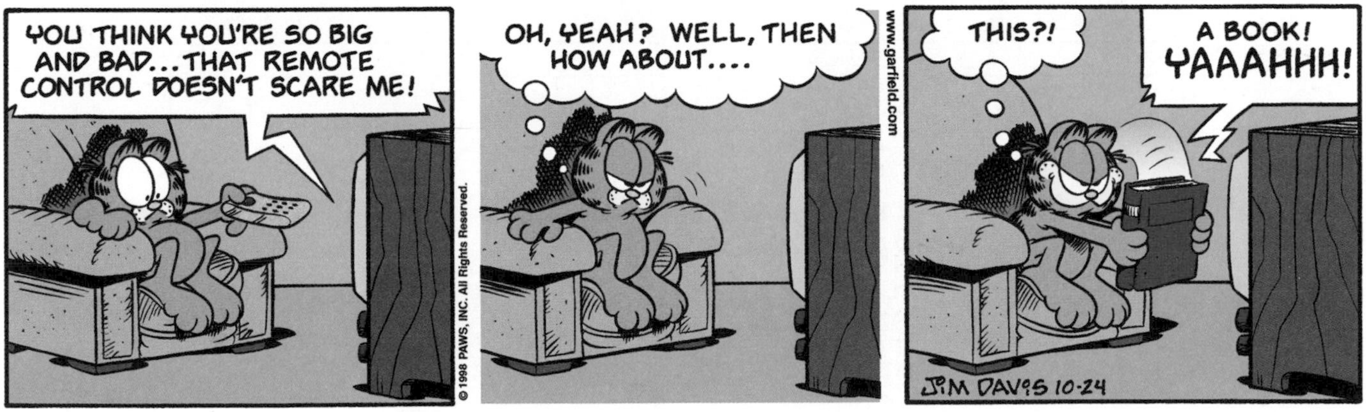
YOU THINK YOU'RE SO BIG AND BAD...THAT REMOTE CONTROL DOESN'T SCARE ME!
© 1998 PAWS, INC. All Rights Reserved.
OH, YEAH? WELL, THEN HOW ABOUT....
www.garfield.com
THIS?!
A BOOK! YAAAHHH!
JIM DAVIS 10-24

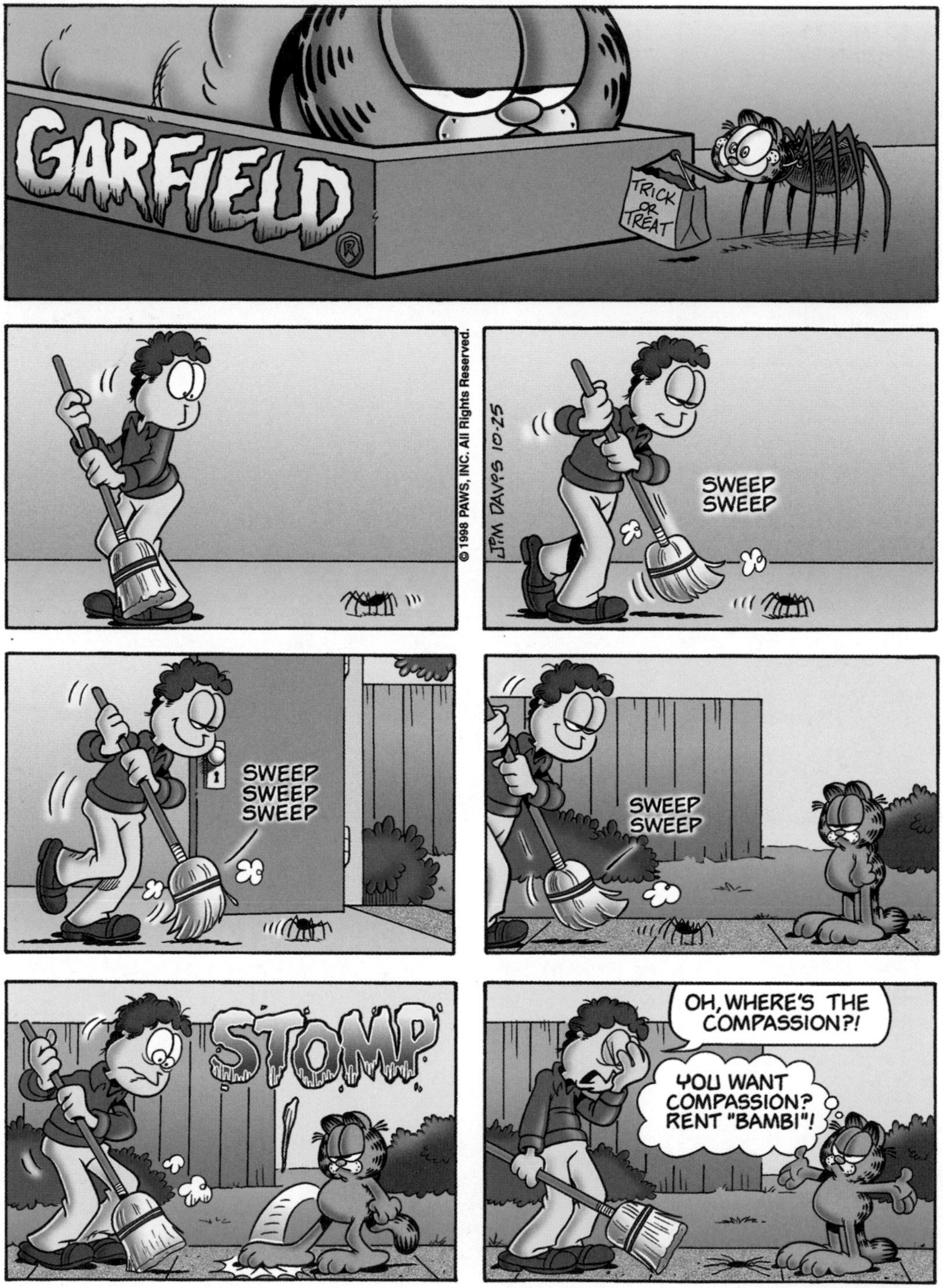
GARFIELD
TRICK OR TREAT
© 1998 PAWS, INC. All Rights Reserved.
JIM DAVIS 10-25
SWEEP SWEEP
SWEEP SWEEP SWEEP
SWEEP SWEEP
STOMP
OH, WHERE'S THE COMPASSION?!
YOU WANT COMPASSION? RENT "BAMBI"!

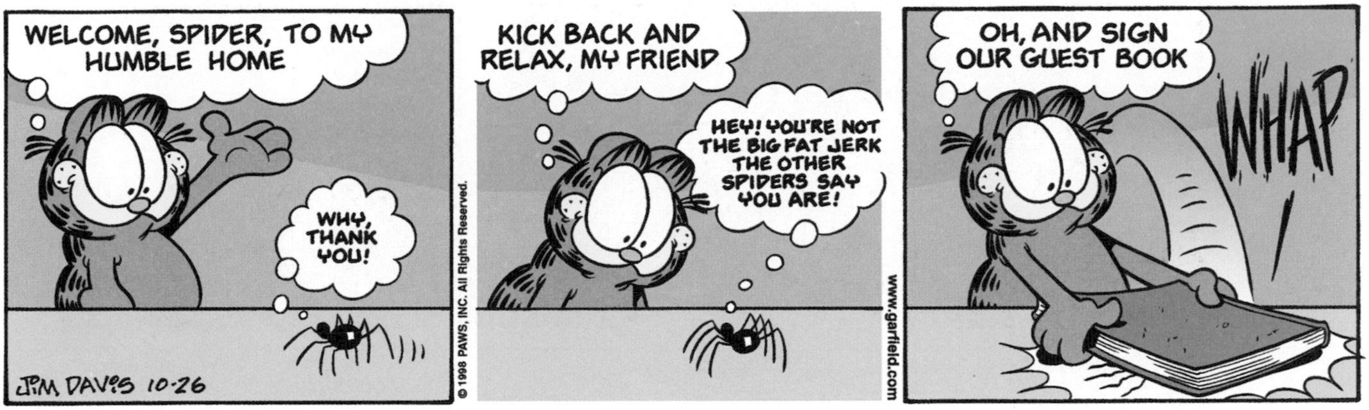
WELCOME, SPIDER, TO MY HUMBLE HOME
WHY, THANK YOU!
JIM DAVIS 10-26
© 1998 PAWS, INC. All Rights Reserved.
KICK BACK AND RELAX, MY FRIEND
HEY! YOU'RE NOT THE BIG FAT JERK THE OTHER SPIDERS SAY YOU ARE!
www.garfield.com
OH, AND SIGN OUR GUEST BOOK
WHAP

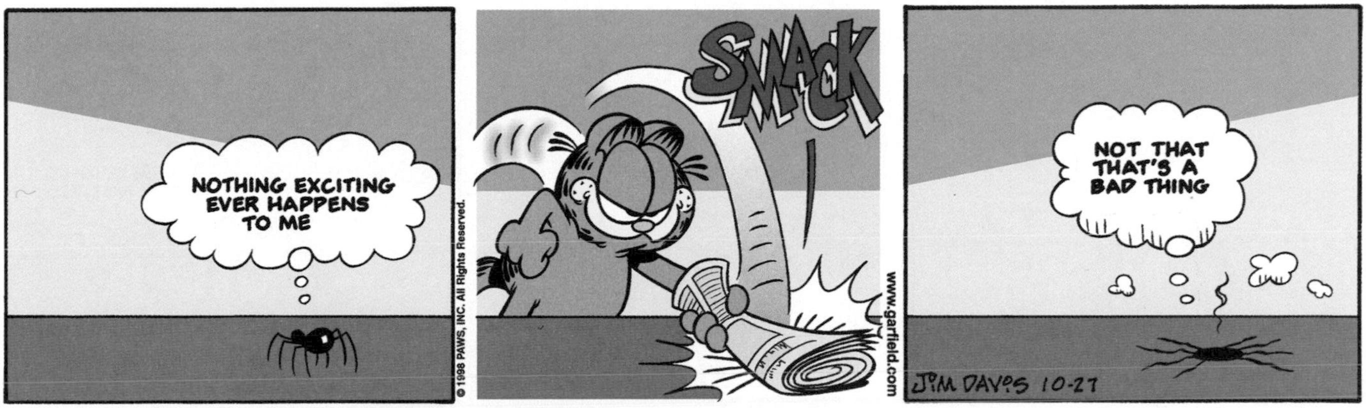
NOTHING EXCITING EVER HAPPENS TO ME
© 1998 PAWS, INC. All Rights Reserved.
SMACK
www.garfield.com
NOT THAT THAT'S A BAD THING
JIM DAVIS 10-27

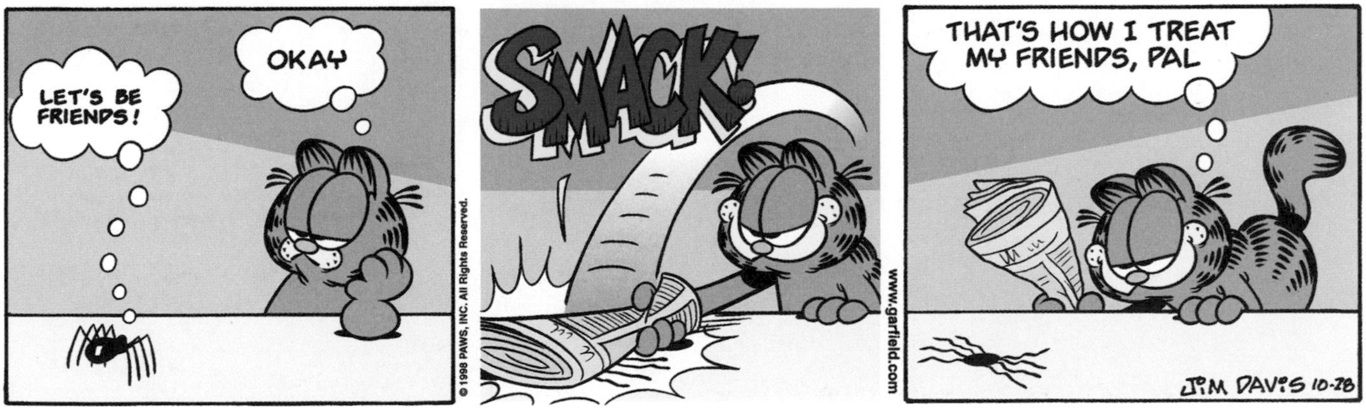
LET'S BE FRIENDS!
OKAY
© 1998 PAWS, INC. All Rights Reserved.
SMACK!
www.garfield.com
THAT'S HOW I TREAT MY FRIENDS, PAL
JIM DAVIS 10-28

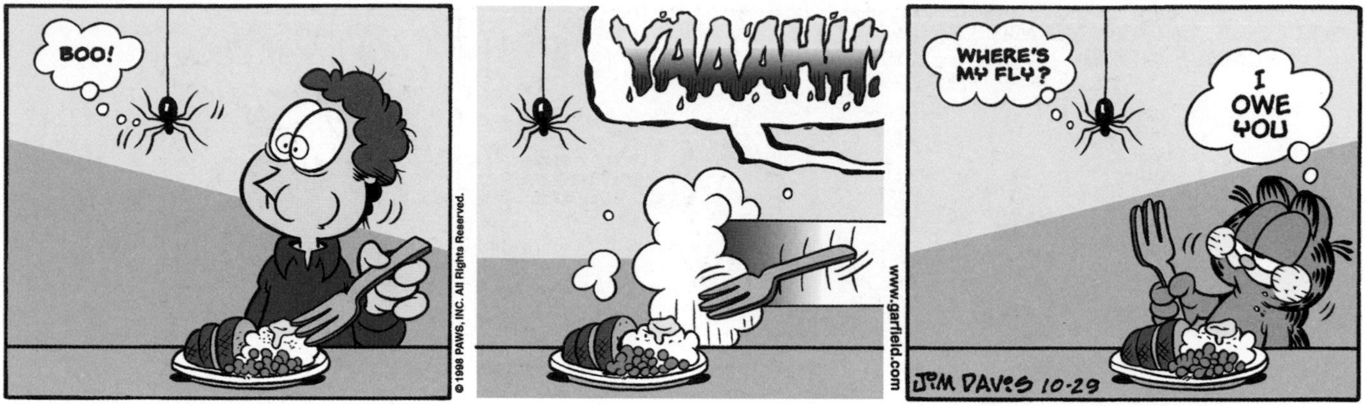
BOO!
YAAAHH!
WHERE'S MY FLY?
I OWE YOU
© 1998 PAWS, INC. All Rights Reserved.
www.garfield.com
JIM DAVIS 10-29

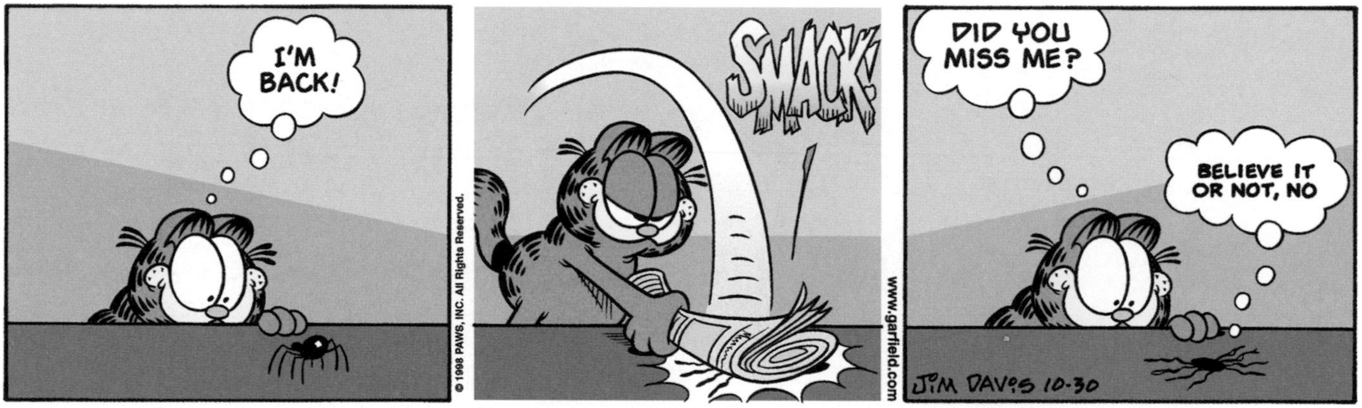
I'M BACK!
SMACK!
DID YOU MISS ME?
BELIEVE IT OR NOT, NO
© 1998 PAWS, INC. All Rights Reserved.
www.garfield.com
JIM DAVIS 10-30

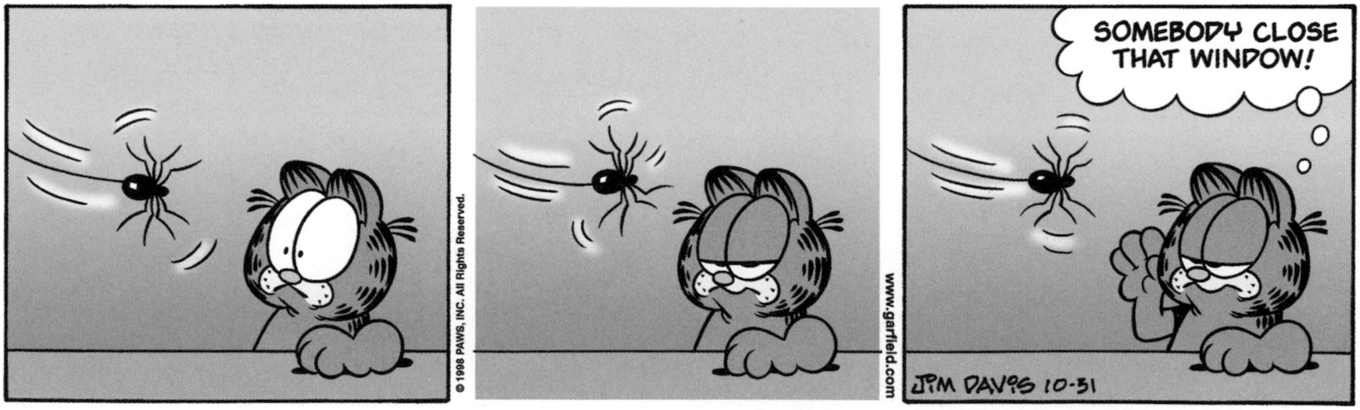
SOMEBODY CLOSE THAT WINDOW!
© 1998 PAWS, INC. All Rights Reserved.
www.garfield.com
JIM DAVIS 10-31

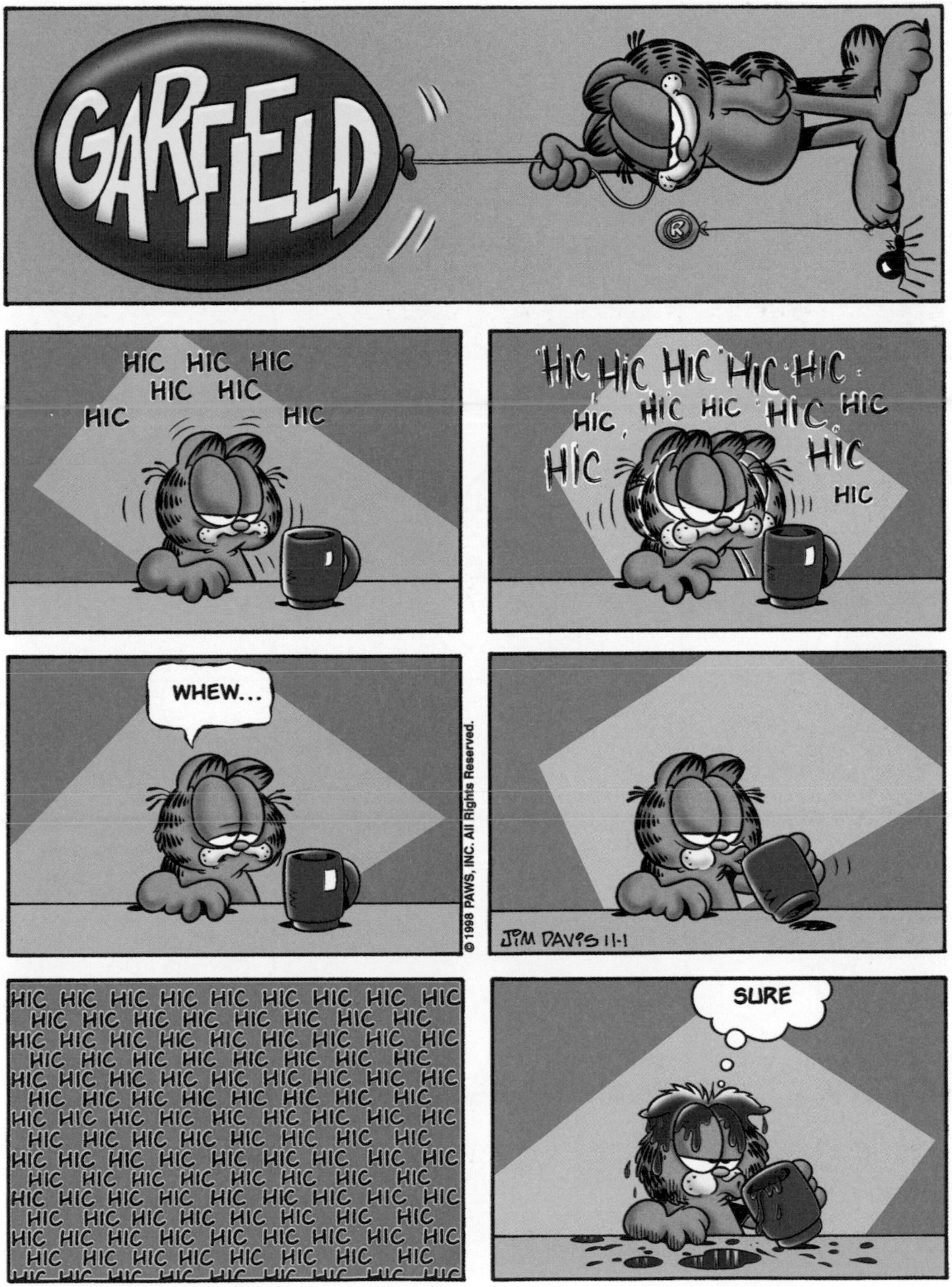
GARFIELD
HIC HIC HIC
HIC HIC
HIC HIC
HIC HIC HIC HIC HIC
HIC HIC HIC HIC HIC
HIC HIC
HIC
WHEW...
© 1998 PAWS, INC. All Rights Reserved.
JIM DAVIS 11-1
HIC HIC HIC HIC HIC HIC HIC HIC HIC
HIC HIC HIC HIC HIC HIC HIC HIC
HIC HIC HIC HIC HIC HIC HIC HIC HIC
HIC HIC HIC HIC HIC HIC HIC HIC
HIC HIC HIC HIC HIC HIC HIC HIC HIC
HIC HIC HIC HIC HIC HIC HIC HIC
HIC HIC HIC HIC HIC HIC HIC HIC HIC
HIC HIC HIC HIC HIC HIC HIC HIC
HIC HIC HIC HIC HIC HIC HIC HIC HIC
HIC HIC HIC HIC HIC HIC HIC HIC
HIC HIC HIC HIC HIC HIC HIC HIC HIC
HIC HIC HIC HIC HIC HIC HIC HIC
HIC HIC HIC HIC HIC HIC HIC HIC HIC
HIC HIC HIC HIC HIC HIC HIC HIC
SURE

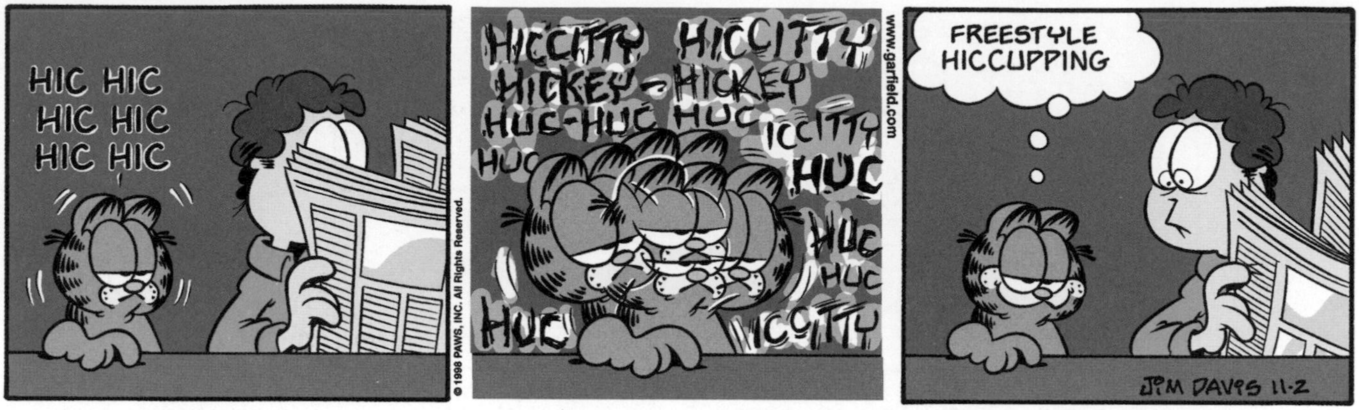
HIC HIC
HIC HIC
HIC HIC
© 1998 PAWS, INC. All Rights Reserved.
HICCITTY HICCITTY
HICKEY-HICKEY
HUC-HUC HUC
ICCITTY
HUC
HUC
HUC
HUC
HUC
ICCITTY
www.garfield.com
FREESTYLE
HICCUPPING
JIM DAVIS 11-2

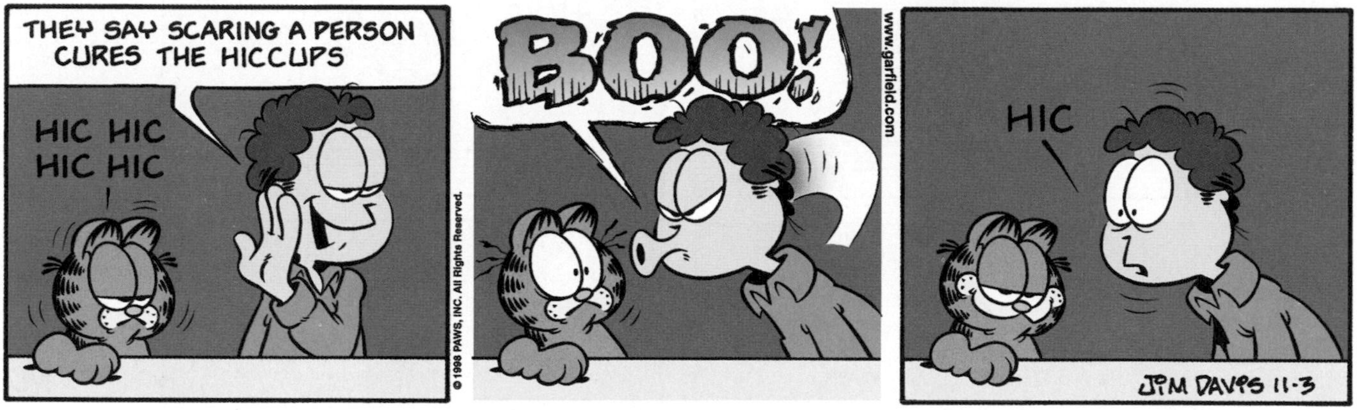
THEY SAY SCARING A PERSON CURES THE HICCUPS
HIC HIC
HIC HIC
© 1998 PAWS, INC. All Rights Reserved.
BOO!
www.garfield.com
HIC
JIM DAVIS 11-3

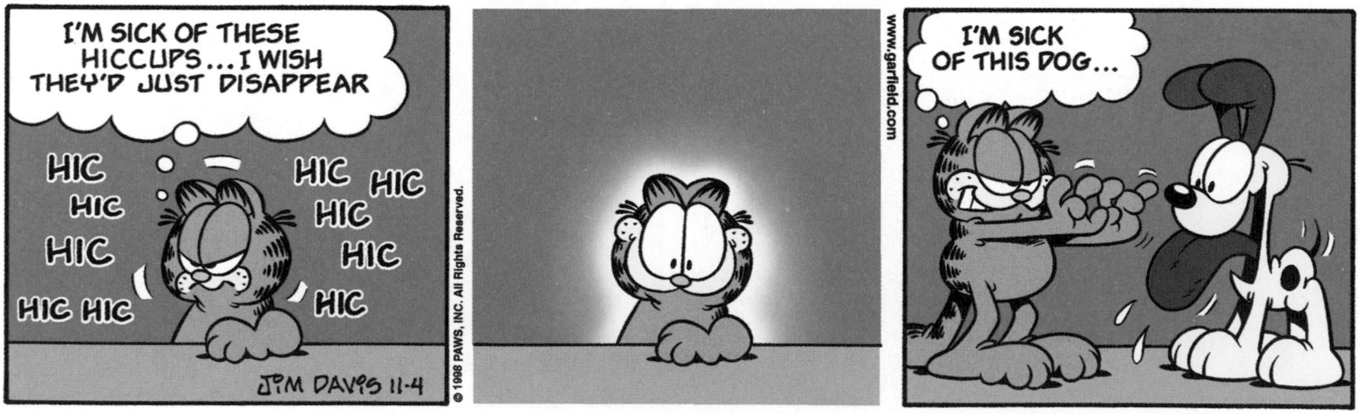
I'M SICK OF THESE HICCUPS... I WISH THEY'D JUST DISAPPEAR
HIC
HIC
HIC
HIC HIC
HIC HIC
HIC
HIC
HIC
JIM DAVIS 11-4
© 1998 PAWS, INC. All Rights Reserved.
www.garfield.com
I'M SICK
OF THIS DOG...

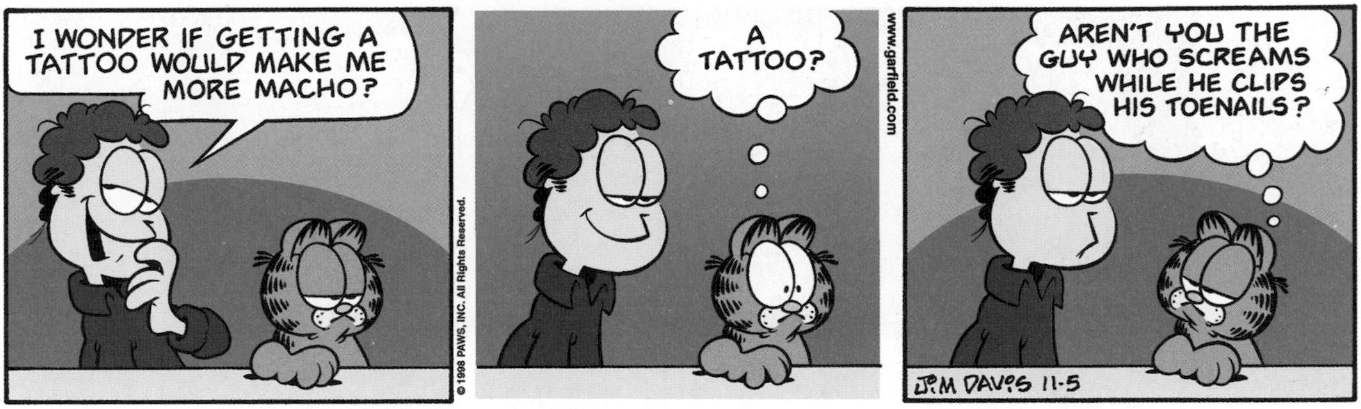
I WONDER IF GETTING A TATTOO WOULD MAKE ME MORE MACHO?
© 1998 PAWS, INC. All Rights Reserved.
A TATTOO?
www.garfield.com
AREN'T YOU THE GUY WHO SCREAMS WHILE HE CLIPS HIS TOENAILS?
JIM DAVIS 11-5

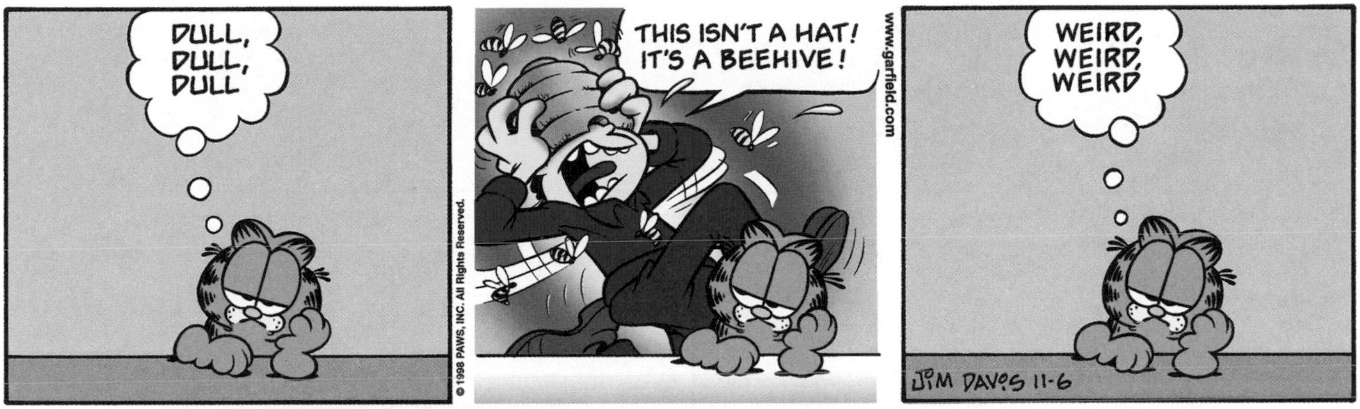
DULL, DULL, DULL
© 1998 PAWS, INC. All Rights Reserved.
THIS ISN'T A HAT! IT'S A BEEHIVE!
www.garfield.com
WEIRD, WEIRD, WEIRD
JIM DAVIS 11-6

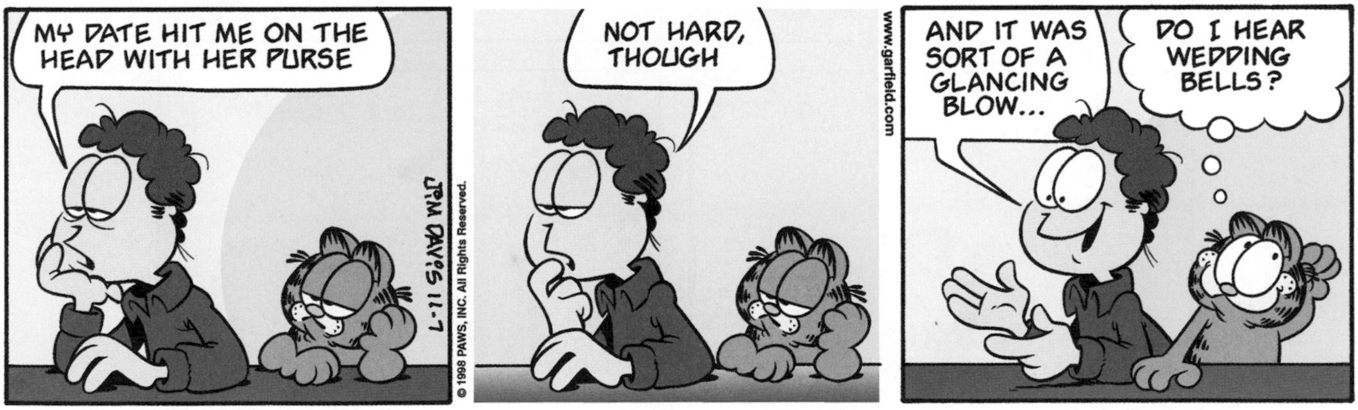
MY DATE HIT ME ON THE HEAD WITH HER PURSE
JIM DAVIS 11-7
© 1998 PAWS, INC. All Rights Reserved.
NOT HARD, THOUGH
www.garfield.com
AND IT WAS SORT OF A GLANCING BLOW...
DO I HEAR WEDDING BELLS?

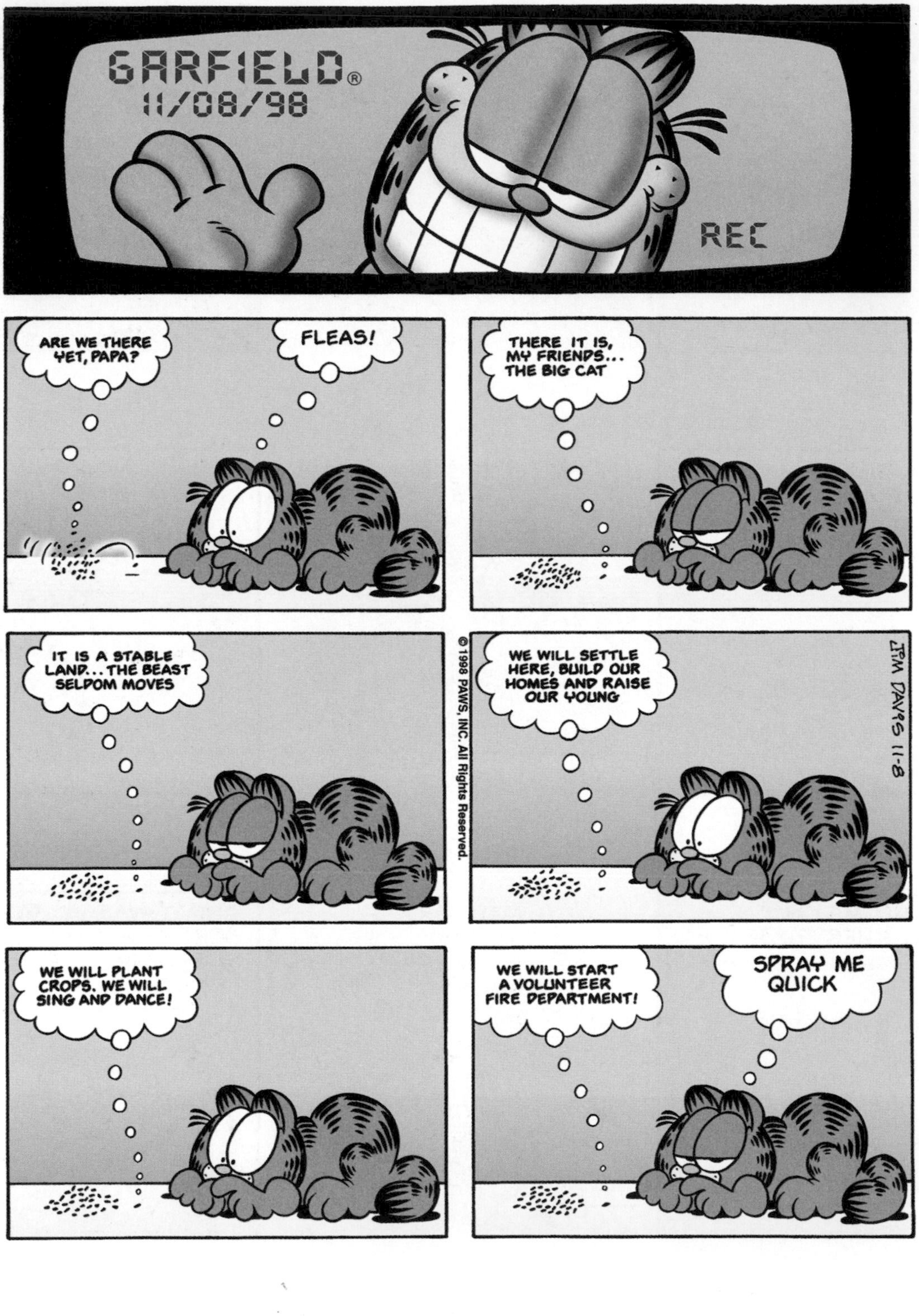
GARFIELD®
11/08/98
REC
ARE WE THERE YET, PAPA?
FLEAS!
THERE IT IS, MY FRIENDS... THE BIG CAT
IT IS A STABLE LAND... THE BEAST SELDOM MOVES
© 1998 PAWS, INC. All Rights Reserved.
WE WILL SETTLE HERE, BUILD OUR HOMES AND RAISE OUR YOUNG
JIM DAVIS 11-8
WE WILL PLANT CROPS. WE WILL SING AND DANCE!
WE WILL START A VOLUNTEER FIRE DEPARTMENT!
SPRAY ME QUICK

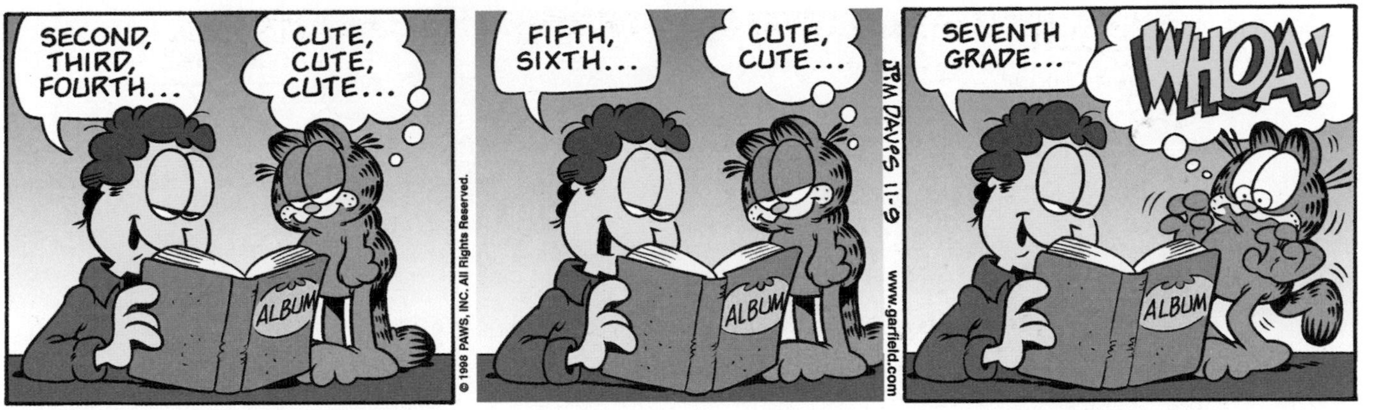
SECOND, THIRD, FOURTH...
CUTE, CUTE, CUTE...
FIFTH, SIXTH...
CUTE, CUTE...
SEVENTH GRADE...
WHOA!
ALBUM
© 1998 PAWS, INC. All Rights Reserved.
JIM DAVIS 11-9
www.garfield.com

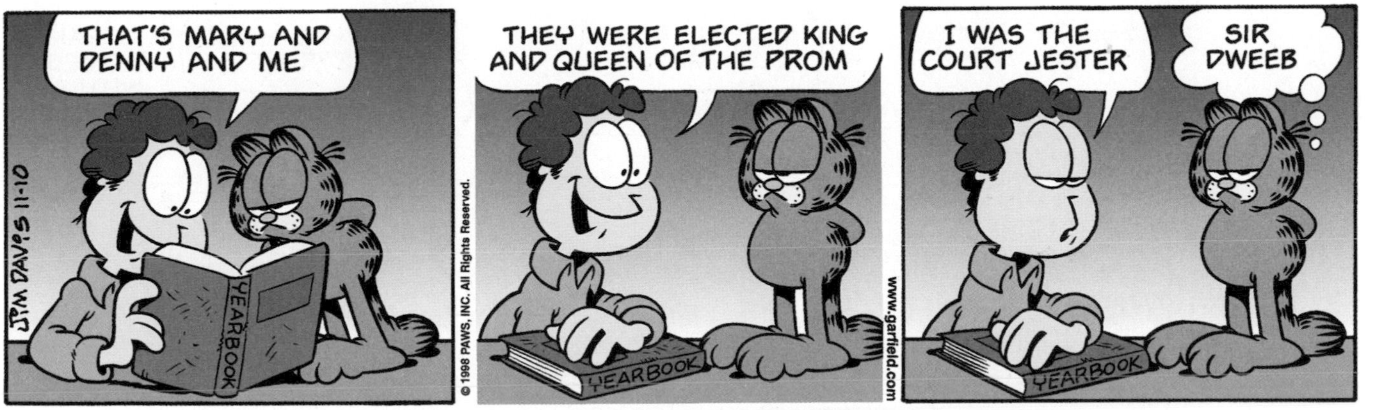
THAT'S MARY AND DENNY AND ME
THEY WERE ELECTED KING AND QUEEN OF THE PROM
I WAS THE COURT JESTER
SIR DWEEB
YEARBOOK
JIM DAVIS 11-10
© 1998 PAWS, INC. All Rights Reserved.
www.garfield.com

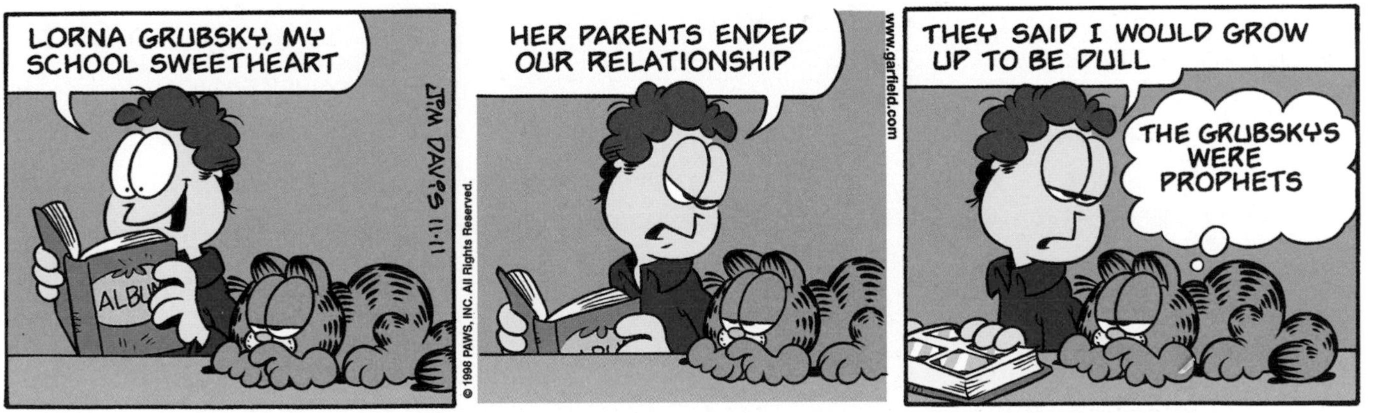
LORNA GRUBSKY, MY SCHOOL SWEETHEART
HER PARENTS ENDED OUR RELATIONSHIP
THEY SAID I WOULD GROW UP TO BE DULL
THE GRUBSKYS WERE PROPHETS
JIM DAVIS 11-11
© 1998 PAWS, INC. All Rights Reserved.
www.garfield.com

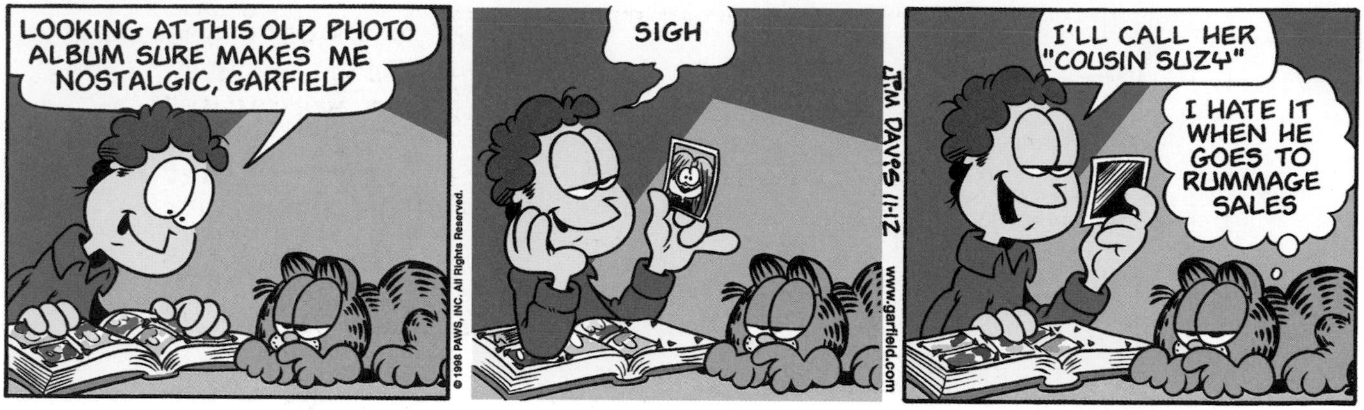
LOOKING AT THIS OLD PHOTO ALBUM SURE MAKES ME NOSTALGIC, GARFIELD
© 1998 PAWS, INC. All Rights Reserved.
SIGH
JIM DAVIS 11-12
www.garfield.com
I'LL CALL HER "COUSIN SUZY"
I HATE IT WHEN HE GOES TO RUMMAGE SALES

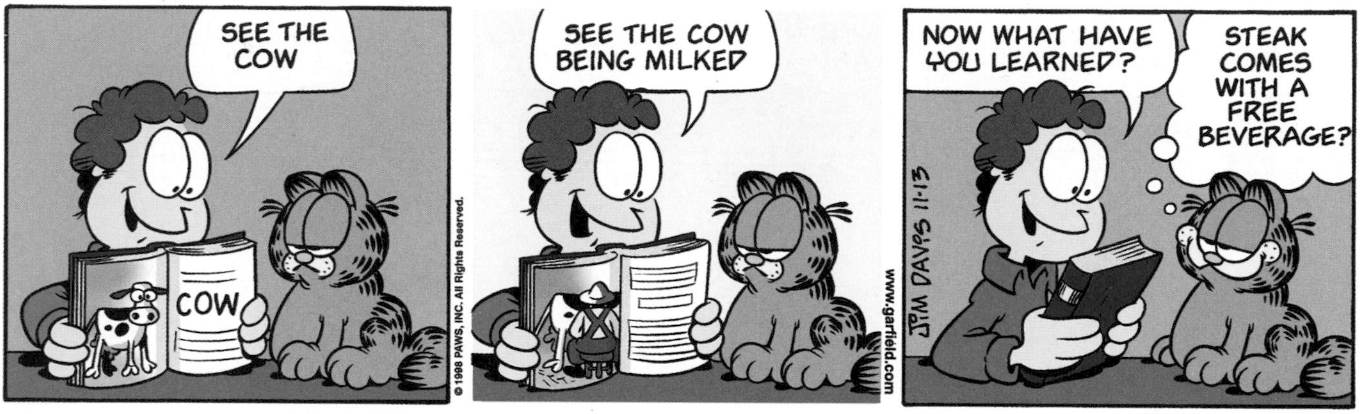
SEE THE COW
COW
© 1998 PAWS, INC. All Rights Reserved.
SEE THE COW BEING MILKED
www.garfield.com
NOW WHAT HAVE YOU LEARNED?
STEAK COMES WITH A FREE BEVERAGE?
JIM DAVIS 11-13

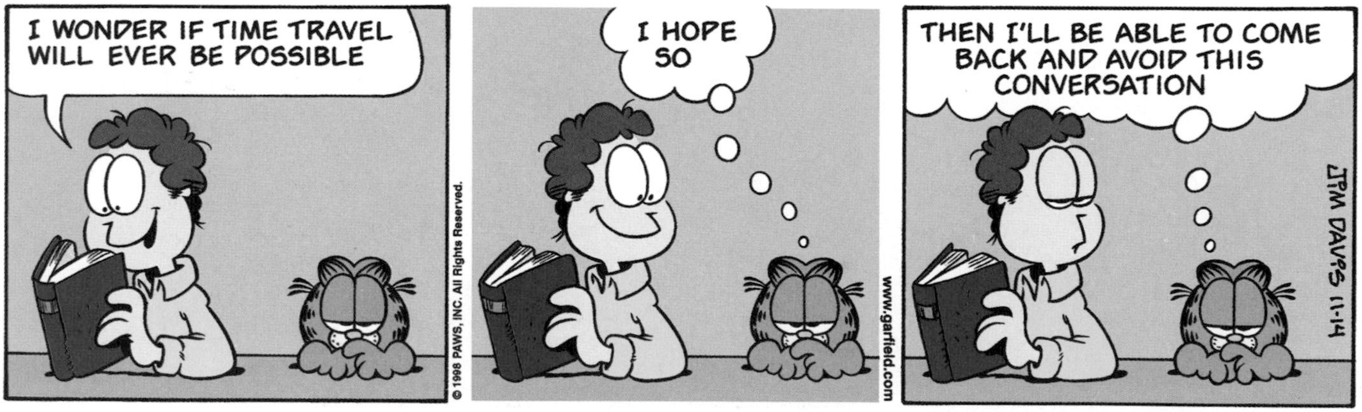
I WONDER IF TIME TRAVEL WILL EVER BE POSSIBLE
© 1998 PAWS, INC. All Rights Reserved.
I HOPE SO
www.garfield.com
THEN I'LL BE ABLE TO COME BACK AND AVOID THIS CONVERSATION
JIM DAVIS 11-14

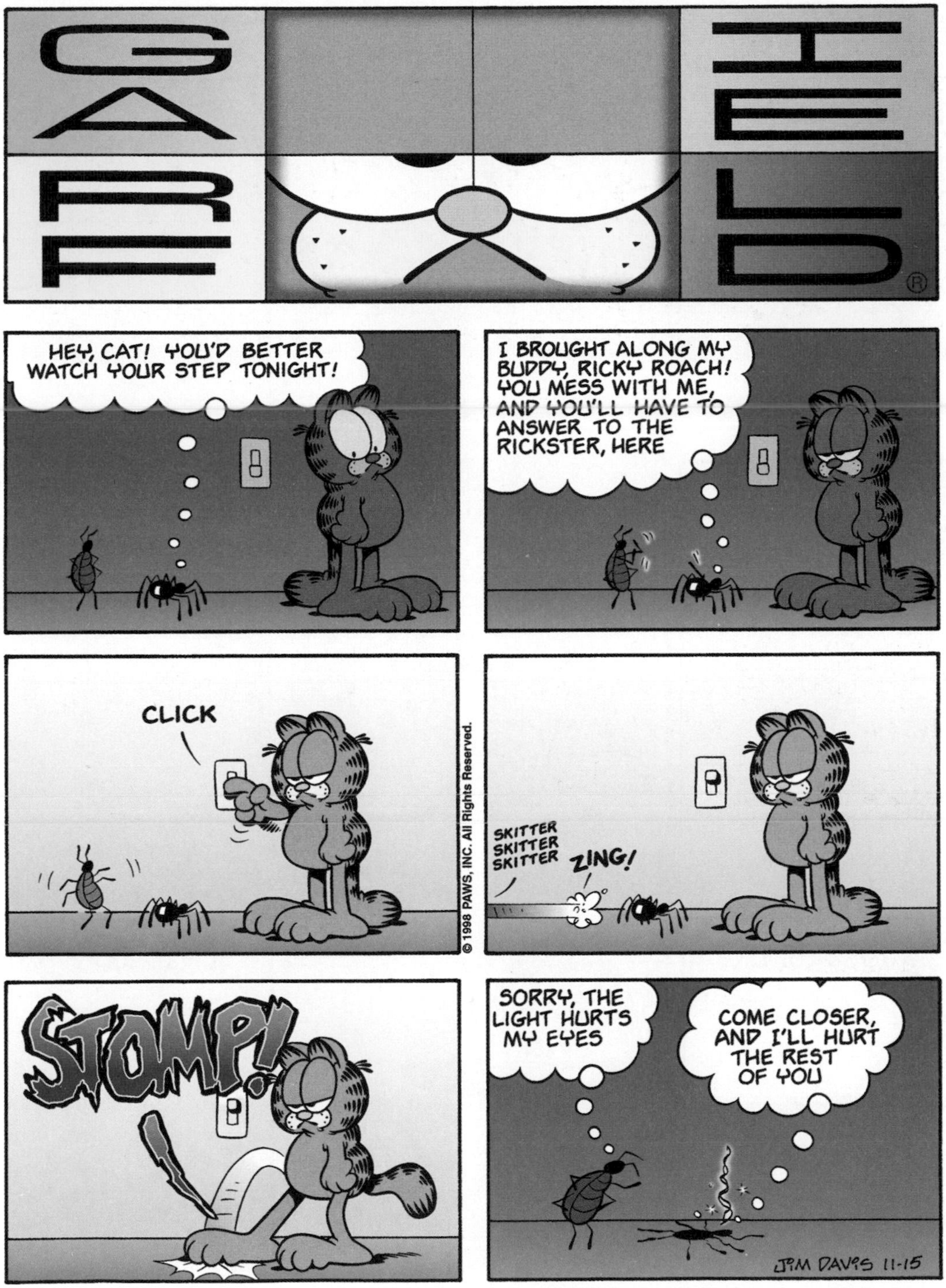
GARFIELD
HEY, CAT! YOU'D BETTER WATCH YOUR STEP TONIGHT!
I BROUGHT ALONG MY BUDDY, RICKY ROACH! YOU MESS WITH ME, AND YOU'LL HAVE TO ANSWER TO THE RICKSTER, HERE
CLICK
© 1998 PAWS, INC. All Rights Reserved.
SKITTER SKITTER SKITTER
ZING!
STOMP!
SORRY, THE LIGHT HURTS MY EYES
COME CLOSER, AND I'LL HURT THE REST OF YOU
JIM DAVIS 11-15

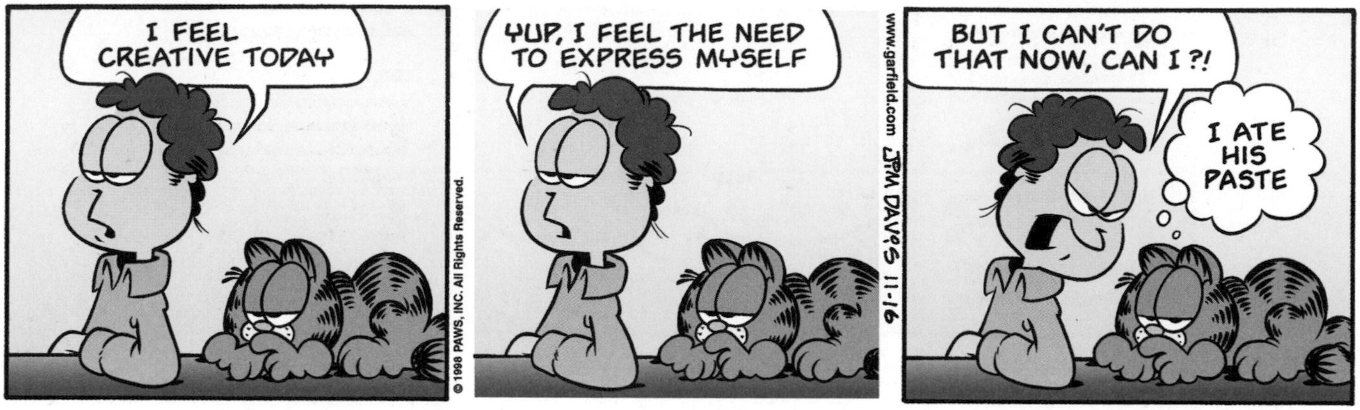
I FEEL CREATIVE TODAY
YUP, I FEEL THE NEED TO EXPRESS MYSELF
BUT I CAN'T DO THAT NOW, CAN I ?!
I ATE HIS PASTE
© 1998 PAWS, INC. All Rights Reserved.
www.garfield.com
JIM DAVIS 11-16

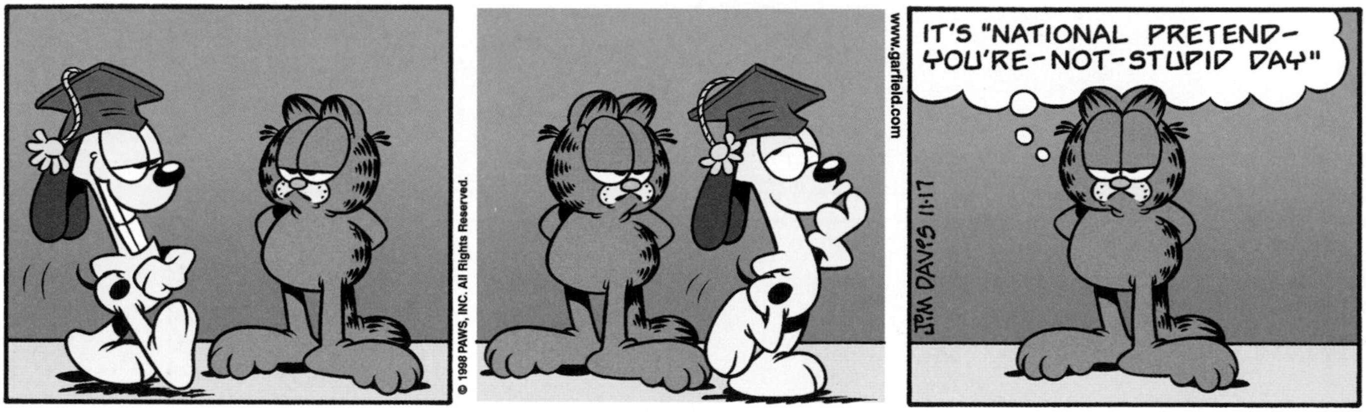
IT'S "NATIONAL PRETEND-YOU'RE-NOT-STUPID DAY"
© 1998 PAWS, INC. All Rights Reserved.
www.garfield.com
JIM DAVIS 11-17

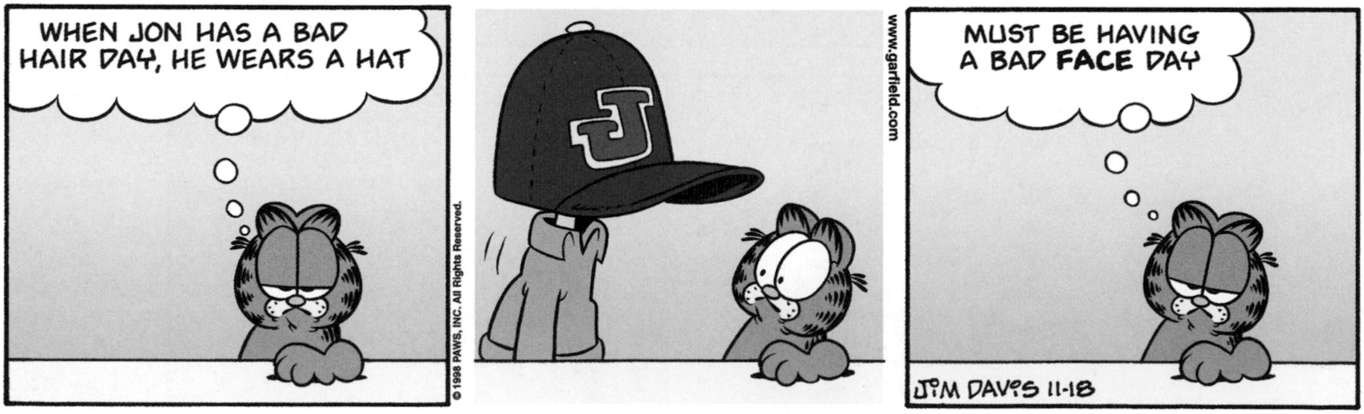
WHEN JON HAS A BAD HAIR DAY, HE WEARS A HAT
J
MUST BE HAVING A BAD FACE DAY
© 1998 PAWS, INC. All Rights Reserved.
www.garfield.com
JIM DAVIS 11-18

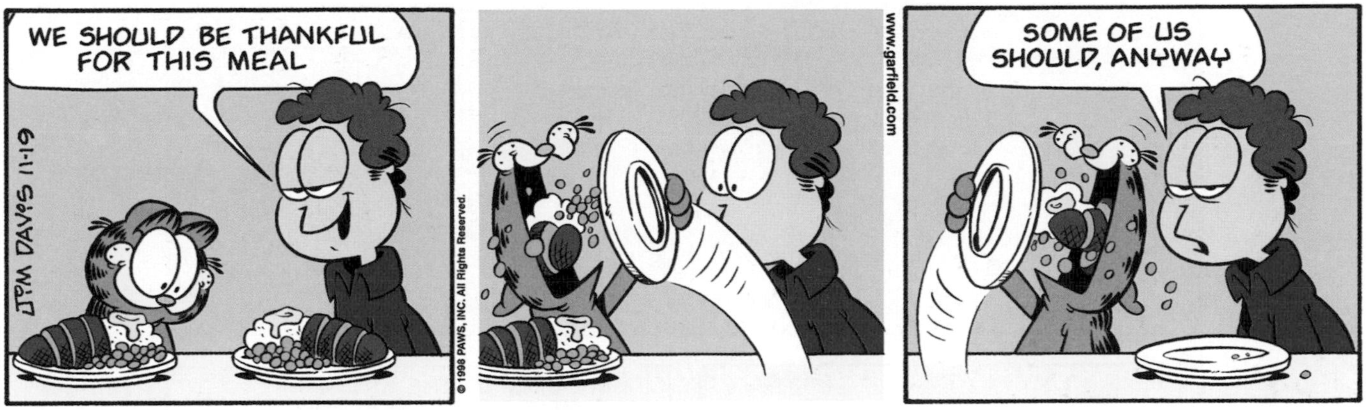
WE SHOULD BE THANKFUL FOR THIS MEAL
JIM DAVIS 11-19
© 1998 PAWS, INC. All Rights Reserved.
www.garfield.com
SOME OF US SHOULD, ANYWAY

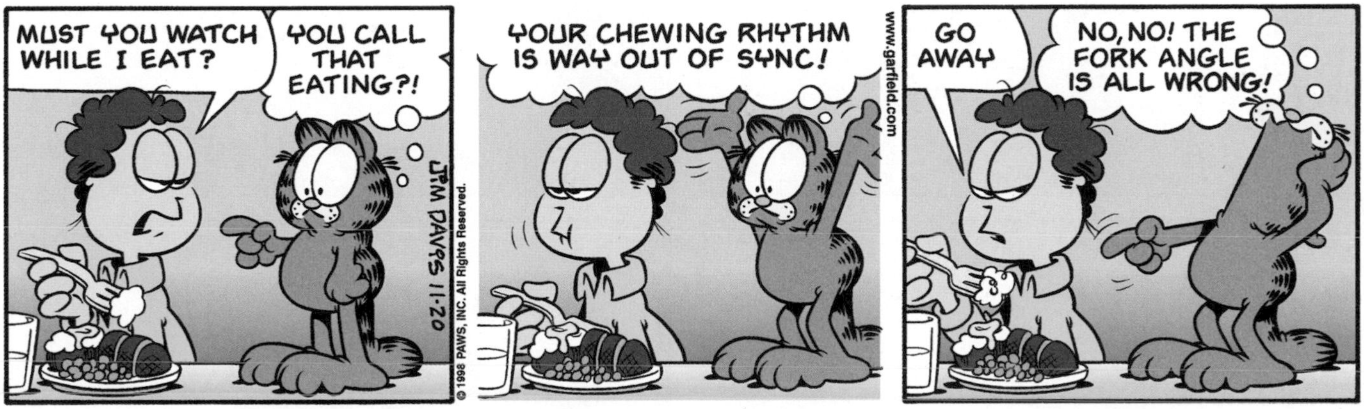
MUST YOU WATCH WHILE I EAT?
YOU CALL THAT EATING?!
JIM DAVIS 11-20
© 1998 PAWS, INC. All Rights Reserved.
YOUR CHEWING RHYTHM IS WAY OUT OF SYNC!
www.garfield.com
GO AWAY
NO, NO! THE FORK ANGLE IS ALL WRONG!

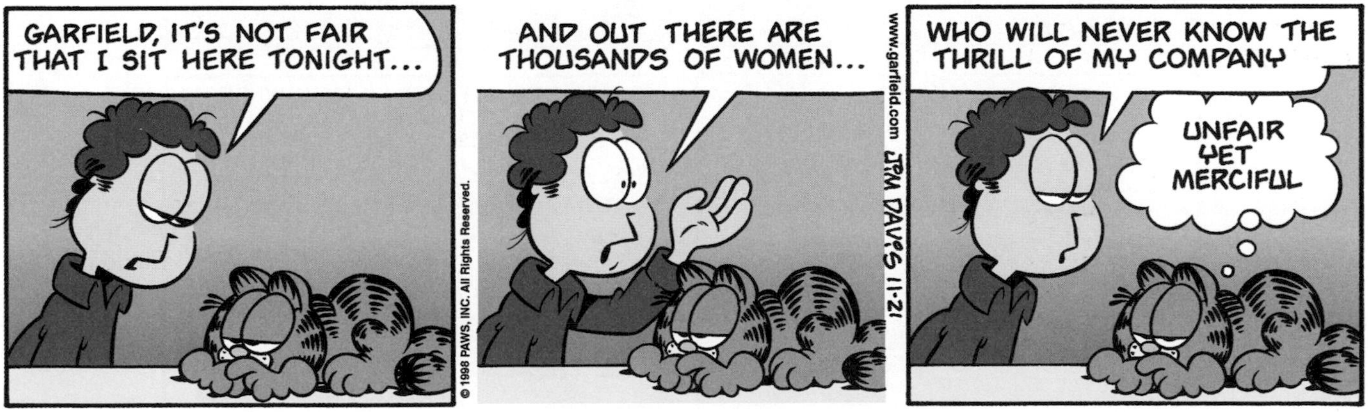
GARFIELD, IT'S NOT FAIR THAT I SIT HERE TONIGHT...
© 1998 PAWS, INC. All Rights Reserved.
AND OUT THERE ARE THOUSANDS OF WOMEN...
www.garfield.com
JIM DAVIS 11-21
WHO WILL NEVER KNOW THE THRILL OF MY COMPANY
UNFAIR YET MERCIFUL

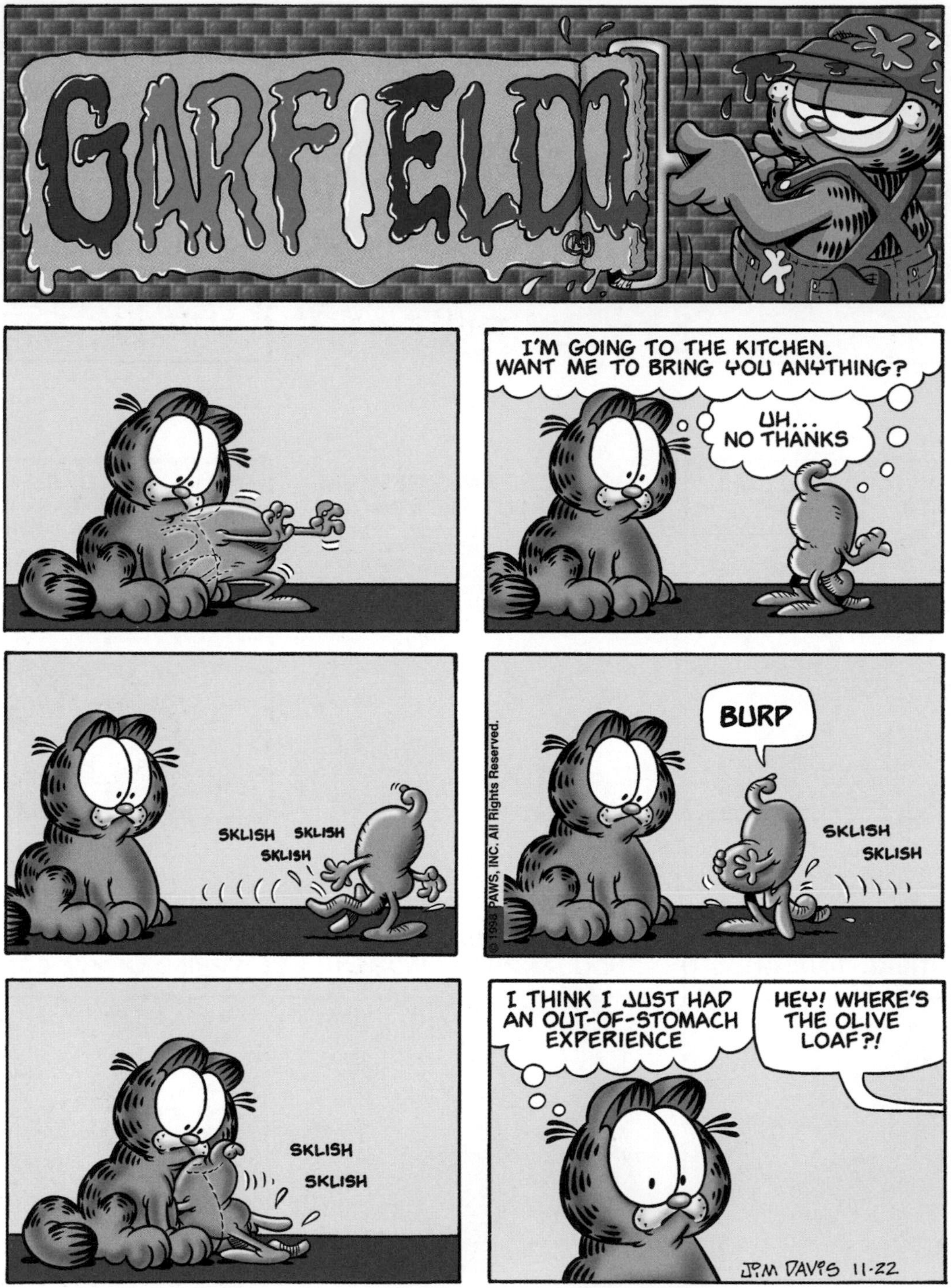
GARFIELD
I'M GOING TO THE KITCHEN. WANT ME TO BRING YOU ANYTHING?
UH... NO THANKS
SKLISH SKLISH
SKLISH
© 1998 PAWS, INC. All Rights Reserved.
BURP
SKLISH
SKLISH
SKLISH
SKLISH
I THINK I JUST HAD AN OUT-OF-STOMACH EXPERIENCE
HEY! WHERE'S THE OLIVE LOAF?!
JIM DAVIS 11-22

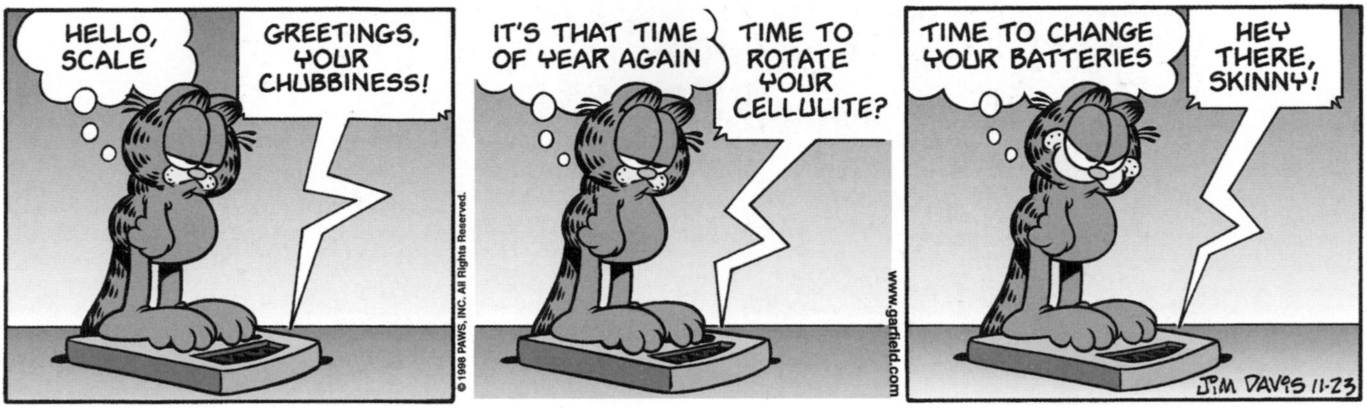
HELLO, SCALE
GREETINGS, YOUR CHUBBINESS!
© 1998 PAWS, INC. All Rights Reserved.
IT'S THAT TIME OF YEAR AGAIN
TIME TO ROTATE YOUR CELLULITE?
www.garfield.com
TIME TO CHANGE YOUR BATTERIES
HEY THERE, SKINNY!
JIM DAVIS 11-23

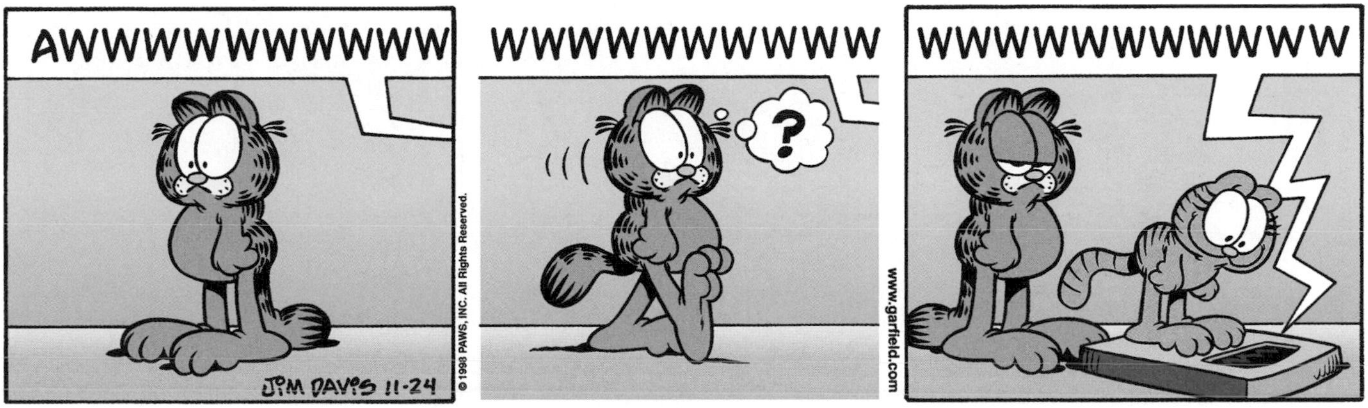
AWWWWWWWWWW
JIM DAVIS 11-24
© 1998 PAWS, INC. All Rights Reserved.
WWWWWWWWWWW
?
www.garfield.com
WWWWWWWWWWWW

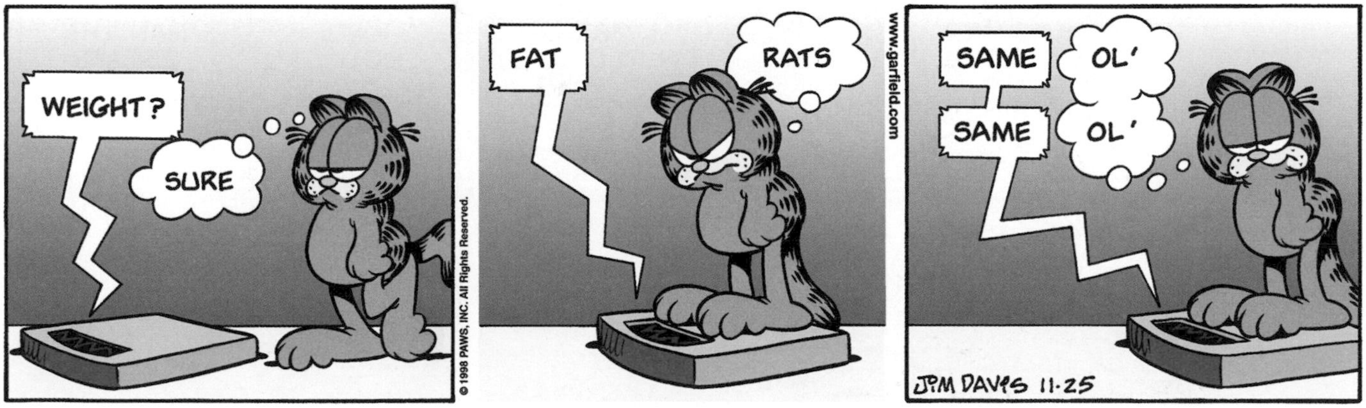
WEIGHT?
SURE
© 1998 PAWS, INC. All Rights Reserved.
FAT
RATS
www.garfield.com
SAME
OL'
SAME
OL'
JIM DAVIS 11-25

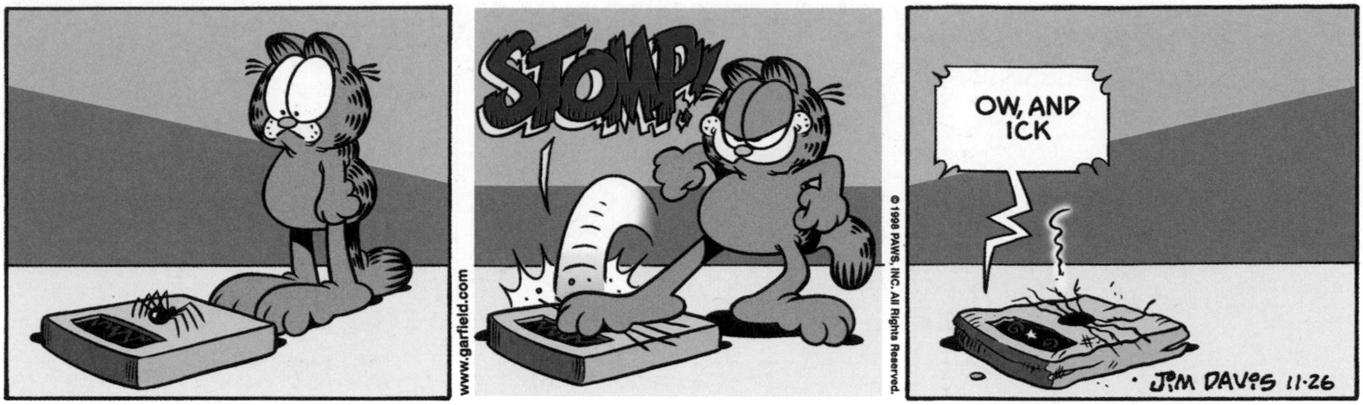
STOMP!
OW, AND ICK
JIM DAVIS 11-26
www.garfield.com
© 1998 PAWS, INC. All Rights Reserved.

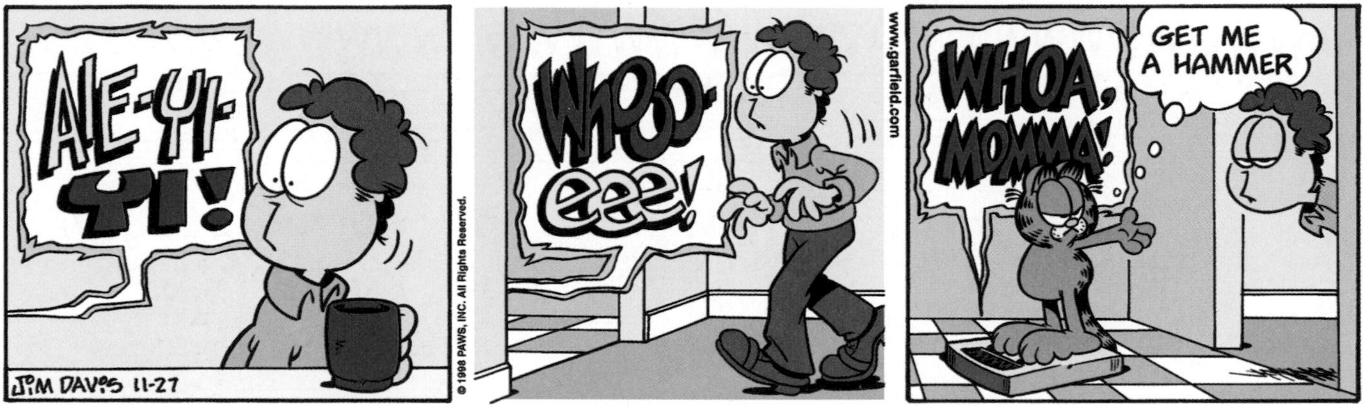
AIE-YI-YI!
JIM DAVIS 11-27
WHOO-eee!
WHOA, MOMMA!
GET ME A HAMMER
© 1998 PAWS, INC. All Rights Reserved.
www.garfield.com

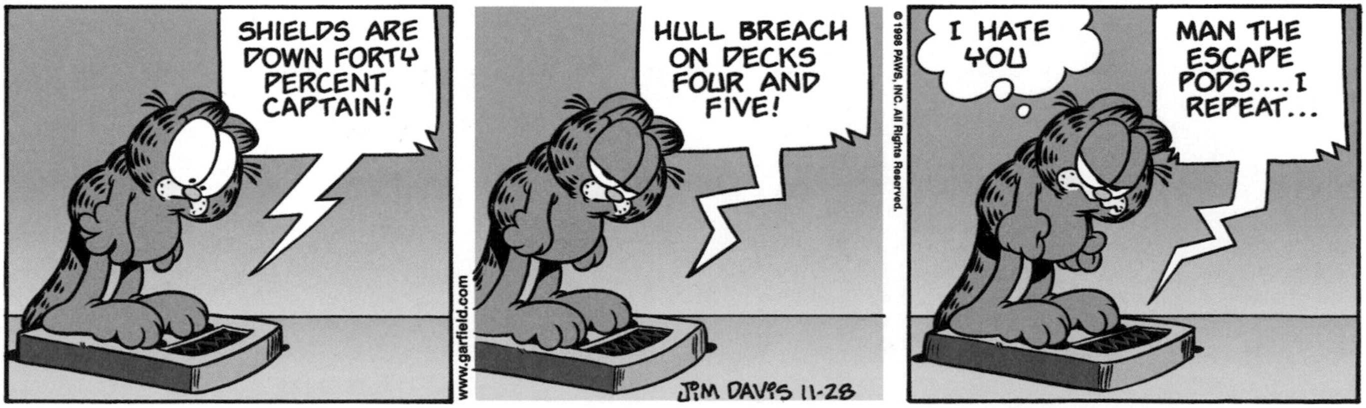
SHIELDS ARE DOWN FORTY PERCENT, CAPTAIN!
HULL BREACH ON DECKS FOUR AND FIVE!
I HATE YOU
MAN THE ESCAPE PODS.... I REPEAT...
JIM DAVIS 11-28
www.garfield.com
© 1998 PAWS, INC. All Rights Reserved.

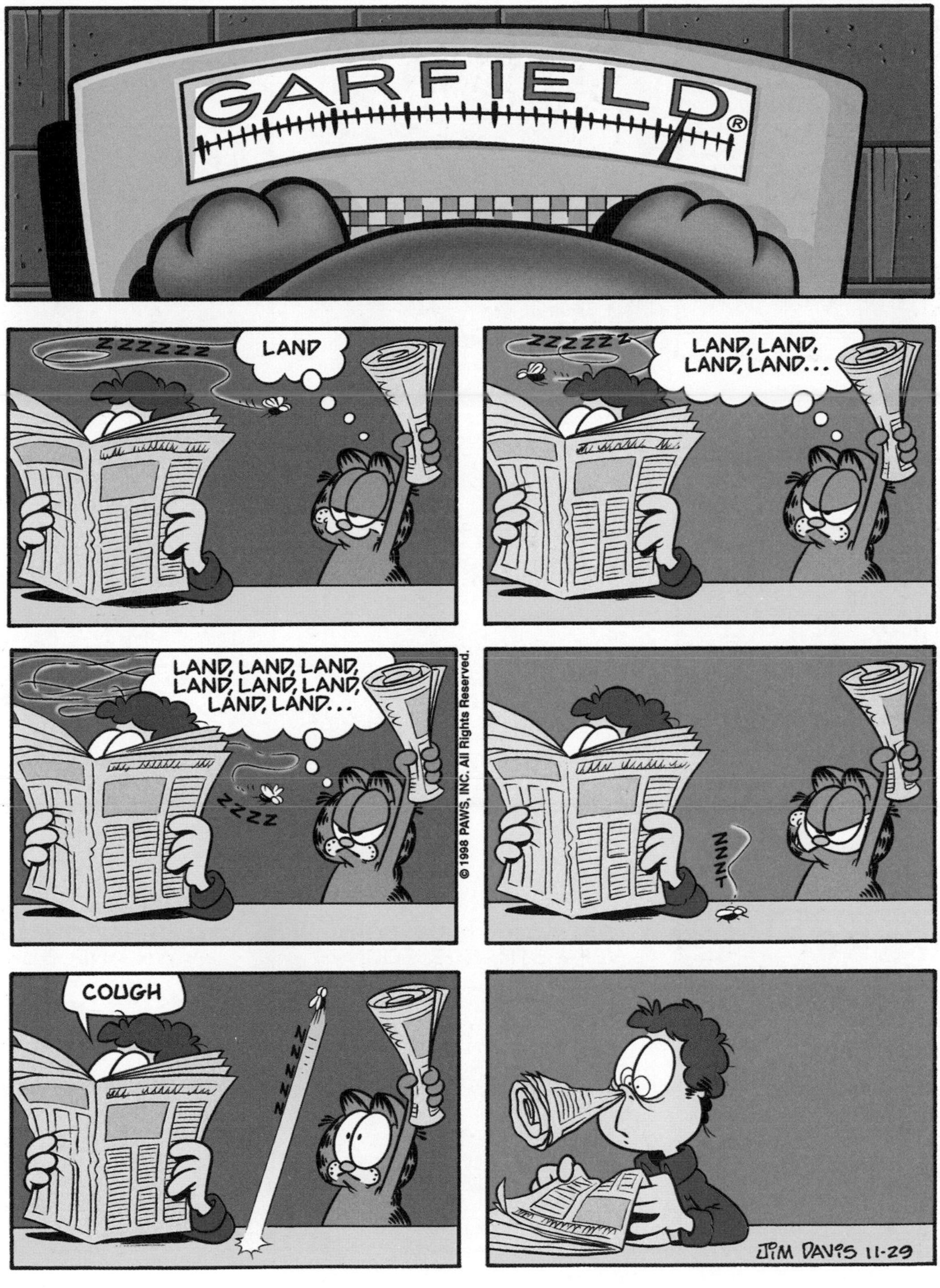
GARFIELD®
ZZZZZZ
LAND
ZZZZZZ
LAND, LAND,
LAND, LAND...
LAND, LAND, LAND,
LAND, LAND, LAND,
LAND, LAND...
ZZZZ
NNNT
COUGH
ZZZZZ
JIM DAVIS 11-29

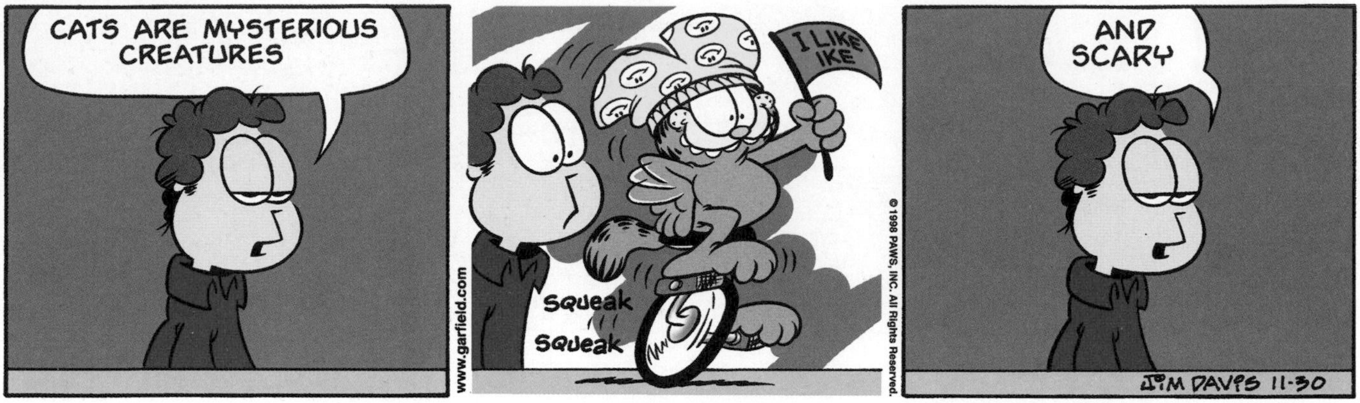
CATS ARE MYSTERIOUS CREATURES
I LIKE IKE
SQUEAK
SQUEAK
www.garfield.com
© 1998 PAWS, INC. All Rights Reserved.
AND SCARY
JIM DAVIS 11-30

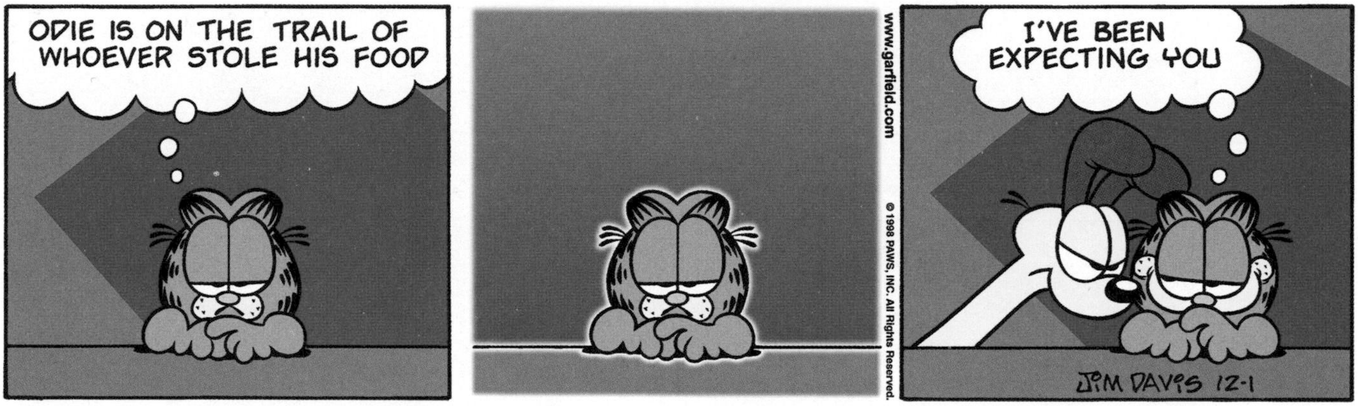
ODIE IS ON THE TRAIL OF WHOEVER STOLE HIS FOOD
www.garfield.com
© 1998 PAWS, INC. All Rights Reserved.
I'VE BEEN EXPECTING YOU
JIM DAVIS 12-1

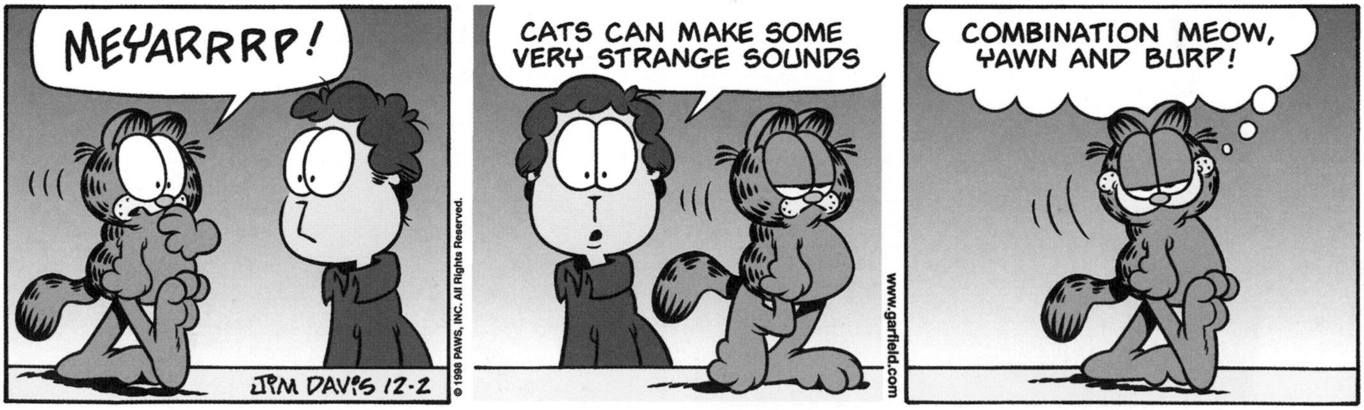
MEYARRRP!
JIM DAVIS 12-2
© 1998 PAWS, INC. All Rights Reserved.
CATS CAN MAKE SOME VERY STRANGE SOUNDS
www.garfield.com
COMBINATION MEOW, YAWN AND BURP!

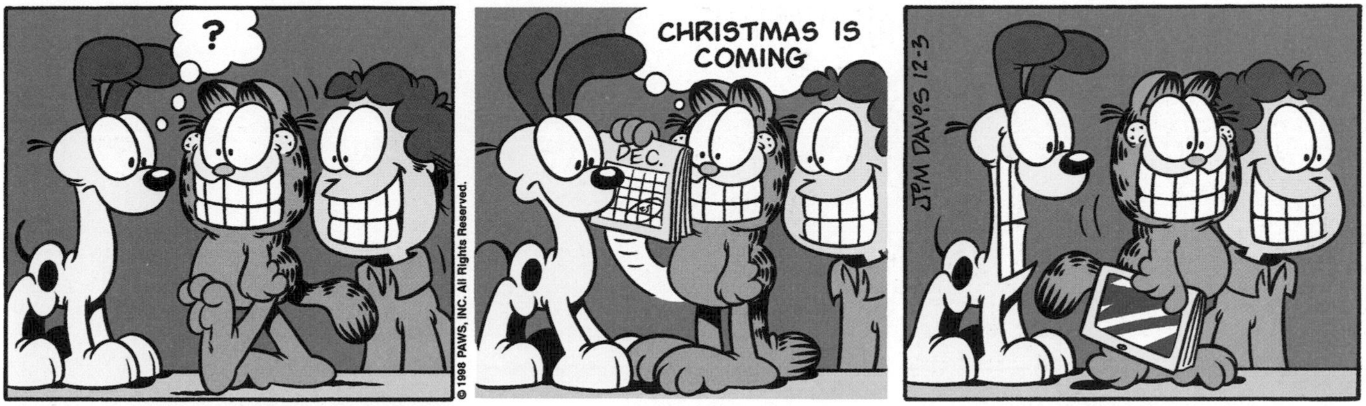
?
© 1998 PAWS, INC. All Rights Reserved.
CHRISTMAS IS COMING
DEC.
JIM DAVIS 12-3

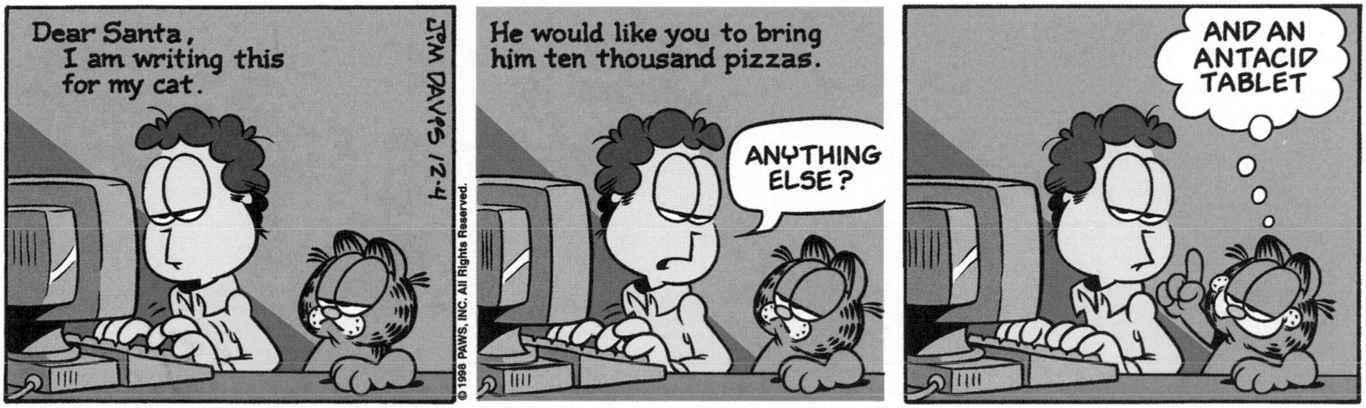
Dear Santa,
I am writing this for my cat.
JIM DAVIS 12-4
© 1998 PAWS, INC. All Rights Reserved.
He would like you to bring him ten thousand pizzas.
ANYTHING ELSE?
AND AN ANTACID TABLET

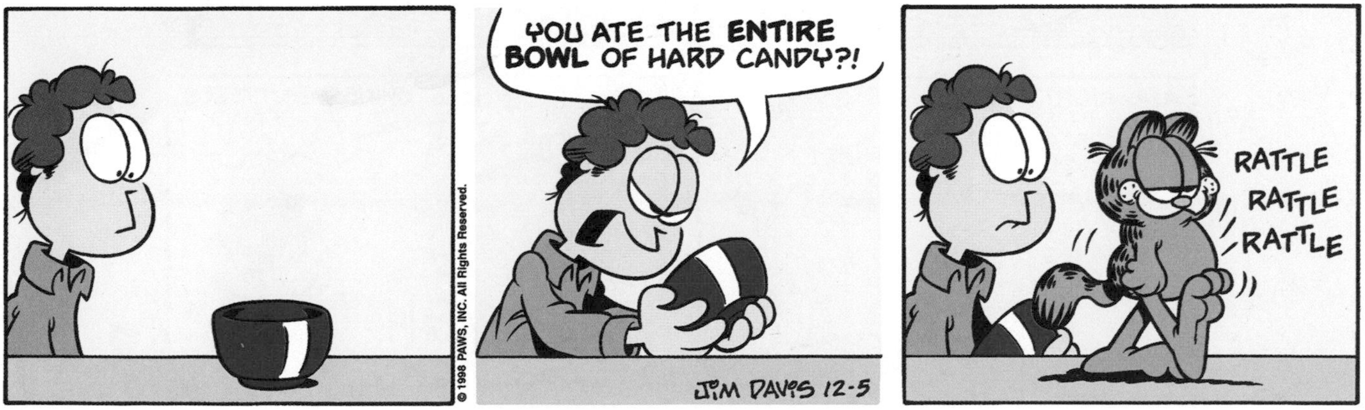
© 1998 PAWS, INC. All Rights Reserved.
YOU ATE THE **ENTIRE BOWL** OF HARD CANDY?!
JIM DAVIS 12-5
RATTLE
RATTLE
RATTLE

OKAY, HERE WE GO....AAANNND...

CRAAASH!

OKAY, OKAY, I KNOW WHAT I DID WRONG... LET'S TRY THAT AGAINNNNN...

WHUMP! KSSSH!! TINKLE TINKLE

ALL RIGHT, WISE GUY...YOU'RE GONNA STAND UP OR ELSE!!

JIM DAVIS 12-6

FUMP CRASH! AAARRRGGHH

CHRISTMAS TREE: 3
JON: 0

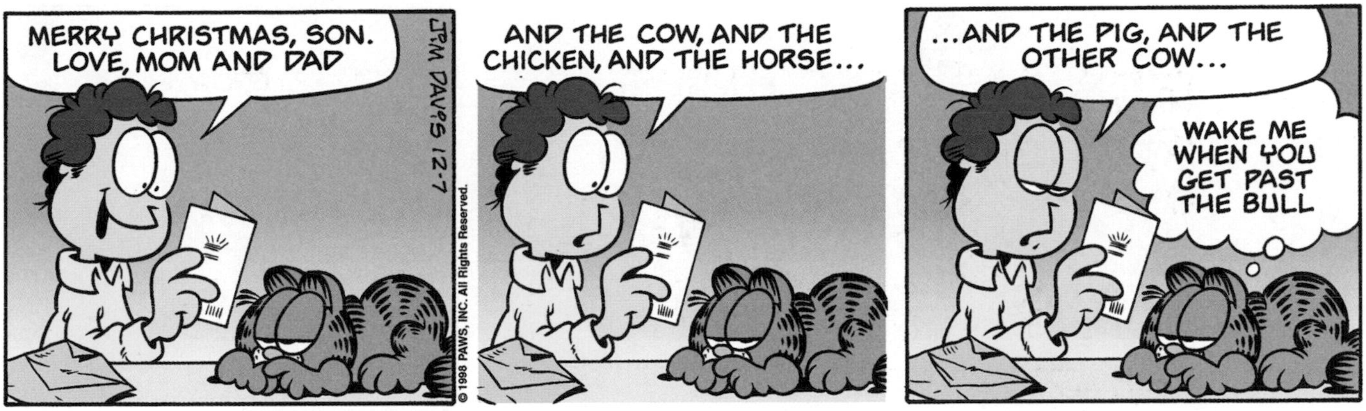
MERRY CHRISTMAS, SON. LOVE, MOM AND DAD
JIM DAVIS 12-7
© 1998 PAWS, INC. All Rights Reserved.
AND THE COW, AND THE CHICKEN, AND THE HORSE...
...AND THE PIG, AND THE OTHER COW...
WAKE ME WHEN YOU GET PAST THE BULL

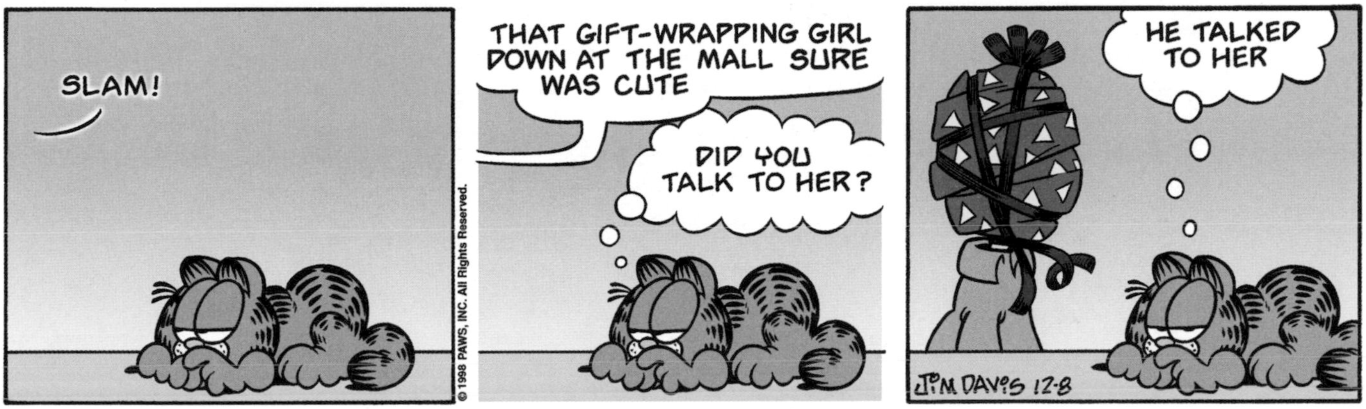
SLAM!
© 1998 PAWS, INC. All Rights Reserved.
THAT GIFT-WRAPPING GIRL DOWN AT THE MALL SURE WAS CUTE
DID YOU TALK TO HER?
HE TALKED TO HER
JIM DAVIS 12-8

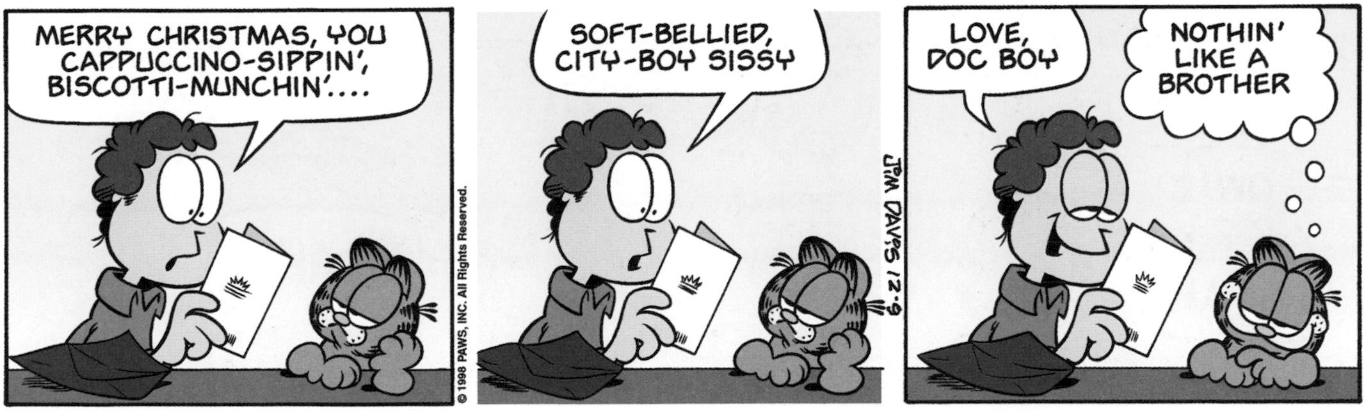
MERRY CHRISTMAS, YOU CAPPUCCINO-SIPPIN', BISCOTTI-MUNCHIN'....
© 1998 PAWS, INC. All Rights Reserved.
SOFT-BELLIED, CITY-BOY SISSY
JIM DAVIS 12-9
LOVE, DOC BOY
NOTHIN' LIKE A BROTHER

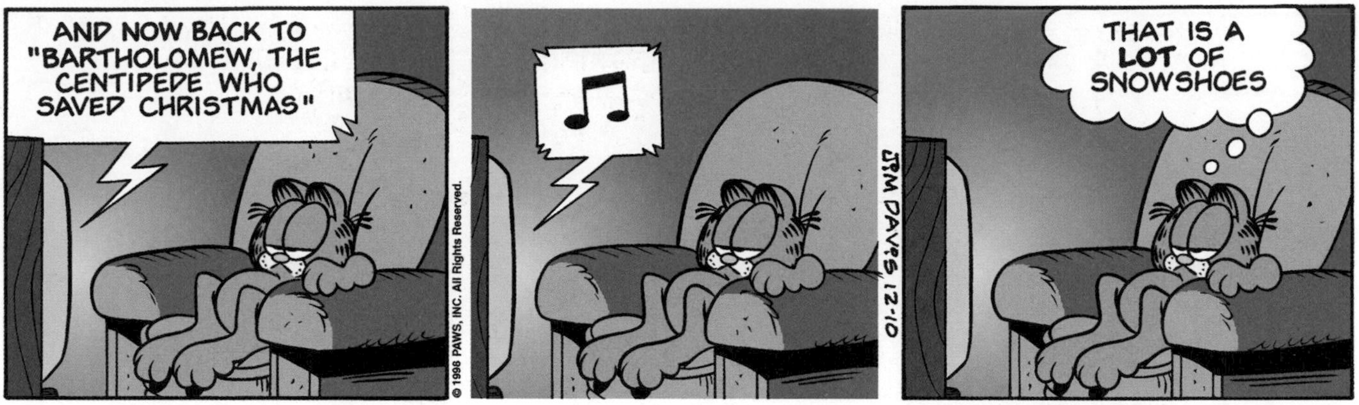
AND NOW BACK TO "BARTHOLOMEW, THE CENTIPEDE WHO SAVED CHRISTMAS"
THAT IS A LOT OF SNOWSHOES
JIM DAVIS 12-10
© 1998 PAWS, INC. All Rights Reserved.

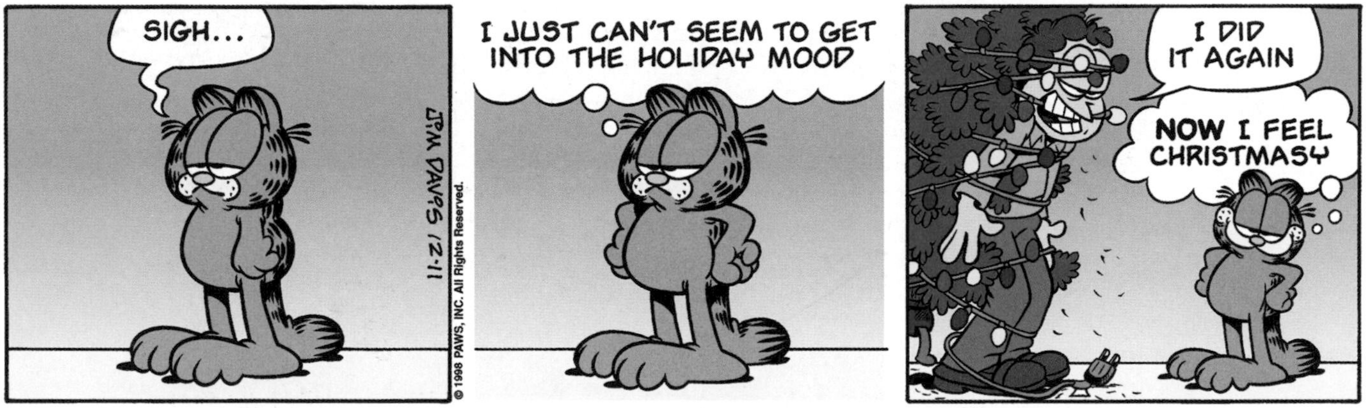
SIGH...
I JUST CAN'T SEEM TO GET INTO THE HOLIDAY MOOD
I DID IT AGAIN
NOW I FEEL CHRISTMASY
JIM DAVIS 12-11
© 1998 PAWS, INC. All Rights Reserved.

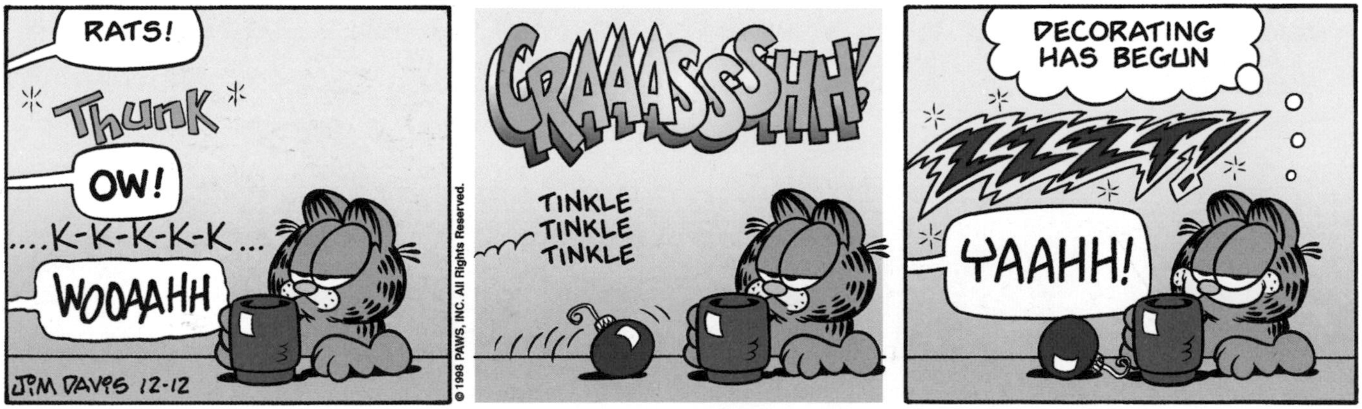
RATS!
Thunk
OW!
....K-K-K-K-K....
WOOAAHH
CRAAASSSHH
TINKLE
TINKLE
TINKLE
DECORATING HAS BEGUN
ZZZT!
YAAHH!
JIM DAVIS 12-12
© 1998 PAWS, INC. All Rights Reserved.

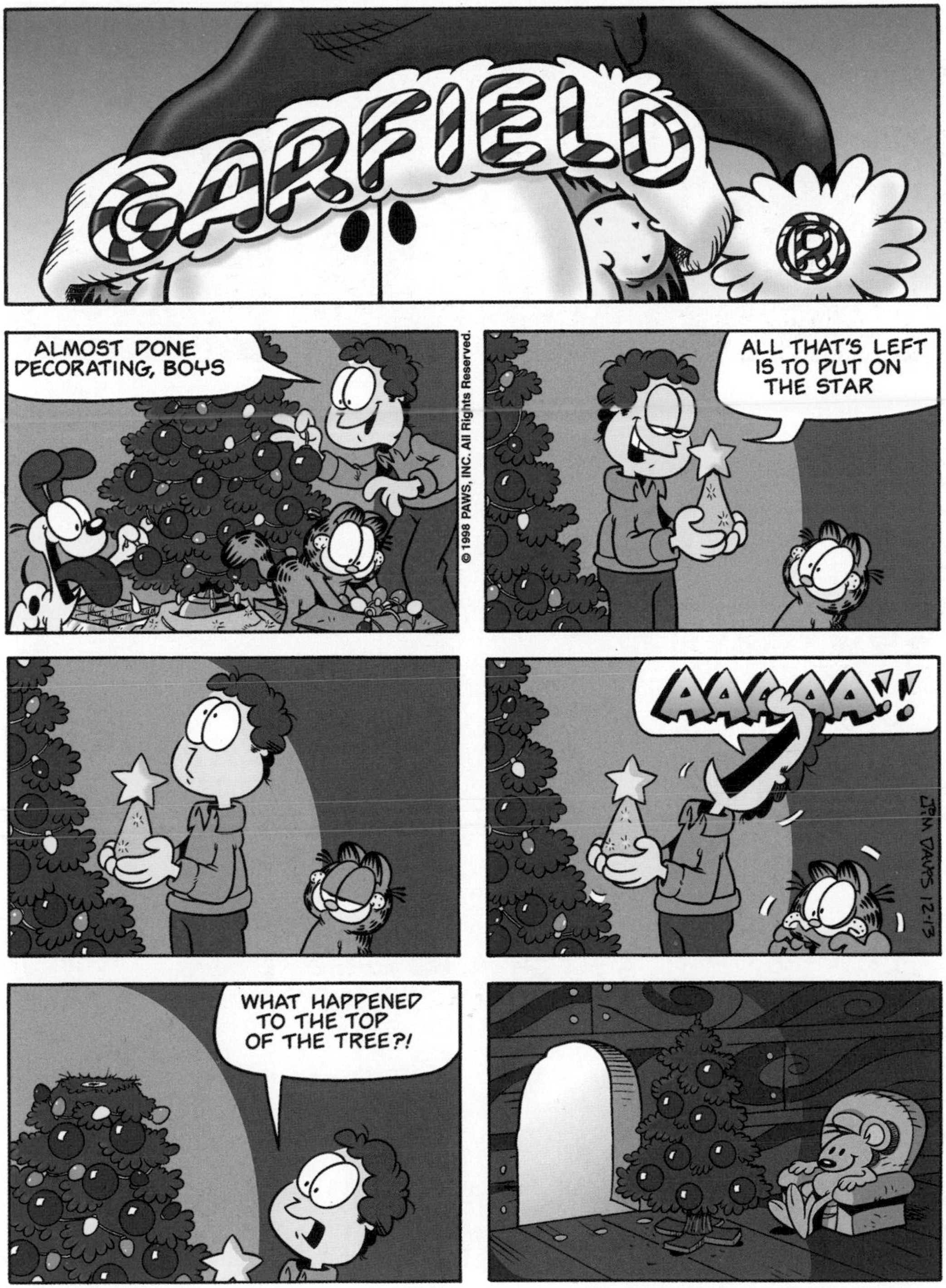
GARFIELD®
ALMOST DONE DECORATING, BOYS
© 1998 PAWS, INC. All Rights Reserved.
ALL THAT'S LEFT IS TO PUT ON THE STAR
AAAAA!!
JIM DAVIS 12-13
WHAT HAPPENED TO THE TOP OF THE TREE?!

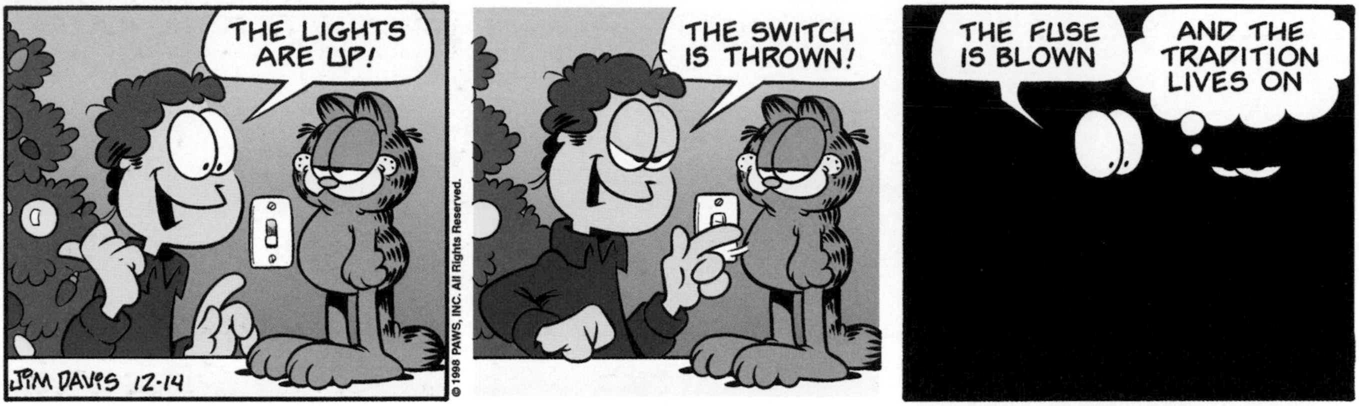
THE LIGHTS ARE UP!
JIM DAVIS 12-14
© 1998 PAWS, INC. All Rights Reserved.
THE SWITCH IS THROWN!
THE FUSE IS BLOWN
AND THE TRADITION LIVES ON

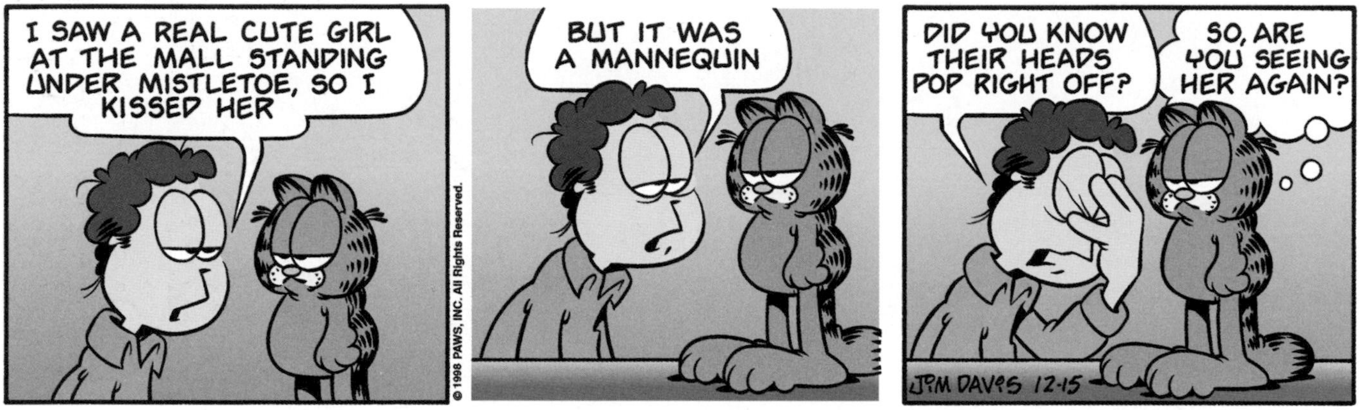
I SAW A REAL CUTE GIRL AT THE MALL STANDING UNDER MISTLETOE, SO I KISSED HER
© 1998 PAWS, INC. All Rights Reserved.
BUT IT WAS A MANNEQUIN
DID YOU KNOW THEIR HEADS POP RIGHT OFF?
SO, ARE YOU SEEING HER AGAIN?
JIM DAVIS 12-15

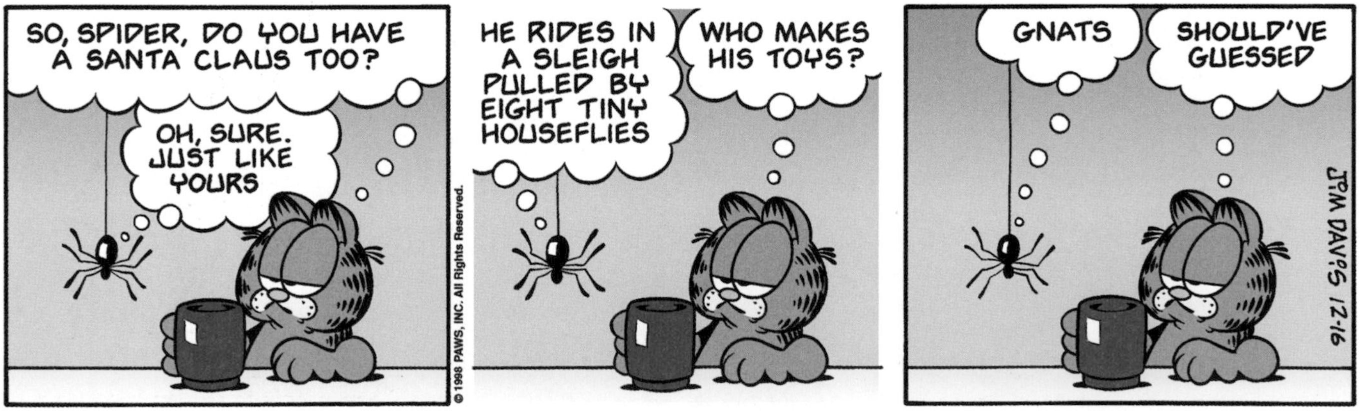
SO, SPIDER, DO YOU HAVE A SANTA CLAUS TOO?
OH, SURE. JUST LIKE YOURS
© 1998 PAWS, INC. All Rights Reserved.
HE RIDES IN A SLEIGH PULLED BY EIGHT TINY HOUSEFLIES
WHO MAKES HIS TOYS?
GNATS
SHOULD'VE GUESSED
JIM DAVIS 12-16

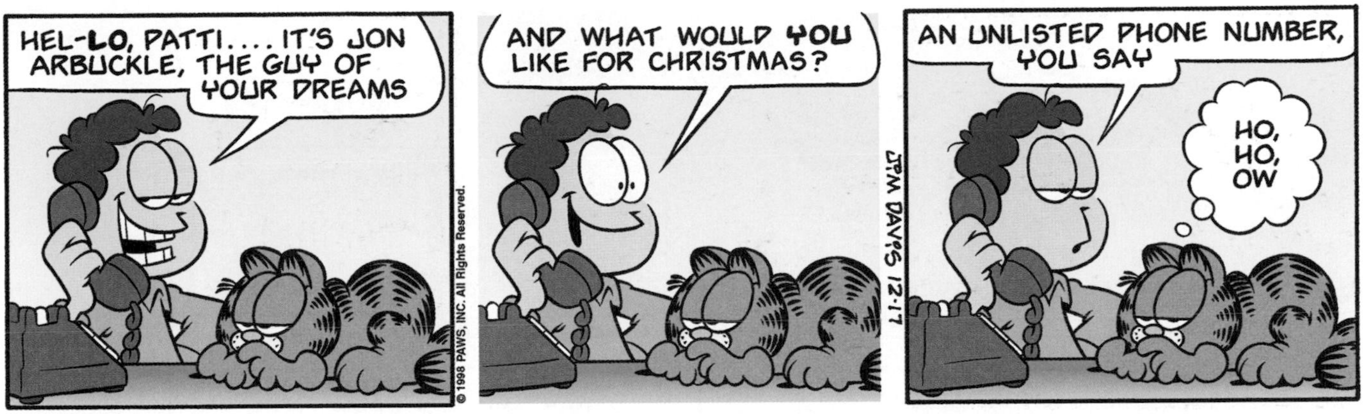
HEL-LO, PATTI.... IT'S JON ARBUCKLE, THE GUY OF YOUR DREAMS
© 1998 PAWS, INC. All Rights Reserved.
AND WHAT WOULD YOU LIKE FOR CHRISTMAS?
JIM DAVIS 12-17
AN UNLISTED PHONE NUMBER, YOU SAY
HO, HO, OW

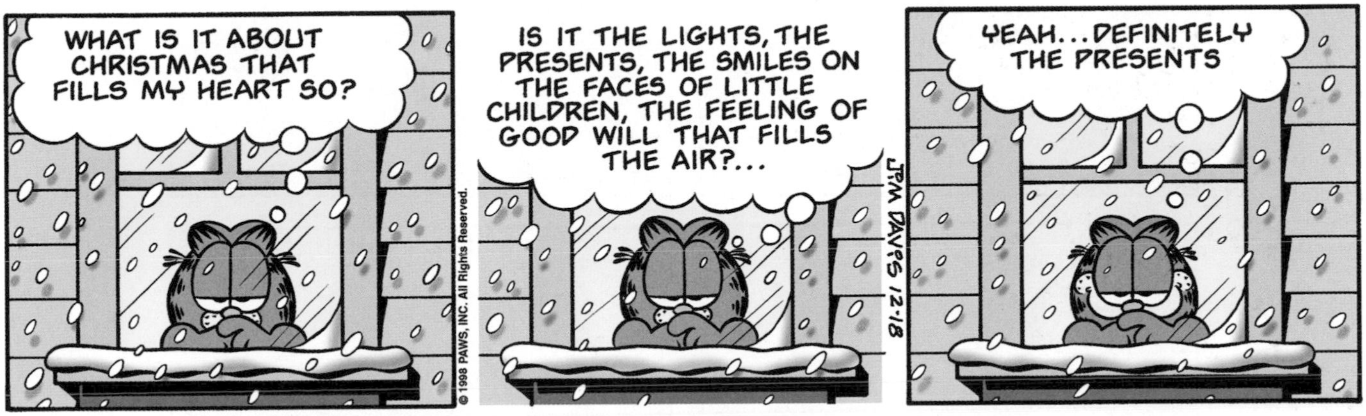
WHAT IS IT ABOUT CHRISTMAS THAT FILLS MY HEART SO?
© 1998 PAWS, INC. All Rights Reserved.
IS IT THE LIGHTS, THE PRESENTS, THE SMILES ON THE FACES OF LITTLE CHILDREN, THE FEELING OF GOOD WILL THAT FILLS THE AIR?...
JIM DAVIS 12-18
YEAH...DEFINITELY THE PRESENTS

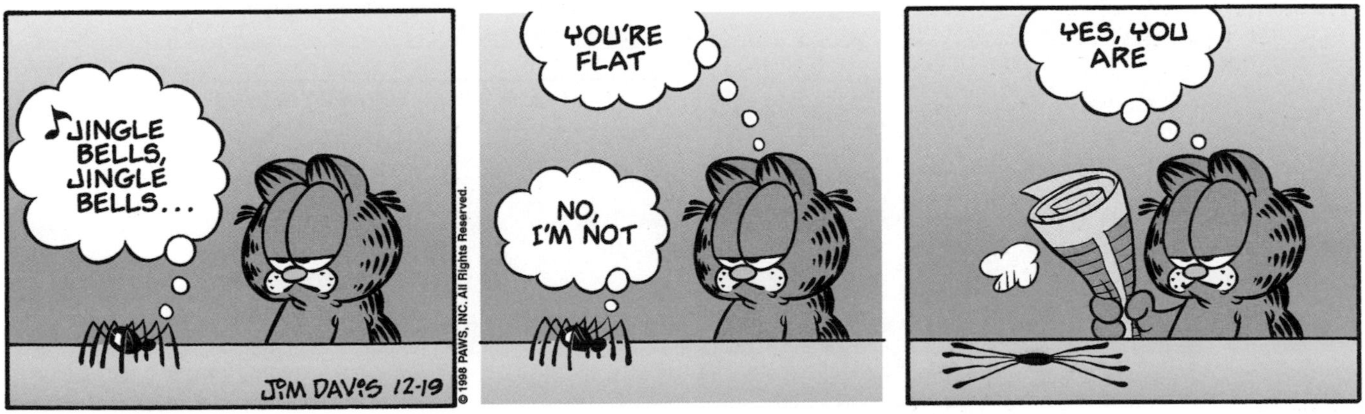
♪JINGLE BELLS, JINGLE BELLS...
JIM DAVIS 12-19
© 1998 PAWS, INC. All Rights Reserved.
YOU'RE FLAT
NO, I'M NOT
YES, YOU ARE

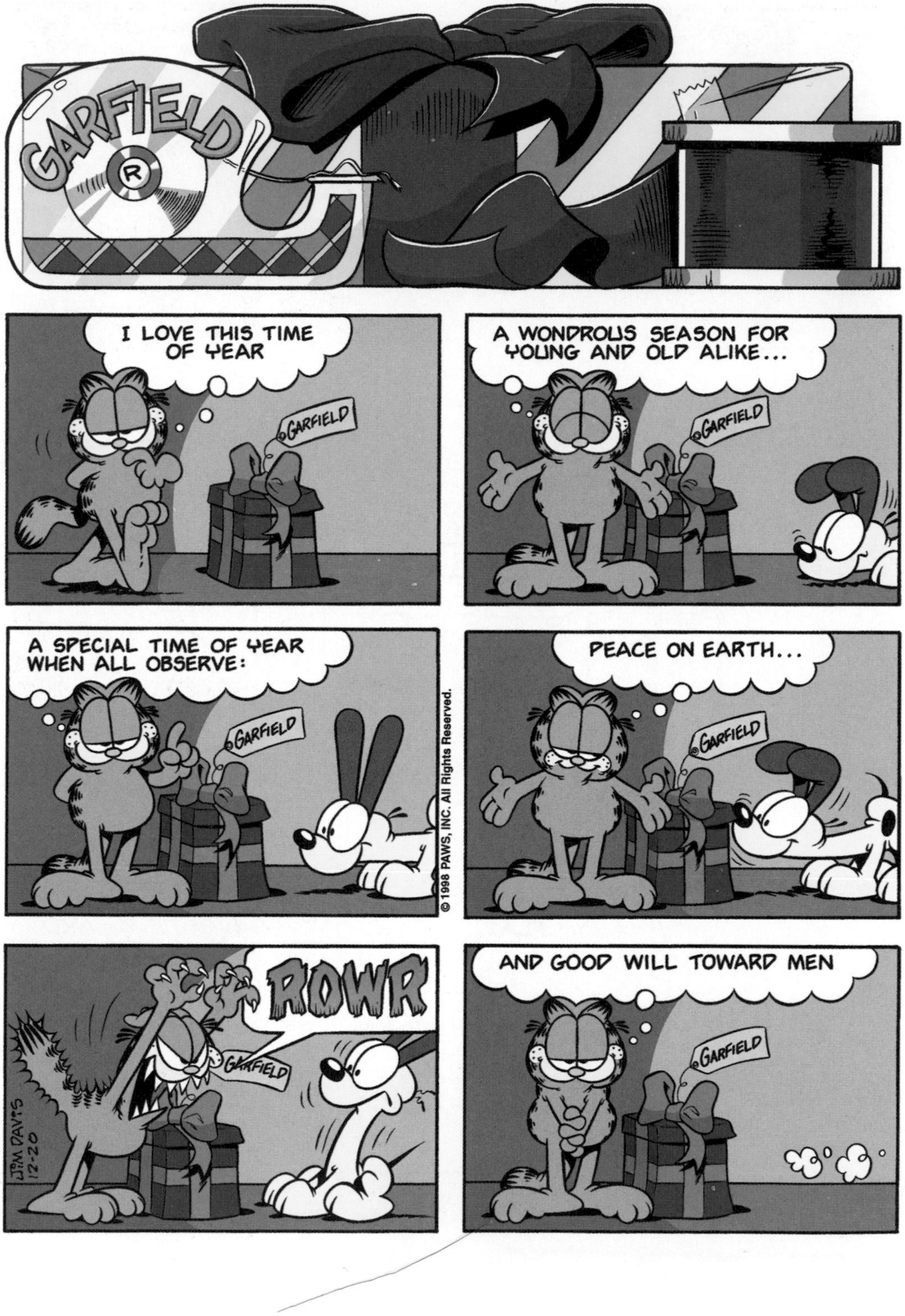
GARFIELD
I LOVE THIS TIME OF YEAR
GARFIELD
A WONDROUS SEASON FOR YOUNG AND OLD ALIKE...
GARFIELD
A SPECIAL TIME OF YEAR WHEN ALL OBSERVE:
GARFIELD
PEACE ON EARTH...
GARFIELD
ROWR
GARFIELD
JIM DAVIS 12-20
AND GOOD WILL TOWARD MEN
GARFIELD

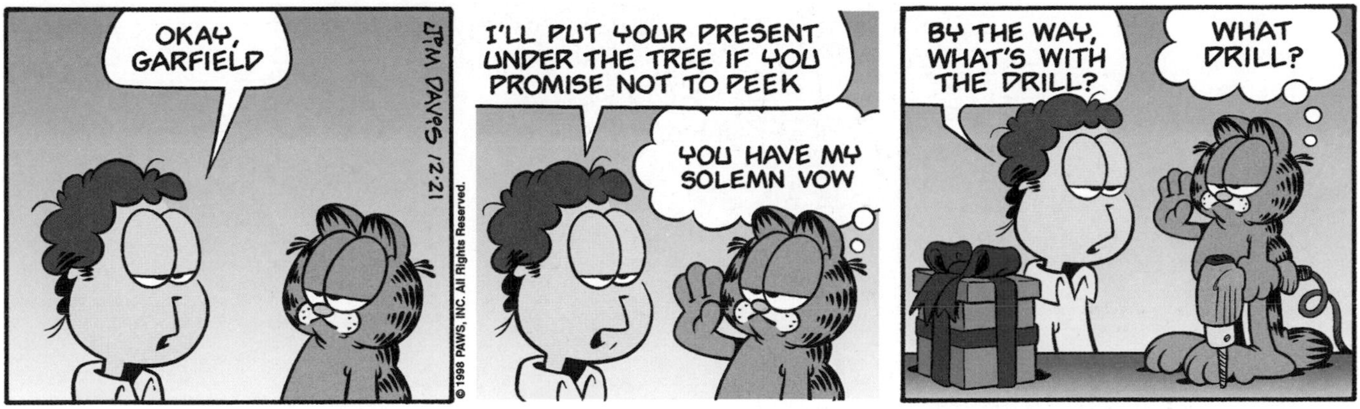
OKAY, GARFIELD
JIM DAVIS 12·21
© 1998 PAWS, INC. All Rights Reserved.
I'LL PUT YOUR PRESENT UNDER THE TREE IF YOU PROMISE NOT TO PEEK
YOU HAVE MY SOLEMN VOW
BY THE WAY, WHAT'S WITH THE DRILL?
WHAT DRILL?

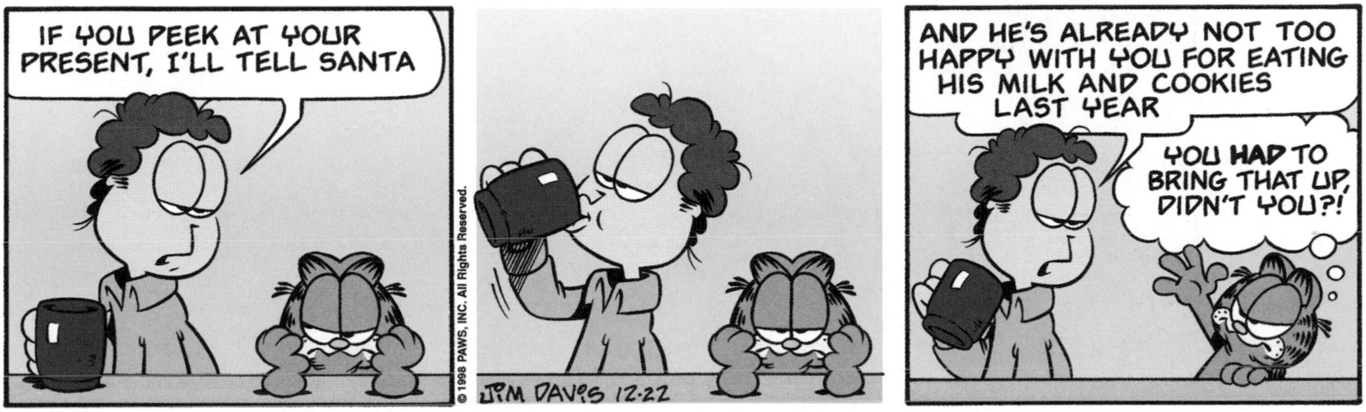
IF YOU PEEK AT YOUR PRESENT, I'LL TELL SANTA
© 1998 PAWS, INC. All Rights Reserved.
JIM DAVIS 12·22
AND HE'S ALREADY NOT TOO HAPPY WITH YOU FOR EATING HIS MILK AND COOKIES LAST YEAR
YOU **HAD** TO BRING THAT UP, DIDN'T YOU?!

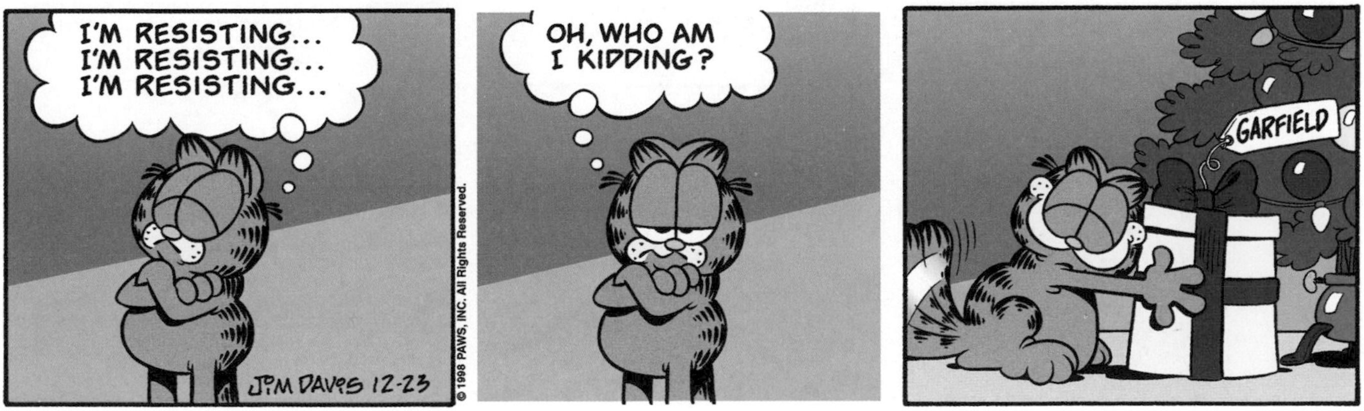
I'M RESISTING... I'M RESISTING... I'M RESISTING...
JIM DAVIS 12-23
© 1998 PAWS, INC. All Rights Reserved.
OH, WHO AM I KIDDING?
GARFIELD

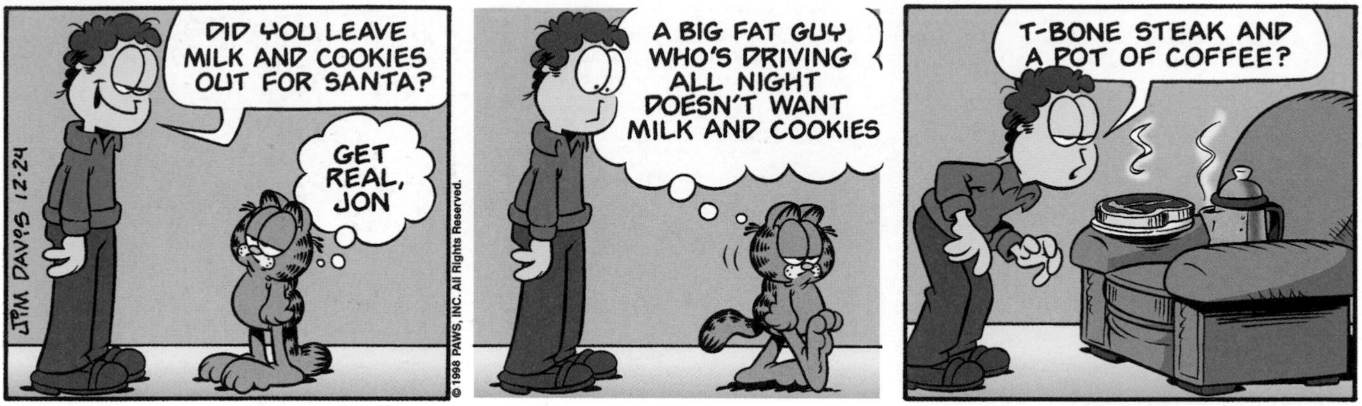
DID YOU LEAVE MILK AND COOKIES OUT FOR SANTA?
GET REAL, JON
A BIG FAT GUY WHO'S DRIVING ALL NIGHT DOESN'T WANT MILK AND COOKIES
T-BONE STEAK AND A POT OF COFFEE?
JIM DAVIS 12-24
© 1998 PAWS, INC. All Rights Reserved.

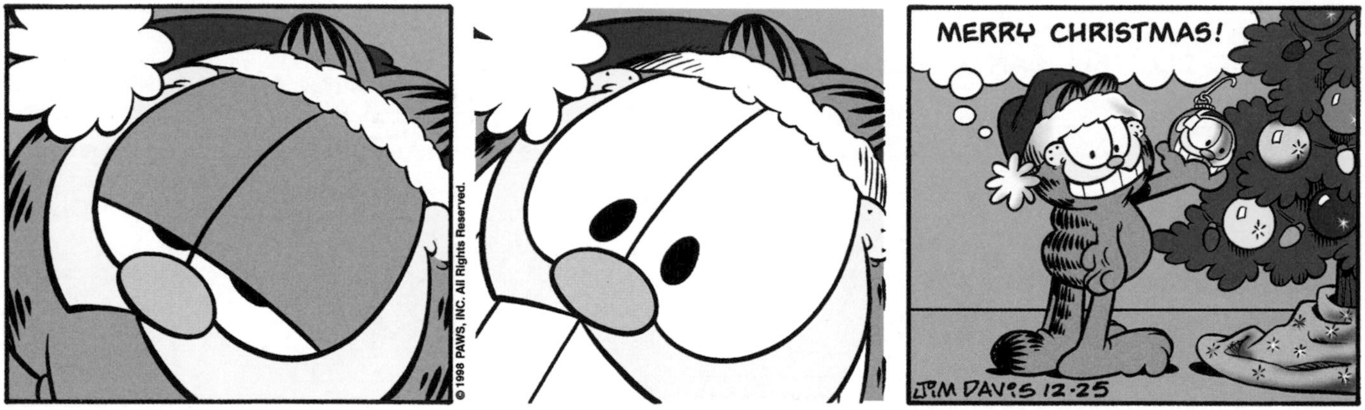
MERRY CHRISTMAS!
JIM DAVIS 12-25
© 1998 PAWS, INC. All Rights Reserved.

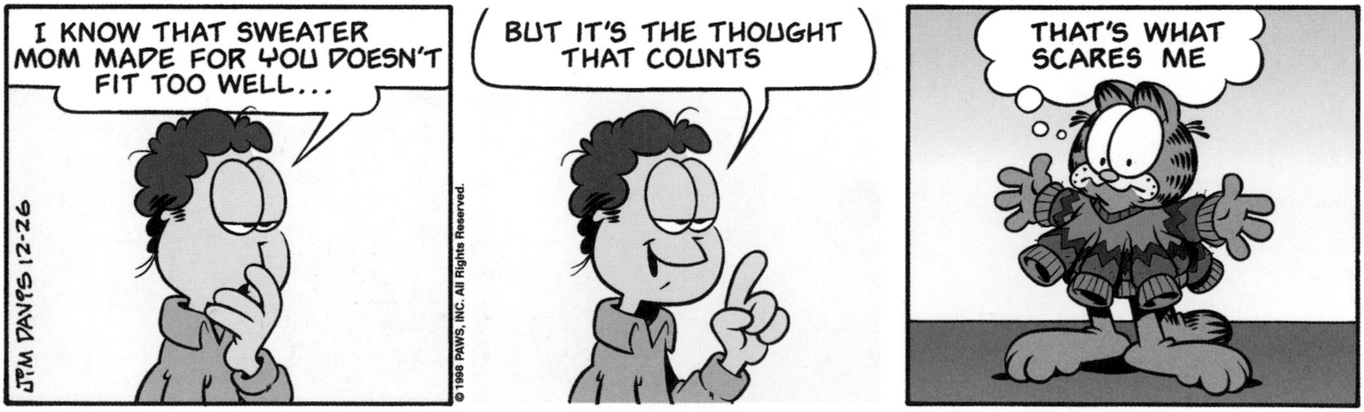
I KNOW THAT SWEATER MOM MADE FOR YOU DOESN'T FIT TOO WELL...
BUT IT'S THE THOUGHT THAT COUNTS
THAT'S WHAT SCARES ME
JIM DAVIS 12-26
© 1998 PAWS, INC. All Rights Reserved.

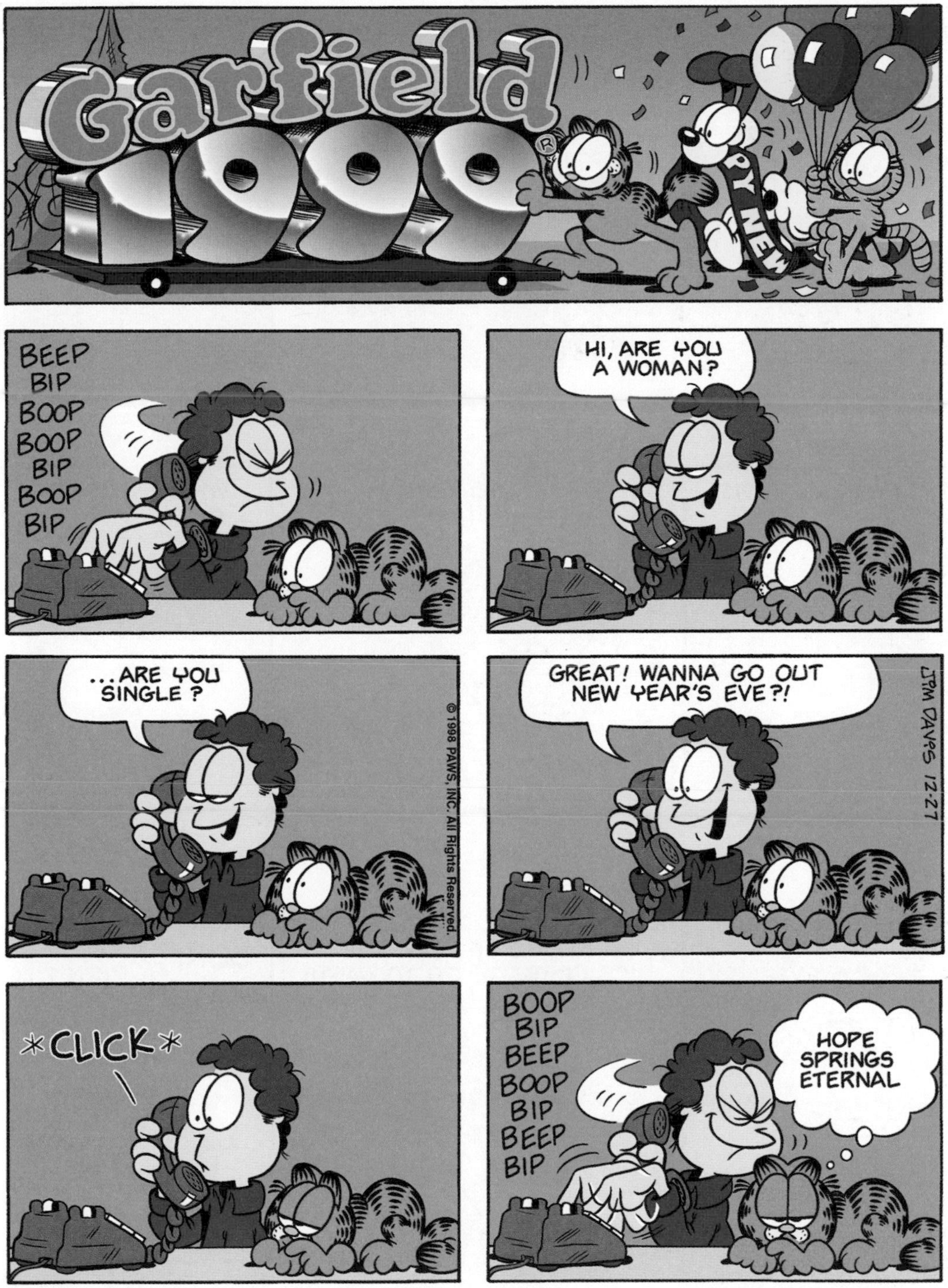
Garfield®
1999
HAPPY NEW
BEEP BIP BOOP BOOP BIP BOOP BIP
HI, ARE YOU A WOMAN?
...ARE YOU SINGLE?
GREAT! WANNA GO OUT NEW YEAR'S EVE?!
JPM DAVPS 12-27
© 1998 PAWS, INC. All Rights Reserved.
CLICK
BOOP BIP BEEP BOOP BIP BEEP BIP
HOPE SPRINGS ETERNAL

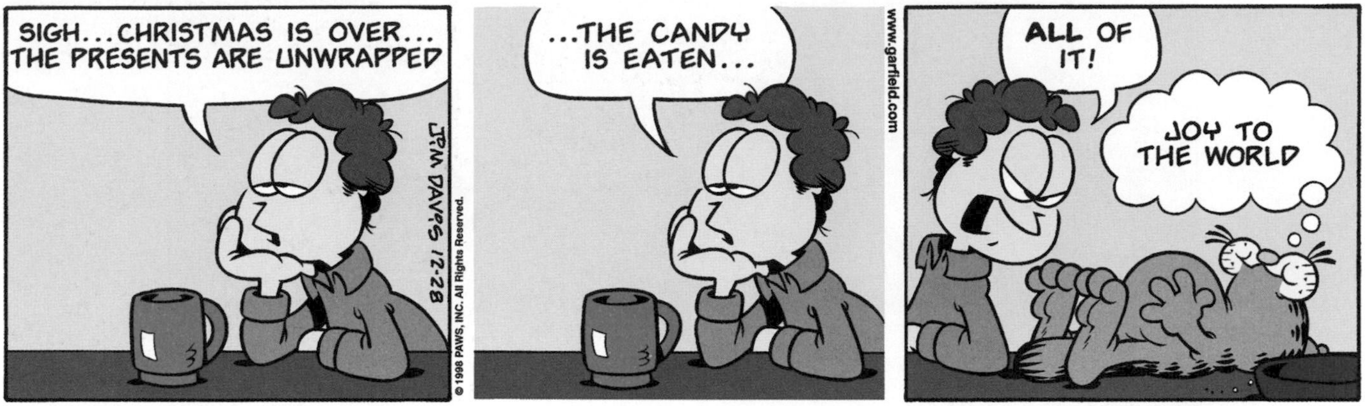
SIGH...CHRISTMAS IS OVER... THE PRESENTS ARE UNWRAPPED
JIM DAVIS 12-28
© 1998 PAWS, INC. All Rights Reserved.
...THE CANDY IS EATEN...
www.garfield.com
ALL OF IT!
JOY TO THE WORLD

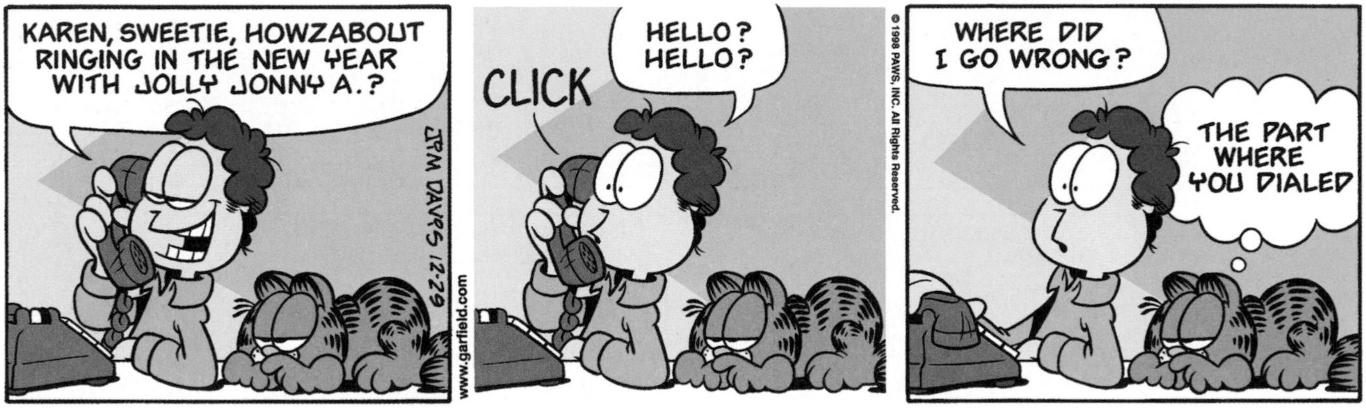
KAREN, SWEETIE, HOWZABOUT RINGING IN THE NEW YEAR WITH JOLLY JONNY A.?
JIM DAVIS 12-29
www.garfield.com
CLICK
HELLO? HELLO?
© 1998 PAWS, INC. All Rights Reserved.
WHERE DID I GO WRONG?
THE PART WHERE YOU DIALED

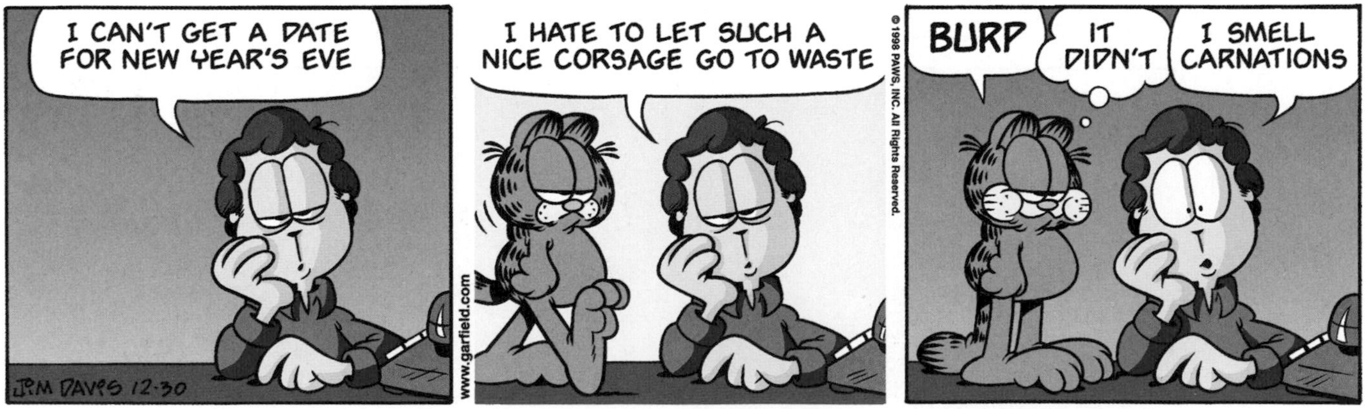
I CAN'T GET A DATE FOR NEW YEAR'S EVE
JIM DAVIS 12-30
www.garfield.com
I HATE TO LET SUCH A NICE CORSAGE GO TO WASTE
© 1998 PAWS, INC. All Rights Reserved.
BURP
IT DIDN'T
I SMELL CARNATIONS

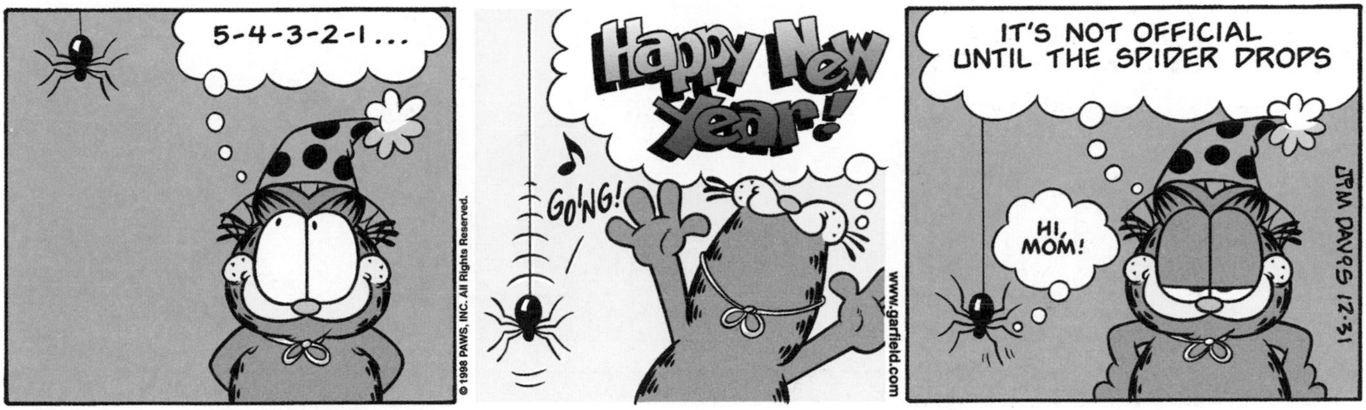
5-4-3-2-1...
Happy New Year!
GO'NG!
IT'S NOT OFFICIAL UNTIL THE SPIDER DROPS
HI, MOM!
JIM DAVIS 12-31
© 1998 PAWS, INC. All Rights Reserved.
www.garfield.com

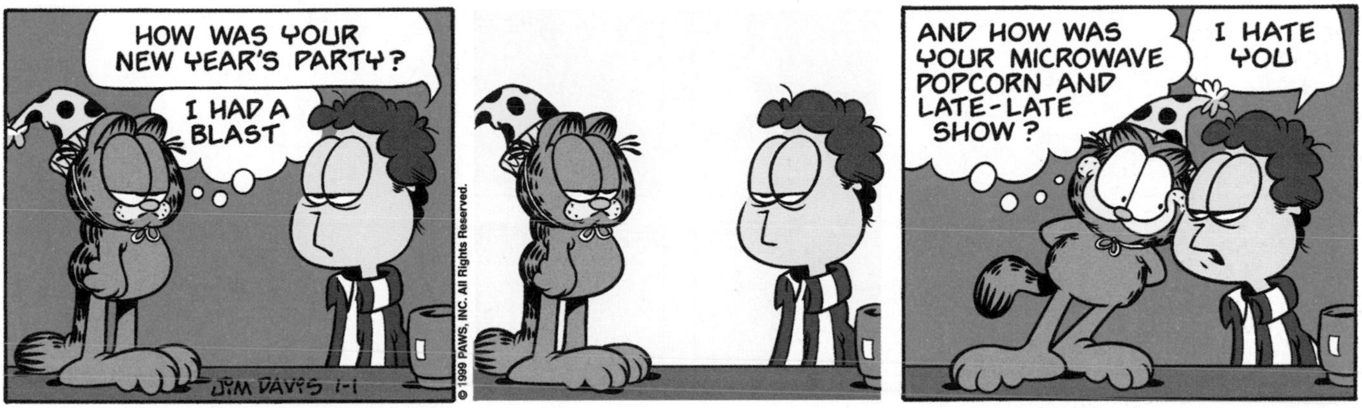
HOW WAS YOUR NEW YEAR'S PARTY?
I HAD A BLAST
AND HOW WAS YOUR MICROWAVE POPCORN AND LATE-LATE SHOW?
I HATE YOU
JIM DAVIS 1-1
© 1999 PAWS, INC. All Rights Reserved.

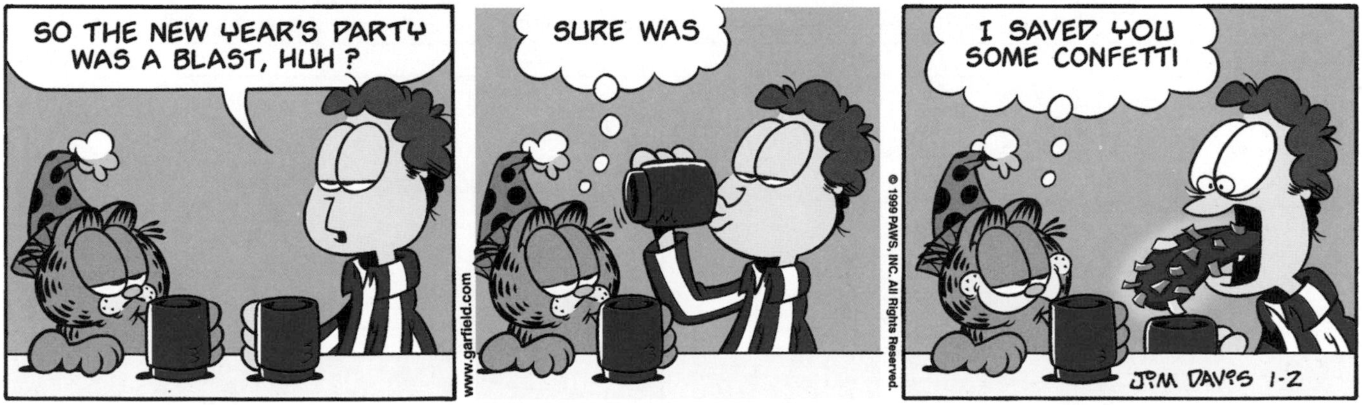
SO THE NEW YEAR'S PARTY WAS A BLAST, HUH?
SURE WAS
I SAVED YOU SOME CONFETTI
JIM DAVIS 1-2
www.garfield.com
© 1999 PAWS, INC. All Rights Reserved.

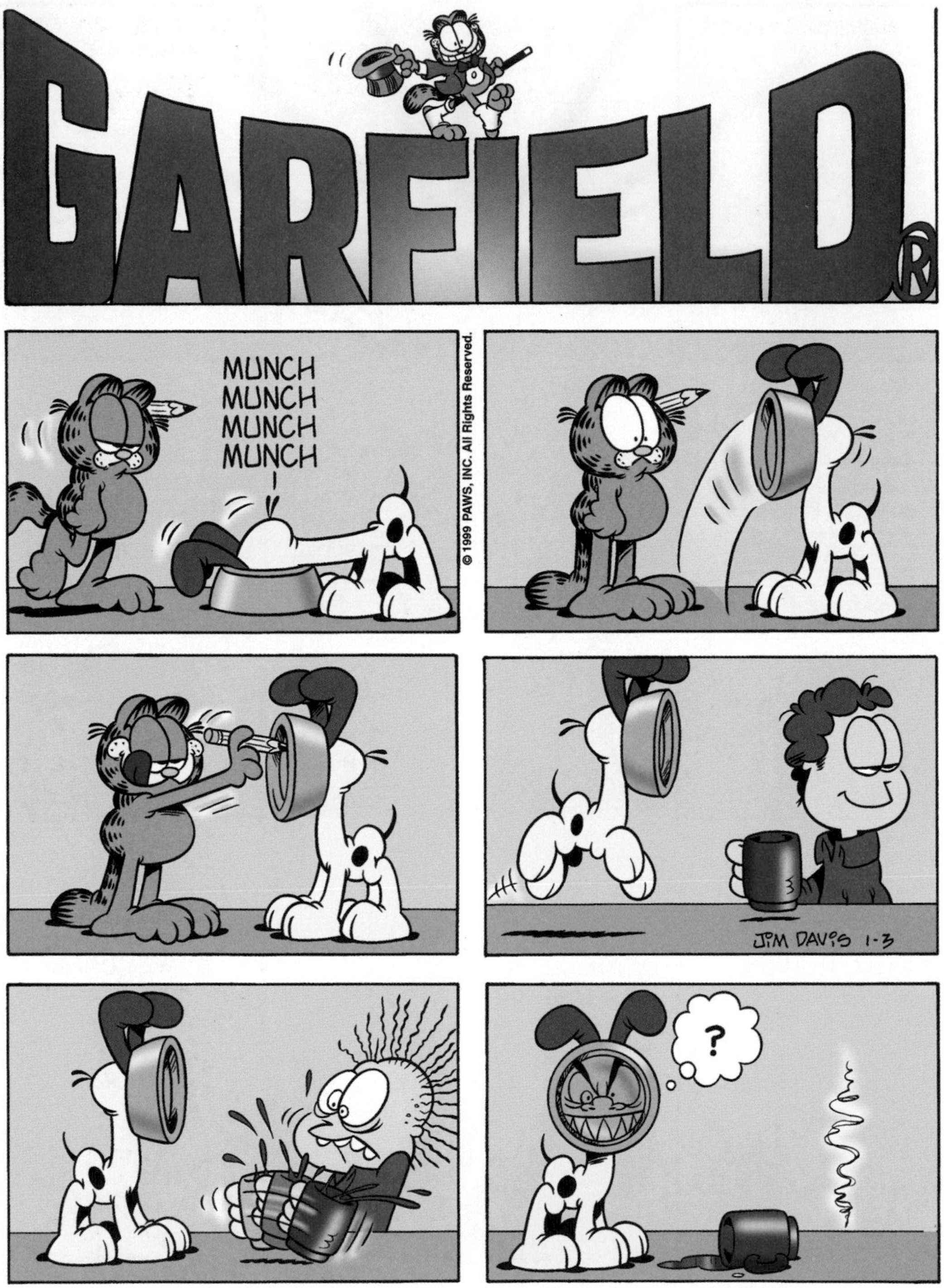
GARFIELD®
MUNCH
MUNCH
MUNCH
MUNCH
© 1999 PAWS, INC. All Rights Reserved.
JIM DAVIS 1-3
?

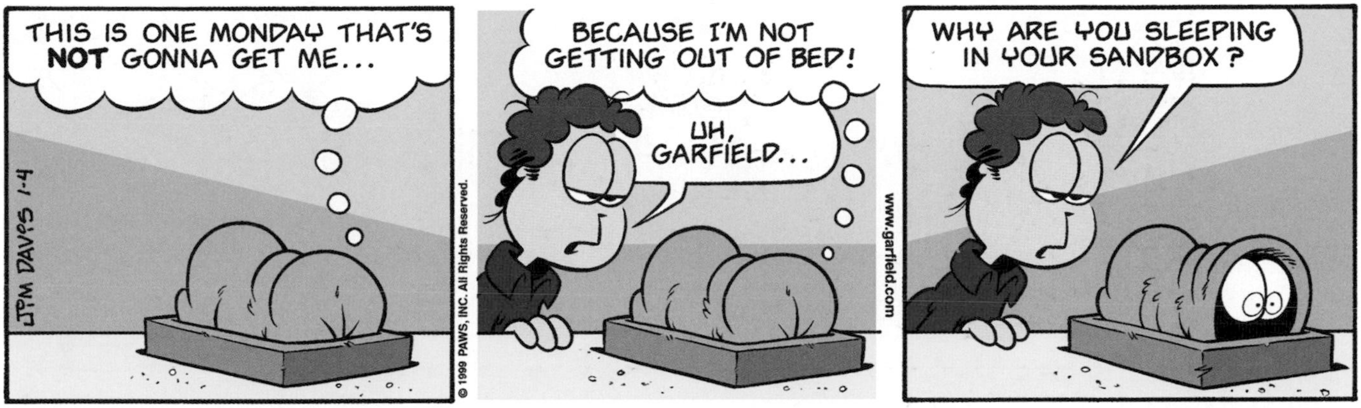
THIS IS ONE MONDAY THAT'S **NOT** GONNA GET ME...
JIM DAVIS 1-4
© 1999 PAWS, INC. All Rights Reserved.
BECAUSE I'M NOT GETTING OUT OF BED!
UH, GARFIELD...
www.garfield.com
WHY ARE YOU SLEEPING IN YOUR SANDBOX?

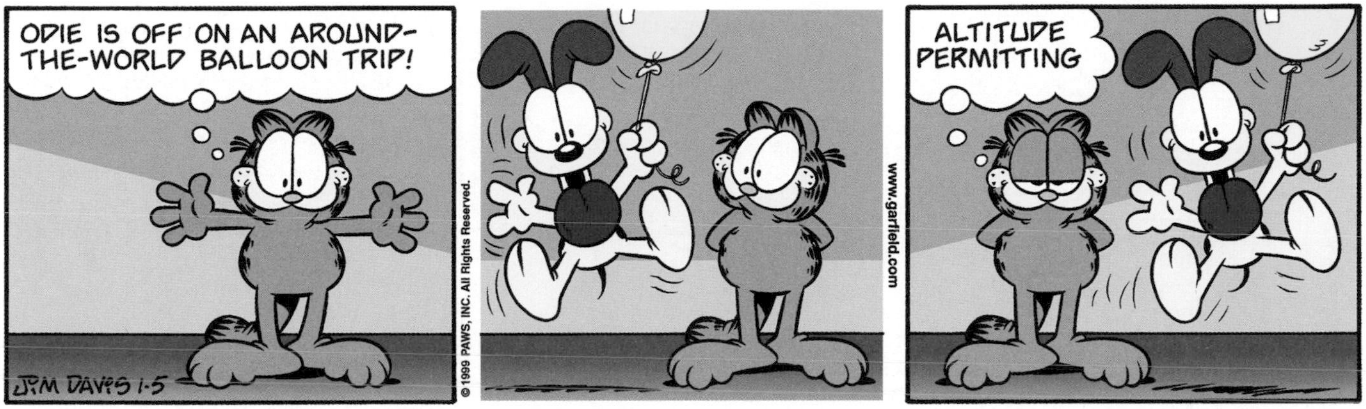
ODIE IS OFF ON AN AROUND-THE-WORLD BALLOON TRIP!
JIM DAVIS 1-5
© 1999 PAWS, INC. All Rights Reserved.
www.garfield.com
ALTITUDE PERMITTING

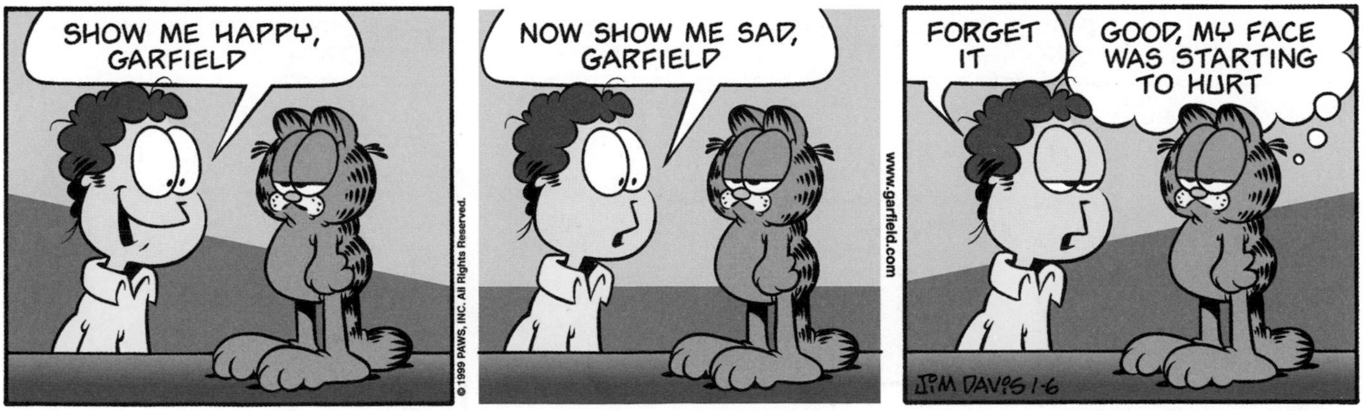
SHOW ME HAPPY, GARFIELD
© 1999 PAWS, INC. All Rights Reserved.
NOW SHOW ME SAD, GARFIELD
www.garfield.com
FORGET IT
GOOD, MY FACE WAS STARTING TO HURT
JIM DAVIS 1-6

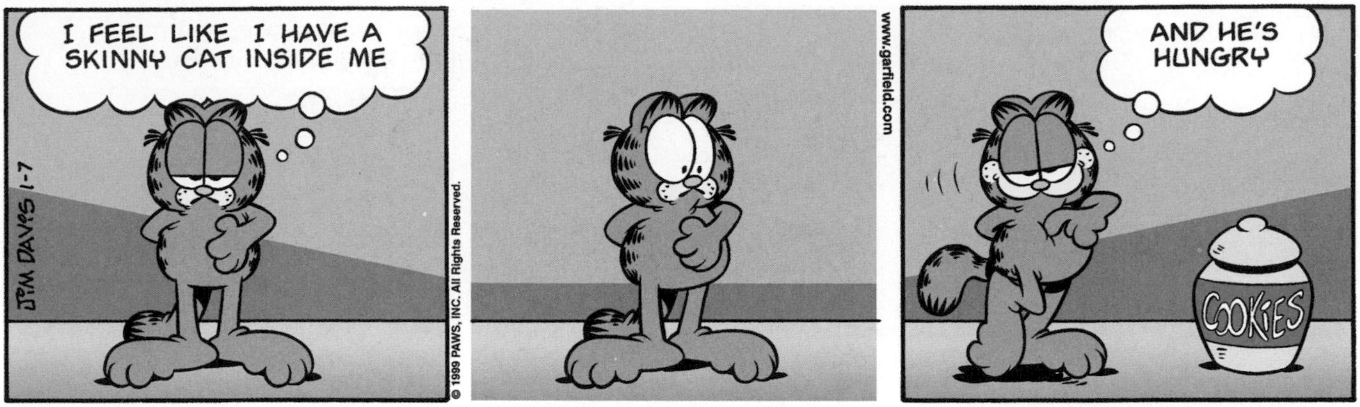
I FEEL LIKE I HAVE A SKINNY CAT INSIDE ME
JIM DAVIS 1-7
© 1999 PAWS, INC. All Rights Reserved.
www.garfield.com
AND HE'S HUNGRY
COOKIES

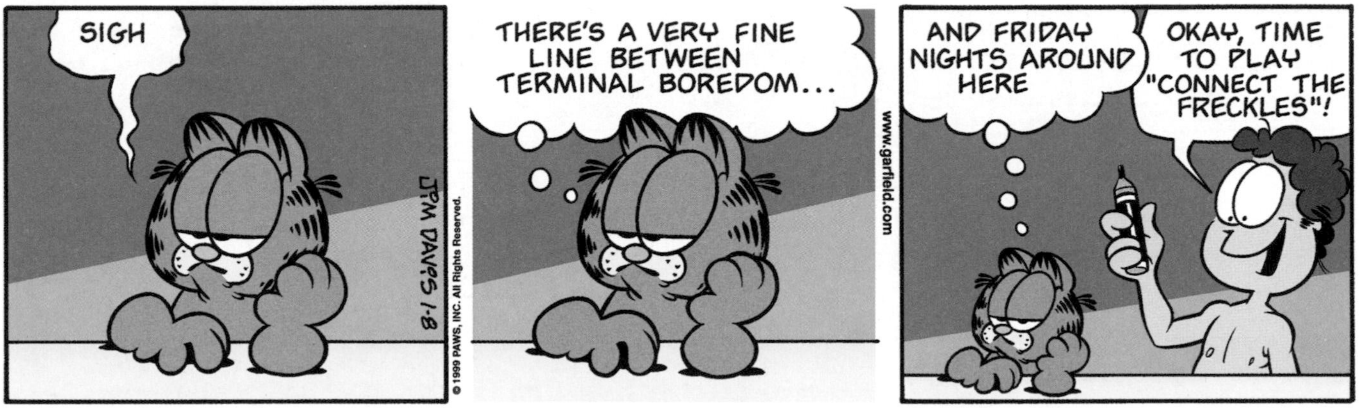
SIGH
JIM DAVIS 1-8
© 1999 PAWS, INC. All Rights Reserved.
THERE'S A VERY FINE LINE BETWEEN TERMINAL BOREDOM...
www.garfield.com
AND FRIDAY NIGHTS AROUND HERE
OKAY, TIME TO PLAY "CONNECT THE FRECKLES"!

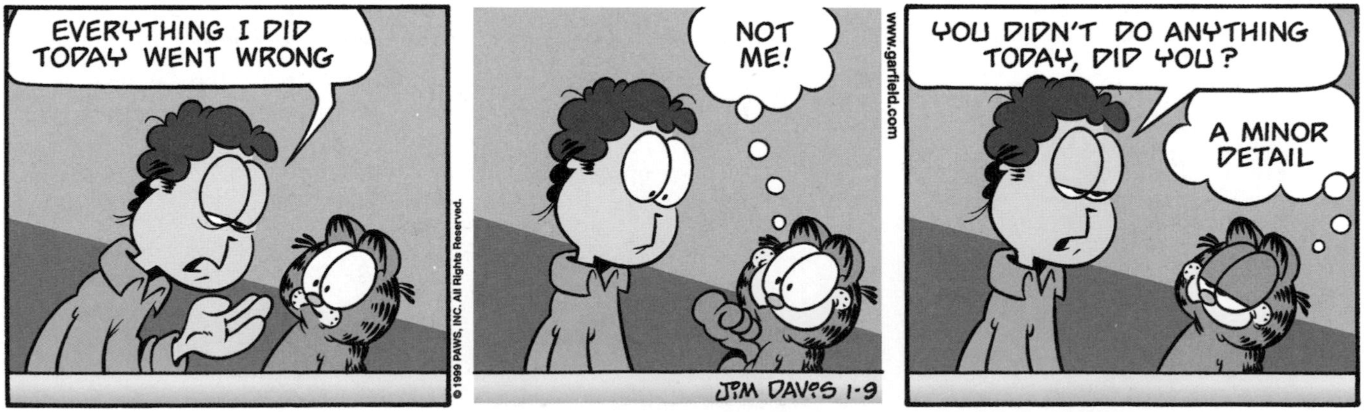
EVERYTHING I DID TODAY WENT WRONG
© 1999 PAWS, INC. All Rights Reserved.
NOT ME!
JIM DAVIS 1-9
www.garfield.com
YOU DIDN'T DO ANYTHING TODAY, DID YOU?
A MINOR DETAIL

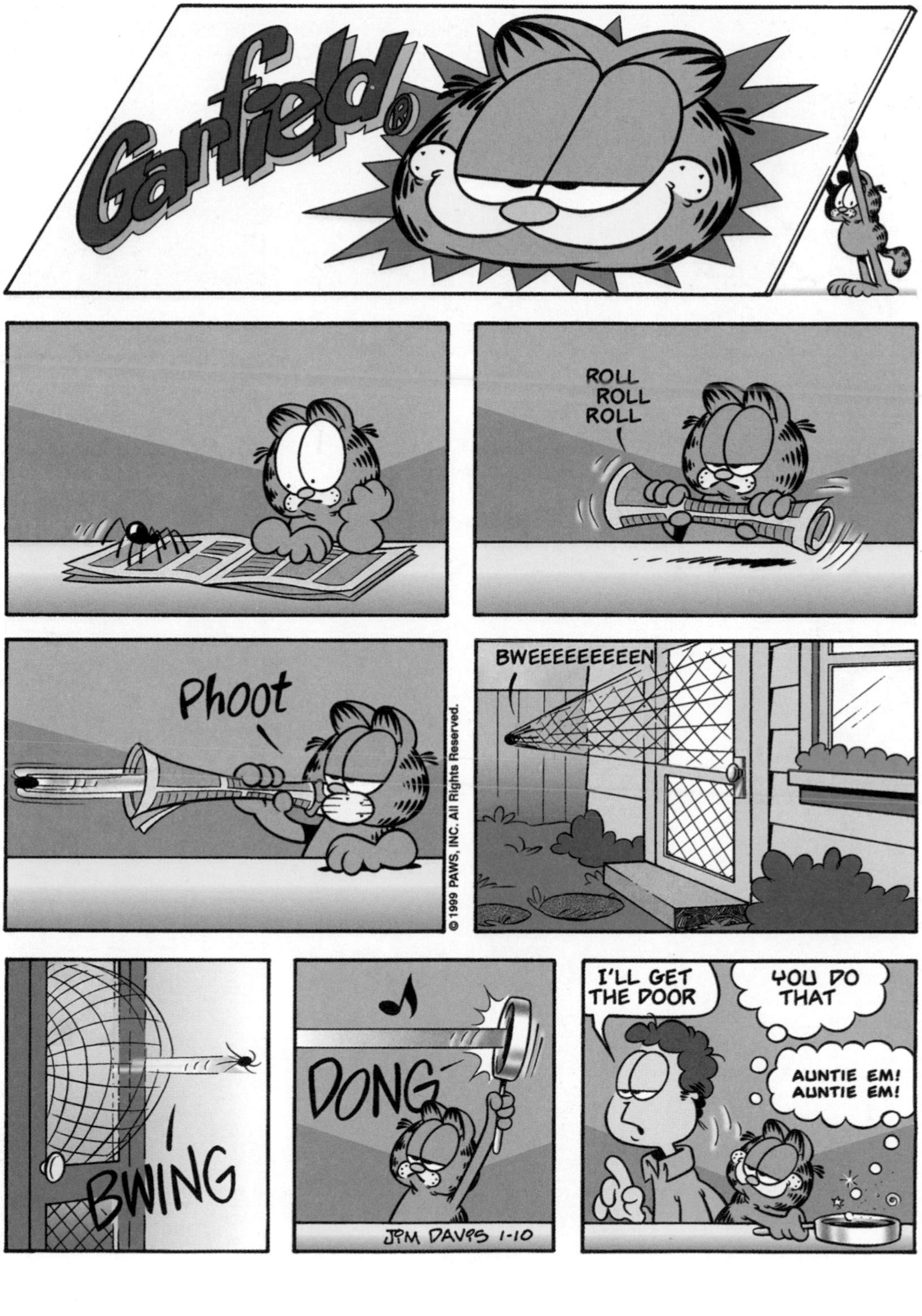
Garfield®
ROLL ROLL ROLL
Phoot
BWEEEEEEEEEN
BWING
DONG
JIM DAVIS 1-10
I'LL GET THE DOOR
YOU DO THAT
AUNTIE EM! AUNTIE EM!

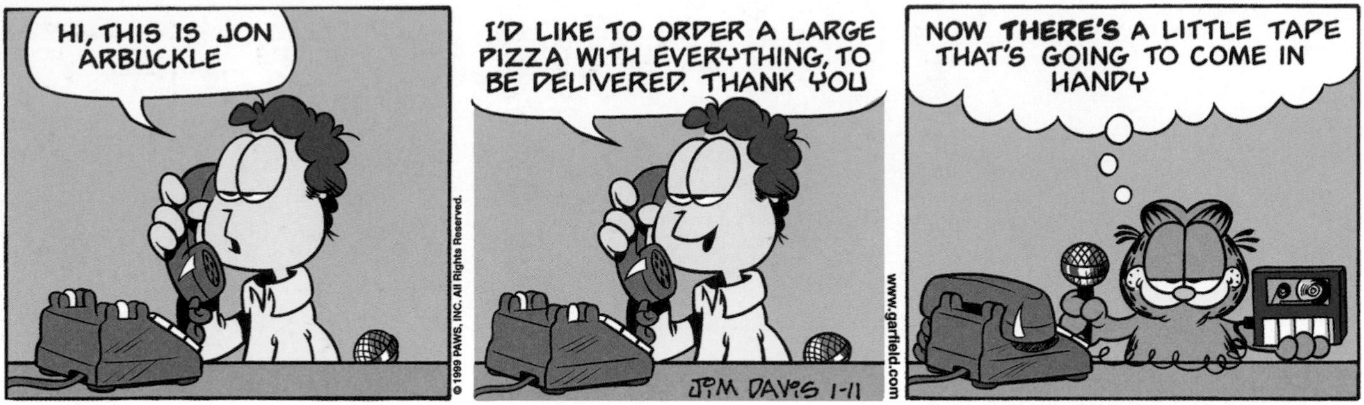
HI, THIS IS JON ARBUCKLE
I'D LIKE TO ORDER A LARGE PIZZA WITH EVERYTHING, TO BE DELIVERED. THANK YOU
JIM DAVIS 1-11
NOW **THERE'S** A LITTLE TAPE THAT'S GOING TO COME IN HANDY
© 1999 PAWS, INC. All Rights Reserved.
www.garfield.com

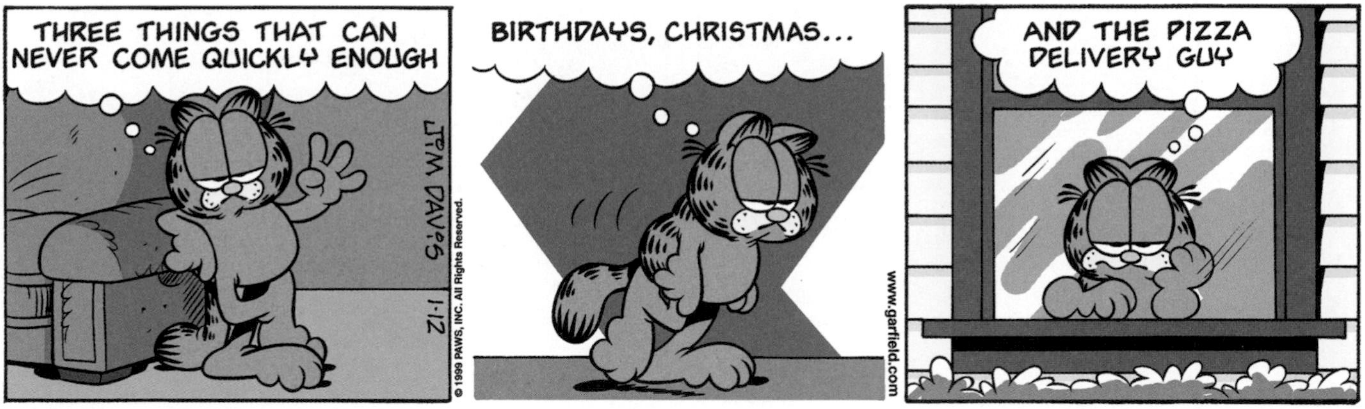
THREE THINGS THAT CAN NEVER COME QUICKLY ENOUGH
JIM DAVIS 1-12
BIRTHDAYS, CHRISTMAS...
AND THE PIZZA DELIVERY GUY
© 1999 PAWS, INC. All Rights Reserved.
www.garfield.com

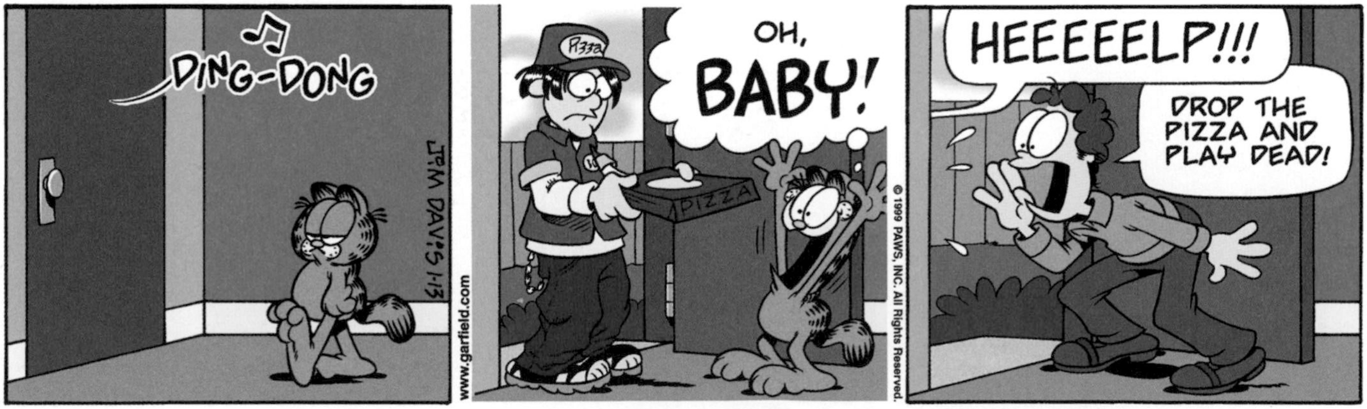
DING-DONG
JIM DAVIS 1-13
OH, BABY!
PIZZA
HEEEEELP!!!
DROP THE PIZZA AND PLAY DEAD!
www.garfield.com
© 1999 PAWS, INC. All Rights Reserved.

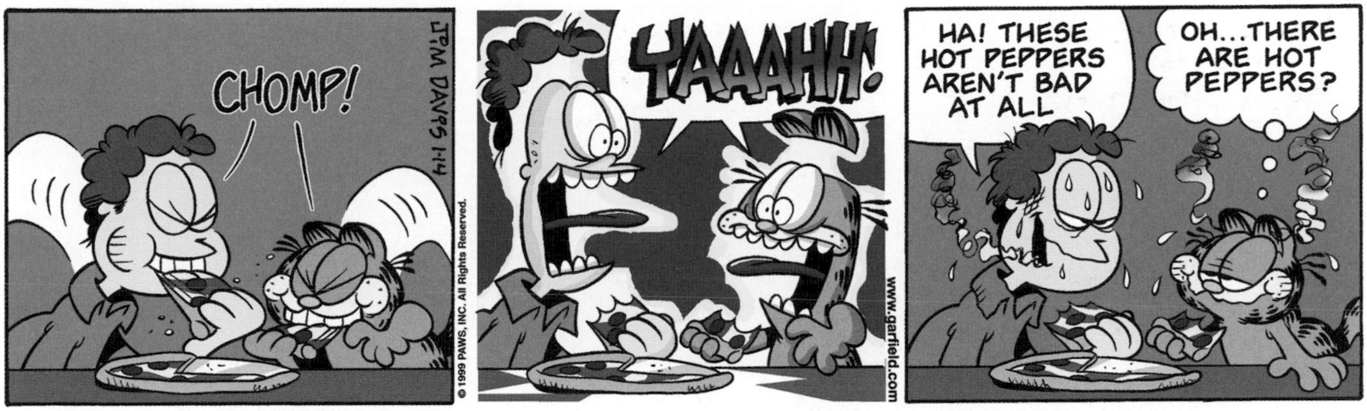
JIM DAVIS 1-14
CHOMP!
© 1999 PAWS, INC. All Rights Reserved.
YAAAHH!
www.garfield.com
HA! THESE HOT PEPPERS AREN'T BAD AT ALL
OH...THERE ARE HOT PEPPERS?

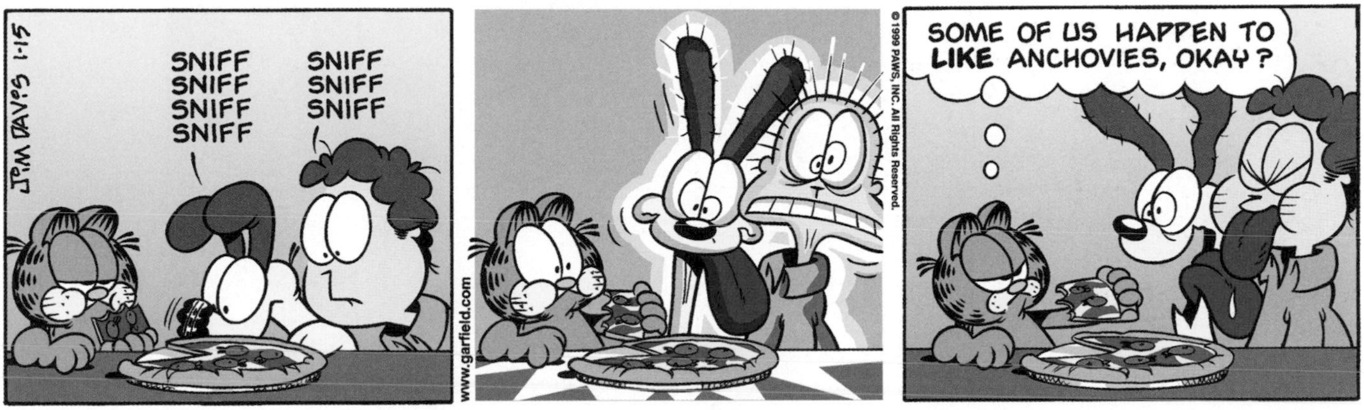
JIM DAVIS 1-15
SNIFF SNIFF SNIFF SNIFF
SNIFF SNIFF SNIFF
www.garfield.com
© 1999 PAWS, INC. All Rights Reserved.
SOME OF US HAPPEN TO LIKE ANCHOVIES, OKAY?

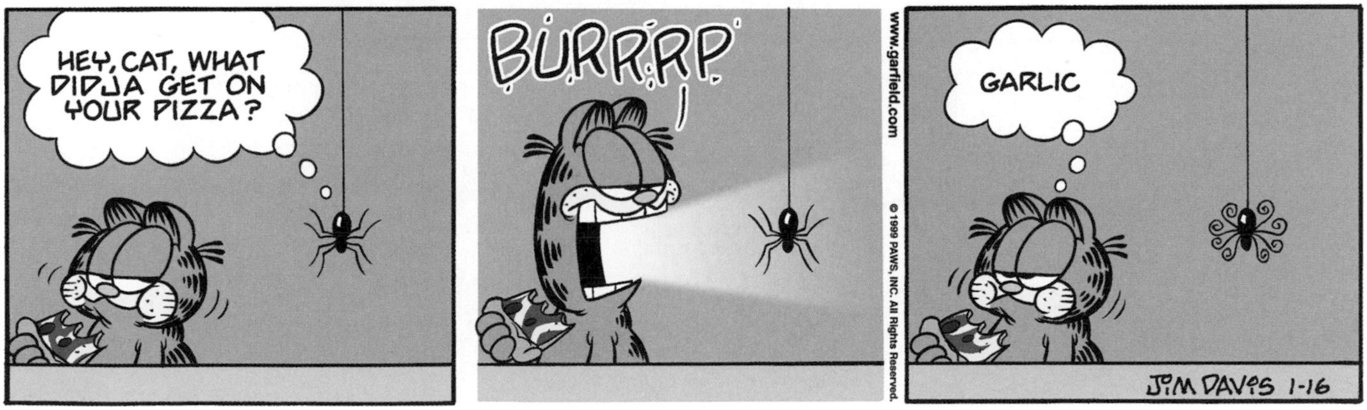
HEY, CAT, WHAT DIDJA GET ON YOUR PIZZA?
BURRRP
www.garfield.com
© 1999 PAWS, INC. All Rights Reserved.
GARLIC
JIM DAVIS 1-16

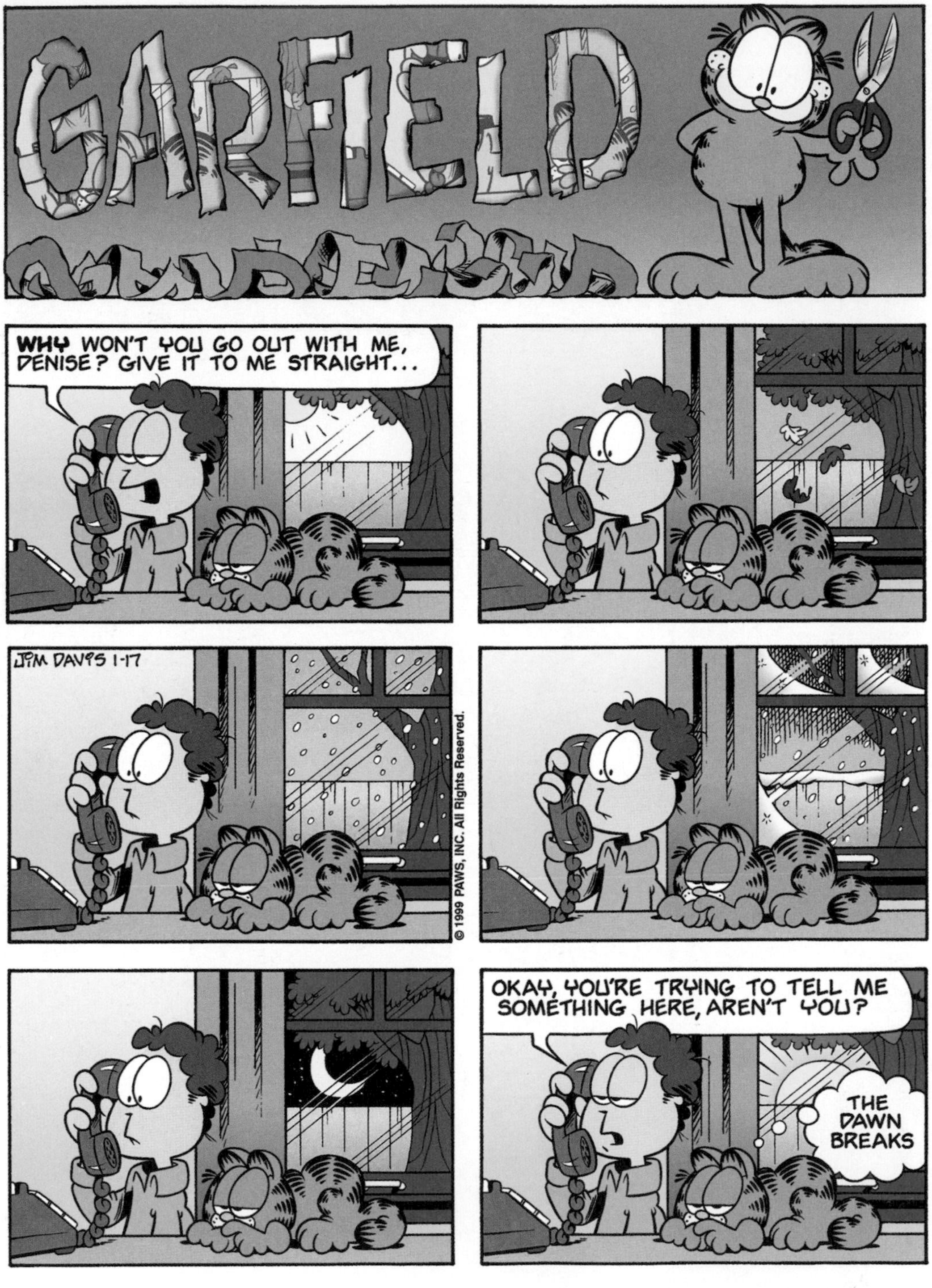
GARFIELD
WHY WON'T YOU GO OUT WITH ME, DENISE? GIVE IT TO ME STRAIGHT...
JIM DAVIS 1-17
© 1999 PAWS, INC. All Rights Reserved.
OKAY, YOU'RE TRYING TO TELL ME SOMETHING HERE, AREN'T YOU?
THE DAWN BREAKS

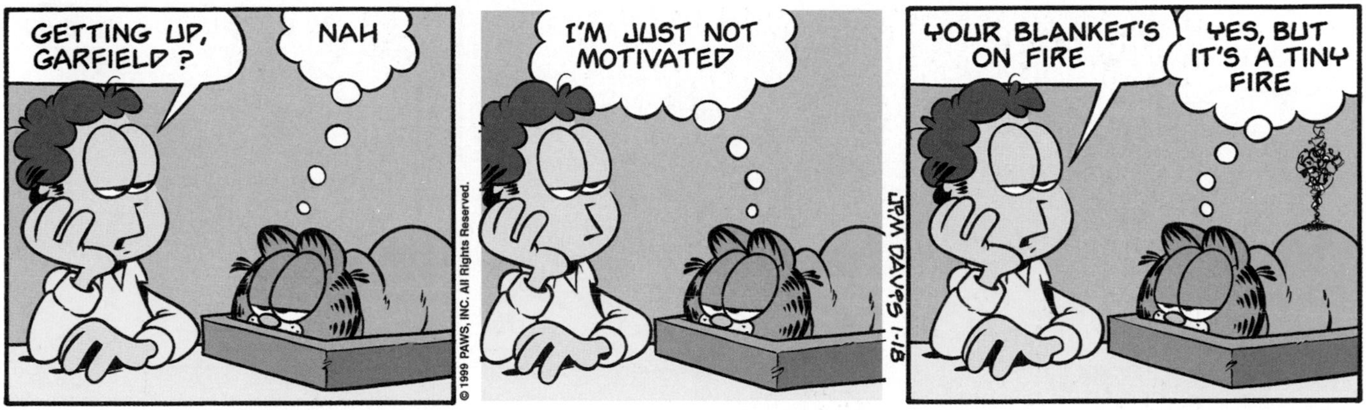
GETTING UP, GARFIELD?
NAH
I'M JUST NOT MOTIVATED
YOUR BLANKET'S ON FIRE
YES, BUT IT'S A TINY FIRE
© 1999 PAWS, INC. All Rights Reserved.
JIM DAVIS 1-18

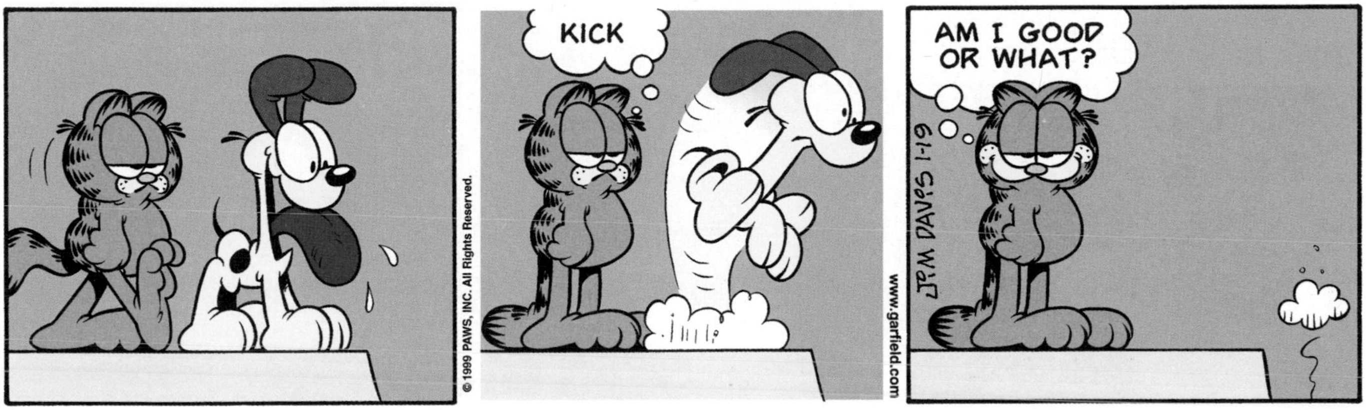
KICK
AM I GOOD OR WHAT?
© 1999 PAWS, INC. All Rights Reserved.
JIM DAVIS 1-19
www.garfield.com

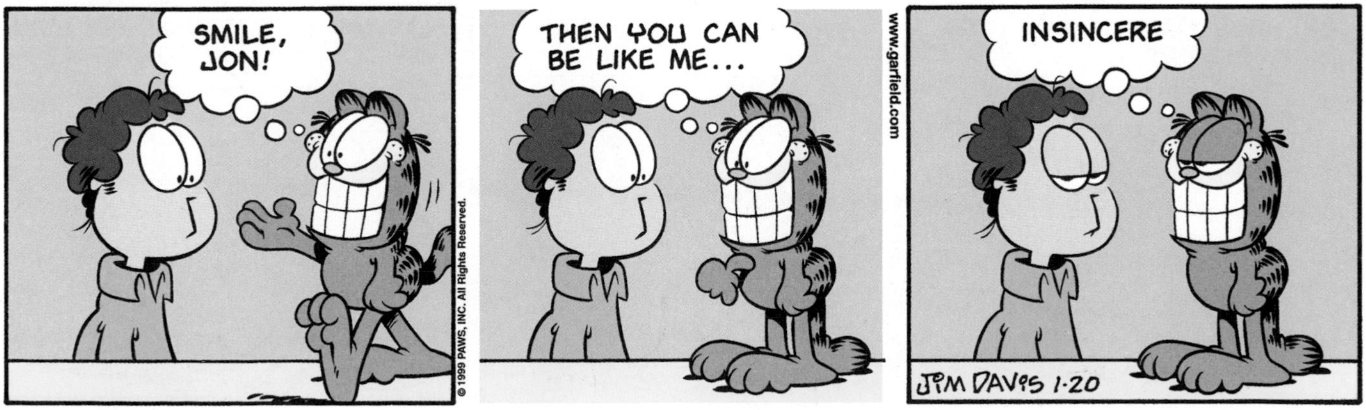
SMILE, JON!
THEN YOU CAN BE LIKE ME...
INSINCERE
© 1999 PAWS, INC. All Rights Reserved.
www.garfield.com
JIM DAVIS 1-20

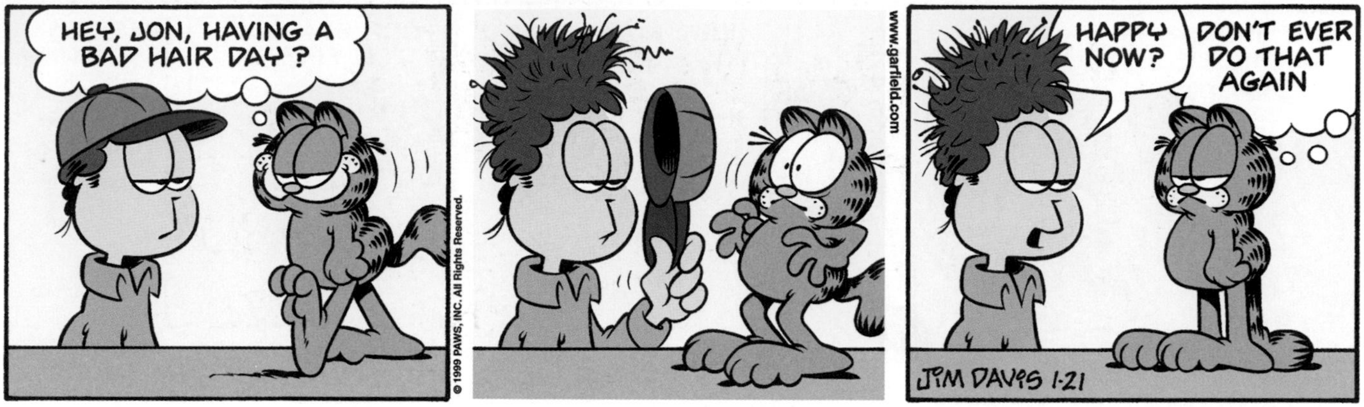
HEY, JON, HAVING A BAD HAIR DAY ?
© 1999 PAWS, INC. All Rights Reserved.
www.garfield.com
HAPPY NOW?
DON'T EVER DO THAT AGAIN
JIM DAVIS 1-21

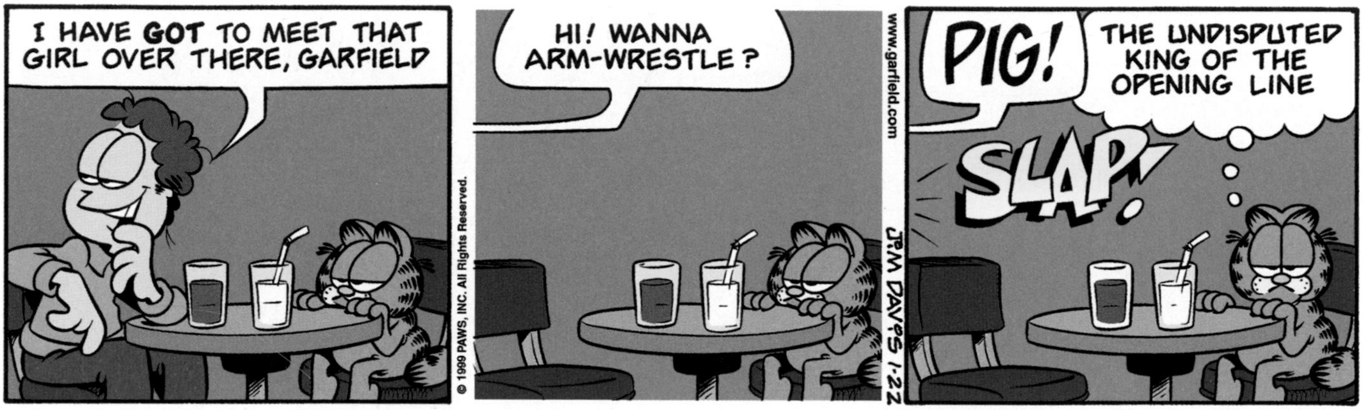
I HAVE GOT TO MEET THAT GIRL OVER THERE, GARFIELD
© 1999 PAWS, INC. All Rights Reserved.
HI! WANNA ARM-WRESTLE ?
JIM DAVIS 1-22
www.garfield.com
PIG!
SLAP!
THE UNDISPUTED KING OF THE OPENING LINE

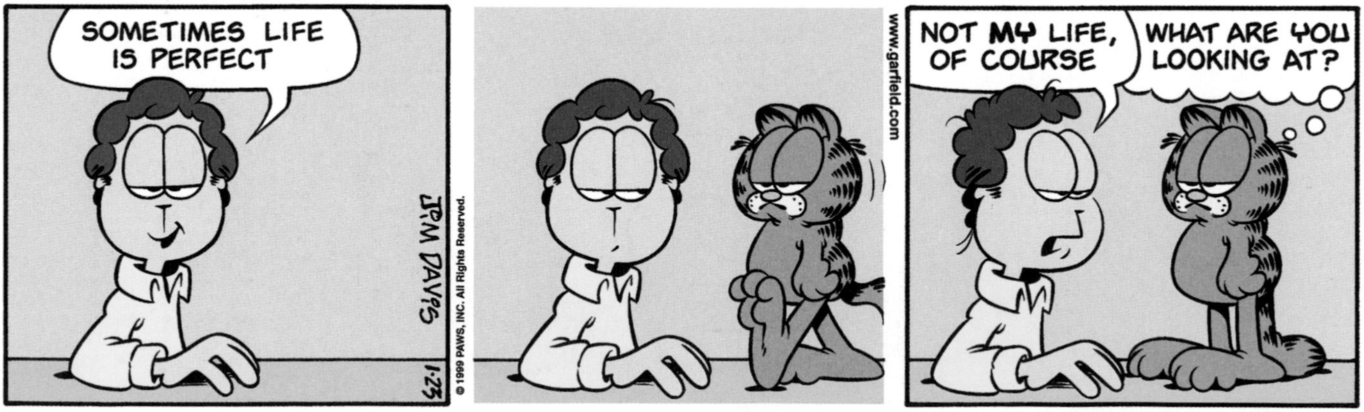
SOMETIMES LIFE IS PERFECT
JIM DAVIS 1-23
© 1999 PAWS, INC. All Rights Reserved.
www.garfield.com
NOT MY LIFE, OF COURSE
WHAT ARE YOU LOOKING AT?

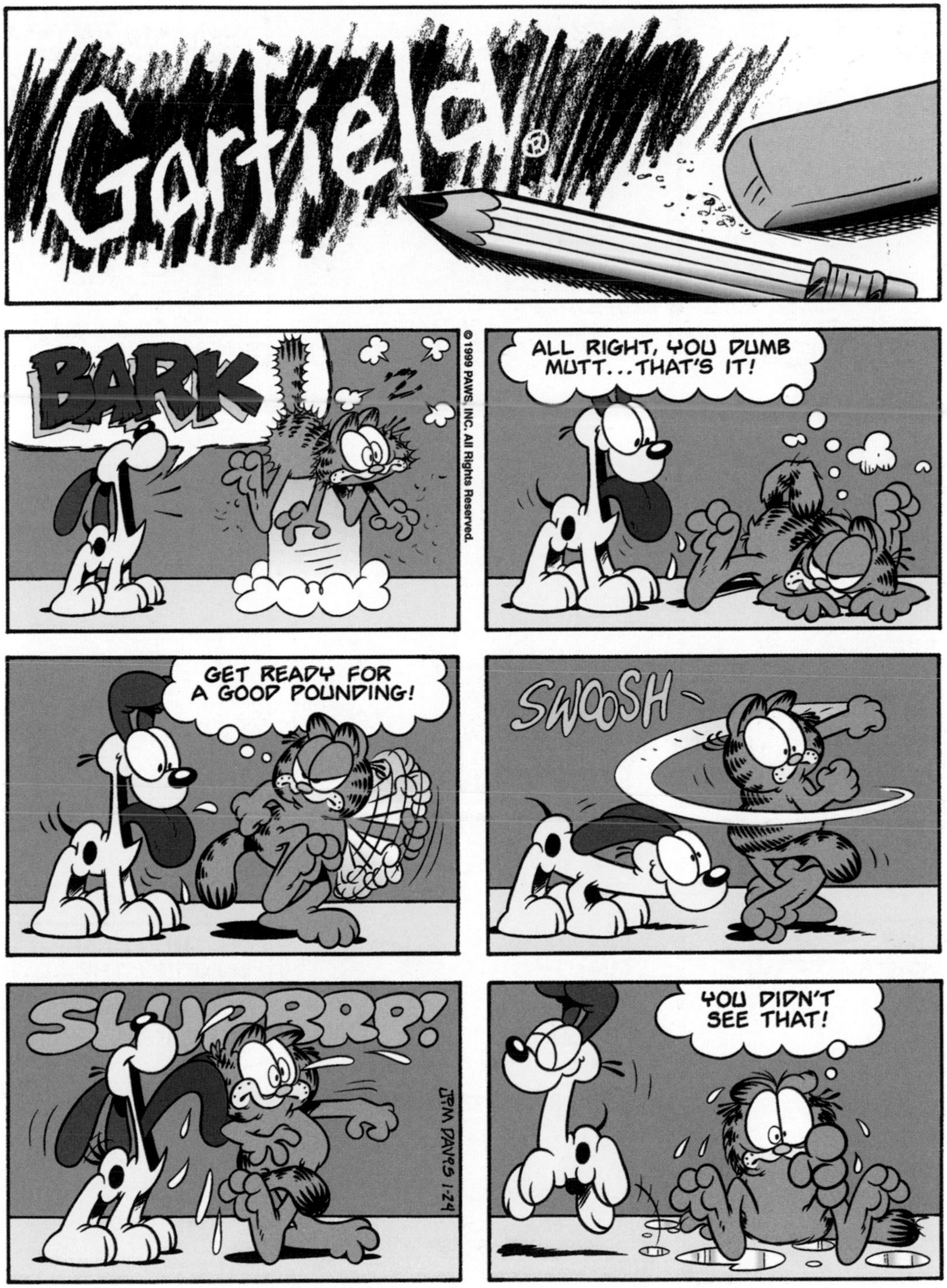

Garfield®
BARK
© 1999 PAWS, INC. All Rights Reserved.
ALL RIGHT, YOU DUMB MUTT...THAT'S IT!
GET READY FOR A GOOD POUNDING!
SWOOSH
JIM DAVIS 1-24
YOU DIDN'T SEE THAT!

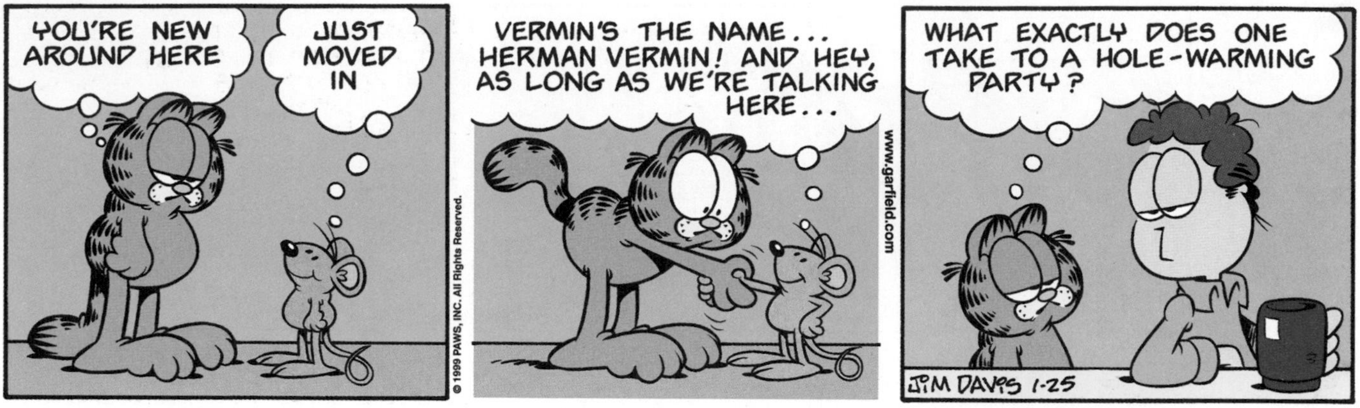
YOU'RE NEW AROUND HERE
JUST MOVED IN
© 1999 PAWS, INC. All Rights Reserved.
VERMIN'S THE NAME... HERMAN VERMIN! AND HEY, AS LONG AS WE'RE TALKING HERE...
www.garfield.com
WHAT EXACTLY DOES ONE TAKE TO A HOLE-WARMING PARTY?
JIM DAVIS 1-25

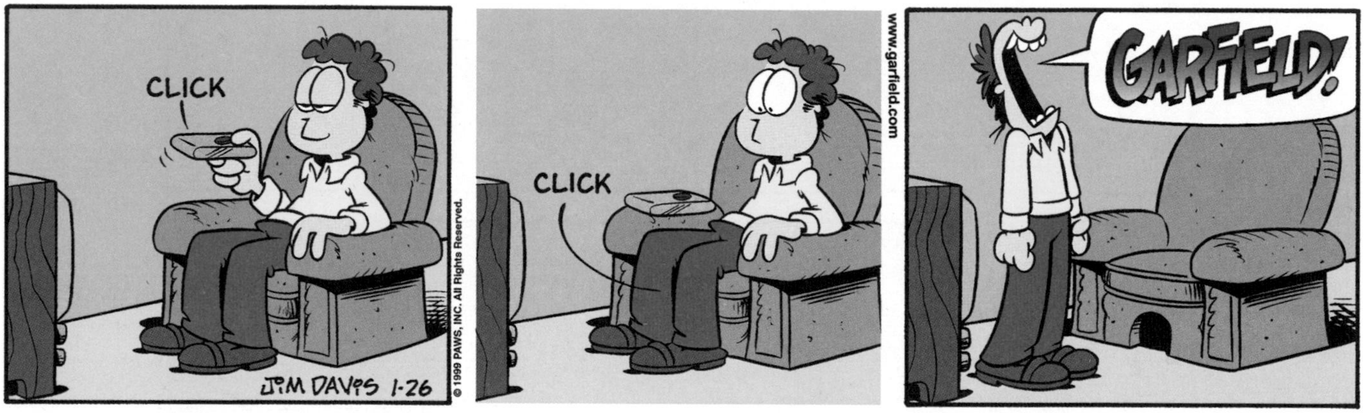
CLICK
JIM DAVIS 1-26
© 1999 PAWS, INC. All Rights Reserved.
CLICK
www.garfield.com
GARFIELD!

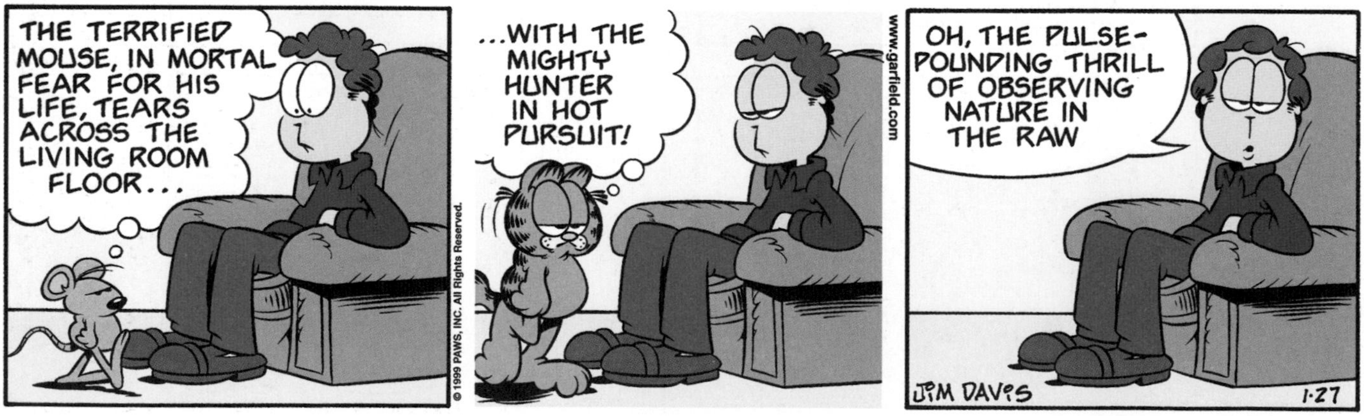
THE TERRIFIED MOUSE, IN MORTAL FEAR FOR HIS LIFE, TEARS ACROSS THE LIVING ROOM FLOOR...
© 1999 PAWS, INC. All Rights Reserved.
...WITH THE MIGHTY HUNTER IN HOT PURSUIT!
www.garfield.com
OH, THE PULSE-POUNDING THRILL OF OBSERVING NATURE IN THE RAW
JIM DAVIS
1-27

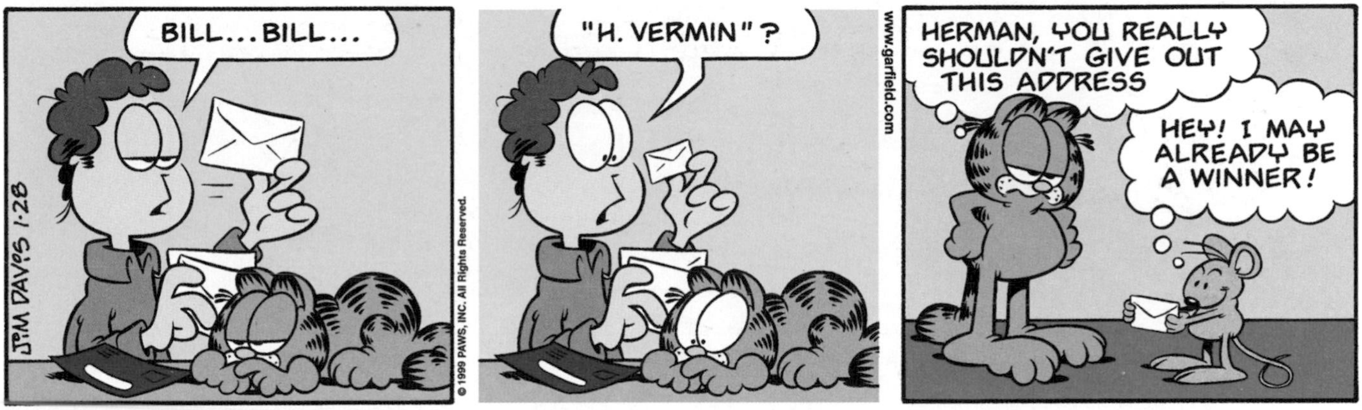
BILL... BILL...
"H. VERMIN"?
HERMAN, YOU REALLY SHOULDN'T GIVE OUT THIS ADDRESS
HEY! I MAY ALREADY BE A WINNER!

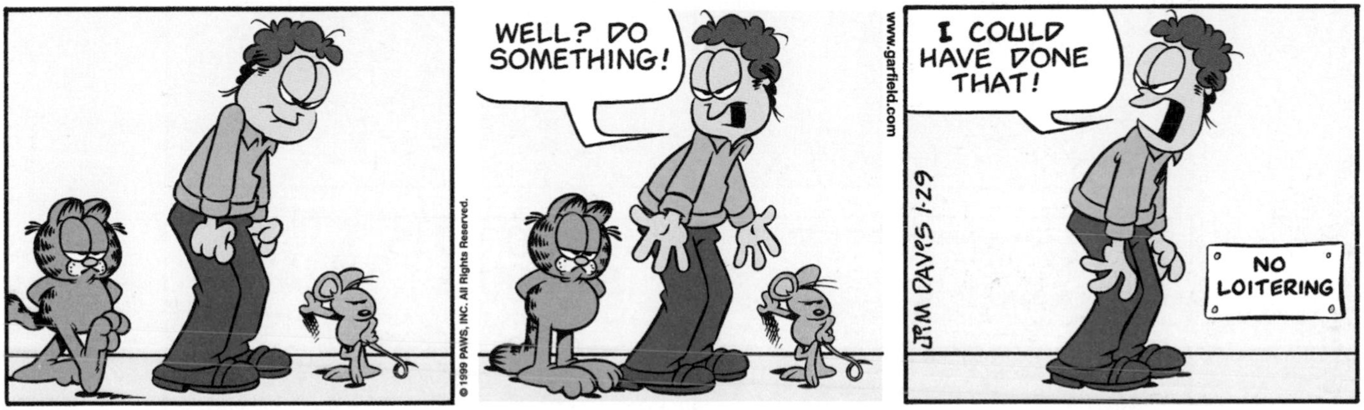
WELL? DO SOMETHING!
I COULD HAVE DONE THAT!
NO LOITERING

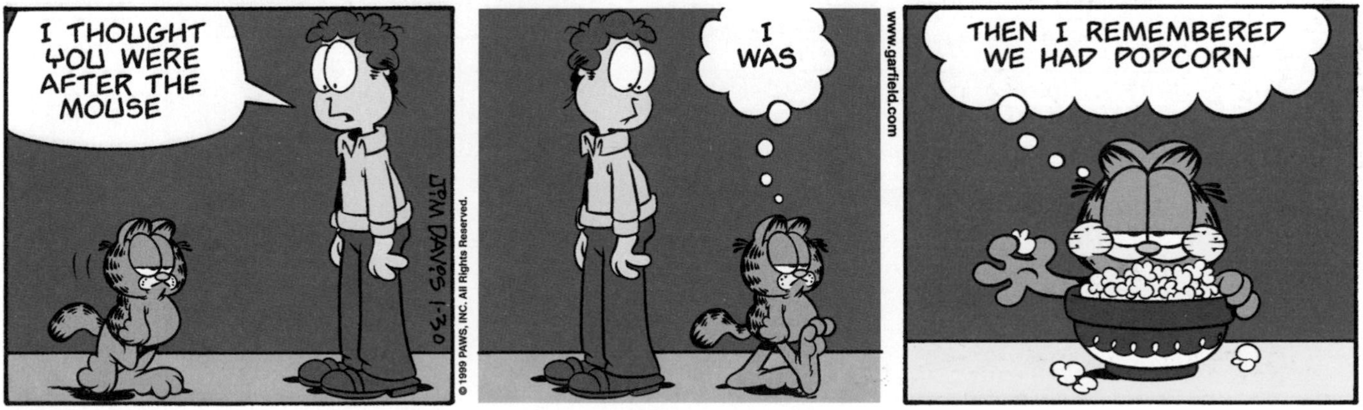
I THOUGHT YOU WERE AFTER THE MOUSE
I WAS
THEN I REMEMBERED WE HAD POPCORN

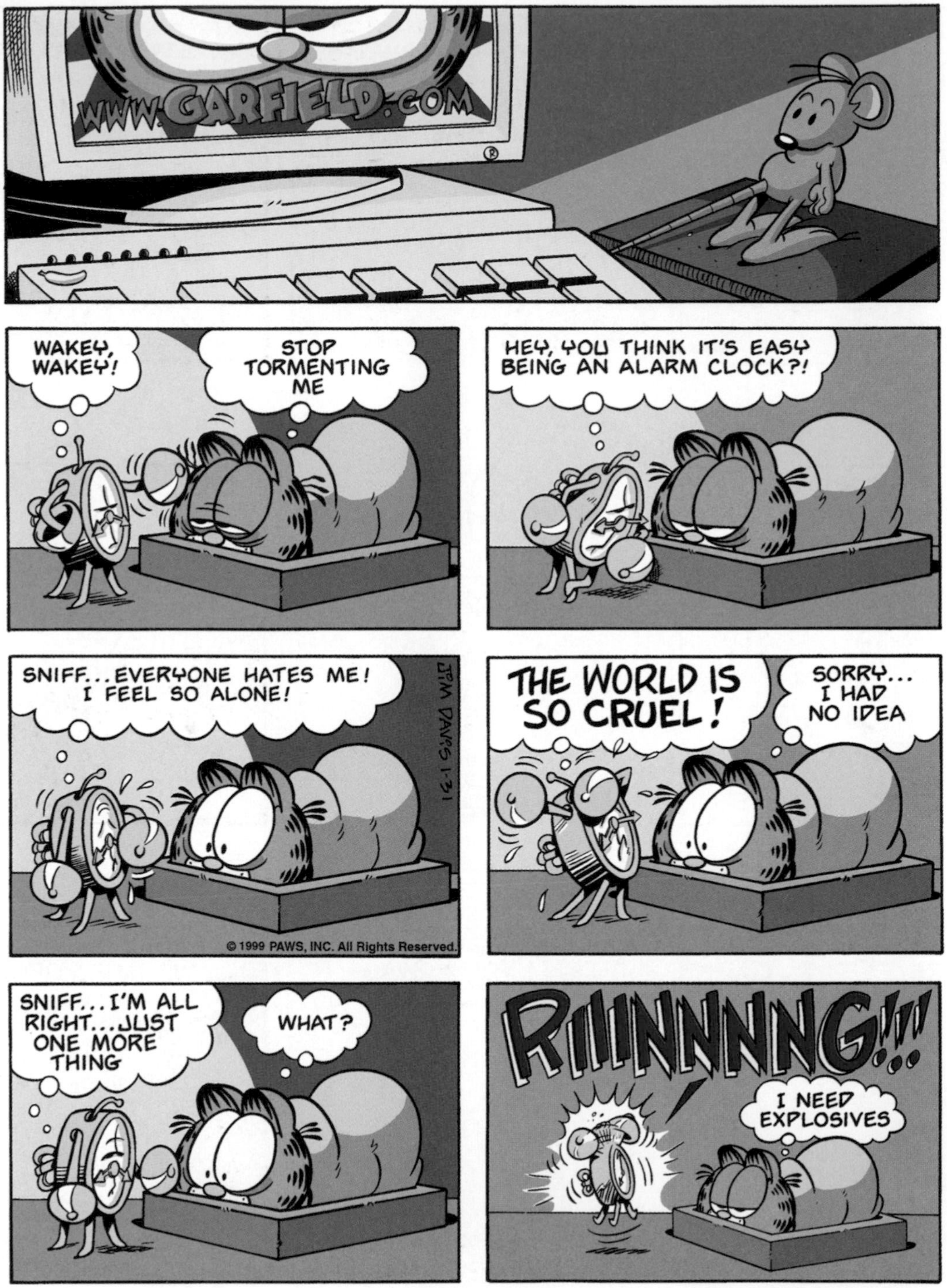
WWW.GARFIELD.COM
WAKEY, WAKEY!
STOP TORMENTING ME
HEY, YOU THINK IT'S EASY BEING AN ALARM CLOCK?!
SNIFF... EVERYONE HATES ME! I FEEL SO ALONE!
JPM DAVIS 1-31
© 1999 PAWS, INC. All Rights Reserved.
THE WORLD IS SO CRUEL!
SORRY... I HAD NO IDEA
SNIFF... I'M ALL RIGHT... JUST ONE MORE THING
WHAT?
RIIINNNNG!!!
I NEED EXPLOSIVES

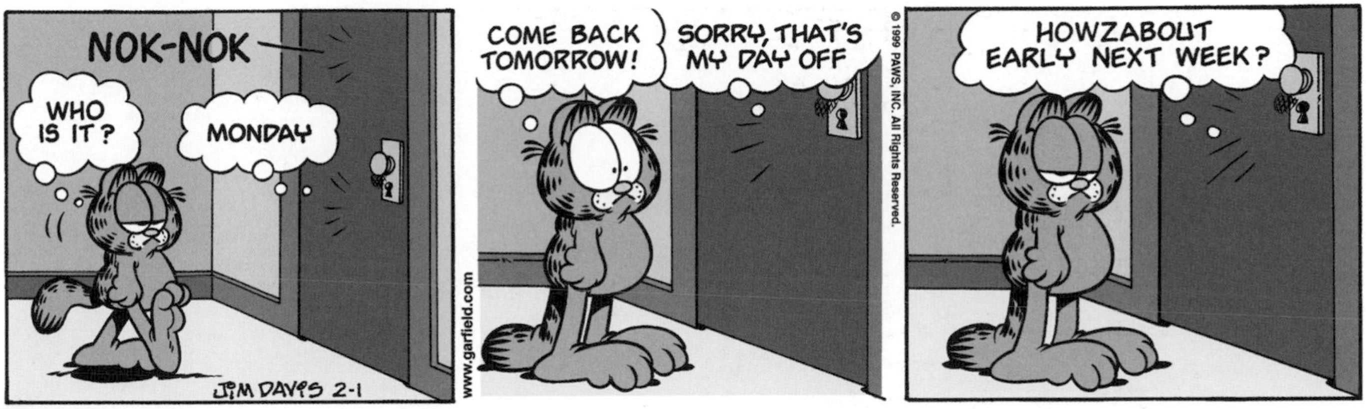
NOK-NOK
WHO IS IT?
MONDAY
JIM DAVIS 2-1
www.garfield.com
COME BACK TOMORROW!
SORRY, THAT'S MY DAY OFF
© 1999 PAWS, INC. All Rights Reserved.
HOWZABOUT EARLY NEXT WEEK?

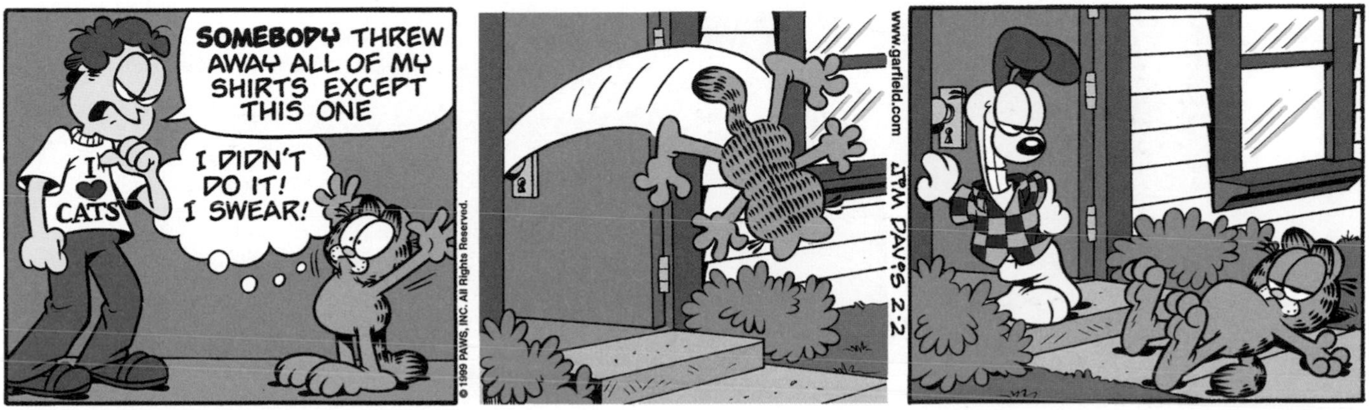
SOMEBODY THREW AWAY ALL OF MY SHIRTS EXCEPT THIS ONE
I ♥ CATS
I DIDN'T DO IT! I SWEAR!
© 1999 PAWS, INC. All Rights Reserved.
www.garfield.com
JIM DAVIS 2-2

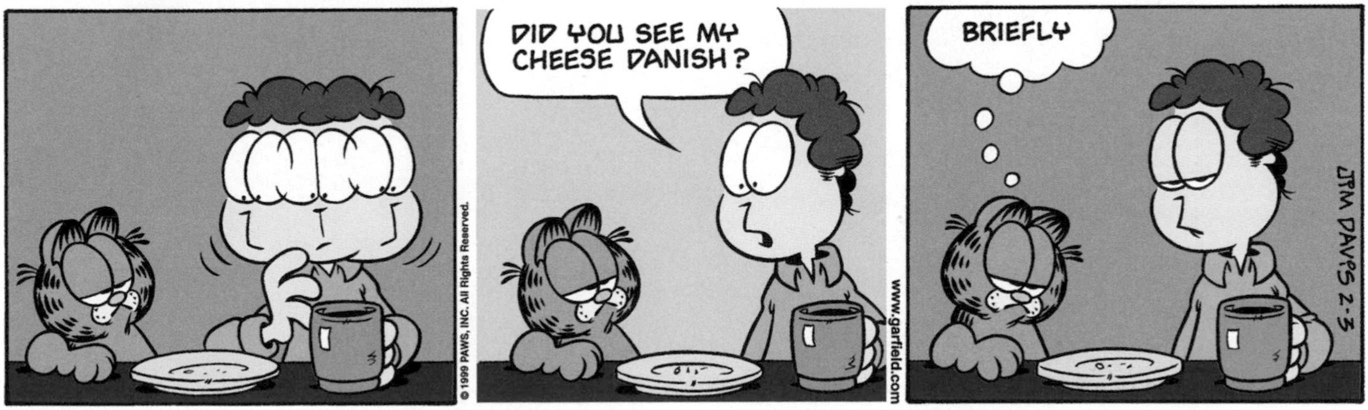
© 1999 PAWS, INC. All Rights Reserved.
DID YOU SEE MY CHEESE DANISH?
www.garfield.com
BRIEFLY
JIM DAVIS 2-3

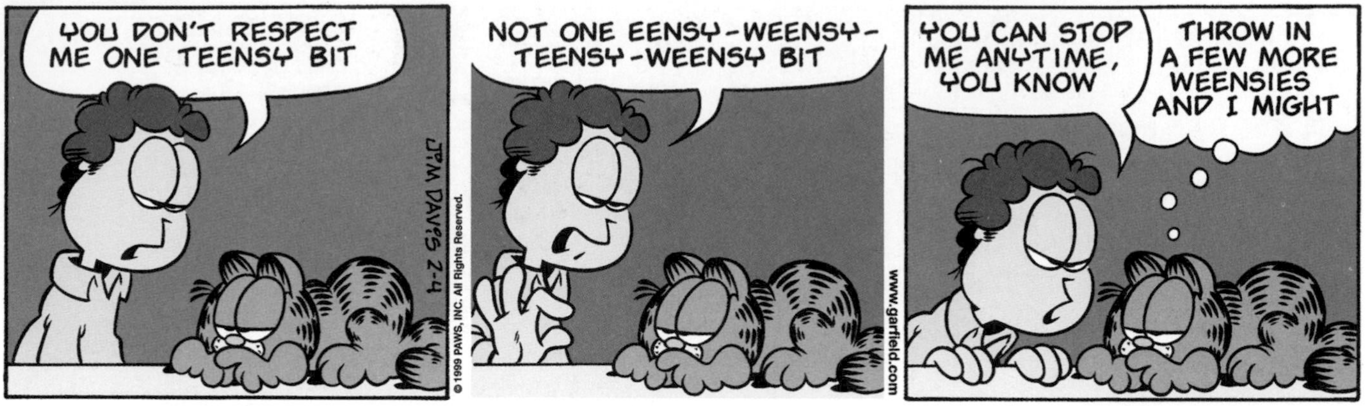
YOU DON'T RESPECT ME ONE TEENSY BIT
JIM DAVIS 2-4
NOT ONE EENSY-WEENSY-TEENSY-WEENSY BIT
© 1999 PAWS, INC. All Rights Reserved.
YOU CAN STOP ME ANYTIME, YOU KNOW
THROW IN A FEW MORE WEENSIES AND I MIGHT
www.garfield.com

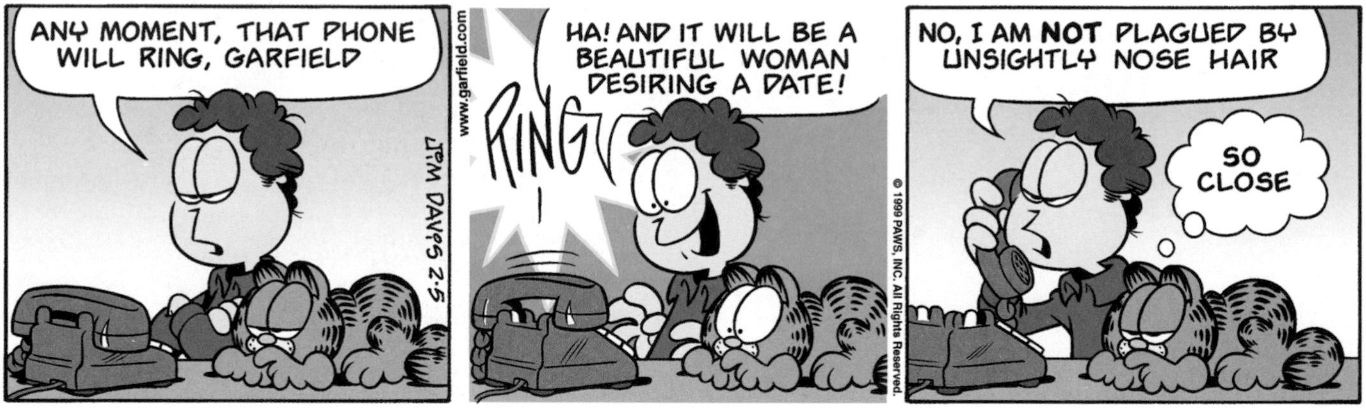
ANY MOMENT, THAT PHONE WILL RING, GARFIELD
JIM DAVIS 2-5
www.garfield.com
RING!
HA! AND IT WILL BE A BEAUTIFUL WOMAN DESIRING A DATE!
© 1999 PAWS, INC. All Rights Reserved.
NO, I AM **NOT** PLAGUED BY UNSIGHTLY NOSE HAIR
SO CLOSE

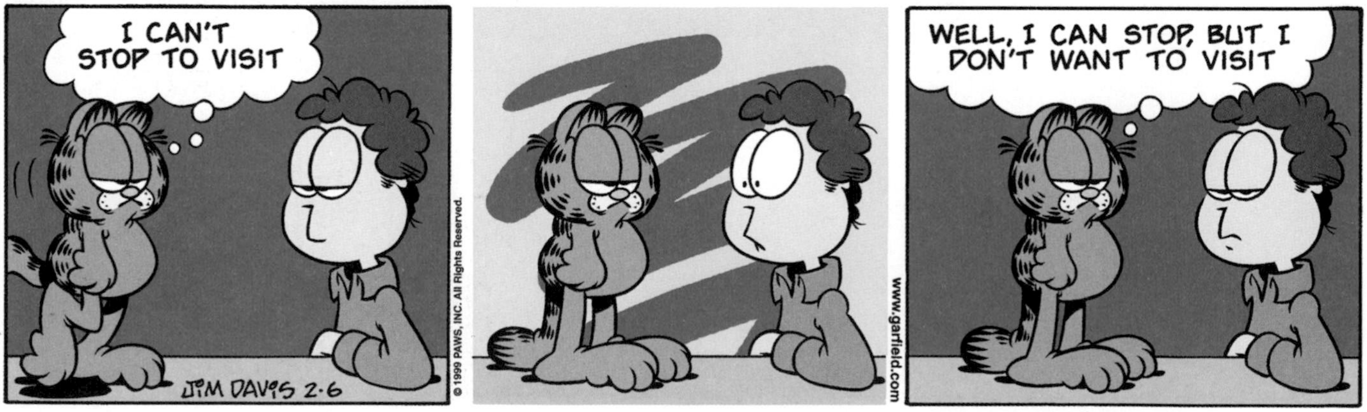
I CAN'T STOP TO VISIT
JIM DAVIS 2-6
© 1999 PAWS, INC. All Rights Reserved.
www.garfield.com
WELL, I CAN STOP, BUT I DON'T WANT TO VISIT

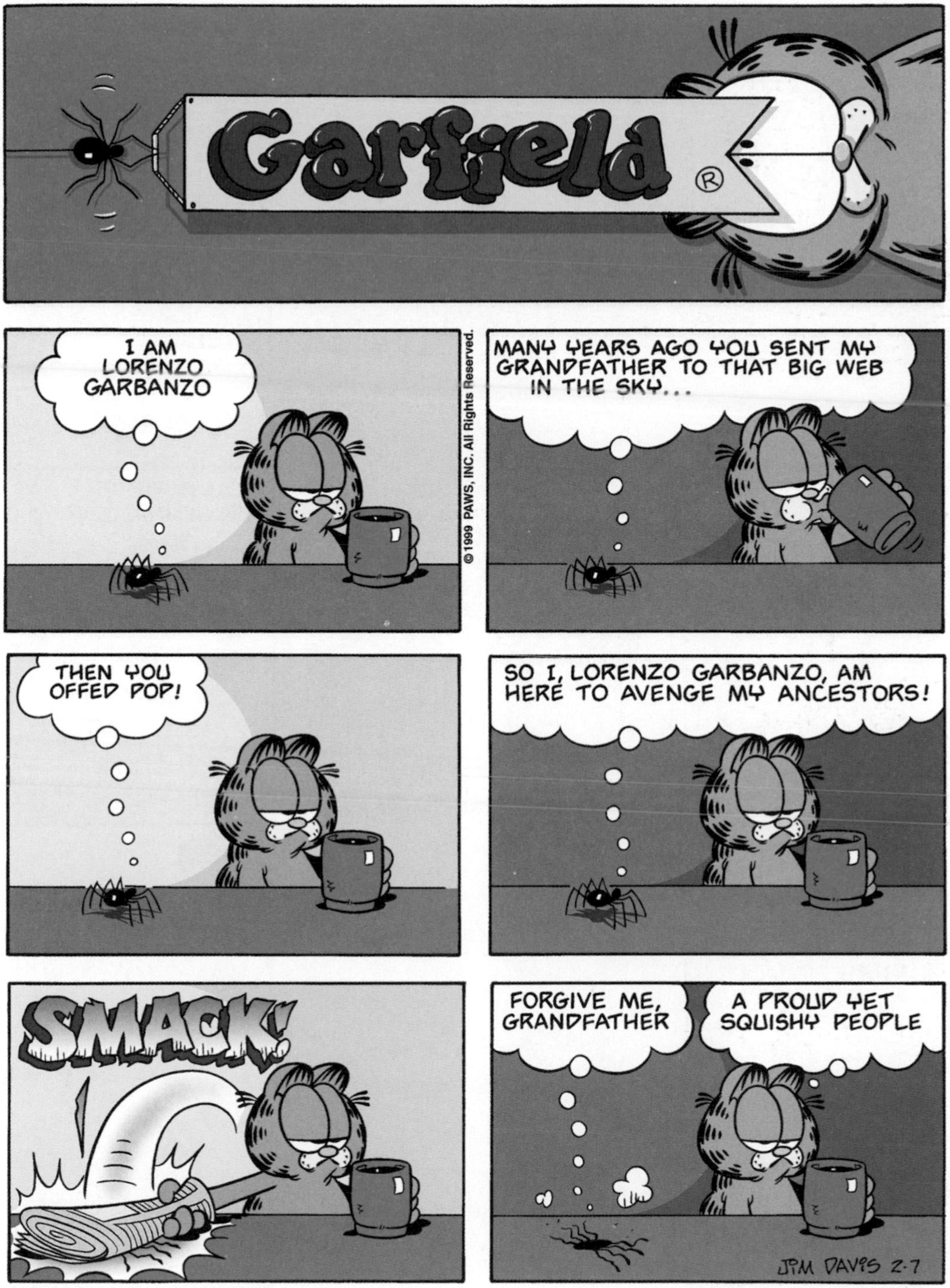

Garfield®
I AM LORENZO GARBANZO
MANY YEARS AGO YOU SENT MY GRANDFATHER TO THAT BIG WEB IN THE SKY...
THEN YOU OFFED POP!
SO I, LORENZO GARBANZO, AM HERE TO AVENGE MY ANCESTORS!
SMACK!
FORGIVE ME, GRANDFATHER
A PROUD YET SQUISHY PEOPLE
JIM DAVIS 2-7

RIIING
JIM DAVIS 2-8
© 1999 PAWS, INC. All Rights Reserved.
HELLO?
I'M BACK
www.garfield.com
HE WHAT?!!
I'M GONE AGAIN

THAT WAS MRS. WOONDUCK
© 1999 PAWS, INC. All Rights Reserved.
HMM...WOONDUCK...
WOONDUCK...HMMM...
WOON-DUCK...HMM...
WOONDUCK...HMM...
www.garfield.com
YOU NOOGIED HER SCHNAUZER
OH YEAH, THE YELLER
JIM DAVIS 2-9

THE COMPLAINTS I GET ABOUT YOU! I'M SURPRISED YOU DON'T HAVE A CRIMINAL RECORD!
JIM DAVIS 2-10
© 1999 PAWS, INC. All Rights Reserved.
www.garfield.com
I DON'T WANT TO KNOW...
THE FOOD'S NOT AS BAD AS THEY SAY

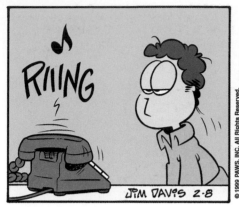

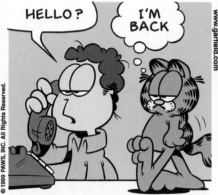

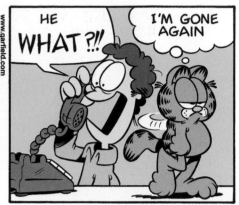

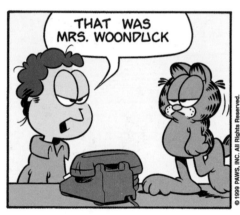

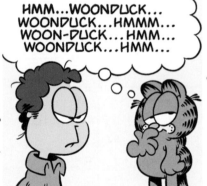

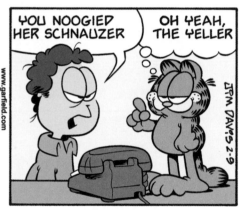

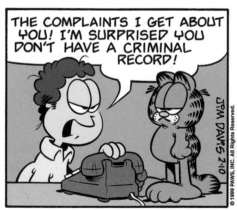

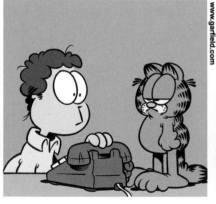

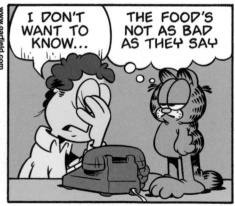

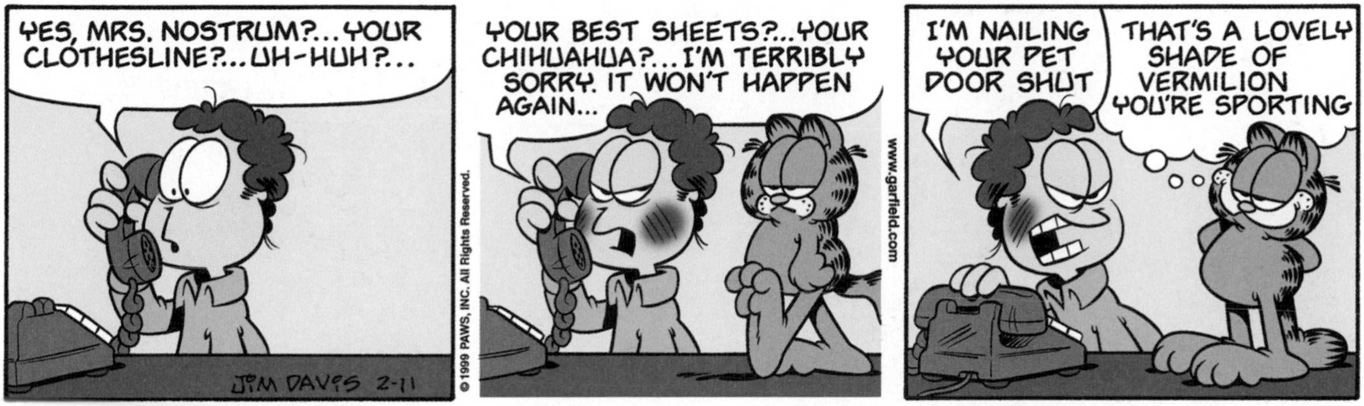
YES, MRS. NOSTRUM?...YOUR CLOTHESLINE?...UH-HUH?...
JIM DAVIS 2-11
© 1999 PAWS, INC. All Rights Reserved.
YOUR BEST SHEETS?...YOUR CHIHUAHUA?...I'M TERRIBLY SORRY. IT WON'T HAPPEN AGAIN...
www.garfield.com
I'M NAILING YOUR PET DOOR SHUT
THAT'S A LOVELY SHADE OF VERMILION YOU'RE SPORTING

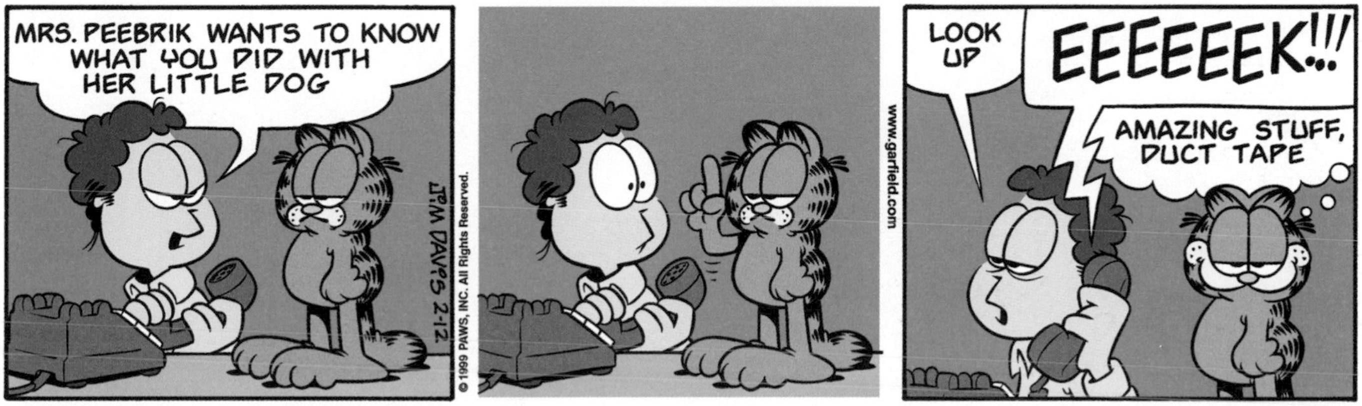
MRS. PEEBRIK WANTS TO KNOW WHAT YOU DID WITH HER LITTLE DOG
JIM DAVIS 2-12
© 1999 PAWS, INC. All Rights Reserved.
www.garfield.com
LOOK UP
EEEEEEK!!!
AMAZING STUFF, DUCT TAPE

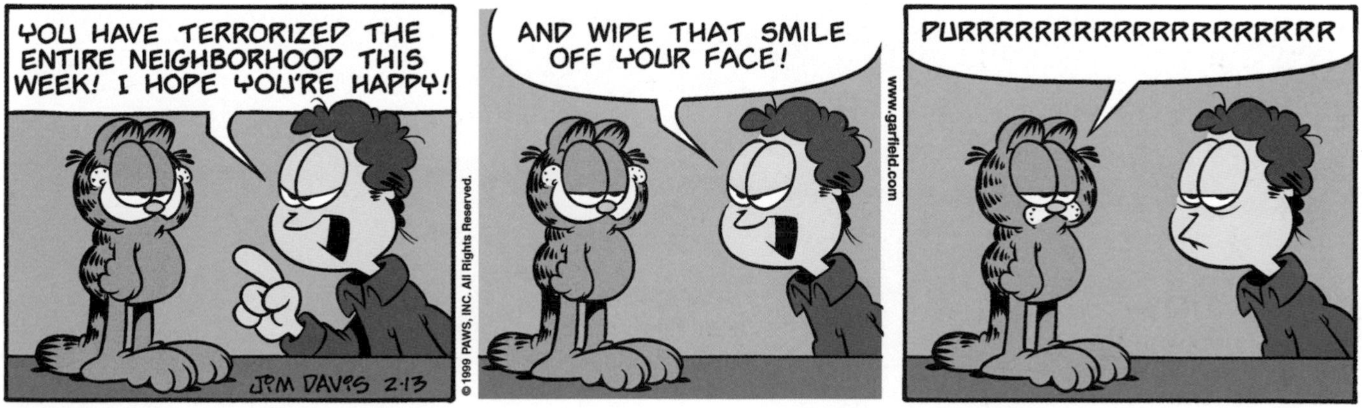
YOU HAVE TERRORIZED THE ENTIRE NEIGHBORHOOD THIS WEEK! I HOPE YOU'RE HAPPY!
JIM DAVIS 2-13
© 1999 PAWS, INC. All Rights Reserved.
AND WIPE THAT SMILE OFF YOUR FACE!
www.garfield.com
PURRRRRRRRRRRRRRRRRRR

REJECTED GARFIELD BOOK TITLES

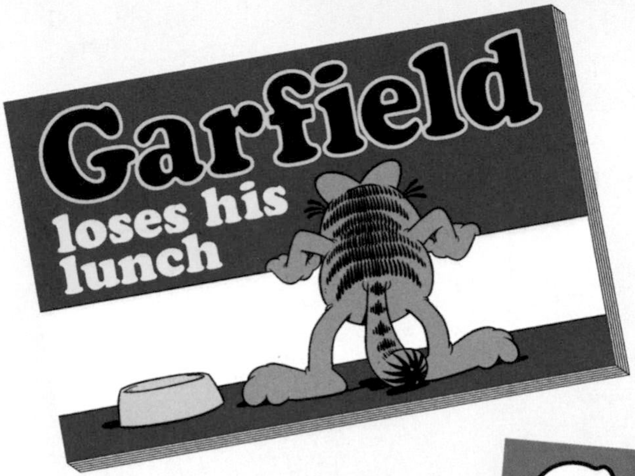
Garfield
loses his lunch

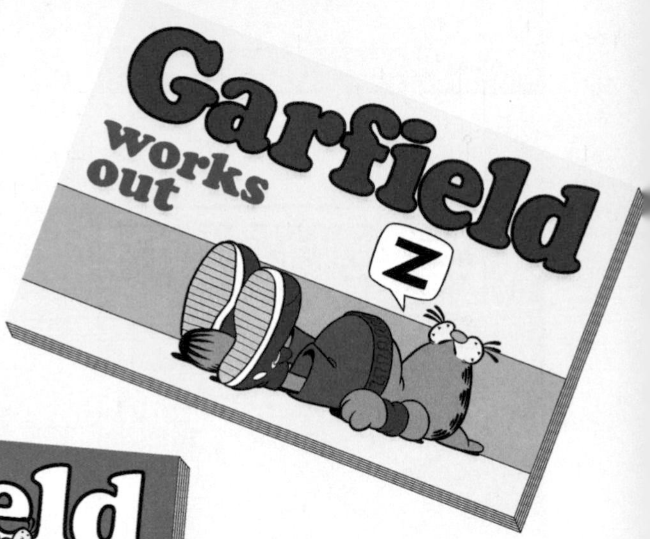
Garfield
works out
Z

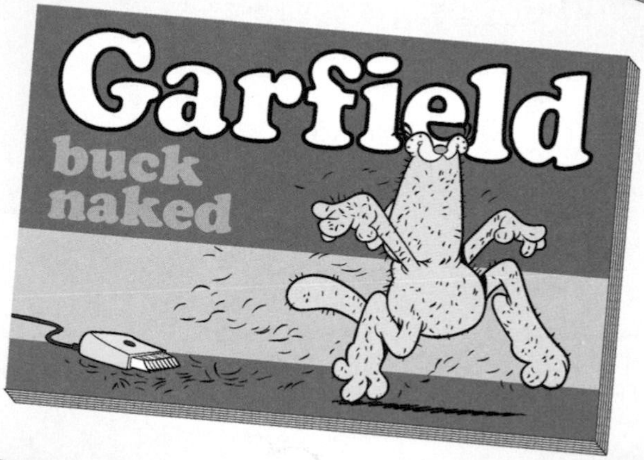
Garfield
buck naked

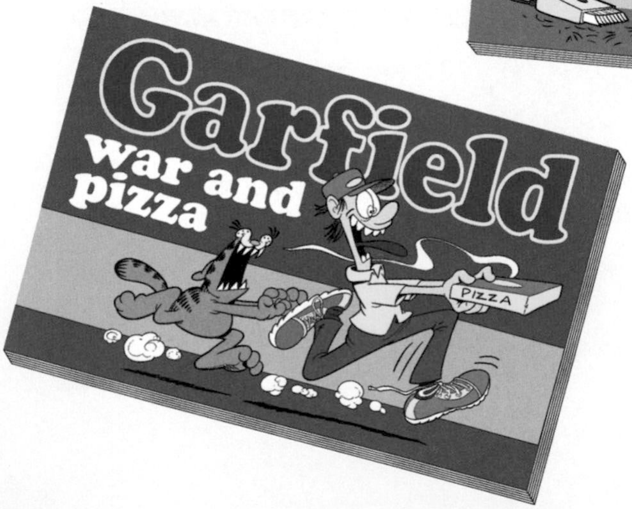
Garfield
war and pizza
PIZZA

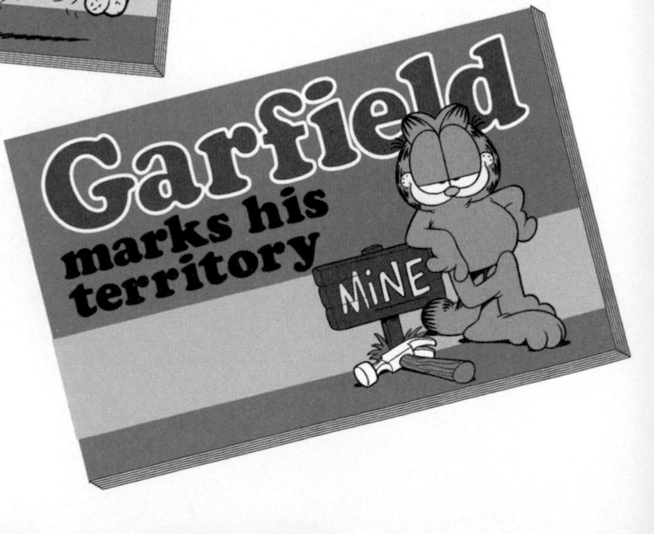
Garfield
marks his territory
MINE

Garfield
hogs the
spotlight

BY JIM DAVIS

Ballantine Books • New York

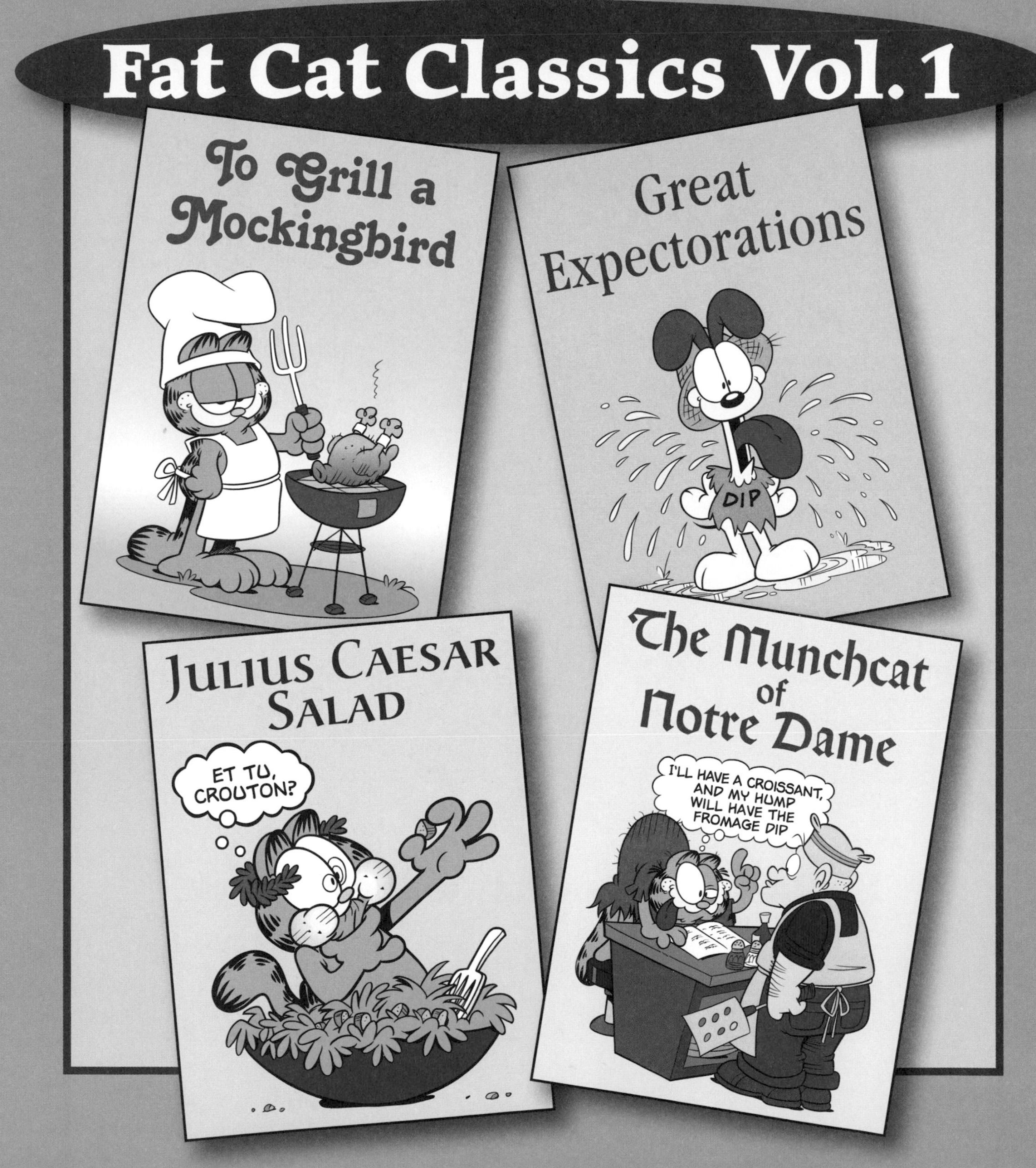
Fat Cat Classics Vol. 1
To Grill a Mockingbird
Great Expectorations
DIP
Julius Caesar Salad
ET TU, CROUTON?
The Munchcat of Notre Dame
I'LL HAVE A CROISSANT, AND MY HUMP WILL HAVE THE FROMAGE DIP

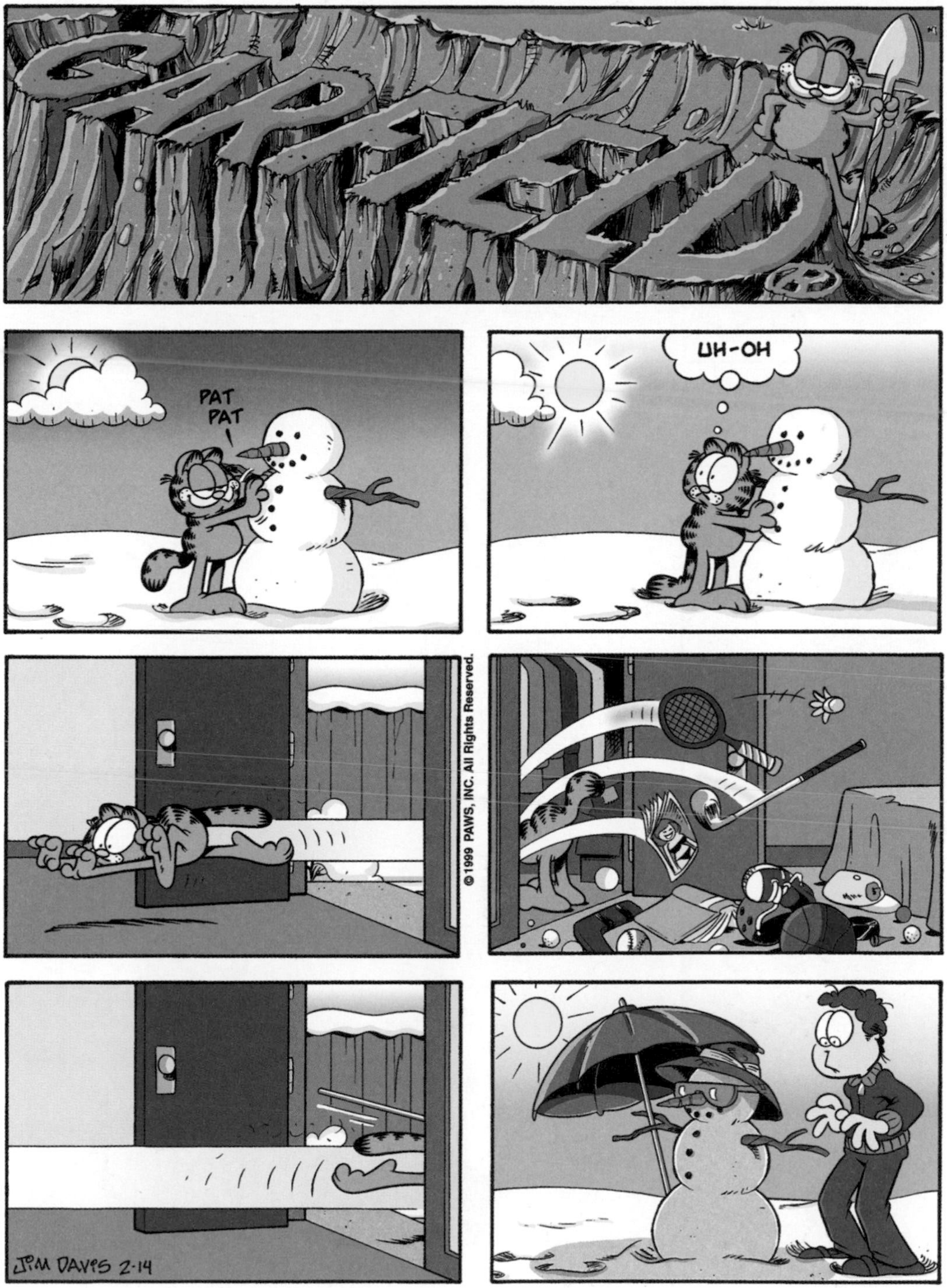
GARFIELD
PAT PAT
UH-OH
© 1999 PAWS, INC. All Rights Reserved.
JIM DAVIS 2-14

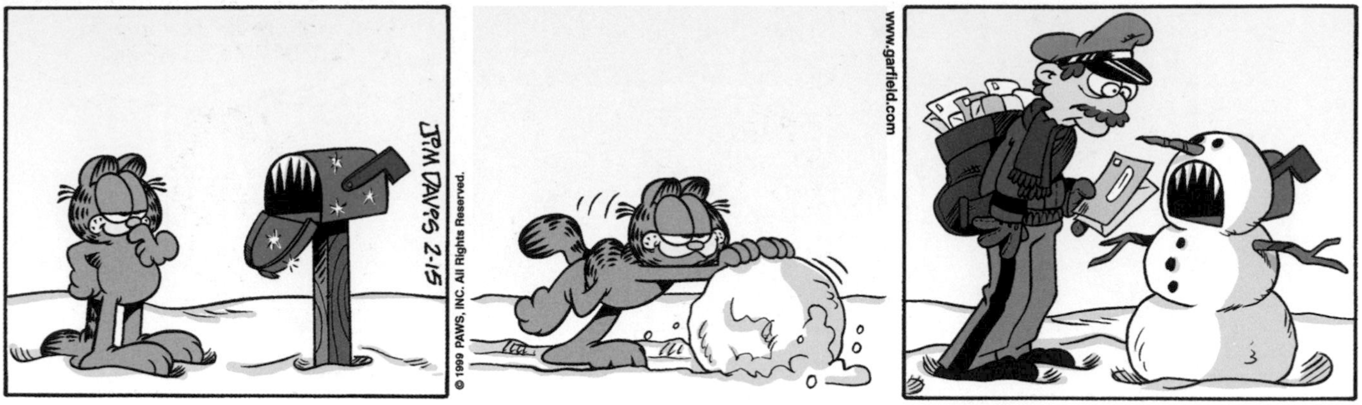
JIM DAVIS 2-15
© 1999 PAWS, INC. All Rights Reserved.
www.garfield.com

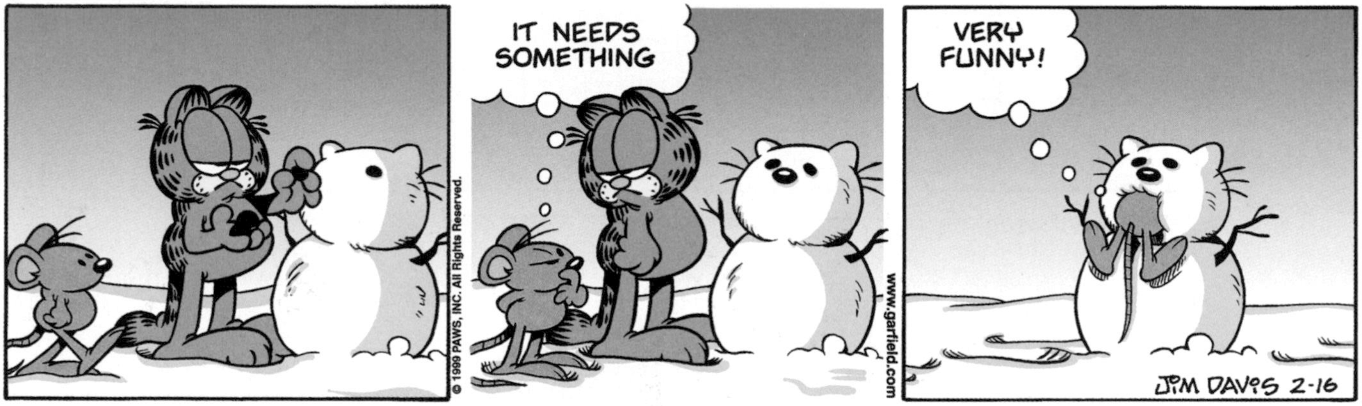
© 1999 PAWS, INC. All Rights Reserved.
IT NEEDS SOMETHING
www.garfield.com
VERY FUNNY!
JIM DAVIS 2-16

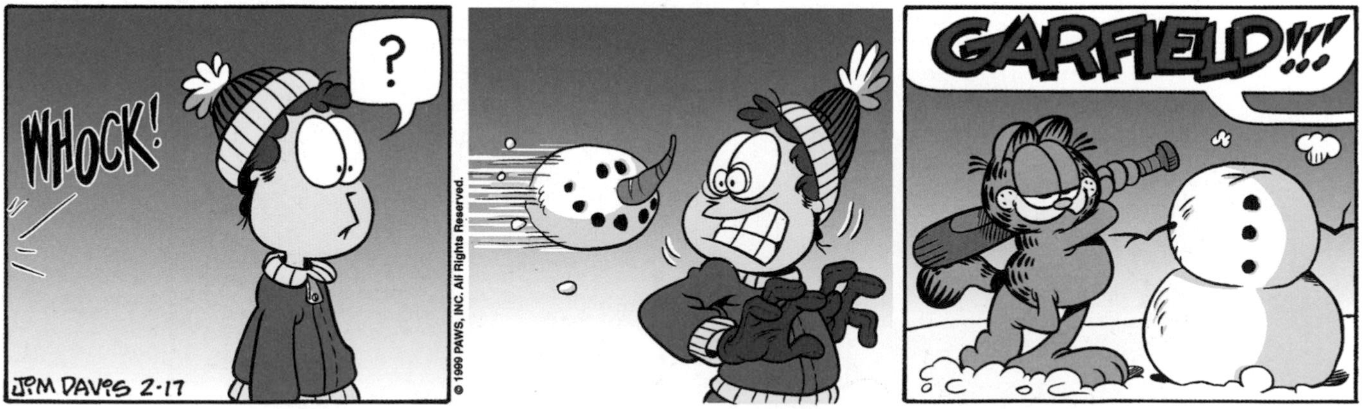
WHOCK!
?
JIM DAVIS 2-17
© 1999 PAWS, INC. All Rights Reserved.
GARFIELD!!!

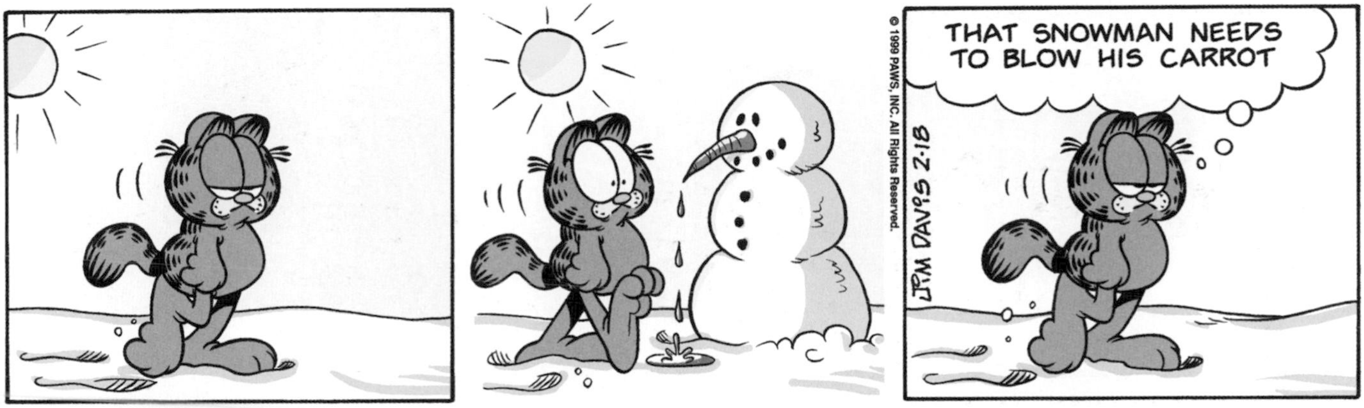
© 1999 PAWS, INC. All Rights Reserved.
JIM DAVIS 2-18
THAT SNOWMAN NEEDS TO BLOW HIS CARROT

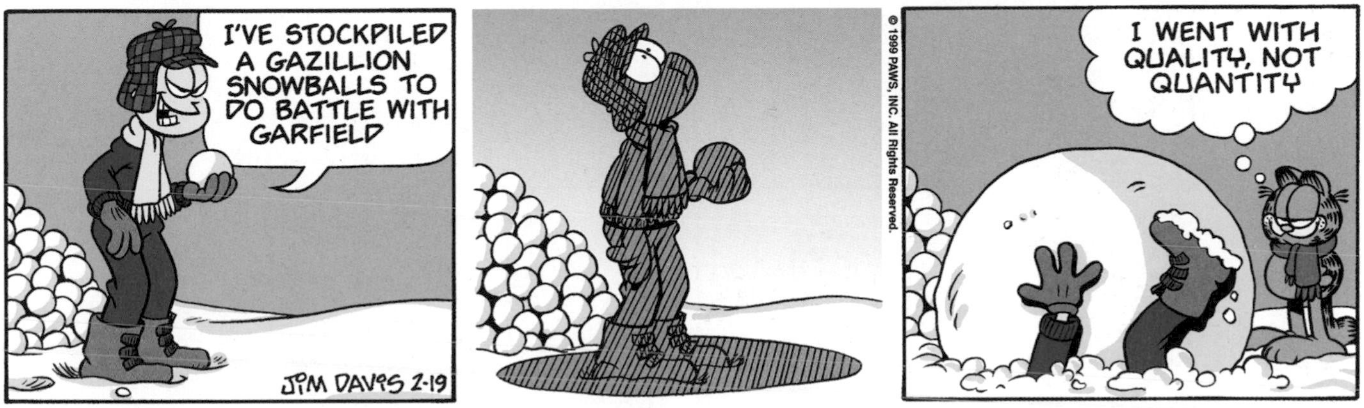
I'VE STOCKPILED A GAZILLION SNOWBALLS TO DO BATTLE WITH GARFIELD
JIM DAVIS 2-19
© 1999 PAWS, INC. All Rights Reserved.
I WENT WITH QUALITY, NOT QUANTITY

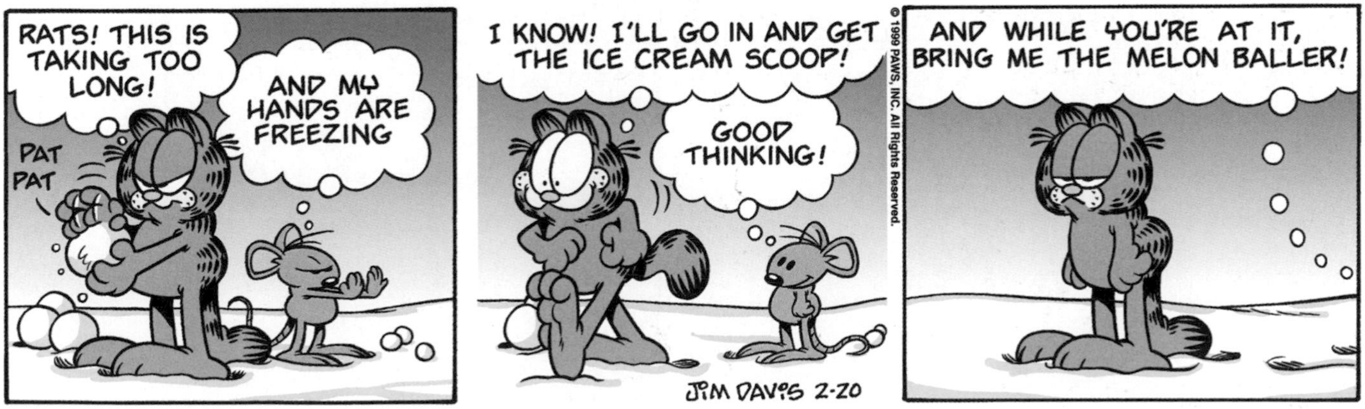
RATS! THIS IS TAKING TOO LONG!
PAT PAT
AND MY HANDS ARE FREEZING
I KNOW! I'LL GO IN AND GET THE ICE CREAM SCOOP!
GOOD THINKING!
JIM DAVIS 2-20
© 1999 PAWS, INC. All Rights Reserved.
AND WHILE YOU'RE AT IT, BRING ME THE MELON BALLER!

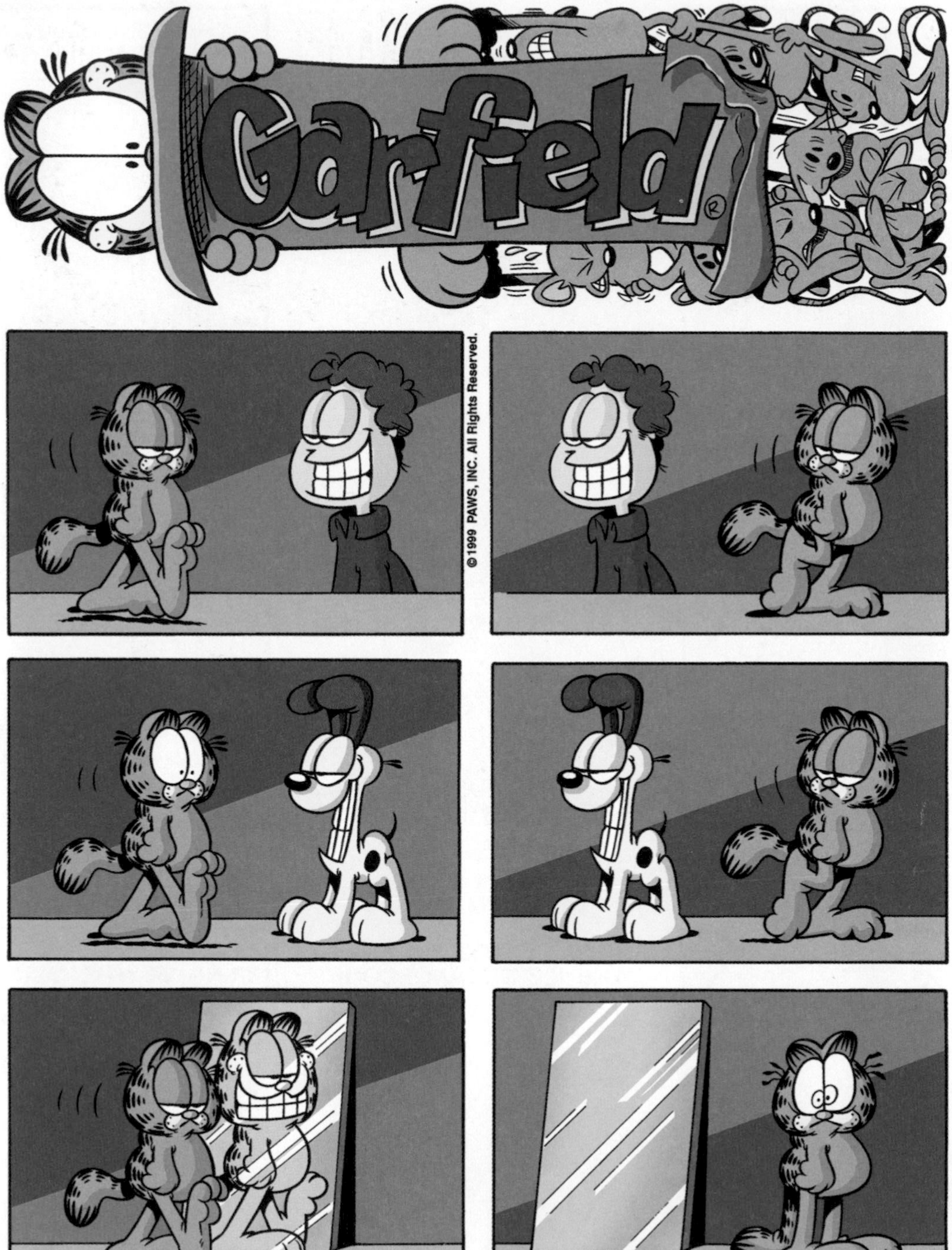
Garfield
©1999 PAWS, INC. All Rights Reserved.
JIM DAVIS 2-21

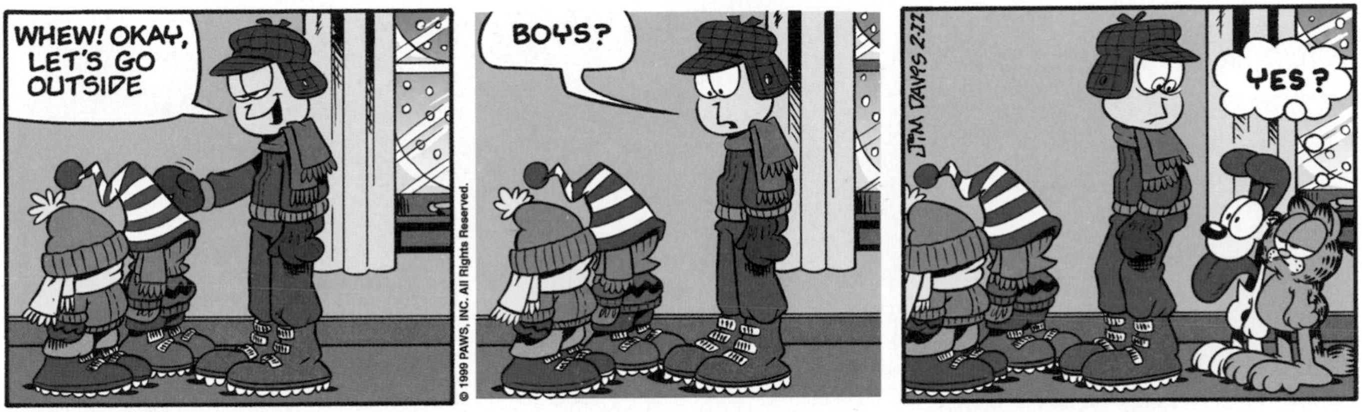
WHEW! OKAY, LET'S GO OUTSIDE
© 1999 PAWS, INC. All Rights Reserved.
BOYS?
JIM DAVIS 2-22
YES?

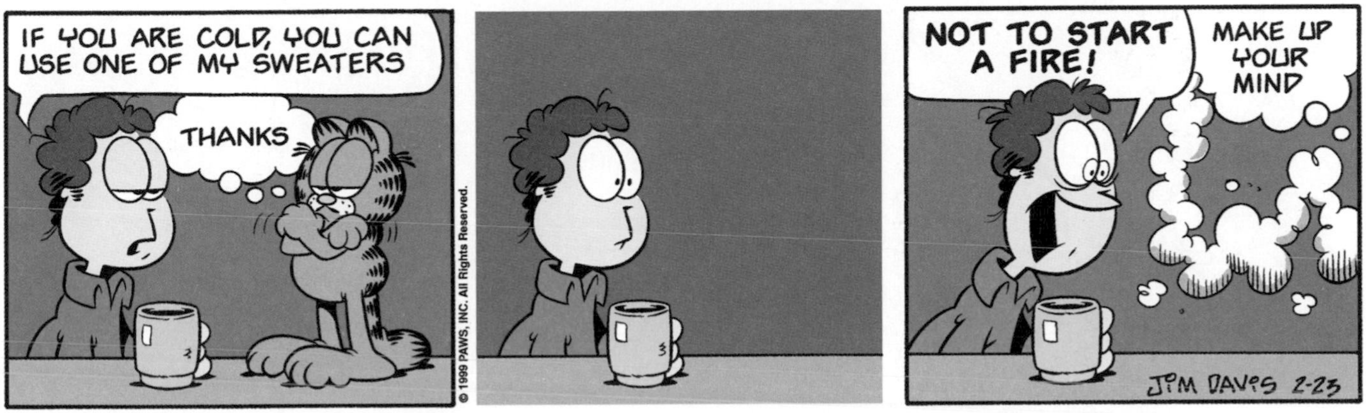
IF YOU ARE COLD, YOU CAN USE ONE OF MY SWEATERS
THANKS
© 1999 PAWS, INC. All Rights Reserved.
NOT TO START A FIRE!
MAKE UP YOUR MIND
JIM DAVIS 2-23

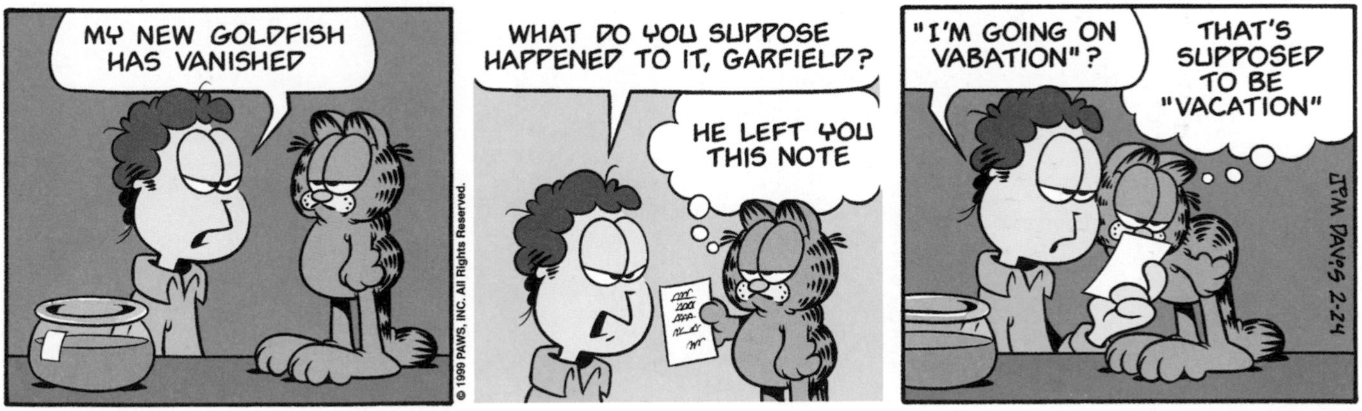
MY NEW GOLDFISH HAS VANISHED
© 1999 PAWS, INC. All Rights Reserved.
WHAT DO YOU SUPPOSE HAPPENED TO IT, GARFIELD?
HE LEFT YOU THIS NOTE
"I'M GOING ON VABATION"?
THAT'S SUPPOSED TO BE "VACATION"
JIM DAVIS 2-24

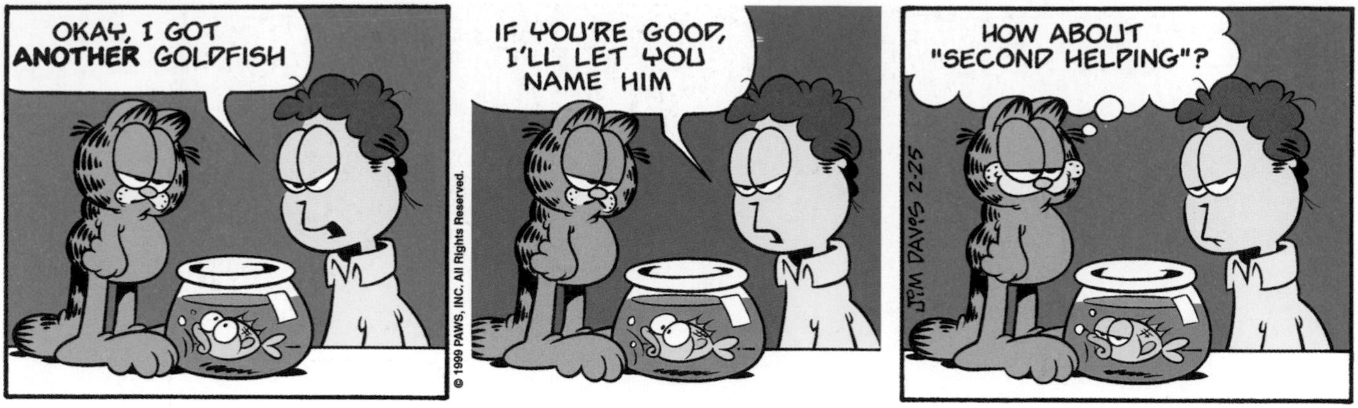
OKAY, I GOT ANOTHER GOLDFISH
IF YOU'RE GOOD, I'LL LET YOU NAME HIM
HOW ABOUT "SECOND HELPING"?
JIM DAVIS 2-25
© 1999 PAWS, INC. All Rights Reserved.

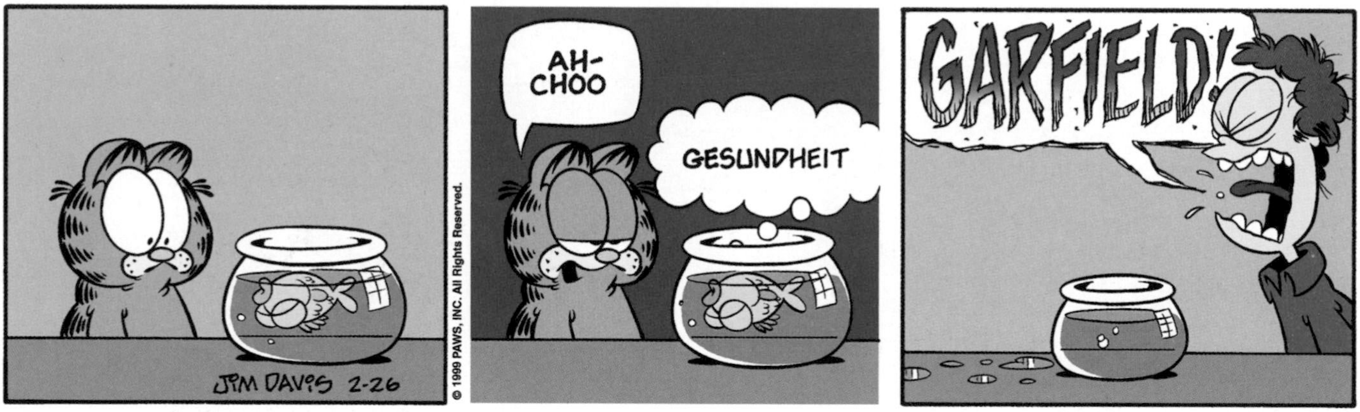
JIM DAVIS 2-26
AH-CHOO
GESUNDHEIT
GARFIELD!
© 1999 PAWS, INC. All Rights Reserved.

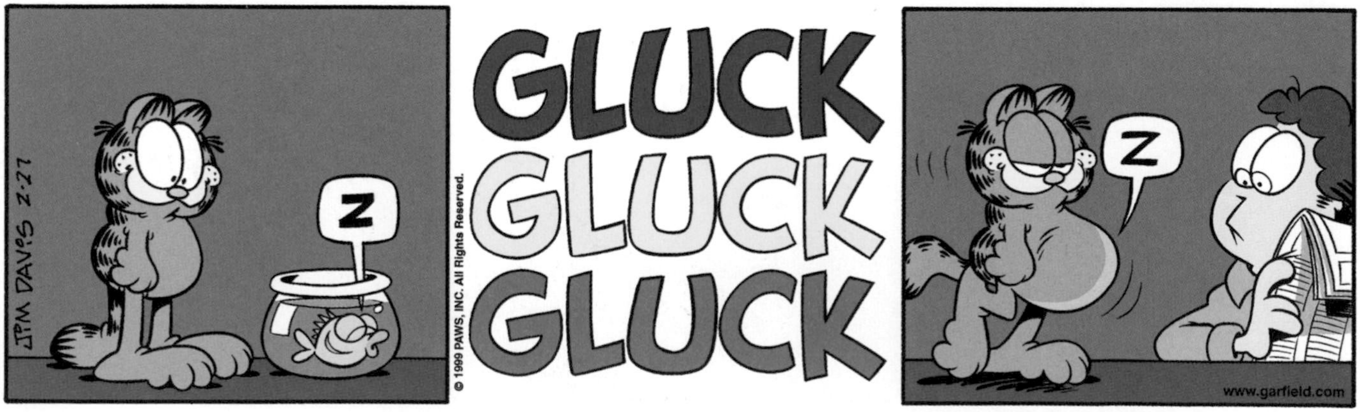
JIM DAVIS 2-27
Z
GLUCK
GLUCK
GLUCK
Z
www.garfield.com
© 1999 PAWS, INC. All Rights Reserved.

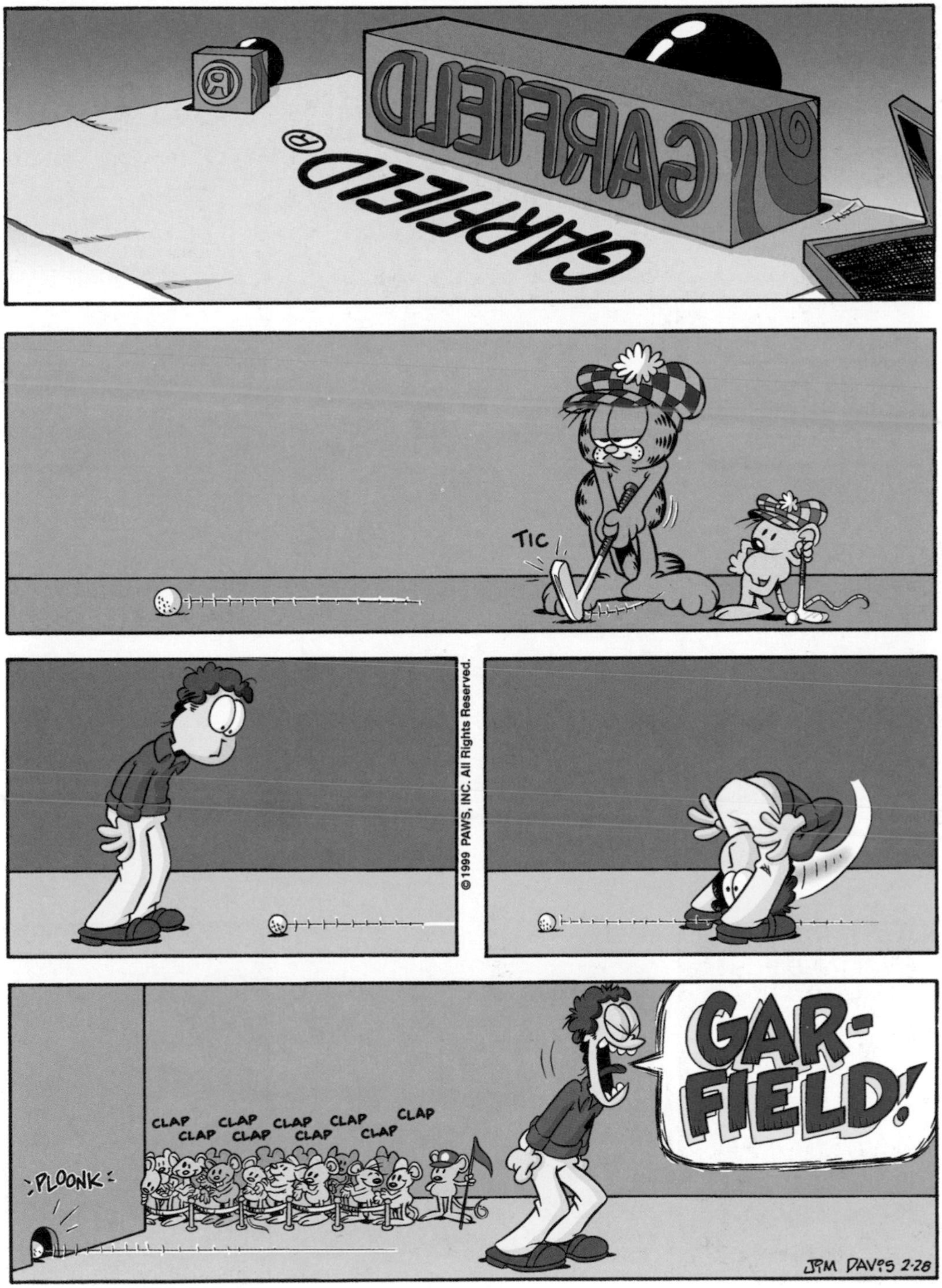
GARFIELD®
TIC
©1999 PAWS, INC. All Rights Reserved.
PLOONK
CLAP CLAP CLAP CLAP CLAP CLAP CLAP CLAP CLAP
GAR-FIELD!
JIM DAVIS 2-28

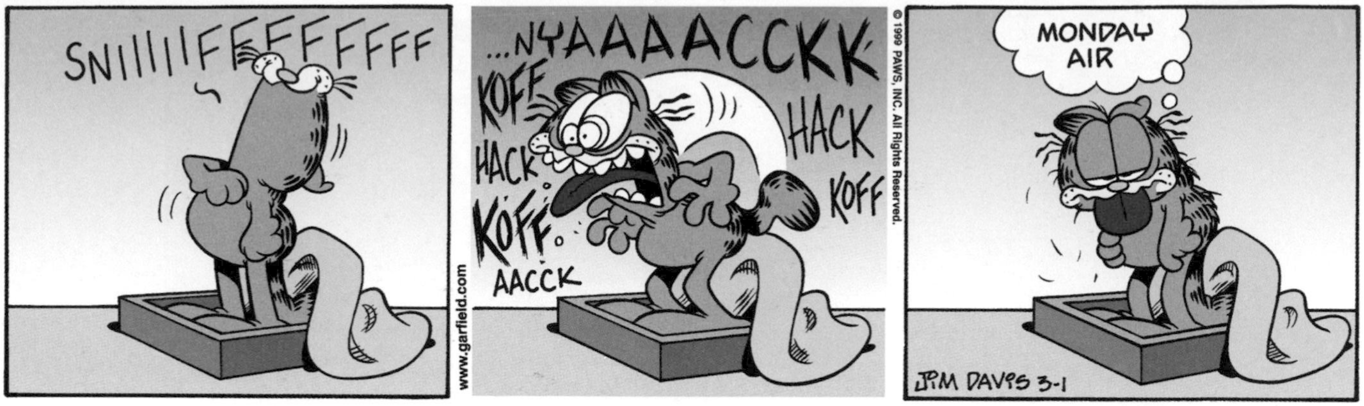
SNIIIIIFFFFFFFFF
...NYAAAACCCKK
KOFF
HACK
KOFF
AACCK
HACK
KOFF
www.garfield.com
© 1999 PAWS, INC. All Rights Reserved.
MONDAY AIR
JIM DAVIS 3-1

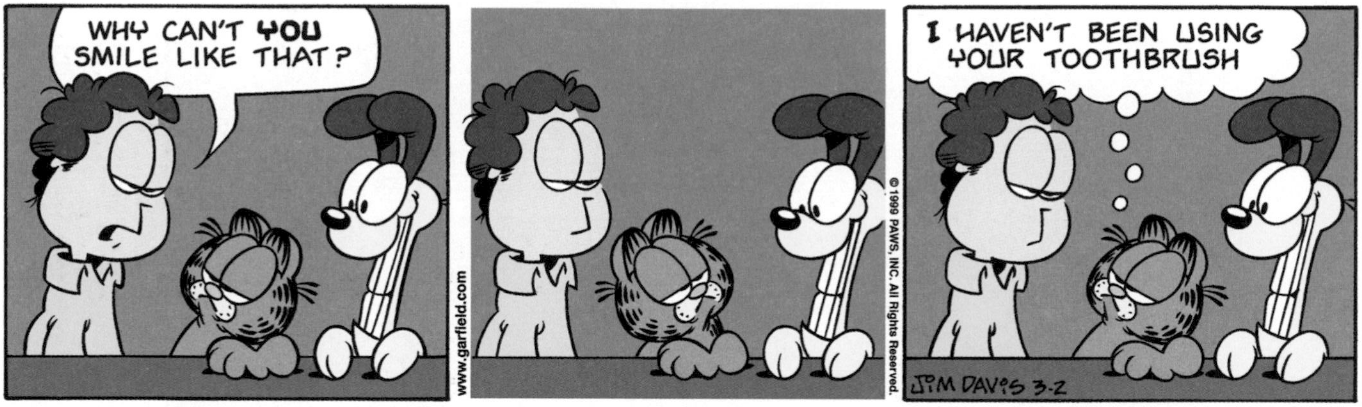
WHY CAN'T **YOU** SMILE LIKE THAT?
www.garfield.com
© 1999 PAWS, INC. All Rights Reserved.
I HAVEN'T BEEN USING YOUR TOOTHBRUSH
JIM DAVIS 3-2

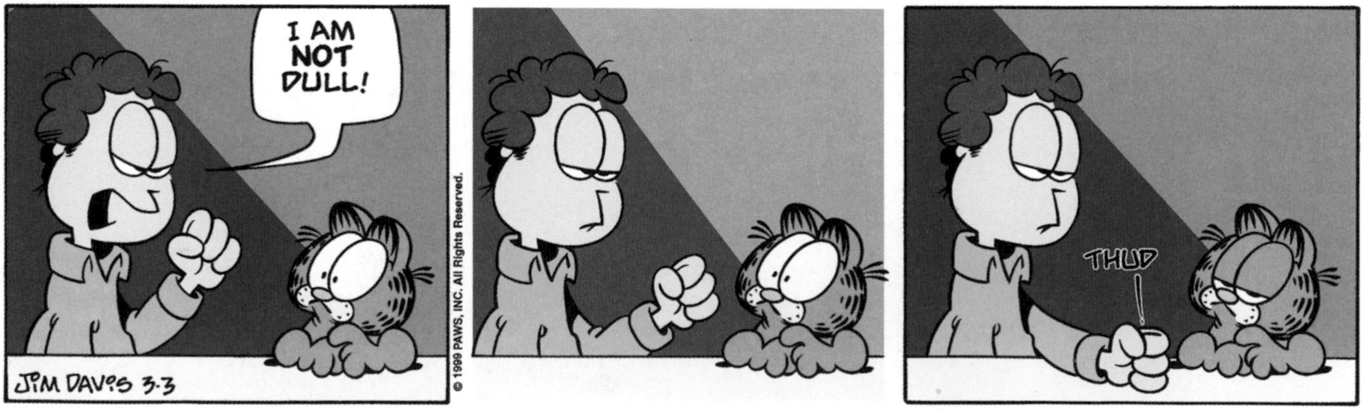
I AM **NOT** DULL!
JIM DAVIS 3-3
© 1999 PAWS, INC. All Rights Reserved.
THUD

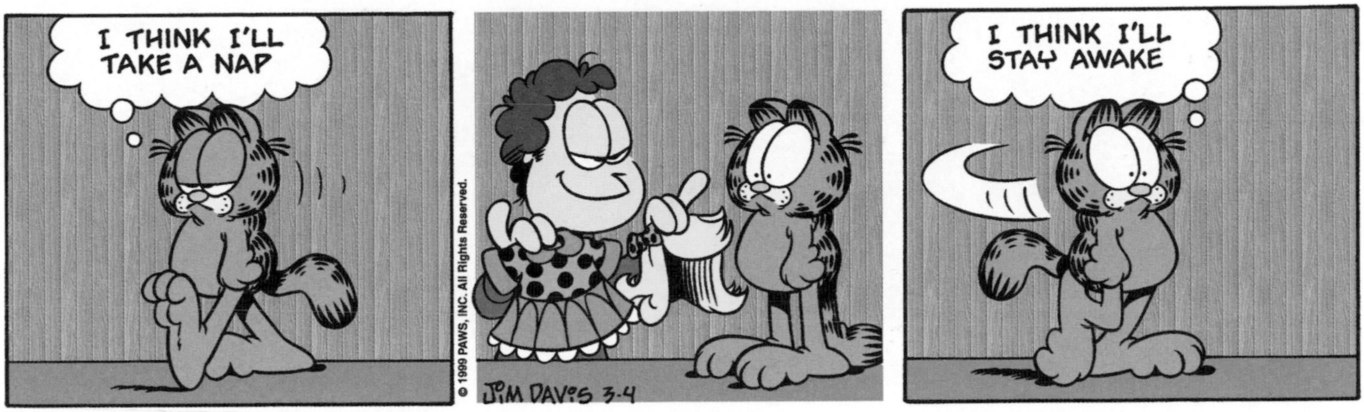
I THINK I'LL TAKE A NAP
I THINK I'LL STAY AWAKE
JIM DAVIS 3-4

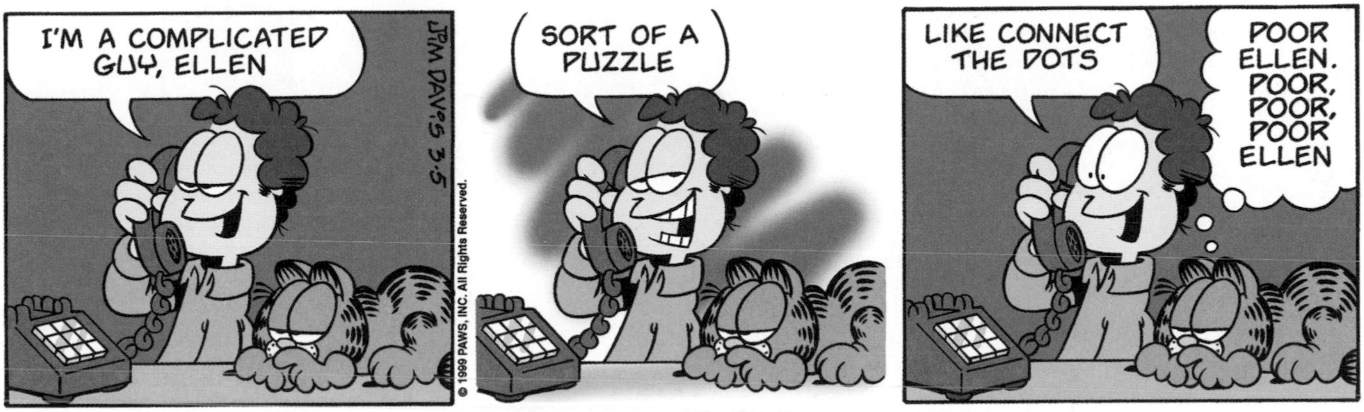
I'M A COMPLICATED GUY, ELLEN
SORT OF A PUZZLE
LIKE CONNECT THE DOTS
POOR ELLEN. POOR, POOR, POOR ELLEN
JIM DAVIS 3-5

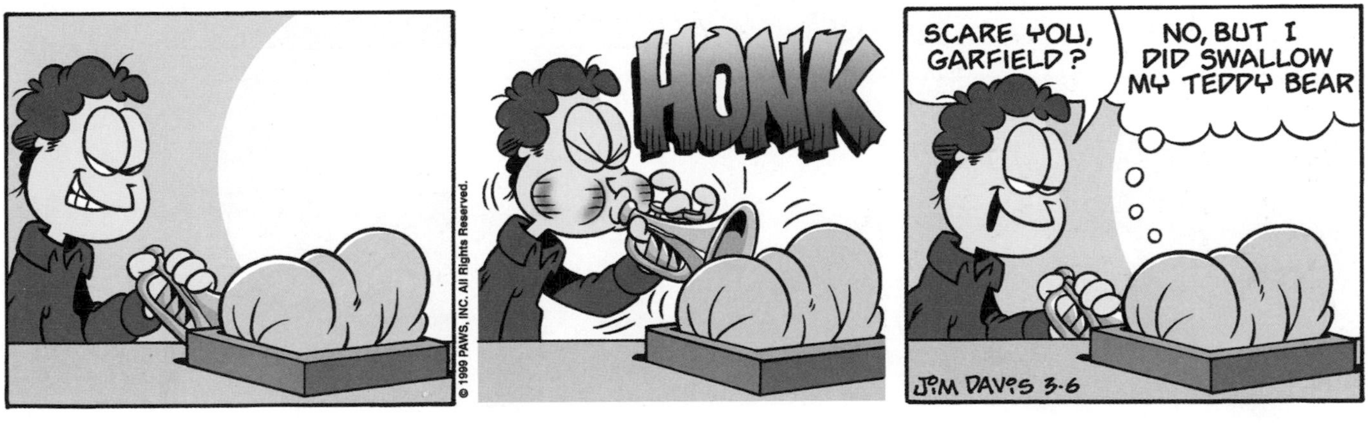
HONK
SCARE YOU, GARFIELD?
NO, BUT I DID SWALLOW MY TEDDY BEAR
JIM DAVIS 3-6

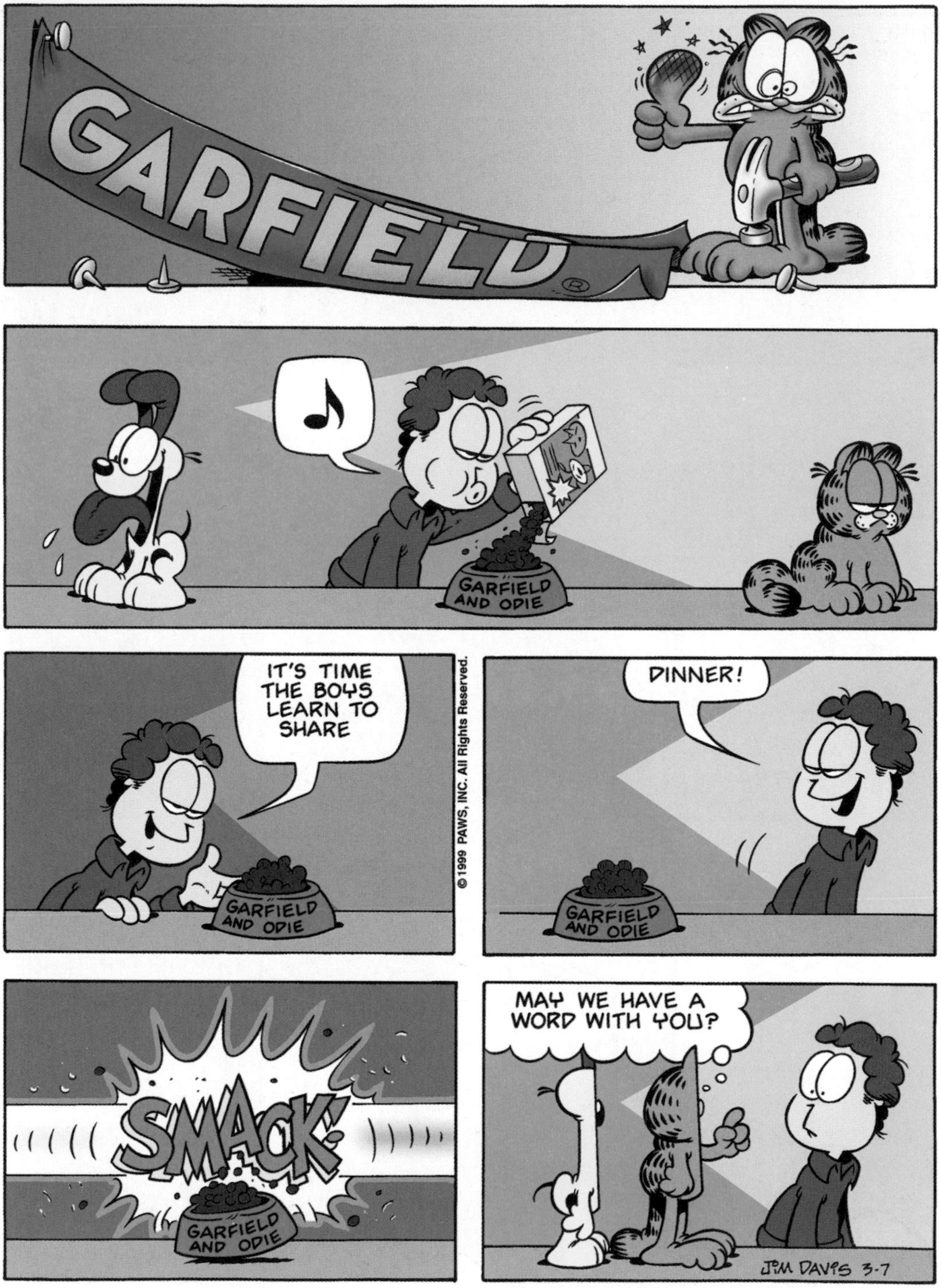
GARFIELD®
♪
GARFIELD AND ODIE
IT'S TIME THE BOYS LEARN TO SHARE
GARFIELD AND ODIE
© 1999 PAWS, INC. All Rights Reserved.
DINNER!
GARFIELD AND ODIE
SMACK!
GARFIELD AND ODIE
MAY WE HAVE A WORD WITH YOU?
JIM DAVIS 3-7

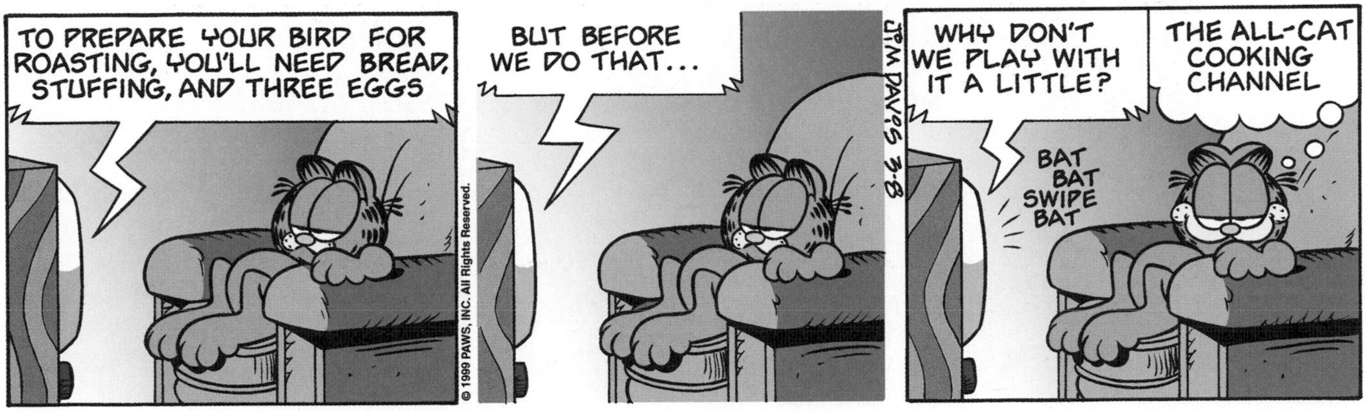
TO PREPARE YOUR BIRD FOR ROASTING, YOU'LL NEED BREAD, STUFFING, AND THREE EGGS
© 1999 PAWS, INC. All Rights Reserved.
BUT BEFORE WE DO THAT...
JPM DAVIS 3-8
WHY DON'T WE PLAY WITH IT A LITTLE?
BAT BAT SWIPE BAT
THE ALL-CAT COOKING CHANNEL

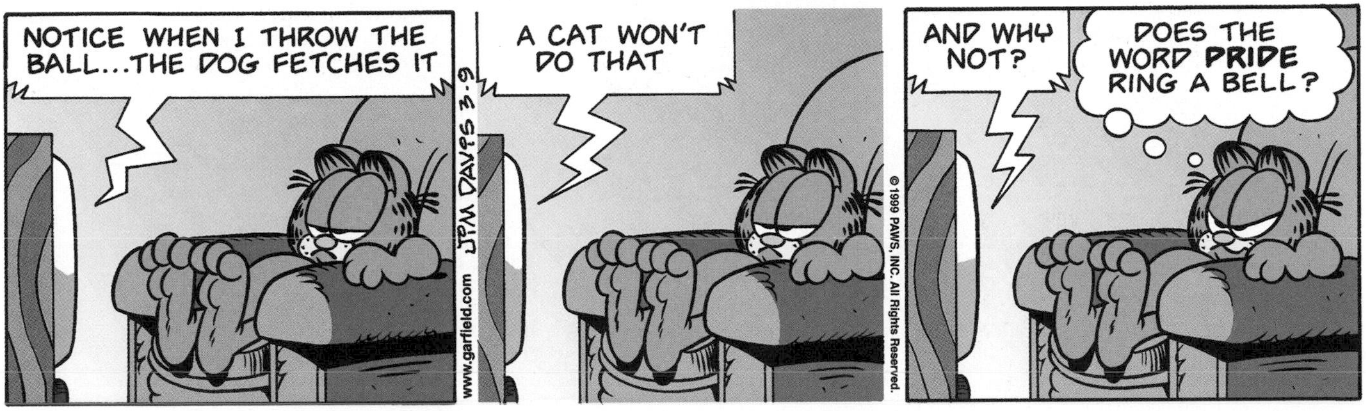
NOTICE WHEN I THROW THE BALL...THE DOG FETCHES IT
www.garfield.com
JPM DAVIS 3-9
A CAT WON'T DO THAT
© 1999 PAWS, INC. All Rights Reserved.
AND WHY NOT?
DOES THE WORD **PRIDE** RING A BELL?

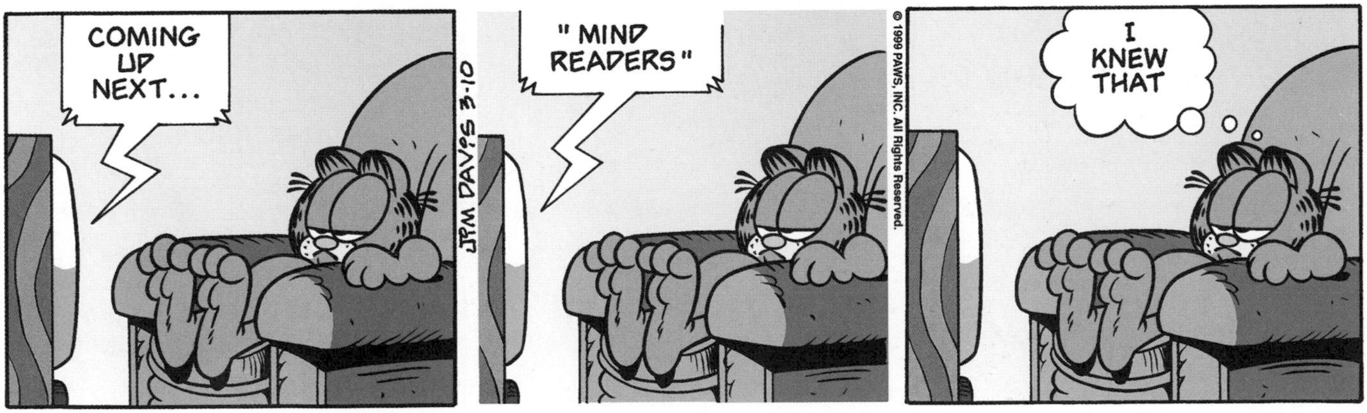
COMING UP NEXT...
JPM DAVIS 3-10
"MIND READERS"
© 1999 PAWS, INC. All Rights Reserved.
I KNEW THAT

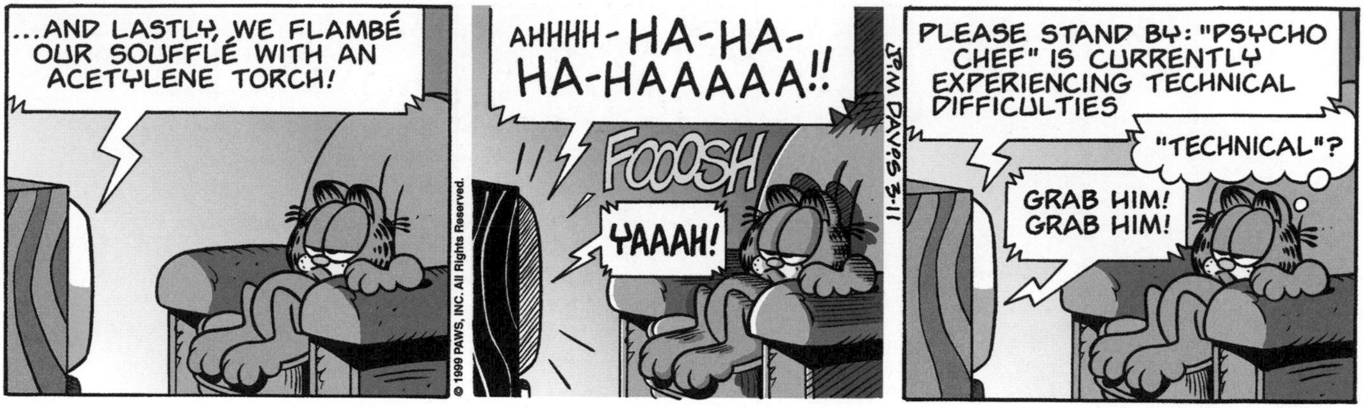
...AND LASTLY, WE FLAMBÉ OUR SOUFFLÉ WITH AN ACETYLENE TORCH!
© 1999 PAWS, INC. All Rights Reserved.
AHHHH-HA-HA-HA-HAAAAA!!
FOOOSH
YAAAH!
JIM DAVIS 3-11
PLEASE STAND BY: "PSYCHO CHEF" IS CURRENTLY EXPERIENCING TECHNICAL DIFFICULTIES
"TECHNICAL"?
GRAB HIM! GRAB HIM!

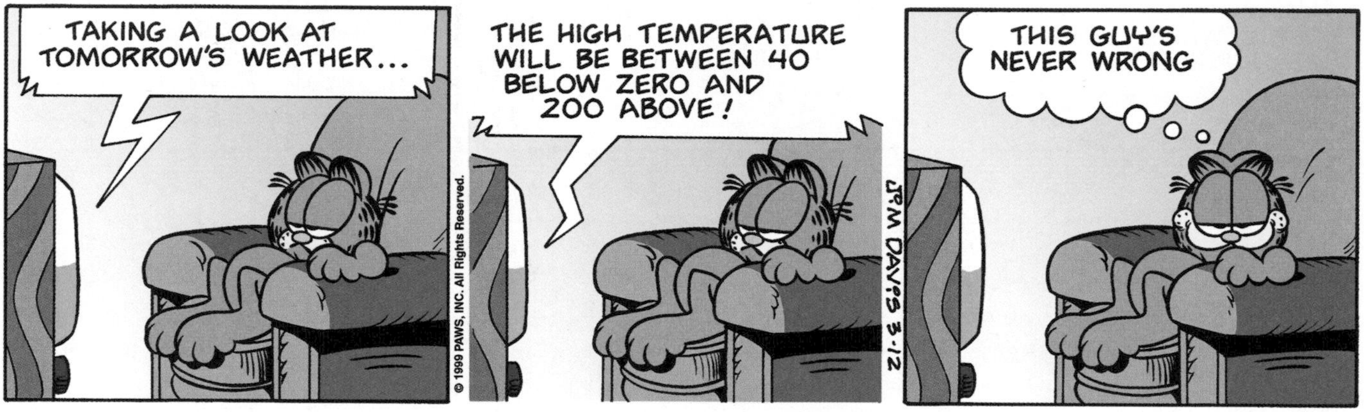
TAKING A LOOK AT TOMORROW'S WEATHER...
© 1999 PAWS, INC. All Rights Reserved.
THE HIGH TEMPERATURE WILL BE BETWEEN 40 BELOW ZERO AND 200 ABOVE!
JIM DAVIS 3-12
THIS GUY'S NEVER WRONG

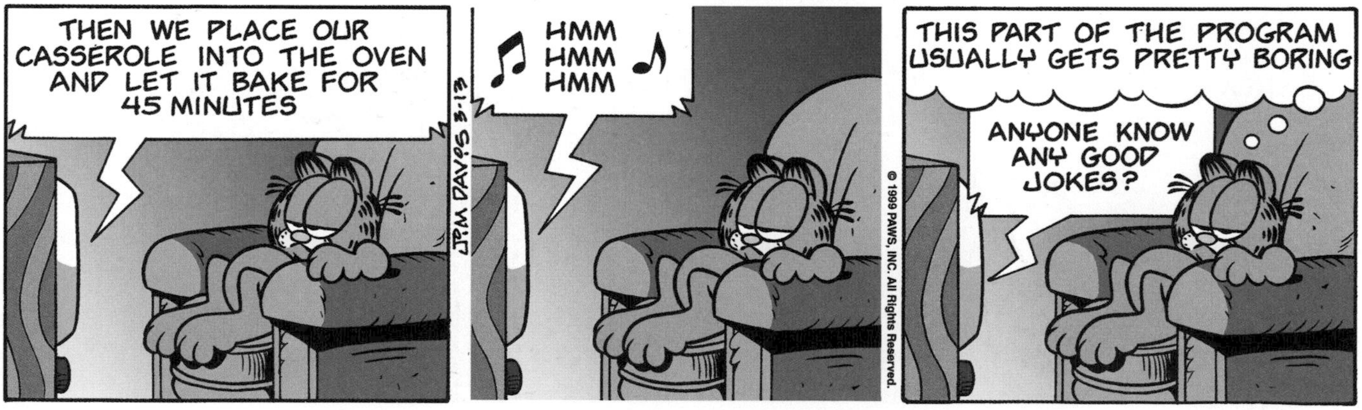
THEN WE PLACE OUR CASSEROLE INTO THE OVEN AND LET IT BAKE FOR 45 MINUTES
JIM DAVIS 3-13
HMM HMM HMM
© 1999 PAWS, INC. All Rights Reserved.
THIS PART OF THE PROGRAM USUALLY GETS PRETTY BORING
ANYONE KNOW ANY GOOD JOKES?

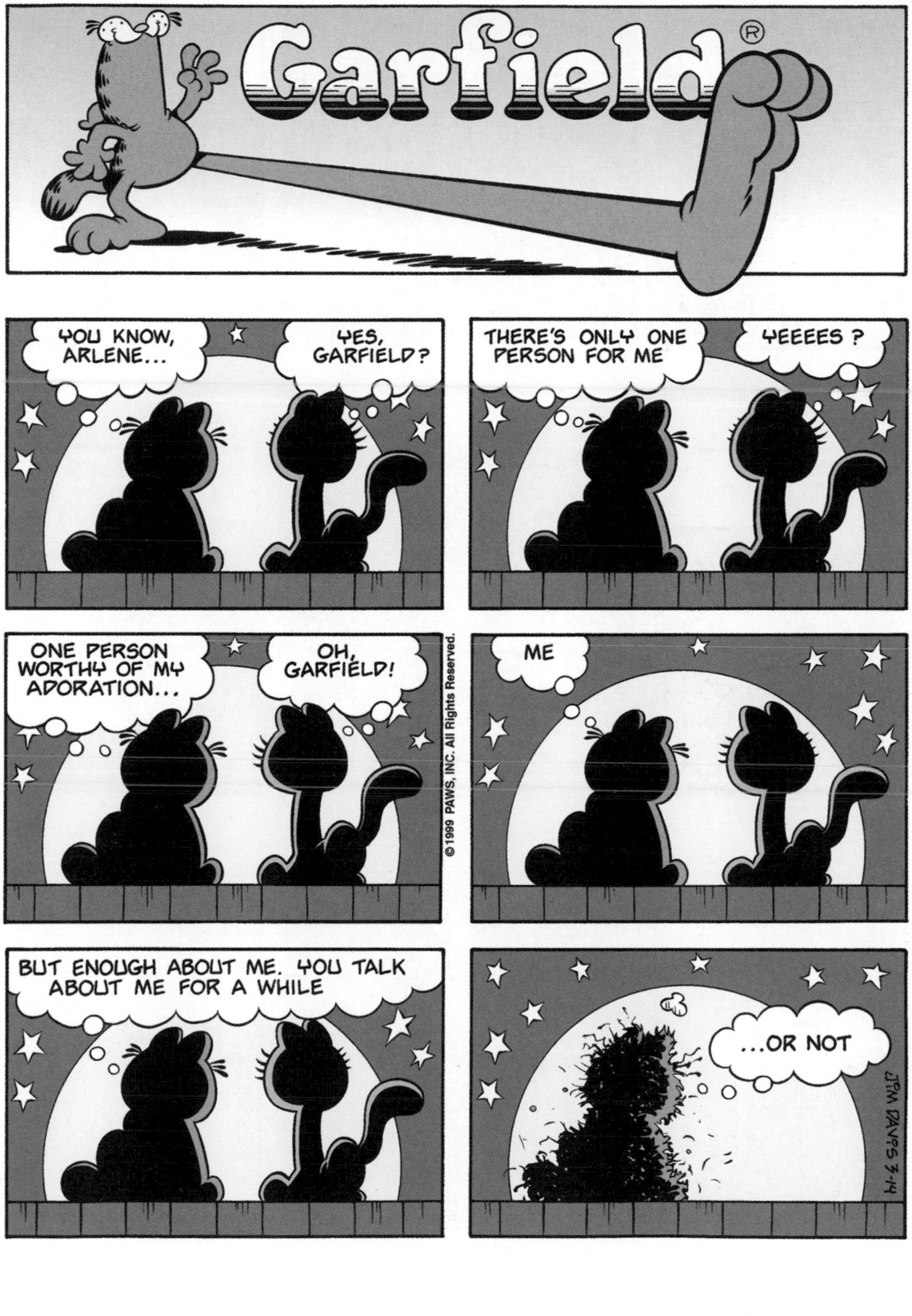
Garfield®
YOU KNOW, ARLENE...
YES, GARFIELD?
THERE'S ONLY ONE PERSON FOR ME
YEEEES ?
ONE PERSON WORTHY OF MY ADORATION...
OH, GARFIELD!
ME
BUT ENOUGH ABOUT ME. YOU TALK ABOUT ME FOR A WHILE
...OR NOT
JIM DAVIS 7-14

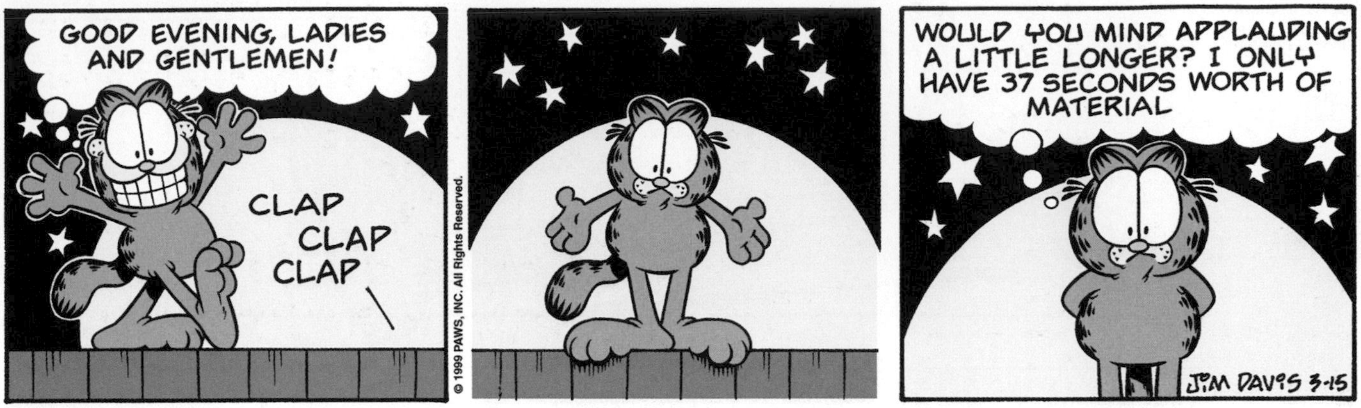
GOOD EVENING, LADIES AND GENTLEMEN!
CLAP CLAP CLAP
© 1999 PAWS, INC. All Rights Reserved.
WOULD YOU MIND APPLAUDING A LITTLE LONGER? I ONLY HAVE 37 SECONDS WORTH OF MATERIAL
JIM DAVIS 3-15

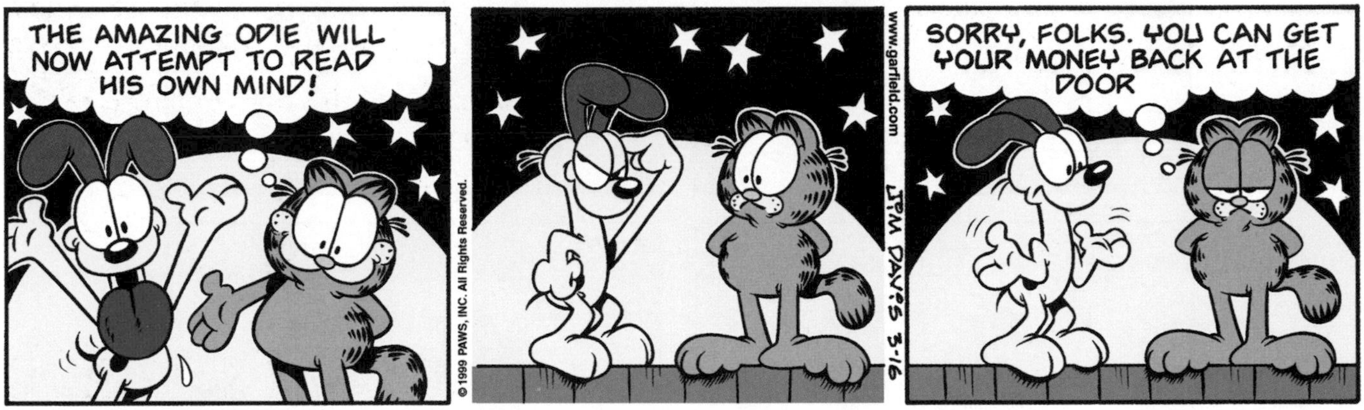
THE AMAZING ODIE WILL NOW ATTEMPT TO READ HIS OWN MIND!
© 1999 PAWS, INC. All Rights Reserved.
www.garfield.com
JIM DAVIS 3-16
SORRY, FOLKS. YOU CAN GET YOUR MONEY BACK AT THE DOOR

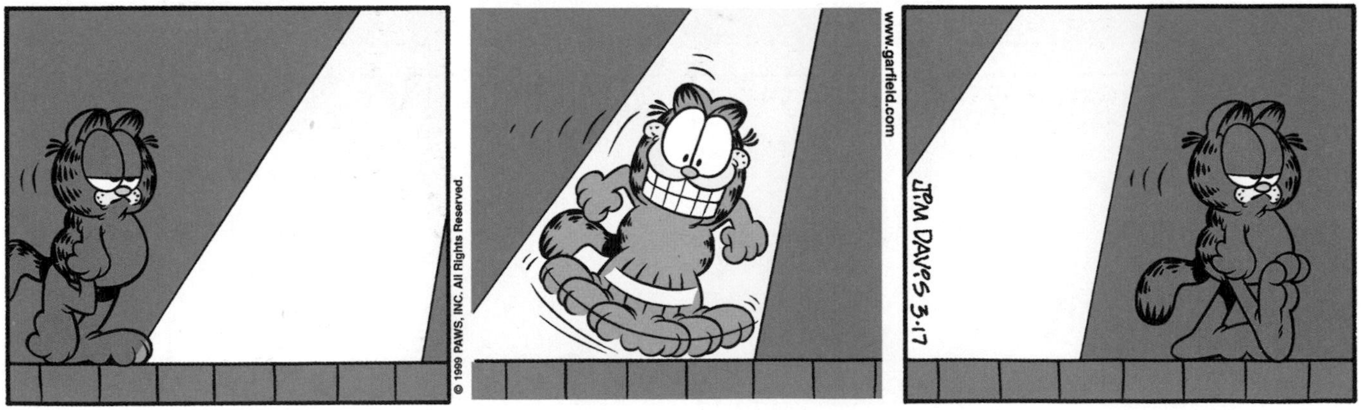
© 1999 PAWS, INC. All Rights Reserved.
www.garfield.com
JIM DAVIS 3-17

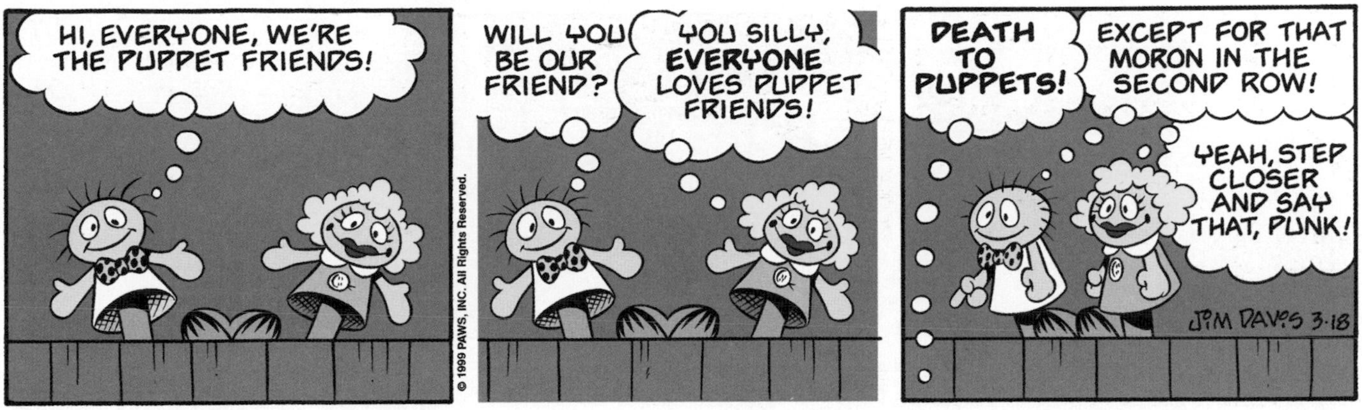
HI, EVERYONE, WE'RE THE PUPPET FRIENDS!
© 1999 PAWS, INC. All Rights Reserved.
WILL YOU BE OUR FRIEND?
YOU SILLY, EVERYONE LOVES PUPPET FRIENDS!
DEATH TO PUPPETS!
EXCEPT FOR THAT MORON IN THE SECOND ROW!
YEAH, STEP CLOSER AND SAY THAT, PUNK!
JIM DAVIS 3-18

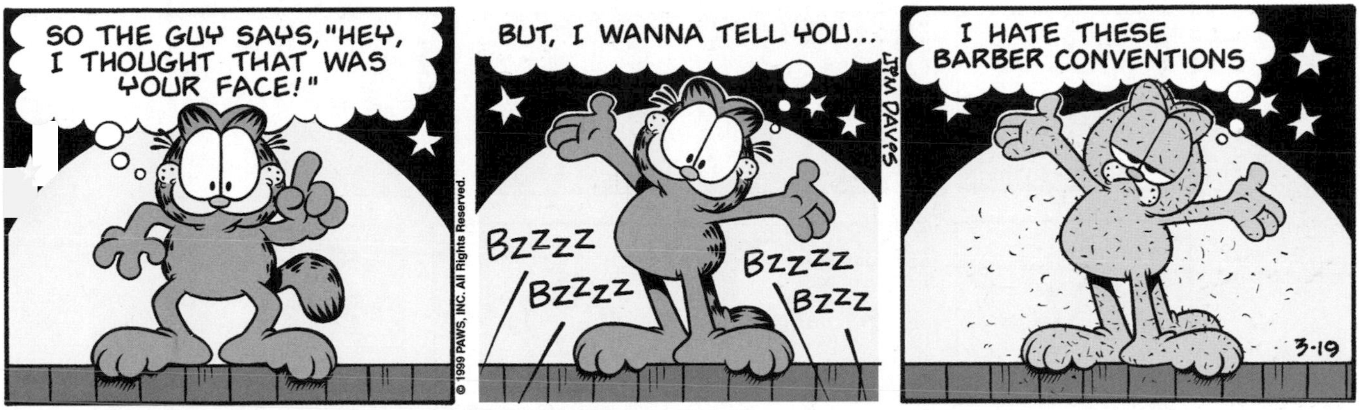
SO THE GUY SAYS, "HEY, I THOUGHT THAT WAS YOUR FACE!"
© 1999 PAWS, INC. All Rights Reserved.
BUT, I WANNA TELL YOU...
JIM DAVIS
BZZZZ
BZZZZ
BZZZZ
BZZZ
I HATE THESE BARBER CONVENTIONS
3-19

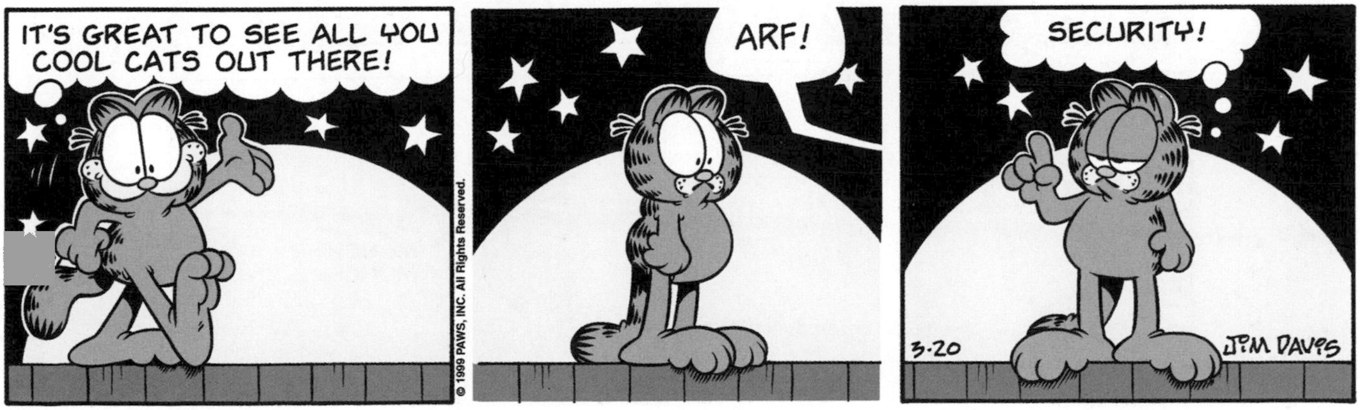
IT'S GREAT TO SEE ALL YOU COOL CATS OUT THERE!
© 1999 PAWS, INC. All Rights Reserved.
ARF!
SECURITY!
3-20
JIM DAVIS

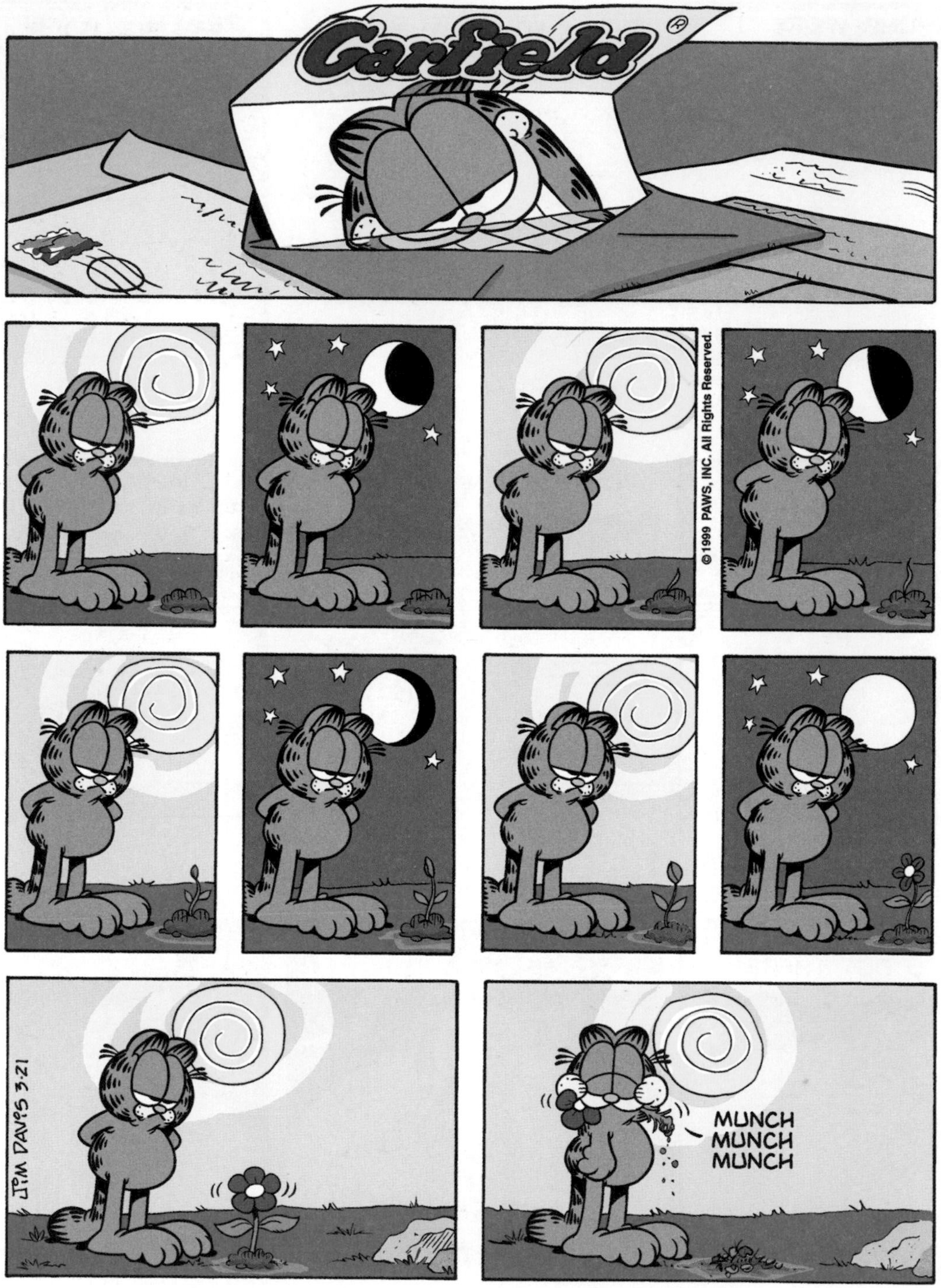
Garfield®
© 1999 PAWS, INC. All Rights Reserved.
JIM DAVIS 3·21
MUNCH
MUNCH
MUNCH

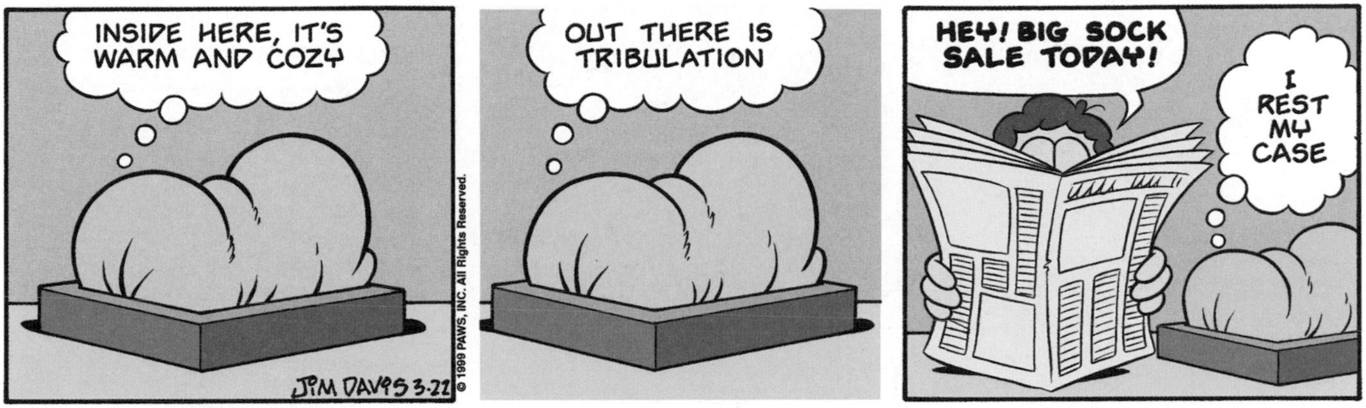
INSIDE HERE, IT'S WARM AND COZY
OUT THERE IS TRIBULATION
HEY! BIG SOCK SALE TODAY!
I REST MY CASE
JIM DAVIS 3-22
© 1999 PAWS, INC. All Rights Reserved.

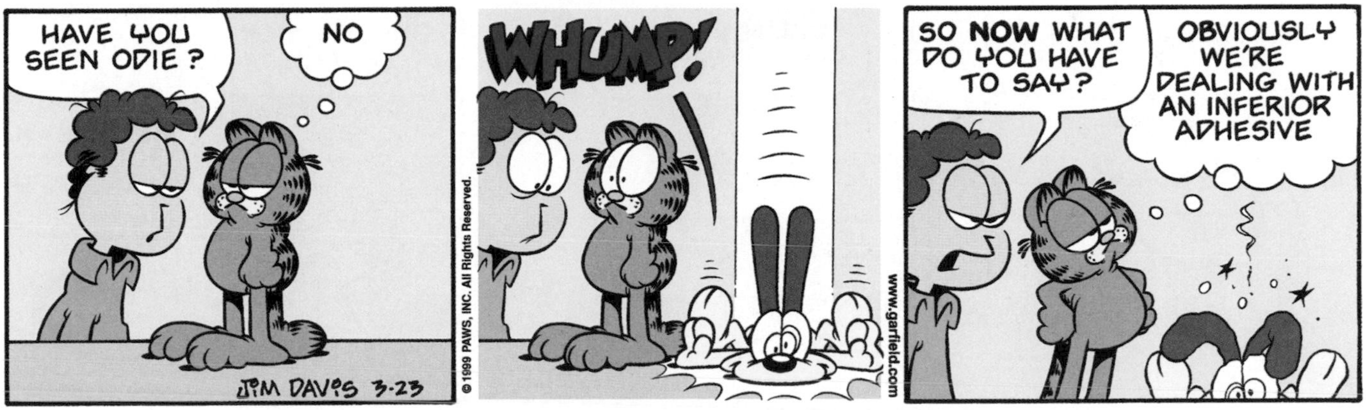
HAVE YOU SEEN ODIE ?
NO
WHUMP!
SO NOW WHAT DO YOU HAVE TO SAY?
OBVIOUSLY WE'RE DEALING WITH AN INFERIOR ADHESIVE
JIM DAVIS 3-23
© 1999 PAWS, INC. All Rights Reserved.
www.garfield.com

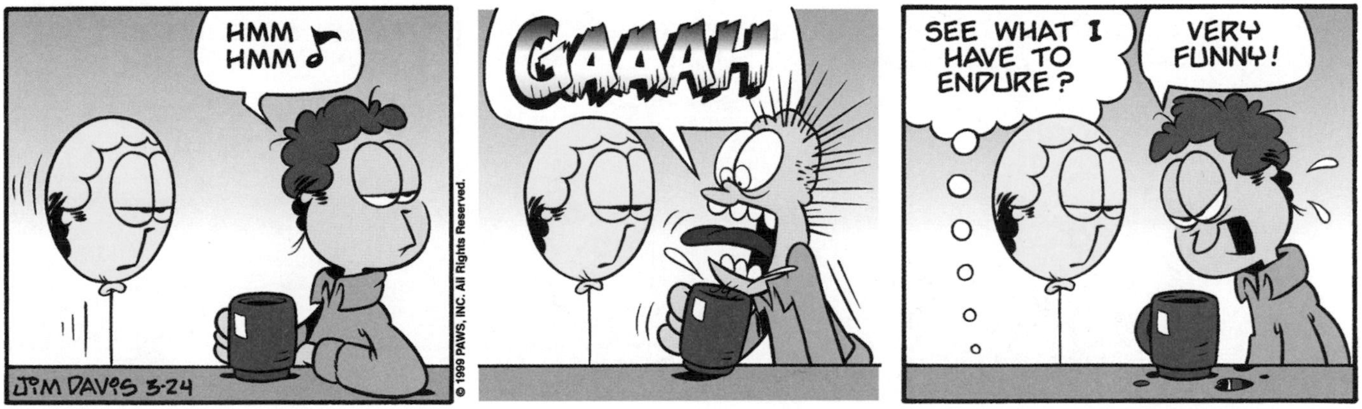
HMM HMM ♪
GAAAH
SEE WHAT I HAVE TO ENDURE?
VERY FUNNY!
JIM DAVIS 3-24
© 1999 PAWS, INC. All Rights Reserved.

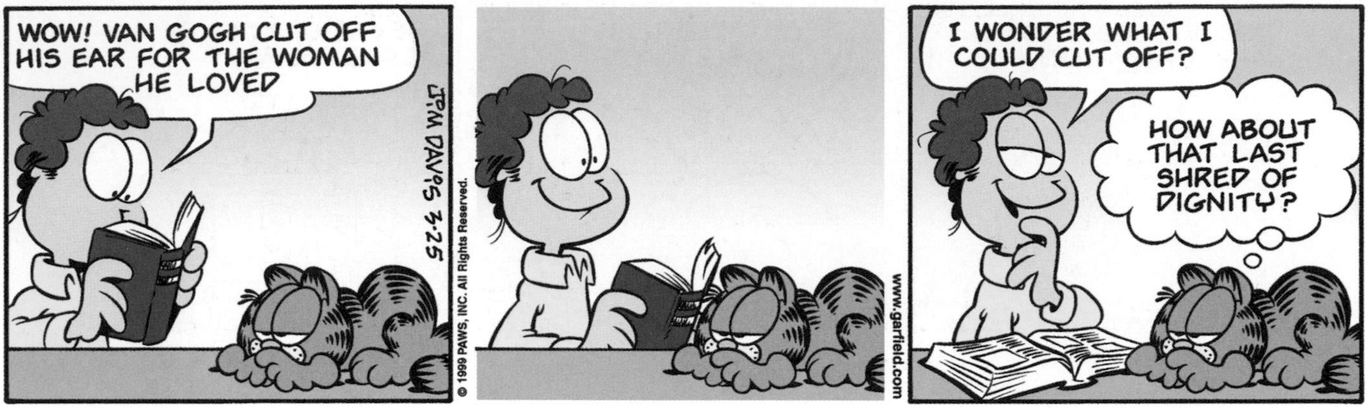
WOW! VAN GOGH CUT OFF HIS EAR FOR THE WOMAN HE LOVED
JIM DAVIS 3-25
© 1999 PAWS, INC. All Rights Reserved.
I WONDER WHAT I COULD CUT OFF?
HOW ABOUT THAT LAST SHRED OF DIGNITY?
www.garfield.com

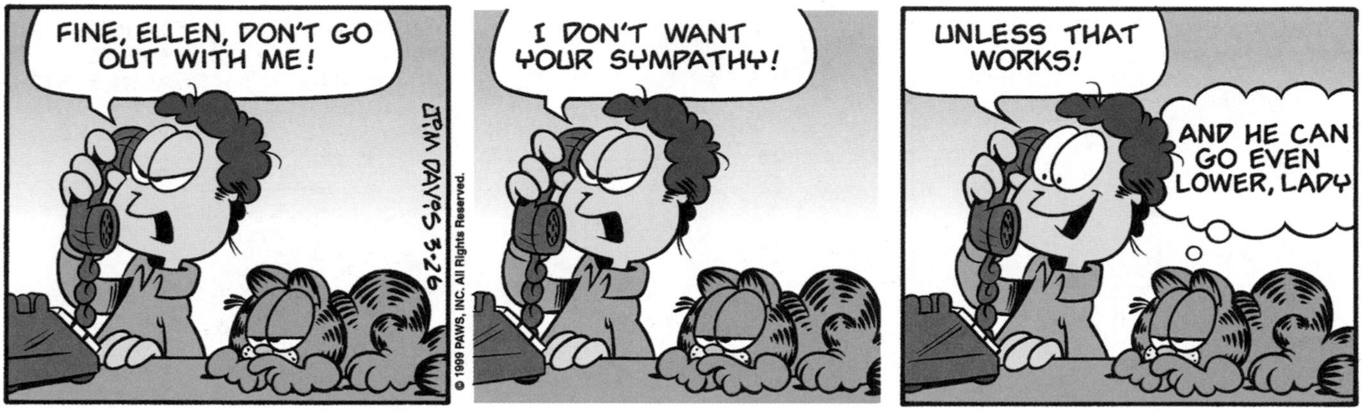
FINE, ELLEN, DON'T GO OUT WITH ME!
JIM DAVIS 3-26
© 1999 PAWS, INC. All Rights Reserved.
I DON'T WANT YOUR SYMPATHY!
UNLESS THAT WORKS!
AND HE CAN GO EVEN LOWER, LADY

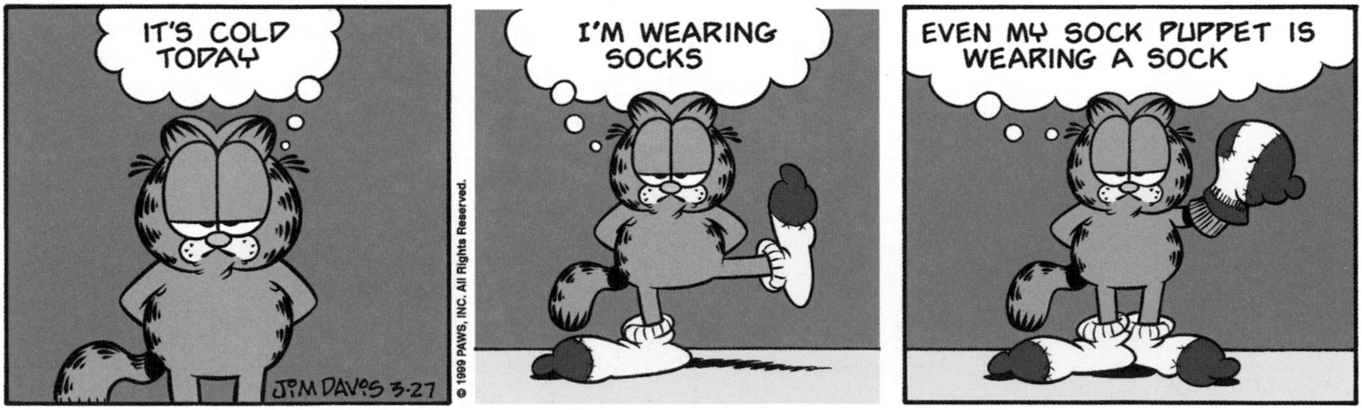
IT'S COLD TODAY
JIM DAVIS 3-27
© 1999 PAWS, INC. All Rights Reserved.
I'M WEARING SOCKS
EVEN MY SOCK PUPPET IS WEARING A SOCK

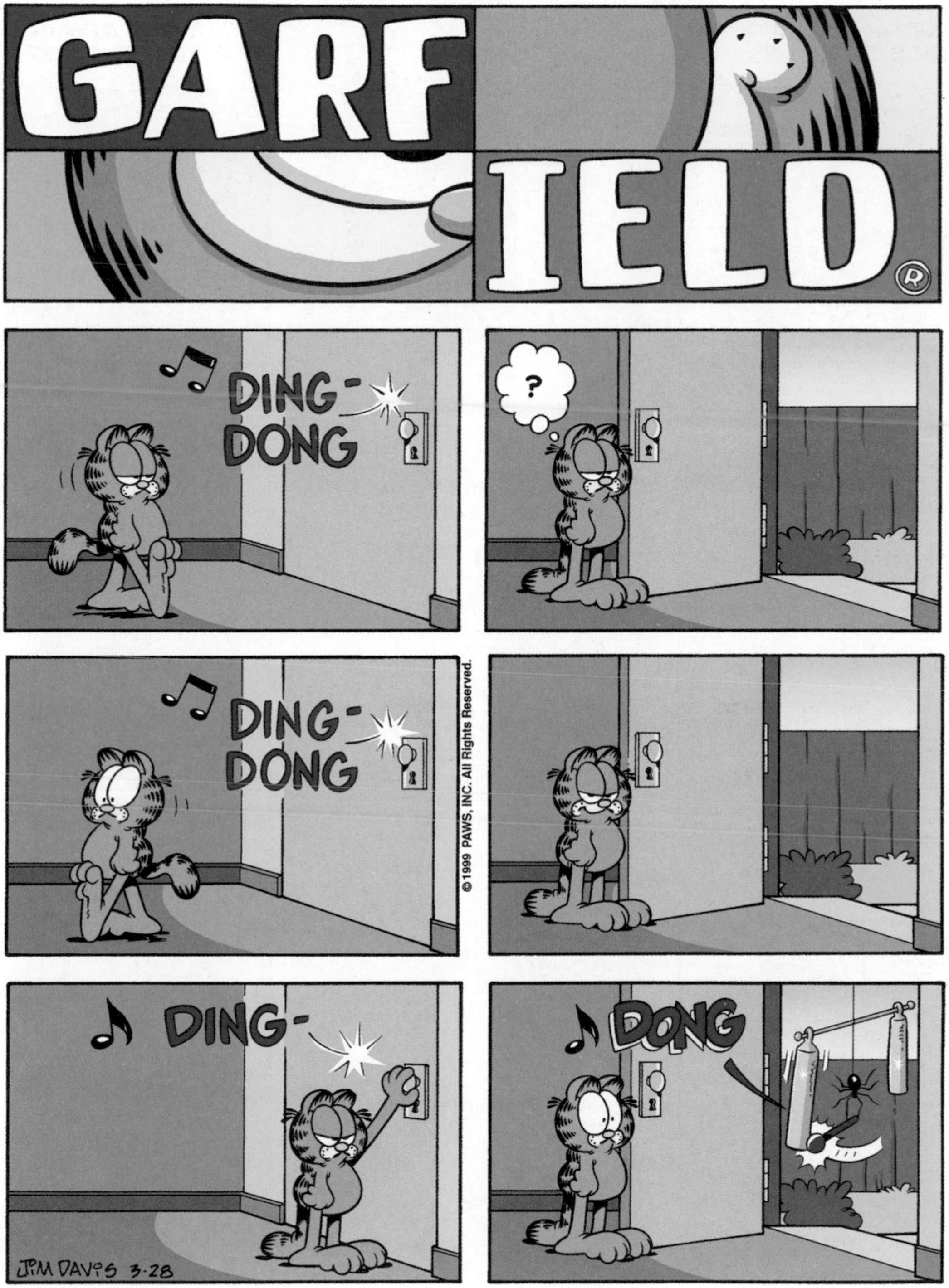
GARFIELD
DING-DONG
?
DING-DONG
DING-
DONG
JIM DAVIS 3-28

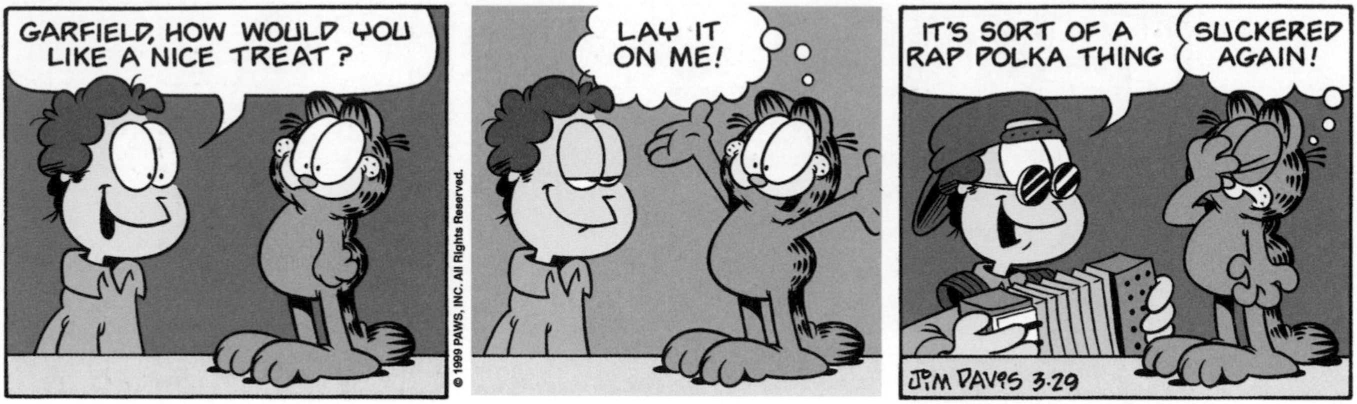
GARFIELD, HOW WOULD YOU LIKE A NICE TREAT?
© 1999 PAWS, INC. All Rights Reserved.
LAY IT ON ME!
IT'S SORT OF A RAP POLKA THING
SUCKERED AGAIN!
JIM DAVIS 3-29

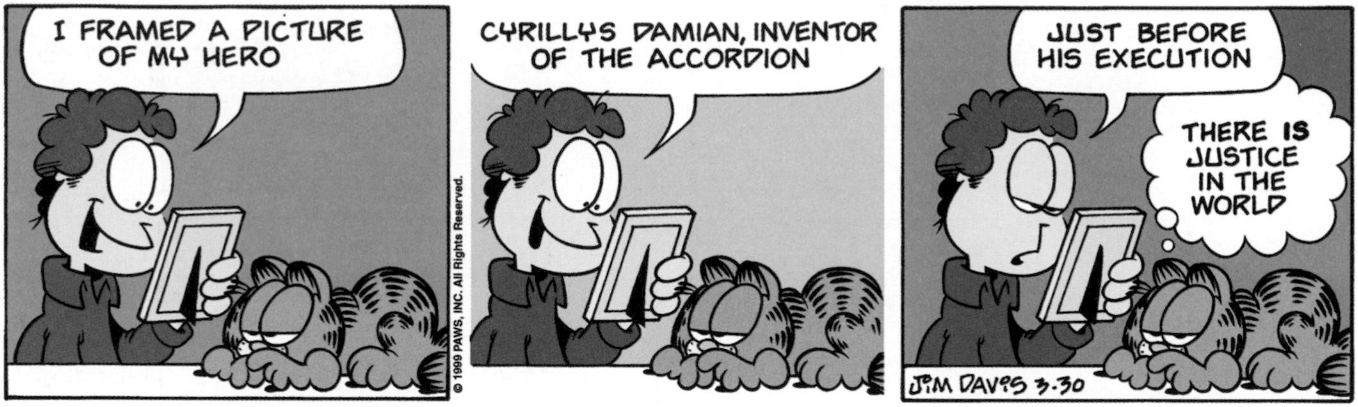
I FRAMED A PICTURE OF MY HERO
© 1999 PAWS, INC. All Rights Reserved.
CYRILLYS DAMIAN, INVENTOR OF THE ACCORDION
JUST BEFORE HIS EXECUTION
THERE IS JUSTICE IN THE WORLD
JIM DAVIS 3-30

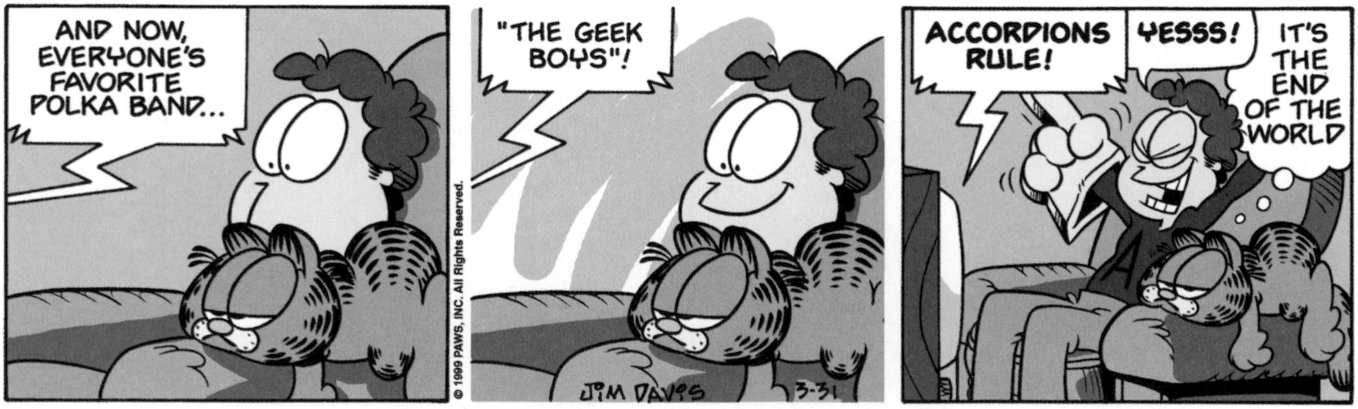
AND NOW, EVERYONE'S FAVORITE POLKA BAND...
© 1999 PAWS, INC. All Rights Reserved.
"THE GEEK BOYS"!
JIM DAVIS 3-31
ACCORDIONS RULE!
YESSS!
IT'S THE END OF THE WORLD

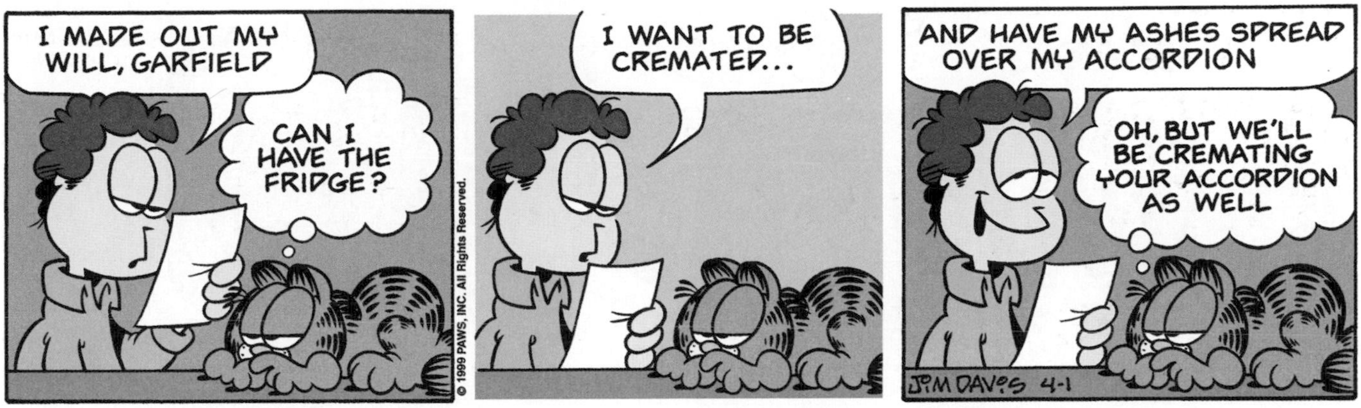
I MADE OUT MY WILL, GARFIELD
CAN I HAVE THE FRIDGE?
I WANT TO BE CREMATED...
AND HAVE MY ASHES SPREAD OVER MY ACCORDION
OH, BUT WE'LL BE CREMATING YOUR ACCORDION AS WELL
JIM DAVIS 4-1

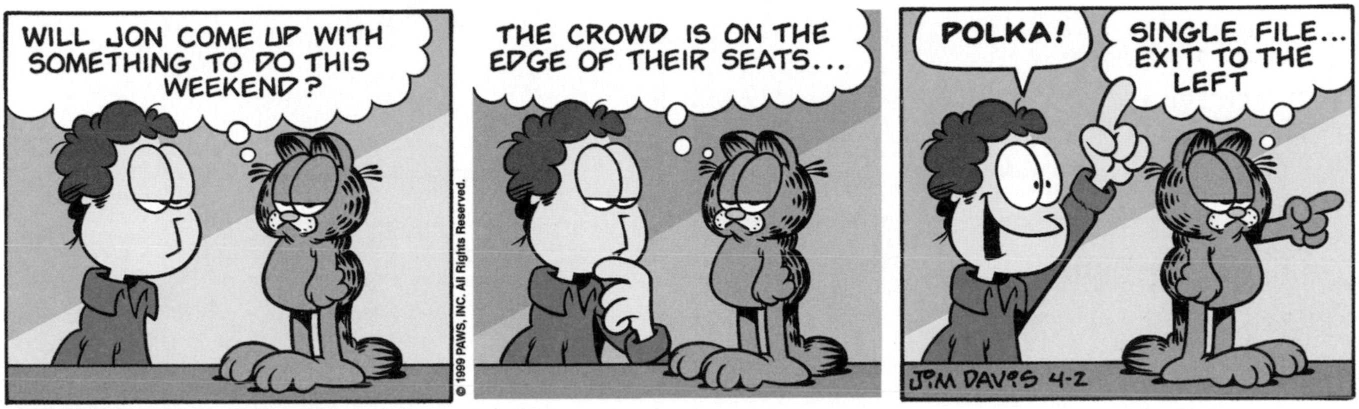
WILL JON COME UP WITH SOMETHING TO DO THIS WEEKEND?
THE CROWD IS ON THE EDGE OF THEIR SEATS...
POLKA!
SINGLE FILE... EXIT TO THE LEFT
JIM DAVIS 4-2

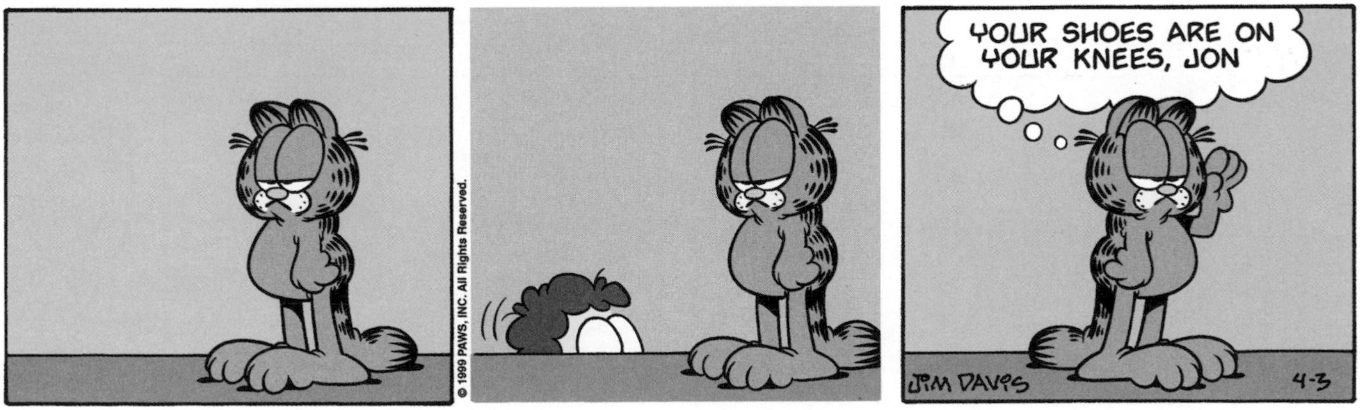
YOUR SHOES ARE ON YOUR KNEES, JON
JIM DAVIS 4-3

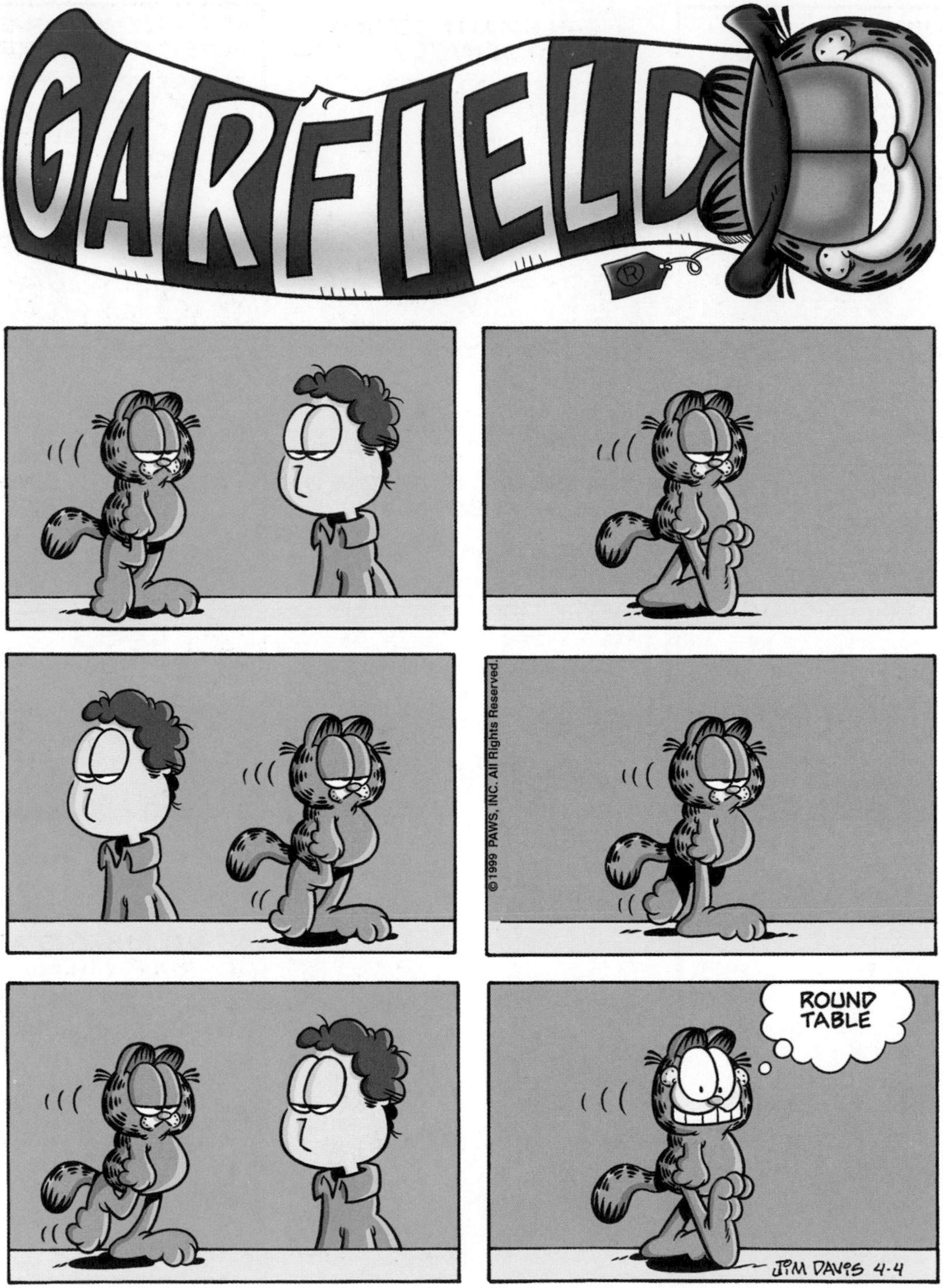
GARFIELD
©1999 PAWS, INC. All Rights Reserved.
ROUND TABLE
JIM DAVIS 4-4

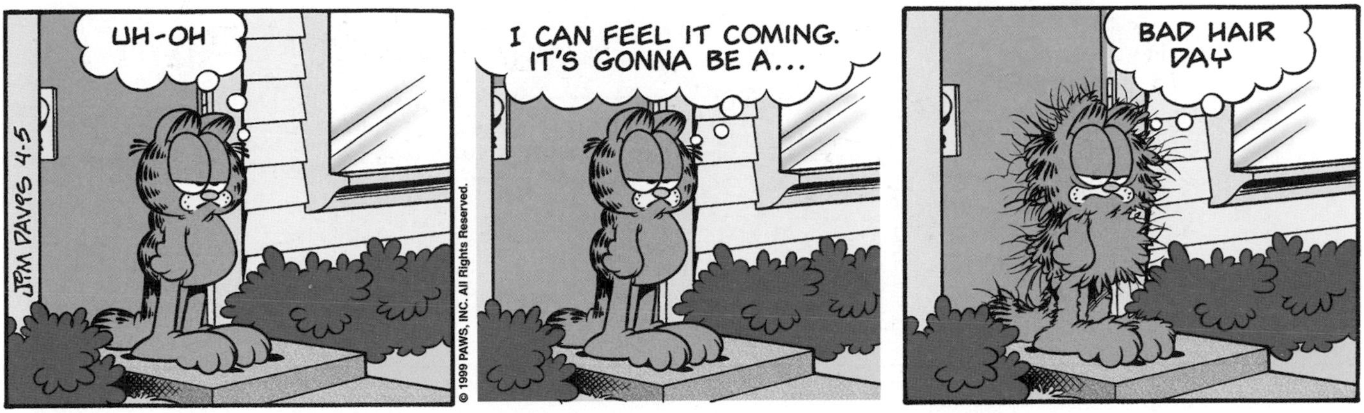
JIM DAVIS 4-5
UH-OH
© 1999 PAWS, INC. All Rights Reserved.
I CAN FEEL IT COMING. IT'S GONNA BE A...
BAD HAIR DAY

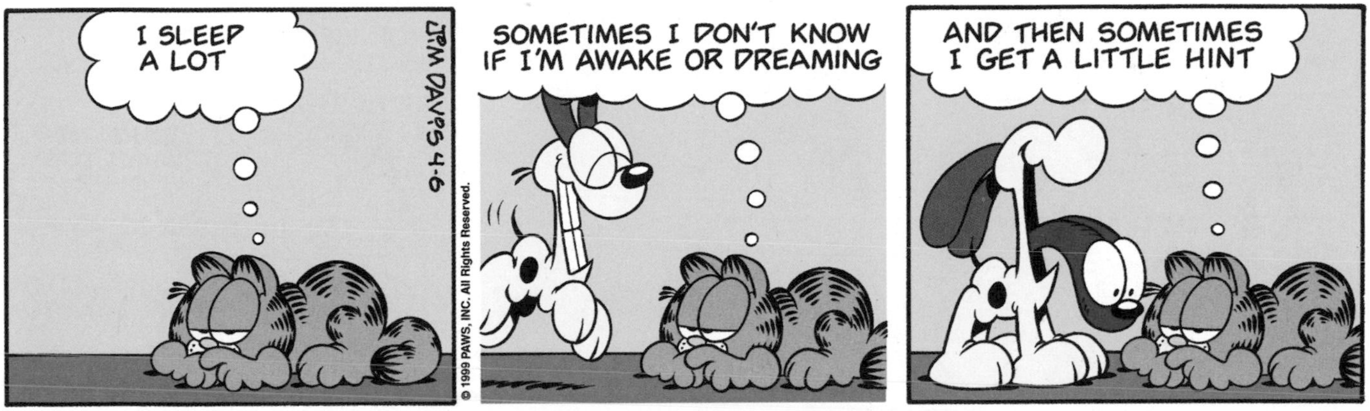
I SLEEP A LOT
JIM DAVIS 4-6
© 1999 PAWS, INC. All Rights Reserved.
SOMETIMES I DON'T KNOW IF I'M AWAKE OR DREAMING
AND THEN SOMETIMES I GET A LITTLE HINT

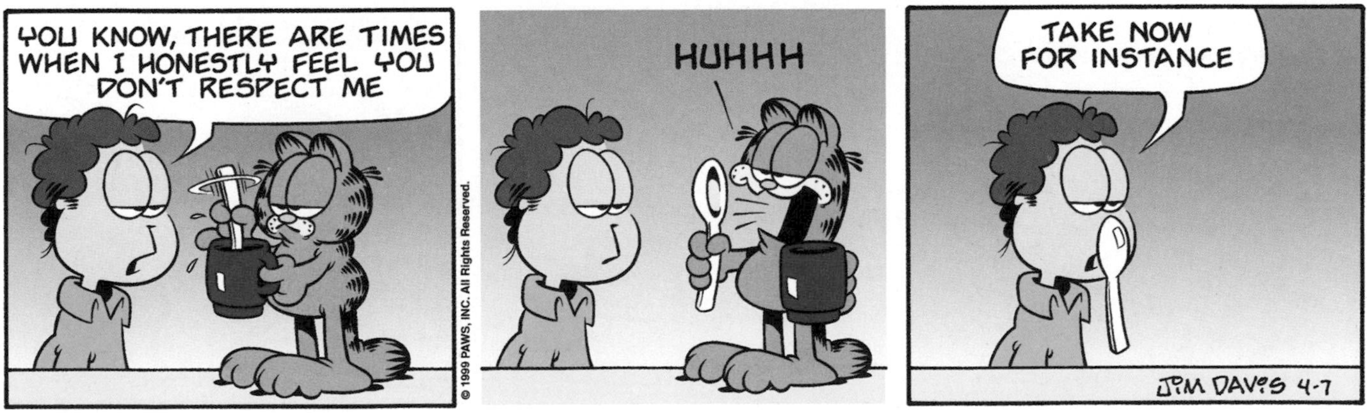
YOU KNOW, THERE ARE TIMES WHEN I HONESTLY FEEL YOU DON'T RESPECT ME
© 1999 PAWS, INC. All Rights Reserved.
HUHHH
TAKE NOW FOR INSTANCE
JIM DAVIS 4-7

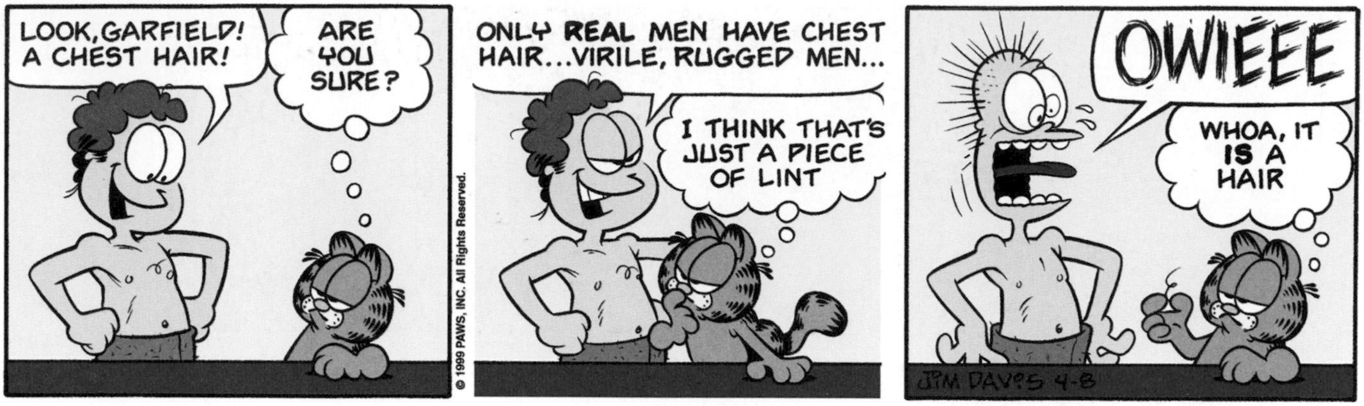
LOOK, GARFIELD! A CHEST HAIR!
ARE YOU SURE?
ONLY REAL MEN HAVE CHEST HAIR...VIRILE, RUGGED MEN...
I THINK THAT'S JUST A PIECE OF LINT
OWIEEE
WHOA, IT IS A HAIR
© 1999 PAWS, INC. All Rights Reserved.
JIM DAVIS 4-8

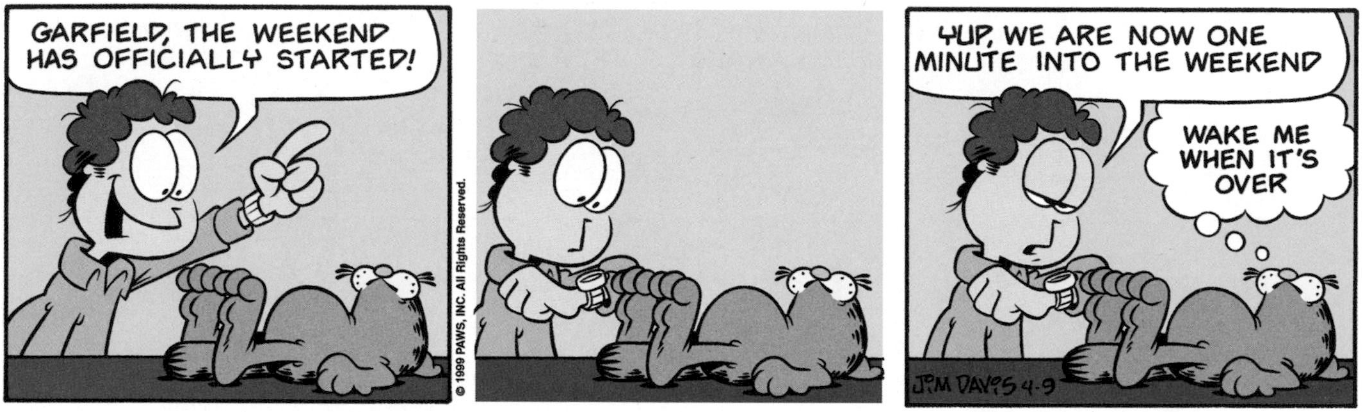
GARFIELD, THE WEEKEND HAS OFFICIALLY STARTED!
YUP, WE ARE NOW ONE MINUTE INTO THE WEEKEND
WAKE ME WHEN IT'S OVER
© 1999 PAWS, INC. All Rights Reserved.
JIM DAVIS 4-9

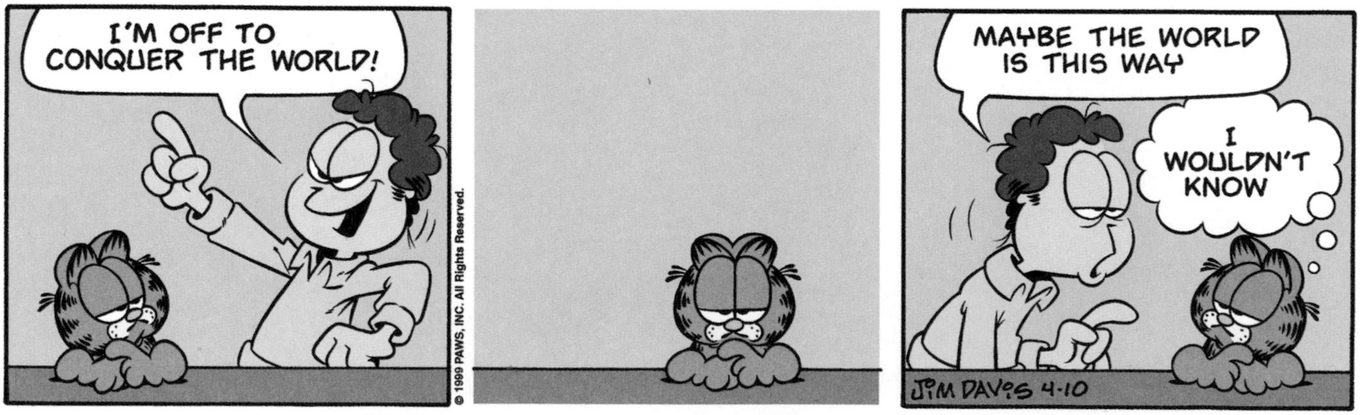
I'M OFF TO CONQUER THE WORLD!
MAYBE THE WORLD IS THIS WAY
I WOULDN'T KNOW
© 1999 PAWS, INC. All Rights Reserved.
JIM DAVIS 4-10

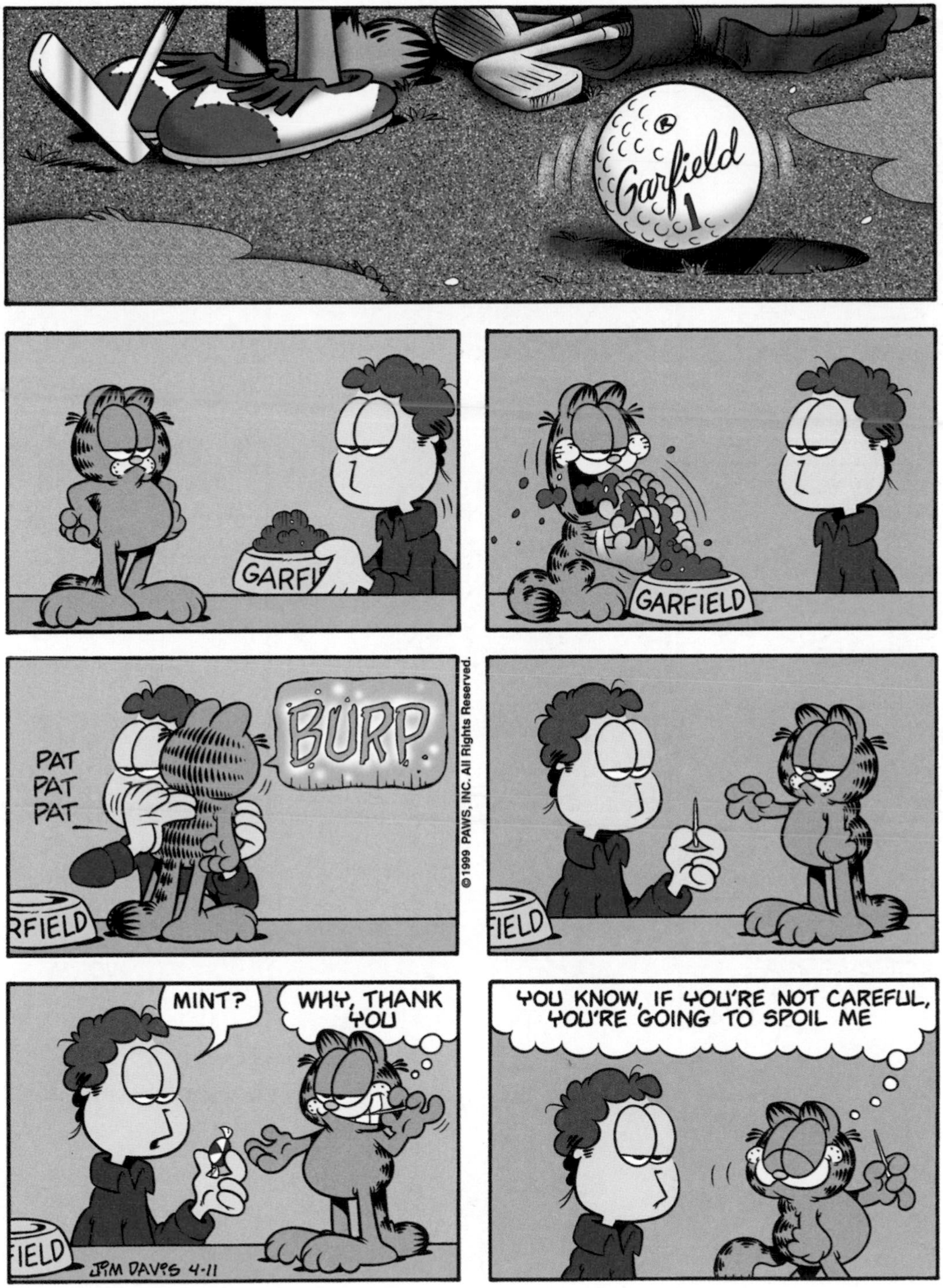
Garfield 1
GARFI
GARFIELD
PAT PAT PAT
BURP
RFIELD
©1999 PAWS, INC. All Rights Reserved.
IELD
MINT?
WHY, THANK YOU
IELD
JIM DAVIS 4-11
YOU KNOW, IF YOU'RE NOT CAREFUL, YOU'RE GOING TO SPOIL ME

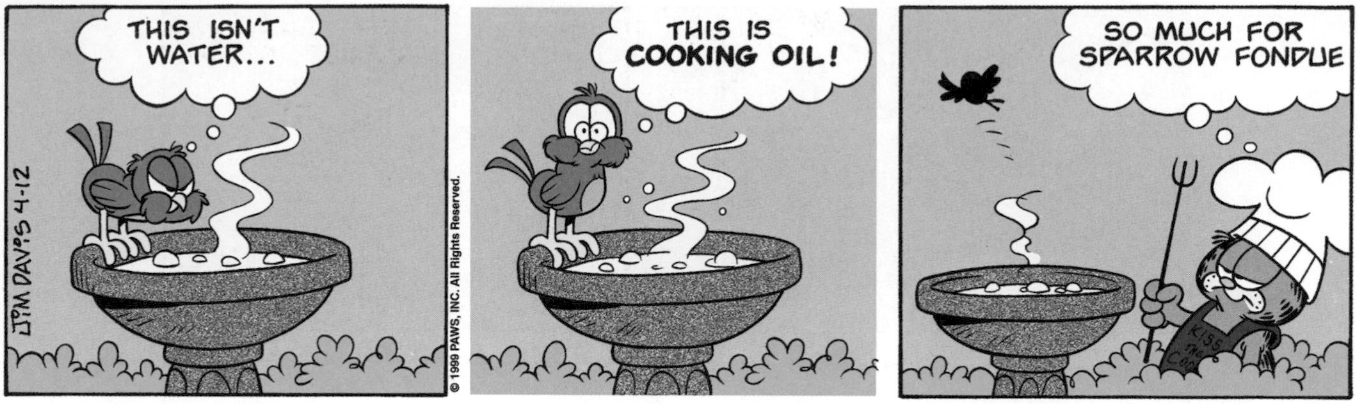
THIS ISN'T WATER...
JIM DAVIS 4-12
© 1999 PAWS, INC. All Rights Reserved.
THIS IS COOKING OIL!
SO MUCH FOR SPARROW FONDUE

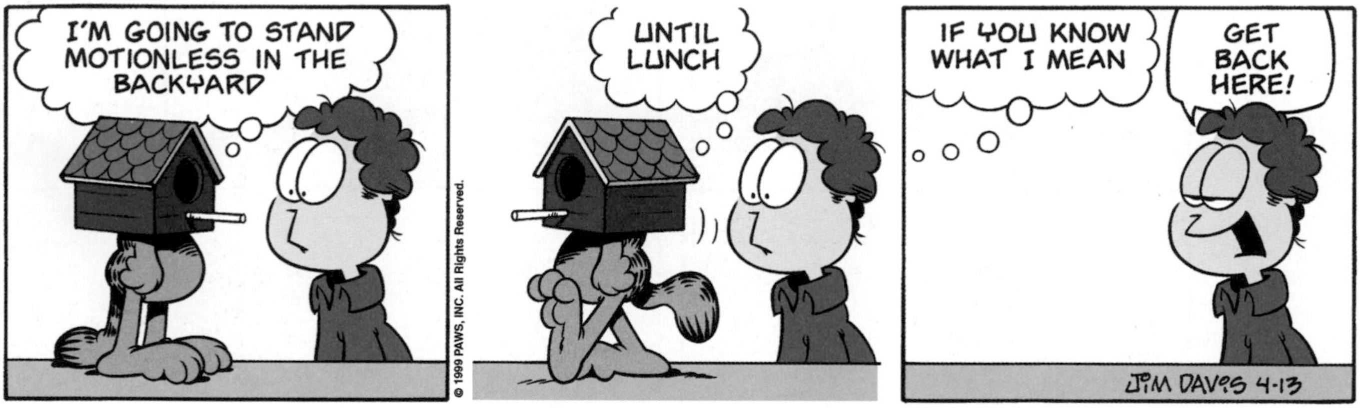
I'M GOING TO STAND MOTIONLESS IN THE BACKYARD
© 1999 PAWS, INC. All Rights Reserved.
UNTIL LUNCH
IF YOU KNOW WHAT I MEAN
GET BACK HERE!
JIM DAVIS 4-13

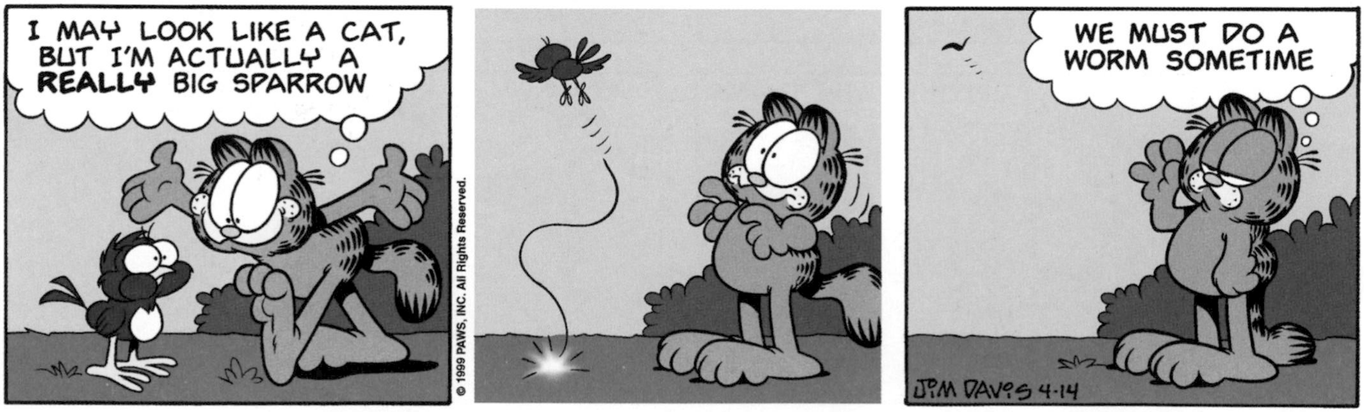
I MAY LOOK LIKE A CAT, BUT I'M ACTUALLY A REALLY BIG SPARROW
© 1999 PAWS, INC. All Rights Reserved.
WE MUST DO A WORM SOMETIME
JIM DAVIS 4-14

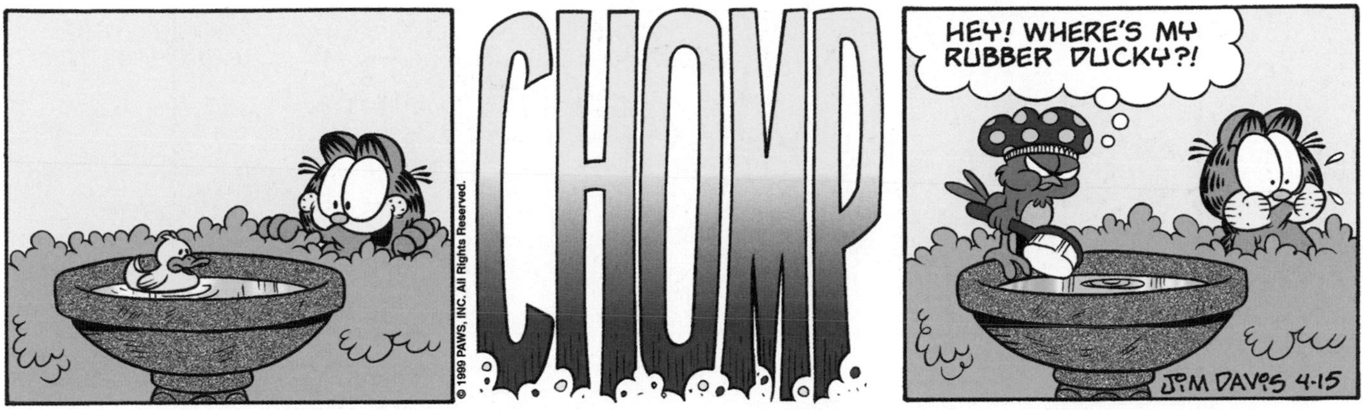
© 1999 PAWS, INC. All Rights Reserved.
CHOMP
HEY! WHERE'S MY RUBBER DUCKY?!
JIM DAVIS 4-15

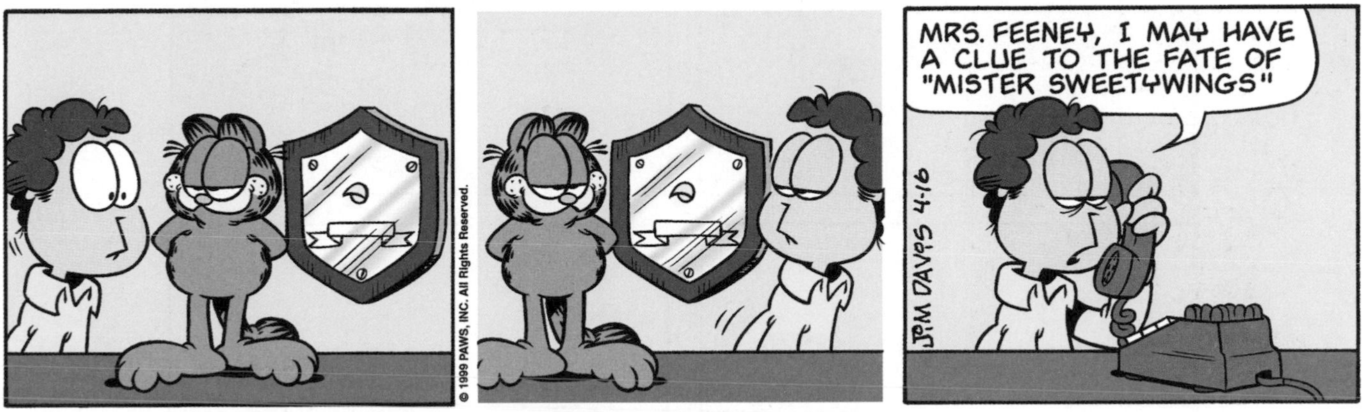
© 1999 PAWS, INC. All Rights Reserved.
JIM DAVIS 4-16
MRS. FEENEY, I MAY HAVE A CLUE TO THE FATE OF "MISTER SWEETYWINGS"

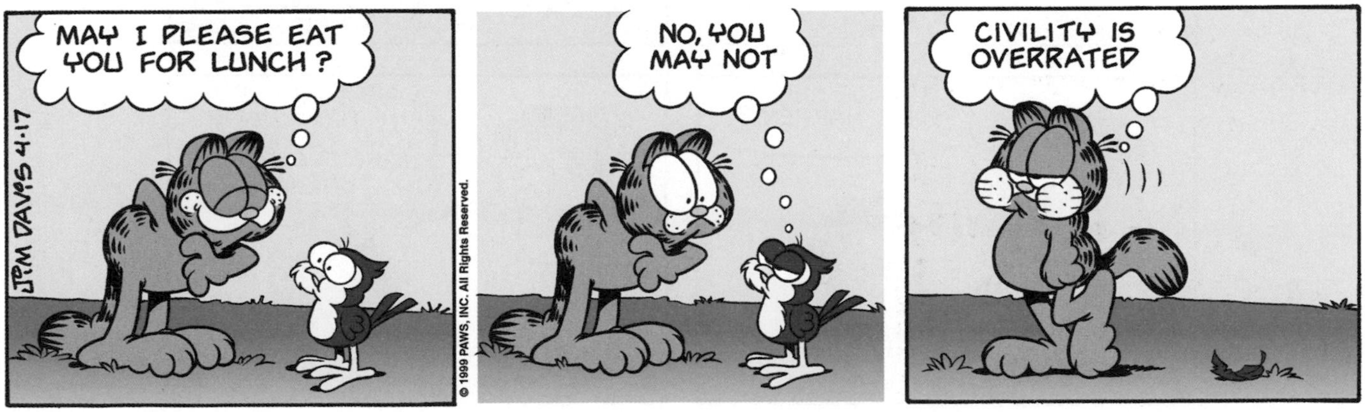
JIM DAVIS 4-17
MAY I PLEASE EAT YOU FOR LUNCH?
© 1999 PAWS, INC. All Rights Reserved.
NO, YOU MAY NOT
CIVILITY IS OVERRATED

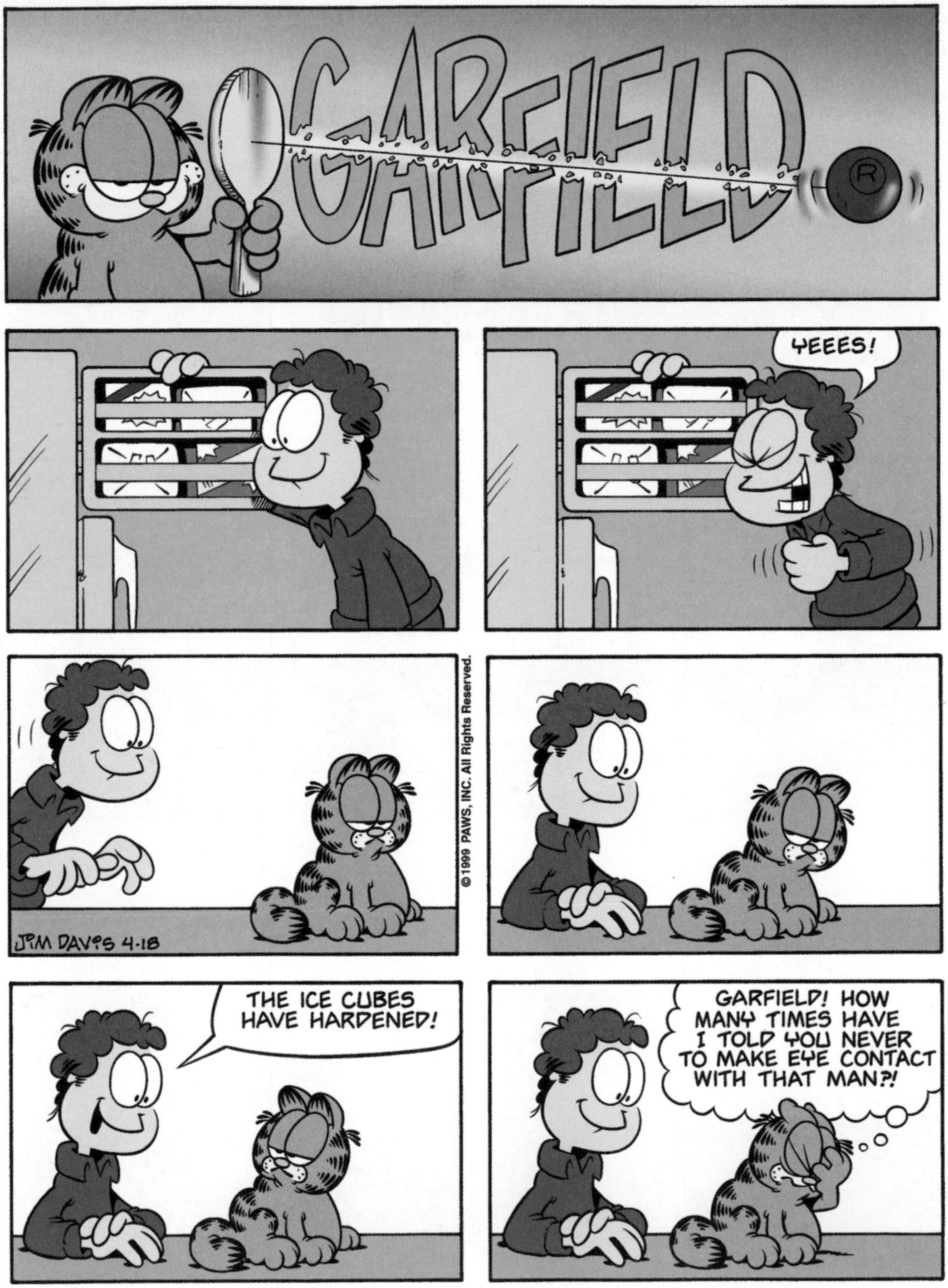
GARFIELD
YEEES!
THE ICE CUBES HAVE HARDENED!
GARFIELD! HOW MANY TIMES HAVE I TOLD YOU NEVER TO MAKE EYE CONTACT WITH THAT MAN?!
JIM DAVIS 4-18
© 1999 PAWS, INC. All Rights Reserved.

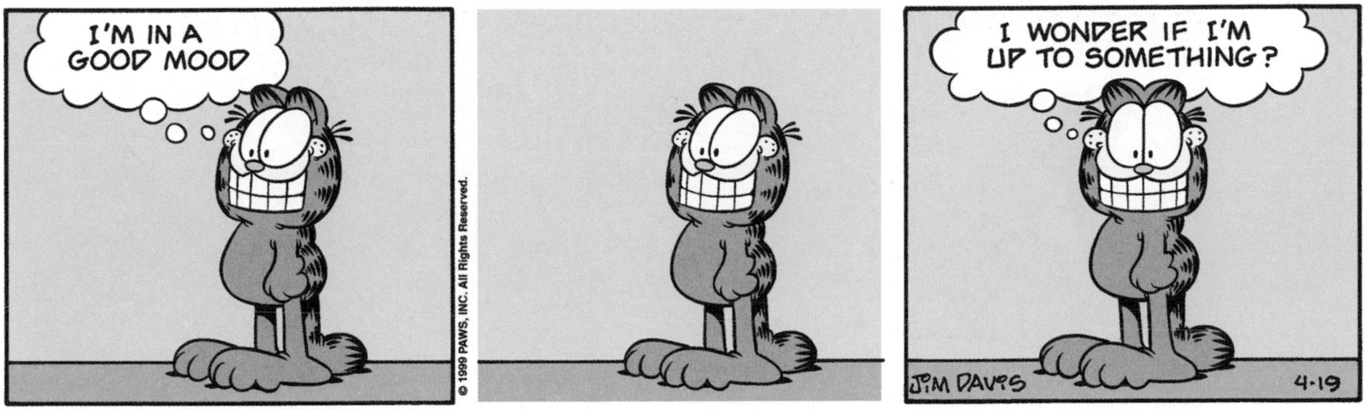
I'M IN A GOOD MOOD
© 1999 PAWS, INC. All Rights Reserved.
I WONDER IF I'M UP TO SOMETHING?
JIM DAVIS
4-19

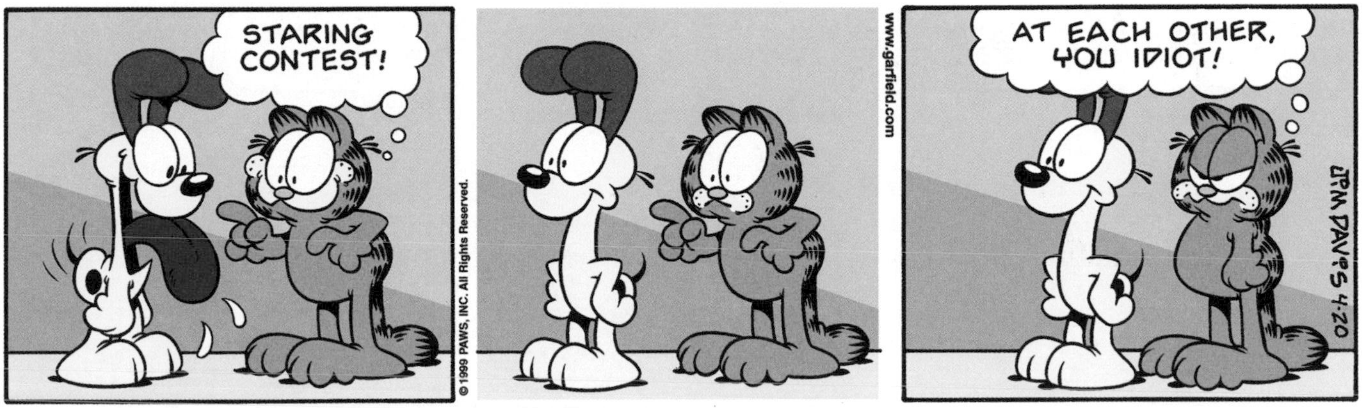
STARING CONTEST!
© 1999 PAWS, INC. All Rights Reserved.
www.garfield.com
AT EACH OTHER, YOU IDIOT!
JIM DAVIS 4-20

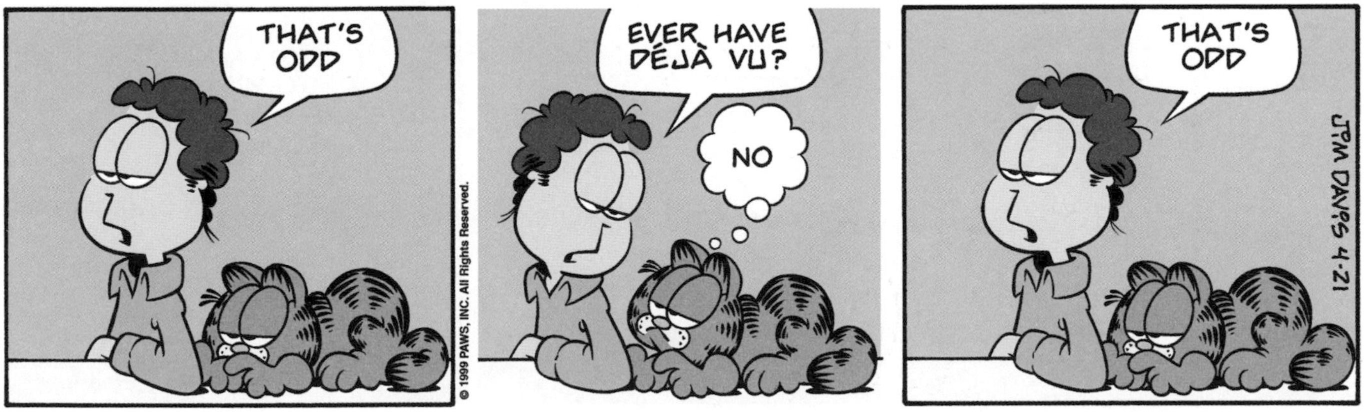
THAT'S ODD
© 1999 PAWS, INC. All Rights Reserved.
EVER HAVE DÉJÀ VU?
NO
THAT'S ODD
JIM DAVIS 4-21

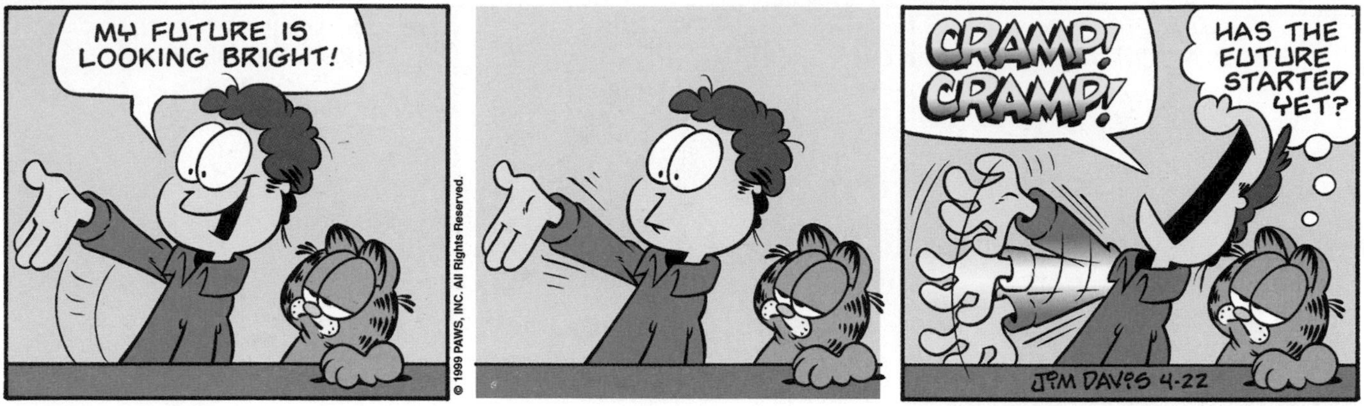
MY FUTURE IS LOOKING BRIGHT!
© 1999 PAWS, INC. All Rights Reserved.
CRAMP! CRAMP!
HAS THE FUTURE STARTED YET?
JIM DAVIS 4-22

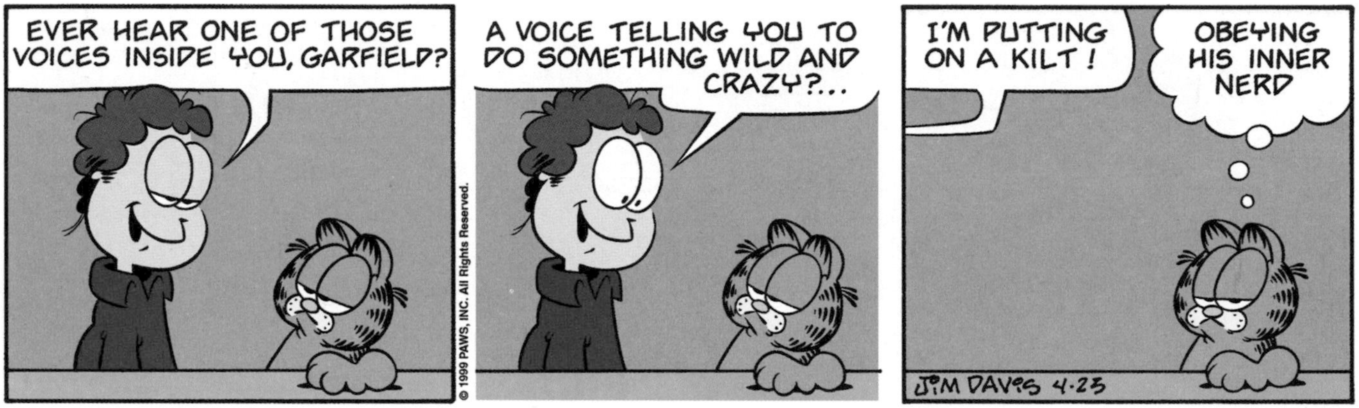
EVER HEAR ONE OF THOSE VOICES INSIDE YOU, GARFIELD?
© 1999 PAWS, INC. All Rights Reserved.
A VOICE TELLING YOU TO DO SOMETHING WILD AND CRAZY?...
I'M PUTTING ON A KILT!
OBEYING HIS INNER NERD
JIM DAVIS 4-23

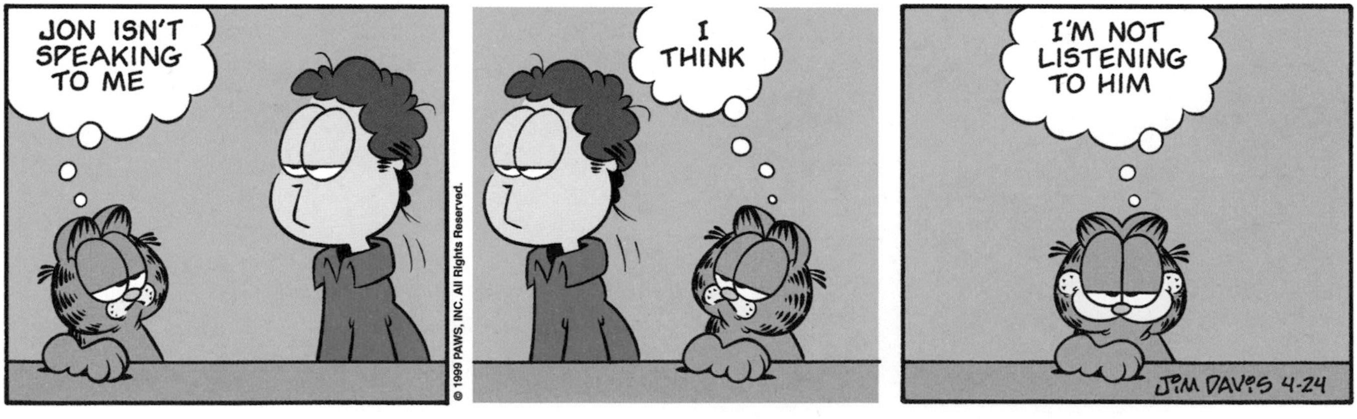
JON ISN'T SPEAKING TO ME
© 1999 PAWS, INC. All Rights Reserved.
I THINK
I'M NOT LISTENING TO HIM
JIM DAVIS 4-24

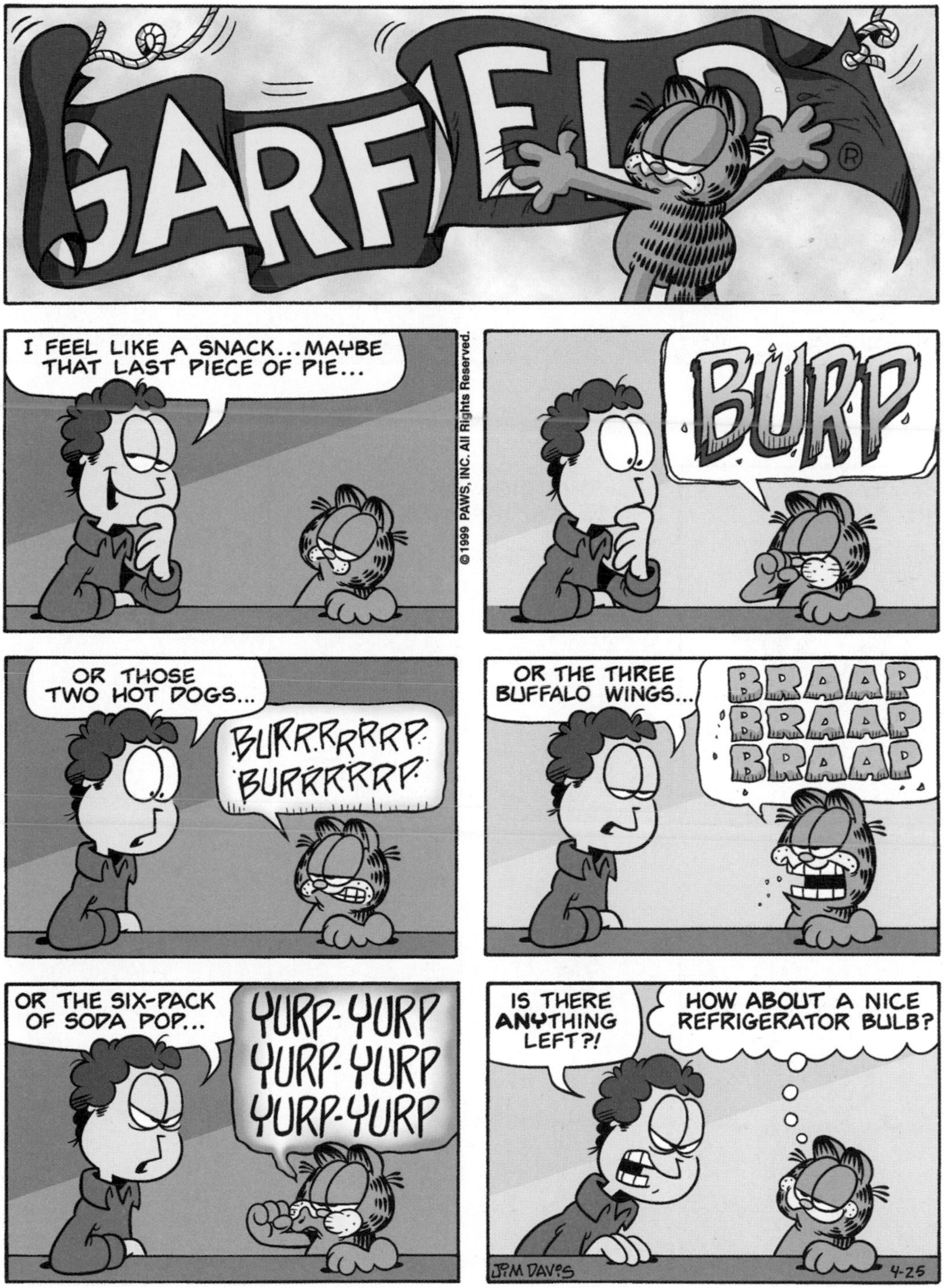
GARFIELD
I FEEL LIKE A SNACK... MAYBE THAT LAST PIECE OF PIE...
© 1999 PAWS, INC. All Rights Reserved.
BURP
OR THOSE TWO HOT DOGS...
BURRRRRRP BURRRRRRP
OR THE THREE BUFFALO WINGS...
BRAAP BRAAP BRAAP
OR THE SIX-PACK OF SODA POP...
YURP-YURP YURP-YURP YURP-YURP
IS THERE ANYTHING LEFT?!
HOW ABOUT A NICE REFRIGERATOR BULB?
JIM DAVIS
4-25

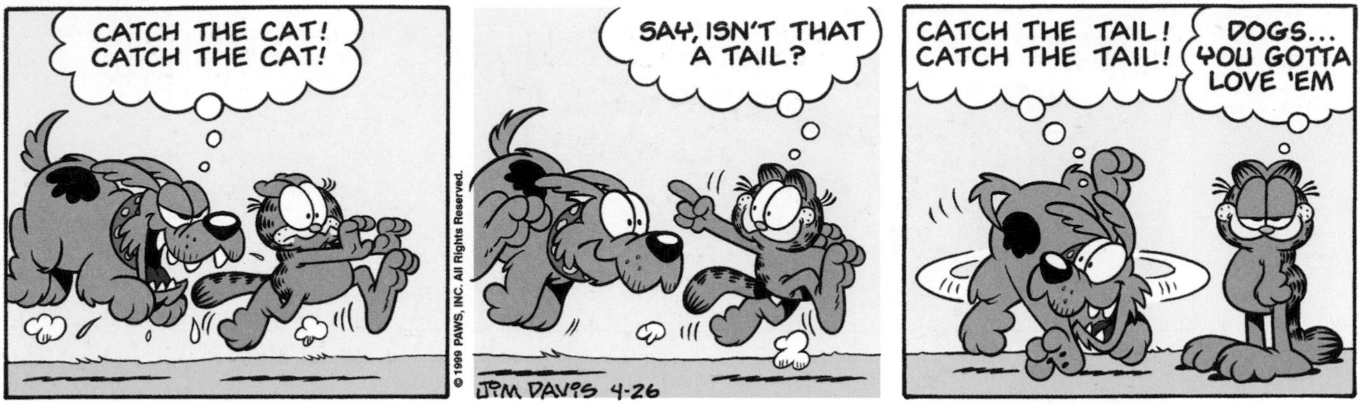
CATCH THE CAT! CATCH THE CAT!
© 1999 PAWS, INC. All Rights Reserved.
SAY, ISN'T THAT A TAIL?
JIM DAVIS 4-26
CATCH THE TAIL! CATCH THE TAIL!
DOGS... YOU GOTTA LOVE 'EM

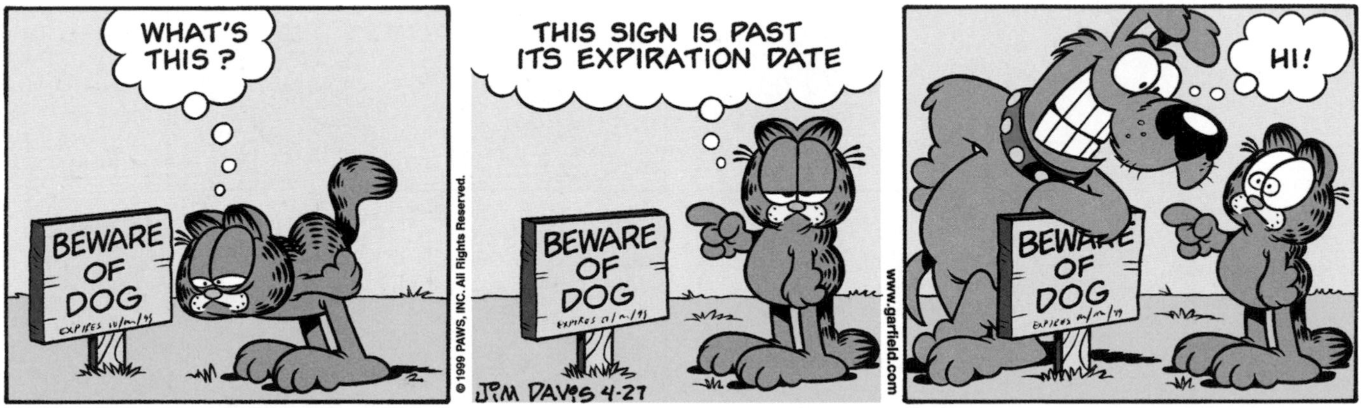
WHAT'S THIS?
BEWARE OF DOG
© 1999 PAWS, INC. All Rights Reserved.
THIS SIGN IS PAST ITS EXPIRATION DATE
BEWARE OF DOG
JIM DAVIS 4-27
www.garfield.com
HI!
BEWARE OF DOG

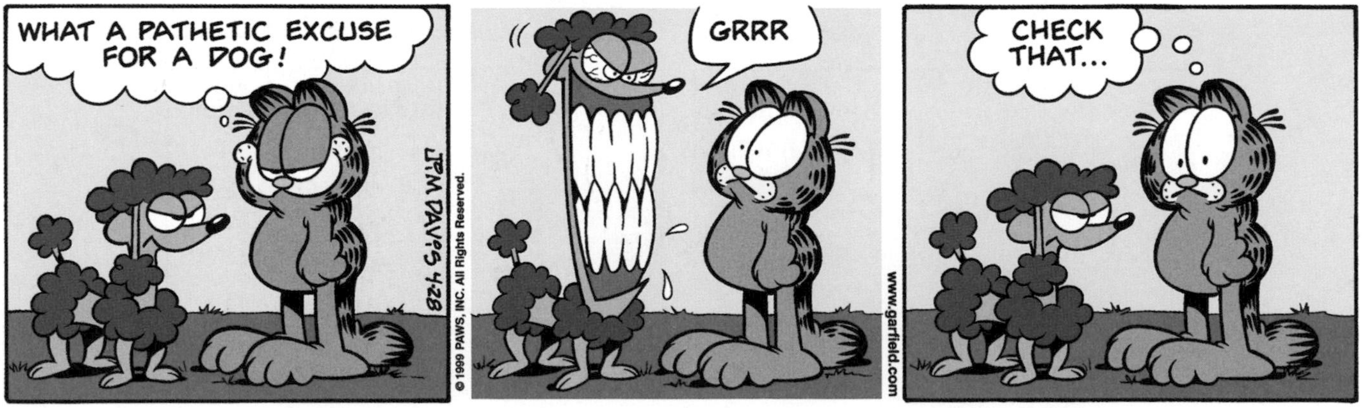
WHAT A PATHETIC EXCUSE FOR A DOG!
JIM DAVIS 4-28
© 1999 PAWS, INC. All Rights Reserved.
GRRR
www.garfield.com
CHECK THAT...

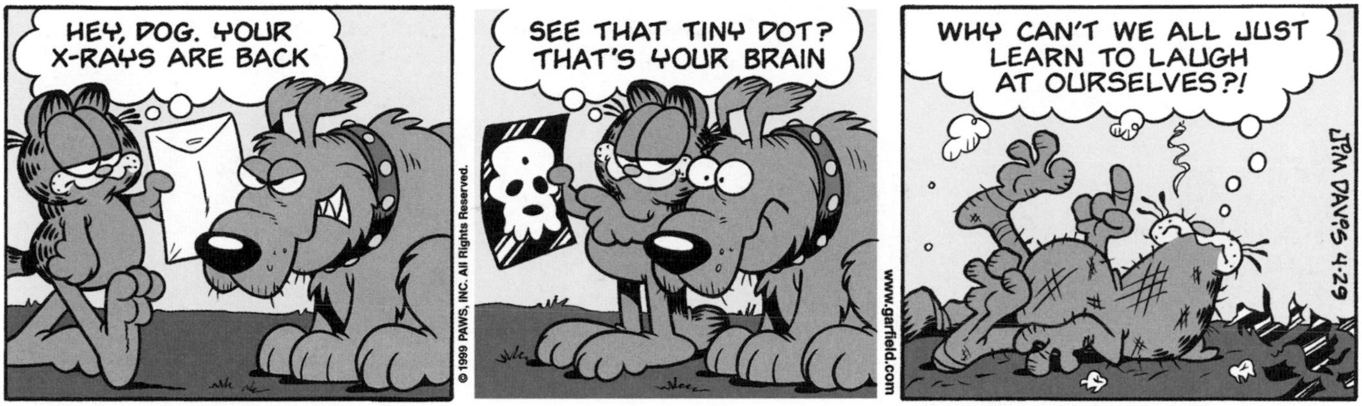
HEY, DOG. YOUR X-RAYS ARE BACK
SEE THAT TINY DOT? THAT'S YOUR BRAIN
WHY CAN'T WE ALL JUST LEARN TO LAUGH AT OURSELVES?!
JIM DAVIS 4-29
© 1999 PAWS, INC. All Rights Reserved.
www.garfield.com

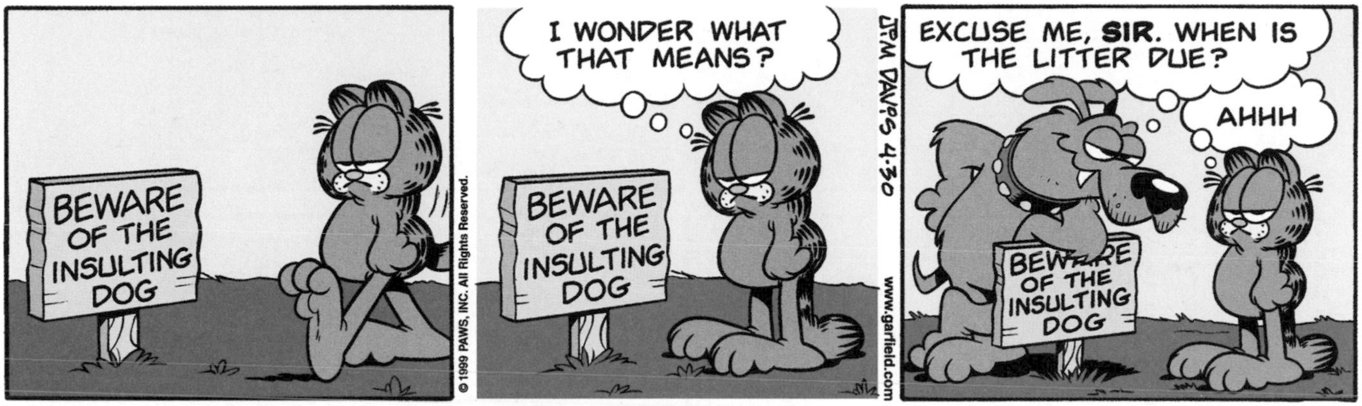
BEWARE OF THE INSULTING DOG
I WONDER WHAT THAT MEANS?
EXCUSE ME, SIR. WHEN IS THE LITTER DUE?
AHHH
JIM DAVIS 4-30
© 1999 PAWS, INC. All Rights Reserved.
www.garfield.com

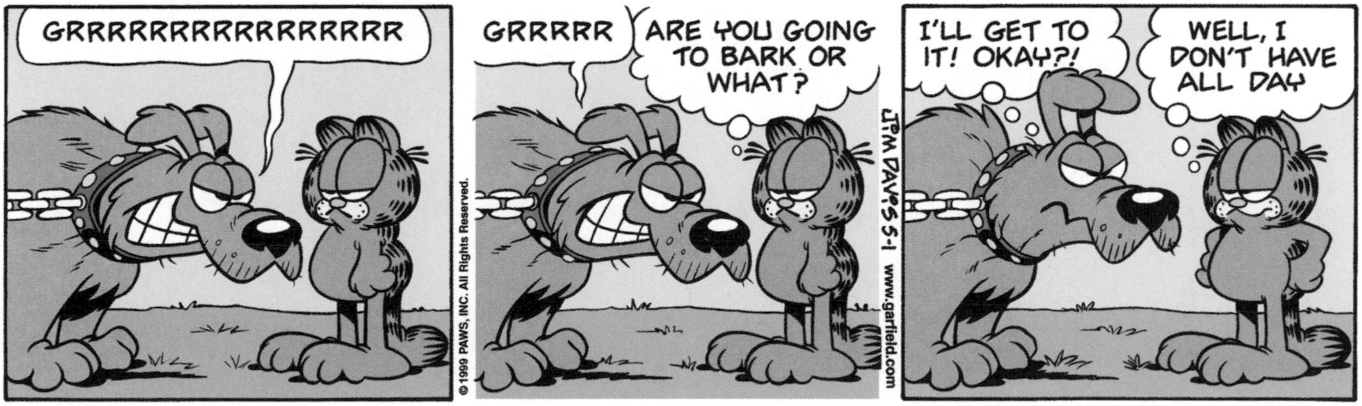
GRRRRRRRRRRRRRRRR
GRRRRR
ARE YOU GOING TO BARK OR WHAT?
I'LL GET TO IT! OKAY?!
WELL, I DON'T HAVE ALL DAY
JIM DAVIS 5-1
© 1999 PAWS, INC. All Rights Reserved.
www.garfield.com

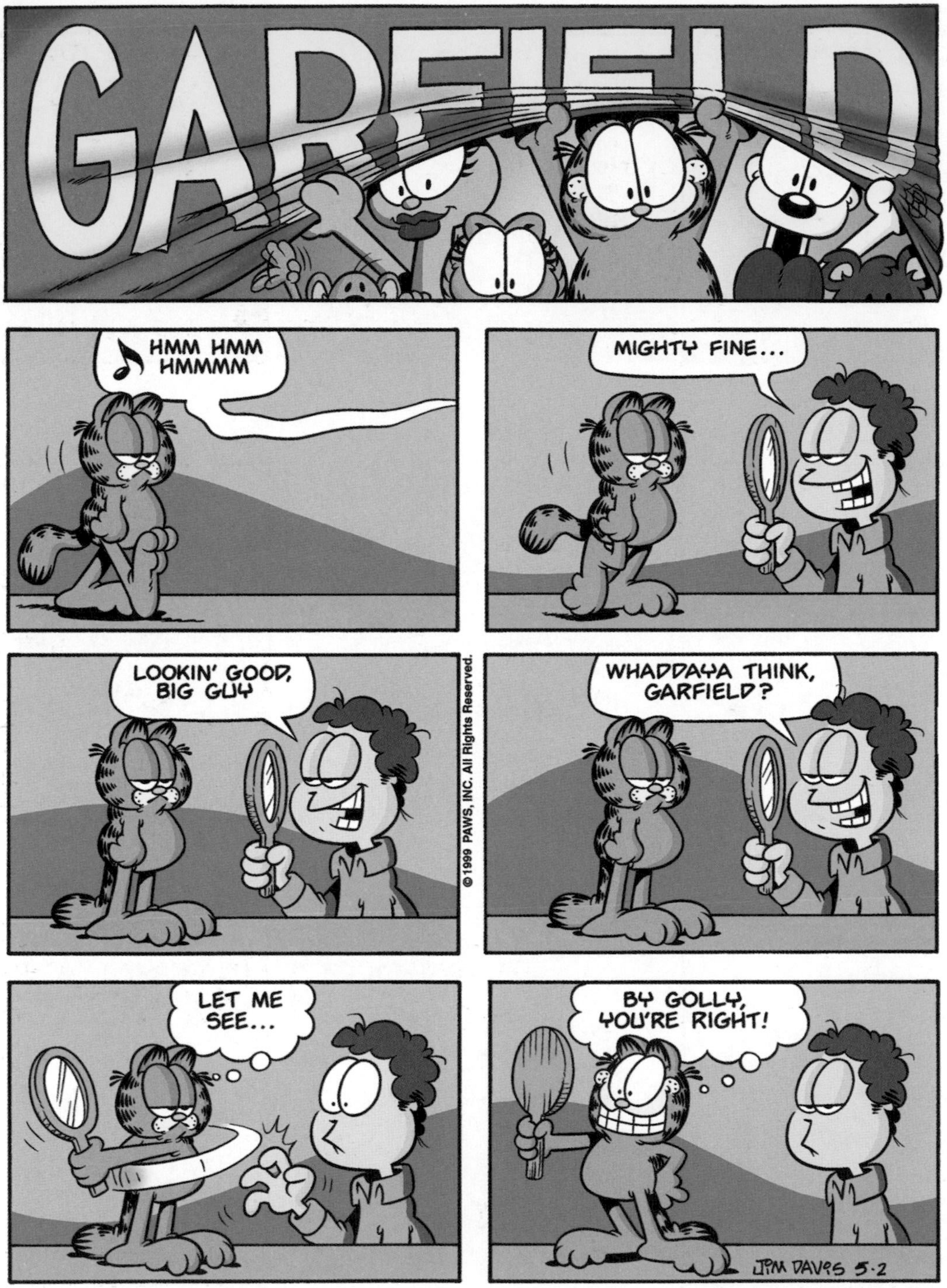
GARFIELD
♪ HMM HMM HMMMM
MIGHTY FINE...
LOOKIN' GOOD, BIG GUY
WHADDAYA THINK, GARFIELD?
LET ME SEE...
BY GOLLY, YOU'RE RIGHT!
JIM DAVIS 5-2

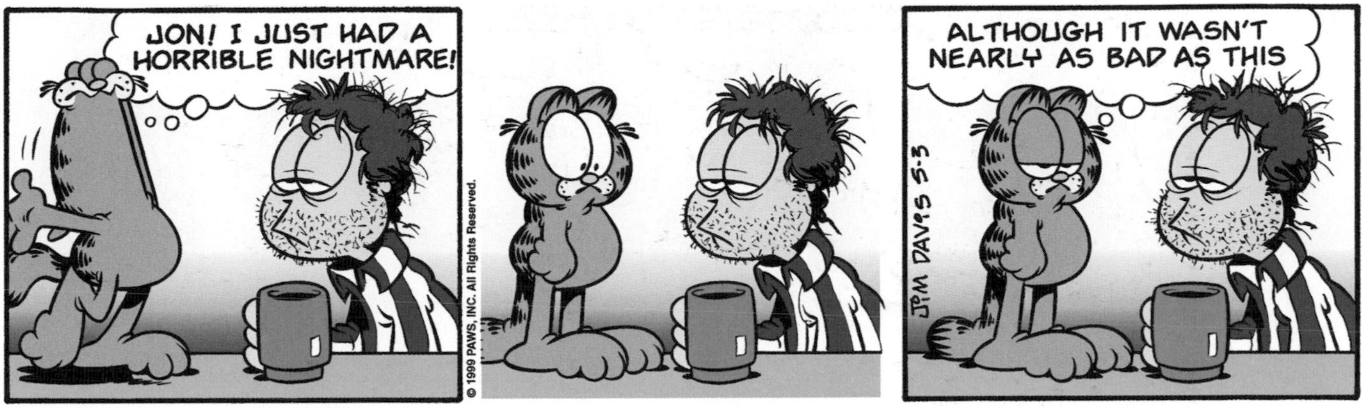
JON! I JUST HAD A HORRIBLE NIGHTMARE!
ALTHOUGH IT WASN'T NEARLY AS BAD AS THIS
JIM DAVIS 5-3

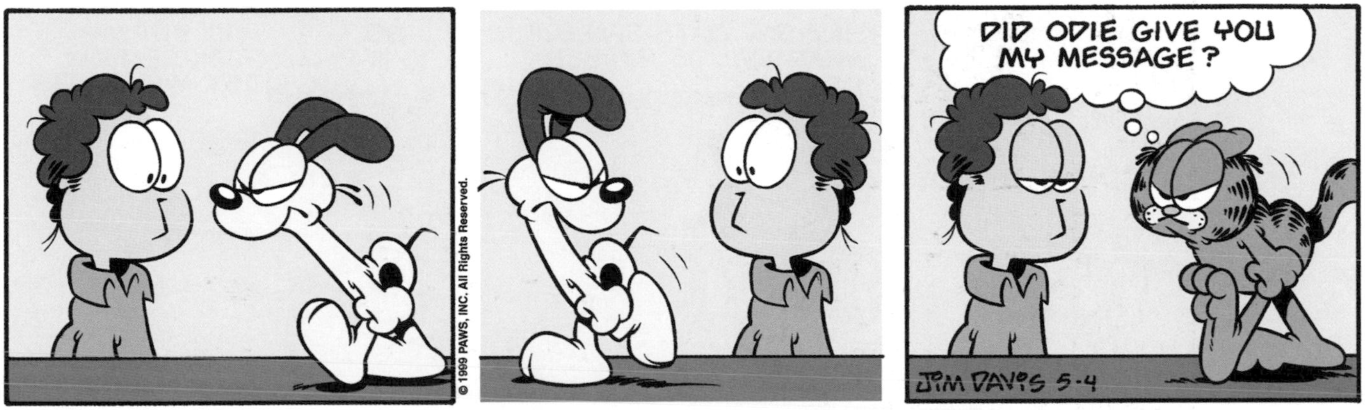
DID ODIE GIVE YOU MY MESSAGE?
JIM DAVIS 5-4

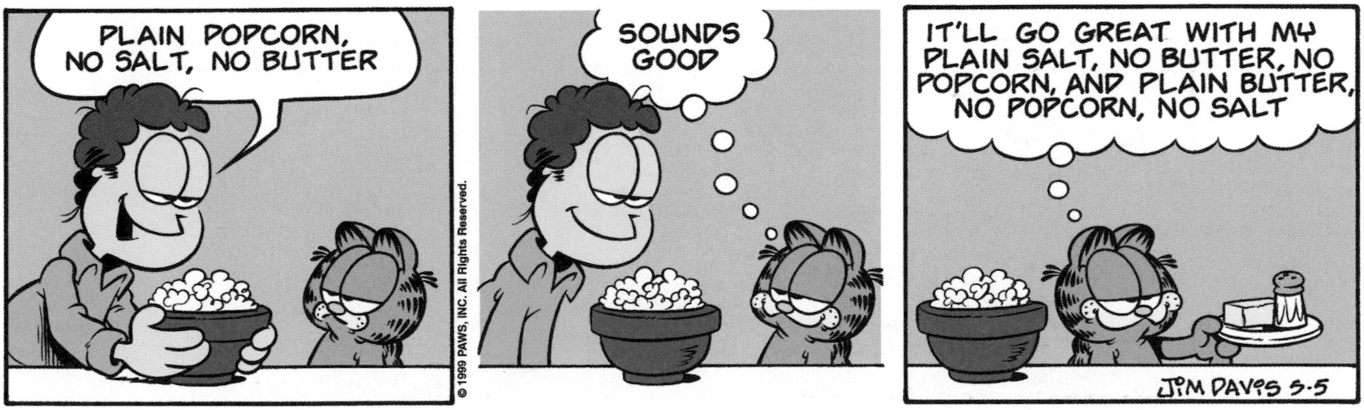
PLAIN POPCORN, NO SALT, NO BUTTER
SOUNDS GOOD
IT'LL GO GREAT WITH MY PLAIN SALT, NO BUTTER, NO POPCORN, AND PLAIN BUTTER, NO POPCORN, NO SALT
JIM DAVIS 5-5

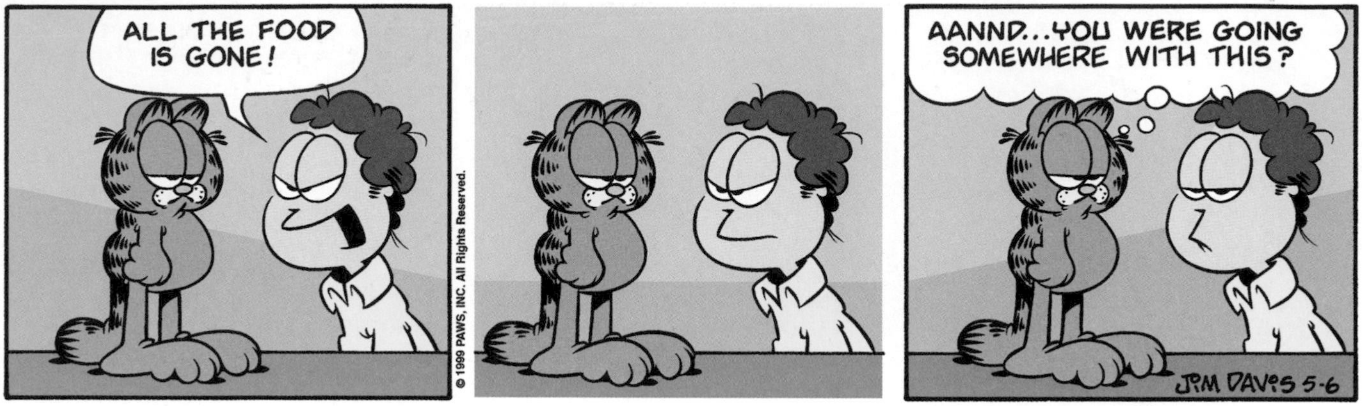
ALL THE FOOD IS GONE!
AANND...YOU WERE GOING SOMEWHERE WITH THIS?
© 1999 PAWS, INC. All Rights Reserved.
JIM DAVIS 5-6

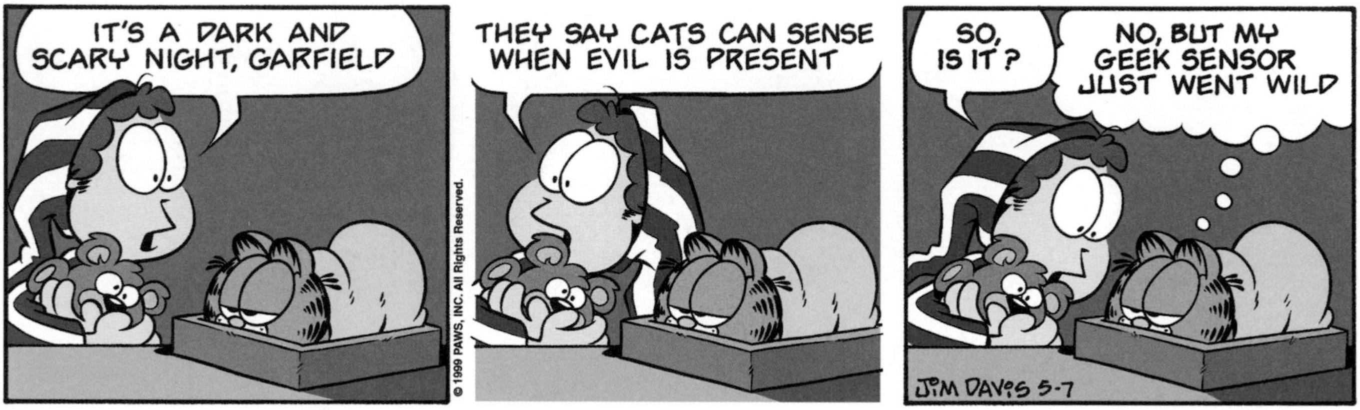
IT'S A DARK AND SCARY NIGHT, GARFIELD
THEY SAY CATS CAN SENSE WHEN EVIL IS PRESENT
SO, IS IT?
NO, BUT MY GEEK SENSOR JUST WENT WILD
© 1999 PAWS, INC. All Rights Reserved.
JIM DAVIS 5-7

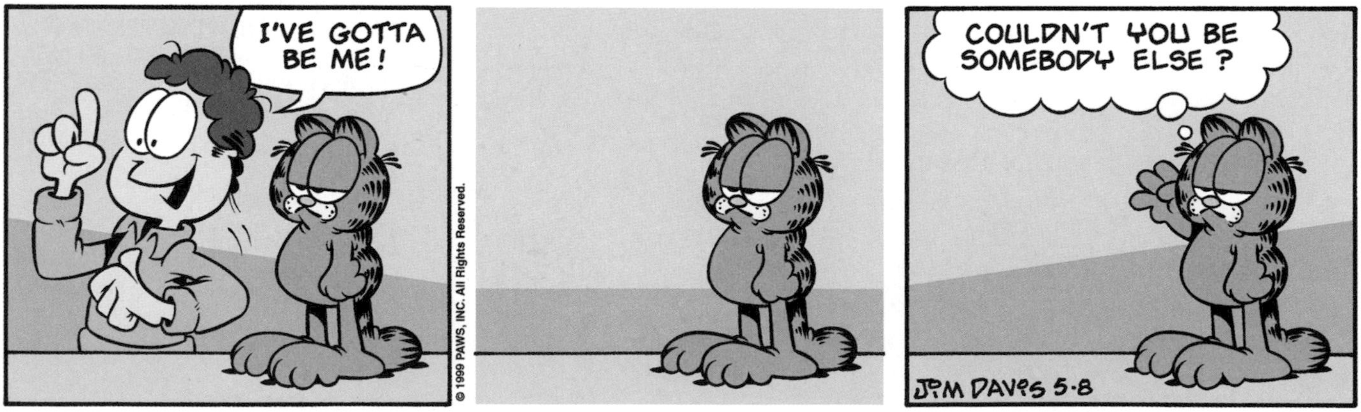
I'VE GOTTA BE ME!
COULDN'T YOU BE SOMEBODY ELSE?
© 1999 PAWS, INC. All Rights Reserved.
JIM DAVIS 5-8

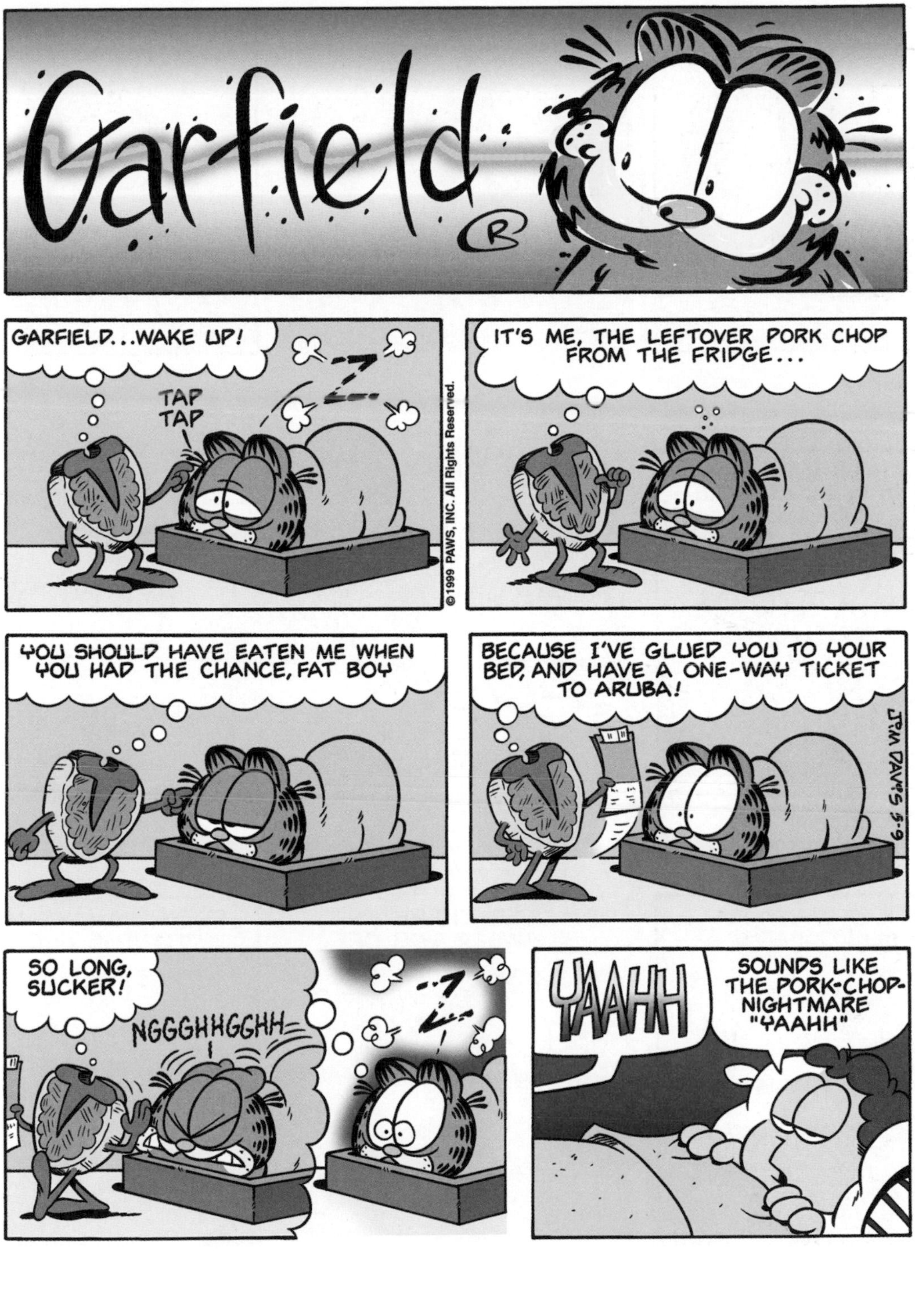
Garfield®
GARFIELD...WAKE UP!
TAP TAP
Z
©1999 PAWS, INC. All Rights Reserved.
IT'S ME, THE LEFTOVER PORK CHOP FROM THE FRIDGE...
YOU SHOULD HAVE EATEN ME WHEN YOU HAD THE CHANCE, FAT BOY
BECAUSE I'VE GLUED YOU TO YOUR BED, AND HAVE A ONE-WAY TICKET TO ARUBA!
JIM DAVIS 5-9
SO LONG, SUCKER!
NGGGHHGGHH
Z
YAAHH
SOUNDS LIKE THE PORK-CHOP-NIGHTMARE "YAAHH"

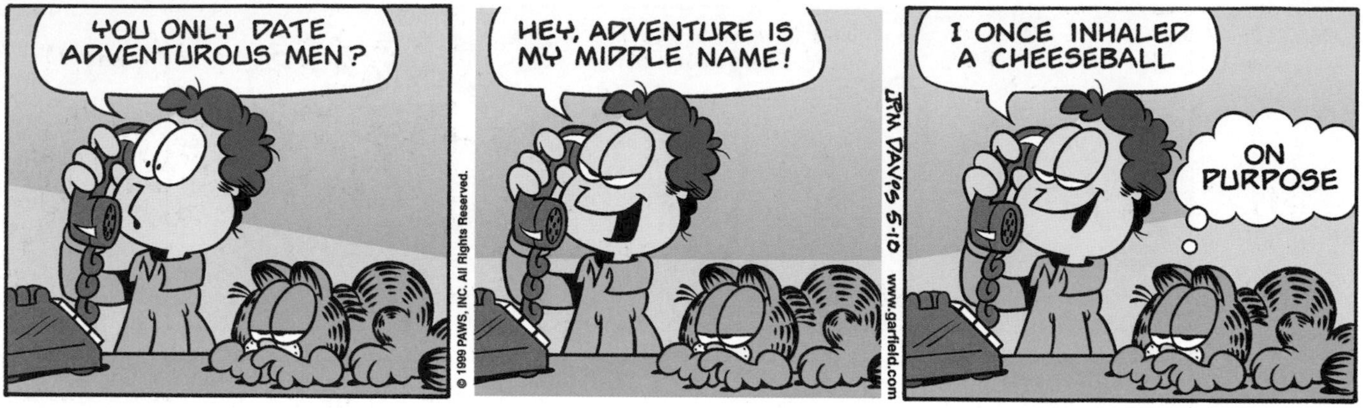
YOU ONLY DATE ADVENTUROUS MEN?
HEY, ADVENTURE IS MY MIDDLE NAME!
I ONCE INHALED A CHEESEBALL
ON PURPOSE
© 1999 PAWS, INC. All Rights Reserved.
JIM DAVIS 5-10
www.garfield.com

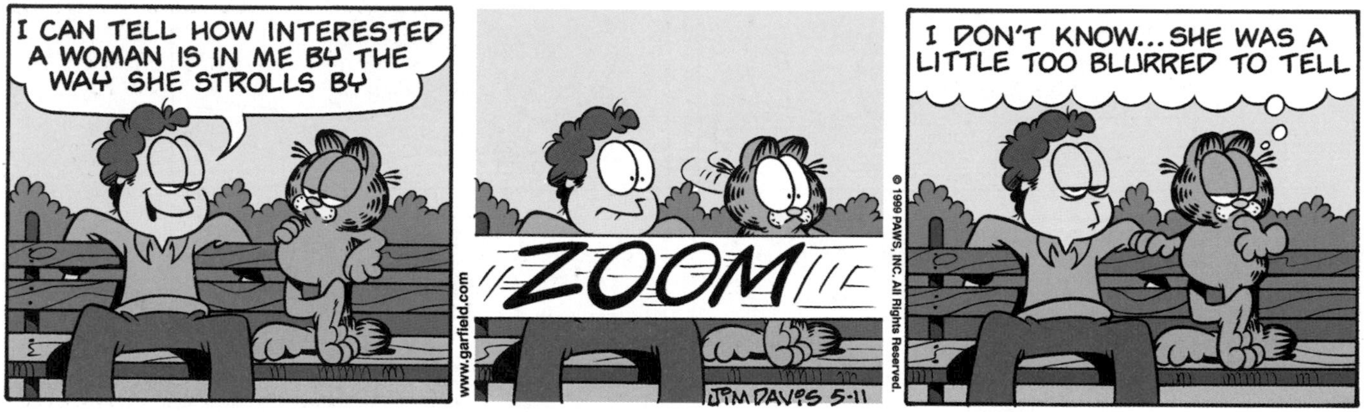
I CAN TELL HOW INTERESTED A WOMAN IS IN ME BY THE WAY SHE STROLLS BY
ZOOM
I DON'T KNOW... SHE WAS A LITTLE TOO BLURRED TO TELL
www.garfield.com
JIM DAVIS 5-11
© 1999 PAWS, INC. All Rights Reserved.

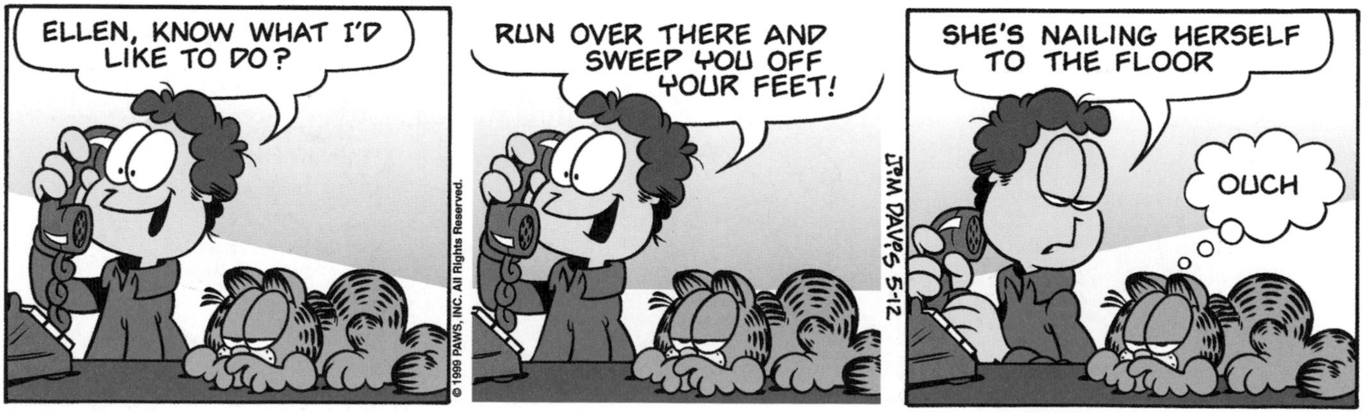
ELLEN, KNOW WHAT I'D LIKE TO DO?
RUN OVER THERE AND SWEEP YOU OFF YOUR FEET!
SHE'S NAILING HERSELF TO THE FLOOR
OUCH
© 1999 PAWS, INC. All Rights Reserved.
JIM DAVIS 5-12

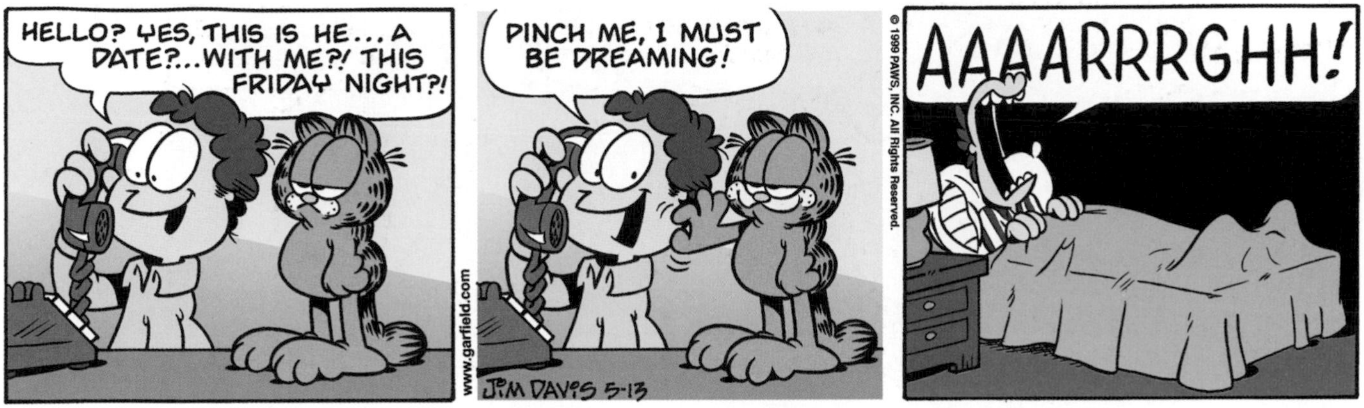
HELLO? YES, THIS IS HE... A DATE?...WITH ME?! THIS FRIDAY NIGHT?!
www.garfield.com
PINCH ME, I MUST BE DREAMING!
JIM DAVIS 5-13
© 1999 PAWS, INC. All Rights Reserved.
AAAARRRRGHH!

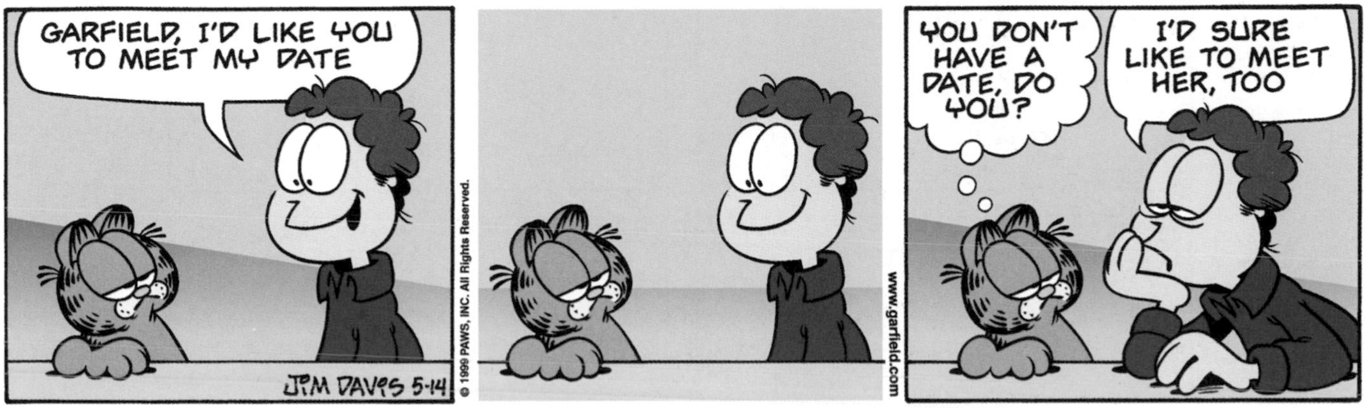
GARFIELD, I'D LIKE YOU TO MEET MY DATE
JIM DAVIS 5-14
© 1999 PAWS, INC. All Rights Reserved.
www.garfield.com
YOU DON'T HAVE A DATE, DO YOU?
I'D SURE LIKE TO MEET HER, TOO

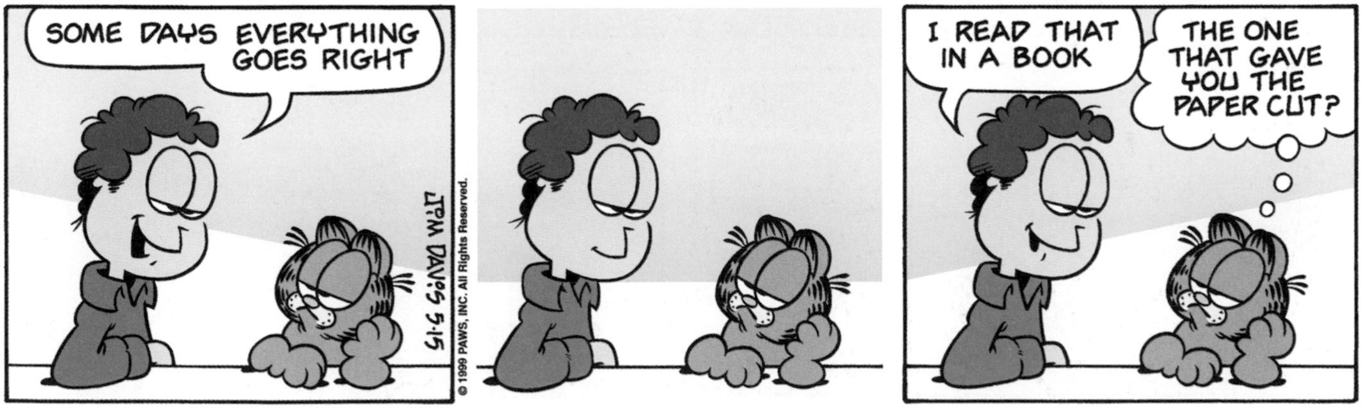
SOME DAYS EVERYTHING GOES RIGHT
JIM DAVIS 5-15
© 1999 PAWS, INC. All Rights Reserved.
I READ THAT IN A BOOK
THE ONE THAT GAVE YOU THE PAPER CUT?

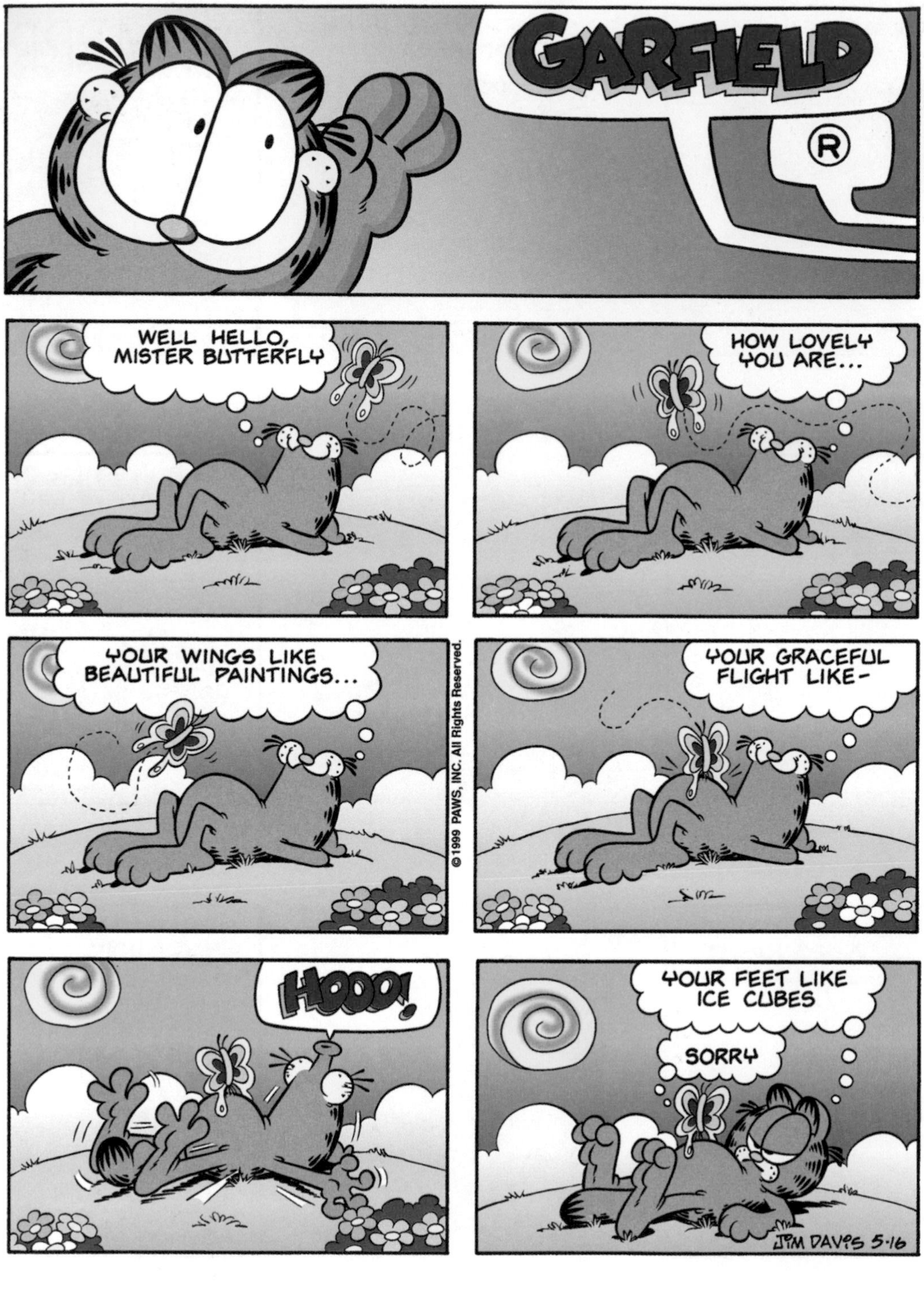
GARFIELD
®
WELL HELLO, MISTER BUTTERFLY
HOW LOVELY YOU ARE...
YOUR WINGS LIKE BEAUTIFUL PAINTINGS...
© 1999 PAWS, INC. All Rights Reserved.
YOUR GRACEFUL FLIGHT LIKE-
HOOO!
YOUR FEET LIKE ICE CUBES
SORRY
JIM DAVIS 5-16

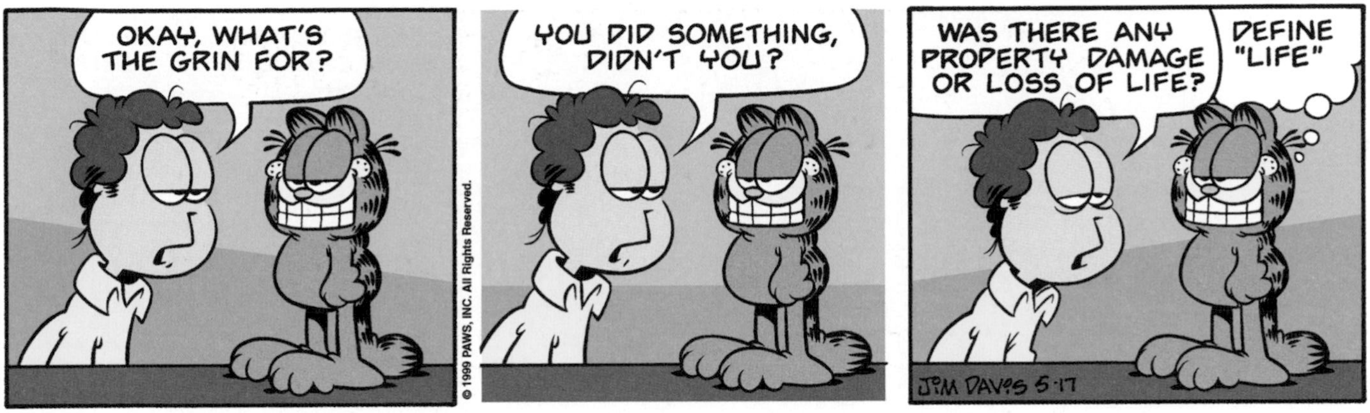
OKAY, WHAT'S THE GRIN FOR?
© 1999 PAWS, INC. All Rights Reserved.
YOU DID SOMETHING, DIDN'T YOU?
WAS THERE ANY PROPERTY DAMAGE OR LOSS OF LIFE?
DEFINE "LIFE"
JIM DAVIS 5-17

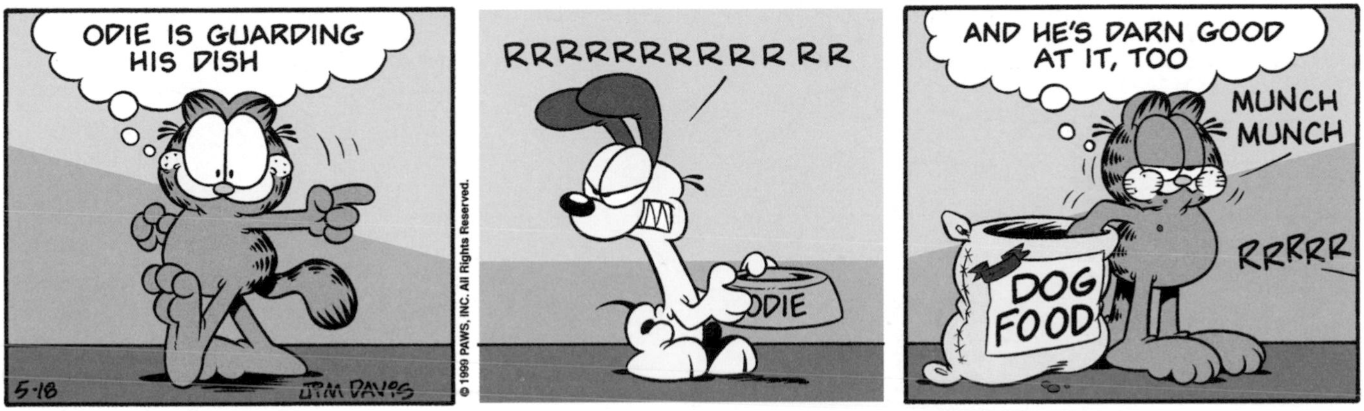
ODIE IS GUARDING HIS DISH
5-18
JIM DAVIS
© 1999 PAWS, INC. All Rights Reserved.
RRRRRRRRRRRRR
ODIE
AND HE'S DARN GOOD AT IT, TOO
MUNCH MUNCH
DOG FOOD
RRRRR

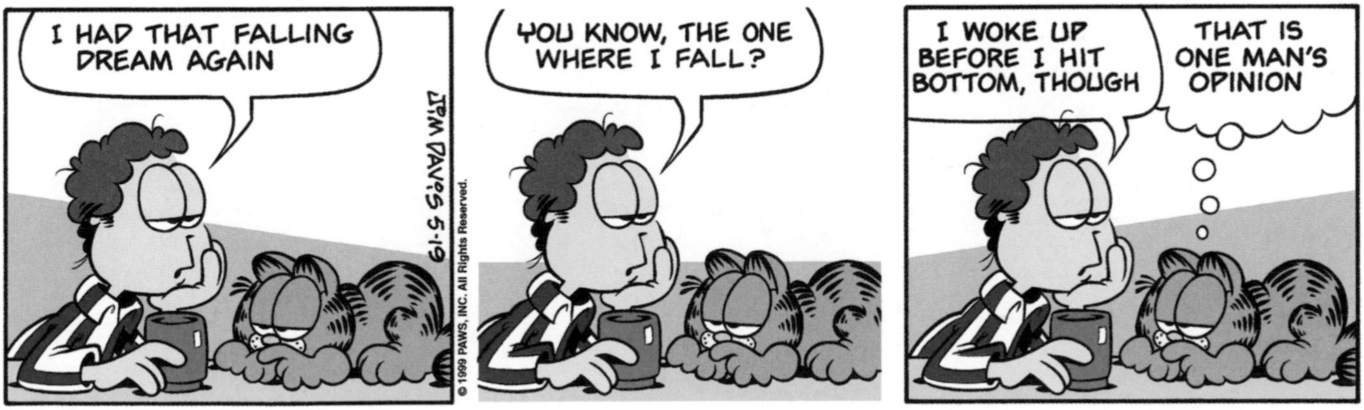
I HAD THAT FALLING DREAM AGAIN
JIM DAVIS 5-19
© 1999 PAWS, INC. All Rights Reserved.
YOU KNOW, THE ONE WHERE I FALL?
I WOKE UP BEFORE I HIT BOTTOM, THOUGH
THAT IS ONE MAN'S OPINION

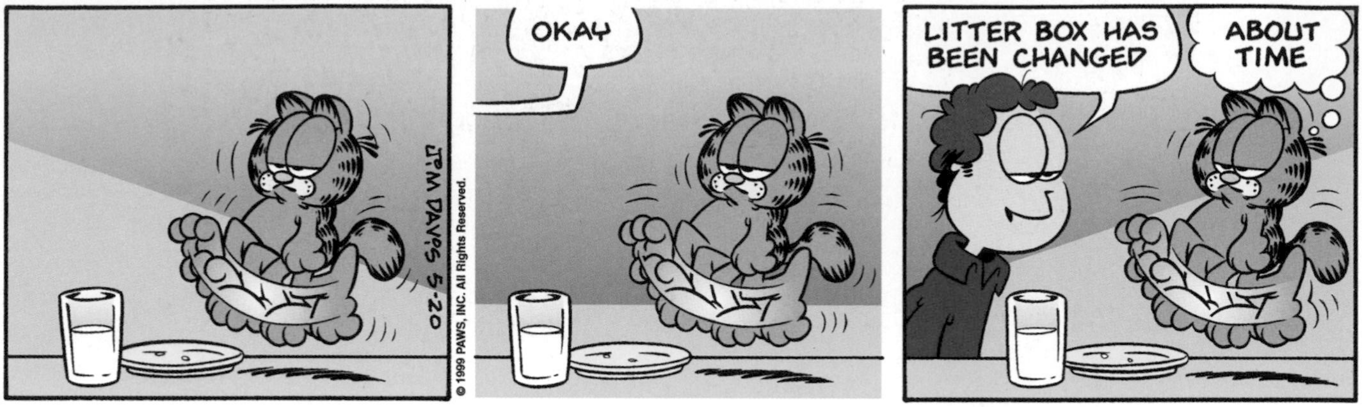
JIM DAVIS 5-20
© 1999 PAWS, INC. All Rights Reserved.
OKAY
LITTER BOX HAS BEEN CHANGED
ABOUT TIME

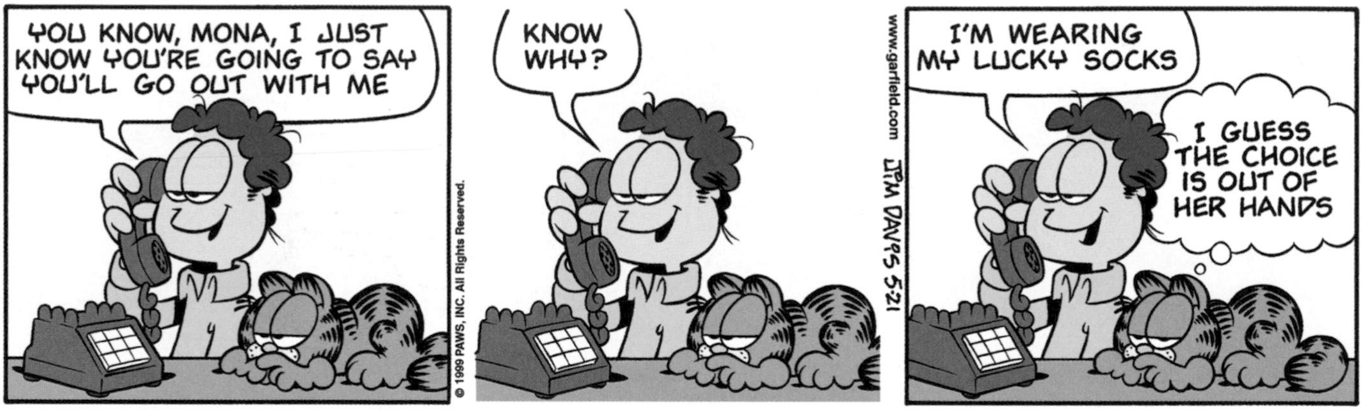
YOU KNOW, MONA, I JUST KNOW YOU'RE GOING TO SAY YOU'LL GO OUT WITH ME
© 1999 PAWS, INC. All Rights Reserved.
KNOW WHY?
www.garfield.com
JIM DAVIS 5-21
I'M WEARING MY LUCKY SOCKS
I GUESS THE CHOICE IS OUT OF HER HANDS

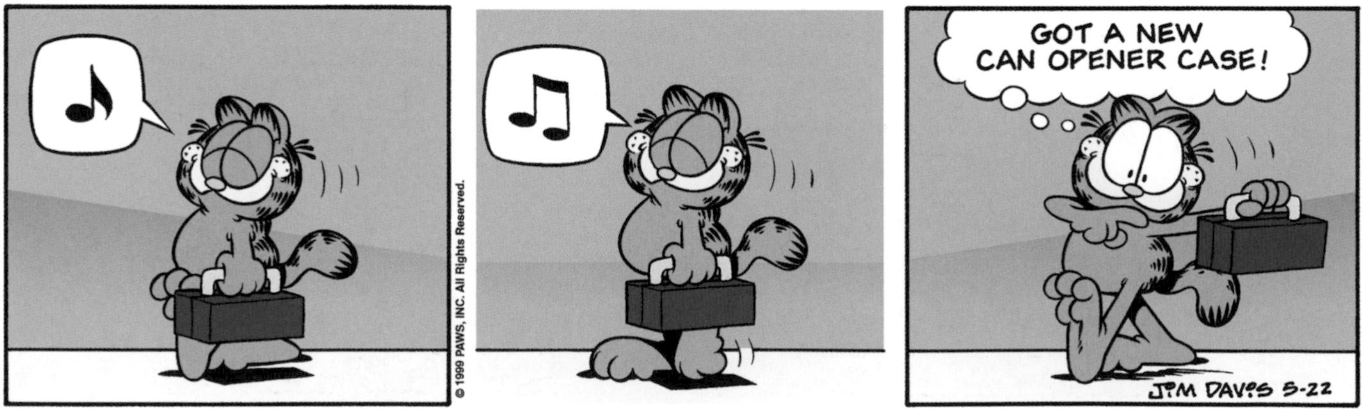
© 1999 PAWS, INC. All Rights Reserved.
GOT A NEW CAN OPENER CASE!
JIM DAVIS 5-22

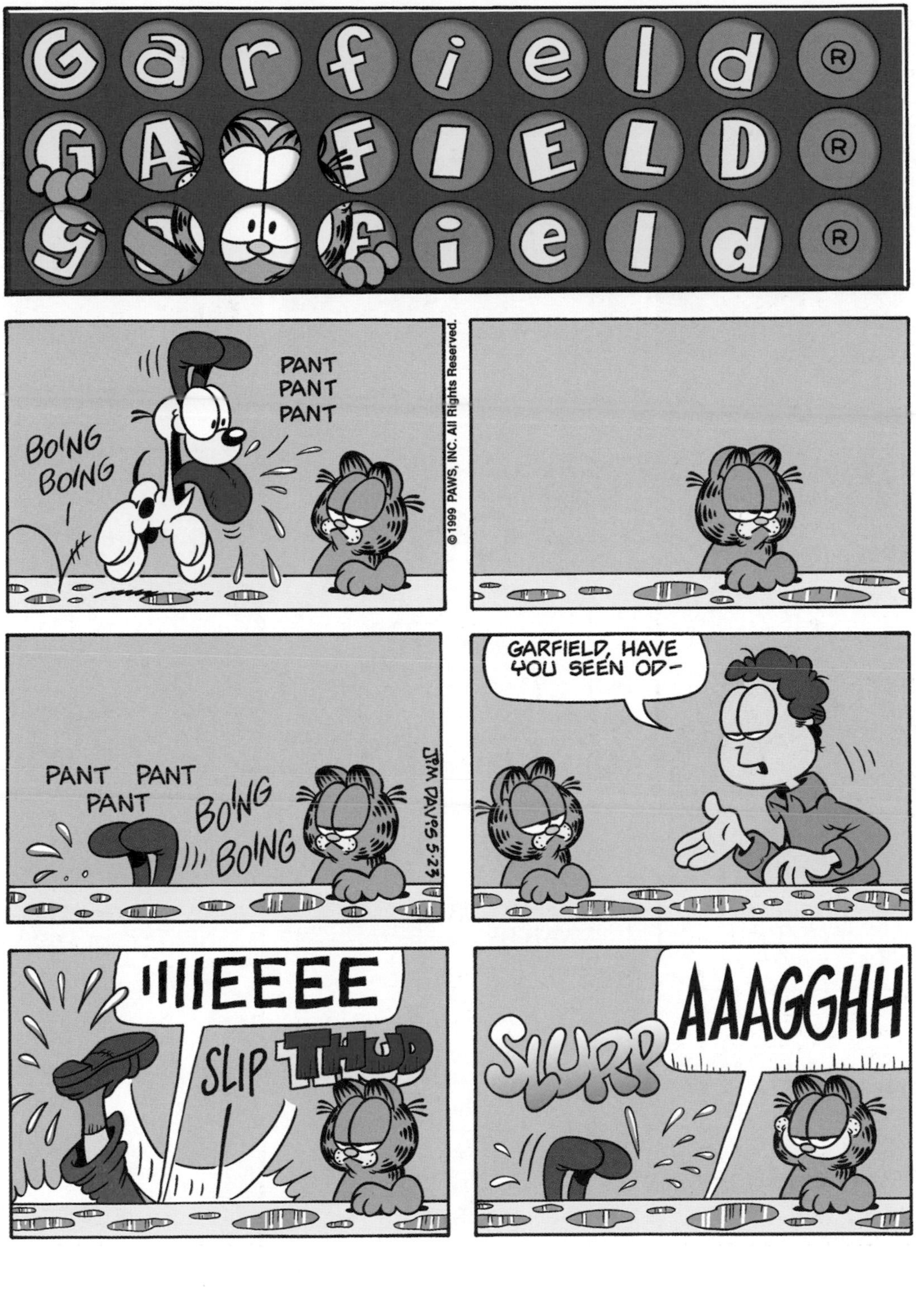
Garfield®
GARFIELD®
Garfield®
©1999 PAWS, INC. All Rights Reserved.
BOING BOING
PANT PANT PANT
PANT PANT PANT
BOING BOING
JIM DAVIS 5-23
GARFIELD, HAVE YOU SEEN OD-
IIIIEEEE
SLIP THUD
SLURP
AAAGGHH

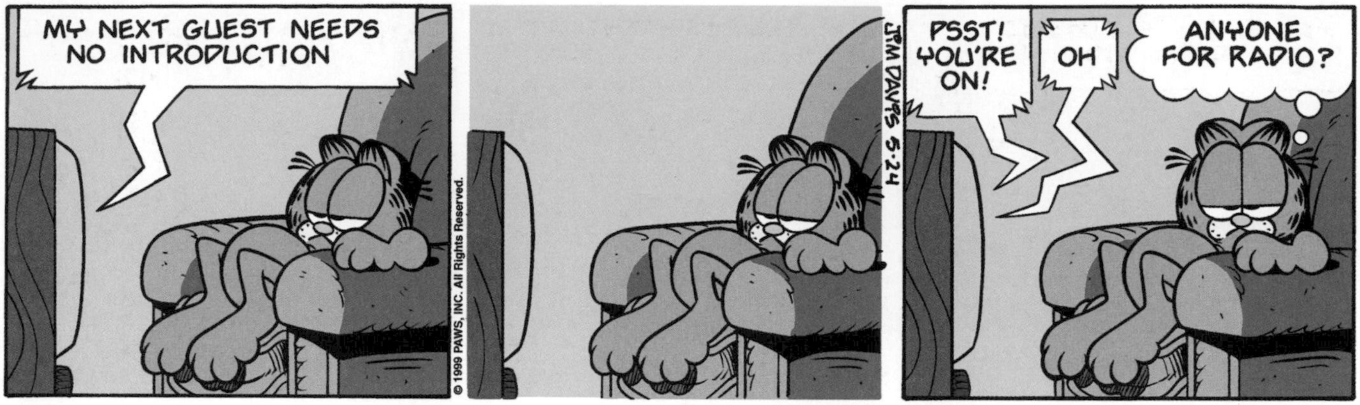
MY NEXT GUEST NEEDS NO INTRODUCTION
© 1999 PAWS, INC. All Rights Reserved.
JIM DAVIS 5-24
PSST! YOU'RE ON!
OH
ANYONE FOR RADIO?

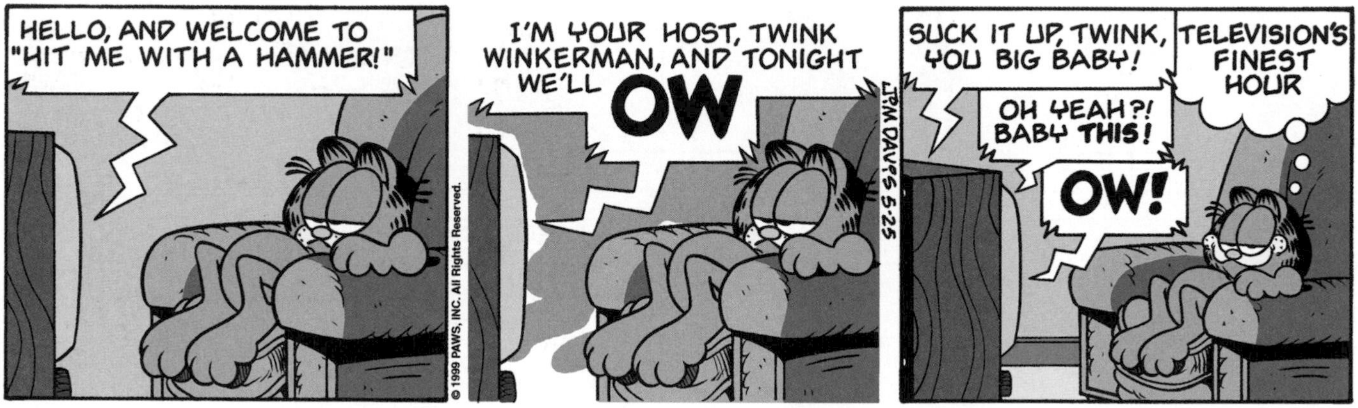
HELLO, AND WELCOME TO "HIT ME WITH A HAMMER!"
© 1999 PAWS, INC. All Rights Reserved.
I'M YOUR HOST, TWINK WINKERMAN, AND TONIGHT WE'LL
OW
JIM DAVIS 5-25
SUCK IT UP, TWINK, YOU BIG BABY!
OH YEAH?! BABY THIS!
OW!
TELEVISION'S FINEST HOUR

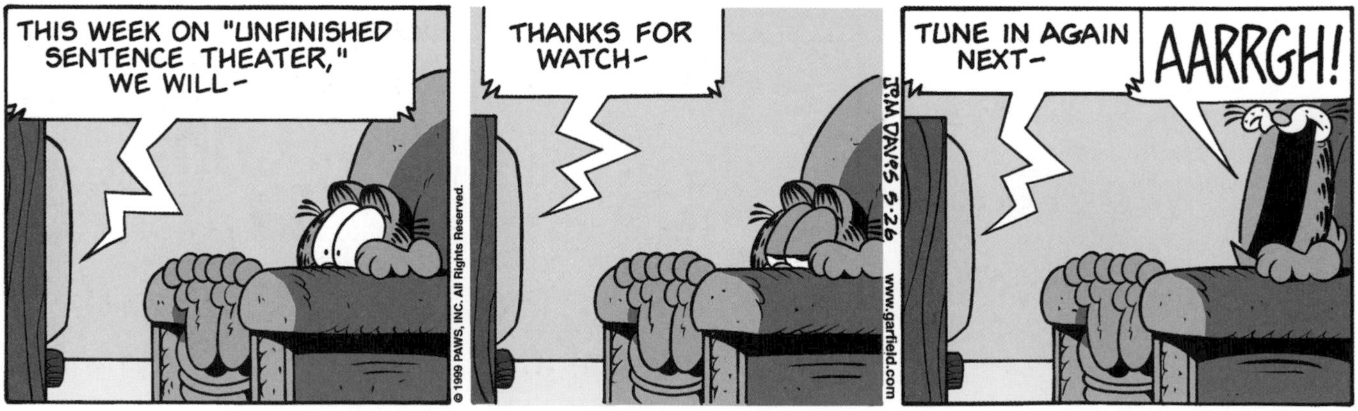
THIS WEEK ON "UNFINISHED SENTENCE THEATER," WE WILL-
© 1999 PAWS, INC. All Rights Reserved.
THANKS FOR WATCH-
JIM DAVIS 5-26
www.garfield.com
TUNE IN AGAIN NEXT-
AARRGH!

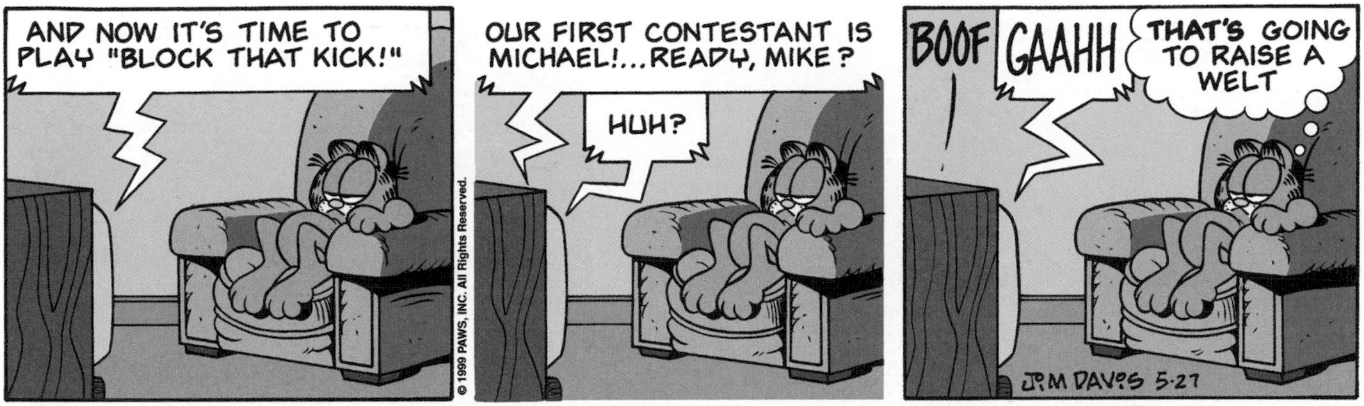
AND NOW IT'S TIME TO PLAY "BLOCK THAT KICK!"
© 1999 PAWS, INC. All Rights Reserved.
OUR FIRST CONTESTANT IS MICHAEL!... READY, MIKE?
HUH?
BOOF
GAAHH
THAT'S GOING TO RAISE A WELT
JIM DAVIS 5-27

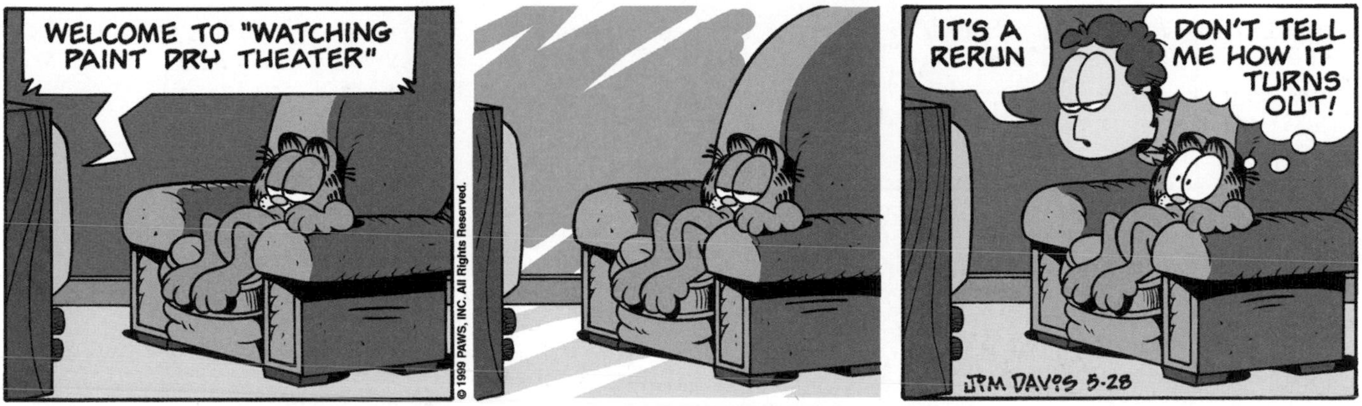
WELCOME TO "WATCHING PAINT DRY THEATER"
© 1999 PAWS, INC. All Rights Reserved.
IT'S A RERUN
DON'T TELL ME HOW IT TURNS OUT!
JIM DAVIS 5-28

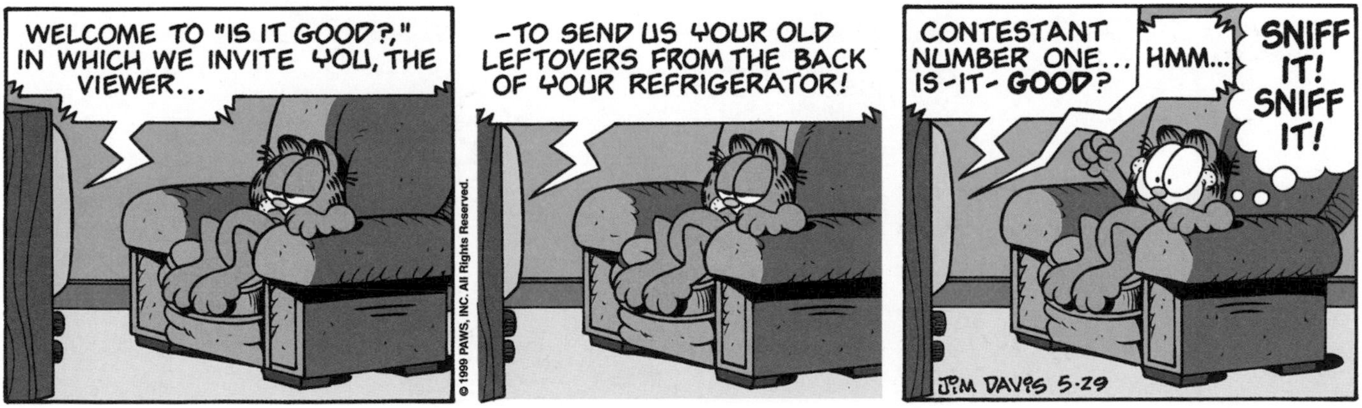
WELCOME TO "IS IT GOOD?," IN WHICH WE INVITE YOU, THE VIEWER...
© 1999 PAWS, INC. All Rights Reserved.
-TO SEND US YOUR OLD LEFTOVERS FROM THE BACK OF YOUR REFRIGERATOR!
CONTESTANT NUMBER ONE... IS-IT-GOOD?
HMM...
SNIFF IT! SNIFF IT!
JIM DAVIS 5-29

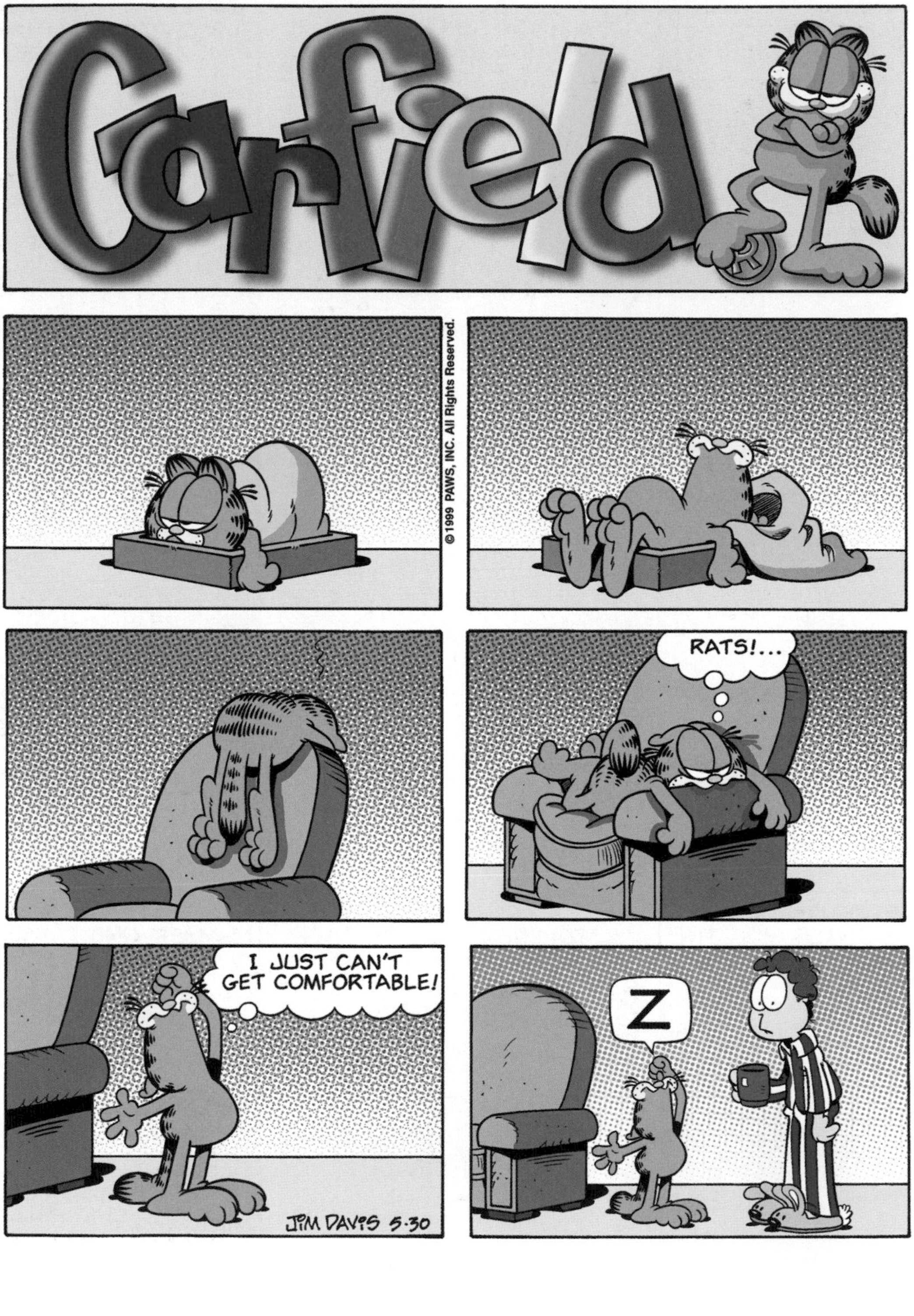
Garfield
© 1999 PAWS, INC. All Rights Reserved.
RATS!...
I JUST CAN'T GET COMFORTABLE!
JIM DAVIS 5-30
Z

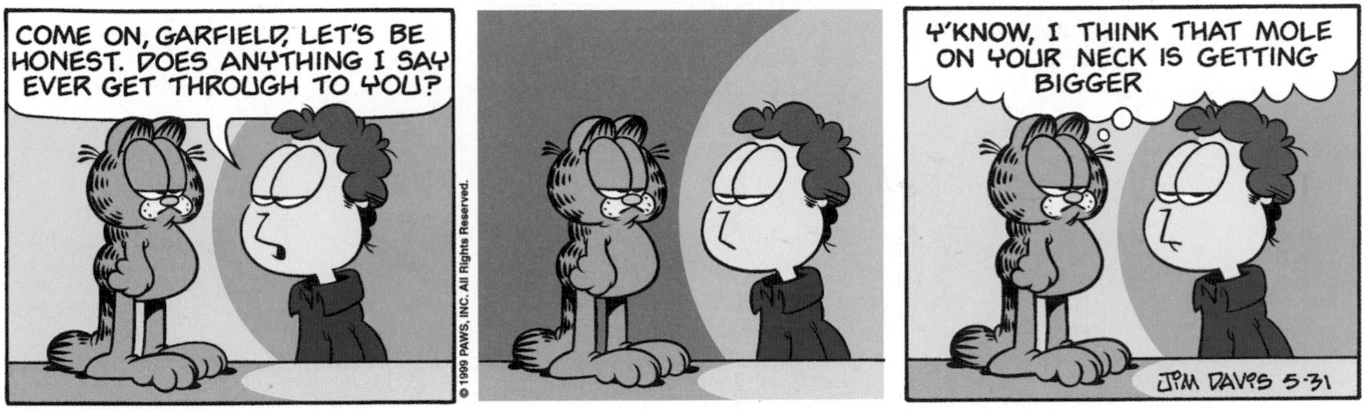
COME ON, GARFIELD, LET'S BE HONEST. DOES ANYTHING I SAY EVER GET THROUGH TO YOU?
© 1999 PAWS, INC. All Rights Reserved.
Y'KNOW, I THINK THAT MOLE ON YOUR NECK IS GETTING BIGGER
JIM DAVIS 5-31

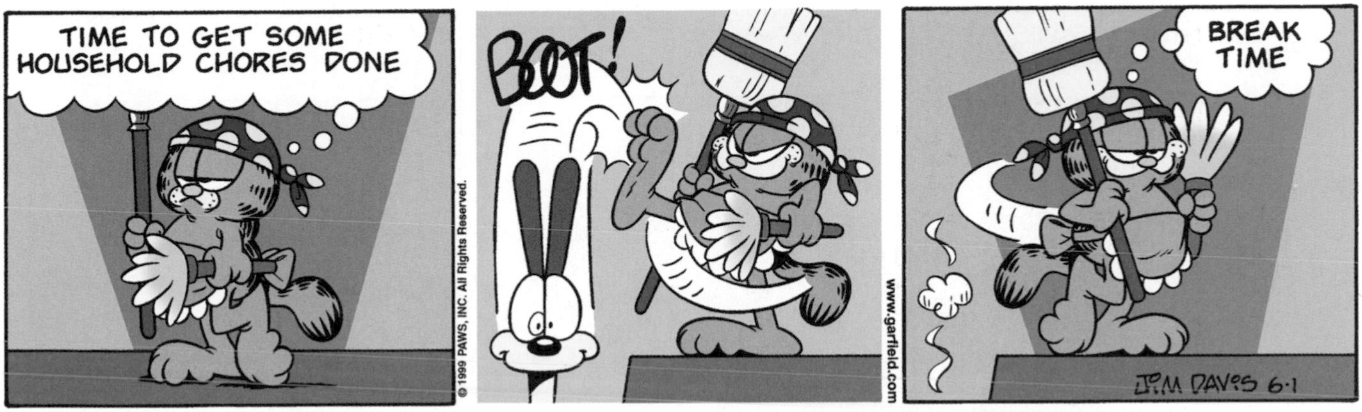
TIME TO GET SOME HOUSEHOLD CHORES DONE
© 1999 PAWS, INC. All Rights Reserved.
BOOT!
www.garfield.com
BREAK TIME
JIM DAVIS 6-1

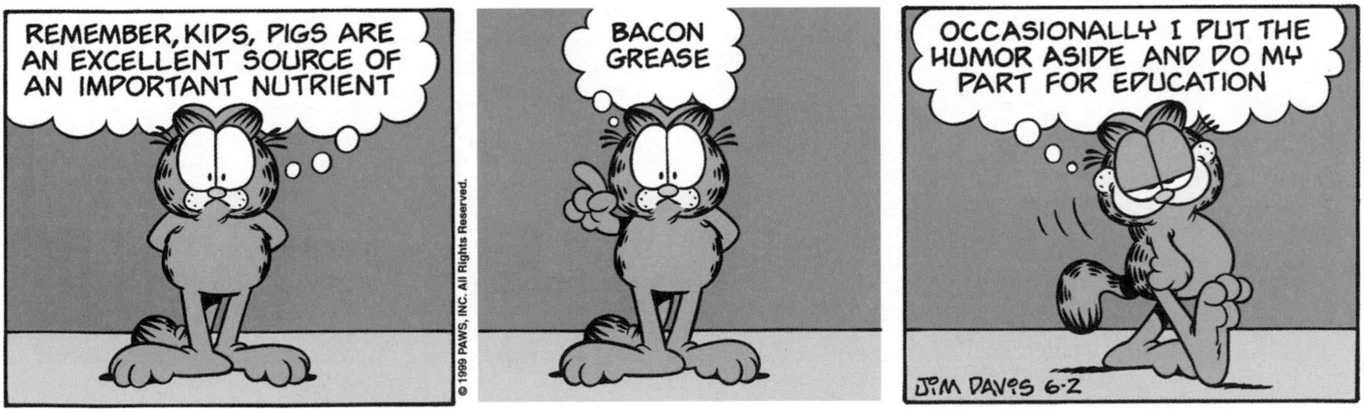
REMEMBER, KIDS, PIGS ARE AN EXCELLENT SOURCE OF AN IMPORTANT NUTRIENT
© 1999 PAWS, INC. All Rights Reserved.
BACON GREASE
OCCASIONALLY I PUT THE HUMOR ASIDE AND DO MY PART FOR EDUCATION
JIM DAVIS 6-2

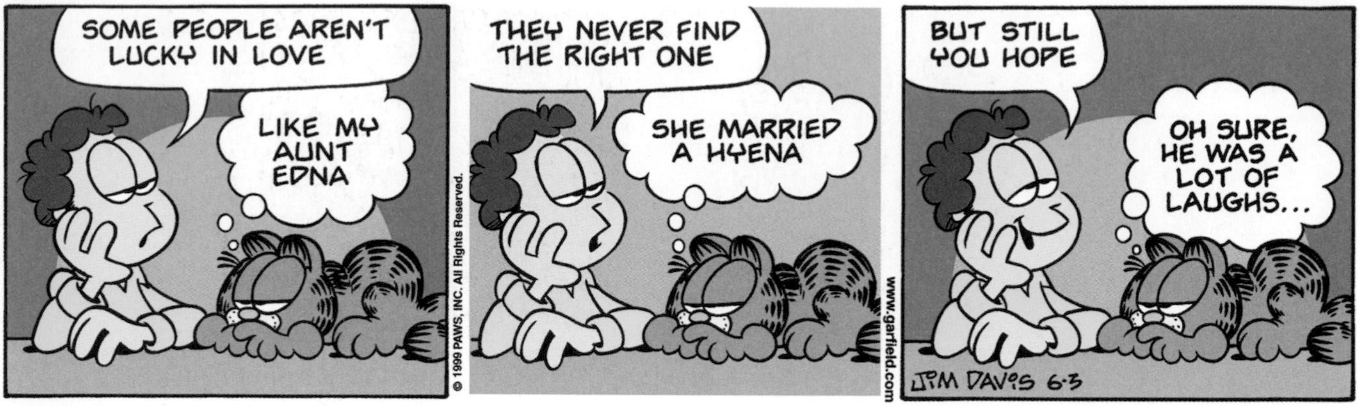
SOME PEOPLE AREN'T LUCKY IN LOVE
LIKE MY AUNT EDNA
THEY NEVER FIND THE RIGHT ONE
SHE MARRIED A HYENA
BUT STILL YOU HOPE
OH SURE, HE WAS A LOT OF LAUGHS...
© 1999 PAWS, INC. All Rights Reserved.
www.garfield.com
JIM DAVIS 6-3

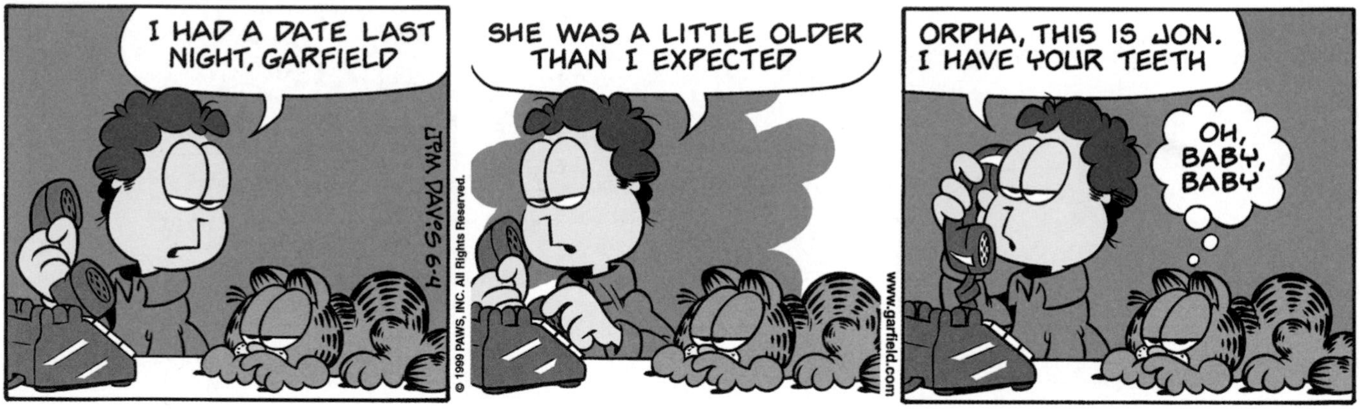
I HAD A DATE LAST NIGHT, GARFIELD
SHE WAS A LITTLE OLDER THAN I EXPECTED
ORPHA, THIS IS JON. I HAVE YOUR TEETH
OH, BABY, BABY
JIM DAVIS 6-4
© 1999 PAWS, INC. All Rights Reserved.
www.garfield.com

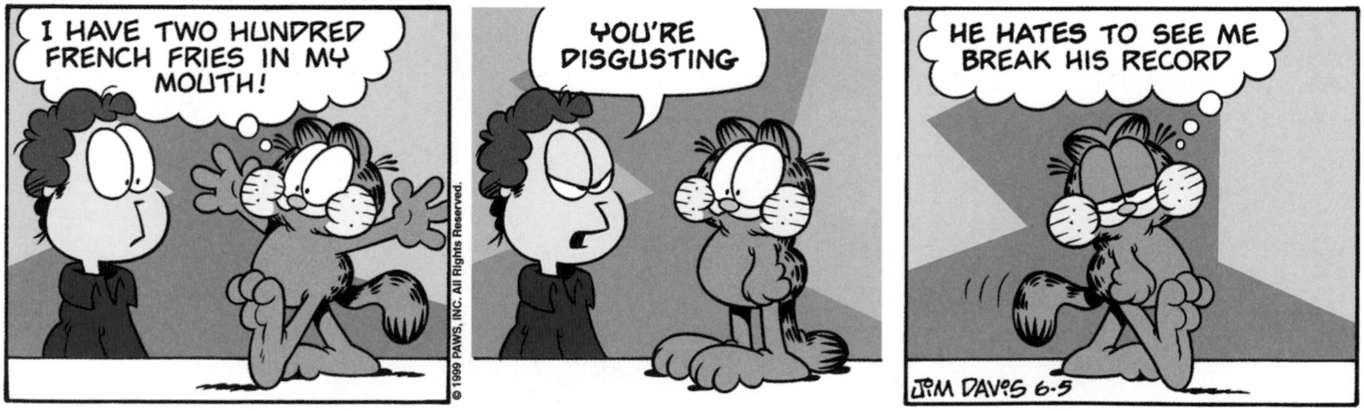
I HAVE TWO HUNDRED FRENCH FRIES IN MY MOUTH!
YOU'RE DISGUSTING
HE HATES TO SEE ME BREAK HIS RECORD
© 1999 PAWS, INC. All Rights Reserved.
JIM DAVIS 6-5

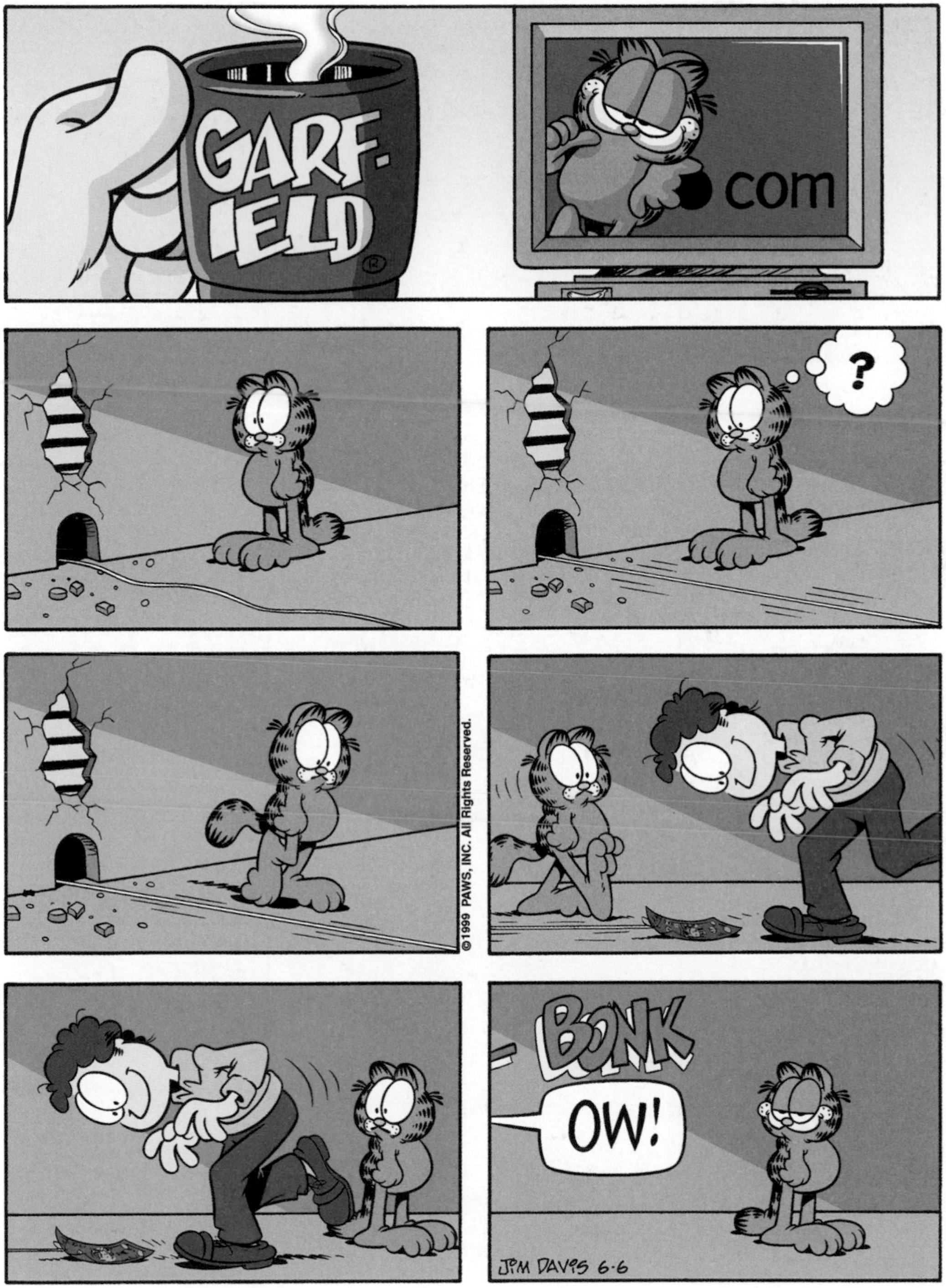
GARF-IELD
com
?
©1999 PAWS, INC. All Rights Reserved.
BONK
OW!
JIM DAVIS 6-6

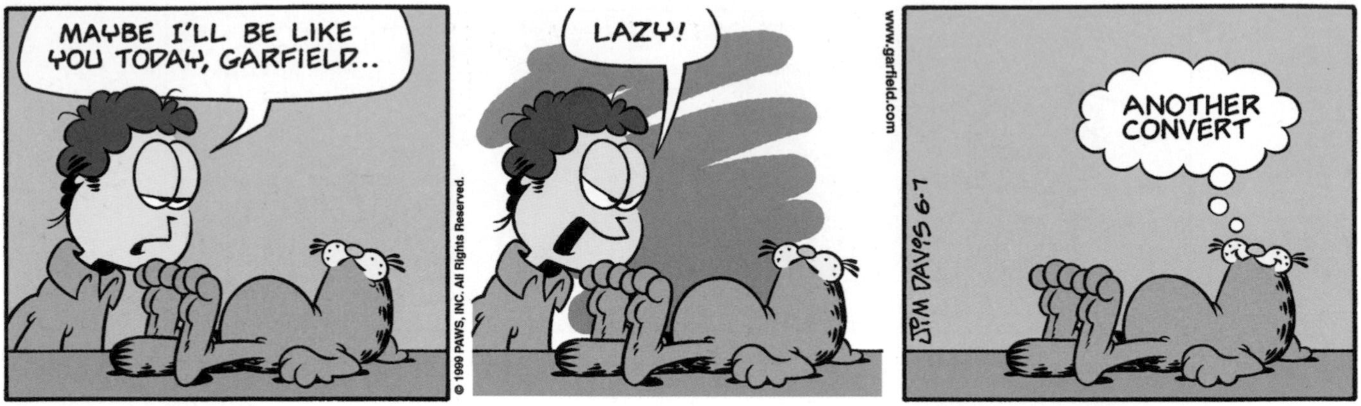
MAYBE I'LL BE LIKE YOU TODAY, GARFIELD...
LAZY!
ANOTHER CONVERT
© 1999 PAWS, INC. All Rights Reserved.
www.garfield.com
JIM DAVIS 6-7

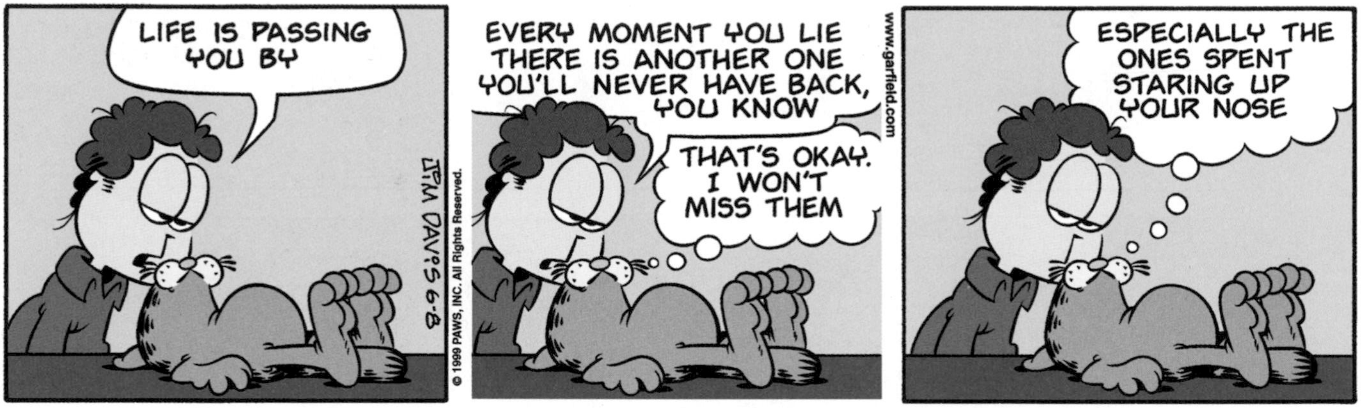
LIFE IS PASSING YOU BY
EVERY MOMENT YOU LIE THERE IS ANOTHER ONE YOU'LL NEVER HAVE BACK, YOU KNOW
THAT'S OKAY. I WON'T MISS THEM
ESPECIALLY THE ONES SPENT STARING UP YOUR NOSE
JIM DAVIS 6-8
© 1999 PAWS, INC. All Rights Reserved.
www.garfield.com

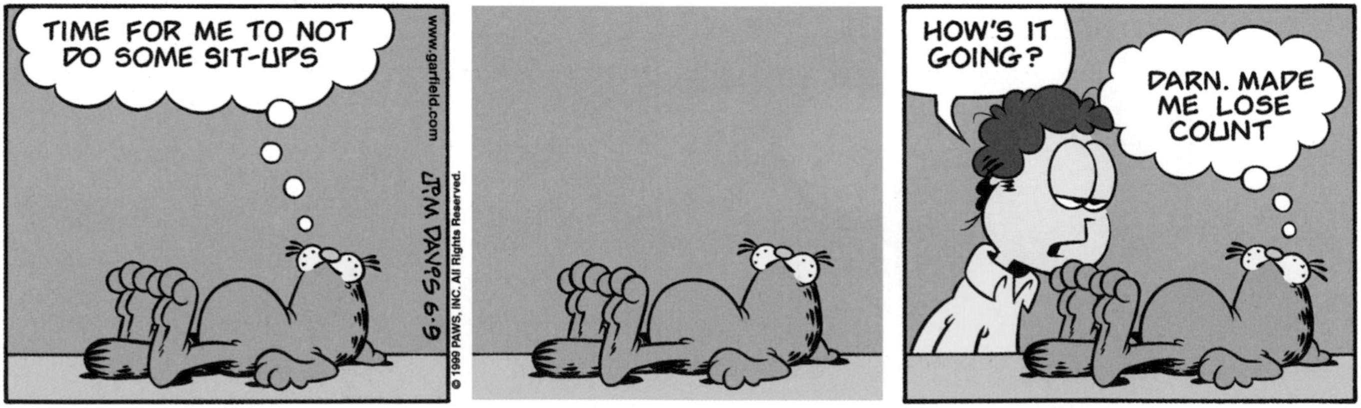
TIME FOR ME TO NOT DO SOME SIT-UPS
HOW'S IT GOING?
DARN. MADE ME LOSE COUNT
www.garfield.com
JIM DAVIS 6-9
© 1999 PAWS, INC. All Rights Reserved.

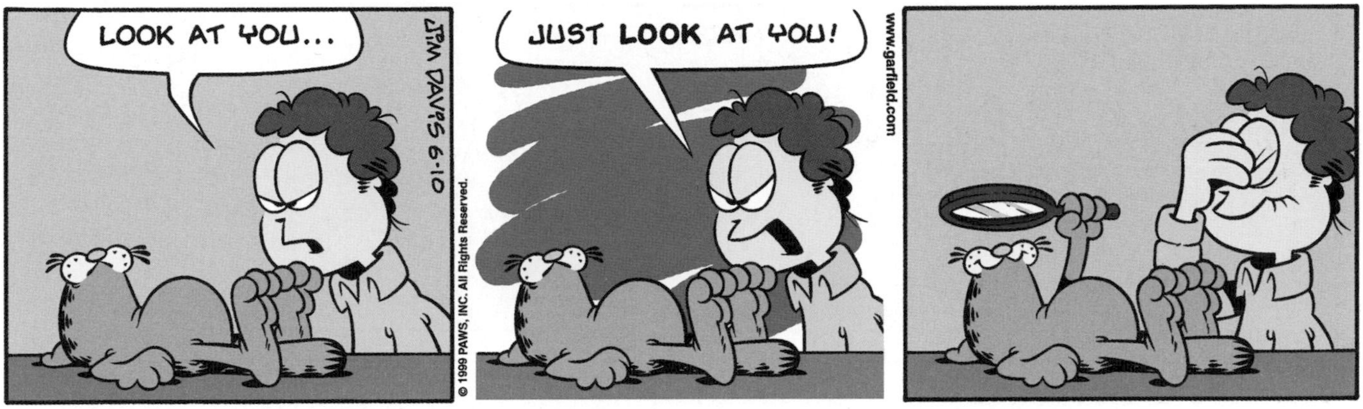
LOOK AT YOU...
JIM DAVIS 6-10
© 1999 PAWS, INC. All Rights Reserved.
JUST LOOK AT YOU!
www.garfield.com

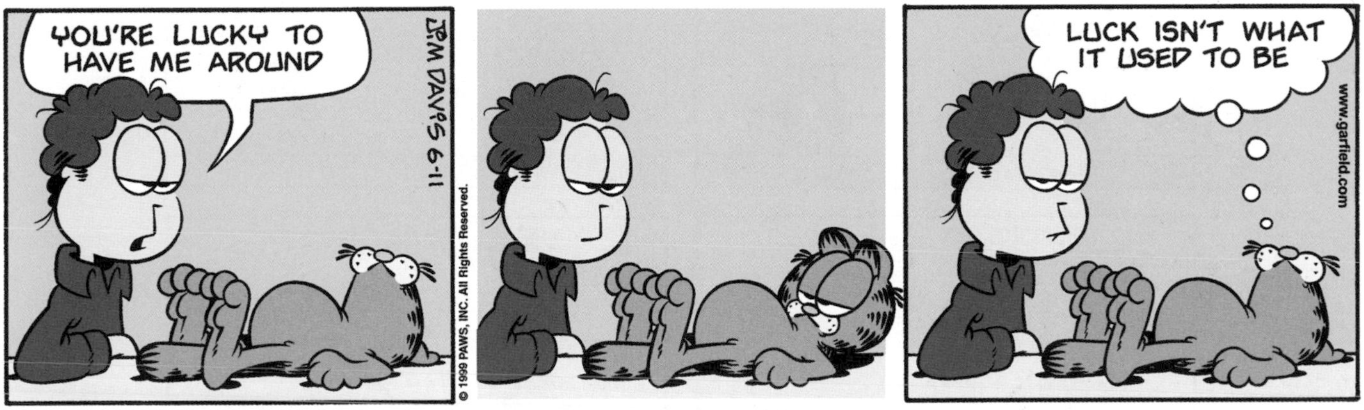
YOU'RE LUCKY TO HAVE ME AROUND
JIM DAVIS 6-11
© 1999 PAWS, INC. All Rights Reserved.
LUCK ISN'T WHAT IT USED TO BE
www.garfield.com

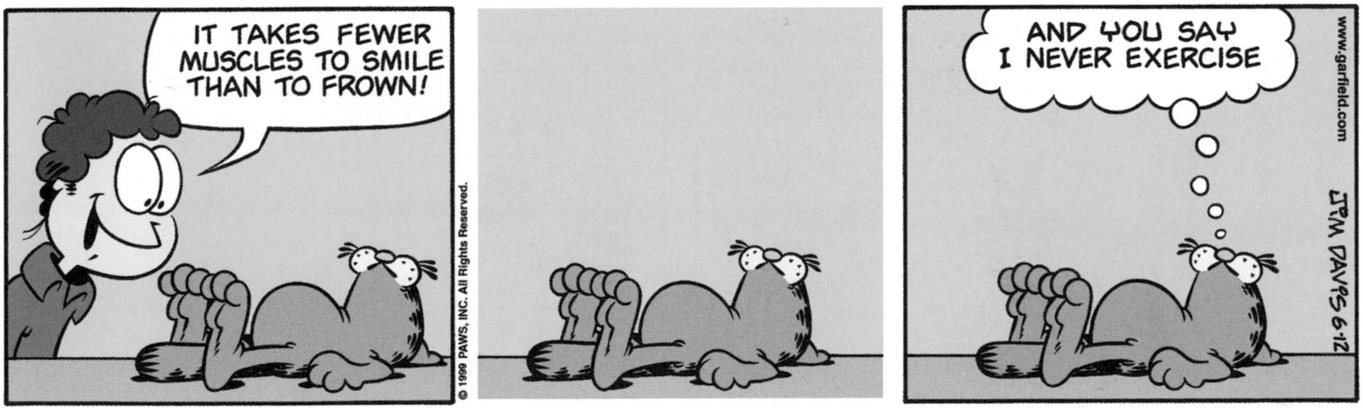
IT TAKES FEWER MUSCLES TO SMILE THAN TO FROWN!
© 1999 PAWS, INC. All Rights Reserved.
AND YOU SAY I NEVER EXERCISE
www.garfield.com
JIM DAVIS 6-12

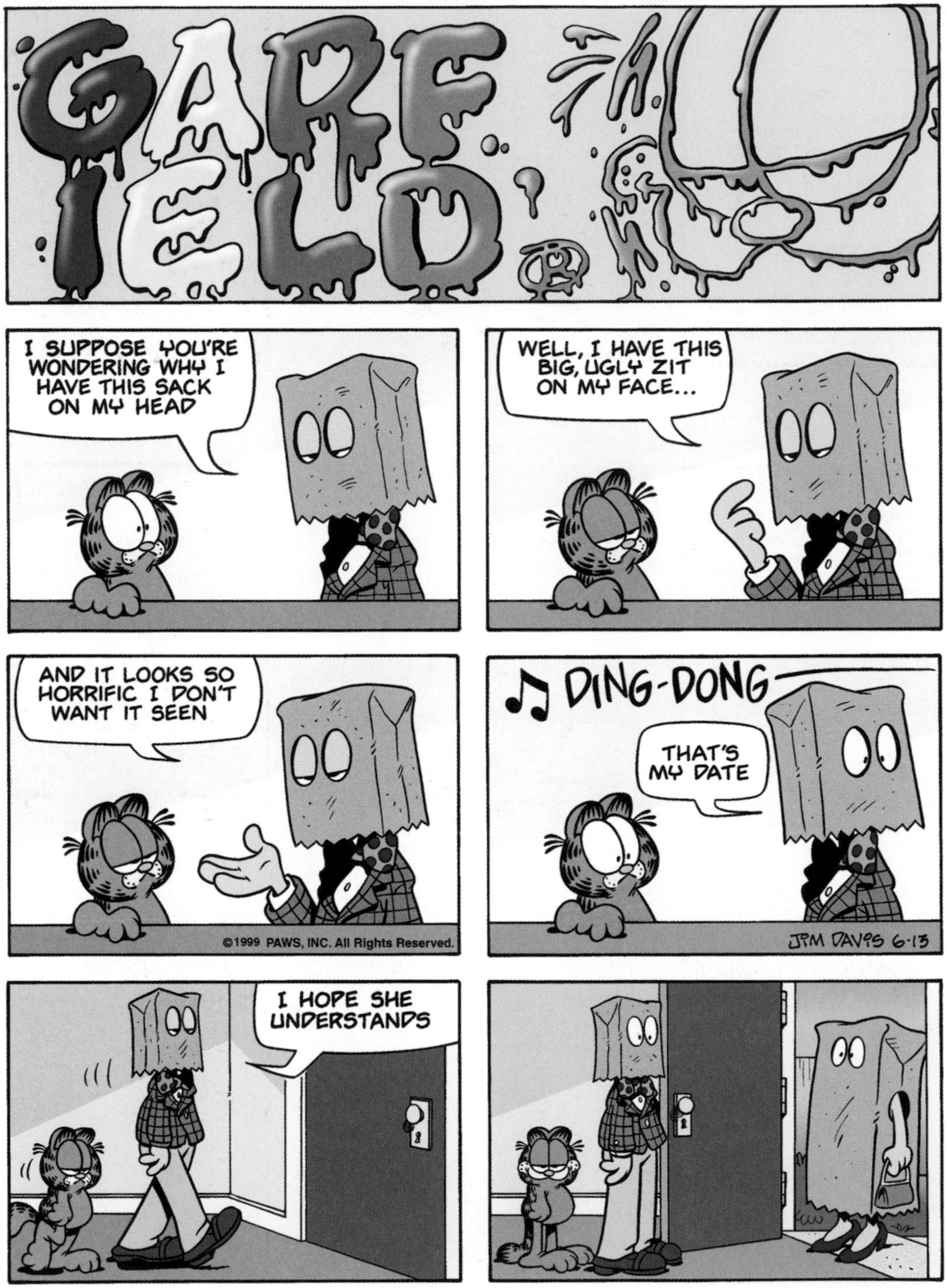
GARFIELD
I SUPPOSE YOU'RE WONDERING WHY I HAVE THIS SACK ON MY HEAD
WELL, I HAVE THIS BIG, UGLY ZIT ON MY FACE...
AND IT LOOKS SO HORRIFIC I DON'T WANT IT SEEN
DING-DONG
THAT'S MY DATE
©1999 PAWS, INC. All Rights Reserved.
JIM DAVIS 6-13
I HOPE SHE UNDERSTANDS

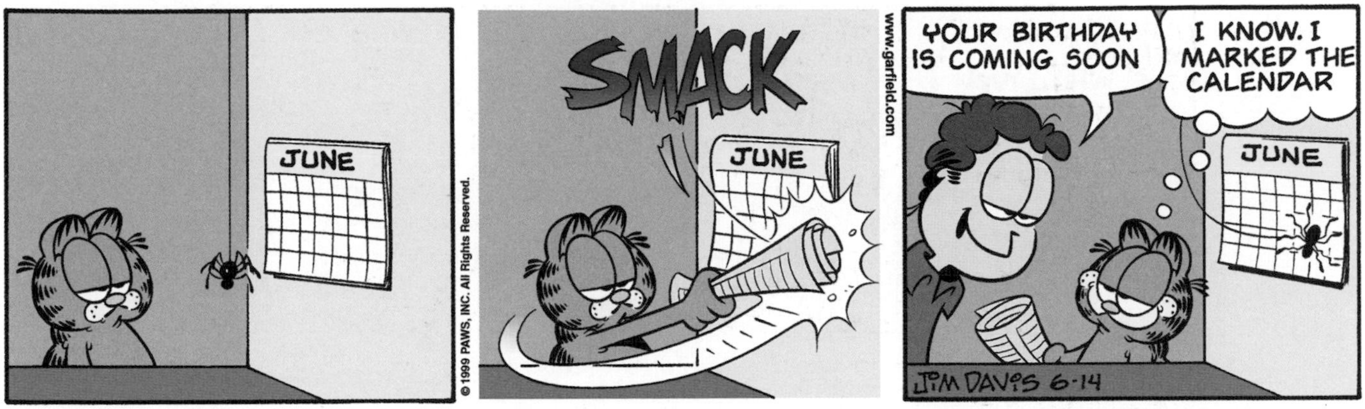
JUNE
SMACK
JUNE
© 1999 PAWS, INC. All Rights Reserved.
www.garfield.com
YOUR BIRTHDAY IS COMING SOON
I KNOW. I MARKED THE CALENDAR
JUNE
JIM DAVIS 6-14

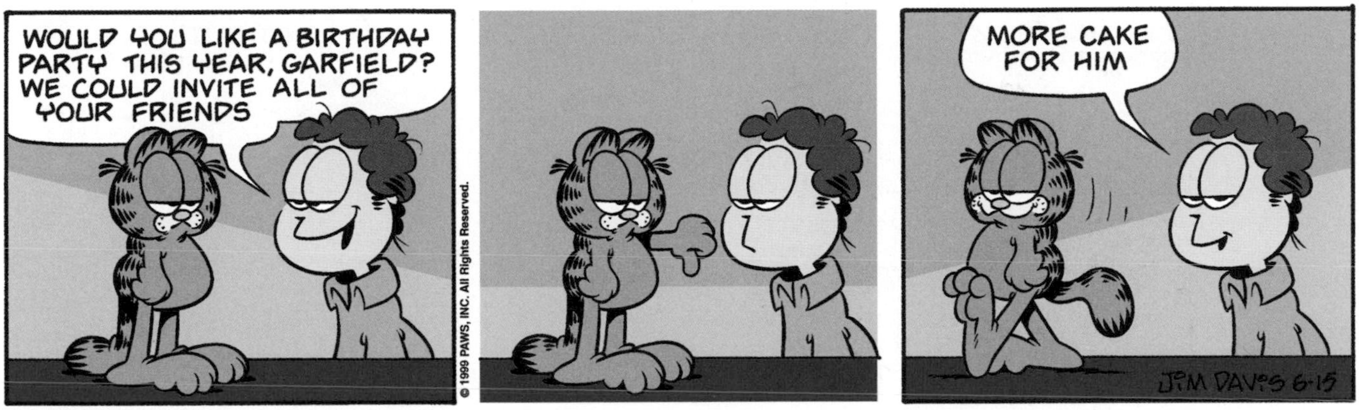
WOULD YOU LIKE A BIRTHDAY PARTY THIS YEAR, GARFIELD? WE COULD INVITE ALL OF YOUR FRIENDS
© 1999 PAWS, INC. All Rights Reserved.
MORE CAKE FOR HIM
JIM DAVIS 6-15

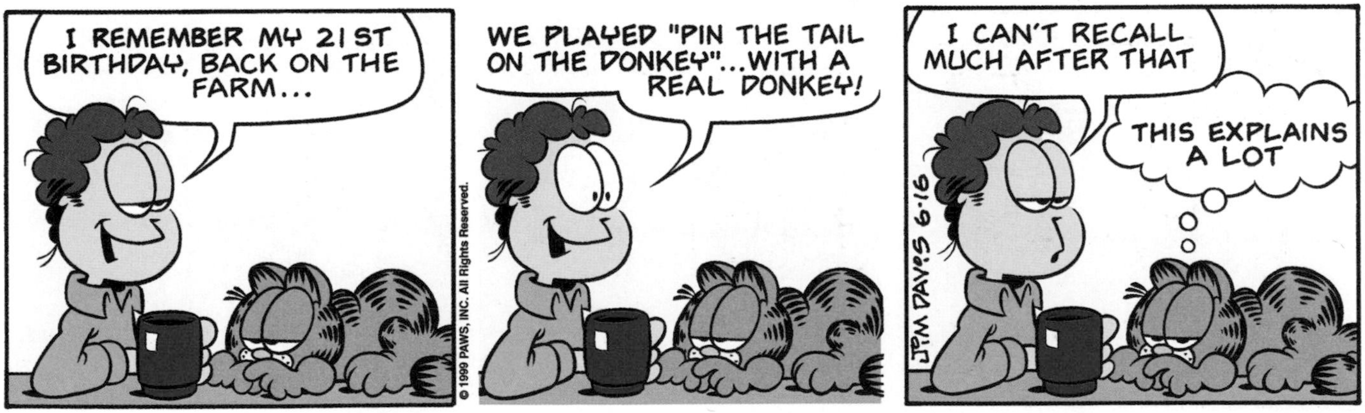
I REMEMBER MY 21 ST BIRTHDAY, BACK ON THE FARM...
© 1999 PAWS, INC. All Rights Reserved.
WE PLAYED "PIN THE TAIL ON THE DONKEY"...WITH A REAL DONKEY!
JIM DAVIS 6-16
I CAN'T RECALL MUCH AFTER THAT
THIS EXPLAINS A LOT

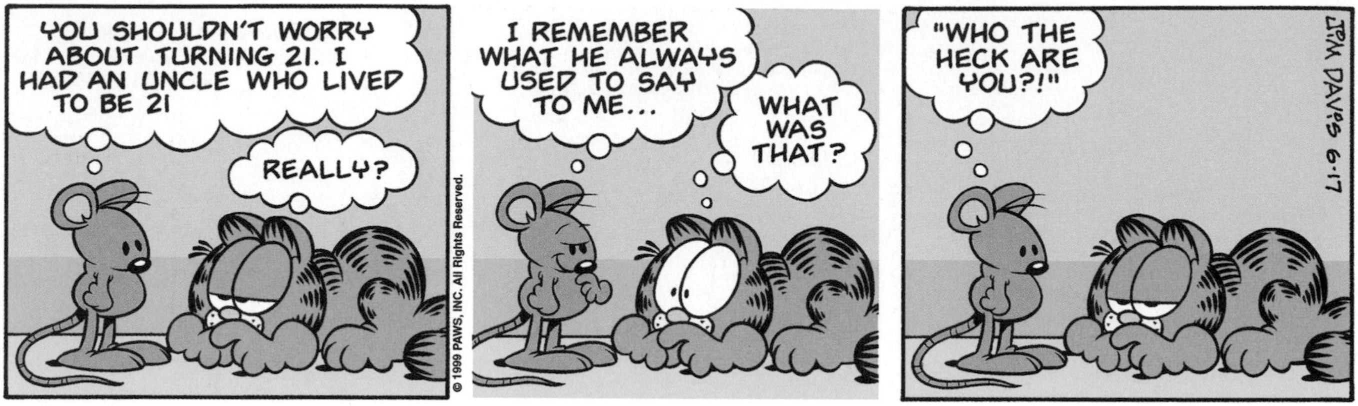
YOU SHOULDN'T WORRY ABOUT TURNING 21. I HAD AN UNCLE WHO LIVED TO BE 21
REALLY?
© 1999 PAWS, INC. All Rights Reserved.
I REMEMBER WHAT HE ALWAYS USED TO SAY TO ME...
WHAT WAS THAT?
"WHO THE HECK ARE YOU?!"
JIM DAVIS 6.17

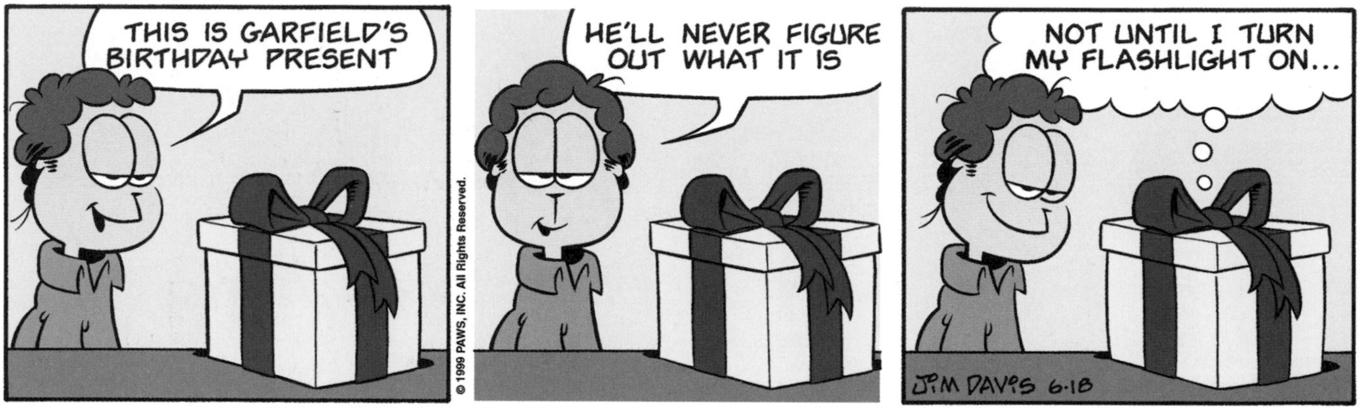
THIS IS GARFIELD'S BIRTHDAY PRESENT
© 1999 PAWS, INC. All Rights Reserved.
HE'LL NEVER FIGURE OUT WHAT IT IS
NOT UNTIL I TURN MY FLASHLIGHT ON...
JIM DAVIS 6.18

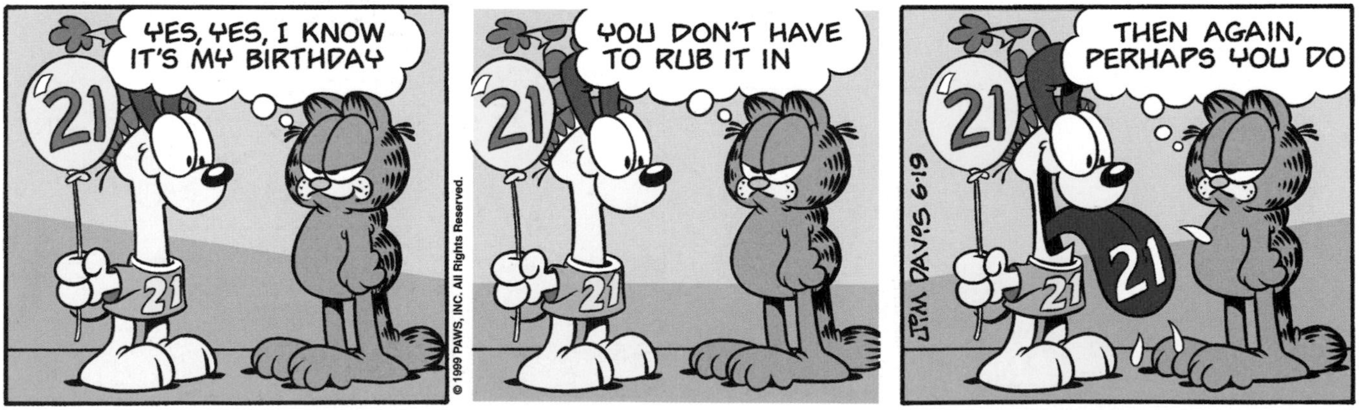
YES, YES, I KNOW IT'S MY BIRTHDAY
21
21
© 1999 PAWS, INC. All Rights Reserved.
YOU DON'T HAVE TO RUB IT IN
THEN AGAIN, PERHAPS YOU DO
JIM DAVIS 6.19

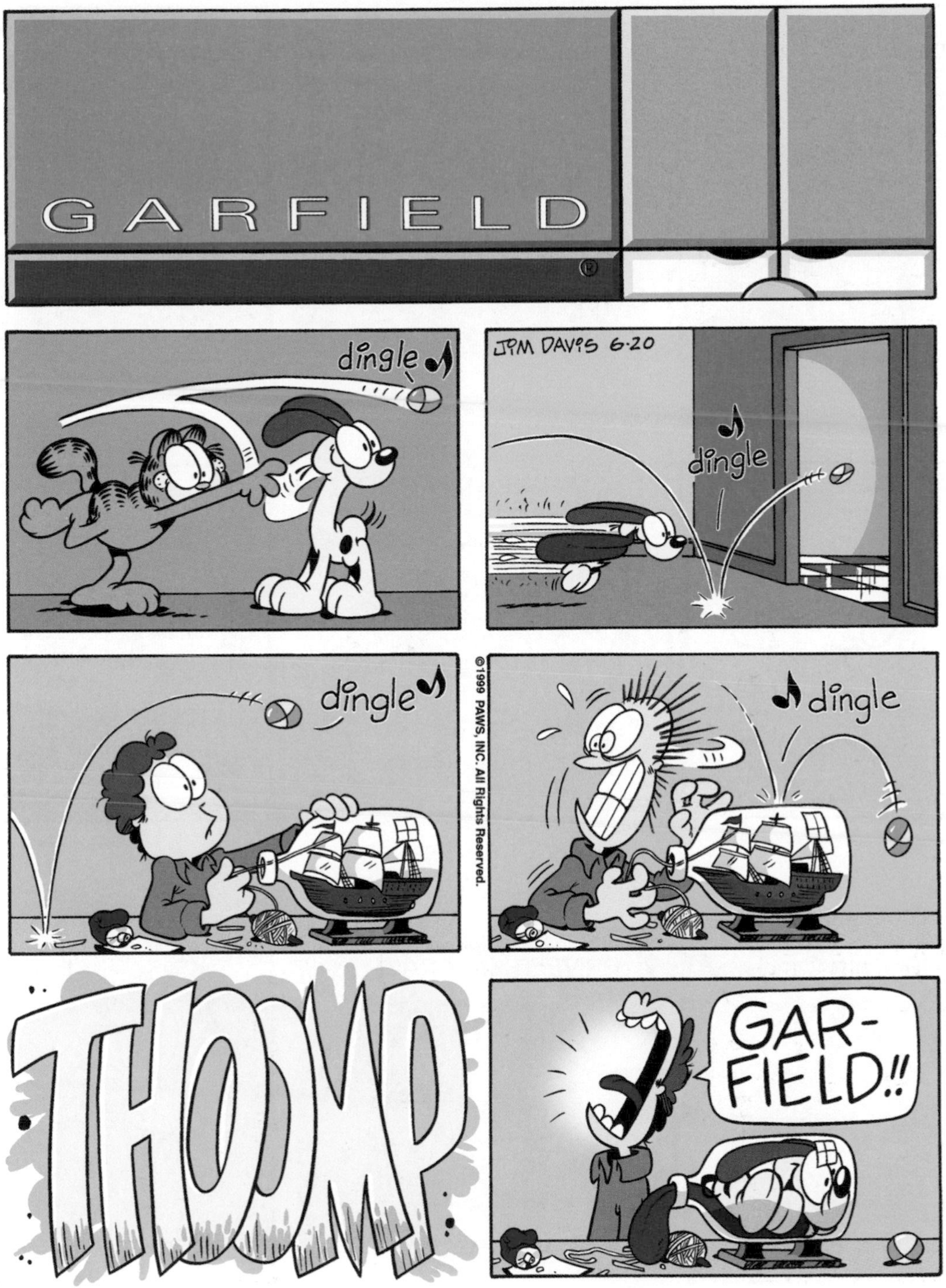
GARFIELD
JIM DAVIS 6-20
dingle
dingle
©1999 PAWS, INC. All Rights Reserved.
dingle
dingle
THOOMP
GAR-
FIELD!!

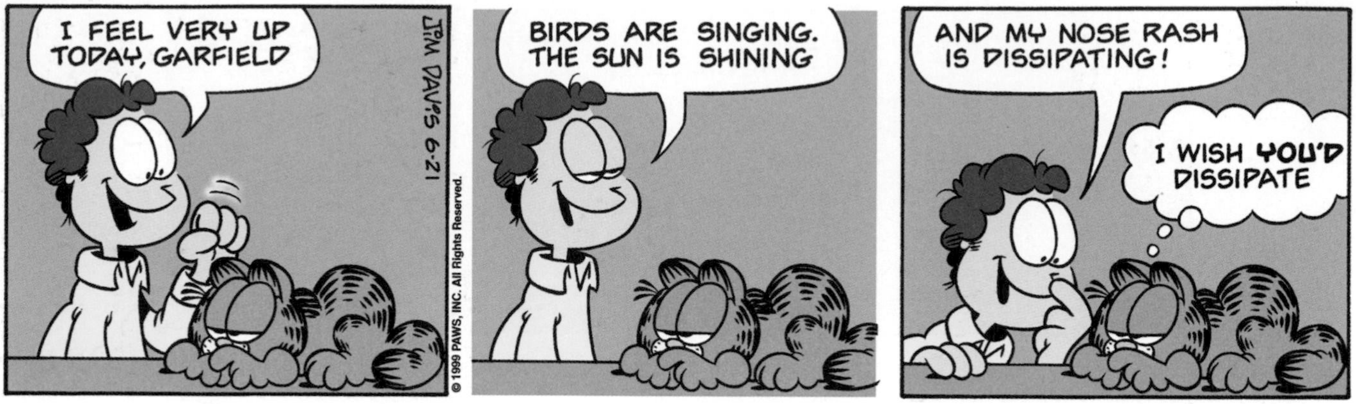
I FEEL VERY UP TODAY, GARFIELD
JIM DAVIS 6-21
BIRDS ARE SINGING. THE SUN IS SHINING
© 1999 PAWS, INC. All Rights Reserved.
AND MY NOSE RASH IS DISSIPATING!
I WISH **YOU'D** DISSIPATE

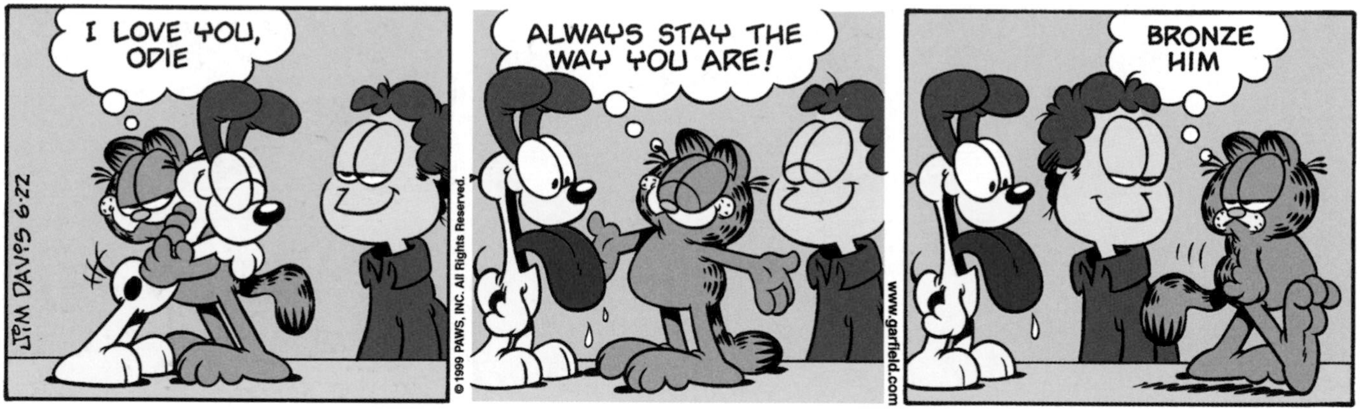
I LOVE YOU, ODIE
JIM DAVIS 6-22
ALWAYS STAY THE WAY YOU ARE!
© 1999 PAWS, INC. All Rights Reserved.
BRONZE HIM
www.garfield.com

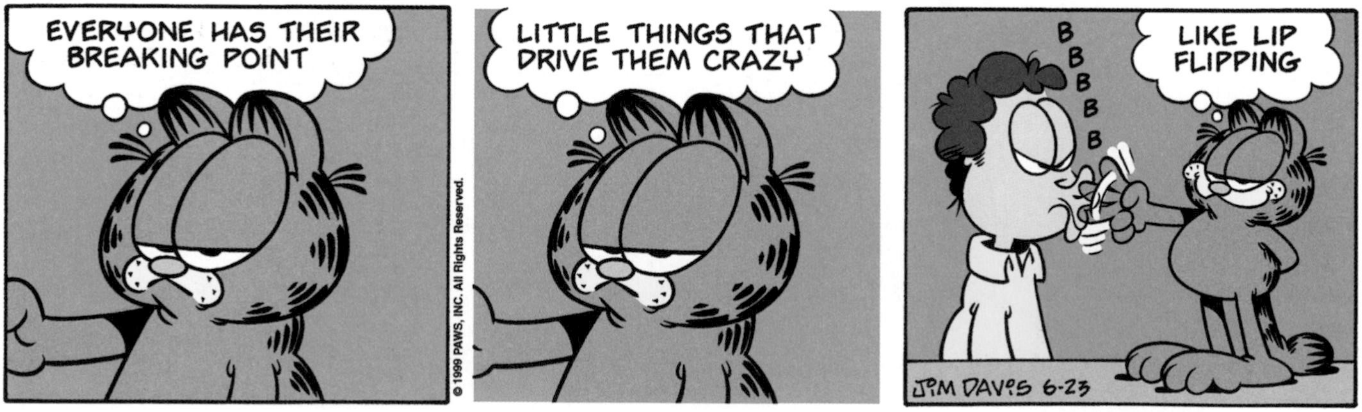
EVERYONE HAS THEIR BREAKING POINT
LITTLE THINGS THAT DRIVE THEM CRAZY
© 1999 PAWS, INC. All Rights Reserved.
B B B B B
LIKE LIP FLIPPING
JIM DAVIS 6-23

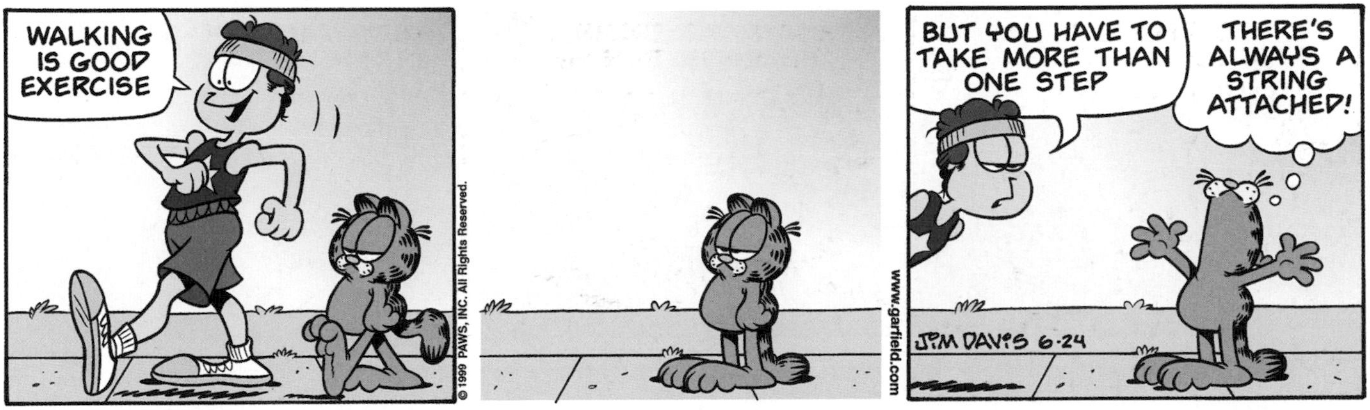
WALKING IS GOOD EXERCISE
© 1999 PAWS, INC. All Rights Reserved.
BUT YOU HAVE TO TAKE MORE THAN ONE STEP
THERE'S ALWAYS A STRING ATTACHED!
www.garfield.com
JIM DAVIS 6-24

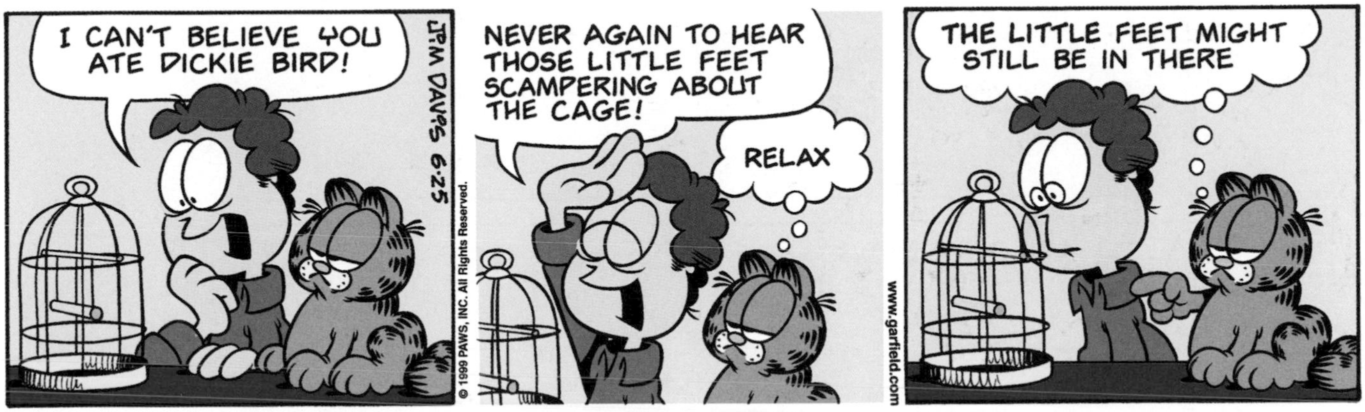
I CAN'T BELIEVE YOU ATE DICKIE BIRD!
JIM DAVIS 6-25
© 1999 PAWS, INC. All Rights Reserved.
NEVER AGAIN TO HEAR THOSE LITTLE FEET SCAMPERING ABOUT THE CAGE!
RELAX
www.garfield.com
THE LITTLE FEET MIGHT STILL BE IN THERE

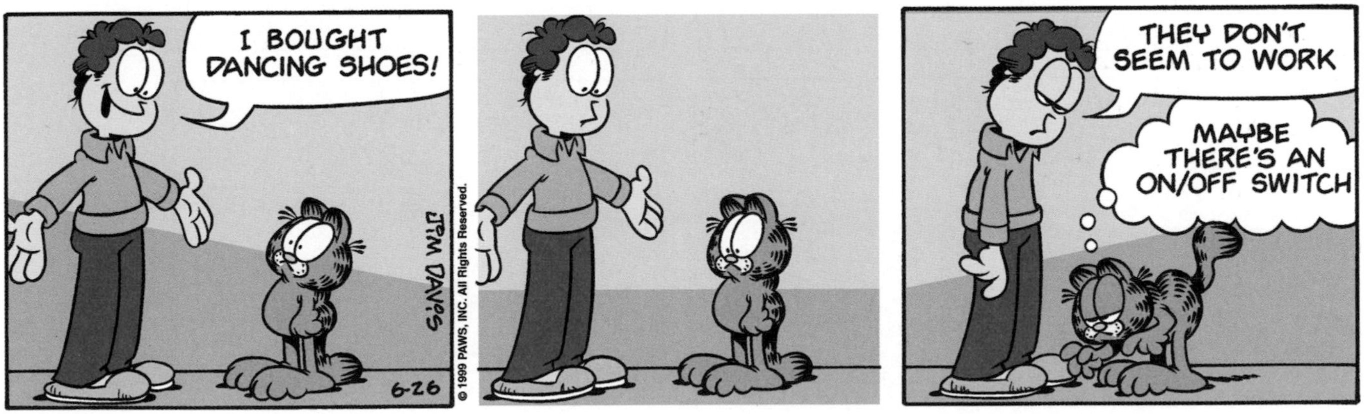
I BOUGHT DANCING SHOES!
JIM DAVIS
6-26
© 1999 PAWS, INC. All Rights Reserved.
THEY DON'T SEEM TO WORK
MAYBE THERE'S AN ON/OFF SWITCH

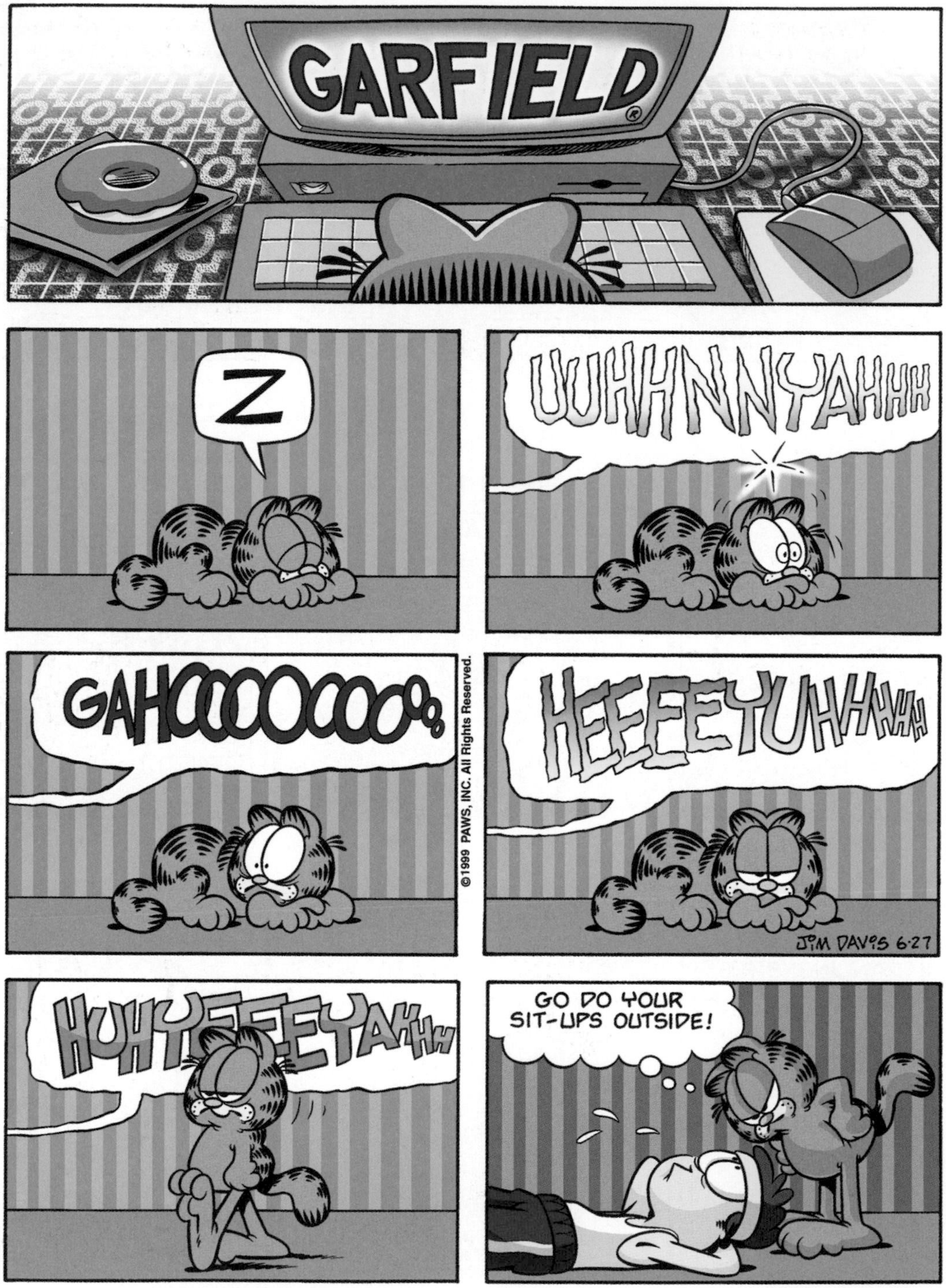
GARFIELD®
Z
UUHHNNYAHHH
GAHOOOOOOOoo
© 1999 PAWS, INC. All Rights Reserved.
HEEEEEYUHHHHH
JIM DAVIS 6·27
HUHYEEEEYAHHH
GO DO YOUR SIT-UPS OUTSIDE!

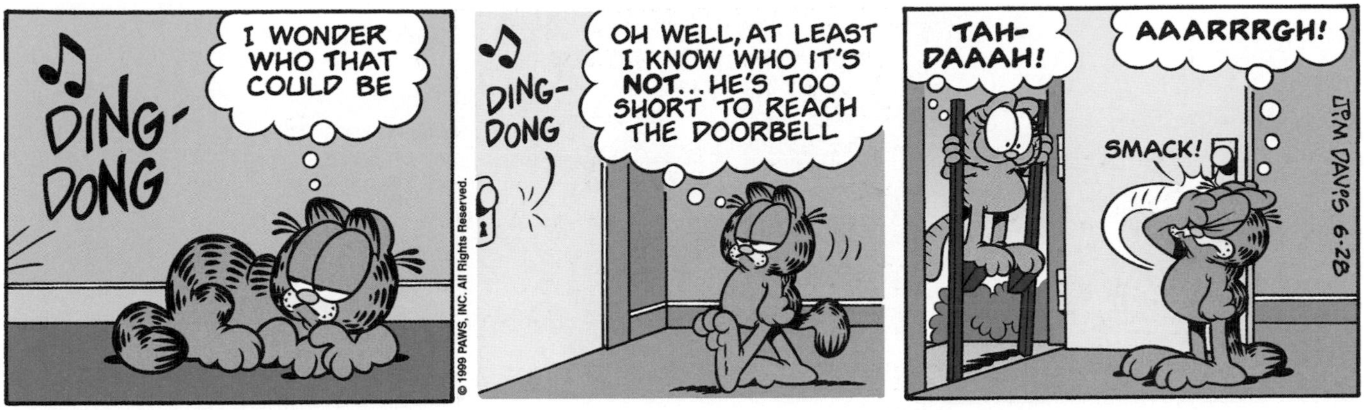
DING-DONG
I WONDER WHO THAT COULD BE
© 1999 PAWS, INC. All Rights Reserved.
DING-DONG
OH WELL, AT LEAST I KNOW WHO IT'S **NOT**... HE'S TOO SHORT TO REACH THE DOORBELL
TAH-DAAAH!
AAARRRGH!
SMACK!
JPM DAVIS 6-28

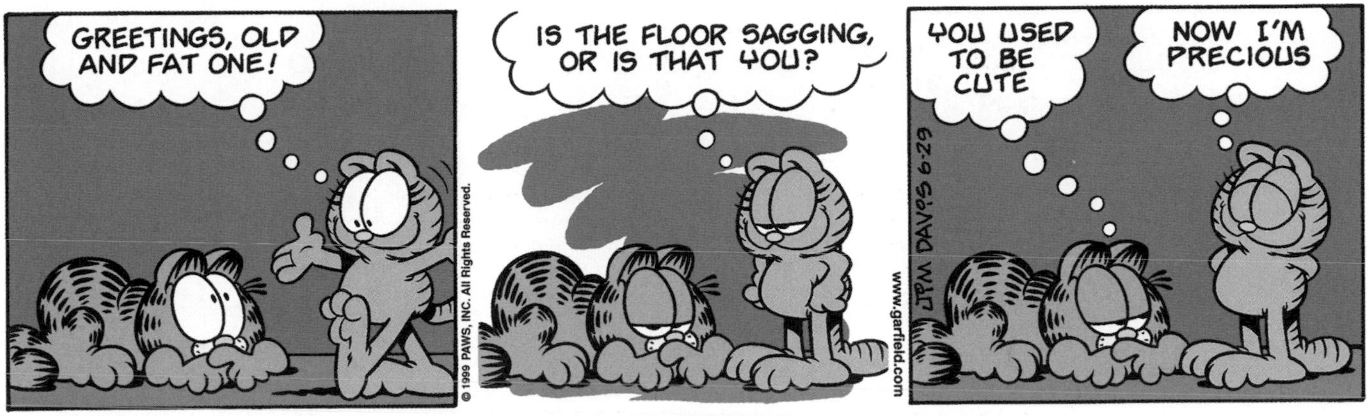
GREETINGS, OLD AND FAT ONE!
© 1999 PAWS, INC. All Rights Reserved.
IS THE FLOOR SAGGING, OR IS THAT YOU?
www.garfield.com
YOU USED TO BE CUTE
NOW I'M PRECIOUS
JPM DAVIS 6-29

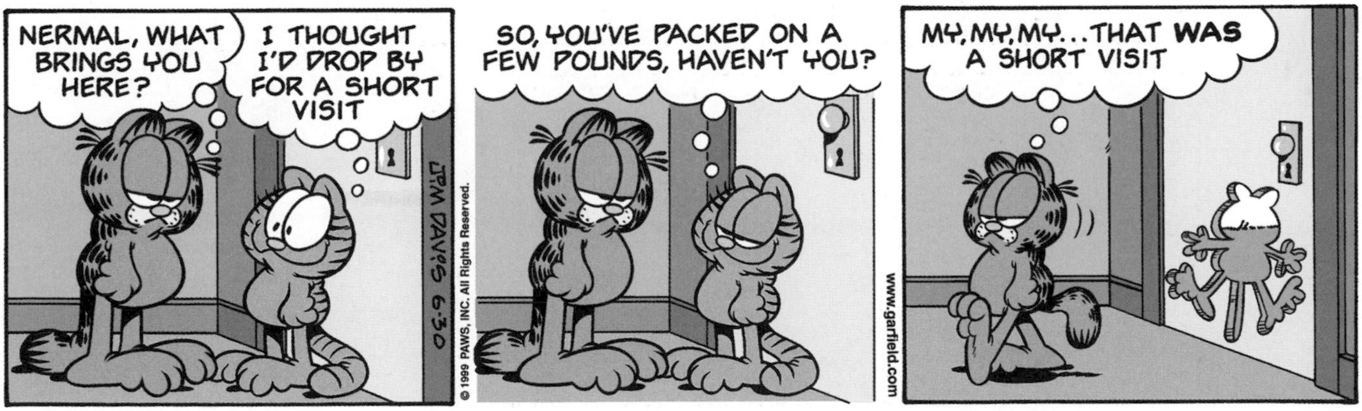
NERMAL, WHAT BRINGS YOU HERE?
I THOUGHT I'D DROP BY FOR A SHORT VISIT
JPM DAVIS 6-30
© 1999 PAWS, INC. All Rights Reserved.
SO, YOU'VE PACKED ON A FEW POUNDS, HAVEN'T YOU?
www.garfield.com
MY, MY, MY... THAT **WAS** A SHORT VISIT

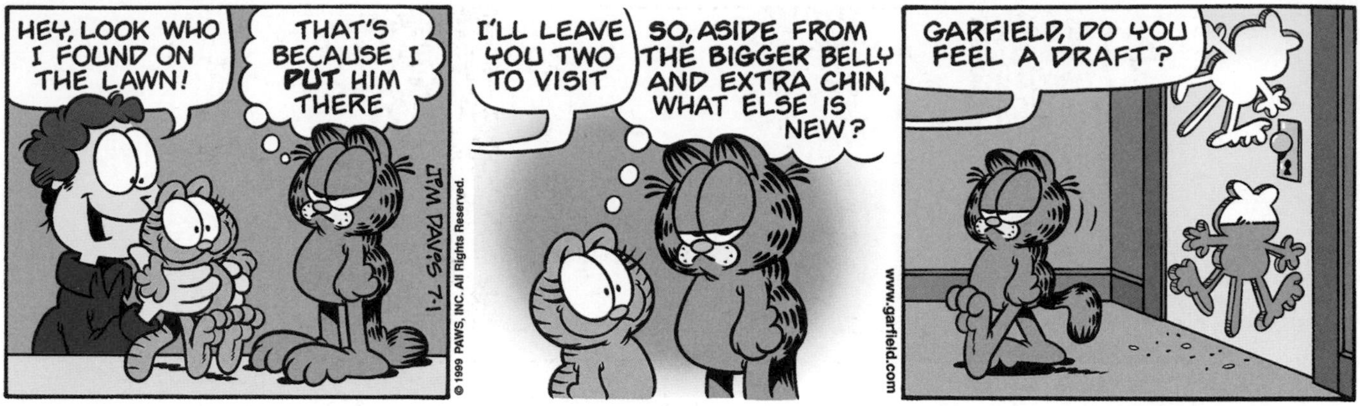
HEY, LOOK WHO I FOUND ON THE LAWN!
THAT'S BECAUSE I PUT HIM THERE
JIM DAVIS 7-1
© 1999 PAWS, INC. All Rights Reserved.
I'LL LEAVE YOU TWO TO VISIT
SO, ASIDE FROM THE BIGGER BELLY AND EXTRA CHIN, WHAT ELSE IS NEW?
www.garfield.com
GARFIELD, DO YOU FEEL A DRAFT?

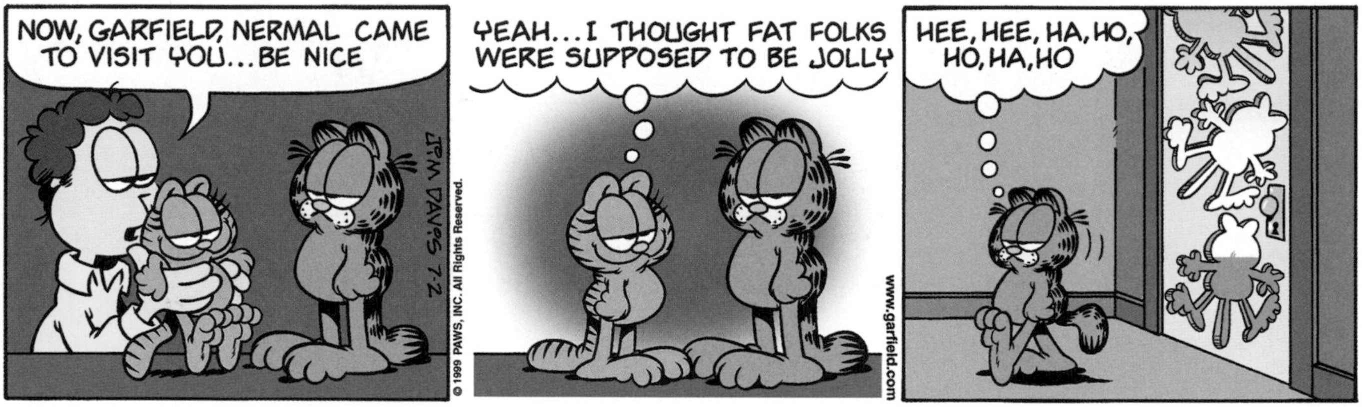
NOW, GARFIELD, NERMAL CAME TO VISIT YOU...BE NICE
JIM DAVIS 7-2
© 1999 PAWS, INC. All Rights Reserved.
YEAH...I THOUGHT FAT FOLKS WERE SUPPOSED TO BE JOLLY
www.garfield.com
HEE, HEE, HA, HO, HO, HA, HO

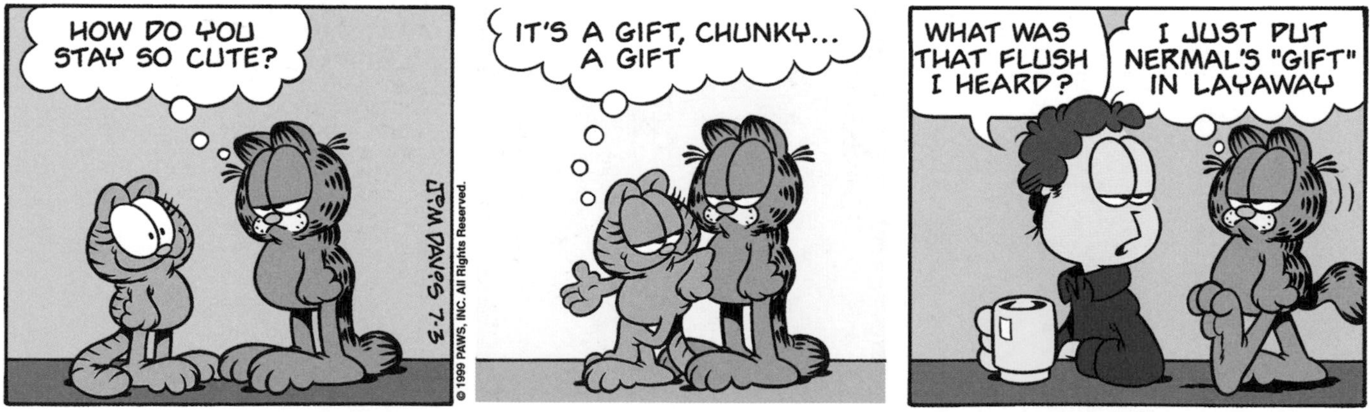
HOW DO YOU STAY SO CUTE?
JIM DAVIS 7-3
© 1999 PAWS, INC. All Rights Reserved.
IT'S A GIFT, CHUNKY... A GIFT
WHAT WAS THAT FLUSH I HEARD?
I JUST PUT NERMAL'S "GIFT" IN LAYAWAY

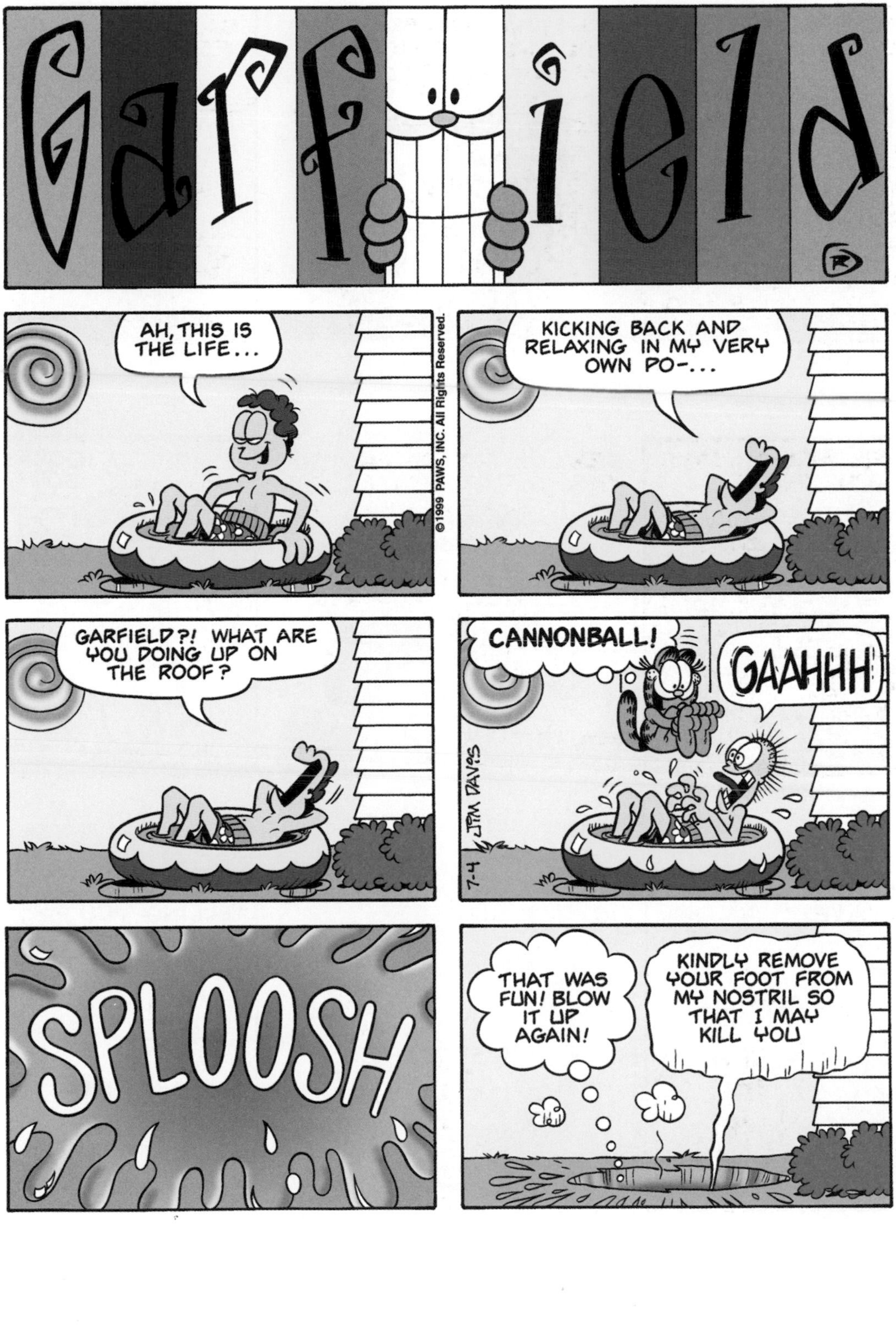

Garfield
AH, THIS IS THE LIFE...
©1999 PAWS, INC. All Rights Reserved.
KICKING BACK AND RELAXING IN MY VERY OWN PO-...
GARFIELD?! WHAT ARE YOU DOING UP ON THE ROOF?
JIM DAVIS 7-4
CANNONBALL!
GAAHHH
SPLOOSH
THAT WAS FUN! BLOW IT UP AGAIN!
KINDLY REMOVE YOUR FOOT FROM MY NOSTRIL SO THAT I MAY KILL YOU

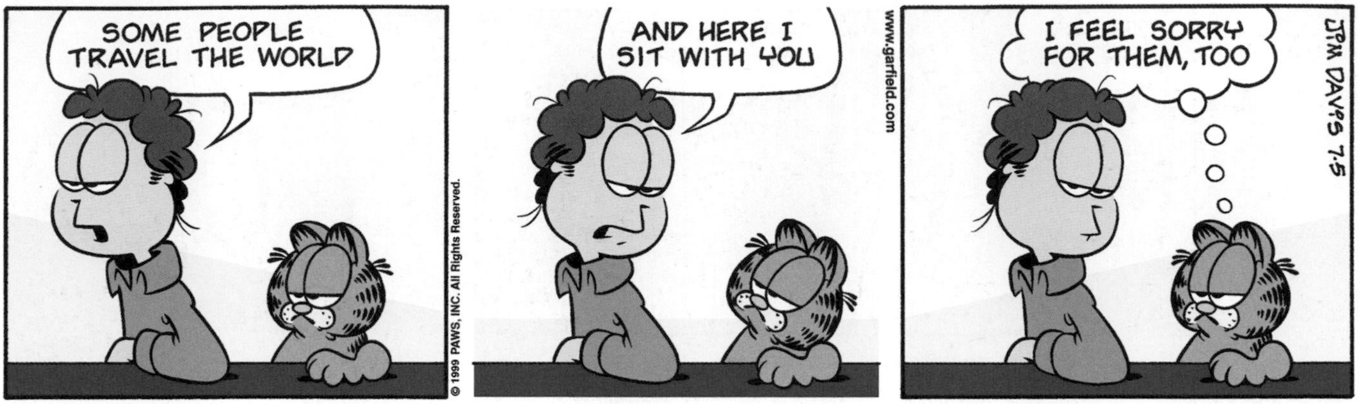
SOME PEOPLE TRAVEL THE WORLD
AND HERE I SIT WITH YOU
I FEEL SORRY FOR THEM, TOO
JPM DAVPS 7-5

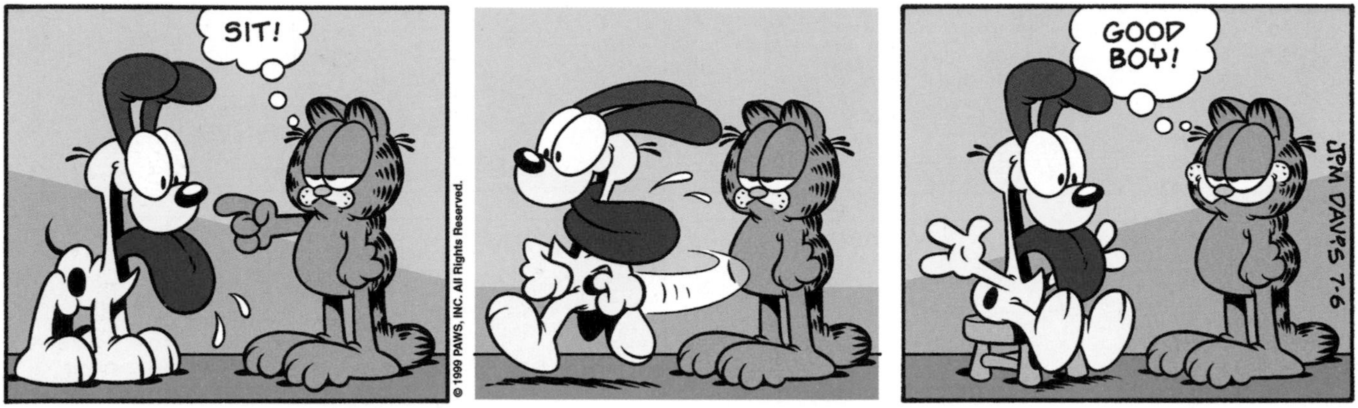
SIT!
GOOD BOY!
JPM DAVPS 7-6

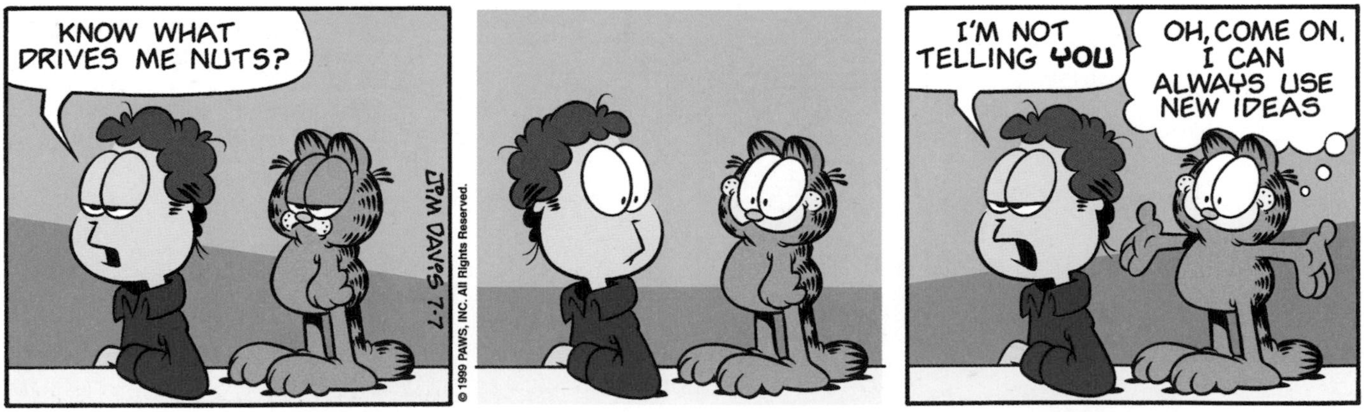
KNOW WHAT DRIVES ME NUTS?
I'M NOT TELLING **YOU**
OH, COME ON. I CAN ALWAYS USE NEW IDEAS
JPM DAVPS 7-7

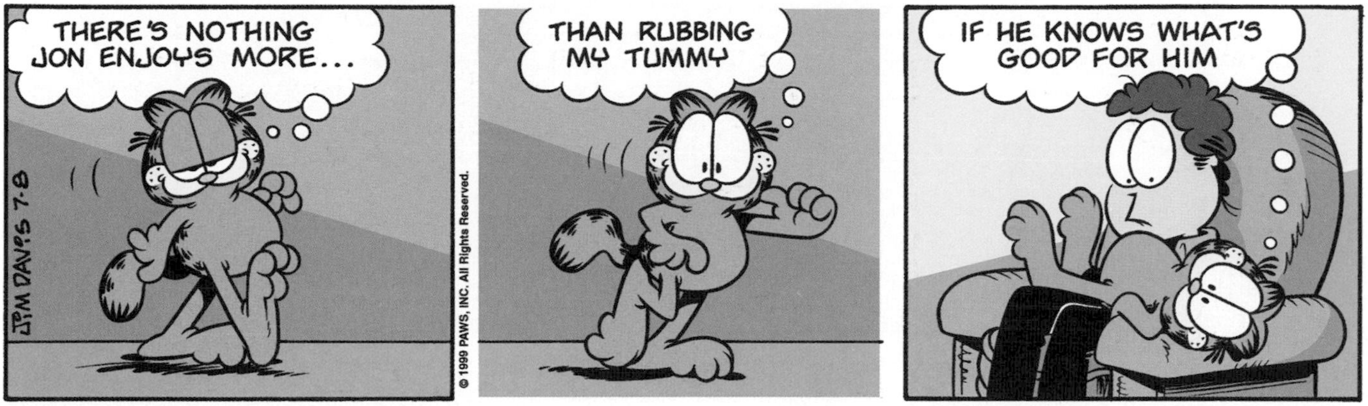
THERE'S NOTHING JON ENJOYS MORE...
JIM DAVIS 7-8
© 1999 PAWS, INC. All Rights Reserved.
THAN RUBBING MY TUMMY
IF HE KNOWS WHAT'S GOOD FOR HIM

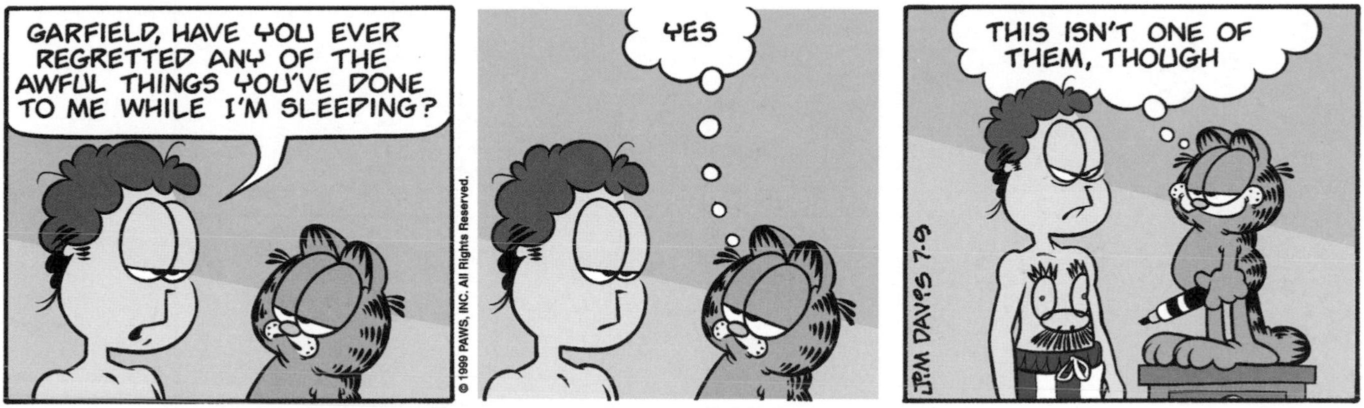
GARFIELD, HAVE YOU EVER REGRETTED ANY OF THE AWFUL THINGS YOU'VE DONE TO ME WHILE I'M SLEEPING?
© 1999 PAWS, INC. All Rights Reserved.
YES
THIS ISN'T ONE OF THEM, THOUGH
JIM DAVIS 7-9

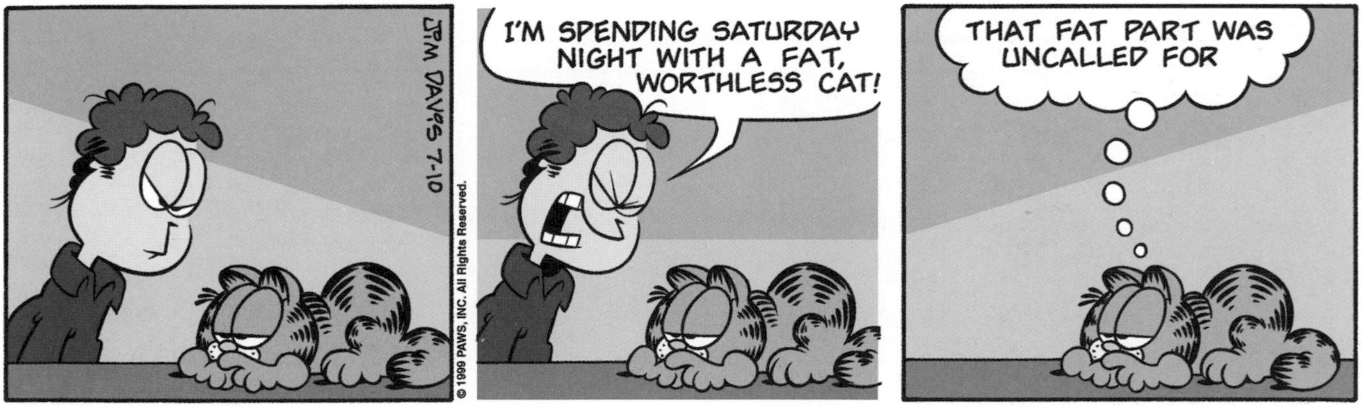
JIM DAVIS 7-10
© 1999 PAWS, INC. All Rights Reserved.
I'M SPENDING SATURDAY NIGHT WITH A FAT, WORTHLESS CAT!
THAT FAT PART WAS UNCALLED FOR

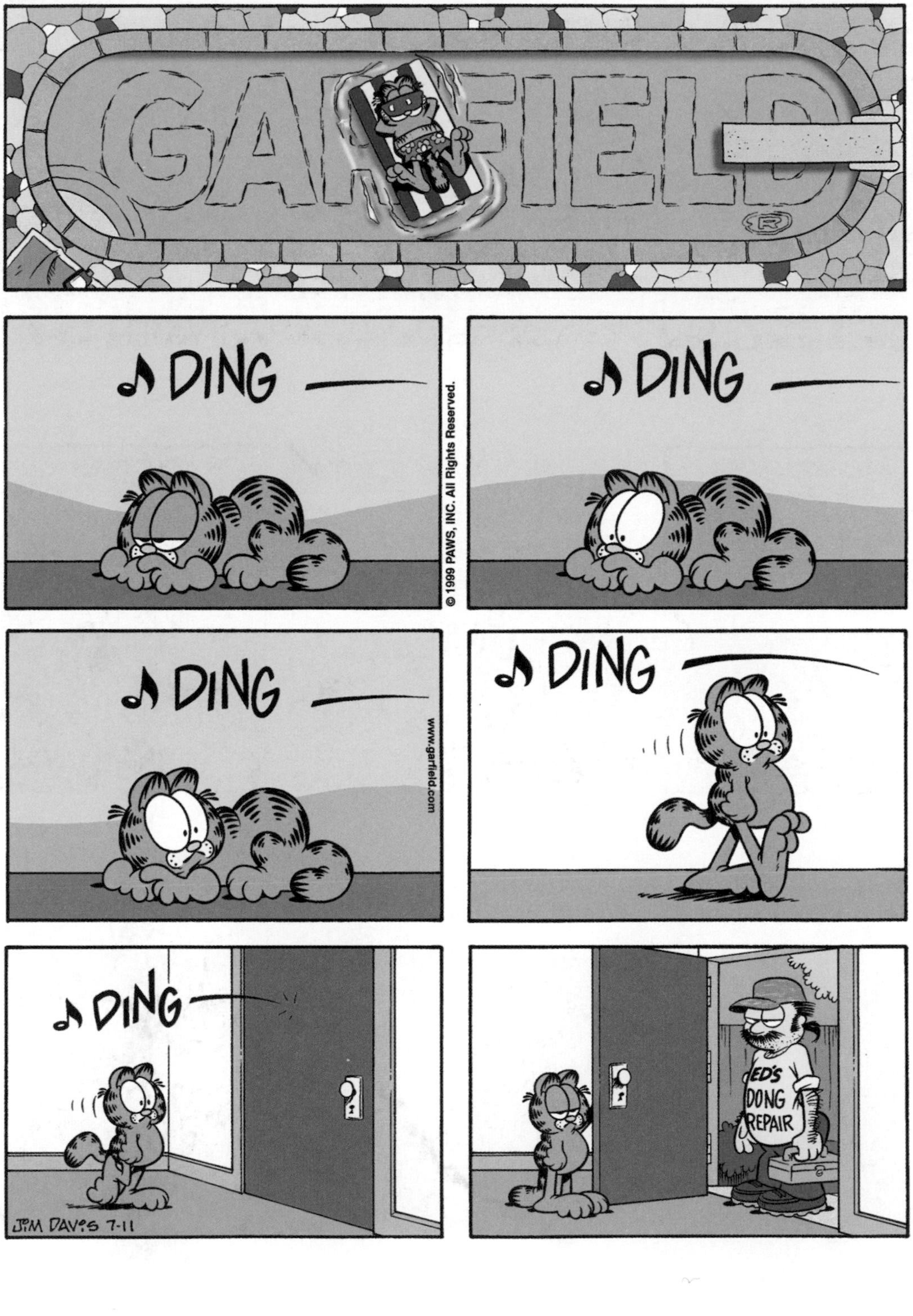
GARFIELD
DING
DING
© 1999 PAWS, INC. All Rights Reserved.
DING
www.garfield.com
DING
DING
JIM DAVIS 7-11
ED'S DONG REPAIR

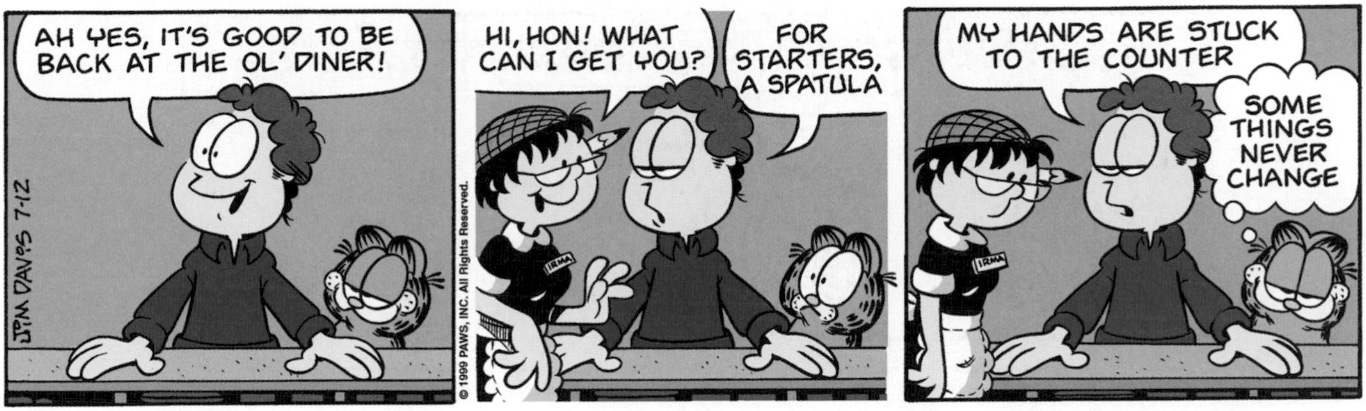
AH YES, IT'S GOOD TO BE BACK AT THE OL' DINER!
JIM DAVIS 7-12
© 1999 PAWS, INC. All Rights Reserved.
HI, HON! WHAT CAN I GET YOU?
FOR STARTERS, A SPATULA
IRMA
MY HANDS ARE STUCK TO THE COUNTER
SOME THINGS NEVER CHANGE

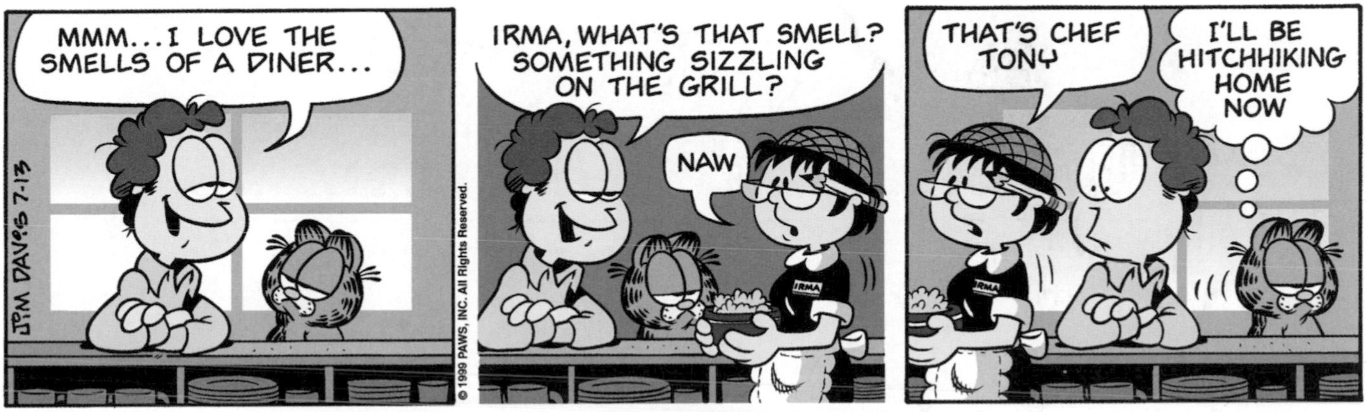
MMM...I LOVE THE SMELLS OF A DINER...
JIM DAVIS 7-13
© 1999 PAWS, INC. All Rights Reserved.
IRMA, WHAT'S THAT SMELL? SOMETHING SIZZLING ON THE GRILL?
NAW
IRMA
THAT'S CHEF TONY
I'LL BE HITCHHIKING HOME NOW

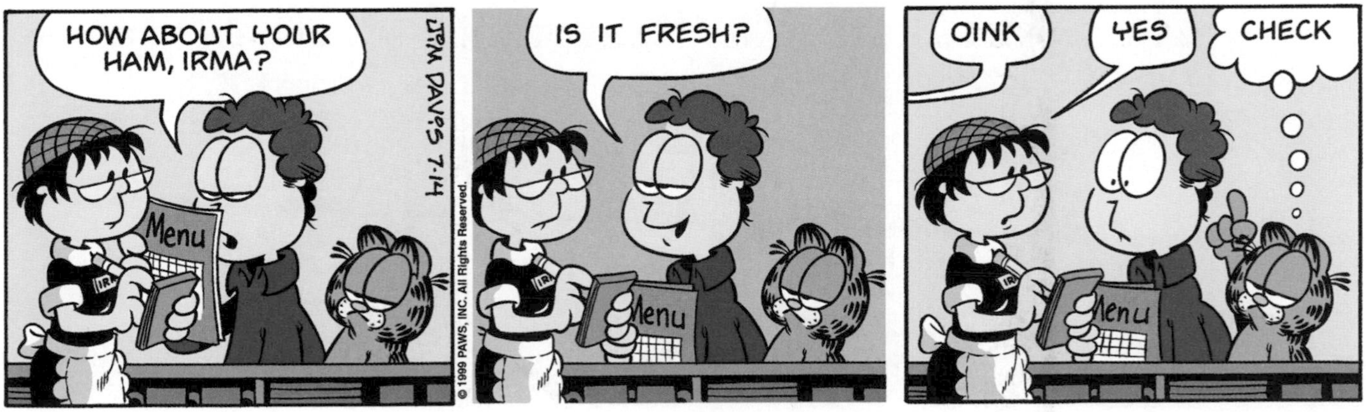
HOW ABOUT YOUR HAM, IRMA?
JIM DAVIS 7-14
Menu
© 1999 PAWS, INC. All Rights Reserved.
IS IT FRESH?
Menu
OINK
YES
CHECK
Menu

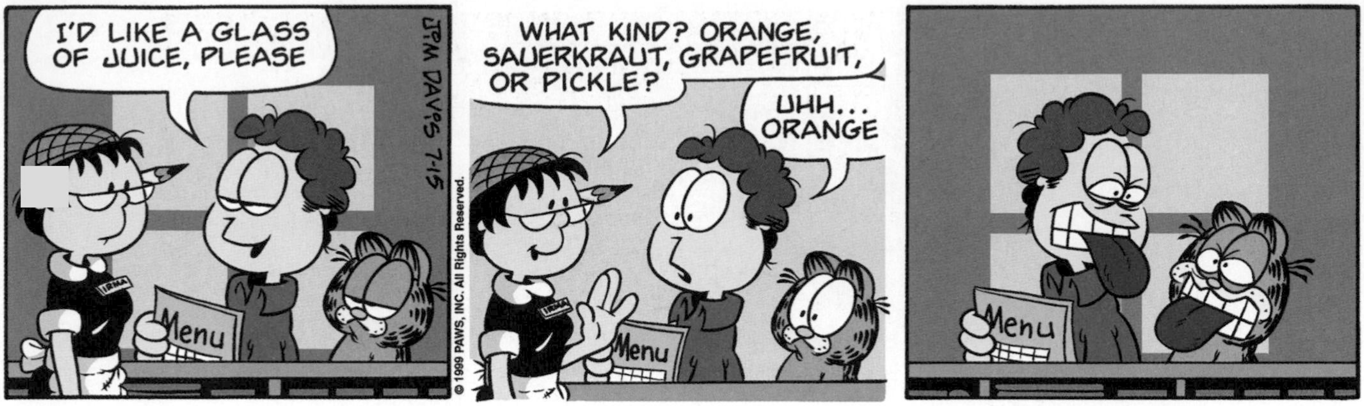
I'D LIKE A GLASS OF JUICE, PLEASE
JPM DAVPS 7-15
© 1999 PAWS, INC. All Rights Reserved.
IRMA
Menu
WHAT KIND? ORANGE, SAUERKRAUT, GRAPEFRUIT, OR PICKLE?
UHH... ORANGE
Menu

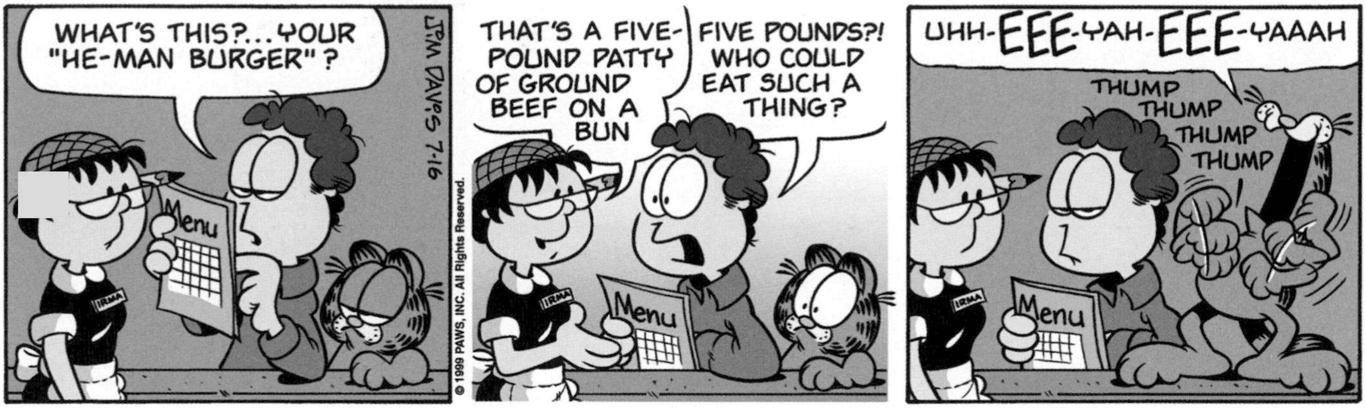
WHAT'S THIS?...YOUR "HE-MAN BURGER"?
JPM DAVPS 7-16
© 1999 PAWS, INC. All Rights Reserved.
THAT'S A FIVE-POUND PATTY OF GROUND BEEF ON A BUN
FIVE POUNDS?! WHO COULD EAT SUCH A THING?
UHH-EEE-YAH-EEE-YAAAH
THUMP THUMP THUMP THUMP

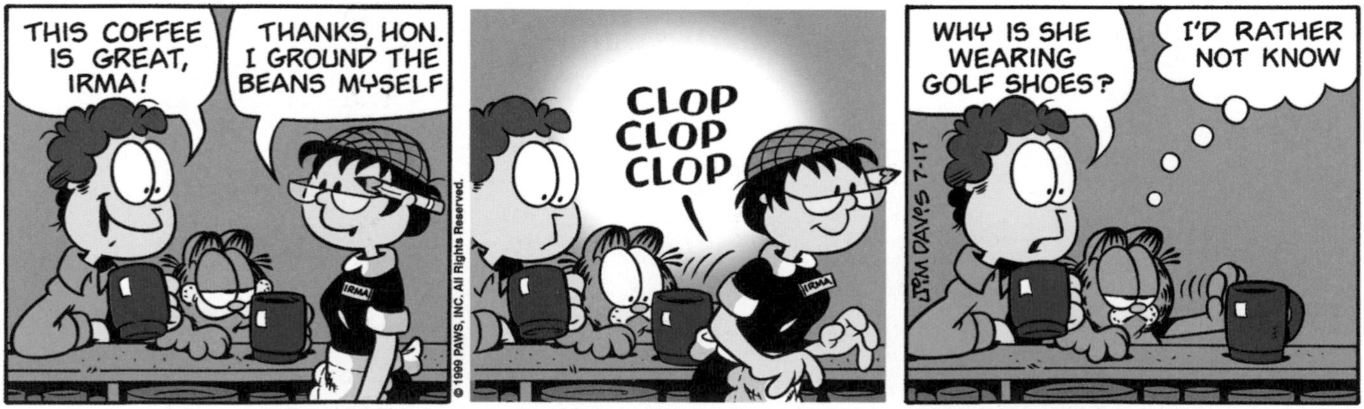
THIS COFFEE IS GREAT, IRMA!
THANKS, HON. I GROUND THE BEANS MYSELF
© 1999 PAWS, INC. All Rights Reserved.
CLOP CLOP CLOP
WHY IS SHE WEARING GOLF SHOES?
I'D RATHER NOT KNOW
JPM DAVPS 7-17

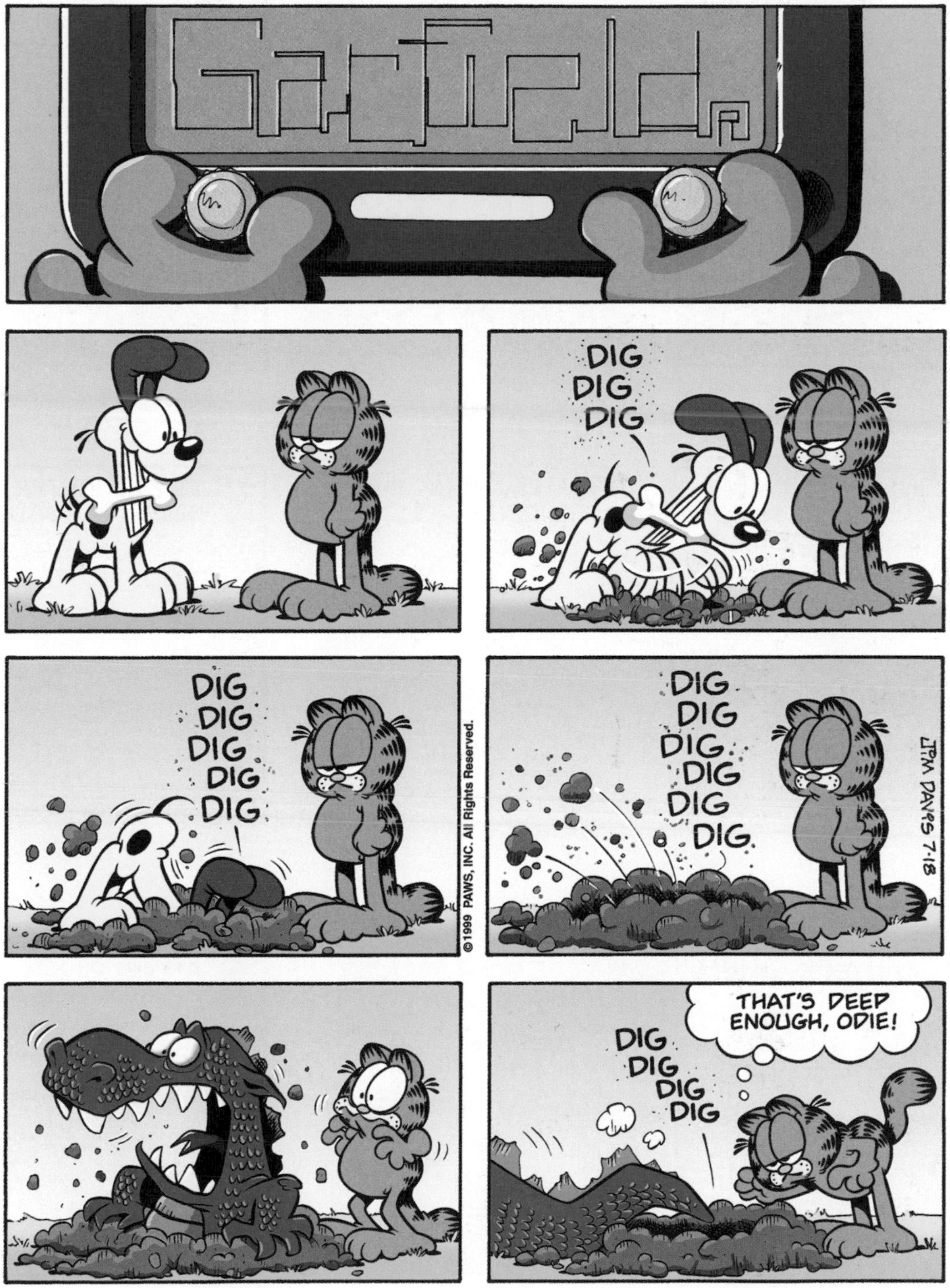
Garfield
DIG DIG DIG
DIG DIG DIG DIG DIG
©1999 PAWS, INC. All Rights Reserved.
DIG DIG DIG DIG DIG DIG
JIM DAVIS 7-18
DIG DIG DIG DIG
THAT'S DEEP ENOUGH, ODIE!

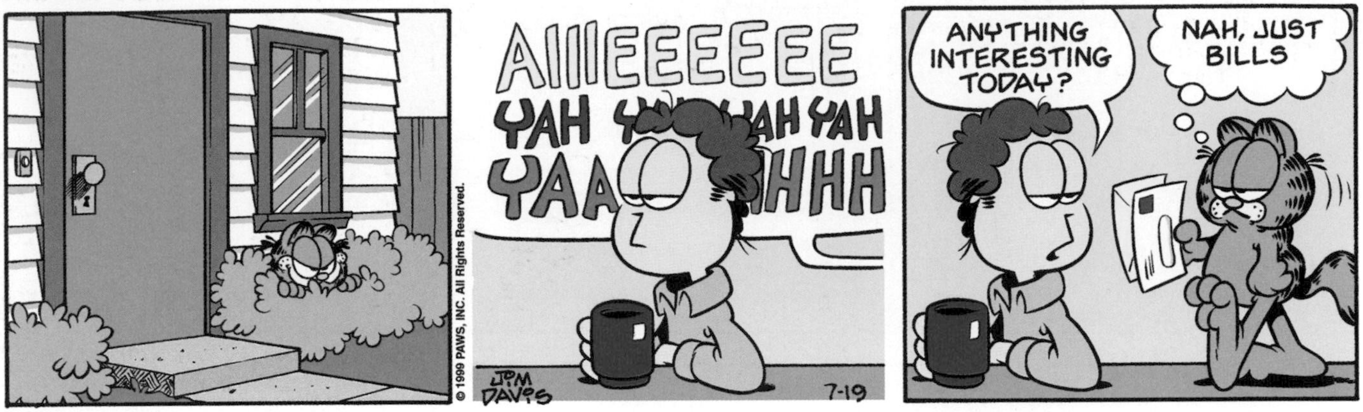
AIIIEEEEEE
YAH
AH YAH
YAA
HHH
© 1999 PAWS, INC. All Rights Reserved.
JIM DAVIS 7-19
ANYTHING INTERESTING TODAY?
NAH, JUST BILLS

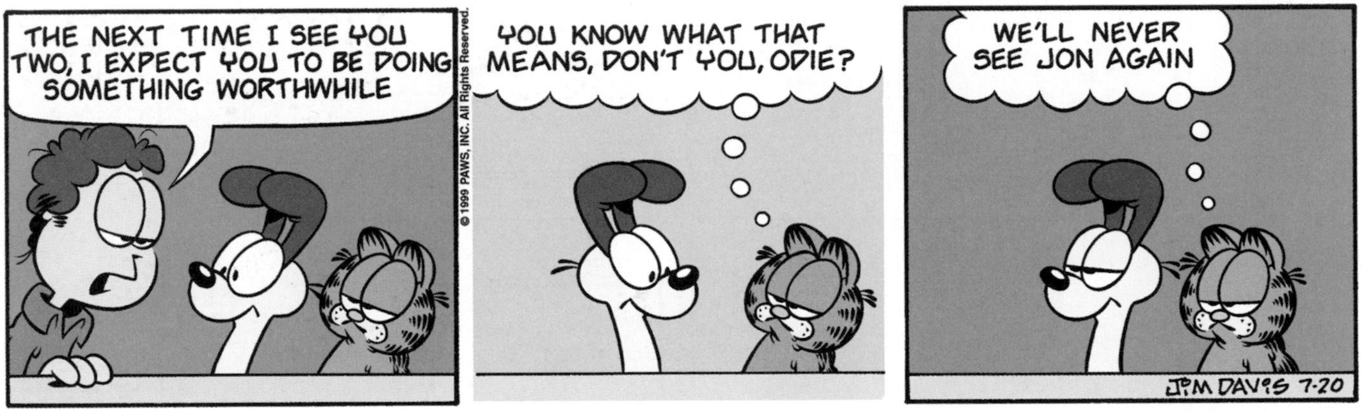
THE NEXT TIME I SEE YOU TWO, I EXPECT YOU TO BE DOING SOMETHING WORTHWHILE
© 1999 PAWS, INC. All Rights Reserved.
YOU KNOW WHAT THAT MEANS, DON'T YOU, ODIE?
WE'LL NEVER SEE JON AGAIN
JIM DAVIS 7-20

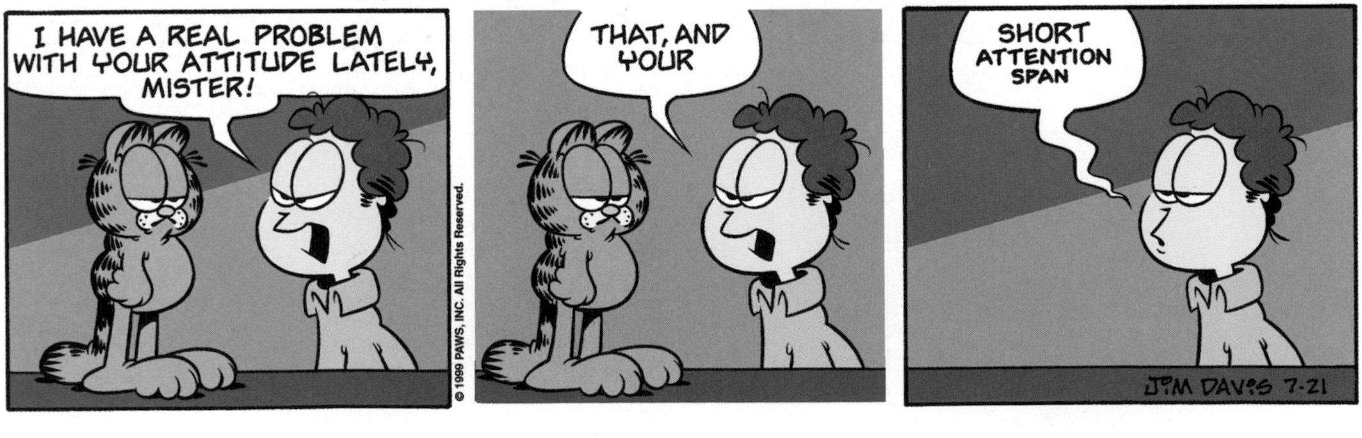
I HAVE A REAL PROBLEM WITH YOUR ATTITUDE LATELY, MISTER!
© 1999 PAWS, INC. All Rights Reserved.
THAT, AND YOUR
SHORT ATTENTION SPAN
JIM DAVIS 7-21

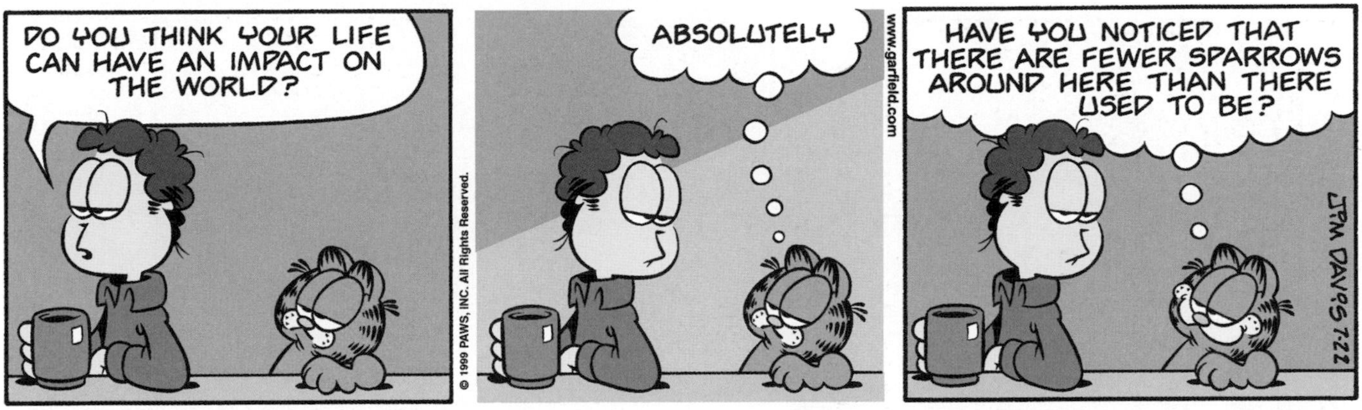
DO YOU THINK YOUR LIFE CAN HAVE AN IMPACT ON THE WORLD?
ABSOLUTELY
HAVE YOU NOTICED THAT THERE ARE FEWER SPARROWS AROUND HERE THAN THERE USED TO BE?
© 1999 PAWS, INC. All Rights Reserved.
www.garfield.com
JIM DAVIS 7-22

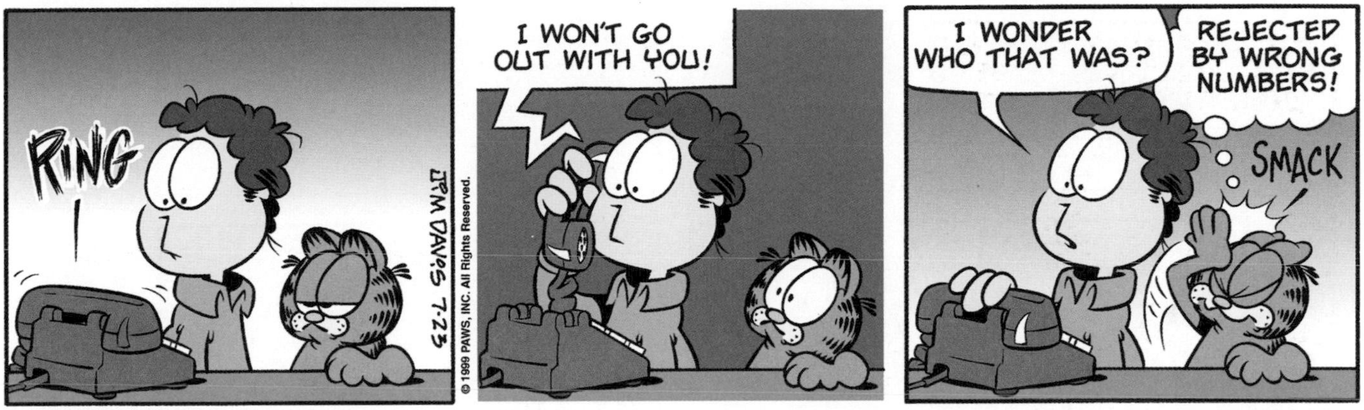
RING
JIM DAVIS 7-23
© 1999 PAWS, INC. All Rights Reserved.
I WON'T GO OUT WITH YOU!
I WONDER WHO THAT WAS?
REJECTED BY WRONG NUMBERS!
SMACK

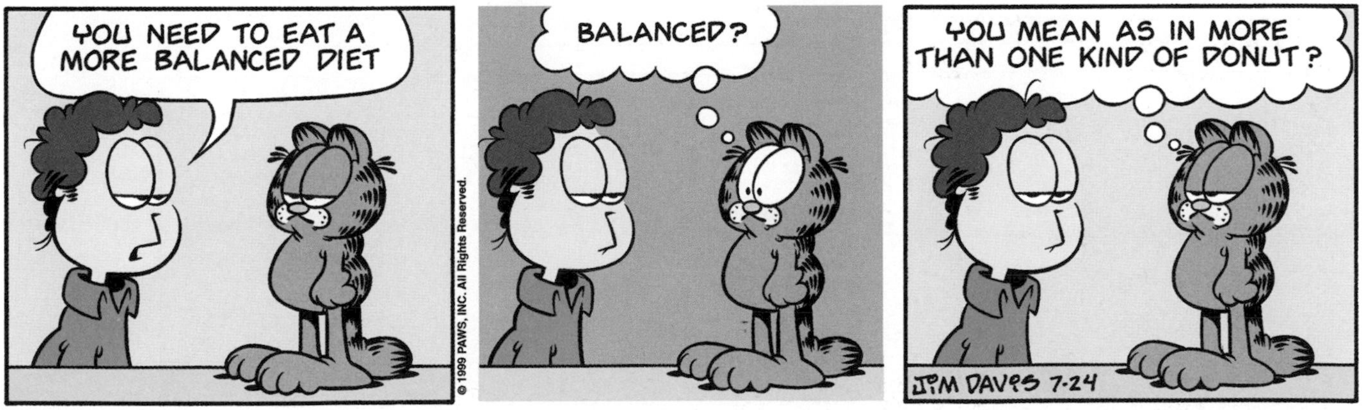
YOU NEED TO EAT A MORE BALANCED DIET
© 1999 PAWS, INC. All Rights Reserved.
BALANCED?
YOU MEAN AS IN MORE THAN ONE KIND OF DONUT?
JIM DAVIS 7-24

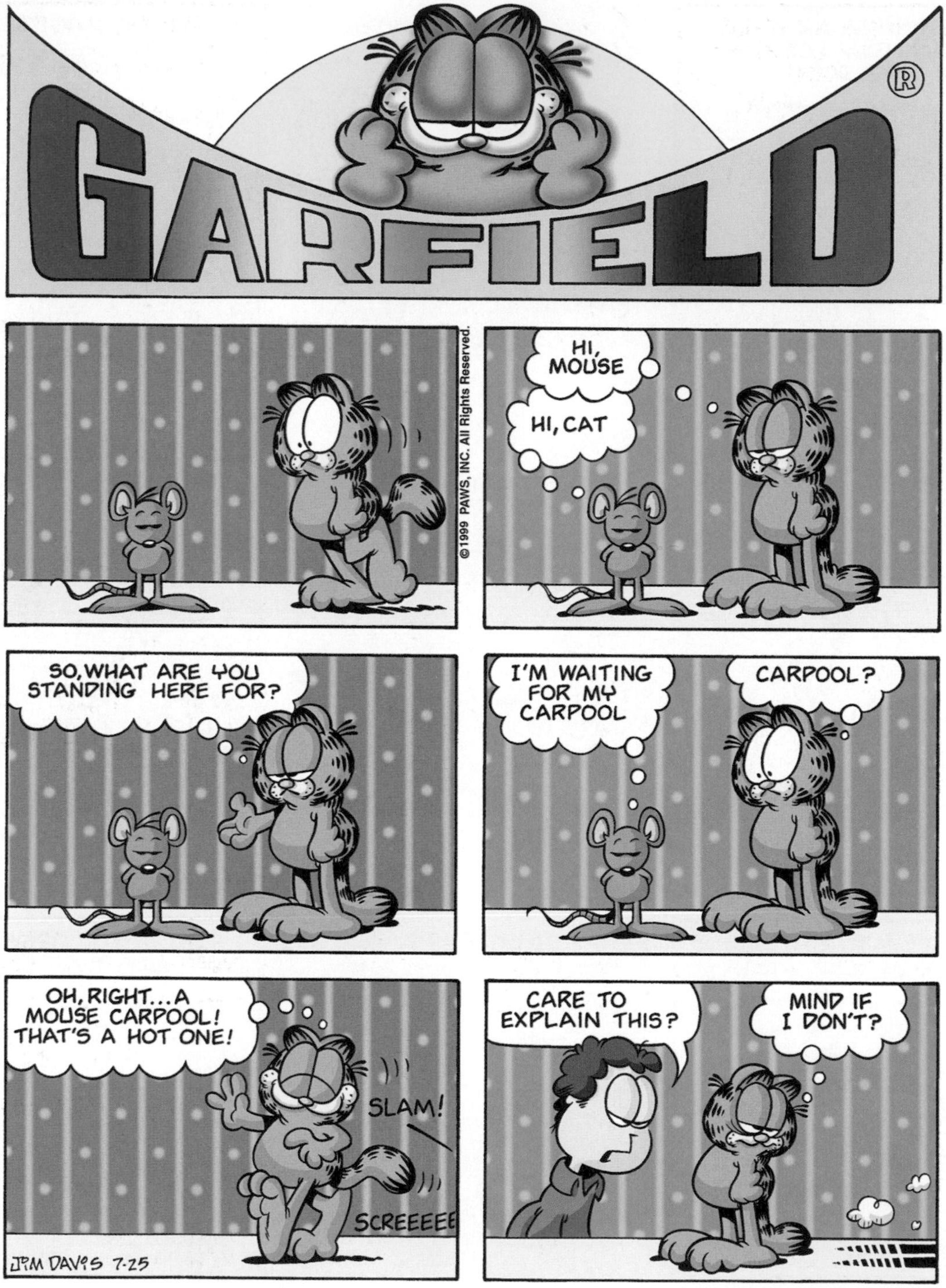
GARFIELD
©1999 PAWS, INC. All Rights Reserved.
HI, MOUSE
HI, CAT
SO, WHAT ARE YOU STANDING HERE FOR?
I'M WAITING FOR MY CARPOOL
CARPOOL?
OH, RIGHT... A MOUSE CARPOOL! THAT'S A HOT ONE!
SLAM!
SCREEEEEE
JIM DAVIS 7-25
CARE TO EXPLAIN THIS?
MIND IF I DON'T?

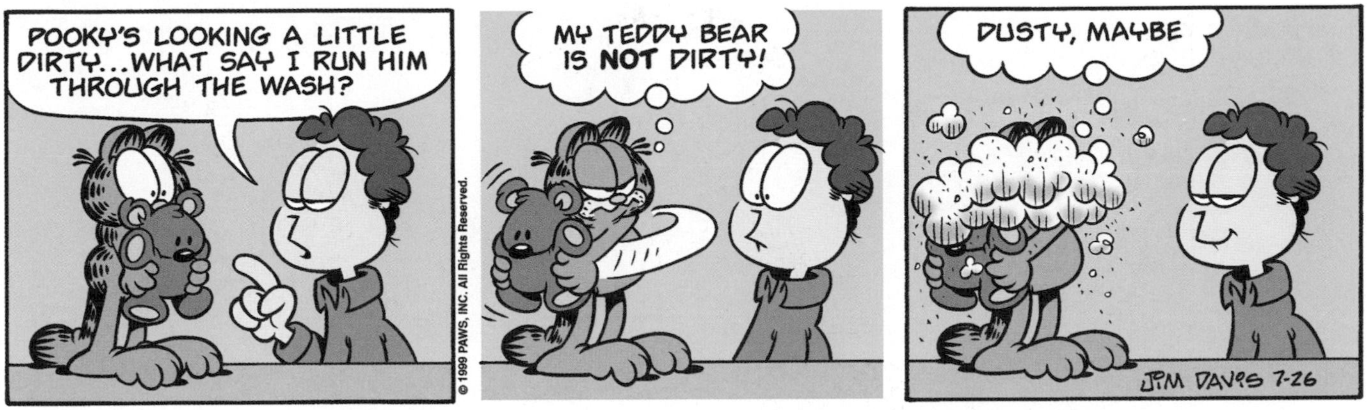
POOKY'S LOOKING A LITTLE DIRTY...WHAT SAY I RUN HIM THROUGH THE WASH?
MY TEDDY BEAR IS **NOT** DIRTY!
DUSTY, MAYBE
© 1999 PAWS, INC. All Rights Reserved.
JIM DAVIS 7-26

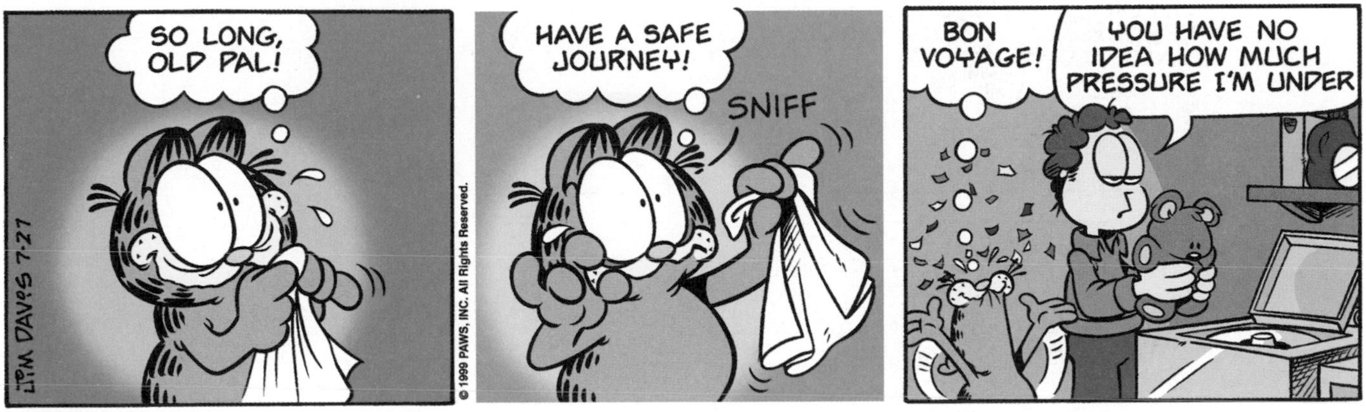
SO LONG, OLD PAL!
HAVE A SAFE JOURNEY!
SNIFF
BON VOYAGE!
YOU HAVE NO IDEA HOW MUCH PRESSURE I'M UNDER
JIM DAVIS 7-27
© 1999 PAWS, INC. All Rights Reserved.

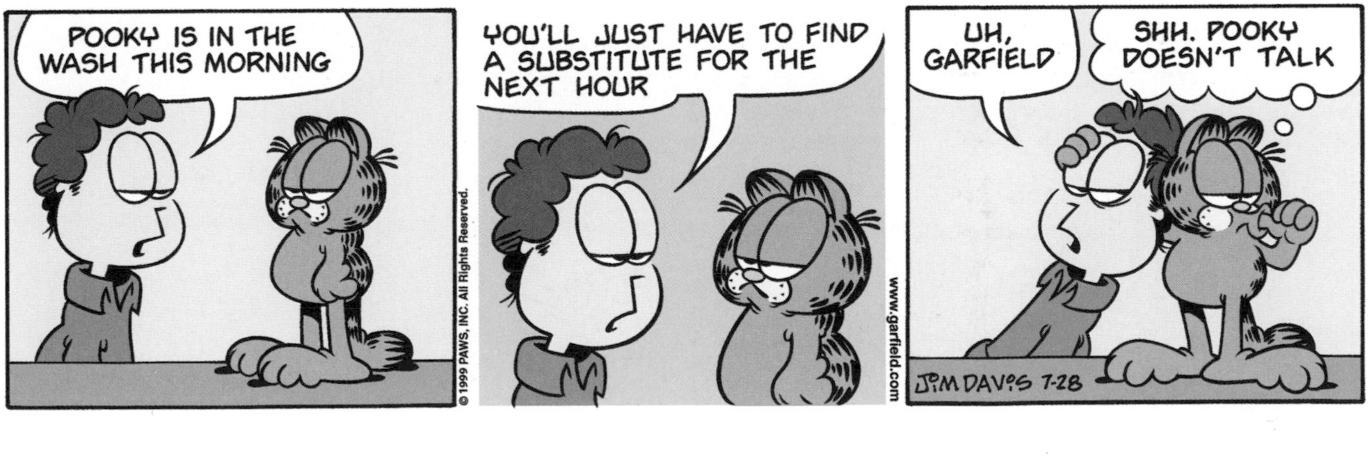
POOKY IS IN THE WASH THIS MORNING
YOU'LL JUST HAVE TO FIND A SUBSTITUTE FOR THE NEXT HOUR
UH, GARFIELD
SHH. POOKY DOESN'T TALK
© 1999 PAWS, INC. All Rights Reserved.
www.garfield.com
JIM DAVIS 7-28

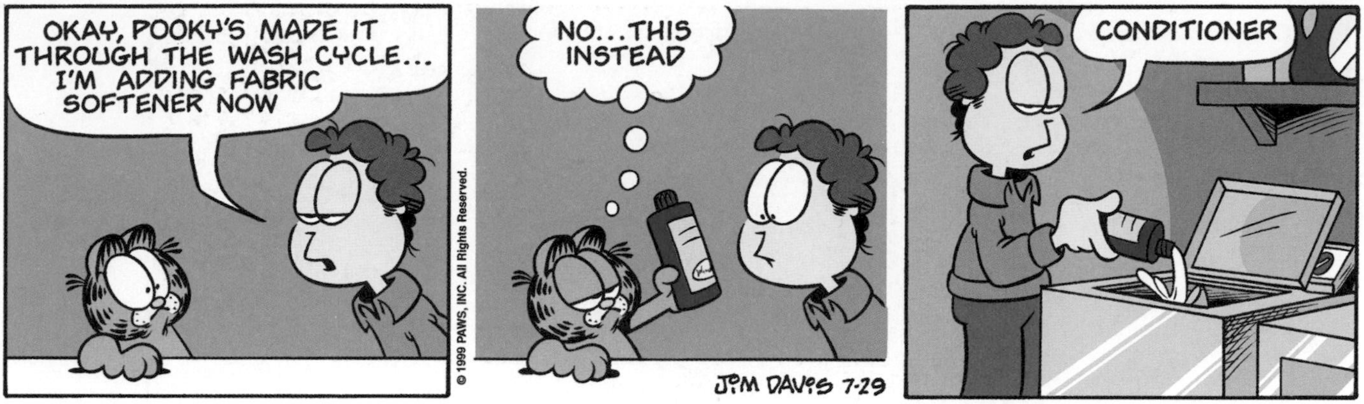
OKAY, POOKY'S MADE IT THROUGH THE WASH CYCLE... I'M ADDING FABRIC SOFTENER NOW
NO...THIS INSTEAD
CONDITIONER
JIM DAVIS 7-29

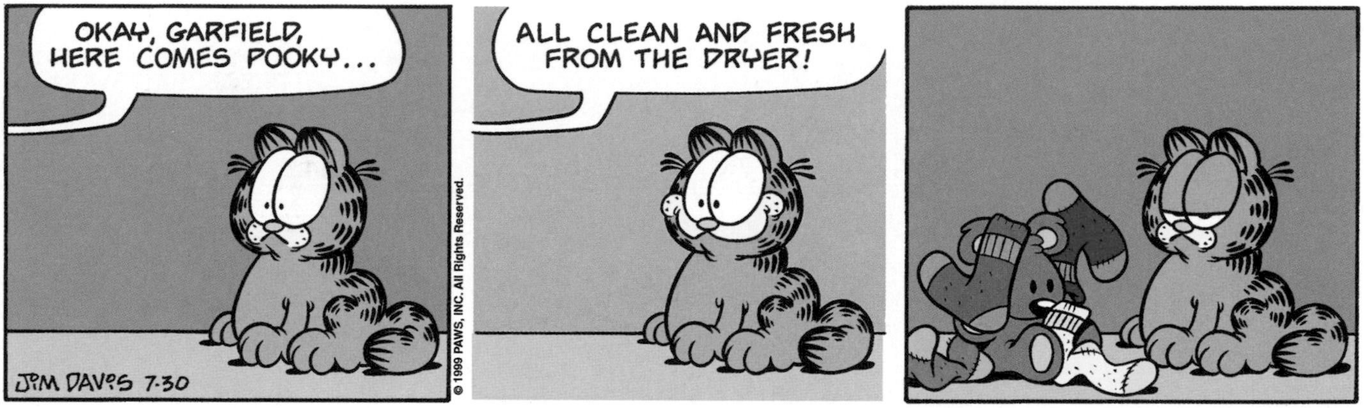
OKAY, GARFIELD, HERE COMES POOKY...
ALL CLEAN AND FRESH FROM THE DRYER!
JIM DAVIS 7-30

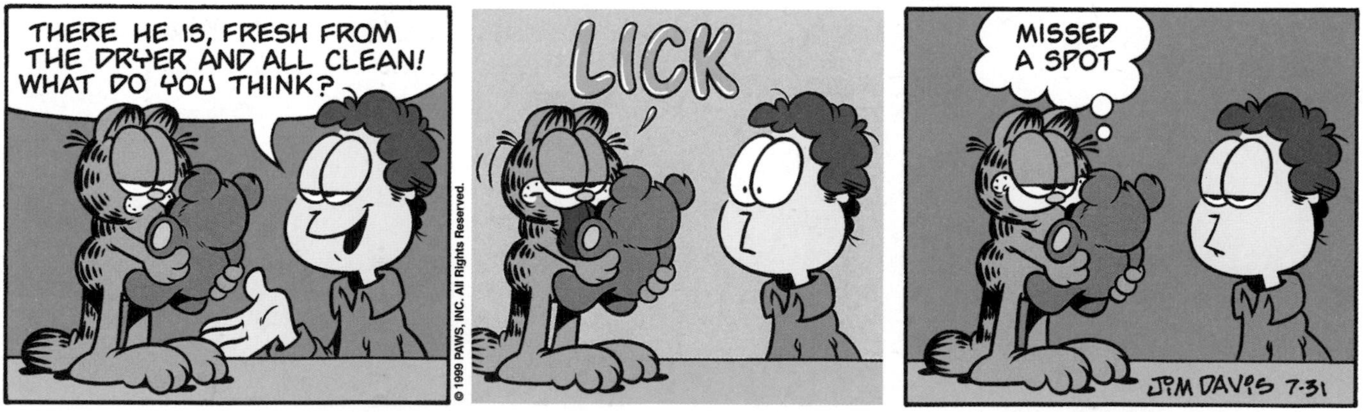
THERE HE IS, FRESH FROM THE DRYER AND ALL CLEAN! WHAT DO YOU THINK?
LICK
MISSED A SPOT
JIM DAVIS 7-31

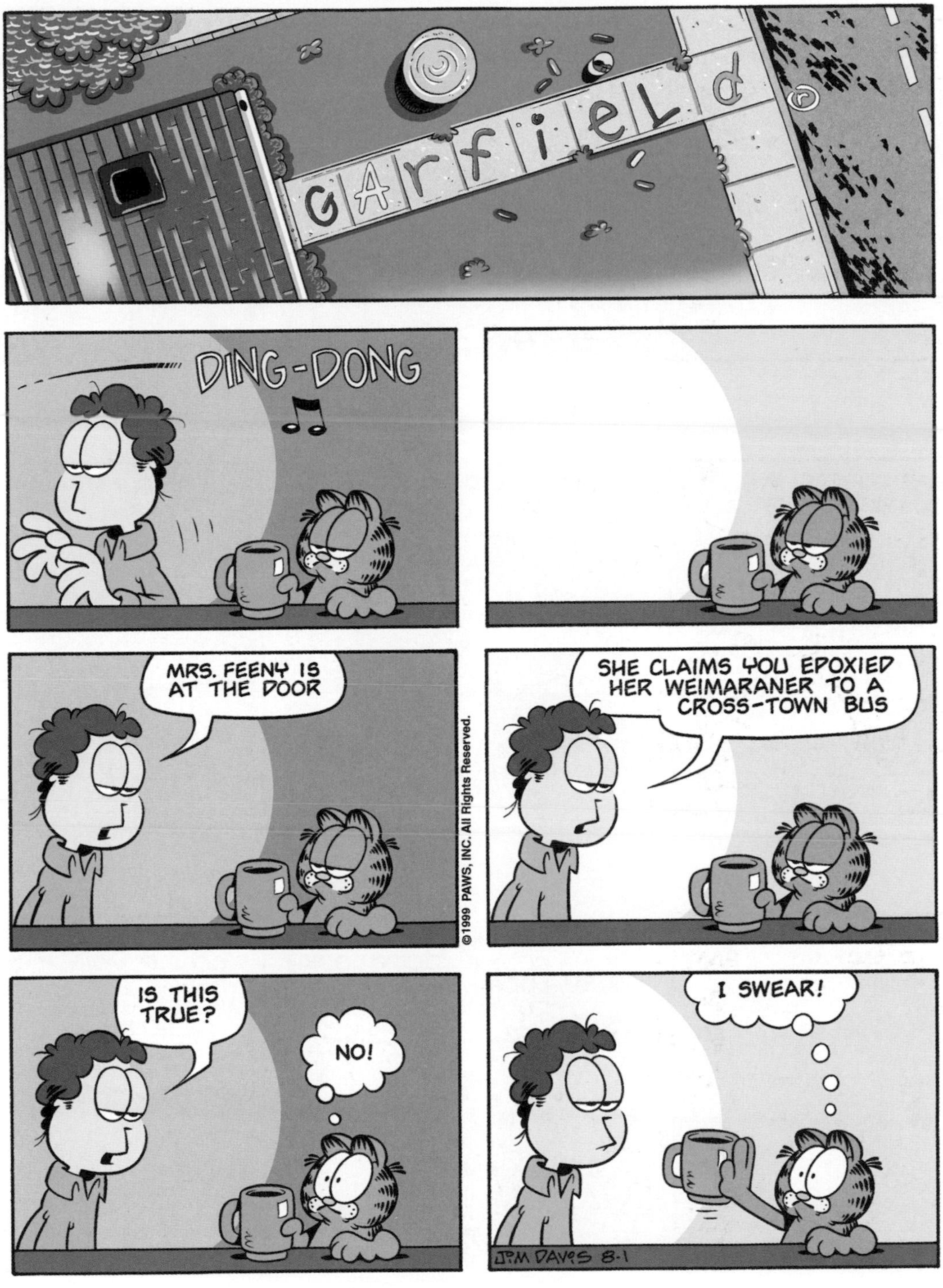
GARFIELD
DING-DONG
MRS. FEENY IS AT THE DOOR
SHE CLAIMS YOU EPOXIED HER WEIMARANER TO A CROSS-TOWN BUS
IS THIS TRUE?
NO!
I SWEAR!
JIM DAVIS 8-1
©1999 PAWS, INC. All Rights Reserved.

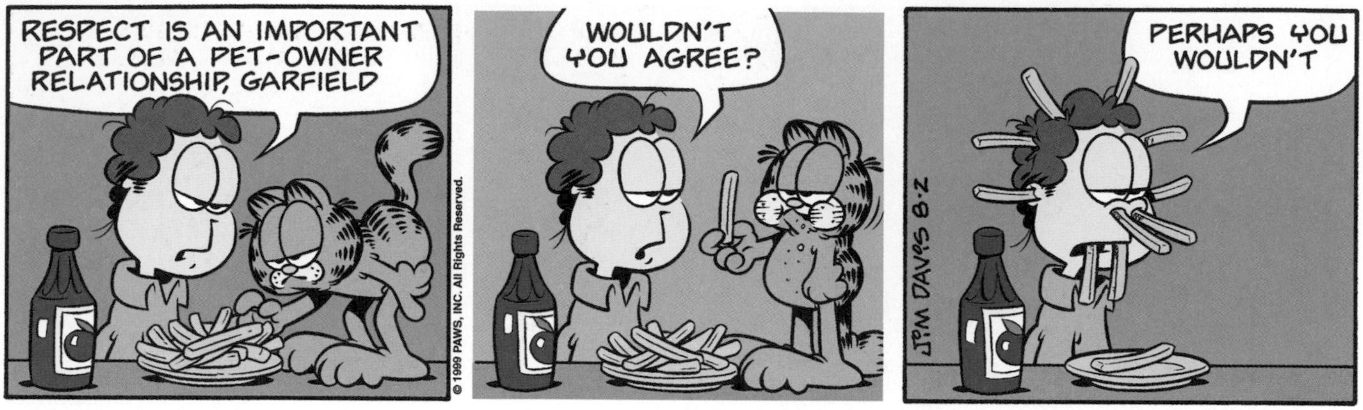
RESPECT IS AN IMPORTANT PART OF A PET-OWNER RELATIONSHIP, GARFIELD
© 1999 PAWS, INC. All Rights Reserved.
WOULDN'T YOU AGREE?
PERHAPS YOU WOULDN'T
JIM DAVIS 8-2

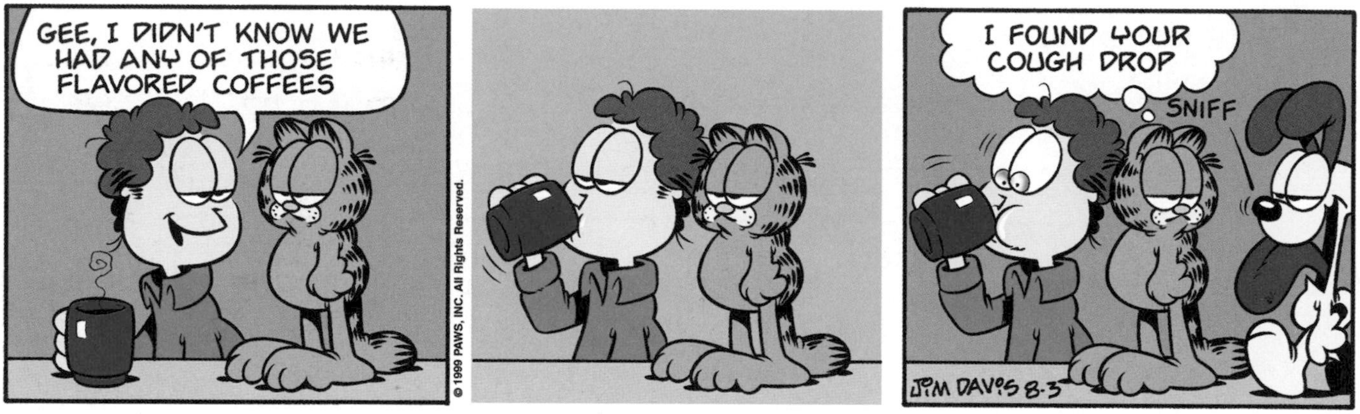
GEE, I DIDN'T KNOW WE HAD ANY OF THOSE FLAVORED COFFEES
© 1999 PAWS, INC. All Rights Reserved.
I FOUND YOUR COUGH DROP
SNIFF
JIM DAVIS 8-3

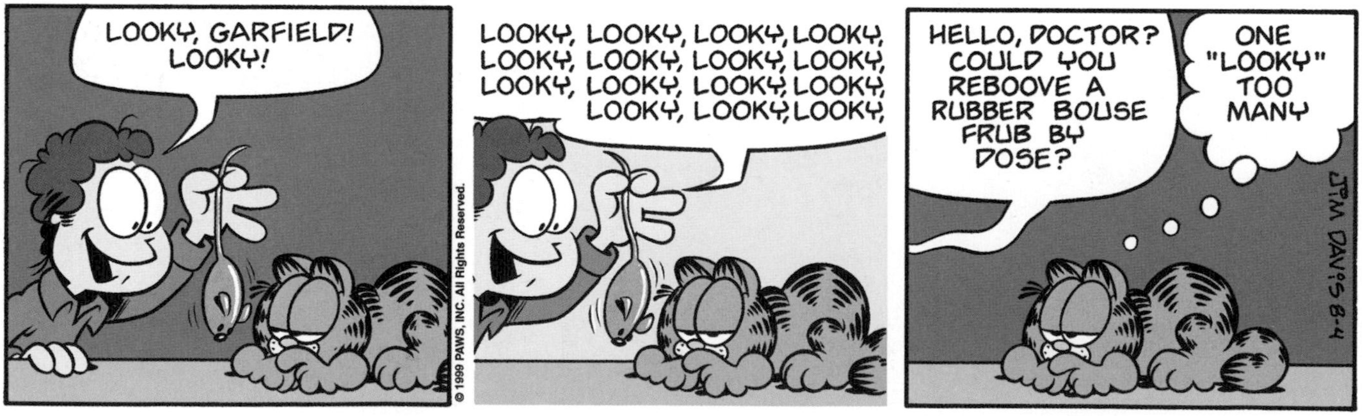
LOOKY, GARFIELD! LOOKY!
© 1999 PAWS, INC. All Rights Reserved.
LOOKY, LOOKY, LOOKY, LOOKY, LOOKY, LOOKY, LOOKY, LOOKY, LOOKY, LOOKY, LOOKY, LOOKY, LOOKY, LOOKY, LOOKY,
HELLO, DOCTOR? COULD YOU REBOOVE A RUBBER BOUSE FRUB BY DOSE?
ONE "LOOKY" TOO MANY
JIM DAVIS 8-4

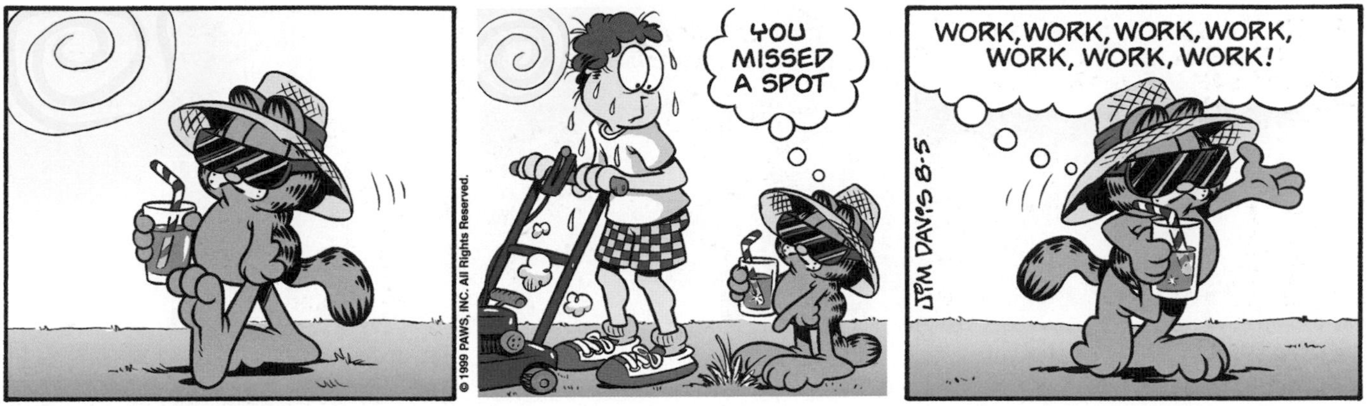
© 1999 PAWS, INC. All Rights Reserved.
YOU MISSED A SPOT
JIM DAVIS 8-5
WORK, WORK, WORK, WORK, WORK, WORK, WORK!

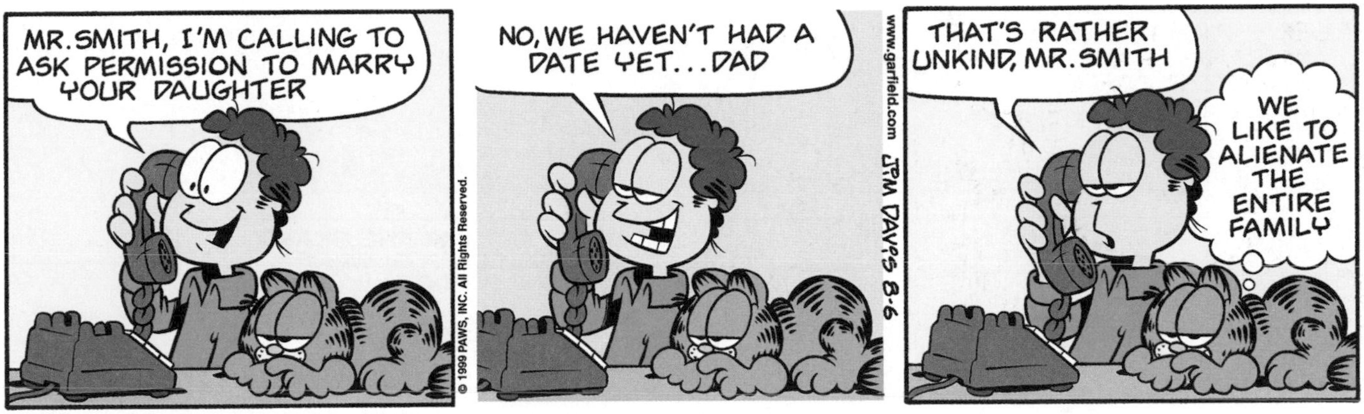
MR. SMITH, I'M CALLING TO ASK PERMISSION TO MARRY YOUR DAUGHTER
© 1999 PAWS, INC. All Rights Reserved.
NO, WE HAVEN'T HAD A DATE YET...DAD
www.garfield.com
JIM DAVIS 8-6
THAT'S RATHER UNKIND, MR. SMITH
WE LIKE TO ALIENATE THE ENTIRE FAMILY

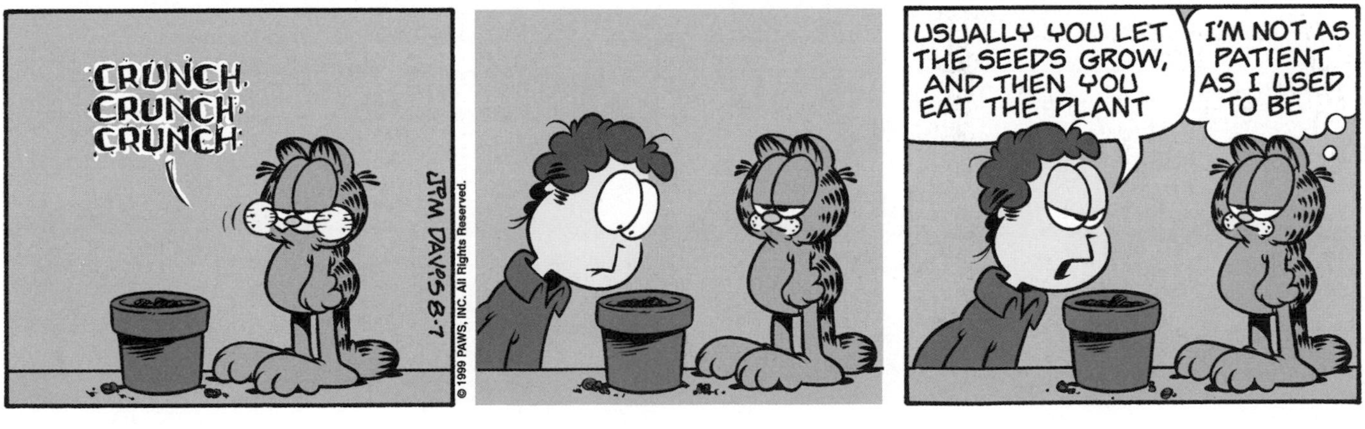
CRUNCH CRUNCH CRUNCH
JIM DAVIS 8-7
© 1999 PAWS, INC. All Rights Reserved.
USUALLY YOU LET THE SEEDS GROW, AND THEN YOU EAT THE PLANT
I'M NOT AS PATIENT AS I USED TO BE

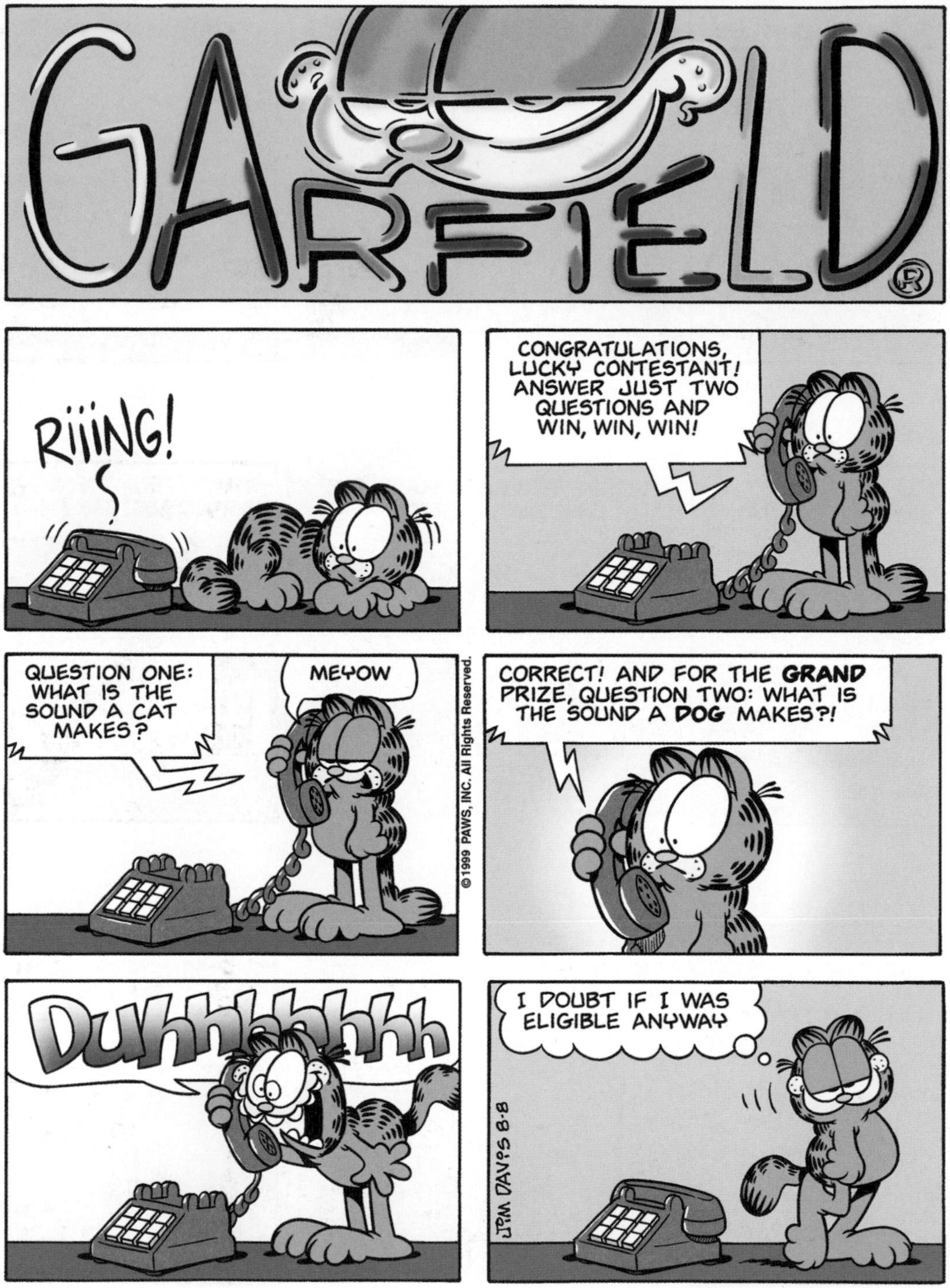
GARFIELD
RiiiNG!
CONGRATULATIONS, LUCKY CONTESTANT! ANSWER JUST TWO QUESTIONS AND WIN, WIN, WIN!
QUESTION ONE: WHAT IS THE SOUND A CAT MAKES?
MEYOW
CORRECT! AND FOR THE **GRAND** PRIZE, QUESTION TWO: WHAT IS THE SOUND A **DOG** MAKES?!
Duhhhhhhh
JPM DAVPS 8-8
I DOUBT IF I WAS ELIGIBLE ANYWAY

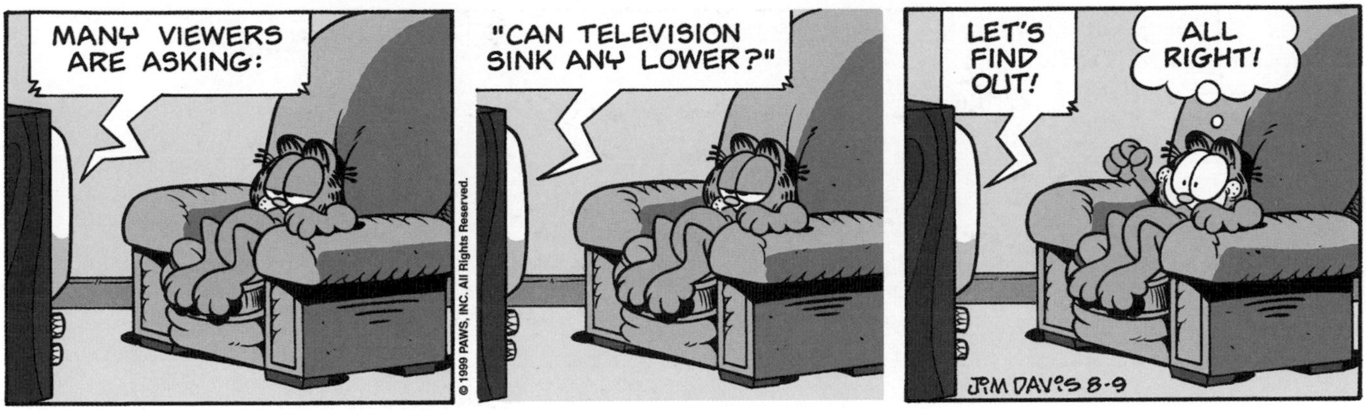
MANY VIEWERS ARE ASKING:
"CAN TELEVISION SINK ANY LOWER?"
LET'S FIND OUT!
ALL RIGHT!
JIM DAVIS 8-9

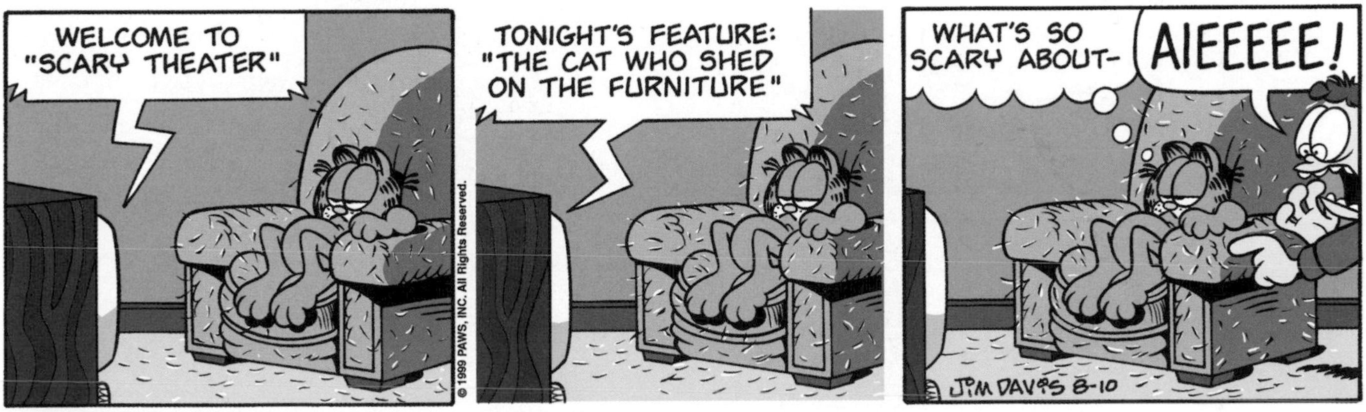
WELCOME TO "SCARY THEATER"
TONIGHT'S FEATURE: "THE CAT WHO SHED ON THE FURNITURE"
WHAT'S SO SCARY ABOUT-
AIEEEEE!
JIM DAVIS 8-10

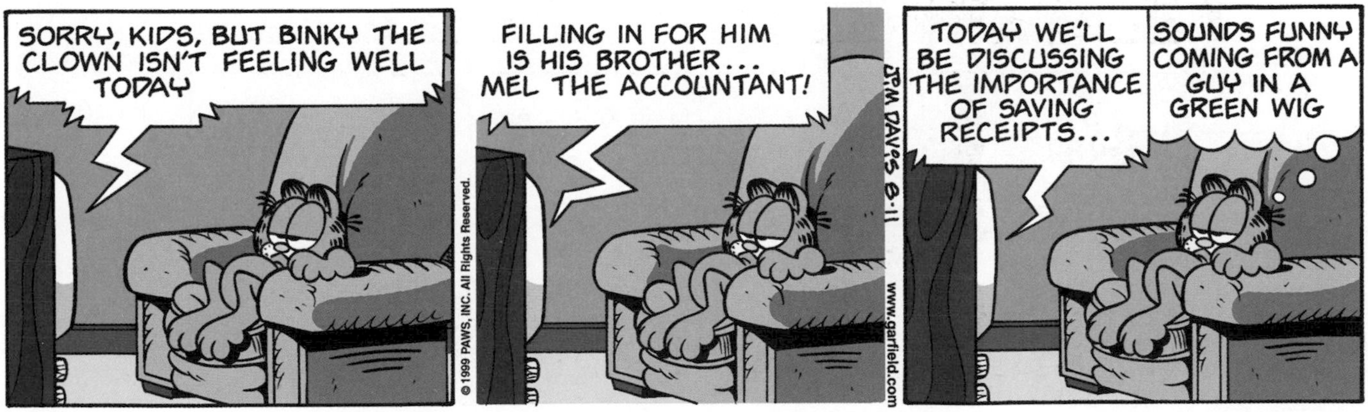
SORRY, KIDS, BUT BINKY THE CLOWN ISN'T FEELING WELL TODAY
FILLING IN FOR HIM IS HIS BROTHER... MEL THE ACCOUNTANT!
TODAY WE'LL BE DISCUSSING THE IMPORTANCE OF SAVING RECEIPTS...
SOUNDS FUNNY COMING FROM A GUY IN A GREEN WIG
JIM DAVIS 8-11

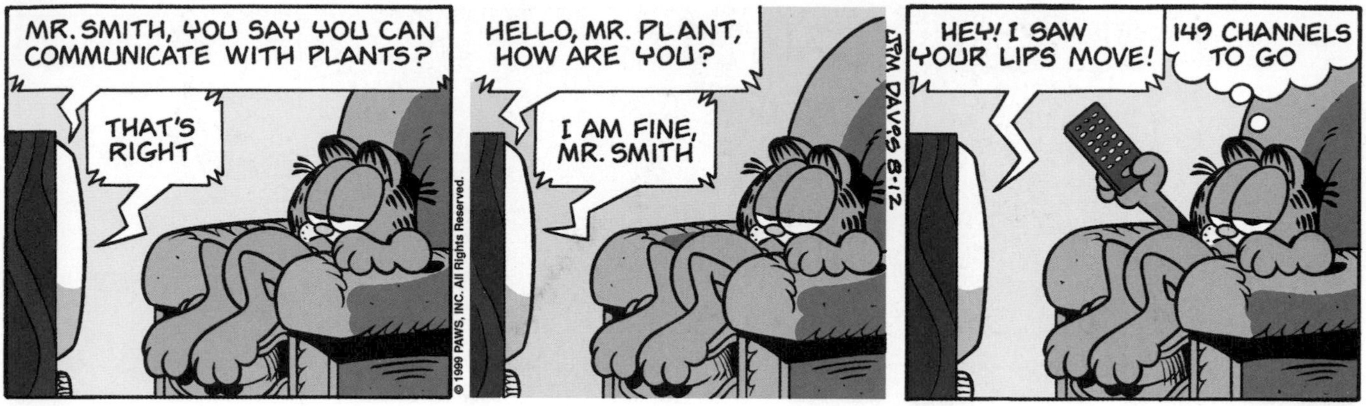
MR. SMITH, YOU SAY YOU CAN COMMUNICATE WITH PLANTS?
THAT'S RIGHT
© 1999 PAWS, INC. All Rights Reserved.
HELLO, MR. PLANT, HOW ARE YOU?
I AM FINE, MR. SMITH
JIM DAVIS 8-12
HEY! I SAW YOUR LIPS MOVE!
149 CHANNELS TO GO

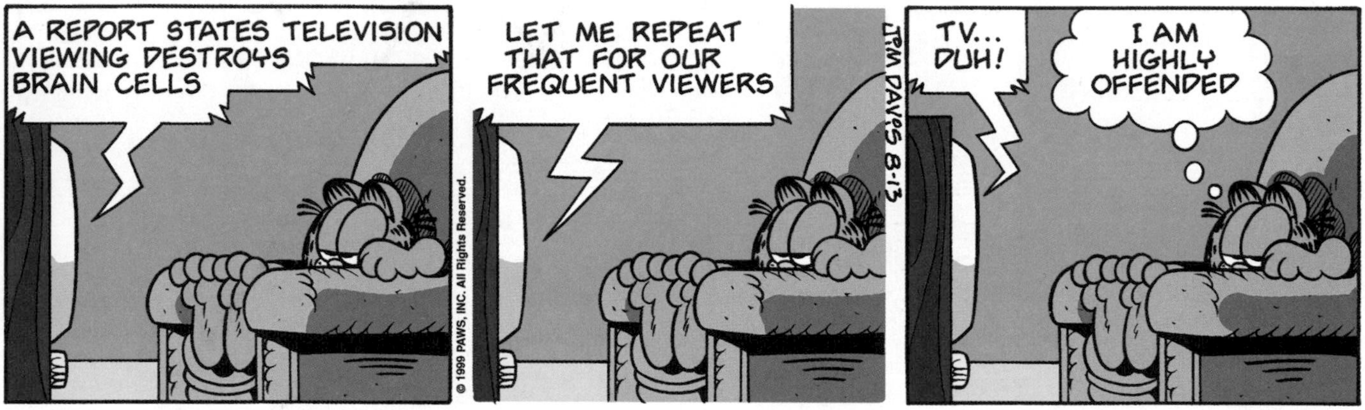
A REPORT STATES TELEVISION VIEWING DESTROYS BRAIN CELLS
© 1999 PAWS, INC. All Rights Reserved.
LET ME REPEAT THAT FOR OUR FREQUENT VIEWERS
JIM DAVIS 8-13
TV... DUH!
I AM HIGHLY OFFENDED

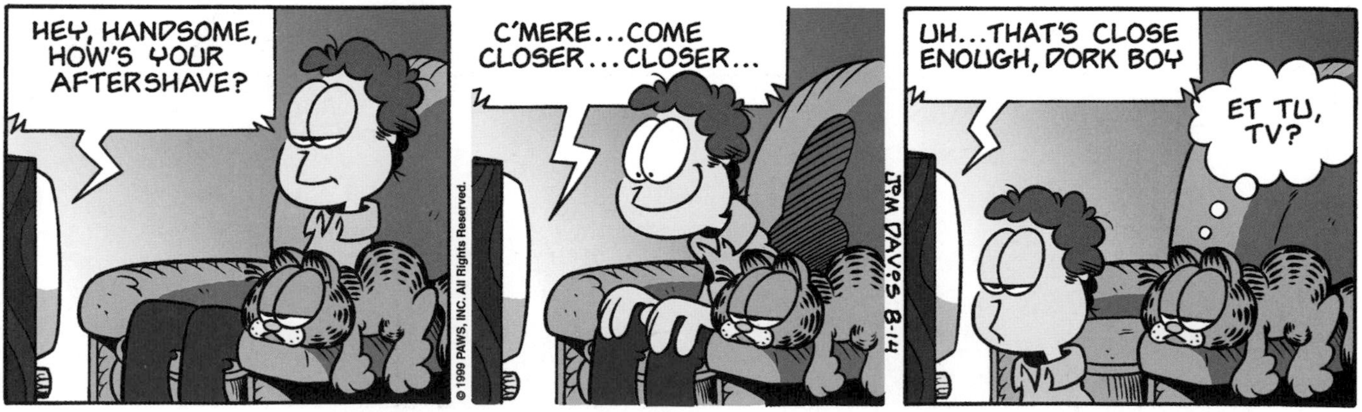
HEY, HANDSOME, HOW'S YOUR AFTERSHAVE?
© 1999 PAWS, INC. All Rights Reserved.
C'MERE...COME CLOSER...CLOSER...
JIM DAVIS 8-14
UH...THAT'S CLOSE ENOUGH, DORK BOY
ET TU, TV?

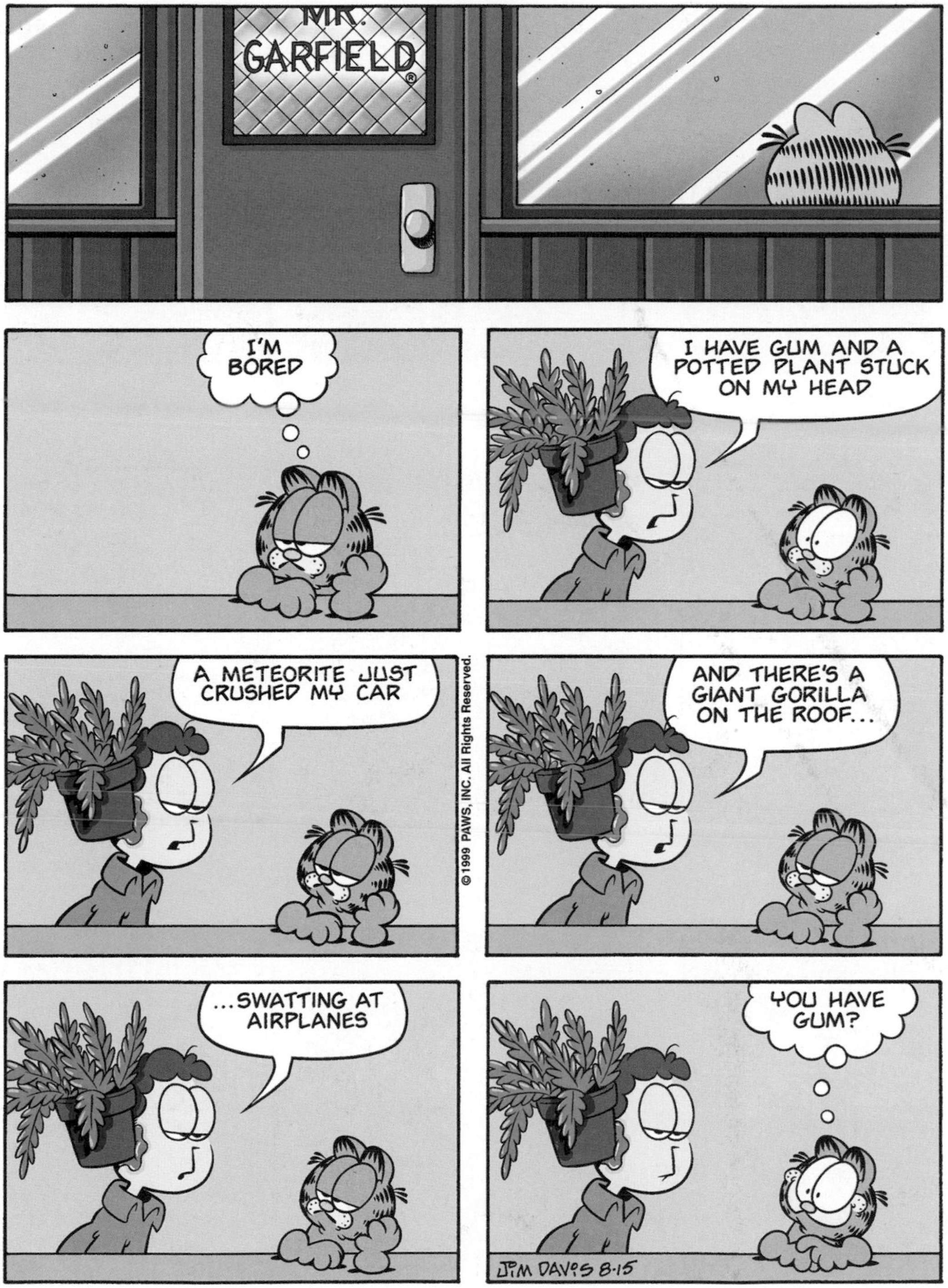
MR.
GARFIELD®
I'M BORED
I HAVE GUM AND A POTTED PLANT STUCK ON MY HEAD
A METEORITE JUST CRUSHED MY CAR
AND THERE'S A GIANT GORILLA ON THE ROOF...
...SWATTING AT AIRPLANES
YOU HAVE GUM?
JIM DAVIS 8-15

© 1999 PAWS, INC. All Rights Reserved.

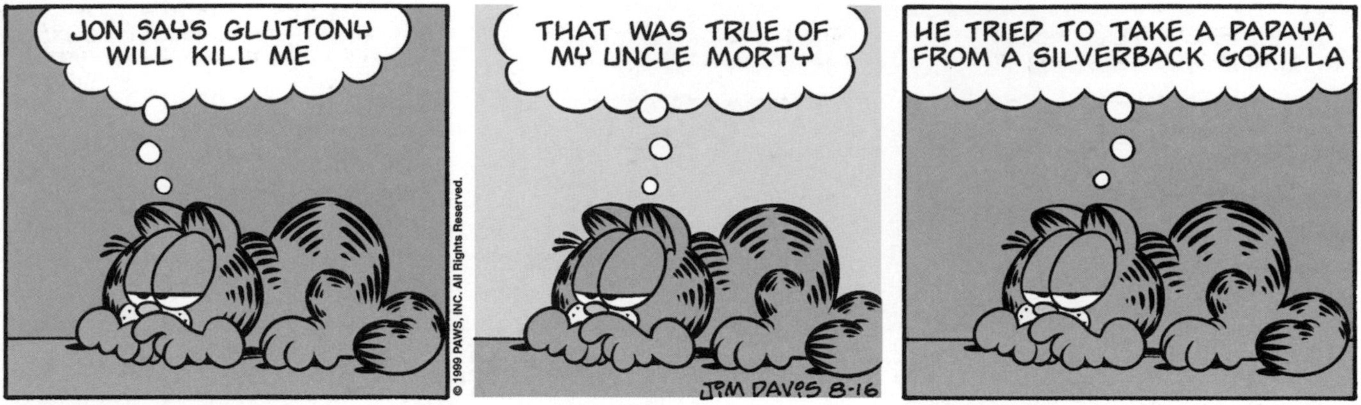
JON SAYS GLUTTONY WILL KILL ME
© 1999 PAWS, INC. All Rights Reserved.
THAT WAS TRUE OF MY UNCLE MORTY
JIM DAVIS 8-16
HE TRIED TO TAKE A PAPAYA FROM A SILVERBACK GORILLA

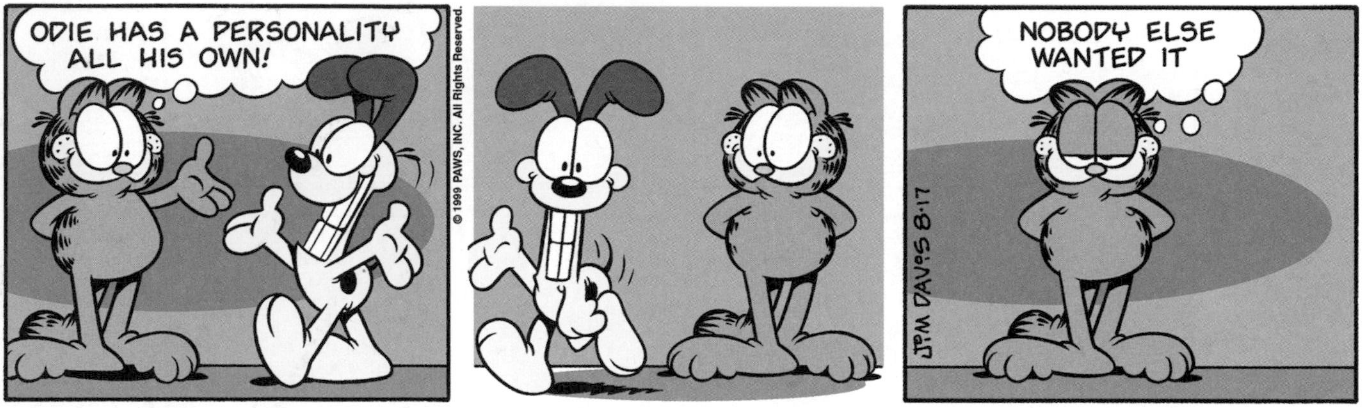
ODIE HAS A PERSONALITY ALL HIS OWN!
© 1999 PAWS, INC. All Rights Reserved.
NOBODY ELSE WANTED IT
JIM DAVIS 8-17

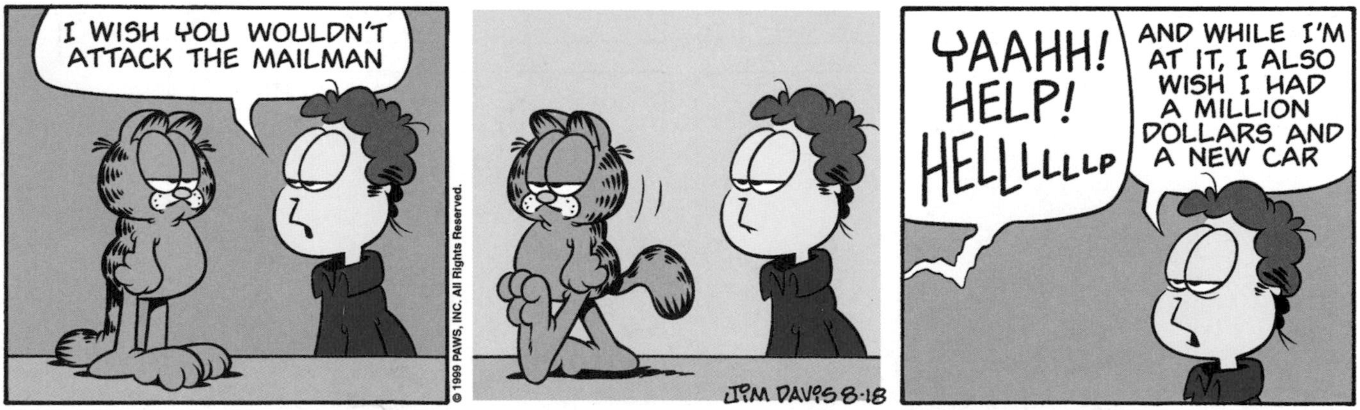
I WISH YOU WOULDN'T ATTACK THE MAILMAN
© 1999 PAWS, INC. All Rights Reserved.
JIM DAVIS 8-18
YAAHH! HELP! HELLLLLLLP
AND WHILE I'M AT IT, I ALSO WISH I HAD A MILLION DOLLARS AND A NEW CAR

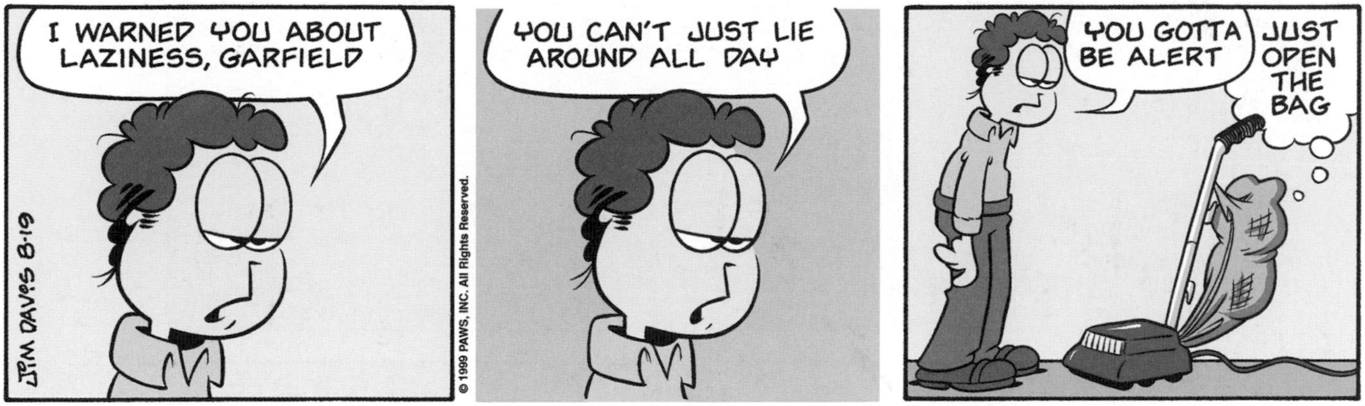
I WARNED YOU ABOUT LAZINESS, GARFIELD
JIM DAVIS 8-19
YOU CAN'T JUST LIE AROUND ALL DAY
YOU GOTTA BE ALERT
JUST OPEN THE BAG

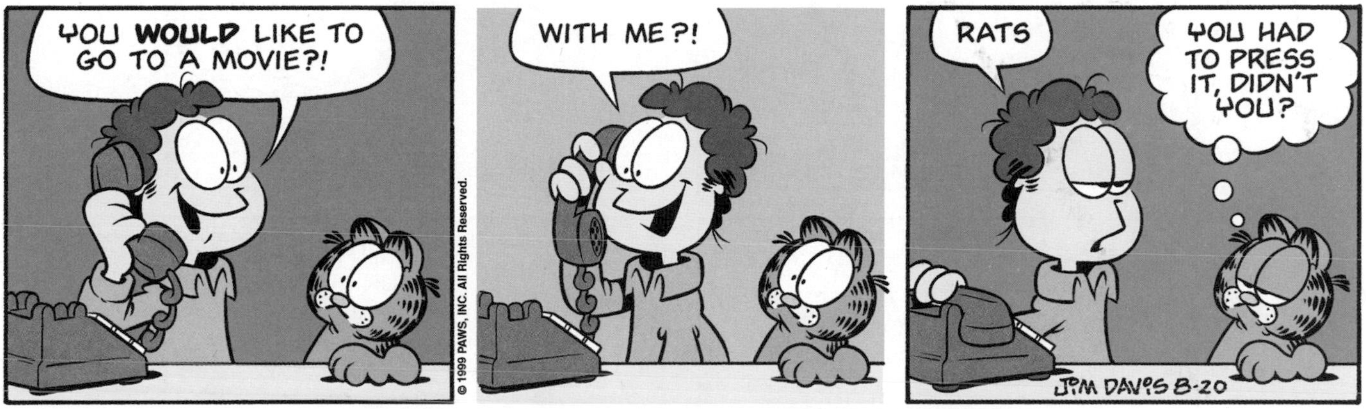
YOU **WOULD** LIKE TO GO TO A MOVIE?!
WITH ME?!
RATS
YOU HAD TO PRESS IT, DIDN'T YOU?
JIM DAVIS 8-20

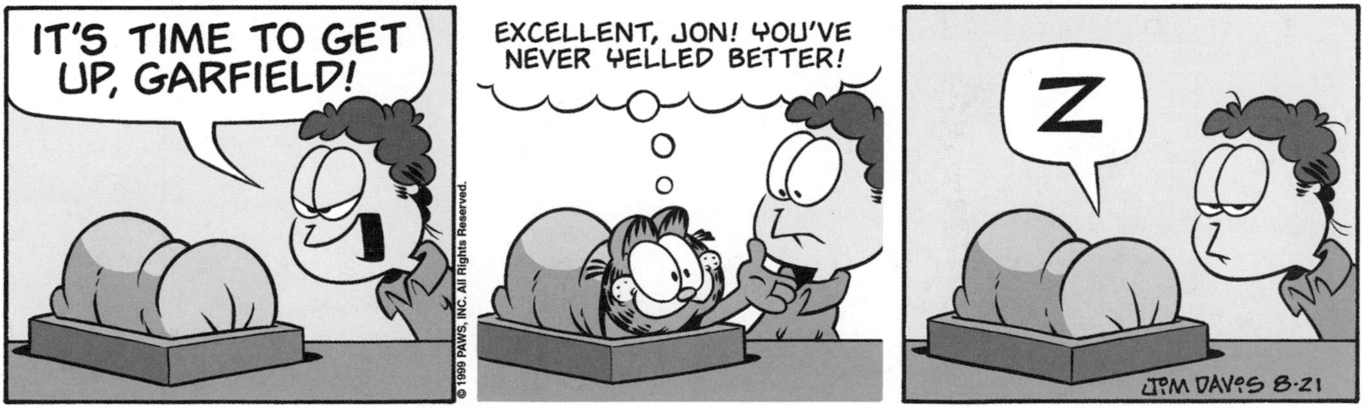
IT'S TIME TO GET UP, GARFIELD!
EXCELLENT, JON! YOU'VE NEVER YELLED BETTER!
Z
JIM DAVIS 8-21

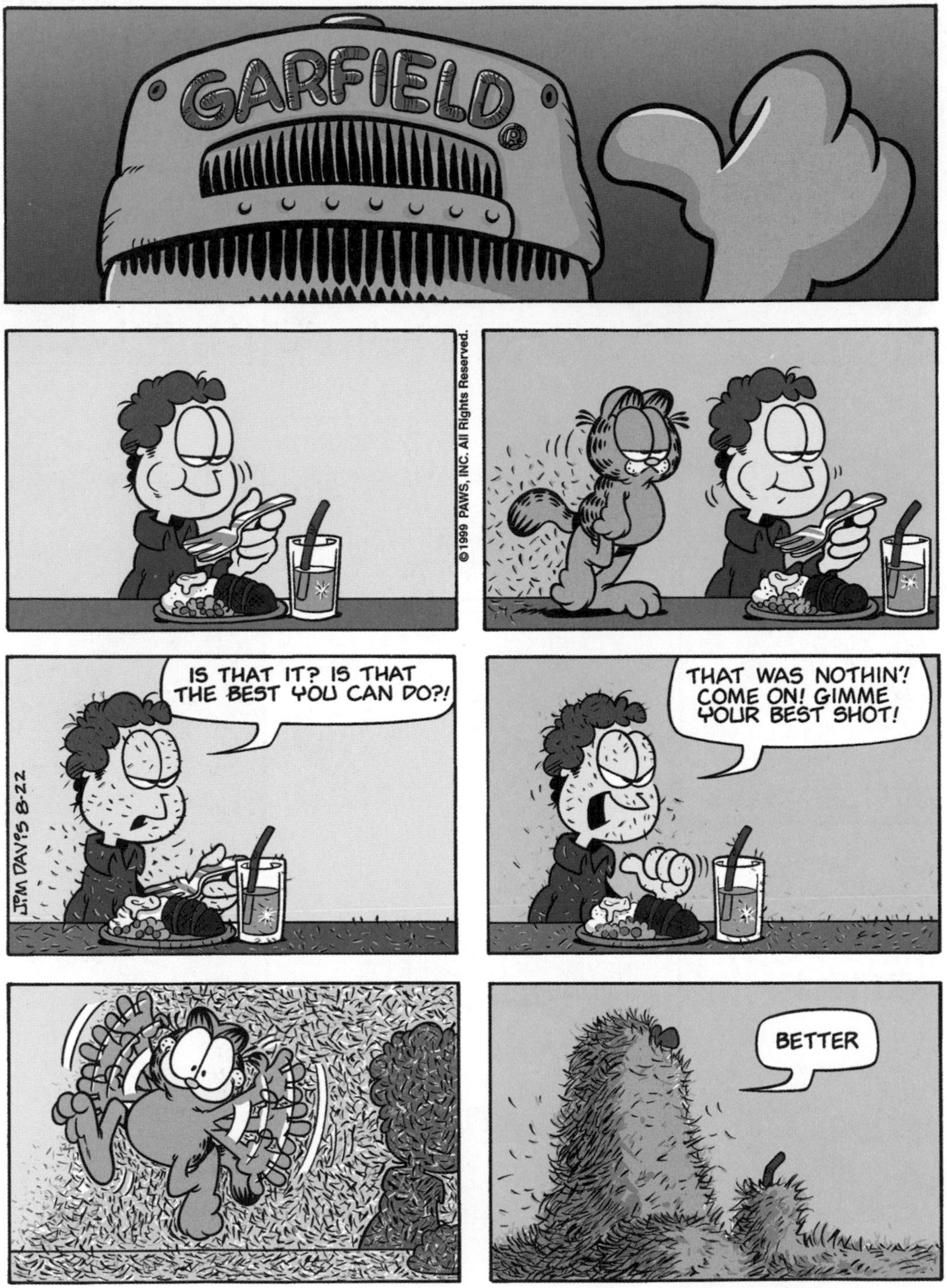
GARFIELD®
©1999 PAWS, INC. All Rights Reserved.
IS THAT IT? IS THAT THE BEST YOU CAN DO?!
JPM DAVIS 8-22
THAT WAS NOTHIN'! COME ON! GIMME YOUR BEST SHOT!
BETTER

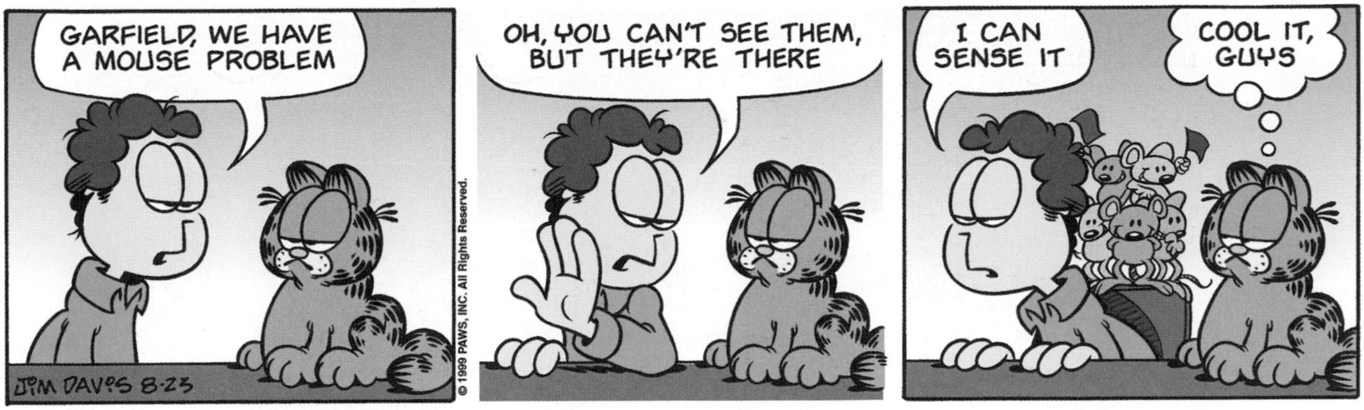
GARFIELD, WE HAVE A MOUSE PROBLEM
JIM DAVIS 8-23
© 1999 PAWS, INC. All Rights Reserved.
OH, YOU CAN'T SEE THEM, BUT THEY'RE THERE
I CAN SENSE IT
COOL IT, GUYS

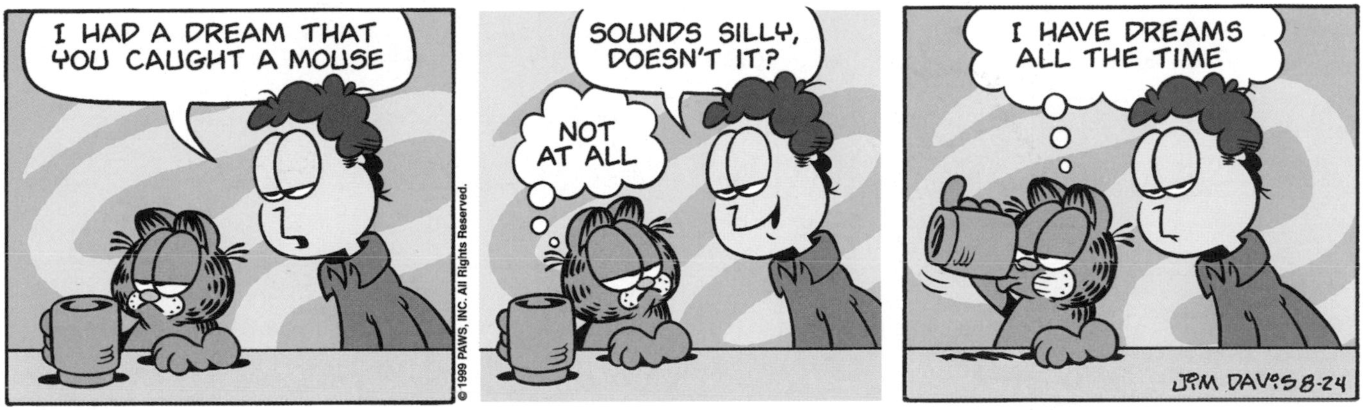
I HAD A DREAM THAT YOU CAUGHT A MOUSE
© 1999 PAWS, INC. All Rights Reserved.
SOUNDS SILLY, DOESN'T IT?
NOT AT ALL
I HAVE DREAMS ALL THE TIME
JIM DAVIS 8-24

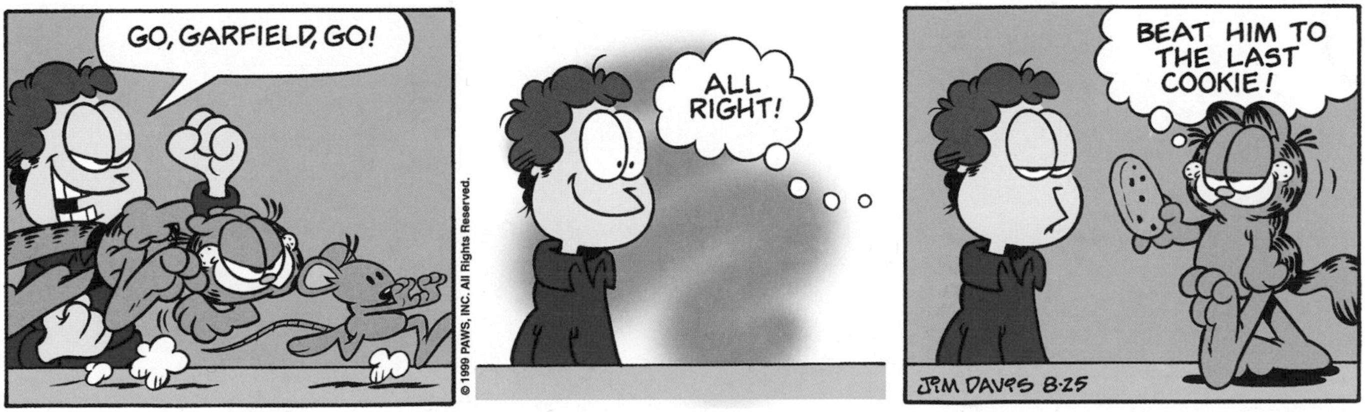
GO, GARFIELD, GO!
© 1999 PAWS, INC. All Rights Reserved.
ALL RIGHT!
BEAT HIM TO THE LAST COOKIE!
JIM DAVIS 8-25

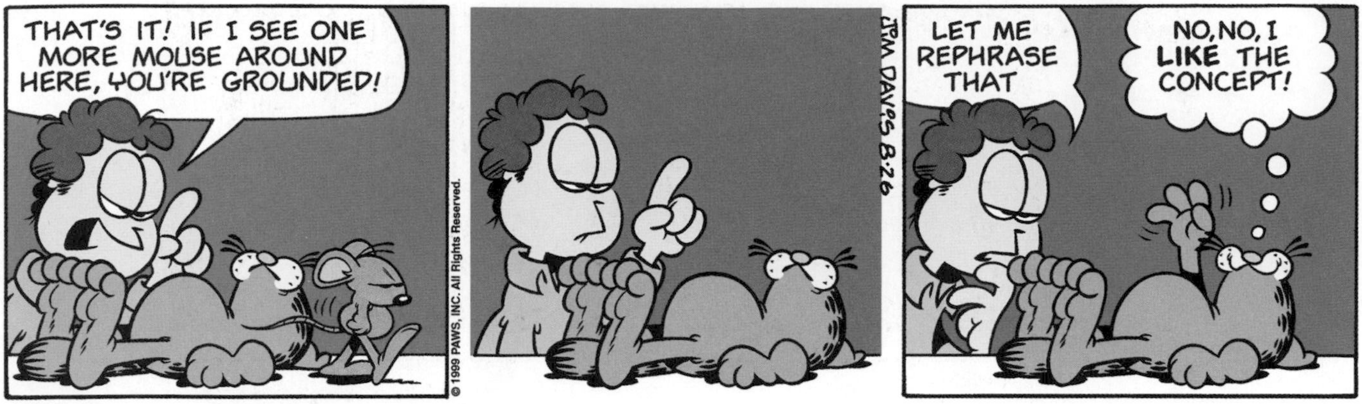
THAT'S IT! IF I SEE ONE MORE MOUSE AROUND HERE, YOU'RE GROUNDED!
© 1999 PAWS, INC. All Rights Reserved.
JIM DAVIS 8-26
LET ME REPHRASE THAT
NO, NO, I **LIKE** THE CONCEPT!

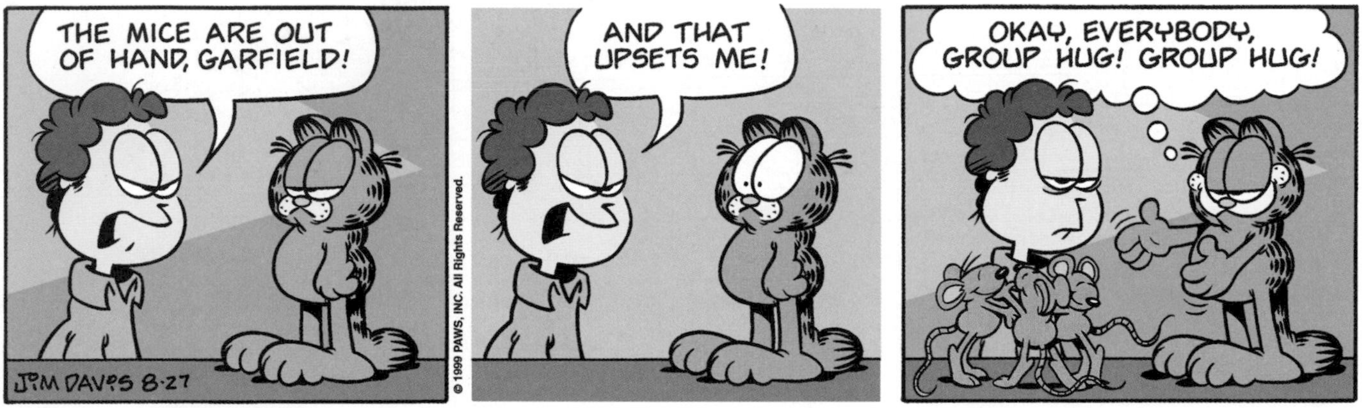
THE MICE ARE OUT OF HAND, GARFIELD!
JIM DAVIS 8-27
© 1999 PAWS, INC. All Rights Reserved.
AND THAT UPSETS ME!
OKAY, EVERYBODY, GROUP HUG! GROUP HUG!

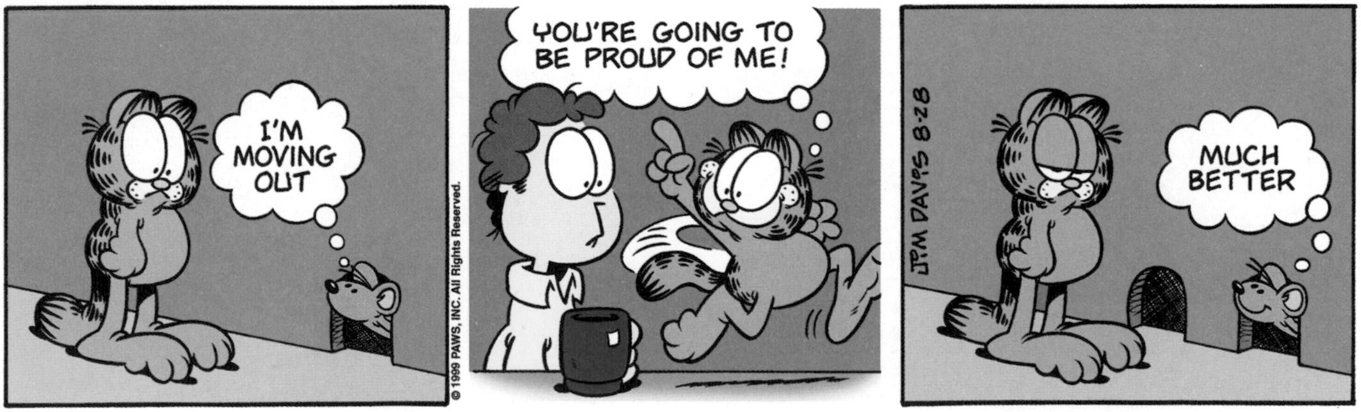
I'M MOVING OUT
© 1999 PAWS, INC. All Rights Reserved.
YOU'RE GOING TO BE PROUD OF ME!
JIM DAVIS 8-28
MUCH BETTER

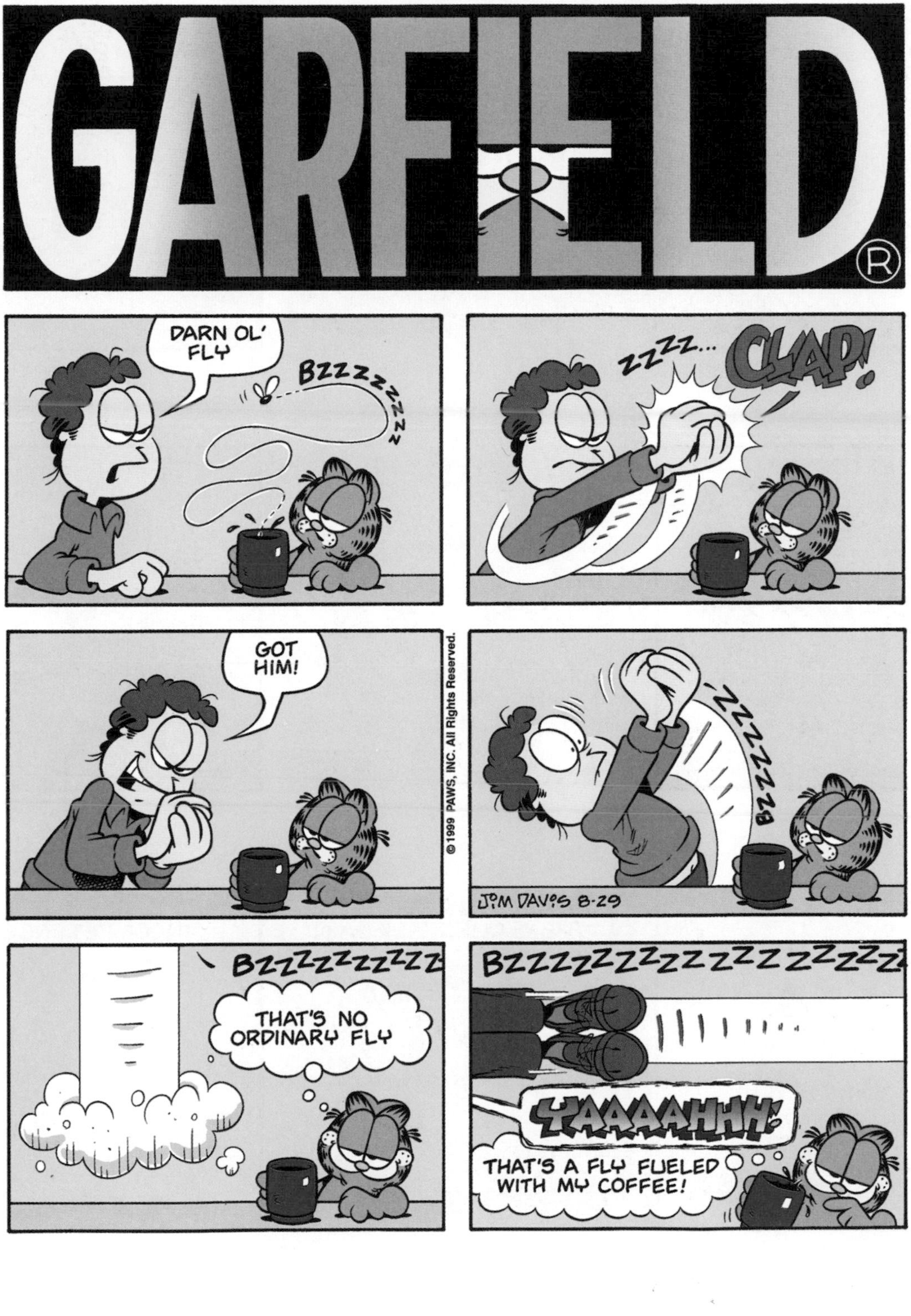
GARFIELD
DARN OL' FLY
BZZZZZZZZZ
ZZZZ...
CLAP!
GOT HIM!
© 1999 PAWS, INC. All Rights Reserved.
BZZZZZZ
JIM DAVIS 8-29
BZZZZZZZZZZZ
THAT'S NO ORDINARY FLY
BZZZZZZZZZZZZZZZZZZ
YAAAAHHH!
THAT'S A FLY FUELED WITH MY COFFEE!

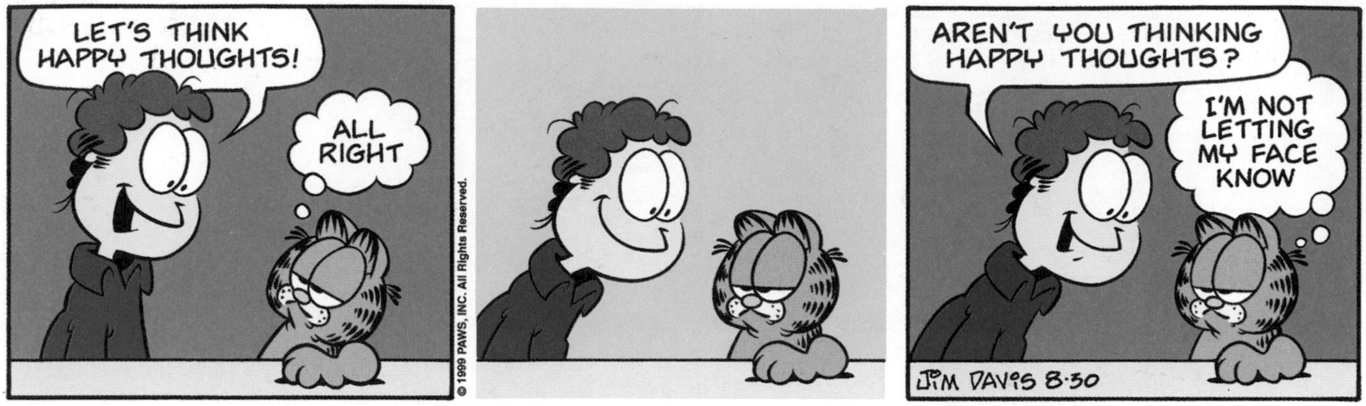
LET'S THINK HAPPY THOUGHTS!
ALL RIGHT
© 1999 PAWS, INC. All Rights Reserved.
AREN'T YOU THINKING HAPPY THOUGHTS?
I'M NOT LETTING MY FACE KNOW
JIM DAVIS 8·30

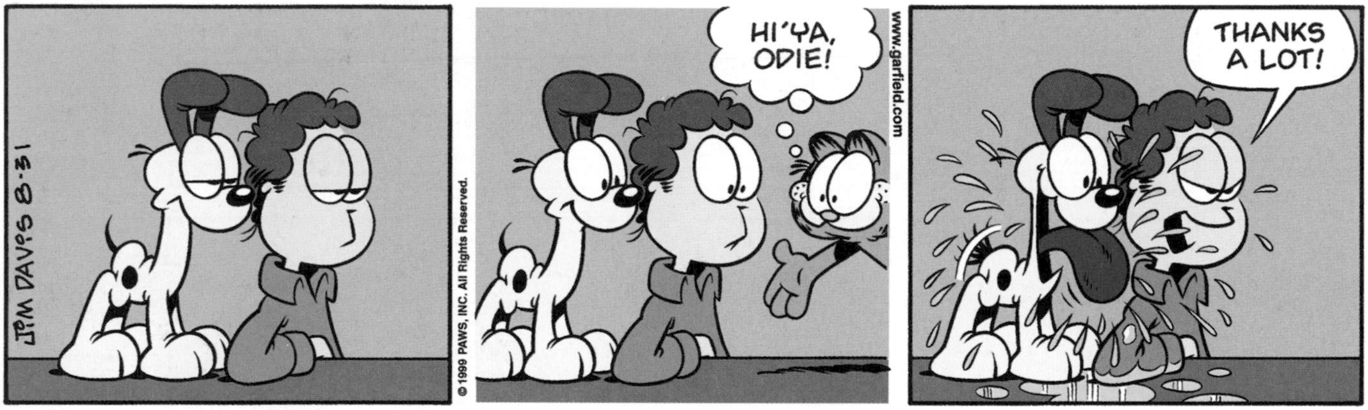
JIM DAVIS 8·31
© 1999 PAWS, INC. All Rights Reserved.
HI'YA, ODIE!
www.garfield.com
THANKS A LOT!

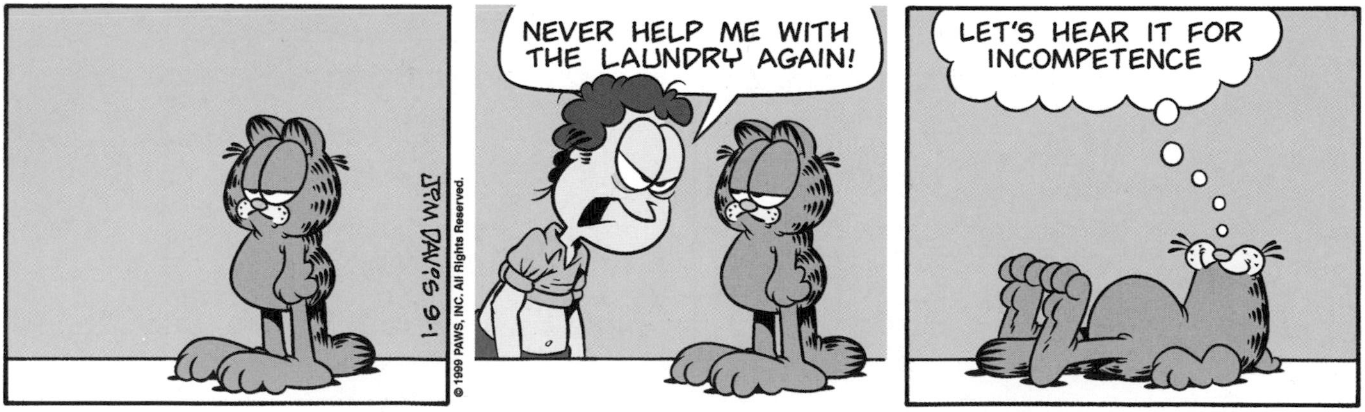
JIM DAVIS 9·1
© 1999 PAWS, INC. All Rights Reserved.
NEVER HELP ME WITH THE LAUNDRY AGAIN!
LET'S HEAR IT FOR INCOMPETENCE

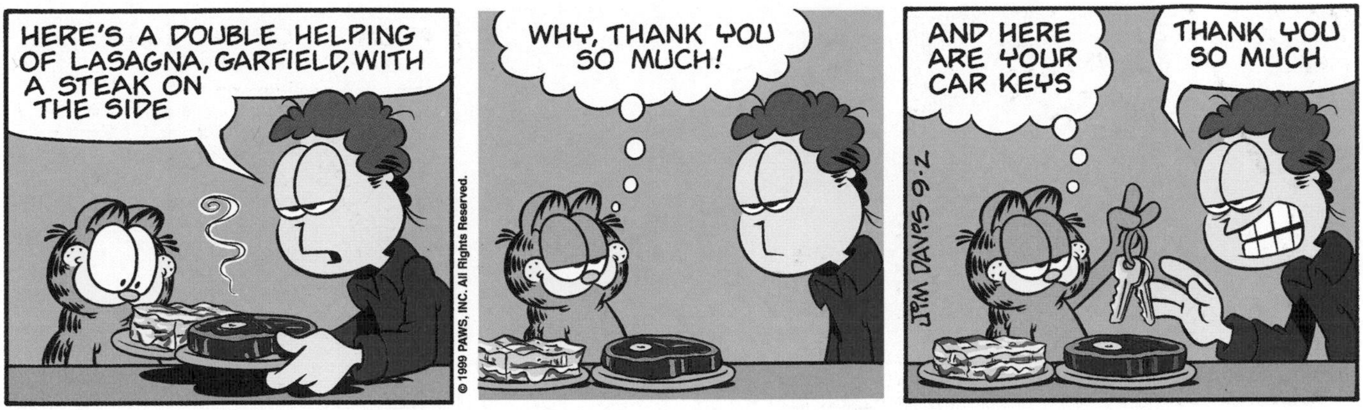
HERE'S A DOUBLE HELPING OF LASAGNA, GARFIELD, WITH A STEAK ON THE SIDE
© 1999 PAWS, INC. All Rights Reserved.
WHY, THANK YOU SO MUCH!
JIM DAVIS 9-2
AND HERE ARE YOUR CAR KEYS
THANK YOU SO MUCH

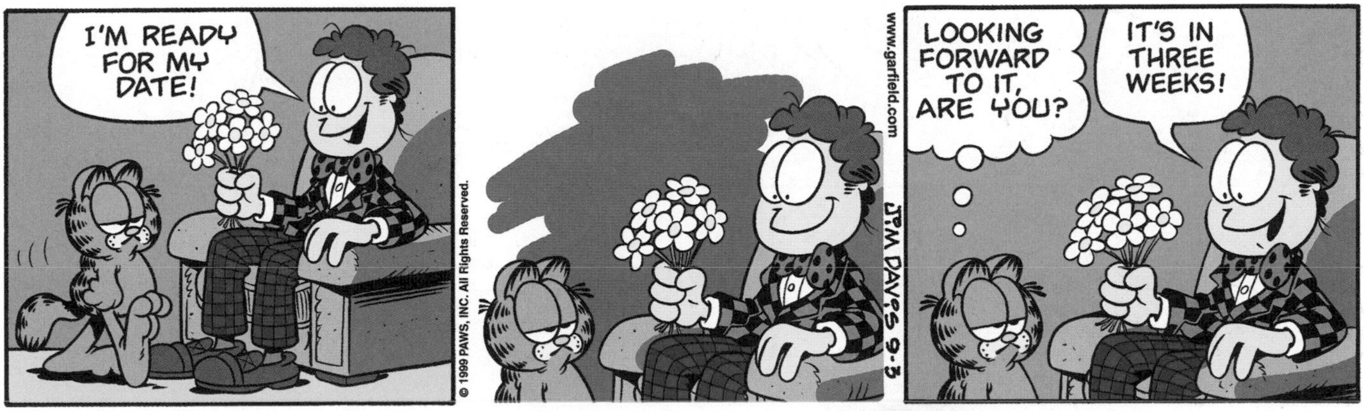
I'M READY FOR MY DATE!
© 1999 PAWS, INC. All Rights Reserved.
www.garfield.com
JIM DAVIS 9-3
LOOKING FORWARD TO IT, ARE YOU?
IT'S IN THREE WEEKS!

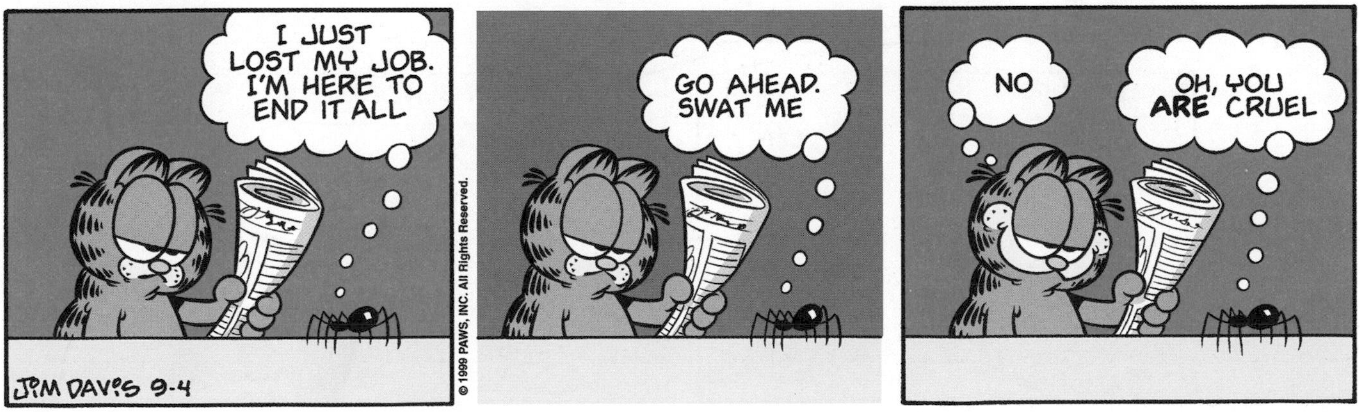
I JUST LOST MY JOB. I'M HERE TO END IT ALL
JIM DAVIS 9-4
© 1999 PAWS, INC. All Rights Reserved.
GO AHEAD. SWAT ME
NO
OH, YOU **ARE** CRUEL

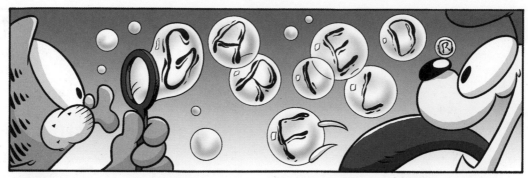

I'M PUTTING THIS CAKE HERE AND TURNING MY BACK

LET'S SEE IF YOU CAN WITHSTAND TEMPTATION

OKAY, MY BACK IS TURNED

BE STRONG, GARFIELD

HEY, FAT BOY. YOU WANNA PIECE OF ME?!

YOU CAN DO THIS

HUH?!

HUH?

SLAP! SLAP!

GARFIELD, GARFIELD, GARFIELD

FORGET IT. YOU WOULDN'T BELIEVE ME ANYWAY

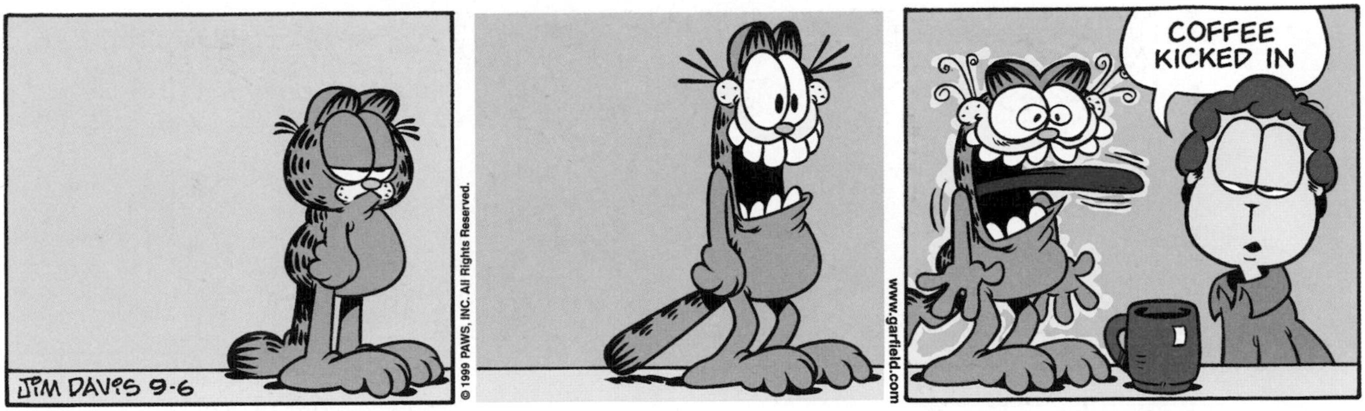
JIM DAVIS 9-6
© 1999 PAWS, INC. All Rights Reserved.
www.garfield.com
COFFEE KICKED IN

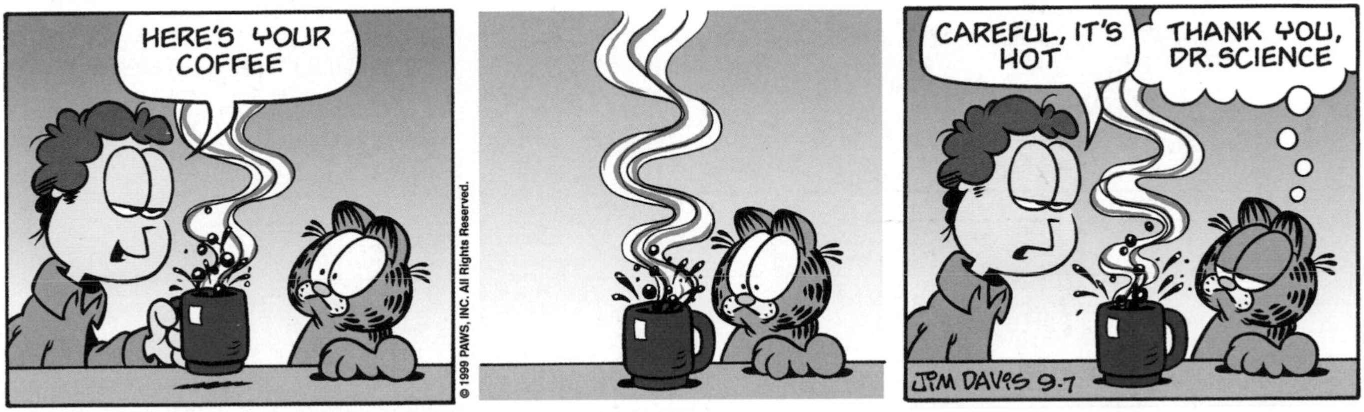
HERE'S YOUR COFFEE
© 1999 PAWS, INC. All Rights Reserved.
CAREFUL, IT'S HOT
THANK YOU, DR. SCIENCE
JIM DAVIS 9-7

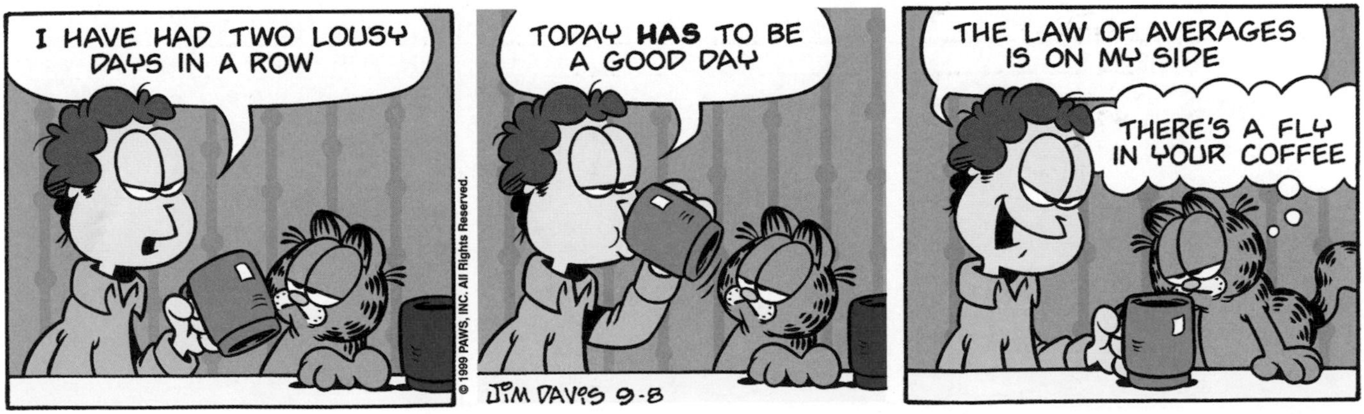
I HAVE HAD TWO LOUSY DAYS IN A ROW
© 1999 PAWS, INC. All Rights Reserved.
TODAY HAS TO BE A GOOD DAY
JIM DAVIS 9-8
THE LAW OF AVERAGES IS ON MY SIDE
THERE'S A FLY IN YOUR COFFEE

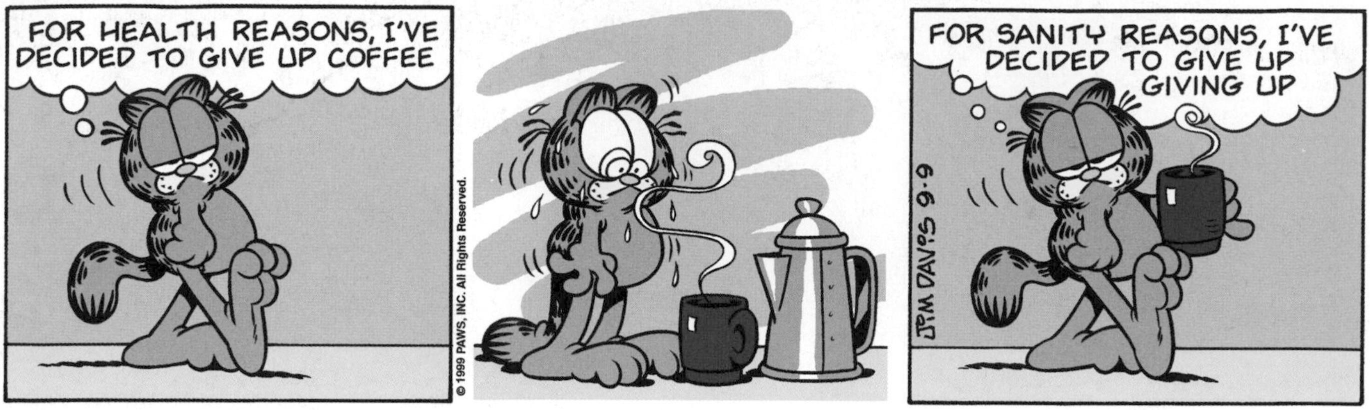
FOR HEALTH REASONS, I'VE DECIDED TO GIVE UP COFFEE
FOR SANITY REASONS, I'VE DECIDED TO GIVE UP GIVING UP
JIM DAVIS 9-9

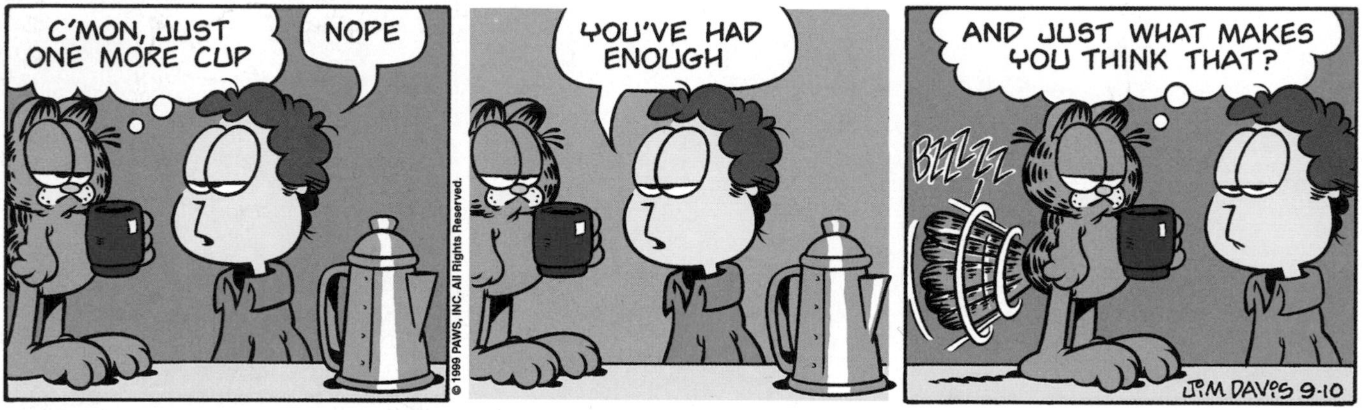
C'MON, JUST ONE MORE CUP
NOPE
YOU'VE HAD ENOUGH
AND JUST WHAT MAKES YOU THINK THAT?
BZZZZZ
JIM DAVIS 9-10

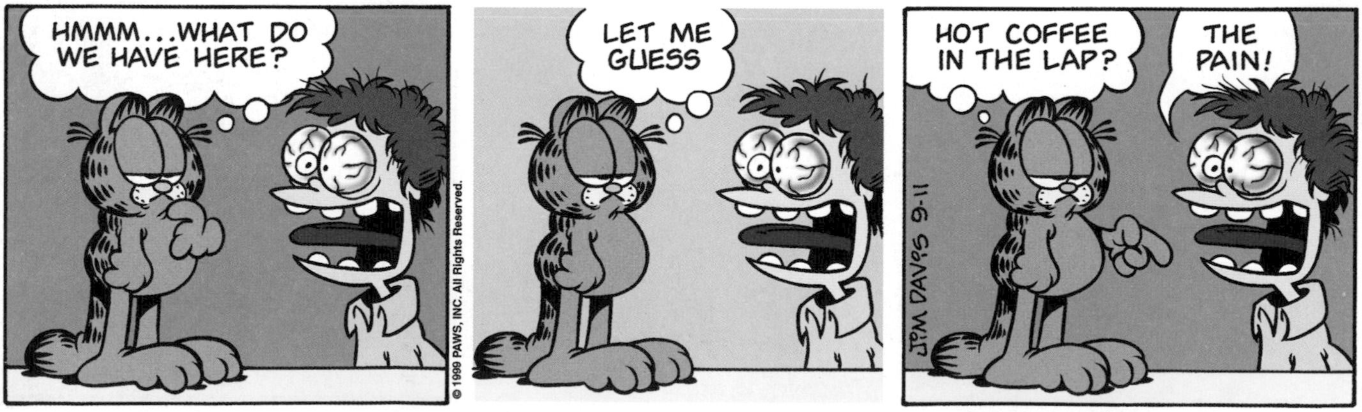
HMMM...WHAT DO WE HAVE HERE?
LET ME GUESS
HOT COFFEE IN THE LAP?
THE PAIN!
JIM DAVIS 9-11

Fat Cat Classics Vol. 2

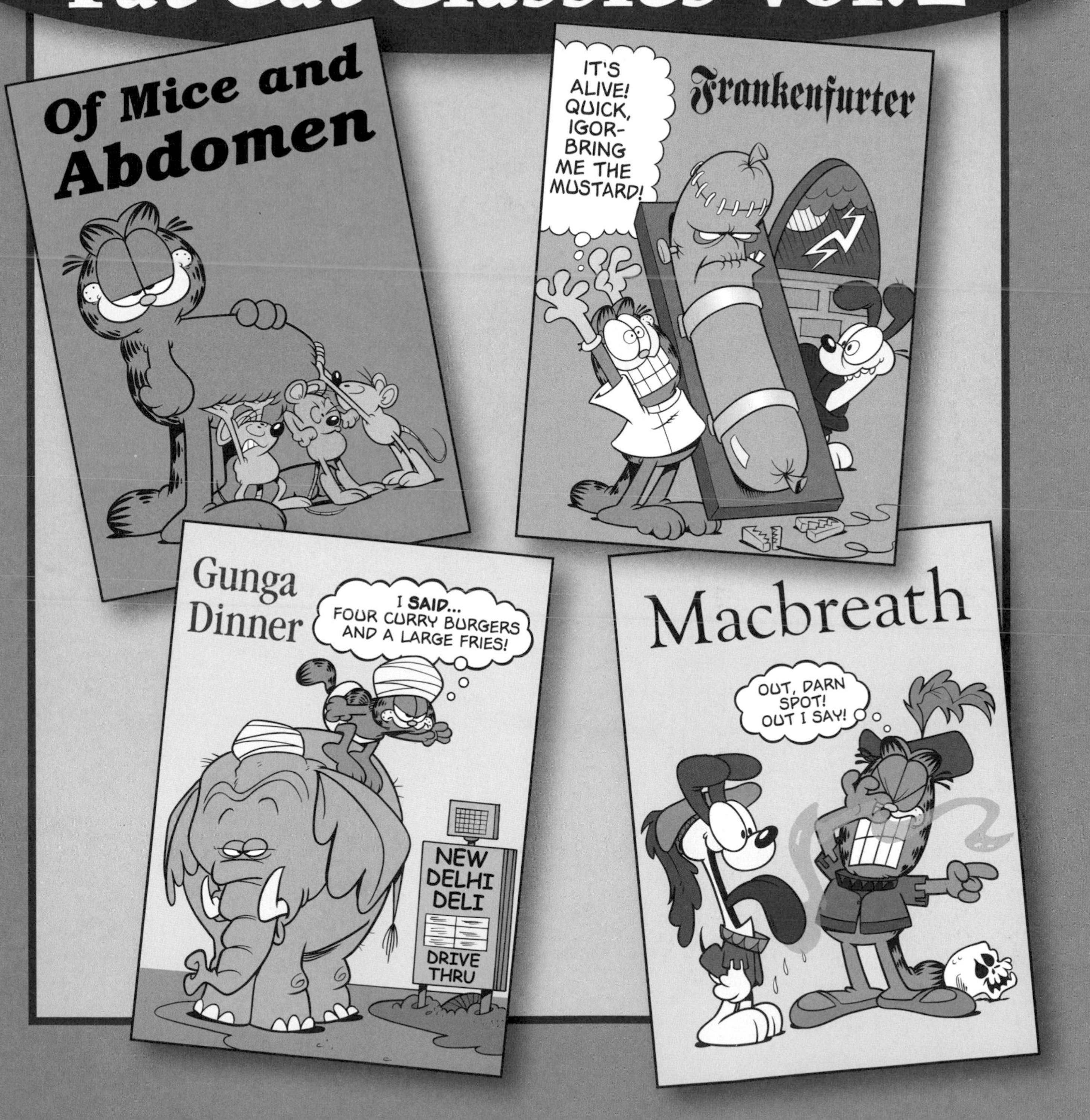
Of Mice and Abdomen
Frankenfurter
IT'S ALIVE! QUICK, IGOR- BRING ME THE MUSTARD!
Gunga Dinner
I SAID... FOUR CURRY BURGERS AND A LARGE FRIES!
NEW DELHI DELI
DRIVE THRU
Macbreath
OUT, DARN SPOT! OUT I SAY!

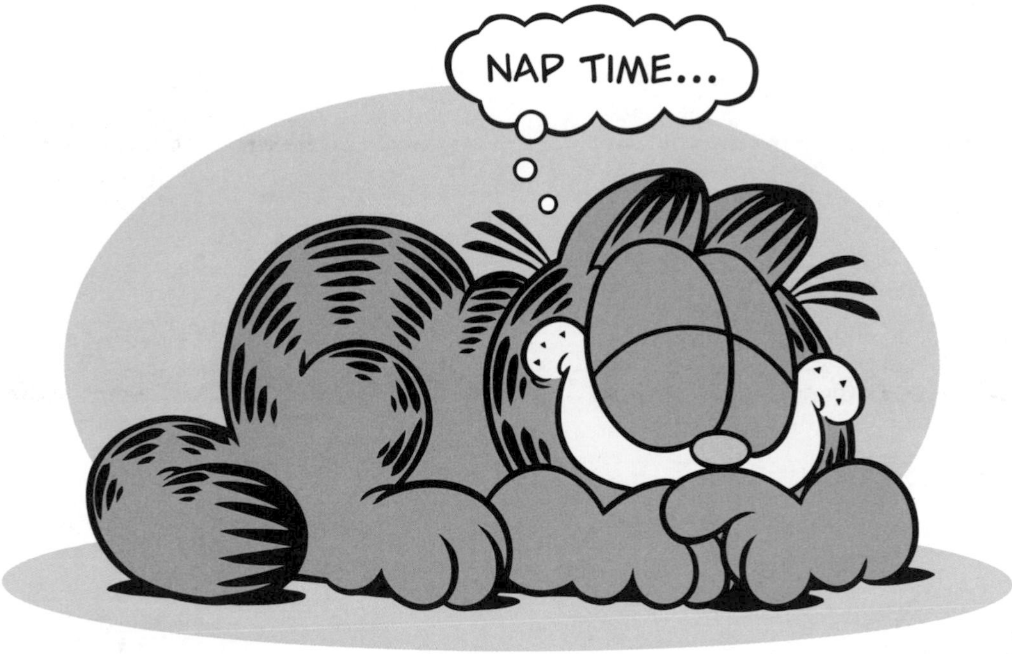
NAP TIME...

Watch. Read. Shop. Play.

DON'T FORGET THE SNACKS!

garfield.com

❋ *Garfield and Friends* and *The Garfield Show*

You can find your favorite episodes of *Garfield and Friends* and *The Garfield Show* on YouTube, Netflix, Cartoon Network, Boomerang, and on demand!

❋ The Comic Strip

Search & read thousands of GARFIELD® comic strips!

❋ Garfield on Social Media

Join millions of Garfield's friends on Facebook, Twitter, and Instagram. Get your daily dose of humor and connect with other fat cat fans!

❋ Shop all the Garfield stores!

Original art & comic strips, books, apparel, personalized products, & more!

❋ Play FREE online Garfield games!

Plus, check out all of the FREE Garfield apps available for your smartphone, tablet, and other mobile devices.

STRIPS, SPECIALS, OR ▓ESTSELLING ▓OOKS . . .
GARFIELD'S ON EVERYONE'S MENU.

Don't miss even one episode in the Tubby Tabby's hilarious series!

DVD TIE-INS

AND DON'T MISS . . .

New larger, full-color format!